GENERAL SOURCES OF
BIRTHS, MARRIAGES
AND DEATHS
BEFORE 1837

Volumes of the *National Index of Parish Registers* already published:

Volume 1. *General Sources of Births, Marriages and Deaths before 1837*. Parish Registers, Marriage Licences, Monumental Inscriptions, Newspapers, Clandestine Marriages, Divorce, Medieval Sources, Other Records, General Bibliography.

Volume 2. *Sources for Nonconformist Genealogy and Family History*. The Three Denominations (Presbyterians, Independents, Baptists), Society of Friends, Moravians, Methodists, Foreign Churches, Other Denominations.

Volume 3. *Sources for Roman Catholic Genealogy and Family History*; with a short section on Jewish Records contributed by Edgar Samuel. Index to Vols. 1, 2 and 3.

Volume 5. *South Midlands and Welsh Border*. Gloucestershire, Herefordshire, Oxfordshire, Shropshire, Warwickshire, Worcestershire.

Volume 12. *Sources for Scottish Genealogy and Family History*. Historical Background, Parish Registers, Ancillary Sources, Nonconformists, Bibliography.

Numbers for further regional volumes (of which there will be at least eight) will be allocated as appropriate.

NATIONAL INDEX OF PARISH REGISTERS VOLUME 1

GENERAL SOURCES OF BIRTHS, MARRIAGES AND DEATHS BEFORE 1837

by

D. J. STEEL

With additional articles by

E. GILLETT   MARY McGUINNESS

E. A. WRIGLEY

Published for the
SOCIETY OF GENEALOGISTS

PHILLIMORE

London and Chichester

Published by
PHILLIMORE & CO. LTD.
Shopwyke Hall, Chichester, Sussex

for the

Society of Genealogists
1976

First published by the Society of Genealogists, 1968
Second impression, 1969
Third, corrected, impression, 1976

ISBN 0 900592 41 9

53787

Printed by photolithography and made in Great Britain
at The Pitman Press, Bath

Contents

FOREWORD

*by Admiral of the Fleet the Earl Mountbatten of Burma,
K.G., O.M., G.C.B., G.C.S.I., G.C.I.E., G.C.V.O., D.S.O.,
President of the Society of Genealogists*

The Society of Genealogists has always been fortunate in having members who are willing to undertake much-needed large-scale work, often far removed from their own particular genealogical interests. This tradition has been continued by Mr D. J. Steel and his voluntary helpers in producing the Society's "Register and Directory," which is already proving of great value to members. Now their "National Index of Parish Registers," the most ambitious of the Society's publications to date, has been made possible by a generous interest-free loan from the Pilgrim Trust.

Genealogists and Local Historians have long felt the need for a comprehensive publication which lists the Parish Registers and Bishop's Transcripts, as well as Roman Catholic and Nonconformist Records. The National Index goes even farther than this, in that the detailed general articles in the introductory volumes, and the General Information sections of each county, contain much miscellaneous information, which genealogists would otherwise have to seek in numerous publications. Not only will the complete index prove a major work of general reference, but the breakdown into groups of counties will provide invaluable handbooks for those whose researches are fairly localised.

In his introduction, Mr Steel emphasises that this work is only a beginning. As further records become available at Record Offices, and are sorted, catalogued and indexed, the National Index will require revision. This publication has, however, paved the way. It is to be hoped that it will inspire others to undertake the revision of particular counties as the need arises.

Mountbatten of Burma

A. F.

GENERAL INTRODUCTION TO THE SERIES

The National Index of Parish Registers evolved from the plan of Mr. J.S.W. Gibson to prepare a new edition of the pre-War Index of Parish Register Copies. His idea was to produce the work, not as previously with the parishes arranged alphabetically throughout the volume, but under counties and with each parish listed whether or not copies of the registers had been made.

The starting date of the original registers was also to be included. This in itself was an ambitious project and without his initiative this Index would have never come into being.

Assisted by the Hon. G.R. Strutt, Mr. Gibson started making a slip index for all parishes and on the slips was entered available information on the starting dates of registers and details of known copies. In 1959 Mr. Gibson appealed for volunteers to assist in checking at the Society of Genealogist's Library, the British Museum Library and elsewhere. By July 1960 drafts had been prepared for Bedfordshire, Berkshire, Buckinghamshire, Cambridgeshire, Cheshire, Dorset and Durham, and slips had been made for all parishes in England and known copies entered. At this point Mr. Gibson found that with his extensive work on Oxfordshire registers it was impossible for him to cope with the Index as well, and passed over the work to Mr. C.W. Field. At approximately the same time I was elected Chairman of the Parish Register Sub-Committee, and agreed to act as Editor of the work.

Work now proceeded rapidly. Mr. Field circularized every library in the country, and entered all printed, typescript and manuscript copies he could locate on to the slips. When work on each county was completed he typed out a provisional list. As almost all my spare time was engaged in the organization of Parish Register transcription, my part was limited to organizing the checks of Mr. Field's lists at the Society of Genealogist's Library and the British Museum Library.

By 1962 work on the list of copies was nearing completion, except for a few counties where particular difficulties had arisen. However, the work done, particularly on starting dates of registers had made it increasingly obvious that except for a few counties there was little reliable information in print on the dates of original registers and less still on the Bishop's Transcripts and I decided to broaden the scope of the project to include this extra material. In July 1962 therefore, I handed over the organization of transcription work to Mr. M.A. Pinhorn in order to concentrate on the National Index.

An excellent team of volunteers was built up and work on all counties progressed simultaneously. Whilst it might have been better to concentrate on one group of counties at a time, I decided against this as so much surveying and depositing of parish registers and sorting and listing of Bishop's Transcripts was going on all over the country that I felt it was better to accumulate all easily accessible existing material, after which it was quite likely that much more would be available on both original parish registers and Bishop's Transcripts, and that the information given would not in the main become out of date so quickly. This indeed proved to be the case. In Warwickshire for example the bulk of the deposits at the diocesan record offices have been made in the last few years. In Kent and Worcestershire the Bishop's Transcripts have only recently been fully listed. The drafts of some counties, such as Hampshire or Dorset were more or less completed two years or more ago but publication was delayed because other counties in the projected volumes were not yet ready. For many counties, such as Norfolk and Gloucestershire the sorting and listing of the Bishops Transcripts is still in progress.

The response of the county Archivists to the project has been superb. List after list of queries has been sent as checks have revealed discrepanices of all kinds and these queries have invariably been dealt with promptly and extremely thoroughly.

So many people have helped with listing and checking that it is almost invidious to single out any for special mention. However, a few have done an enormous volume of work over a prolonged period. Mr. F. M. Barrell over a period of four years has done a large part of the checking at the Society of Genealogists and has continually helped with tricky queries. Miss D. I. Lloyd, Mrs. D. Perry, Mr. F. L. Leeson, Mr. A. D. Francis, and many others have done extensive work on listing and checking for many counties at the Society of Genealogists, the Public Record Office, the British Museum and the National Register of Archives. In addition, almost every county has had its dedicated helper or helpers who has assisted in the listing of registers or Bishop's Transcripts. Mr. A. J. Willis circularized Hampshire incumbents at his own expense, a generous contribution to the work, and many others have put in an enormous amount of time and effort. Thus Mr. P. C. Withers personally examined page by page the eighty per cent of Berkshire registers deposited at the County Record Office and circularized the incumbents holding the remainder, Mr. C. P. Neat has forwarded list after list of Northumberland and Durham registers and Mr. C. M. Turner listed in detail all Warwickshire deposited registers. Lack of space precludes the mention of more names here, but all are mentioned in the acknowledgements at the front of each county section, regrettably a quite inadequate recognition of their services.

Mr. Field in the meantime made slips for all Welsh parishes, and completed the work of preparing the original county drafts, and since 1962 my mother Mrs. A.E.F. Steel has been working full-time on this project, sorting co-ordinating and listing information from all sources, typing correspondence and, since 1964, preparing rough drafts for all counties.

In 1965 the work moved into its penultimate phase. This involved the circulatization of all Anglican clergy on whose registers reliable information had not been obtained from elsewhere, of Church Secretaries of every Nonconformist Church founded before 1837 for which registers could not be traced, of 600 Methodist Circuits Superintendents and of nearly all Parish Priests of Catholic Churches founded before 1837. The dates and parishes included in Boyd's Marriage Index were added and Mr. J.R. Cunningham of the Church of Jesus Christ of Latter Day Saints very kindly put at my disposal the records of the extensive microfilming on which the church has been engaged. With the assistance of Edward Milligan Archivist of Friends' House, Euston, an attempt was made to identify Quaker surrendered registers, the catalogue of surrendered registers being totally unreliable. Furthermore, from the excellent records at Friends House information was abstracted on the composition of the Monthly Meetings at various times and the administrative history of every Quaker Meeting House. This item took over a year of irregular visits to Friends' House, Euston, to complete.

By January 1966, the preparation of the County lists was almost complete, and work was commenced on the General Articles for volumes 1, 2 and 3, and on the General Information sections of those counties it was considered most convenient to publish first. Here again I received more help than I could possibly have anticipated, and I should like to express my gratitude to those who have contributed articles to the first two volumes, to those authors and publishers who have allowed published material to be used, and to the very large number of people who assisted with the General Articles in volumes 1, 2 and 3 or the County prefaces, and in the Scottish volume (12).

It is intended that the General Volumes should serve not only as an introduction to the Series, but also as a standard work of reference on sources of births, marriages and deaths.

* * * * * * * * *

General Information Section of each County

These county prefaces include information on Record Repositories, Original Registers, Bishop's Transcripts, Modern Copies,

Marriage Indexes, Marriage Licences, Nonconformist and Catholic
Registers, Regimental Registers, pre-1837 Newspapers, Publishing
Societies, other local Societies and a bibliography. The only item
which may cause any mild surprise is the newspapers, which have been
included as the information is often not readily accessible and these
may be a useful source for Births, Marriages and Deaths. Only
newspapers of which a fairly consecutive series for a few years or
more exists have been included. Every effort has been made to ensure
that the information on local Societies is as up to date as possible.
The county bibliographies do not claim to be comprehensive, and list
only some of the more important printed works of genealogical
interest. For reasons of space, local histories have normally been included only when these contain specifically genealogical material,
though of course any local history may prove invaluable to the
genealogist. Information on Wills has not been included as this is more
than adequately covered by Mr. A.J. Camp's book "Wills and their
Whereabouts" (1974) or by "Wills and Where to Find Them" by J.S.W. Gibson
(1974).

One point which may surprise users of the index is the repetition
of material in two or more county prefaces even if they appear in the
same volume. This particularly applies to Bishop's Transcripts and
Marriage Licences where one diocese, such as Lichfield, may extend
over several counties. However, this has been done so that each county
section is an entirely self contained unit, thus leaving the way clear
for the publication of individual counties should this be decided upon
at any future date. Occasionally where the information given is fairly
detailed and lengthy, only a summary has been given in the preface to
another county which has only a few parishes in that diocese.

Parish Registers

The basic aim has been to cover only registers dating before 1837.
Parishes founded after 1837 have therefore not normally been entered,
unless they were previously chapelries of another parish and kept
separate registers. However, where the registers of pre-1837 parishes
have been deposited at a County Record Office or elsewhere, the
terminal dates are given even if these are long after 1837, but of
course deposited registers of parishes formed after 1837 have not been
included, an illogical but unavoidable distinction. In the case of
Original Registers still with the incumbent, the starting dates are
normally given with a + sign meaning "onwards". In practice this
invariably means "beyond 1837". In the case of Original Registers,
but not Bishop's Transcripts it normally indicates that entries continue from the date listed up to the present.

It is important to remember that the index gives only a summary of
the registers. Duplicate and overlapping registers have therefore

normally been ignored. An effort has been made to include registers of Banns, but returns made for the National Register of Archives or completed circulars returned to me have often been deficient in that respect and no guarantee can be made that where no Banns register is listed, one does not exist. The dates given for Banns include all Banns whether they are in a separate register or in a combined register with the marriages.

Bishop's Transcripts

The amount of information it has been possible to include with regard to the Bishop's Transcripts varies considerably from county to county. This is partly because many records have not been fully sorted and listed and partly because the degree of completeness of the Transcripts themselves varies. In some counties it has been possible to show every missing year, in others only four year gaps have been noted and in others only ten year gaps. In the case of one or two counties, such as Gloucestershire, the only information given is the date of the first transcript. It is most important that users of this index should read the section on Bishop's Transcripts in the relevant County preface to familiarise themselves with the degree of detail recorded for that particular county.

When the + sign is used after Bishop's Transcript dates, it indicates that the transcripts continue beyond 1837, but unlike Parish Registers, it must be borne in mind that they do not normally continue beyond the 19th Century.

Modern Copies

An attempt has been made to include all known copies whether Printed, Typescript, Manuscript, Photostat or Microfilm in libraries and record repositories in England and Wales. Repositories outside England and Wales have not normally been included with the solitary exception of the Genealogical Society of the Church of Latter Day Saints, Salt Lake City, Utah, U.S.A. whose collection is so vast that American users of this book may find it handy to have some indication that there is a copy there. However, a word of warning is necessary. The Church is microfilming registers and Bishop's Transcripts at such a rate that if no copy at Salt Lake City is listed it does not necessarily mean that one does not exist. Any list including Mormon material is bound to be out of date before it is printed.

In the case of a printed volume it may be assumed that there is a copy in the British Museum Library and, unless otherwise stated, in the Society of Genealogists' Library. There is normally also a copy at Salt Lake City. Except in the case of very rare books it may safely be assumed that the County Library has a copy and more often than not, the County Record Office.

Every attempt has been made to keep the list of typescript and manuscript copies up to date and as regards copies in the Society of Genealogists' Library, each county list is up to date at the time of going to press. In the case of other libraries and repositories however, it has not been possible to recircularize them all, so it is quite possible that copies deposited recently may not have been included.

In using modern copies the attention of readers is drawn to the general article on the subject which points out some of the many pitfalls. In compiling the index every effort has been made to overcome one of these – the possibility that the "copy" may consist of extracts only. Every parish register copy in the Society of Genealogists' library has been examined to check on this, and this point was emphasized in the questionnaires sent out to libraries. Normally extracts have been excluded except in cases where they are substantial or else the original register from which they were taken has since disappeared. In these cases the word *Extracts* or the abbreviation *Extr.* has been used. In spite of all precautions, however, it is more than likely that many extracts have slipped through disguised as complete copies. Difficulty has sometimes arisen in that a copy has in the past sometimes been described as "Extracts" when in fact it gives an accurate *summary* of every entry as with most copies, or when it contains a complete copy of a restricted number of years. These have been included in the index as ordinary copies.

Nonconformist Chapels and Catholic Churches

Urban chapels and churches have been included at the end of the list of Anglican parishes for each town – Catholic churches first and then Nonconformist chapels. In the case of London and Middlesex this has involved several separate sections.

Rural chapels and churches have normally been listed under the Anglican Parish. In many cases however, the place in which they were situated is better known that the Anglican parish, or they drew their Congregations from several Anglican parishes and the entry has been made under the place name with a suitable cross reference under the relevant Anglican Parish. In the case of Nonconformist or Catholic churches which were founded before 1837 but which did not surrender registers, the starting date of registers in church hands is noted even if these are after 1837. Copies made at the time of the surrender of the original registers have been listed under OR rather than Cop as frequently fresh entries were added to these after 1837.

Whenever the information has been easily accessible an attempt
has been made to include every known Nonconformist chapel and Catholic
Mission or Church in existence before 1837 whether registers are known
or not. In the case of existing Nonconformist Churches, many Church
Secretaries failed to return completed questionnaires, and the name
and foundation church have been entered with the cryptic phrase "No
information". When a "nil return" has been made, the phrase "No
registers known" has been used. In the case of pre-1837 Nonconformist
chapels now no longer in existence, as with most other information,
the thoroughness of the listing varies to some degree from county to
county, and whilst it is true that further research would bring to
light many unlisted defunct chapels, the time has simply not been
available to explore this subject thoroughly. However, all denominational Unions and Associations were approached in an effort to locate
any registers.

Roman Catholics

In the case of many Catholic Missions and Churches covering a wide
area cross references have been put in for the principal Anglican
parishes mentioned in the registers. All Dioceson Archivists and
Bishops' Secretaries have been asked if they held any registers.

Independents

This designation has been used throughout except when an existing
church is referred to for the location of registers when the more
familiar "Congregationalist" (or the abbreviation 'Cong') has been
used, e. g. Minister, X Cong. Ch.

Baptists

It is important to bear in mind that the abbreviation 'C' is used
here for adult Baptisms. Except in a few counties it has not been
possible in the time available to distinguish between General Baptist
and Particular Baptist churches, although these were of course
entirely separate denominations.

Methodists

An entry has normally been made under the Circuit heading listing
known churches within the Circuit in 1837 and any circuit registers
and referring readers to any individual church which kept registers.
Under the name of the Church, the circuit to which it belonged in
1837 is listed. Sometimes more detail on the administrative history
is given.

Society of Friends (Quakers)

An entry has been made for each Monthly Meeting, listing meeting houses within it at various periods and any Monthly Meeting registers. It is then necessary to consult the entries for individual meeting houses to discover if there were additional registers, though when only one or two isolated meeting houses within the Monthly Meeting kept registers these have been indicated. Under the name of each meeting house is the Monthly Meeting to which it belonged at various times, to which reference should be made to discover whether registers exist.

Composition of Volumes

In December 1966 publication began with Volume 5 which covers the South Midlands and Welsh Border. Since then the three introductory volumes, covering generally the Anglican, Nonconformist, Roman Catholic and Jewish sources of pre-1837 births, marriages and deaths, have appeared, as well as a separate volume of general material on Scotland. Further regional volumes are at an advanced stage, but their final composition depends on various factors which make it impossible to forecast ahead with certainty.

* * * * * * * * *

The National Index does not make any claims to be regarded as a definite work. It aims only to provide Genealogists with a reference work of a practical nature which gives some indication of the records available. New deposits of registers are continually being made at Record Offices and new copies – especially those by members of the recently proliferating local family history societies – are being made at a considerable rate. Moreover although much checking and rechecking has been done to try and eliminate errors, many of the figures for original registers may be incorrect, being often based on inadequate or out-of-date returns. Corrections will be gratefully received from readers by the General Editor, c/o the Society of Genealogists.

In conclusion I should like to thank the Pilgrim Trust for making an interest-free loan to cover the cost of publication, the printers Sir Isaac Pitman and Sons Ltd., Bath, for their kindness in dealing with many small problems which became apparent only at the printing stage, and the staff of the Society of Genealogists for their co-operation. Most of all, however, I would like to thank Mr. C.W. Field and many others who have done a great deal of work on the National Index project over the years. Lack of space precludes the mention of their names here, but all are listed in the acknowledgments at the front of each county section. Lastly I remember with gratitude the help of my mother, the late Mrs. A.E.F. Steel who unfortunately died before the full fruits of her labour had appeared in print.

D.J. Steel

PREFACE TO VOLUME I

The three introductory volumes of the National Index of Parish
Registers have been designed to perform a dual function: to make the
information given in the remaining volumes more intelligible and
secondly to serve as a general work of reference on the Sources of
Births, Marriages and Deaths. Thus, though they are not in any way
intended as a substitute for the standard genealogical manuals, consideration has been given throughout to the practical needs of
genealogists and local historians as well as to an examination of the
subject from the more academic point of view. Sometimes, as in the case
of the article on *"Parish Registers and the Genealogist"* it has been
possible largely to isolate the practical advice from the general
background knowledge. More frequently, however, the two aspects have
been combined in the same article.

Although the original intention was that there would be only one
general volume, the amount of material became so considerable that it
was found necessary to split it into three. Any such division must be
to some extent arbitrary, but this volume deals with General Sources:
Parish Registers, Marriage Licences, Newspapers, Clandestine Marriages,
Divorce and Medieval Records, whereas more specialized sources are dealt
with in Volume 2: the Nonconformist Denominations; and Volume 3: Roman
Catholics and Jews, and the Register of Births at the Heralds' College
(in which the bulk of the registrations were of Moravians, Roman Catholics and Jews). However it must be emphasised that the division is for
convenience only. There must be very few who have not direct ancestors
in one of these groups, and hardly a family in the country which has not
had some Nonconformist members. So the three introductory volumes at
least are able to be regarded as integral parts of the same work and a
combined index to all three forms part of volume 3. A separate volume
covers general materials on Scotland (Vol. 12, already published),
and comparable material on Wales will be included in the Welsh volume.

Sources of Births, Marriages and Deaths are, together with
Census Returns and Wills the most important records for the genealogist.
In many cases it is possible to construct a pedigree from them alone.
This, however, is a barren exercise. Genealogy has little value unless it is used to provide basic material for family history, local
history or historical demography, yet though all family historians
are also genealogists, the converse is by no means true; many
genealogists seem satisfied with a pedigree well documented with dates
of baptism, marriage and burial and the writing and proving of a Will

and little else. The family historian must use records of all kinds and be familiar with the Social history of the relevant period. Only then do the lives, occupations and movements of one's ancestors become intelligible. This volume includes a bibliography listing some of the books and articles which the family historian may find useful for setting his family in its social context. It may be argued that however desirable such a bibliography might be in a general work on family history, it is out of place in a work devoted to Sources of Births, Marriages and Deaths. However, the Sources are worthless if one does not know where to look. Thus it is hoped that through studies in social history and other related subjects, such as historical demography, local history and above all, historical geography the searcher will be able to discover what factors in the broader picture were likely to influence his own family. When one has traced a pedigree back to the earliest known ancestor in one parish, it is often quite unnecessary to undertake a vast and possibly unsuccessful search of thirty neighbouring parishes trying to seek his place of origin. As is emphasized in the article on *"Parish Registers and the Genealogist"* the location of roads, market towns and rivers were important, but so too were wage rates, enclosures, the relative cost of rents, the location of industries, the other estates or business interests of the lord of the manor and the policy of the overseers in particular areas or parishes. Thus, even taking the narrowest view, a knowledge of national and local social history not only throws light on the way our ancestors lived; it is indispensable for the very loca- tion of their vital records. Other subjects too may perform a similar function. A. J. Willis describes how on discovering an ancestor was a pipe maker, he used a geological map to discover the nearest deposits of pipe-clay.[1]

The bibliography therefore devotes as much space to related sub- jects, as it does to specifically genealogical and archive material, much of which already appears in other bibliographies, such as those of Miss M. Kaminkow or Gerald Hamilton-Edwards[2] which the enthusiastic genealogist will already have on his bookshelves. Works specifically on subjects on which there are articles in this volume have been listed not in the general bibliography, but at the end of the relevant article, or in the case of all Parish Register material (where further division would be undesirable) as Appendix I to the article on *'Form and Content'*. Further specialised bibliographies are appended to articles in Volumes 2 and 3.

---

[1] *Genealogy for Beginners*
[2] *In Search of Ancestry*

As with work on the Index itself, I am greatly indebted to the large number of people who have assisted in some way with the writing of this volume. Their names are given elsewhere, but particular mention must be made of those who have contributed entire articles: Miss. M. McGuinness, Mr. E. Gillett and Dr. E. A. Wrigley, and to those authors and publishers who have allowed copyright material to be reproduced – W. E. Tate and the Cambridge University Press for material from *"The Parish Chest"*, Miss Rosemary ffoliott for permission to use extracts from her article *"Matched and Dispatched"* in the *"Irish Genealogist"* and Lionel M. Munby for permission to use material appearing originally in the *"Amateur Historian"*. Above all I must express my gratitude to D. E. Gardner and F. Smith and their publishers, Bookcraft Ltd., Salt Lake City, Utah, U.S.A. for permission to make use of material from their invaluable three volumed work *"Genealogical Research in England and Wales"*.

For this corrected reprint, I am most grateful to Mr Anthony Camp for his revision of the sections on custody of, access to, and fees for personal searches in parish registers, pages 129–134; to the staff of the Society of Genealogists for checking and up-dating references to National Record Repositories (pages xx and xxi); and to Mr. Jeremy Gibson for help throughout the volume.

See also the lists at the beginning of the "General Information"
section of each county.

P.R.O. – The Public Record Office, Land Registry Building, Portugal
Street, London WC2A 1LR (Mon.–Fri., 9.30 – 5; Sat., 9.30 – 1),
holds the bulk of the Nonconformist registers of the whole
country and a certain number of Catholic Registers, mainly from
the North of England; also Census records. The main building,
in Chancery Lane (hours as for Land Registry Building, Sat.,
Round Room only) houses pre-1858 probate records of the Prerogative Court of Canterbury (P.C.C.). Prior application (to Chancery Lane) for reader's ticket necessary.

S.G. – Library of the Society of Genealogists, 37 Harrington Gardens,
London SW7 4JX (tel. 01-373 7054) (Tues., Fri., 10 – 6; Wed.,
Thurs., 10 – 8; Sat., 10 – 5; closed Sun. and Mon.) holds the
largest single collection in this country of Printed, Typescript
and Manuscript copies as well as a vast amount of other genealogical material. The library is open to non-members on payment of
a search fee dependent on time spent – rates obtainable on request

B.M. or Brit. Mus. – Department of Western Manuscripts, British Museum
Library (or British Library), London WC1B 3DG (Mon. – Fri., 10 –
4; Sat., 10 – 12). Reader's ticket necessary, adviseable to phone
first to order material.

G.L. – Guildhall Library, Basinghall Street, London EC2P 2EJ (Mon. – Sat.
9.30 – 5; Cloakroom closed Sat.) holds many London Original Parish
Registers and a large number of copies of registers of many
counties, especially those made by the late W.H. Challen.

General Register Office, St. Catherine's House, Kingsway, London WC2B 6JF
(Mon. – Fri., 9.30 – 4.30). Civil registration records of births
marriages and deaths in England and Wales since 1837. At present
also holds Regimental Registers and some other specialised material of relevance to the genealogist, but these records may eventually be transferred to the P.R.O.

Principal Probate Registry, Somerset House, London WC2R 1LP (Mon. – Fri.
10 – 4.30). This now houses only post-1857 probate records of
England and Wales.

N.R.A. – National Register of Archives, Quality House, Quality Court,
Chancery Lane, London WC2A 1HP (Mon. – Fri., 9.30 – 5) has detailed information on Parish Registers and all other archives
which have been inspected.

H.L. – House of Lords Record Office, Houses of Parliament, London SW1A
    0AA (Mon. – Fri., 9.30 – 5.30).

C of A – College of Arms, Queen Victoria Street, London. The Library
    holds many copies of Parish Registers, but is not open to the
    public.

Bod. – Bodleian Library, Oxford OX1 3BG (term; Mon. – Fri., 9am – 10pm,
    Sat. 9 – 1; Vac.: Mon. – Fri., 9 – 7, Sat., 9 – 1).

B.I. – Borthwick Institute of Historical Research (University of York),
    St. Anthony's Hall, Peaseholm Green, York YO1 2PW (Mon. – Fri.,
    9.30 – 1, 2 – 5). Essential to make prior appointment; fees are
    charged.

N.L.W. – National Library of Wales, Aberystwyth. (Mon. – Fri., 9.30 – 6;
    Sat., 9 – 5).

Phil. Ms. – Manuscript copies of Parish Registers formerly in the pos-
    session of Phillimore & Co. These are now housed by the Trustees
    of the Marc Fitch Fund, Kingston House, Kingston Gorse, Sussex
    BN16 1SF, to whom application to view may be made. A fee is
    normally charged.

Religious Denominations (prior appointment necessary in all cases)

Church of England – Lambeth Palace Library, London SE1 7JU (Mon. – Fri.,
    10 – 4.15)

Roman Catholics – Archbishop's House, Westminster, London SW1P 1QJ

Nonconformists – Dr. Williams's Library, 14 Gordon Square, London WC1A
    0AG (Mon., Wed., Fri., 10 – 5; Tues., Thurs., 10 – 6.30)

Baptists – Baptist Union Library, Baptist Church House, 4 Southampton
    Row, London WC1B 4AB (9.30 – 5)

Congregationalists – Congregational Union of England and Wales, Memorial
    Hall, Farringdon Street, London EC4 (Mon. – Fri., 10 – 4)

Society of Friends (Quakers) – Friends' House, Euston Road, London NW1
    2BJ (9.50 – 5.30) holds consolidated digests of all surrendered
    Quaker registers.

Presbyterians – Presbyterian Historical Society of England, 86 Tavistock
    Place, London WC1H 9RT (Tues., 10.30 – 12.30; Fri., 1.30 – 4)

Unitarians – Unitarian Church Headquarters, Essex Hall, Essex Street,
    London WC2.

Huguenots – Huguenot Library, University College, Gower Street, London
    W1 (not open to non-members of the Huguenot Society).

Jews – Jewish Museum, Woburn House, Upper Woburn Place, London WC1H 0EP.
    (Mon. – Thurs., 9 – 5; Fri., 9.30 – 1)

In recent years a number of these societies have been formed throughout the country. As the addresses of Hon. Secretaries are somewhat ephemeral anyone wishing to contact any of them is recommended to write c/o Society of Genealogists, 37 Harrington Gardens, London SW7 4JX, and their letters will be forwarded. Moreover the Federation of Family History Societies (also c/o Society of Genealogists) will be pleased to provide up-to-date information on newly-formed societies.

Bath Heraldry Society

Berkshire Family History Society

Birmingham and Midland Society for Genealogy and Heraldry

Bristol and Avon Family History Society

Cheshire Family History Society

North Cheshire Family History Society

Essex Society for Family History

The Hampshire Genealogical Society with separate sections in
North Hampshire
The Isle of Wight

Kent Family History Society

Leicester Family History Circle

Macclesfield Heraldry Society

Manchester and Lancashire Family History Society

Genealogical Society of the East Midlands

Northumberland and Durham Family History Society

Norfolk and Norwich Genealogical Society

Rossendale Society for Genealogy and Heraldry

Somerset and Dorset Family History Society

Sussex Family History Group

Suffolk Genealogy Society

West Surrey Borders Family History Society

The York Society
Yorkshire Archaeological Society, Family Studies Section

The Scottish Genealogy Society

The Heraldic and Genealogical Society of Wales

NATIONAL SOCIETIES

See also lists for Nonconformists, Scotland and Wales in Volume 2.

Genealogy etc.

Society of Genealogists, 37, Harrington Gardens, London, S.W.7.
Institute of Heraldic & Genealogical Studies, Northgate, Canterbury.
Society of Antiquaries, Burlington House, Piccadilly, London, W.1.
Society of the Friends of St. George's and the Descendants of the Knights of the Garter. Curfew Tower, Windsor Castle, Windsor, Berks.

Archives

British Records Association. The Charterhouse, London, E.C.2.
Society of Archivists. Herts Record Office, County Hall, Hertford.
Business Archives Council. 9, King's Bench Walk, London, E.C.4.

Publishing Societies

British Record Society. Dept. of History, University of Keele, Staffs.
Anglo-Norman Text Society. Sec. Miss E.A. Francis, 41, Brookside, Headington, Oxford.
Harleian Society. 79, Duke Street, London. W.1.
Pipe Roll Society. Sec. Dr. Patricia M. Barnes, P.R.O. London, W.C.2.

Heraldry

Heraldry Society. 28 Museum Street, London WC1A 1LH
Institute for Heraldic & Genealogical Studies, Northgate, Canterbury, Kent.

Historical Societies – General

Historical Association. 59, Kennington Park Road, London, S.E.11.
Royal Historical Society . 96, Cheyne Walk, London, S.W.10.

Religious History

See also *Catholics*, *The Three Denominations*, *Methodists*, *Huguenots & Walloons*, and *Jews* all in Volumes 2 and 3.

> *Church Historical Society*. S.P.C.K, Holy Trinity Church, Marylebone Road, London, N.W.1.
>
> *Ecclesiastical Historical Society*. St. Ann's Vestry Hall, Church Entry, Carter Lane, London, E.C.4.
>
> *English Church History Society*. Sec. C.L.H. Spratt, c/o Barclay's Bank, 41, Castle Street, Liverpool.

Economic History

> *Economic History Society*. London School of Economics, Aldwych, London, W.C.2.
>
> *British Agricultural History Society*. Department of Agriculture, The University, Reading, Berks.

Army & Navy

> *Military Historical Society*. c/o Imperial War Museum, Lambeth Road, Lambeth, S.E.1.
>
> *Society for Army Historical Research*. Library, War Office, London, S.W.1.
>
> *Navy Records Society*. c/o Royal Naval College, London, S.E.10.

Theatre

> *British Theatre Museum Association*, Leighton House, 12 Holland Park Road, London, W.14.

Indexing

> *Society of Indexers*, 3, Western Mansions, Western Parade, Barnet, Herts.

Overseas

In general these are beyond the scope of this index, but one has been included, viz: -

S.L.C. – Genealogical Society of the Church of Jesus Christ of Latter Day Saints, Salt Lake City, Utah, U.S.A.
This holds the largest collection of genealogical material in the World.

PREFACE

Parish Registers are undoubtedly the most important single genealogical source. However, numerous difficulties are likely to arise in
using them, and most genealogists are probably not thoroughly familiar
with the background knowledge which not only makes the use of them far
more interesting but which at times proves indispensible.

The article on the *History* of the Registers has been kept fairly
short as this is covered at considerable length in the standard works
on the subject, particularly J.S. Burn *History of Parish Registers of
England* (1862 edn), R.E. Chester Waters *Parish Registers in England*
(1887) and Dr. J.C. Cox *The Parish Registers of England* (1910). With
the exception of *Mediaeval Registers* the greater part of the *History*
has been condensed from pages 46 to 50 of W.E. Tate's *The Parish Chest*
(Cambridge University Press 1946 and edns. New edition now (1967) in
the press) which has also been cited from time to time in the articles
on *Bishop's Transcripts* and *Form and Content*. I am grateful to Mr.
Tate and the publishers for permission to use the work. The Appendix
to the *History* article deals in detail with the various attempts that
have been made to secure the better preservation of Parish Registers.
It is almost incredible that after more than a century of continuous
disquiet, little has been done to ensure that these priceless records
are properly looked after, and all genealogists should be concerned
with securing legislation on the subject.

The main pitfalls in using registers are dealt with in the article
entitled *Parish Registers and the Genealogist*. In writing this article
I encountered several items on which further research is necessary
before any statements can be made with confidence. One which does not
seem to have been noticed before in any genealogical work is the question as to how far, following the calendar change of 1752 people amended
their dates of birth – moving them forward 11 days to accord with the
New Style. This could have unfortunate repercussions when a date of
birth is already known and a search is requested for the baptismal
entry. Other questions such as the extent to which births were unregistered in the early years of Civil Registration have been the subject
of interest from time to time but have not been fully resolved. Lacking the time for a thorough study of primary sources I have been able
only to marshall the available evidence and opinions.

3

The importance of not treating parish registers in isolation but of using them in strict conjunction with other sources may to many genealogists seem to hardly need stressing. However, in my experience it is surprising how many genealogists, while paying lip service to the principle seem baffled when they run into difficulties, such as the presence of a number of families of the same name or inability to trace marriages, whereas the raw material for overcoming these difficulties is often already close at hand.

Most other matters of interest with regard to original registers are dealt with in the article entitled *Form and Content.* Here I must acknowledge again my debt to my four principal predecessors in this field, – R. Bigland (1764) J.S. Burn (1829 and 1862) R.E. Chester Waters (1887) and Dr. J.C. Cox (1910) and the reader will find that they are cited fairly frequently. However, the half-century since the publication of Dr. Cox's work has seen the birth of the *Genealogists' Magazine,* the *Amateur Historian, Family History, Archives, Journal of the Society of Archivists* and many other useful periodicals, and the discoveries and observations of numerous genealogists, antiquarians and archivists more often than not either lie completely forgotten in the past issues of these (as well, of course, as the venerable *Notes and Queries* which was started in 1849) or else have never been published at all. This article has therefore aimed at being as far as possible a statement of present knowledge on the subject. Inevitably the decision whether to include material in this article or in *Parish Registers and the Genealogist* has been sometimes rather arbitrary. However, where topics such as *Spelling,* the *Calendar change* of 1752 *Adult Baptisms* or *Post-1837 registers* clearly merit inclusion in both, they have been treated fully in one and more briefly in the other, with a suitable cross reference. In *Form and Content* and its appendices will be found further unresolved questions. Were the majority of clandestine marriages due to parental opposition or merely because the *marriage mongers* offered a cheaper service than the local vicar? To what extent and at what periods and places did the poorest class not bother to go through any form of marriage ceremony at all? There are also many aspects of the alias and of naming customs which have not been fully examined. The appendices to the *Form and Content* article attempt to deal with these and other questions which while of general genealogical interest rather than arising solely from the use of parish registers are nevertheless important in interpreting correctly information which may be found in them and giving some guidance on where to look if it is not.

The article on *Modern Copies* to some extent supplements *Parish Registers and the Genealogist* although again some overlapping has proved inevitable. Misreading of entries has proved not only a pitfall for the searcher, but for the copyist as well. In both these articles and occasionally elsewhere by kind permission of the authors and publishers,

4

use has been made of material from *Genealogical Research in England and Wales* by D.E. Gardner and F. Smith (*published Bookcraft Ltd, Salt Lake City, Utah U.S.A.*) The early part of the article overlaps the Appendix to the *History* article. Parish Register transcription has always been closely associated with the preservation of the original registers, and in the nineteenth century many strenuous efforts were made to ensure that the originals were placed in safe custody and that copies were made at public expense.

It is to be hoped that the article on *Modern Copies* will encourage more members of the Society of Genealogists to undertake much needed transcription work. In recent years there has been a great increase in the number of transcribers, but apart from the extensive microfilming of the Church of Jesus Christ of Latter Day Saints, it is probably true to say that the bulk of transcriptions are still made by a fairly small group of devoted workers. Many genealogists seem quite content to make use of the labours of others without fulfilling their moral obligation to make some contribution. At the same time, whilst stressing the importance of transcription, this article gives a word of warning against relying too much on copies. Not infrequently these are inaccurate or incomplete or both.

The article on *Bishop's Transcripts* to a large extent breaks fresh ground. No complete study of this subject seems to have been published before, though again, my work has to a large extent been editorial – bringing together small items of information or observations which have appeared in numerous books and articles.

Parish Registers are of course of value to the historian as well as to the genealogist, for they frequently contain references to events of local or national importance. Since this work is concerned only with *Sources of Births, Marriages and Deaths* these have not been included in the *Form and Content* article, and readers are referred to chapter VIII of J.S. Burn's *History of Parish Registers in England*, to chapters 8-12 of Dr. Cox's *The Parish Registers of England*[1] or to the shorter summary in W.E. Tate's *The Parish Chest*.[2] Apart from historical notes and the *briefs*, also often of considerable historical interest, parish registers may also contain further material of more direct value to the genealogist. Lists of Parishioners are sometimes found. Most commonly, these are lists of those who subscribed to oaths of loyalty (e.g. in 1642 or 1715) or of those who in times of crisis such as the Napoleonic Wars joined the local militia. Lists of dissenters or papists are also occasionally found.

An extremely interesting development in recent years has been the use of the entries of baptisms, marriages and burials for the study of

---

[1]   Chapter viii *Accidents*, ix *Plague and other Sickness*, x *Historical*, xi *Storms, Frosts and Fires*, xii *Olla Podrida* (numerous miscellaneous items)

[2]   Interesting items will also be found in *N + Q* Ser 6 vol 2 pp.288-9, 375. vol 10. p.337.

historical demography. Of course population statistics have always been largely based on parish registers, but the work of the *Cambridge Group for the History of Population and Social Structure* goes much further than this and hinges on Family Reconstitution – the reconstruction of every family in numerous representative parishes to firstly obtain accurate statistics for, and secondly discover the reasons for regional or occupational variations in such matters as age at marriage, number of children, illegitimacy – in short the whole pattern of human behaviour. This exciting work, which should be of interest to every person concerned with the wider implications of genealogical research, is outlined by Dr. E.A. Wrigley in the article on *"Parish Registers and the Historian"*. Parish Registers are also being used by the Cambridge Group in other ways. Another member – Dr. Roger Schofield has begun work on a survey of minimal literacy using the signatures or marks in post-Hardwicke registers as his main source.

In conclusion, I should like to thank A.J. Willis, E. Roe, T.F. Allen, C.R. Humphery-Smith and W.E. Tate for reading through preliminary drafts of several of the articles in this section and for offering useful comments and suggestions for their improvement.

I. HISTORY

Mediaeval Registers

In Mediaeval times there were no official parish registers. However, for some years before the Reformation monastic houses, especially the smaller ones, and parish priests had developed the custom of keeping informal registers of the births and deaths in the leading local families.

Thus Dr. J.C. Cox points out. [1]

"In the highly interesting fourteenth century chartulary of the Chantries of Crich, Derbyshire, there are entries of the exact deathdays of various members of the Wakebridge family and their connections from 1344 to 1368 inserted in the calendar. [2]

The twelfth Century obituary of the Priory of Cistercian nuns at Wintney, Hants, printed by Hearne in 1729, abounds in entries of the death-days not only of prioresses and sisters of the convent, but also a variety of benefactors both lay and clerical. There are also two most notable and exceptionally full obituaries extending far beyond the actual monastery, in connection with the Derbyshire Abbey of White Canons at Beauchief. [3]

The records of a serious dispute between the parishioners of St. Helen's, Abingdon, and the ancient Benedictine Abbey of that town, which came to a head in 1396, incidentally show that an exact register of the sixty seven persons buried in the new cemetery of St. Helen's from its opening in 1391 had been duly kept." [4]

In the fly leaf of the Chartulary of St. John of Jerusalem [5] from 1492 to 1500 is the following entry of marriage:

"Memor^d. The iij^{de} day of Novembre the xviij yere of Kynge Henry the Eighth, w^{t}in the howse of Sancte Johns Clerkenwell in the Buttery of the same my Lorde Thomas Docwra Prior ther beyng the same tyme present John Docwra sone and heire of Thomas Docwra of Kyrkeby Kendall, in the countie of Westmland, gentilman beyng of the age of xviij yeres and more and Margaret Turpyn, second daughter and heire of Edward Turpyn now departed of the Countie of Leyceyter gentilwoman, beyng of the full age of xiii yeres and more, of ther mere fre will and mynde w^{t}oute fere, drede or compulsion of any man the said John toke unto his wiffe the forseid

---

[1] Dr. J.C. Cox *The Parish Registers of England*, p. 236.
[2] Harl.Ms 3669. See Dr. Cox's *Churches of Derbyshire* IV, 36-47.
[3] See *Victoria County History of Derbyshire*, vol ii. 68.
[4] *Victoria County History of Berks*, vol ii. 56-57.
[5] Lansdown Ms.

Margaret, and the seid Margaret toke unto hire husband the forseid John and thereunto each to other plighted and gave ther feythe and trew the desiryng and requyrynge witnesse for the same Thomas...anie... Elizabeth Chomley Rowland Brae Thomas Chicheley John Docwra Thomas Larke and Willyam Bardesey with divers others at that time beyng present".[6]

Baptisms, Marriages and Burials were sometimes recorded in Missals and Psalters. Thus, in *Proofs of Age*, there are references such as the following.

"37 Ed. III — Roger de Broderegge recollects the day, because Agnes, his wife died on the following Sunday, and the day of her death is enrolled in the Missal at Slinfold Church"

"Because his brother, William Elcham, married on that day, and is enrolled in the Missal of Clithurst Church"

"Because Joan, his wife, died that day, and the day of her death is enrolled in the Psalter of Midhurst"

"25 Ed. III — Because Alice, his wife was buried that day in the said Church and the day of her death was enrolled in the Calendar of the Missal".[7]

Nevertheless, until the end of the fifteenth Century, the keeping of registers was entirely a personal matter for the individual parish priest, but the difficulties which arose in trying to prove ages or establish descent made a more general system imperative. The first such system in Western Europe was established in Spain. In 1497 Cardinal Ximenes exerted all his influence to secure that firstly throughout his own province of Toledo, then through all Western Europe, there should be a proper registration of baptisms.

Thomas Cromwell's Injunctions 1538.

In 1535 and 1536 a notion gained ground in England that the Vice-Gerent, Thomas Cromwell, intended to introduce some such registration system here. There was popular suspicion that any scheme of the sort. would be found to have fiscal connections, and it was not until 5 September 1538, after the final suppression of the Pilgrimage of Grace and the Lincolnshire Rising, which this rumour had helped to foment, that Cromwell ventured to issue his mandate. This ordered every parson, vicar, or curate to enter in a book every wedding, christening and burial in his parish, with the names of the parties. The parish was to provide a "sure coffer" with two locks, the parson having the custody of one key, the wardens that of the other. The entries for the proceeding week were to be made each Sunday after service in the presence of one of the wardens. The mandate was enforced under a penalty of 3s. 4d. to be applied towards the repair

---

[6] cited in J.S. Burn *History of Parish Registers in England* (1862 edn) p. 168.
[7] J.S. Burn op. cit. p. 11 footnote.

of the church.

These entries were generally made upon paper, sometimes upon loose sheets. The majority of paper books were destroyed when the entries were copied up into parchment books in 1598. Nevertheless, a few do survive such as those of Staplehurst, Kent, Banbury, Oxon and Great Berkhamsted, Herts.

Cromwell's injunction was repeated by Edward VI in 1547 with the modification that in future any fine should be given to the poor. Edward's order was re-enacted the same year in the Canterbury visitation articles. In 1555 and 1557 Cardinal Pole required the bishops in their visitations to see that the names of sponsors were duly entered in the registers of baptisms. In 1559, soon after her accession, Queen Elizabeth repeated Cromwell's edict in more rigorous terms.

Constitution of Canterbury Province 1597.

Abortive registration bills were introduced in Parliament in 1563 and 1590, and on 25 October 1597 a provincial constitution of Canterbury, approved by the Queen in 1598, ordered that parchment registers should be purchased by each parish, and that all names from the older (usually paper) registers should be copied therein from the beginning, 'but especially since the first year of her Majesty's reign'. This time it was ordered that entries should be made as before, on Sundays, but in the presence of *both* wardens. Every page was to be subscribed by them as well as by the minister, and it was ordered that the coffer should have a third lock, the minister and each warden to have a key. The entries of the past week were to be read out each Sunday after service. Finally, it was provided that the churchwardens of each parish should, within a month after Easter each year, transmit to the Diocesan Registry a transcript of the register entries for the preceding year.

The canons of 1603 include an order based on the constitution of 1597-8, with the modification that the period during which the church-wardens were ordered to send in their transcripts was altered to within a month of Lady Day. The order as to public reading of entries was not repeated, but the injunctions as to the three locks of the coffer and the recording of entries in the registers on Sundays were reiterated in the canon.

Apparently, scriveners i.e. skilled writing clerks were employed in the larger parishes to transcribe the paper books on to parchment, but in the smaller parishes the transcription was done by the clergy, who often recorded the fact in the transcript. However, the church-wardens' accounts at All Hallows, Hoo, Kent show that in some cases the registers were transcribed at "the office", probably that of the Diocesan Registrar. As a rule the transcripts were well written, but

9

the transcribers generally welcomed the limit of the first year of
Elizabeth, treating it as a maximum instead of a minimum, and omit-
ting all entries prior to 1558. They ignored all except those of
baptisms, marriages, and burials, and often standardised and
truncated these, as can be seen from the paper books which have
survived, such as that of Great Berkhamsted, Herts. As noted above
the original paper books were usually destroyed. The continuance of
one handwriting for many years at the beginning of a parchment
register is evidence of transcription from an earlier (usually the
paper) book, but in many instances it is evident that the transcripts
were made long after 1603.

Some parishes such as Burton Latimer, Northants, Barming, Kent
and Nursted, Kent procured, not parchment books but narrow strips
of membranes, which were stitched together to form a roll.

It is a matter of some debate whether on balance the 1597
Constitution did more good than harm. On the one hand the intention
was to ensure that registers were better kept, and indeed whatever
view one takes of post-1598 registers, it is possible that, but for
the 1597 injunction their state might have been worse. Furthermore,
it did try and ensure that a second security duplicate was made
which in innumerable cases is now the only copy extant. However, on
the other hand the vague wording of the act which ensured in practice
the wilful destruction of nearly all existing registers with the
fuller details they contained and the complete loss of so many entries
between 1538 and 1558 and perhaps some dating back to the fifteenth
century, was a disaster unparalled in the whole history of Parish
Registers.

The Civil War and the Commonwealth.

The period of the Civil War and the Commonwealth was one of
ecclesiastical anarchy, which seriously affected parish registers.
The Long Parliament abolished the royal supremacy and made itself
the supreme judge in ecclesiastical matters. Many clergy were ejected
in 1643, on refusal to take the Covenant, more in 1645 when the
Prayer Book was forbidden and most of those who had so far retained
their benefices were ejected by the Committees of Triers established
by Cromwell in 1653 to examine every candidate for a benefice.

On 6 Dec. 1644/4 Jan 1645, the same ordinance which substituted
the 'Directory' for the Prayer Book required that each parish or
chapelry in the country should provide a 'fair Register Book of
Velim' wherein were to be recorded the dates of baptisms as before,
plus the dates of births and the parents' names. The regulations as
to marriage entries remained unchanged. but it was ordered that each
burial entry was to record also the date of death. The Civil War being
then in progress, there are very few parish registers in which

these directions were observed. Much more important changes were
introduced by an act pased in 1653 by Barebone's Parliament. By this,
the government took away from the ministers not merely the custody
of the registers but even the solemnisation of the marriage ceremony
itself. The latter of these functions was entrusted to the justices,
the former to a new secular official, the *Parish Register* (sic),
elected by all the ratepayers in a parish and sworn before, and
approved by, a magistrate. Sometimes the minister of the parish was
elected *Register*. In other parishes the parish clerk was chosen. All
registration functions were entrusted to these officials at a fee of
12d. per birth and baptism, and 4d. per death and burial. Two con-
tiguous or intermixed parishes were sometimes amalgamated for
registration purposes. Some parishes entirely ignored the new legislation. With the establishment of civil marriage, all other marriages
were made illegal, a rider which was omitted when this act was confirmed in 1657. In many places, fron then until the end of the
Commonwealth, marriages were celebrated by magistrate and *Register*
jointly. The legality of the Commonwealth Civil Marriages was confirmed by statute after the Restoration. A common feature of the
registers at this time is the entry of dates of birth and of banns
or "publication of intent" as they were called, as well as, or instead
of, those of baptism and of marriage by a Justice of the Peace.

Generally, however, the outstanding feature of the registers during
the Interregnum is the haphazard and half-hearted fashion in which
they were kept at any rate until 1653, and sometimes throughout the
whole period. In and after 1660 it is quite usual to find entries
explaining the lacunae in the registers, especially those from about
1642 to the beginning of civil registration 1653. Archdeacon Fearon
notes,[8] however, that in Hampshire the *Registers* generally did their
work well.

The Restoration.

With the Restoration, the bishops and clergy who survived
returned to their sees and benefices. By 1660 there were many people
who were unbaptised; the Office for "The Ministration of Baptism to
such as are of riper years" was drawn up and approved by Convocation
in 1661, and a number of adult baptisms appear in the registers from
1660.

Acts for Burial in Woollen.

The first act ordering burial in woollen was passed in 1666 in
order to encourage the wool trade. In 1678 a second act was passed,
with more stringent regulations, ordering the production of an

---

[8] W.A. Fearon and W.E. Williams *Parish Registers and Parochial
    Documents in the Archdeaconry of Winchester* (1909).

11

affidavit signed by a magistrate.[9] In 1680 a concession was made allowing the affidavit to be signed by a minister.

Registration of Births 1680.

In 1680 parents were ordered to register with the clergy the birth of every child and to pay a fee of 6d., but the act was generally neglected.

Tax on Marriages, Births and Burials, 1694.

In 1694 Parliament granted the Crown, for a quinquennial period "for carrying on the war against France with vigour" a duty of 2s. per birth, 2s.6d. per marriage and 4s. per burial of all non-paupers, with a sliding scale rising to £30 for the birth of the eldest son of a duke, £50 for a duke's marriage and £50 for his burial.[10] An act, of the following year laid down that a fine of 40s was to be imposed on parents who failed to notify the rector or vicar within five days of the birth of a child, and he was to record them for a fee of 6d, under a like penalty. It was specially provided that a birth should not be exempt from tax merely because the parents failed to have the child christened, but nevertheless in many parishes such births were not registered, and presumably no tax was paid. In other parishes, however, there is clear evidence that the parson in his capacity of tax-collector looked up the neglectful parishoner and collected the tax, plus, one hopes, his sixpenny fee. How little the acts were regarded may be judged from the fact that in 1705 it was thought necessary to pass an act of indemnity on behalf of the clergy who had neglected to obey these provisions, and who, in consequence, were liable to colossal fines. In 1702-3 a committee of Convocation drew up a list of ecclesiastical offences notoriously requiring remedy, in which irregularity in keeping the registers is prominent. Another act was passed in 1711 ordering the keeping of proper register books with ruled and numbered pages. Many such registers were started, but the act was generally ignored and no efforts were made to ensure that its provisions were kept.

Lord Hardwicke's Marriage Act, 1753.

Until the year 1753 a marriage was valid[11] if performed by a priest even without banns or licence, although the parties were liable to censure, and the priest to heavy legal penalties. Such penalties were useless where the priest had neither liberty nor benefice to lose,

---

[9]   For the effect of these acts on the burial registers, see *Form and Content*, pages 72-73.

[10] There were also taxes on Bachelors and childless widowers which necessitated parish censuses. See *Other Records: Some Brief Notes* p.334.

[11] For discussion on the validity of marriages celebrated other than in the Anglican Church, see *Clandestine Marriages* pages 292-294, 315, *Form and Content* page 62 and *Roman Catholics* in Volume II.

so legal marriages were performed by disreputable priests, especially by those imprisoned in the Fleet for debt. Clandestine and scandalous marriages were also performed in churches or chapels which had real or pretended exemption from the jurisdiction of the bishop. Entries may be found in most registers of the marriage of persons neither of whom resided in the parish.[12] This laxity was dealt with by Lord Hardwicke's Act of 1753, entitled "An Act for the better preventing of clandestine marriages", of which the principal provisions were (1) that every marriage should be by licence or banns; (2) that the ceremony should be performed in the parish where one of the parties resided, and (3) that the record should be kept "in proper books of vellum or good and durable paper" to be provided by the churchwardens. The entries were to be signed by the parties and witnesses, and were to follow a prescribed form, and the registers were to be "carefully kept and preserved for public use". This is the origin of the Hardwicke marriage registers, the first to consist of bound volumes of printed forms. Forms for banns and marriages could be obtained in separate volumes or a combined volume could be used containing banns forms at the beginning followed by those for marriages, or the two could be combined in each entry. Where separate banns volumes were kept, these have often since disappeared.

Legalisation of Marriages in recently built Churches or Chapels 1781.

The Hardwicke Act had specified that for a marriage to be valid it must be solemnised in a church or chapel where banns had been theretofore usually published. In 1781 the Court of King's Bench annulled a marriage made in a chapel erected in 1765. An Act was therefore passed directing that all marriages solemnised before 1st August 1781 in any church or public chapel erected since 1753 should be valid and the registers should be received as evidence in all courts.

This Act also affected the location of registers in that it specified that the registers of all marriages solemnised in chapels should within twenty days be removed to the parish church of the parish in which such a chapel was situated to be kept with the marriage register of the parish.

The Stamp Act 1783.

The Stamp Act of 1783 granted to the Crown a stamp duty of threepence upon every parish register entry of a burial, marriage, birth, or christening, the officiating minister who collected the duty being allowed a commission of 10 per cent for his trouble. Two

---

[12] For a fuller examination of this subject, see *Clandestine Marriages* pages 313-314.

years later this act was extended to cover Nonconformists. This legislation – the second attempt to use the registers for fiscal purposes – remained in force only until 1794 when it was repealed.

Rose's Act 1812.

In 1812 an act known as *Rose's Act* was passed "for the better regulating and preserving Parish and other Registers of births, baptisms, marriages and burials in England". It is printed in full at the beginning of the baptismal registers issued in 1813. It ordered registers of baptisms, marriages and burials to be kept in every parish, such registers to be printed in a prescribed form, provided by the King's Printer in the first instance, and afterwards by the churchwardens. The registers were to be kept in the custody of the incumbent in a dry, well-painted iron chest. The minister who performed the ceremony was to sign each entry of baptism or burial within seven days, and parchment copies of the entries were to be made annually and sent to the registrar of each diocese. These were to be preserved by him in a safe building, carefully arranged and thoroughly indexed. Persons making false entries or altering, damaging or destroying the registers were made liable to transportation for fourteen years. No other penalty was provided but yet, by a curious lapse, provision was made that one half of the fines or penalties should go to the informer, and the remainder to the poor of the parish, or to such charitable purposes as the bishop might direct. The act also ordered lists of all extant register books to be sent to the bishop of the diocese.

The 1812 Act also directed that the Bishop and Chancellor should before 1st Feb. 1813 make a survey of the places where parish registers were kept, and report their opinion to the Privy Council upon the most suitable mode of remunerating the officers employed in each Registry for their additional trouble and expense in carrying out provisions of the Act. Only one report was made viz from the Diocese of Lichfield and Coventry which recommended that the remuneration to the officers in each Registry should be paid out of the County rate.

This act ended the parchment registers and introduced the familiar books which are devoid of entries recording other events of interest. The sending in of Bishop's Transcripts, though still by no means invariably observed became more regular from now on but little effort was made to implement the act's injunctions with regard to their cataloguing and indexing. [13]

---

[13] For a fuller treatment of this subject see article on *Bishop's Transcripts*, page 173.

General Registration Act, 1836.

In 1836, just on three hundred years after Thomas Cromwell had instituted registration of baptisms, marriages and burials, the State passed the General Registration Act instituting civil registration of births, marriages and deaths. This act left the Parish Registers of baptisms and burials in the forms provided by Rose's Act and authorised the issue from the office of the Registrar-General of the marriage registers bound in green cloth which are now in use. Copies of the marriage entries were to be sent each quarter to the District Registrar, and through him to the Registrar-General. Since the passing of this act Parish registers no longer have a unique value as the sole written evidence of births, marriages or deaths and certificates of entries in them are seldom required for civil purposes.

APPENDIX.   THE PRESERVATION OF REGISTERS

Apart from the negligence which occurred almost universally with
regard to the entering of data in the registers,[1] most parish registers
seem to have been treated with scant respect at any time in their history. Conscientious clergy and clerks abounded, of course but the careful custody of generations was frequently undone by one negligent
holder, and fortunate indeed was the parish which sooner or later did
not suffer in this way.

The loss of registers had already started even before 1598. At
Kirton in Lindsey, Lincs. according to a note in the earliest extant
register the register is missing since one "Vicar was maryed and
deprived and ye next incumbent kep one that non can fynd"[2].
J.S. Burn quotes numerous illustrations of the wilful destruction or
mutilation of registers,[3] and some of these were summarized by
R.E. Chester Waters as follows:

> "They were cut up for patterns by tailors and lacemakers, mutilated by
> collectors of autographs, and sold for waste paper, almost without remon-
> strance, except from a few indignant antiquaries. The parchment books suf-
> fered more than the paper ones from the greater number of uses to which the
> materials could be turned. In one parish in Sussex they were cut up by the
> clergyman into slips, which he used as labels for addressing baskets of
> game; and when Mr. Bell inquired for the early registers at Christchurch,
> in Hampshire, for the purpose of producing them in the House of Lords as
> evidence in the Huntingdon peerage case, he found that they had been con-
> verted into kettle-holders by the wife of a former curate. It may safely be
> affirmed that the negligence of the eighteenth century was more destructive
> than the civil wars of the seventeenth."[4]

The surprising thing is, not that so many registers have disappeared but that so many still survive. It seems to have been the normal
practice for the registers to have been kept by the clerk, but this was
quite illegal. In one lawsuit the parish register had been seen at the
home of the clerk. It was held that as the 1812 Act directed registers
to be kept by the clergyman, the evidence was inadmissible.[5] If this
decision seems a little harsh one must remember that the inadequate
custody of registers has enabled a considerable number of forged entrie

---

[1]   See *Form and Content* pp 27–32.
[2]   W.E. Tate *The Parish Chest* p.44.
[3]   *History of Parish Registers in England* (1862 edn) Chap.3.pp.40-64.
[4]   R.E. Chester Waters. *Parish Registers in England* (1887) p.95.
[5]   *Doe d Arundell v Fowler.* N & Q 4th Ser. 1 p.199 1868.

16

to be made from time to time. Perhaps the most notorious were those described at a trial at Liverpool in 1886 when 50 forged entries had been made in the registers of Preston, Kirkham, Poulton, and Lytham and the Bishop's Transcripts for Preston, Kirkham and Penwortham, not to mention three entire forged Marriage Bonds.[6]

Listing of Registers

The first attempt to secure a census of Parish Registers was Rose's Act of 1812. This ordered that lists of parish registers were to be sent by each incumbent to the Bishop. However, nothing was done to enforce this. J. Rickman, Clerk of the House of Commons after consultation with J.S. Burn prevailed on the authorities to include in the 1831 Census the compilation of a list of all register books in England and Wales with the dates of commencement and termination of each. This revealed enormous recent losses:

> On a comparison of the dates of the Sussex registers seen by Sir W. Burrell between 1770 and 1780 and of those returned as the earliest in the population returns of 1831, the old registers in no less than 29 parishes had in the interval disappeared, whilst during the same half century, nineteen old registers had found their way back to the proper depository.[7]

Nevertheless the government, which had gone to considerable expense to obtain fairly reliable statistics on the loss of registers, did nothing whatever to stop it. In 1910 Dr. J.C. Cox lamented:

> "There is alas, no doubt whatsoever that there has been shocking carelessness with regard to the safe custody of parish registers since the 1831 return was compiled. There were at that time 772 registers beginning in 1538; there are now (1910) we believe 656."[8]

No further government census of parish registers has even been taken, though of course surveys have been made of many counties through the initiative of local societies, the religious authorities, archivists, or private individuals. In 1872 a bill for a further census of parish registers moved by Lord Romilly in the Lords[9] failed to gain enough support even though Bishop's Transcripts and Marriage Licences were not included.[10]

However, genealogists have been rightly less concerned with

---

[6] See T.P. Earwaker *A Lancashire Pedigree Case* (Warrington 1887). Other forgeries are described in *N & Q* Vol. 155 pp. 352-354, 376, 463 and 7th Ser. I p. 243.

[7] W. Durrent Cooper *N & Q* 1st Ser. I p. 443 (1850).

[8] Cox *The Parish Registers of England* (1910) p. 239 Examples of carelessness have been frequently given in *Notes and Queries*. e.g. 2nd Ser. Vol. 3 pp. 321-3.

[9] *N & Q* 4th Ser. p. 251.

[10] Their inclusion in the proposed survey was strongly urged in *N & Q* 4th Ser. 5 pp. 464, 504, 606.

maintaining accurate records of registers in ecclesiastical hands than with removing them altogether from the custody of the clergy.

Agitation for Further Legislation

An Act of Parliament to secure the centralization of parish registers has been the constant aim of genealogists and antiquarians and hardly a year went by in the second half of the 19th century without some correspondence on the subject in the columns of *Notes and Queries*. The most favourable opportunity was of course missed in 1836 when Civil Registration was instituted and a commission set up to examine the question of authentication and centralization of Nonconformist registers, whose recommendations were subsequently carried out. [11] The reasons why parish registers were left untouched are uncertain. Certainly the act was passed largely as a result of a campaign waged by the Nonconformists who achieved all they wanted. T.P. Taswell-Langmead observed: [12]

> The Act however was not passed without strong opposition and the government may possibly have hesitated to provoke additional hostility by proposing to deprive the parochial clergy of the custody of the old registers or the idea of collecting these registers into a central depository in London may not then have presented itself.

However, the need for further legislation was immediately apparent. In 1850 there was a letter addressed to R. Monckton Milnes Esq. M.P. *on the Condition and unsafe State of the Ancient Parochial Registers in England and the Colonies.* [13] In 1857 a correspondent in *Notes and Queries* optimistically suggested:

> If Parliament should decide upon having all the parish registers from 1538 to 1837 deposited in some metropolitan office, the books as they arrived should be, for convenience of reference, arranged in counties alphabetically and the parishes also in alphabetical order under the counties to which they belong, the missing registers being as far as practicable supplied by the diocesan transcripts: the books should also be forthwith numbered and paged and the necessary particulars transcribed for the indexes..... [14]

He continued with a detailed scheme for their indexing! However little has changed in a century, and today we might still say:

> It now only remains to be decided whether these public registers shall be allowed to continue scattered over the country, inaccessible to the public and liable to be falsified, lost, stolen, burnt or otherwise destroyed, or whether they shall be all collected and secured in a central office and rendered easily accessible to the present and future generations. [15]

---

[11] See *Nonconformist Registers - A General Survey* in Volume II.
[12] *N & Q* 4th Ser. 1 p.198.
[13] *N & Q* 1st Ser. i p.407.
[14] W.H.W.T. *N & Q* 2nd Ser. Vol.3 p.324.
[15] *ibid* p.324.

The following year T.P. Taswell-Langmead proposed that the Society of Antiquaries and other archaeological societies should get a petition to Parliament praying that a committee be appointed to examine the state of parochial records and to report on the feasability of transferring their custody to the Master of the Rolls.

> "My plan would be to deposit the whole of the original registers in the Record Office, Chancery Lane..... two authenticated copies of each being made, one to be deposited in the respective parishes and the other for the inspection of the public..... at the Record Office." [16]

J.S. Burn continued to agitate for legislation:

> "The late Bishop Blomfield, the late Sir James Scarlett and the late Lord Lyndhurst have each of them been convinced of this necessity..... It will be no little honour to any peer whether spiritual or temporal or any Member of our new House of Commons to take up a subject which has been entertained by such names..... and I trust..... that such a member may be found this Session for no time should be lost." [17]

Others denounced the inefficiency of the clergy in violent terms:

> "Nine vicars out of every ten, in spite of their self-sufficiency and nineteen church wardens out of every twenty, by their ignorance and pigheadedness are not fit to have the keeping of such books, as all experience has proved over and over again. " [18]

The anomalous position of the Anglican registers as compared with the Nonconformist registers was pointed out:

> This is manifestly unfair..... the birth or death of the one individual was registered at the time in the proper legal manner with a view to preserve a record of the event for the behalf of posterity, while in the other case the event was knowingly registered in such a manner as not to be legal evidence at the time..... Yet the latter registration is now in a more favourable position that the former. [19]

Most correspondents were agreed that centralization was the best policy, but differed on how the financial position of the incumbent should be safeguarded. Charles Rogers proposed that incumbents should have the custody of the registers for 20 years, [20] and Henry Moody that a proportion of the search fees should go to the incumbent. [21] In 1872 John Maclean proposed that a copy should be made of each register for the incumbent. [22] Finally in 1882 there seemed a reasonable hope that Parliament would take action. A *Parish Register Preservation Bill* provided that

---

[16] T.P. Taswell-Langmead. *N & Q.* 2nd Ser. Vol.6. p.380 (1858).
[17] J.S. Burn. *N & Q* 3rd Ser. Vol.9. p.243 (1866).
[18] P. Hutchinson. *N & Q* 4th Ser. 1. p.38 (1868).
[19] T.P. Taswell-Longmead *N & Q* 4th Ser. 1. p.199.
[20] *N & Q* 4th Ser. 2. p.20. (1868).
[21] *ibid* p.114.
[22] *N & Q* 4th Ser. 9. p.315.

> "every existing register of an earlier date than July 1st 1837 and also
> every transcript thereof remaining in any diocesan registry, shall after
> the passing of this Act be under the charge and control of the Master of
> the Rolls, and shall be removed by his warrant to the Record Office."

Unfortunately private members' bills tended to suffer the same fate
then as now, but R.E. Chester Waters optimistically predicted:

> "Although the exigencies of public business prevented the subject being
> discussed during the late session, there is little doubt that a similar
> Bill with some modifications will sooner or later receive the sanction
> of Parliament." [23]

However, a further bill introduced in 1887 by W.C. Borlase was also
dropped and when in 1894 the *Parish Councils Bill* transferred to the
custody of parish councils all documents hitherto deposited with the
parish clerk, parish registers were specifically excluded. [24] An amendment to remove pre-1837 registers to the Public Record Office after
parish councils had made authenticated copies was ruled to be beyond
the scope of the bill. In 1904, even Lord Salisbury failed to secure
the passage of a *Local Records Bill* which included Parish Registers.

Had the parish registers been centralized in 1882 or 1894 as the
Nonconformist registers were in 1840, a large number of subsequent
losses would have been avoided, for until recent years, the twentieth
century custodians have taken little better care of the registers than
their predecessors. Not only must Dr. Cox's figure now be further considerably reduced, but large numbers of later registers have also disappeared. In spite of increased record consciousness in the 20th
Century the pace of loss has continued unabated due to several factors.
There has been the usual proportion of losses or damage through fire,
flood, theft and damp and many urban registers were destroyed in the
Second World War. Much more disastrous, however, has been the amalgamation of parishes, which has often meant that the registers have been
even less efficiently supervised than before. Furthermore, a smaller
proportion of the clergy now have the inclination or the time for
antiquarian interests. The type of Victorian country parson, who was
more likely to be found inspecting Neolithic remains than visiting his
parishioners is now a rarity. Almost certainly this represents an
unqualified gain for the church, but it was such men who were the
backbone of many local antiquarian societies which have since become
defunct, and, of course, who took the greatest care of the records in
their own custody. Even deliberate destruction has sometimes been of
recent date. A correspondent in *Notes and Queries* in 1902 reported:

> "I asked for a complete copy of that certificate of marriage. The reply
> comes back that the original registers, up to a certain date late in the
> eighteenth century, have been recopied and then destroyed. The copies

---

[23] R.E. Chester Waters *op.cit.* p.98.
[24] See *Parish Councils & Parochial Records*, N & Q 8th Ser. 5. pp.61-63.

omit the names of the witnesses and other matter not judged material, the object seemingly having been to reduce the number of volumes to be stored. The destroyed registers have therefore been replaced by a record taken from them, or purporting so to have been, which contains at the head of each page a note of the year and then in two columns the precise date of the particular marriage in one column and the names of the couple·who were married on the corresponding line in the adjoining column. Each page of this list is signed by the curate and the two church wardens at foot, as having been examined and found correct."[25]

Mr. J.H. Matthews commented:

"It is monstrous that records of such priceless value as church registers should be left in any custody but that of the Master of the Rolls. They are perishing by the dozen every year."[26]

Between 1905 and 1916 the *Joint Committee of Convocation of Canterbury* produced four reports on *The Collection and Custody of Local Ecclesiastical Records*[27] which achieved nothing, and in 1927 the *Registers Commission of the Church Assembly* produced a report. They decided that parishes would generally desire to continue to be custodians of their own registers, declared themselves against any compulsory centralization and expressed their belief that:

"existing conditions though suseptible of much improvement indicate almost universal alertness on the question of the value of old registers."

Nevertheless, in order to prevent loss, neglect or misuse they made the following suggestions: [28]

"There ought to be frequent and periodic occasions when these possessions should be produced to the satisfaction of persons in authority and compared with the list in the terrier or inventory. For example: (a) The churchwardens having been responsible for the registers during a vacancy, whenever a clerk is inducted to a benefice there should be a formal handing over of the registers, after comparison with the terrier, which the new incumbent should then sign in token of having received them. (b) When an archdeacon or a rural Dean pays a visit of inspection to a parish on behalf of the Bishop, the visitor should inspect the registers and annotate the terrier accordingly. (c) These comparisons of the lists with the actual possessions should, if possible, take place in the presence of the churchwardens and of as many members as may be of the parochial church council. (d) If, for good reason, the registers are not kept either in the church or in the parsonage, the person who takes charge of them should give a receipt for them, which should remain in the custody of the parochial church council.
On the supposition that such periodic inspection reveals a case of loss or neglect or ill usage, power should be given to the Bishop, after consideration of the facts reported to him, either to order the removal

[25] *N & Q* 9th Ser. 9. p.168-9. (1902).
[26] *ibid.* p.337.
[27] **Nos. 393, 403, 441, 498.**
[28] This summary is reproduced from *Gen. Mag.* Vol.4, No.3. Sept 1928. p.62. The report is discussed in *N & Q* Vol.152. p.343.

of the registers (except those actually in use) to the diocesan registry or other central repository, or to order a particular register, or more than one, to be repaired or rebound at the expense of the parochial church council. If the incumbent and the parochial church council resolve that their registers had best be resigned into the keeping of the diocesan registry (or other local record office), the Bishop should be empowered to give an order for the transfer. In such case it would be equitable that the parson of the parish concerned should be credited with his due proportion of any fees for searches or for certificates. On the other hand, it should be possible for the parson, on being approached by historical students, to certify that, as far as he is concerned, he is willing that facilities for study should be given without charge.

It is clear that authority must be given to the Bishop to insist on the provision of a sufficiently strong and a sufficiently commodious chest or safe wherever a parish decides that its registers shall not be centralised. Similar recommendations are made with regard to insisting on due care being taken by the parochial church councils of ancient documents and to reposing power in the Bishop to order their removal to some central repository in cases of neglect."

As regards registers still held by the incumbents, these recommendations seem to have borne little fruit and losses have continued. The *Parochial Registers and Records Measure* of 1929 was in many respects disappointing. Few of the Registers Commission's recommendations were implemented. No system of inspection was laid down and there was no provision for the safe custody of the Bishop's Transcripts and Marriage Licences. [29] However, it did empower the bishops to establish one or more record offices at which incumbents could deposit registers and this has almost certainly prevented many losses. In fact the Bishop was empowered to compel deposit when he felt this was necessary. In many dioceses county record offices have been approved as diocesan record offices, and the 1962 *Local Government (Records) Act* made it clear that record offices could accept non-public records. In some counties such as Warwickshire, there has recently been such a vigorous policy of centralization that further losses of registers are unlikely. Of course centralization too has its dangers, as the destruction of the *Four Courts* in Dublin in 1922 bears witness, but when every modern precaution against loss or damage is taken, the odds against mass destruction are fairly high. The importance of ensuring that parish registers are kept in safe custody cannot be over-emphasised. Every year fresh losses are reported and a large number have come to light as a result of the work done on compiling the *National Index*.

In the years since this Appendix was written much attention has been given to improving the security and preservation of registers, very many more of which are anyway now deposited in local record offices, and there is reason to hope that such deposit, or at least custody in a modern air-conditioned safe, may shortly become mandatory.

---

[29] For more detailed criticism of the Measure see *N & Q* 155. pp. 75-76 (1929).

II. PARISH REGISTERS – FORM AND CONTENT

A. GENERAL

In the amount of detail given in Parish Registers, England was very much behind several European countries. In *Spain*, the registers had an alphabetical index, and contained ancestral details. In *Switzerland*, the Baptismal register gave the place of the marriage of the parents, and the maiden name of the mother appeared in both the baptismal and the burial registers. *Austria* and *Prussia* were even more particular. The day and hour of the birth had to be entered in the baptism register. In the mortality register full particulars of identification were compulsory, together with details of the cause of death.[1] After the Revolution the most advanced country of all was *France*, with its 40,000 civil registrars, but the previous church registers are even more defective than those of England,[2] and the civil registers of Paris were destroyed during the Commune. Of course the comparative inferiority of English registers can be exaggerated, and it must not be presumed that registration systems on the Continent were universally popular. However, the suspicion in the 1530's that parochial registration was required mainly for fiscal purposes was probably never fully allayed, and though exceptions abounded, by and large, it is probably true to say that registration was unpopular or treated lightly by parishioners, clerks and clergy. In these circumstances, it is perhaps surprising, not that so many registers have been lost, but that so many survive, and that these, on the whole, give a considerable amount of information.

Starting Dates

According to the *Parish Register Abstract* of 1831 there were 40 registers beginning before 1538. This would not seem inherently unlikely. Like the Catholic priests during the penal period,[3] most parish priests

---

[1] L.O. Henderson *"Parish Registers"*, Amateur Historian, Vol.4. No.6. Winter 1959-60.

[2] Nevertheless, as laid down by the *Council of Trent* November 1563, these invariably contain the names of godparents at Baptism. For examples, see R. Bigland. *Observations on Marriages, Baptisms and Burials are preserved in the parochial registers* (1764) p.32.

[3] See *Roman Catholics* in Volume II.

of the Old Faith must have kept entries in their missals, bibles or office books – at least for the living generations in their cure – simply to remind themselves of consanguities and spiritual relationships. [4] References to such records are frequently found in *Proofs of Age* and elsewhere. [5]

Nevertheless, although records of baptisms, marriages and burials were undoubtedly kept before the Reformation, Dr. Cox's investigations of the claims in the *Parish Register Abstract* reduced the figure of pre 1538 registers from 40 to 18 with the caveat that "this list ought possibly to be reduced by one or two. [6]

In a few cases the parish priest in 1538 transcribed at the beginning of the newly ordered official register some of the recent entries from his parochial note-book. Of the six instances quoted by Dr. Cox as being transcripts of earlier registers, [7] one at least is an error. He cites the register of *Tipton*, Staffs (ostensibly beginning in 1513) as "by far the most remarkable of these early instances." However, the 1513 date arises from a mis-reading on the part of the transcriber of 1598, and the correct date should be 1573. [8]

At the commencement of the register of *St. George, Botolph Lane* which commences in 1547 are 22 entries taken from tombs dating from 1390 to 1410, [9] which are undoubtedly the earliest entries in any parish register.

These apart, the earliest known entries are in the register of *Alfriston*, Sussex. The first entry is a marriage dated 10th July 1506. There are five marriages dated 1504, three dated 1505 and then no more until 1547. The baptisms begin in 1538 (with a gap 1540-1555 except for 3 entries for 1547) and the burials in 1547 (with a gap to 1558). [10] The transcriber of 1598 clearly copied, not a pre-1538 register, but one begun later. R.W. Muncey comments [11]

"These early entries may probably have been taken from entries made in an old service book, or from an old account book in which marriage fees

---

4   Mediaeval restrictions on marriage for reasons of consanguinity were far stricter then than those later laid down in the Anglican Prayer-book. Marriages of third or fourth cousins could be declared invalid if they had been performed without a dispensation. Spiritual relationships were contracted through god-parents, and the church's attitude to these was equally strict. See *Divorce and Annulment* p. 323.

5   For a fuller discussion of this subject and examples see *History* pp 7–8. Ma further examples are given in C.E. Ewen *History of Surnames of the British Isles* pp. 418-9.

6   J.C. Cox *The Parish Registers of England* (1910) p. 239.

7   *ibid* p. 237.

8   See *Staffs Hist.Coll.* Vol. X pt. 2 p. 134 and introduction to the printed register (Staffs Parish Register Socy.) p. iii.

9   *N & Q* 6th Ser. Vol. 2, p. 18. Curiously this register is not mentioned by Cox or any of the other authorities on Parish Registers.

10 *N & Q* 9th Series Vol. ii p. 490 (1898).

11 *The Romance of Parish Registers* p. 8.

may have been entered, or more probably they are merely the answer to enquiries made by the vicar among some of his oldest parishioners as to when and where they were married, and so entered as the first marriages under the new order of things."

The register of *Perlethorpe*, Notts, begins:

"The Register of all suche as have bynne Christened, maryed and buryed in the parish of Parlthorp Thow' sbye since the yeare 1528."[12]

The register of *Carburton*, Notts. is similarly worded, and the use of the word *since*, as Dr. Cox points out, shows that the entries were a compilation and not entered year by year.

Thus, it is not really accurate to refer to all these registers as pre-1538 registers. It is probable that the early entries in several others[13] were retrospective entries made in 1538, and it is unlikely that there are more than a handful which genuinely antedate 1538. At first sight this seems surprising, as one would have assumed that a fair proportion of personal notebooks kept by priests would have been copied up into the registers in 1538. However, the vast majority of missals and office books were destroyed at the Reformation. Many were taken abroad and it is possible that a number of mediaeval English entries of this kind may survive in Continental Catholic libraries, including the Vatican Library.[14]

The Transcripts of 1598

Another reason for the complete absence of pre-16th century entries is that nearly all surviving 16th century registers are the transcripts made in 1598, and doubtless pre-1538 entries in many registers, together

---

[12] Cox. *op. cit.* pp. 237-8.

[13] The remaining pre-1538 registers noted by Dr. Cox are *Altham*, Lancs. (1518), *Ashperton*, Herefordshire (1521), *Elsworth*, Cambs. (1528), *Stoke Hammond*, Bucks. (1534), *Wolverton*, Bucks. (1535), *Kirton*, Notts. (1535), *West Clandon*, Surrey (1536), *Parkham*, Devon, *Kingsbury*, Warwickshire, *Snaith*, Yorks., *Somersal Herbert*, Derbyshire, *Eling*, Hunts., *Fairstead*, Essex, *Shrawley*, Worcs. (all 1537). To this list may be added *St. James, Garlickythe*, London (1535).

[14] In 1934 a Mr. Townend, an Australian wrote to the editor of the *Genealogists' Magazine* saying that when in Rome in 1884 he was assured by officials of the Vatican Library that there were pre-Reformation English registers in the Vatican (Gen. Mag. Vol.6. No.10. June 1934 p.434.) and later added (p.565) that the party of which he was a member was shown some of these ancient registers through the influence of the Earl of Carlisle. This provoked an official statement from Monseigneur Angelo Mercati, Prefect of the Archives at the Vatican (Gen. Mag. Vol.7. p.21) that 'there are no Papal registers of pre-Reformation, Births, Marriages etc at all.' However, it is not impossible that the party of which Mr. Townend was a member was shown a few pre-Reformation missals or even rough note books with English entries which may have given rise to the legend of vast numbers of "Papal Registers."

perhaps with all other entries before 1558 were ignored by the copyist
Dr. Cox lists 656 registers beginning in 1538 and a further 205 beginning in 1539 although these figures must now be somewhat reduced. It i
curious that some counties have a much higher proportion of early registers than others. Thus in *Worcestershire* about a quarter of the registers begin in 1538 or 1539 and it would seem likely that when the
Constitution of 1597[15] was put into operation the Bishop of Worcester
gave a general directive for registers to be copied from 1538. In most
counties, however, the transcribers welcomed the limit of the first
year of Elizabeth as a maximum instead of a minimum and ignored all
entries before that date. Furthermore they usually omitted not only
religious, social or historical comments in the original paper registers but often personal information as well. Thus an entry in the
transcript of *St. Dunstan's West*, London, reads:

"1560-1, Feb 17. Mr. Rithe buried"

The old paper book adds:

"a benchar of Lyncolnes Yne buryed out of the newe brycke byldynge, beyng
in owre p'ishe, the hether syde of Lyncolnes Yne."[16]

In accordance with the Injunctions of 1598 the transcripts are normally
signed at the foot of every page by the minister and churchwardens of
the year in which the copy was made.[17] A few of the 1598 transcriptions
were on parchment strips sewn together to form a roll.[18]

The majority even of the 1598 transcripts have since disappeared
and it is not uncommon for the existing registers of a parish to com-
mence after the starting dates of the Bishop's Transcripts.

Later Transcripts

Many registers were recopied for one reason or another at various
times in the 17th and 18th centuries. One of the earliest of these
post-1598 transcriptions was at *Stepney*. In the Stepney Parish Vestry
Minutes appears the following entry:

"At a vestrye holden the 14th Decemb[r] 1613 in the vestrye in the
Church It is agreed in maner folowing..... Also yt is agreed that where-
as there is much of the Register unrecorded as well for Christnings
Mariages and Burialls where through much hurt may arise, that therefore
Peter Wright If he like yt shall haue foure pounds for the full recording
of all that is yet unrecorded vnto the time of the death of Jhon
Brockbanke late clerke and keper of the Registye of if he shall make

---

[15] See *History* p. 9.

[16] R.E. Chester Waters. *Parish Registers in England* p. 10. Also cited by Cox.
      op. cit. p. 17.

[17] Lack of information on this subject caused some antiquarians of the last
      century to make absurd attributions of longevity to some ministers and
      churchwardens! See R.E. Chester Waters. *op. cit.* p. 10.

[18] See *History* p. 10.

refusall thereof then the Churchwardens to provide some other who for
theaforesaid summe shall faithfully transcribe all that is to be found
into the severall perchm^t bookes and they the Churchwardens to see that
the same be perfectlye finished by the feast of Easter next ensuing." [19]

The Keeping of the Registers
Clerk's Rough Notebooks

All sixteenth century registers and many of the seventeenth and
eighteenth centuries are therefore secondary texts. However, it is not
generally appreciated that seventeenth and eighteenth Century parish
registers are very frequently copies of a primary text, probably a
memorandum book kept for the purpose. Thus at *Cartmel*, Lancashire, in
the period 1724 to 1751, baptisms were entered up for a whole year,
then the marriages and lastly the burials, after which the cycle was
repeated for the next year. The three sets of entries follow each other
without any gaps and therefore the register was written up once a year.
Other cases are known where the writing up was done monthly and sometimes quarterly. Such book-keeping could only be done from notes or
memoranda made at about the time of the ceremonies themselves. Portions
of such notes have sometimes survived; thus there are two paper volumes
at *Warrington*, Lancs. described as "duplicates" a Curate's Paper
Book at *Harpenden*, Herts. several pages at *Cartmel*, and a single page
at *Walton*, (near Liverpool). Detailed comparison establishes beyond-
doubt that the official parchment register is indeed a copy of the
paper notes. Not only are the latter more detailed, the copyist having
exercised the functions of an editor, suppressing minor details or even
whole entries but also he has made mistakes such as telescoping
together the first half of one entry to the second half of the next one.
In the *Cartmel* Register is the entry:

1769 Aug 5 Richard Maychell or Wraysholme buried.

The paper original adds

"lunatick; poison'd by eating nightshade berries".

Again 1769:

"July 11 John Hadwen of Lindale, buried",

The copyist had suppressed:

"aged 24, drown'd bathing near Holme" [20]

This custom of copying entries into the register from a rough note
book seems to have been widespread in the 18th century over most of the

---

[19] Hill and Frere. *Memorial of Stepney Parish.* Curiously the preface states
that the registers date from 1579 and are perfect!
[20] Dr. D.R. Dickinson *The Value of Bishop's Transcripts and some notes on
Parish Registers.* Gen. Mag, Vol,ix, No.6, June 1952 p.212-213.

country and probably occurred to some extent throughout the entire period from 1538 to 1837. For this practice the Act of 1538 and the Canons of 1603 were partly to blame. Canon LXX emphasises the provision of the 1538 Act

"And for the safe keeping of the said book, the churchwardens, at the charge of the parish shall provide one sure coffer with three locks and keys, whereof the one to remain with the minister, and the other two with the churchwardens severally, so that neither the minister without the two churchwardens, nor the churchwardens without the minister, shall at any time take that book out of the said coffer. And henceforth upon every Sabbath day, immediately after morning or evening prayer, the minister and churchwardens shall take the said parchment book out of the said coffer and the minister, in the presence of the churchwardens, shall write and record in the said book the names of all persons christened, together with the names and surnames of their parents, and also the names of all persons married and buried in that parish in the week before, and the day and year of every such christening, marriage and burial, and that done, they shall lay up that book in the coffer as before. "

If this injunction was properly complied with, it made inevitable either the keeping of a rough register or omissions and errors due to lapse of memory. In point of fact, where a rough register was kept, the entries were usually copied up much less frequently than weekly and it is clear that such a system made omissions due to carelessness and for-getfulness more likely. In 1651 the Vicar of *Carshalton*, Surrey dis-claims responsibility for several vacant years in the register and claims:

"The special ground of that pretermission ought to be imputed to Richard Finch the parish clerke, whose office it was by long proscription to gather the ephemeris, or dyary of the dayly passages and to exhibit them once a yeare to be transcribed into this registry; and though I often called upon him agayne and agayne to remember his chardje and he always told me that he had the accompts lying by him....."[21]

In the neighbouring parish of *Mitcham* the clerk kept a similar rough note-book and this has survived. A comparison with the parish register shows:

"In many cases, as might be expected, entries made by the former are omit-ted by the latter, and vice versa. But where entries are found in both, they often disagree in the matter of dates, and sometimes even in the christian names, the surnames, or the relationship of the parties con-cerned."[22]

Sometimes discrepancies between two surviving lists of entries defy

---

[21] The full text of this interesting entry is printed in Cox – *op.cit* p.20. Cox uses this quotation to illustrate the irregularities of the Interreg-num, but curiously fails to draw attention to its importance in showing the manner in which registers were written up.

[22] *Gen. Mag.* Vol.7 No.3 p.109.

explanation. In the oldest register of *North Cadbury*, Somerset, folios
99 and 100 both purport to give the entries for the year 1695. Folio
99 is a loose sheet of parchment which has been attached to the preceding folio by the wrong edge. Folio 100 is written in a much more
clerkly hand. There is an incredible collection of discrepancies. The
dates rarely correspond at all, more detail is sometimes given on folio
100 and many names in one list are not in the other.[23] Similarly the
clerk's register at *Winslow*, Bucks. records entries entirely different
from those in the parish register.[24]

Sometimes a new and more efficient incumbent copied up into the
register entries he found in a paper register. Thus in the register of
Wilbye, Northants. appears the following memorandum:

> "Feb 25 1767 This day I transcribed into the three following leaves of
> Parchment all the Articles of Births, Baptisms and Burials during the
> years 1756, 1757, 1758, 1759, 1760, 1761, 1762, 1763, 1764, 1765, 1766, which
> I found entered in a paper register of Baptisms and Burials of this parish
> of Wilbye, viz all that have happened since I have been Rector of this
> Parish; and after a very exact Collation of this copy with the said
> Originals, I hereby declare it to be very correct and perfect.
> Thomas Percy Rector of Wilbye."[25]

Sometimes the Vicar himself appears to have kept the rough notebook. Thus in 1766, the Vicar of *Chatham*, Kent, observes in a letter
that

> "the entries are chiefly brought from the Minute Book, carefully kept in
> the Vestry room, and it cannot be supposed that there should be any
> material variation in the case"[26]

A similar book was kept at *St. Margaret's Rochester*, but a great
many entries were omitted in the copying into the register.

Loose Notes

Some clerks did not even use rough registers but wrote the entries
on odd slips of paper with the idea of writing them in at some later
date. R.E. Chester Waters observes:

> "This is so well known to historical students, that they habitually make
> search among the church records for the original memoranda, when they
> examine the registers for a literary purpose."[27]

As with a rough notebook, the entries might be abbreviated when entered
up. Thus, the register of *St. Saviour's, Southwark* gives:

---

[23] I. Fitzroy James. *The Reliability of Parish Registers*. Gen. Mag. Vol.9.
p.130, where all the entries on the two lists are printed in full.

[24] H. Southam *N & Q* Vol.155. p.158.

[25] W.W.S. *N & Q* 3rd Ser. Vol.5. p.244. Thomas Percy was the author of the
"Reliques of English Poetry."

[26] J.S. Burn *The History of Parish Registers in England* (1862 edn) p.51.

[27] *op.cit.* p.85.

"1608. Laurence Fletcher, a man, bur. in the church, 12 Sept.
"1625. Mr. John Fletcher, a man, bur. in the church, 29 Aug."

The original entries of these burials, in the unbound sheets still preserved in the vestry, run thus:

"1608. Laurence Fletcher, a player, the king's servant, bur. in the church 12 Sept., with an afternoon's knell of the great bell "
"1625. John Fletcher, a poet, bur. in the church, Aug. 29."[28]

Sometimes the parish register contains even more defective data. In the register of *Rochdale*, Lancs. the name of the wife is frequently not given in a marriage entry (the Latin abbreviation *cu. ux.* being substituted) or the Christian name in a burial. M.H. Dodds suggested that this was due to notes kept by the clerk merely as an aide-memoire ("*John Smith married* ", "*Thomas Brown's child baptized*") and that he subsequently forgot the details. [29]

Such notes might never be entered in the register in any form. Thus in the register of *St. Peter's Dorchester*:

"1645. In twelve months there died 52 persons whose names are not inserted, the old clark being dead who had the notes."[30]

This practice explains why entries are often found in Bishop's Transcripts but not in the register. In these cases it would appear that when the Bishop's transcripts came to be written at the end of the year the loose slips were transcribed in their proper order on the parchment. Meanwhile in the parish register more baptisms, marriages and burials had been entered and so the entries on the slips, although they appear on the Bishop's transcripts were never written up in the register and the slips were subsequently lost.

Ironically, both the keeping of the clerk's rough register and the use of rough notes on separate slips of paper sometimes occur with the best kept registers as well as with the worst. Sometimes professional scriveners were employed to write up the register making some such system unavoidable. Where the clerk himself wrote up the registers, if he took good care of them and prided himself on his penmanship, he might be reluctant to take the register to the church, which would increase the wear and tear, and furthermore, the facilities for writing at the church might be far from ideal. If his notes were forgotten until after other ceremonies had taken place, the clerk might prefer to omit them rather than enter items out of order "spoiling" his register and advertising his previous lapses.

The custom of keeping rough registers or notes was specifically

---

[28] *ibid* p.85.
[29] *N & Q* Vol.169. p.156. (1935).
[30] R.E. Chester Waters *op.cit.* p.83.

forbidden by *Rose's Act* of 1812 which directed:

> " That after the solemnisation of baptism or burial, the Rector etc shall as soon as possible, enter in a fair and legible handwriting, in a proper Register Book, the several particulars described in the schedules, and sign the same; and in no case (unless prevented by sickness or other unavoidable impediment) later than within seven days after the ceremony of any such baptism or burial shall have taken place "

However clearly this clause in the Act was, like the sending in of Bishop's Transcripts, frequently ignored. J.S. Burn, writing in 1829 comments:

> " The practice of the clerk keeping notes, and the clergyman making up his Register Book therefrom once a year, is still in use, notwithstanding the third section of the last Act: in the parish of St. Clement Danes, London, the entries were often made in the waste book in pencil. An affidavit being required in 1829, of the entry of a burial in this Register, it was found to be in pencil; and after waiting two months to see it properly entered in ink, the deponent was obliged to swear to the copy from the pencilled entry. And in another parish, the clerk demands a fee for causing his memoranda to be entered in the Register Book "[31]

The Legal Position

A Clerk's rough notes or register would seem to have no validity as legal evidence, even when they are clearly more authentic than the parish register. In the case of May v May:

> " It appeared that a Register Book was kept in the parish, into which the entries of baptism were made every three months, from a Day Book, into which they were made at the time, or in the course of the morning. In the Day Book were put the letters B.B., which were said to signify base-born, but these letters were not inserted in the Register Book. A majority of the judges present, on a trial at bar, were of the opinion that there could not be two registers in the parish, and that the Register Book, being the Public Book, was to be considered as the original entry, from which evidence was to be given, and that it could not be controlled or altered by anything appearing in the Day Book, the entry in which appeared to be merely a private memorandum kept for the purpose of assisting the clerk in making up the registers."[32]

Such an omission may have been deliberate rather than accidental arising from a well intentioned but mistaken charity on the part of the clerk. However, clerk's daybooks have been used to discount the legal validity of the parish register entry itself, although in agreement with it in every particular. In 1828 an ejectment cause was tried at the Worcestershire Spring Assizes, and the question was whether the defendant, Aaron Bray was the legitimate son of his father.

> "On the part of the defendant, the Register of Baptisms of the parish of Castlemorton for 1776 was produced, which contained an entry of baptism of

---

[31] J.S. Burn *op.cit.* p.50 (footnote).
[32] *May v May* 2 Strange p.272. *N & Q* 1857 p.323.

Aaron, the son of John Bray, and Elizabeth his wife, on the 6th February 1776. It appeared, however, that the entry was in the handwriting of the Revd. Dr. Smith, and that he did not become Minister of the parish till 1777; that during the years 1775 and 1776, the then incumbent of the parish was very infirm and that the then clerk entered on slips of paper an account of the baptisms etc, and his memoranda, which had been preserved, were produced, and there was no doubt that Dr. Smith had made from them the entries in the Register Book. It was objected that neither the Register nor the memorandum was admissible in evidence; but Mr. Baron Vaughan received them. Upon a motion, however, for a new trial, Mr. Justice Bayley said, "the register ought not to have been received in evidence. Register should be made up promptly, and by the person whose duty it is to make them up. The Register of Baptism, in this case purports to bear the date 6th February 1766, but it was not made up till June 1777, and then it was made up, not by the person who was the minister of the parish at the time of baptism, or by a person who appeared at that time to have any connexion with the parish, but by one, who afterwards became the minister of the parish. It must be taken, therefore, that he made this entry after the death of the minister of the Parish who was present at this baptism. He was recording a fact therefore, not within his own knowledge, but one of which he received information from the clerk."

The court, therefore, held that neither the Register nor the Clerk' Memorandum was admissible in evidence, and the rule for a new trial was made absolute accordingly.[33]

Thus the decision in this case contradicts the generally held legal opinion that Parish Register entries necessarily have legal validity.

That omissions in registers were often intentional, even in the 19th Century is shown by the evidence of Mr. William Durrant Cooper in 1833 before the Select Committee appointed to enquire into the question of registration. He reported that

"a parish clerk said it was usual for him and not the clergyman to take an account of burials and he entered them in a little sixpenny memorandum book, thus "A.B. Is". If the fee were paid at the time, no name would be put into his book, he only booked what was due to him and the Clergyman entered in the Register at the end of the year from his Memorandum Book."[34]

Although vast numbers of clerical errors in parish registers must have remained uncorrected to baffle the future genealogist,[35] occasionally one finds a note of correction. In *Barnstaple* Parish Registers is recorded the baptism on 23rd Nov. 1794 of William son of John and Elizabeth Ley. A note has been added:

"The William was an error for John and was corrected 29th June 1843 by the Vicar in the presence of the father "[36]

---

[33] *8 Barn and Cres* 813 Cited by J.S. Burn *op.cit.* p.261 footnote 2.
[34] Burn *op.cit.* p.44.
[35] See *Parish Registers and the Genealogist* p.140.
[36] *Barnstaple Parish Register* ed. Thomas Wainwright p.212.

Gaps

Most registers have gaps during the period of the Civil War and the Commonwealth, partly from the disruption caused by the war and partly from the ejection of so many of the incumbents and the vacancies thereby caused. However, apart from this major gap entries were often not noted for periods of years or were very irregularly kept. Dr. Burn quotes innumerable examples of lacunae in registers caused, not by subsequent loss, but by the failure to record entries at the time, or from the loss of rough notes which were made.[37] Sometimes negligence in the keeping of parish registers finds its way into the ecclesiastical courts, or, during the Commonwealth period even into the civil courts as in the following case:

"At the Quarter Sessions held at Kirbymoorside Jan. 17 1655/6. Trespasses acknowledged: Rob. Henley of Sinnington, Parish Register, for betraying his trust, and abusing the register books committed unto him, and deceiving the people (submitted etc and to loose his place)"[38]

The inability to rely on the parish registers was constantly felt by the Courts. In 1751 Anne wife of Thomas Lewis was on trial for perjury.

"She remembered the day Lawler lay in her house, particularly by this, she having buried a female child that day in St. Anne's parish etc. The register keeper produced the register, and upon examining it, there was no such child buried by that name in the month of May; but upon his cross examination he said he set down such names as were brought to him, but could not determine whether all are the true names of persons buried there, and likewise could not depose he never did omit setting down a name after the burial through hurry or mistake."[39]

Amount of Detail Given

The amount of detail given varies a great deal from register to register. Not infrequently one finds the vicar or clerk has added his opinion of the persons concerned:

Shillingstone, Dorset. 1742 Jan.1. David Pitman and Mary Haskell, a rogue and a whore, married.[40]

Occasionally, there may be an attempt at malicious humour:

Sea Salter, Kent. 1734. John Ponney of Canterbury, huntsman to that ancient Corporation of Cuckolds, and Elizabeth Johnson daughter of the Devil's Vicegerent, commonly called a Bailiff, were trammell'd at the Cathedral of Sea Salter, April 26.[41]

---

[37] *op.cit.* Chap.III pp.40-64.
[38] *North Riding Record Soc. Publications* Vol.5 p.203.
[39] *Proceedings in King's Commissions of the Peace, Oyer and Terminer and Gaol Delivery for City of London.* Old Bailey 16, 17, 18, 19, 21 Oct. 25 Geo.II Lond. 1751 p.315 *N & Q* 9th Ser. IV p.149.
[40] Cited by Chester Waters *op.cit.* p.84.
[41] *ibid.* p.83. J.S. Burn *op.cit* pp.166-167.

Some omissions were by design rather than negligence:

> Tunstall, Kent. 1557. Mary Pottman nat. and bapt. 15 Apr. Mary Pottman nat
> and bapt. 29 June. Mary Pottman sep. 22 Aug. From henceforward I omit the
> Pottmans. [42]

The respective amount of detail given in entries of baptisms, marriages
and burials is examined later under their separate headings. As has been
pointed out in some registers the names of the brides are omitted in
marriages,[43] and the use of nicknames in burial entries was almost commonplace. [44] The mode of keeping the registers depended entirely upon
the efficiency or eccentricity of the individual vicar or clerk. It
is not unknown to even find entries written in cipher. In the register of *Cleator*, Cumberland is an entry which begins:

> J182t1   B1982   f3631   G5632673.....

Here the vowels and liquids have been replaced by figures (1 = a, 2 = e
3 = i etc). The transcription reads:

> Janeta Barne filia Gulielmi Barne Curati de Cleater primo die mensis
> Januarii Baptizata fuit anno predicto 1745. [45]

and at Iver, near Uxbridge, Middlesex:

> Jno Pontifex and 188 B58Y48 [Ann Bunyon] wis 719932D [married] J17 [Jan]
> 17 1767 at London. [46]

Though negligence in recording Baptisms and Burials continued unabated
until the printed forms of 1813 and to a lesser extent right up to
Civil Registration in 1837, the standard of recording marriages
improved after the passing of the *Hardwicke Act* in 1753. Nevertheless
even the printed forms were not always properly completed, the classic
example being that of *Feltham*, Middlesex where, observes Dr. Burn:

> "the contracting parties certainly made their marks, yet the clergyman
> had not written either of their names against those marks, so that as it
> would be an utter impossibility to throw any light on the subject by the
> marks, it would be equally impossible by anything on the face of the entry
> to prove whose marriage was solemnised." [47]

It is of interest to note that as early as 1593 a printed form for
parish registers was prepared, as is shown by the following entry in the
Registers of the Stationers' Company for 26 Feb. 1592/3:

> "Thomas Purfoote thelder and Thomas Purfoote the yonger Entred for their
> Copie under thande of Master Stirrop The Register Booke, or Applicacon of
> the Blanck Almanack to the true and orderlie keepinge of the Register book

---

[42]   *ibid* p.83.
[43]   For example, *Rochdale* Lancs. *See above* p.
[44]   *See below* pp 69–70.
[45]   H. Aiken *N & Q* Vol.157 p.134 (1929).
[46]   *"An Old Church Fee Book"*. *The Times* 10 Sept. 1929. cited by L.R.M. Strach
        N & Q 157 p.214.
[47]   Burn *op.cit.* pp.45–46.

of weddinges Christeninges and Buralls accordinge to the Queene's Iniunctyons....."[48]

Had this been used we would have been spared the negligent and irresponsible entries of many of the clerks and clergy, but at the same time a great deal of interesting and useful information found in parish registers would doubtless have been excluded.

Of course, it is very easy to paint too black a picture; there are many parish registers which were extremely well kept for quite considerable periods. In particular, 18th century parish registers in areas containing Government establishments are particularly well kept as the incumbent's certificate of baptism was required for admission to Government posts. [49]

In general in the 16th century in most parishes marriages and burials were intermingled, though sometimes when they were recopied in 1598 they were started in three different parts of the register. In some of the larger parishes (e.g. *St. Minver's, Cornwall*) two separate books were kept, one for baptisms and the other for marriages and burials. One of the best kept 16th Century registers was that of *Achurch*, Northants when Robert Browne the Puritan separatist was vicar. Between 1591 and 1631 the register is ruled into three columns for baptisms, marriages and burials. Place of residence is invariably given in the marriages and relationships in the burials. [50] Though normal later, this information was not by any means invariably given in registers of this early date. On the other hand the mother's name is not given in the baptisms.

Duplicate Entries

These are sometimes found and there is a variety of different explanations. Clearly a marriage might be entered in the registers of the parishes of both the parties. For example the marriage of Henry Blake and Loveday Holman 15th June 1619 appears in the registers of *Lanreath* and of *Braddock*, Cornwall. [51] In the case of a burial, the funeral service might be held in one church and the interment in the churchyard of another, as was doubtless the case with regard to Mary, Lady Drake the first wife of Sir Francis Drake whose burial on 25th Jan. 1582/3 was entered in the registers of *St. Andrew's Plymouth* and of *St. Budeaux*. [52]

---

[48] Arber. *Registers of the Company of Stationers* Vol. 2. p. 269.

[49] For example the registers of *Stoke Damerel*, Devon in which parish was Devonport Dockyard. C.E. Welch. *Nonconformist Registers*. Journal of Soc. of Archivists Vol. II. No. 9. p. 413.

[50] F. Cater. *Robert Browne and the Achurch Parish Register*. Trans. Cong. Hist. Soc. Vol. 3. p. 127.

[51] *N & Q* 9th Ser. 4 p. 482. Duplicate entries were especially frequent during the Commonwealth period. *See below,* pp 60–61.

[52] On duplicate burials see *Times Lit. Suppl.* 12 May 1921 P. 308 23 June, 1921 p. 404, 30 June, 1921 p. 421.

Duplicate baptismal entries are more difficult to explain. Sometimes where the dates disagree, the entries may represent a private baptism and subsequent reception into the church, but where the dates are the same it may be that in a case of plurality the incumbent made entries in one register only and the relevant entries were subsequently recopied into the register of the other parish.

Latin

Most early registers are in Latin. The use of Latin was generally discontinued before the accession of Charles I[53] and during the Commonwealth ceased altogether. It was occasionally resumed after the Restoration.[54] In the register of *Clyst St. George,* Devon is the entry:

9° Georgie 2^{di}, 1735,6. The Law now forbids ye Keeping any Records in Latin.[55]

The vicar was however mistaken. In 1731 an act had been passed that all proceedings in *Courts of Justice* should be in English. This did not extend to Parish Registers, but few English registers appear to have been still kept in Latin at this late date.

The Latin terms most frequently used were:

for baptised – *baptizatus erat; renatus erat; consignatus baptismo; perfusus baptismo;*[56]

for married – *nupti erant; copulati sunt in matrimonio; contraxerunt matrimonium; conjuncti fuere; mariti fuerunt; alligati fuerunt; connubio juncti erant;*

for buried – *sepultus erat.*

Christian names were usually Latinized[57] but not normally Surnames, even when there was an exact Latin equivalent.[58] This was in conformity with the accepted legal practice of the time. Earlier – in the 11th, 12th and 13th centuries – Latinization of surnames was normal. However, this could cause considerable ambiguity. Coke commented:[59]

"It is not safe in writs, pleadings, grants etc to translate surnames into Latin. As if the surname of one be Fitzwilliam or Williamson if he translate him Filius Willi, if in truth his father had any other Christian

---

[53] In the register of *All Saints, Derby* is the entry on May 16 1610 "I see no reason why a register for English people should be written in Latin" However, entries in Latin continued to be made.

[54] In Welsh registers Latin tended to be used later. See *Welsh Registers* in Vol. II.

[55] J.S. Burn *op.cit.* p.61; *N & Q* Ser. 2, Vol.II p.8.

[56] For *illegitimacy* see under *Baptisms,* below p.50.

[57] A list of these is given in Appendix IV *Christian Names* pp.110–112.

[58] *Smith* would be used rather than *Faber.*

[59] *Coke on Littleton* (1658) p.3a. Cited by C.E. Ewen *History of Surnames in the British Isles* pp.394-5.

than William, the writ etc shall abate, for Fitzwilliam or Williamson is
his surname, whatsoever Christian name his father had; therefore the lawyer never translates surnames."

The most common words for status were; *eques* and less frequently *miles*[60]
(knight) *armiger* (esquire) and *generosus* (gentleman). Where the register
is in Latin the Latin names of trades sometimes appear in the burials.[61]
Miscellaneous memoranda, particularly those of a personal nature are
frequently entered in Latin or occasionally in Greek even when the rest
of the register is in English.

Spelling

Spelling fluctuates enormously in the registers, partly because
there was no fixed orthography and partly because the persons concerned
were often illiterate, and the vicar or clerk spelt surnames phonetically.[62] Moreover, the clerks themselves were often men of very little
education, as is shown in the burial entry in 1687 of George Villiers
Duke of Buckingham in the register of *Kirkby Moorside*, Yorkshire:

Georges vilaus Lord dooke of bookingham bur 17. April.[63]

Christian names too, were often distorted 'beyond recognition, particularly if the name were an unusual one. C.E. Ewen cites some
extreme examples:

" A woman baptized by the unusual name of *Delariviere* was married as
Dillamoretta; another named *Sigismunda*, according to an entry of her
marriage had become *Sydgistermondayer*, and *Irene* was buried in Geldeston
Churchyard as *Iearenery*"[64]

With some of the more usual Christian names, although the spelling was
more standardised, the most common forms were not those used today.
Thus *Agnes* was spelt (and pronounced) *Annis*, *Annys* or *Annais* and *Alan*
was spelt *Aleyn*.[65]

The Civil War and the Commonwealth

As has been pointed out, the Civil War period is defective in most
registers. Many registers were destroyed and others lost when the
parish was without an incumbent. Due to the lack of a minister or
because the minister was not willing to use the *Directory* as laid down

---

[60] *Eques* was used by the Heralds and *Miles* by the legal profession.
[61] For a glossary of these see Appendix to article on *Marriage Licences*.
pp. 239–244.
[62] For a fuller examination of this question see *Parish Registers and the
Genealogist* pp. 138–140.
[63] Cited by J.S. Burn *op.cit.* p.135 and R.E. Chester Waters *op.cit.* p.85.
[64] *op.cit.* p.xii.
[65] For more information on this subject see Appendix IV. *Christian Names*
p.106.

by the Act of 1644/5 many children were not baptized at all.[66] With
the appointment of the Civil *Registers* in 1653[67] in many cases clergy
failed to hand over the registers to the new officials who started a
new register which might not be handed back to the incumbent at the
Restoration. Sometimes the *Registers* failed to part with the parish
registers themselves. However, in many cases the parson or his clerk
was appointed *Register*[68] and in others the clergy seem to have carried
on much the same as before. An anonymous clerical correspondent to
Notes and Queries commented:

> "I think it will be found that a large number of the parochial clergy
> continued to keep their own registers, particularly in country parishes
> in spite of the Act which in many places would be thoroughly unpopular.
> In such parishes a *register* would be appointed pro forma, but his office
> would by common consent remain a sinecure; his chief concern being his
> fees, which under the Act were 12d for a marriage, 4d for a birth and 4d
> for a burial."

He continued:

> "This is the case with my own register. From 1650-1681 each year is
> signed *Stephen Rant minister* with signatures of churchwardens for the time
> being. In one instance only is the name of the *register* signed, namely in
> the first year of his appointment and then after and in addition to the
> signatures of the minister and churchwardens. As the Act was for the
> registration of births and not baptisms, the date of the birth as well as
> of the baptism is given from 1654, after which period the date of the
> birth is omitted – another proof of the disregard paid to the Act."[69]

The vicar of *Clyst St. George*, Devon, whether he was appointed *Register*
or whether he was able to carry on without undue restriction, certainly
retained the custody of his registers throughout the Commonwealth
period and made no secret of his Royalist sympathies. The year 1649 is
styled

> "Anno primo post decollationem Regis Caroli primi"

and the same wording is continued until 1660 which is styled

> "Anno 12 mo Caroli Regis Secundi"[70]

Many of the *Registers* were men of little education. In 1660 there is
a note in the register of *North Runcton*, Norfolk:

> ..... and so it came to passe that persons of no learning for many places
> were chosen by ye parish and ministers declined the office."[71]

As we have seen, in one case at least the *Register* was brought

---

[66] See under *Baptisms*, below pp. 48–49.
[67] See *History* p. 11.
[68] See J. S. Burn. *N & Q* 3rd Ser. Vol. 3. p. 239 (1869)
[69] E. V. *N & Q* 3rd Ser. Vol. 3. p. 296. (1863).
[70] *N & Q* 3rd. Ser. Vol. 3. p. 191. (1863).
[71] *N & Q* Ser. 1, 1 p. 103 (1849).

before the Civil Courts for inefficiency.[72] However, many of the
Registers undoubtedly performed their functions efficiently, and sometimes one finds the register better kept during this period than before
or after.[73]

Between 1653 and 1660, *births* were entered rather than *baptisms*
and frequently *proclamations of marriage* (i.e. banns) rather than the
marriages themselves.[74]

The Calendar – Old Style (O.S.) and New Style (N.S.)

Until 1752 in England the beginning of the year was normally ·
reckoned from 25th March, although a few registers[75] even before this
date begin each year at 1st January. For the calculation of the Leap
Year however, the Civil Year was used, as is shown by the following
entry:

1699 Ellinora Baxter vid. sepult vigesimo nono ffebruaris.[76]

In 1751 the Gregorian Calendar or *New Style* (NS) was adopted by
act of Parliament.[77] The cumulative error of about eleven minutes too
many in each year throughout the centuries had by then amounted to
eleven days. To correct this excess, eleven days were omitted in 1752.
What would have been the *3rd* September being called *14th* September. At
the same time the first day of January, the beginning of the historical
year, the old Roman civil year was made the official beginning of the
year in England for both civil and ecclesiastical purposes. Thus the
day after the 31st December 1751, which by the old custom could have
normally been styled " *1751*" sometimes " *1751/2* " and occasionally
1752 was in fact to be known as *1st January 1752*, and so on henceforward, according to the usage familiar to us nowadays.[78]

By the act of 1751, although special provision was made that
solemn days of thanksgiving, fasting and humiliation (e.g. Guy Fawkes

---

[72] *See above*, p.33.

[73] Archdeacon Fearon notes that in Hampshire the *registers* generally did
their work well. *Parish Registers and Parochial Documents in the
Archdeaconry of Winchester* (1909).

[74] For a detailed consideration of these topics see *Baptisms* below pp.48–49
and *Marriages* below pp.59–61.

[75] e.g. *Whelton*, Northants. See Cox, *op.cit.* p.23.

[76] L. Griffith. *Gen. Mag.* Vol.2. No.3 p.78. (Sept 1926) See letters of Evelyn
Young and William McMurray *Gen. Mag.* Vol.2. No.4. p.105. (Dec.1926). This
has caused some confusion. Thus in *N & Q* 4th Ser. 10 p.326 (1872) Robert
Holland cites four parish register entries where 29th February had been
put in error for 1st March. However, two of these were for 1639 and 1659
which were in fact leap years. The other two (1582 and 1671) were
undoubtedly errors.

[77] 24 Geo.II.c.23.

[78] In modern transcripts of entries between 1st January and 25th March of
any year before 1752 both the old style and the new style years are
often given. e.g. 23rd January 1727/8.

Day) were to be kept on the same nominal days as before;[79] all birth-days were altered by 11 days as far as the law was concerned:

> "No person or persons whatsoever shall be deemed or taken to have at-
> tained the said Age of one and twenty years or any other such Age as
> aforesaid or to have completed the Time of any such Service as aforesaid
> until the full number of years and Days shall be elapsed in which such
> Person or Persons respectively would have attained such Age, or would
> have completed the Time of such Service as aforesaid in case this Act had
> not been made.[80]

Robert Pierpoint observes:

> Whether private celebrations of such anniversaries took place on the
> statutory dates or on the nominal dates would be a matter of personal and
> domestic concern.[81]

However, George III was born on 24th May 1738. After the change in the calendar, his birthday was always celebrated on 4th June. It seems likely that the royal lead was almost universally followed.[82] Thus John Wesley born 17th June 1703 recognised 28th June (NS) as his anniversary. It may well be that when a definite date of birth is available from records (e.g. Naval or Military records) that it has been so adjusted. The searcher may thus seek the baptismal entry start-ing from that date, whereas in fact the baptism took place a week or more before.

Effect on the Registers of the 1783 Stamp Act[83]

The mode of carrying out the provisions of the Act varied con-siderably from parish to parish. For example in Essex, at *Little Waltham* the right hand page was stamped with embossed stamps and the entries were spaced to fit the stamps. The opposite page was used for persons for whom no duty was paid. At *Broomfield* certificates from the collector were entered in the register. At *Mashbury*, in the reg-ister of burials was entered " *tax paid 3d*" and at *Little Leighs* is the reference " *inspected by I. Smitheman*" but no notice of payment.[84] In the registers of *Hawarden*, Flintshire appears the entry:

---

79 Robert Pierpoint. *N & Q* 10th Ser. 4 p.73-4. This did not however apply
to the celebration of the Accession of Geo. II (11th June 1727 OS). In
1753 it was celebrated on 22nd June. Similarly the dates of public
ceremonies were changed. The swearing in of the Lord Mayor at Westminster
had been on 29th October (OS). In 1752 it took place on 9th November (NS).

80 It was however made clear with regard to contracts and ages of persons
that the first year after the Act came into force was to be a full year
for each person and contract and not a year less 11 days.

81 *N & Q* 11th Ser. 111. p.475.

82 Some extracts from a Family Bible to illustrate the amending of dates of
birth are given in *Parish Registers and the Genealogist* p.141.

83 See *History* pp.13-14.

84 O.W. Tancock. *N & Q* 8th Ser. 8. p.332.

Oct 1783. "On the 2nd of this month the act commenced which layeth a duty of threepence upon every registry of a Burial except a Pauper's".

Between then and 1794 many burials are marked *paupers*,[85] and one cannot but suspect that a charitable incumbent so marked as many as he dared. Doubtless in many parishes clergy remitted the tax wherever they thought this would cause hardship and the description *pauper* between those years may not mean that the person was on actual relief.[86]

B. BAPTISMS

In general the words *Baptisms* and *Christenings* are used indiscriminately, though the latter does sometimes refer to reception into the church·after private baptism.[87] In the register of *Walton in Gordano*, Somerset from 1778 to 1781 the curious word *crossings* is used, and no doubt there were other local variants. It is rare for dates of birth as well as baptism to be entered in the registers until the Commonwealth period, but in the 16th century baptism was normally within three days of birth and often as in Mediaeval times on the same day or the following day. Camden commented[88]

"Most nations since Christianity celebrated baptism on the eighth day after birth, only our Ancestors in this Realm until later time baptized and gave names the very birth day or next day after, following therein the counsel of St. Cyprian in his 3 Epistle Ad Finem."

Certainly in *Chislet*, Kent, it was customary to baptize on the actual day of birth.[89] However, the Prayer Book directs that children should be baptized on the first or second Sunday next after their birth, or a Holy-day falling between. In a Family Bible of the 18th century of a Shropshire family, baptisms were entered as well as births, and there seems to have been a favourite baptism day, the majority of a family of about 10 children being baptized on the same day of the same month in different years.[90] Clearly the interval between birth and baptism varied from time to time and place to place.

Baptismal Certificates

Many official records contain baptismal certificates which are invaluable when one has no idea of the parish of origin or if the

---

[85]   Waldegrave Brewster *N & Q* 6th Ser. Vol.3. p.94.
[86]   To the best of my knowledge no comparison of registers and surviving records of poor relief during this period has yet been made. I would be interested to receive any information on this point. [D.J.S.]
[87]   See *Private Baptisms*, below pp. 46—47.
[88]   *Remains Concerning Britain* Cited by H. Southam N & Q 146 p.82 (1924).
[89]   Cox *op.cit.* p.40. Out of 15 Baptisms in 1544, 13 were baptized on the day of birth; in 1545, 8 out of 11, and in 1546 all 16.
[90]   G.S. Gibbons. *N & Q*. 146. p.121 (1924).

registers are missing. From 1789 onwards and with a few earlier ones
from 1777 the Navy Board copies of *Lieutenants' Passing Certificates*
have filed with them the baptismal certificate which the candidate had
to produce to prove he was at least twenty years of age. In the Public
Record Office there are two manuscript indexes to these certificates.
One was compiled by Miss E.H.B. Fairbrother and covers the years 1777
to 1832 and includes information from the baptismal certificates. The
other compiled by Miss P. Schrader covers the years 1789-1818.[91]
Ordinands' Papers also contain baptismal certificates.[92]

Information Given in a Baptismal Entry

The amount of information given varies considerably. Before 1813,
normally the Christian name and the surname of the child are given, with
the Christian names of the parents. Sometimes, particularly in early
registers no parentage is entered. Thus the register of *St. Bridget's
Chester* gives no parentage between 1560 and 1583, and thereafter gives
only the father's name[93]

There are many entries in the register of *Wrotham*, Kent where even
the child's surname is not given.

1580 Elizabeth, the Daughter of [left blank] was baptized ye 29th of
October[94]

On the other hand one occasionally finds minute detail. The clergy
often gave special attention to the entries of their own children, as
for example at *Staplehurst*, Kent:

"1549, June 9. This day being Whitsonday (wherein the Booke of the
Common Prayer and Administration of the Sacraments and other rite and
ceremonie of the Churche, after the use of the churche of Englande begon
to be executed), ther was first baptized Marie, the daughter of Richard
Beseley, Parson of this Paryshe Churche, borne the last Thursday, hora
fere quinta ante meridiem of his lawfull wif Jane, who were maryed the
year before, and in the first day that the holly Comvnion in the English
tonge (after thorder that now it was here mynystered), ther bothe with
others most humblye and devoutlie comvnicating the same. The Parson
christined his owne childe."[95]

When registering their own children (and less frequently those of
others) 16th century clergy might include astrological information.

St. Edmunds, Dudley, Worcs.

"1539. Samuell, son of Sir William Smithe Clarke, Vicare of Duddly, was
born on Friday morninge, at 4 of the clock, beinge the xxviij day of
February, the signe of that day was the midle of Aquaris ♌; the signe

[91] Gerald Hamilton Edwards. *In Search of Ancestry* (1966) p.89.
[92] See A.J. Willis *"Winchester Ordinations"* Vol.1.
[93] J.S. Burn *op. cit.* p.94
[94] *ibid* p.95.
[95] Cited by R.E. Chester Waters *op. cit.* p.35.

of the monthe ♓ ; the plenet of that day ♀ ; plenet of the same ower ☿ and the morow-day, whose name hath continued in Duddly from the conqueste."[96]

Throughout the period of parish registers, on occasions the father's occupation might also be given:

St. Giles Cripplegate 1582. Adam sonne of Nicolas Wilson, Minstrell, bapt. 18 Nov.

St. Oswald's Durham 1640, 14 Feb. Ann, dau. of Thomas Forcer, Virginall Master bapt.

However, this is hardly of assistance if the child's name is omitted!

"The Son of Janken, the Shepherd, baptized."[97]

More commonly merely the status of the father is given (e.g. *Gent, Esq*). After 1694 when a sliding scale of fees was introduced[98] one sometimes encounters an estimate of the father's financial position. Entries such as the following appear in many baptismal and burial entries in the registers of *Shottisbrooke*, Berks:

Rudye the son of James Finmore, Curate of ye Parish and Thomasine his wife was born April 14th 1699 and baptized April ye 15th. Reputed not worth 600 1.[99]

Occasionally one finds entries which have been annotated with biographical information.

Braintree, Essex

"Anno 1580 April 2 was baptized Joseph Mann son of Joseph Mann. Mem. That the said Joseph Mann, the son in the year 1631 did lay open the street called New Street and also built the New Cross at his own proper costs and charges and afterwards sold the same to the Right Hon. Robert Earl of Warwick for the sum of 600 1 being then bailiff to the said Earl of the town of Braintree.[100]

In some registers, particularly in East Anglia, the maiden name of the mother is given:[101]

Redgrave cum Botesdale, Suffolk.
1793 5th January. Mary daughter of James and Susannah Roper (Musk).[102]

In 1553, by Cardinal Pole's mandate the names of sponsors were to be entered in the baptismal register. These had probably already been

---

[96] J.S. Burn *op.cit.* p.80.
[97] *ibid.* p.80, but neither the register nor the date is given.
[98] See *History* p.12.
[99] *N & Q* 2nd Ser. Vol.7. p.498. (1859).
[100] E. Blencowe. *N & Q* 6th Ser. Vol.10. p.337.
[101] In Scottish registers it is almost invariably given. See *Scottish Registers* in Volume 12, p. 74
[102] Cited by D.E. Gardner and F. Smith *"Genealogical Research in England and Wales* p.144.

included in many parishes since 1538, but were omitted when the registers were re-copied in 1598. In most parishes the entry of godparents
probably ceased on Elizabeth's accession, though they were by no
means exceptional even in the 17th century[103] and in the cases of
the nobility and gentry, the godparents being of high rank were
often given throughout the registers.

A particularly curious case is the register of *Thornbury*,
Gloucestershire, where full details of godparents are given from the
commencement of the registers in 1538 until 1641, but the names of the
infants' parents are never given.

In some Lancashire, North Yorkshire and Durham registers from about
1765 very full genealogical information was given.

At *Lowick*, Lancs. the double page of the folio register is ruled
into five columns, giving: (1) The child's name;   (2) the father's name
and descent;   (3) the mother's name and descent;   (4) the date of birth;
(5) the date of baptism. Thus:

> 1. Sarah Redhead.   2. William Redhead of Moss, tanner, son of Matthew
> Redhead of Woodyeat, yeoman by Izabel his wife daughter of William
> Colton of Morebeck in Kirkby, yeoman. 3. Jane Redhead daughter of Edward
> Watterson of Bridgfield, tanner by Alice his wife daughter of Samuel
> Turner of Stenton, yeoman.   4. Born 14 March 1779. Baptised 22 March 1779.

Unfortunately the entries only extend from July 1778 to April
1780 (12 entries) and from August 1789 to March 1791 (18 entries).
Three Burial entries in 1778 are similar, recording three generations."[104] At *Eston*, Yorkshire, precisely the same degree of information was given in a consecutive form:

> 24, Sept. 1777 Sarah Robinson, daughter of John Robinson, farmer of Eston
> and son of William Robinson of Normanby, farmer; by Sarah his wife who
> was ye daughter of William Clement late of Normanby, a taylor. The child's
> mother's name is Ann Robinson, daughter of Thomas Bulmer of Eston, a
> carpenter by Elenor his wife the daughter of Thomas Hutton a weaver of
> Stainton. Born 16 Sept 1777.[105]

Since the information given corresponds so exactly, one may infer that
it was as a result of a largely ineffective episcopal recommendation.[106]
However in 1798 Shute Barrington Bishop of Durham gave detailed instructions of a slightly less ambitious, but still extremely thorough
nature. Certainly his standards were far higher than those of the
framers of either the *Rose Act* of 1812 or the *Births, Marriages and
Deaths Act* of 1836. Thus in all registers of parishes within the
Diocese of Durham between 1798 and 1813 more information was given

---

103   Cox. *op.cit.* quotes numerous examples, some continuing to 1624 or 1625.
104   *Gen. Mag.* Vol.7. p.425.
105   D.E. Gardner & F. Smith *op.cit.* Vol.I p.145.
106   I have been unable to trace this [D.J.S.].

than at any time subsequently as the following examples will show.

All Saints. Newcastle on Tyne:

July 15 1801 Edmund Reed born 10th June 2nd son of Edmund Reed miller native of Norfolk by his wife Hannah daughter of John Pile gardener of Norwich.

Rothbury, Northumberland:

Oct. 14 1804 Sarah Ainsley of Rothbury born 22 August 3rd daughter of George Ainsley tailor native of this parish by his wife Catherine daughter of Andrew Dryden native of Widdrington.

The order of the child in the family is a useful piece of information, but care must be exercised, as it is possible that in some cases the numbering of the children may be continued into a second marriage.[107] In the country as a whole, however, only for two periods are dates of birth regularly entered, as well as those of baptism – in the Commonwealth, and in some parishes for several years after 1783.[108] After 1813, with the use of the printed forms, the information given in a baptismal entry was standardised for the whole country. Columns are filled giving date of baptism, Christian names of the child, parents' Christian names, father's surname, father's abode and profession and by whom the ceremony was performed. Frequently one finds that the margin was used to record date of birth.

Private Baptisms

It has always been recognised in ecclesiastical law that a layman can baptize in an emergency. The midwife was especially enjoined not to neglect baptism in the presence of witnesses if there was any chance of the child dying before the priest could arrive.[109] After Private Baptism, whether by cleric or layman, the child, if it happened to survive, was duly received in church later on. Thus, Elizabeth Barrett Browning was baptized privately at Coxhoe Hall, Kelloe, Durham soon after birth on March 6th 1806. When her brother Edward Barrett Moulton Barrett was baptized, his sister was received, and the parish register entry reads:

"Elizabeth Barrett Moulton Barrett, first child of Edward Barrett Moulton Barrett Esq., of Coxhoe Hall, native of St. James's Jamaica, by his wife Mary, late Clarke of Newcastle-on-Tyne born March 6th 1806 and admitted February 10th 1808."[110]

In the stress and excitement of a dangerous delivery a mistake might well occur as to the sex of the child, and incidents are recorded of

---

[107] For an example See *Parish Registers and the Genealogist*, p.144.

[108] e.g. *Askham*, Notts. Cox *op.cit.* p.41.

[109] In fact to this day both medical and nursing students receive during their training instruction in the canonical requirements for valid Christian baptism.

[110] H. Askew *N & Q*. 146. p.140.

girls being baptized by boys' names and vice versa. Mr. W.E. Tate suggests[111] it was possibly to avoid awkward cases of this kind that midwives often baptized children as *Creature* or *Creatura Christi* which would serve equally well for either sex.[112] However the more likely explanation was that the midwife feared the child would die before the parents had decided how it should be named.

The custom of private baptism was much abused in the 18th century, particularly in London where private baptisms were very common, and the celebration of the sacrament was made the occasion of something of a social function. This is reflected in the existence for some London churches of separate registers of private baptisms.[113] The word *christened* may sometimes indicate a private baptism.

Usually, however, private baptisms were entered in the ordinary register with the words *baptised privately*. In such cases the vicar sometimes made his record on slips of paper, presumably with the intention of copying them up later. Such slips have on occasion been found at the bottom of a parish chest with no corresponding entries in the register.

Sometimes the expression *half-baptised* occurs. Thus in an Oxfordshire register, against two baptismal entries, of different families appears the marginal note " *both these children were half baptised.*"[114] Rev. C. Chitty pointed out that it is a well-known expression for *baptised privately* in country districts and wondered, if, in this case the children died before they could later be brought to the church.[115] In this connection it is important to point out that the word *christened* although usually synonymous with *baptized* was often used for receiving into the church subsequent to a private baptism. Thus a Family Bible records

"Wm Collison born 8 March 1788 at half past 5 o'clock in ye Eveng. privately baptizd 6 April 1788 and Christened 28 May 1788 at ye parish Church ".[116]

However, even the second ceremony might be at home, for a later entry in the same Bible reads:

"John Collison born 9 May 1790 at half an hour after eight o clock at

---

111 *The Parish Chest* p.59.
112 For examples see Chester Waters *op.cit.* p.36.
113 e.g. *St. Luke, Old St.*, London. See *Parish Registers and the Genealogist.* p.137.
114 H.J. Willis. *Gen. Mag.* Vol.II. No.9 March 1953 p.314.
115 *Gen. Mag.* Vol.II. No.10 June 1953 p.350. The view of Rev. D.D. Bailey cited there, that the expression indicates the public reception of a child into the Church *after* having been privately baptised is possible, but unlikely. However more research is clearly needed to fully clarify in what circumstances the expression was used.
116 *N & Q.* 146. p.140.

night. privately baptizd by Mr. Embry the 27th June 1790 and Christened
at their own house 20 Octr 1791 Sponsors etc.

It would seem likely that the importance of the *Christening* was largely
social rather than theological – an opportunity for relatives and
friends to sponsor the child and be present at a party. [117] Thus, a
series of diaries written in Lincolnshire between 1820 and 1840 record
children of a good family who were *baptized* on the Sunday after birth,
but *christened* sometimes a year later and the sponsors are mentioned
at the second ceremony, when there was a christening party. In one
case a child of 18 months and the next baby of 6 months were *christened*
together. [118]

Missing Baptisms.

In the period before 1662 when many of the Puritans were incumbents,
omissions in the baptisms may be due to religious reasons. Many parents
and some of the clergy objected to infant baptism and other incumbents
would satisfy themselves of the *worthiness* of the parents before they
would baptize a child. [119] Conversely in the Civil War period many
Laudian clergy refused to baptize according to the *Directory*. [120]

With the increase of private baptisms in the 18th century, many
clergy, in an effort to combat the practice refused to make an entry
in the register until the child had been brought to church. On occasion
the parish church could not be used:

> *Ayleston*, Leics:
> "1639, March 8. Was baptised at Enderby, Henrye, the Sonn of Henrye
> Taylor, of Lubsthorp, Mason, and of Prudence his Wife, by reason of a
> grate flood hindering passage to our church."[121]

The majority of omissions are however probably the result of carelessness, of the preference of the parents for another minister or of the
fact that parents were dissenters. As has been pointed out, negligence
is always a factor to be taken into consideration. [122] When another
church was nearer than the parish church, parents would often prefer it:

> "About the year 1776, there appears to have been an objection by the
> parishioners of Chatham, against the christening of children belonging to
> the parish of Gillingham, at their Church, the Minister of Chatham in his
> defence, attributed the circumstance more to the importunity of the parents,
> who lived nearer Chatham than their own Parish Church, than to his wish,
> and stated that the letter "G" or "Gillingham" was set against those

---

[117] This of course was largely the case even when *baptism* and *christening*
were synonymous. For the cost of christenings See Burn *op.cit.* pp. 74-75.
[118] G.S. Gibbons *N & Q.* 146. p. 121 (1924).
[119] J.S. Burn *op.cit.* p. 76. He cites Bishop Kennett as his authority.
[120] *See below* p. 49.
[121] J.S. Burn *op.cit.* p. 83.
[122] *See above* pp. 27-30.

entries, and that all bastards were properly distinguished."[123]

The thoroughness with which the births of dissenters were entered in the registers varied considerably from time to time and place to place. For some years after the Act of 1694[124] births of dissenters were regularly entered in many parishes often on separate lists.[125] Occasionally baptisms performed by Dissenting Ministers or Roman Catholic priests are recorded, as in the following entry at *Southam, Warwick*.

> 10 June 1810 Charles Coles baptized by the Rev. Mr. Merelland a Roman priest.

However, in the period 1662-1837 as a whole, it is probable that the majority of births of dissenters escaped entry in the parish registers.[126]

Adult Baptisms

Adult Baptisms are not uncommon and it is important to remember that there may be no indication in the registers that the persons baptized were adults, as in the following example:

> *Wanlip*, Leics. Samuel and Matthew, sons of John Woodcock by Elizabeth his wife were baptized 3rd Sept. 1699.[127]

In the majority of cases the person concerned had been a dissenter – probably a Quaker or less frequently a Baptist. Baptism could take place at any age:

> *Thurcaston*, Leics.
> "Nov. 19, 1763. John Cragg of Thurcaston, an adult, in his 75th year, being bed-rid, was privately baptized at his own request. N.B. His Father and Mother had been rigid Anabaptists."[128]

The Civil War and the Commonwealth

Exceptions to the generalization that adult baptisms are normally of former dissenters are most frequently found after the Restoration. During the Civil War and Commonwealth period, as a result of the disorders of the time, many infants were not baptized at all and some of

---

[123] J.S. Burn. *op.cit.* p.83 (footnote) See *Parish Registers and the Genealogist* p.136.

[124] See *History* p.12.

[125] The description *Anabaptist* would seem to have been used for Quakers as well as Baptists. See *Society of Friends* in Volume II.

[126] For more information on this subject see *The Three Denominations Society of Friends* and *Roman Catholics* all in Volume II.

[127] For a fuller treatment of this subject and for the evidence that the persons in this example were adults see *Parish Registers and the Genealogist* p.145.

[128] J.S. Burn. *op.cit.* p.83.

these were baptized as adults after the Restoration.

Collegiate Church of Westminster

"Dnell Pead, one of the King's Scholars, ab^t 16 y^{rs} of age, was bapt^d by the Deane publickly in the font newly set up, Apr. 18. 1663."[129]

Failure to be baptized during the Civil War and Commonwealth period was not always because the parish was without a minister. Some clergy refused to baptize according to the *Directory* as laid down by the act of 1644. Thus, at *East Peckham,* Kent:

1648. Upon the third of June the following infants all born in the parish of Brenchley were baptized in this parish Church by an order granted from Sir John Sedley, Knight and Baronett, Sir John Rayney and Sir Isaac Sedley, Knights:

"Whereas complaints have often been made unto us by many of the principal inhabitants of the Parish of Brenchley, that they having desired Mr. Gilbert, minister of the said Parish to baptize their children and according to the Directorie offered to present them before the congregation, he hath neglected or refused so to do, whereby divers infants remain unbaptized, some of them above a year old, expressly contrary to the said Directorie.

We do therefore order that the parents of such children do bring them into the Parish Church of East Peckham where we desire that Mr. Topping, minister of the said parish, would baptize them according to the sayd Directorie; they acquainting him with the day they intend to bring them beforehand.

Dated ye 25th of May 1648 John Sedley
                              John Rayney
                              Isaac Sedley."[130]

From 1645 entries occur of baptisms with the rite of *pouring or sprinckling of water"* in church but not in what the *Directory* described as *places where Fonts in the time of Popery were unfitly and superstitiously placed.*

With the appointment of the Civil *registers* in 1653, [131] births rather than baptisms were entered. However, as has been pointed out[132] many of these registers have been lost.

Illegitimate Children

Although some churches kept a special bastard register, [133] more usually baptisms of illegitimate children are found scattered among the baptisms of lawful children. Illegitimacy is indicated sometimes with the brutal frankness of a legal term, often by a more agreeable euphemism.

---

[129] J.S. Burn. *op.cit.* p.92.
[130] *N & Q* Ser. 1, 1. p.42 (1849).
[131] See *History* p.11.
[132] *Above* p.38.
[133] Such a register was kept at Edgmond, Salop from 1797 to 1828. For more information on other documents relating to bastardy see *Other Records-Some Brief Notes* pages 347–350.

Some of the terms denoting illegitimacy are:- **Latin:** *Filius populi,*
natus ex fornicatione, filius meretricis, filius vulgi, filius terrae,
filius fornicatoris, filius unicuscujusque, filius scorti, filius
adulterinus.

The word *nothus* was sometimes used to indicate the illegitimate
child of a gentleman by a plebeian mother and sometimes the illegitimate child of a married woman. In many parishes it was, however, used
indiscriminately of all illegitimate children. **English:** *Base, bastard,*
base-born, son of the people, son of an harlott, begotten in adultery,
a scape begotten child, begotten in fornication, lanebegot, a merry
begot, a byeblow.

The term, *natural child* did not always, or indeed generally imply
illegitimacy. Mr. D. Maclean points out:-

> A child born of its parents in wedlock is properly described as their
> *natural and lawful child,* natural because he was born in the course of
> nature; lawful because he was born in wedlock. He may also be properly
> described as their *natural child* in contra distinction to lawful children
> who are not naturally born to them i.e. to those children acquired by one
> of them, so to speak, by marriage, commonly called step-children or by
> adoption. A child born out of wedlock is also properly described as the
> *natural child* of his parents, but the use of this phrase is in itself no
> evidence of bastardy at least up to the end of the 18th Century. For in
> the affidavits which supported applications for marriage licences through-
> out the century in the Diocese of Chichester, documents in which are in-
> corporated the *consents* of parents in the case of minors, *natural and*
> *lawful* was the usual phrase in which the relationship of the parent and
> child is described. Often the phrase is shortened to *natural* but there
> is no reason to suppose that this is anything more than an abbreviation
> of the usual description. [134]

Nevertheless the term was certainly used in parish registers with
its modern connotation by 1673 as the following entries in the register of *Keighley,* Yorks, show:-

> 1649/50 Jan 9 Baptism
>   Basterd. Christo: base child of Christo: Clapham and Ann Clapham.
> 1673 Burial Aug 24
>   Christopher ye naturell son of Christo and Ann Clapham was buried. [135]

In this connection Mr. MacLean points out:-[136]

> Personally, I always regard with some suspicion allegations of bastardy
> in parish registers of the late 17th Century, when the names of both
> parents are given. Many a parson did not hesitate to describe as bastards
> the children of those who had gone through a form of marriage of which

---

[134] *Gen. Mag.* Vol. 5. p. 250.
[135] Cited by Lord Farrer *Gen. Mag.* Vol. 5 p. 176. Two earlier instances of the
       modern usage from other sources are cited by R. J. Beevor *Gen. Mag.* Vol. 5
       p. 217, but the former of these is discounted by Mr. D. MacLean, Vol. 5.
       p. 250.
[136] *Gen. Mag.* Vol. 5. p. 250.

he did not happen to approve.[137] In burial registers there is evidence
of this feeling, when a woman is described as "the pretended wife" of
her husband, and one has noticed cases in which the offending word has
been scored out by a later and more charitable hand.

However, whilst many cases of alleged illegitimacy might be of dissenters or Roman Catholics, in general Mr. MacLean's suspicion is
probably unjustified. It is true that in earlier registers it was
very common in cases of illegitimacy to record only the father's name,
as in the following examples from the registers of *St. Andrew,
Newcastle-on-Tyne*.

> 1634 Feb 13 Margaret sup.d. [supposed daughter] to Richard Richardson.
> Sureties – Charles Robson, Margaret Thompson and Margaret Maddison.
> It was borne under a wayne befor Richard Aplyes dore in a morning
> in a sore frost and snow..... [More details given].
>
> 1640 Feb 22 Andrew supposed s to Rande Atkinson workman very bas begott
> for he is the [4?] bastor that he hath by that woman.
>
> 1641 May 30 Margaret suposed daughter to Capten William Abernathe one of
> the Skotes Arme he hath a wif of his owne in Scotland the mothers
> nam is Margaret Powr.[138]

However, by the late 17th century it was general for both parents to
be given as in the example cited earlier. In fact a notice occurs in
a Hertfordshire register to the effect that after Aug. 1634 it was
required by Act of Parliament that the names of both parents should
be entered in all baptisms.[139] The later practice of giving only the
mother's name (with perhaps a postcript naming the *reputed father*)
seems to have come into general use only in the 18th century.[140]

There was considerable prejudice against the baptism of illegitimate children. Many probably remained unbaptised, or, if baptised were
not registered. Sometimes the reluctance to baptise bastards came from
the clergy:

> *Ulcomb*, Kent.
>
> "Jeremias, filius scorti de Hedcorne, baptizatus' fuit 18mo die Decembris
> 1608. This child was born in the fields as was reported, but whether in
> Hedcorne or in Ulcombe is not justly known; yet they of Hedcorne would
> not suffer it to be baptized there, although often offered, so it was
> above 3 months unbaptized, as the woman said who brought it."[141]

and sometimes from the laity. In the Vestry Minutes of *St. Saviours
Southwark* appears in 1613

> "That the Minister shall be turned out at the pleasure of the Vestry and
> that he shall not baptize any bastard, without half a day's notice, to be

---

[137] e.g. A Roman Catholic Marriage ceremony. See *Roman Catholics* in Volume II.
[138] Cited by Richard Welford *N & Q*. 8th Ser. 1 p.223.
[139] F.C. Cass *N & Q*. 7th Ser. 4 p.109.
[140] See also Section on *Foundlings and Workhouse Children* in Appendix III.
Surnames pp.96–98.
[141] J.S. Burn *op.cit.* p.86. W.E. Tate (*The Parish Chest* p.196) cites a
similar case at Merton, Surrey in 1723 and attributes this to a
mistaken belief that baptism gave a legal settlement in the parish.
However, the prejudice against the baptism of bastards clearly long
ante-dated the Settlement laws.

Nurse Children

Baptisms or Burials of Nurse-children (usually spelt *Norschilde*) are fairly common in the registers of the Home Counties. There were children put out to nurse with people in the country. Most of these were illegitimate or waifs and the vast majority died in infancy or childhood.[143] Often no parentage is given in the registers.

Negro Servants

Adult Baptisms of Negro servants are not infrequent in parish registers particularly in country districts, thus emphasizing the comparative size of the 18th Century Negro population in this country, which some estimates place as high as 30,000. In the registers of *Lancaster* there are 12 entries of baptisms of adult negroes between 1759 and 1764.[144] The Negroes are generally described by some such term as *" a Blackamoor"*, *" an African"*, *" a black"*, *" a blackboy"*. These descriptions are seldom found in marriage entries but it may be assumed that many of these servants contracted mixed marriages and their descendants were absorbed into the population.[145] The following baptismal entry occurs in the register of *Midgham*, Berks:

October ye 11 daughter frances of Liddey and Steeven Tegg a Black.

and in the churchwardens' accounts for August 1st 1762 appears

To a coffin for Ste Teggs Wifes Black Child which her husband supposed to be a Bastard and on that account compeled her to bring it on the parish Charge.

After the founding of the East India Company, the baptisms of Indians are occasionally found, as in the following entry from *Bishop Wearmouth*; Durham:

"March 27, 1695, a person aged about 20 years, a Tawny, borne at the Bay of Bengal, in the East Indies, and being taken captive by the English, in his minoritie, was (after due examination of himself and witnesses) baptized, and named John Weremouth, by me.   T.O.., Curate." [146]

Post 1837 Births

Many persons were unregistered in the early years and their baptisms must still be sought in the parish registers. A correspondent

---

142 *ibid.* p.83. footnote.
143 Cox *op.cit.* p.67-8.
144 T. Canon Hughes. *N & Q.* Vol.160 p.80.
145 I would be most interested to hear of any descent which can be traced from one of them [D.J.S.].
146 Cited by J.S. Burn *op.cit.* p.81.

to *Notes and Queries* pointed out in 1868: [147]

> "I do not think the registers sent to Somerset House have as yet supplied the place of our parochial registers. First because in a large town, unless (in case of a birth) the father of the child takes the trouble to give notice to the registrar, no entry is made. Secondly because it is optional whether or not he enter the child by any name, and if he does enter a name it may be entirely changed when the child is baptized and entered in the parish register."

He continued that he registered a child without submitting a name, asked to add the name later and was refused unless a baptismal certificate was produced. He announced his intention of not registering any further children. This evoked a fierce correspondence. A Superintendent Registrar confirmed that "unless a parent felt the importance of registering his child's birth, a Registrar may never hear of it." [148] There was considerable discussion whether a name could be conferred before baptism; [149] one correspondent pointed out that "a person's name is that by which for the time being he choses to call himself" [150] and another pointed out that Registrars normally do insist on a name begin given. [151] It was also alleged that some clergy were making a serious and apparently successful attempt to prevent the civil registration of births:

> "G.W.M. doubts if I ever heard of a clergyman preventing a child's name being entered in the register of the birth. I can assure him that I have not only heard of numerous such cases, but of clergymen preventing any register of the birth at all, and wrongfully and untruly telling the parents it was unnecessary as the register of baptism was sufficient.... At another trial a clergyman considered it incumbent upon him to explain a handbill he had affixed to the church doors and which the parent stated had induced him to refuse to register his child's birth." [152]

Another important point raised concerned the registration of illegitimate births:

> "In Scotland illegitimate births are registered with as great regularity as legitimate ones. But in England it seems to me impossible that this can be the case. Such births are naturally kept as quiet as possible – the parent very rarely feels the importance of registering the birth of such a child; so that it is, I think pretty nearly certain that in England the registrar must never hear of many such births." [153]

It seems likely that in the early years at least one birth in seven

---

[147] G.W.M. 4th Ser. Vol.2. p.262.
[148] *ibid* p.282.
[149] *ibid* p.611.
[150] G.W.M. 4th Ser. 3. p.64. On this point See *Change of Name* in Appendix IV to this article, pp.124–127.
[151] W.H.S. 4th Ser. 3. pp.386-88.
[152] W.H.W.T. *N & Q* 4th Ser. 3. p.249.
[153] *N & Q.* 4th Ser. II. p.542 (1868).

was unregistered.[154]

Apart from unregistered births, it must also be borne in mind that although a name has been registered, this may be changed at baptism. Thus at a Lambeth Inquest 11 Feb 1924 a witness stated she was registered as *Emily Sophia Jane* and christened *Emily Charlotte Elizabeth*. The latter was held to be her true name.[155] Furthermore, in the case of children registered merely as *"male"* or *"female"* the baptismal register is the sole source of their names. In all, it cannot be assumed that post-1837 baptismal registers are of little genealogical importance.

C. MARRIAGES

Normally, of course, the English marriage took place, and still takes place, by banns, and until 1837 marriages (except those of Jews and Quakers) without banns could in general be *lawfully* celebrated only in virtue of licences issued by the Bishop or archdeacon or his surrogate, or by one of the archbishops.[156]

When a marriage was by licence, this is normally, even before 1753, indicated in the registers, and the marriage licence, giving considerably more information than the parish register entry can therefore usually be fairly easily traced. In general the middle and upper classes tended to get married by license and the poorer classes by banns. In the 18th century, Horace Walpole says:

> "Publication of banns was already an established ordinance, but totally in disuse except amongst the inferior people who did not blush to obey the law."[157]

One must however beware of over generalizing. Many lower class people were married by licence, particularly in the peculiar jurisdictions where the fees charged were probably lower than the fee charged for marrying in the parish church.[158]

Although marriages received the blessing of the church and state only if celebrated by banns or licence, both canon law and the ancient Common Law of England were agreed that no formal ceremony, secular or ecclesiastical was necessary to the making of a valid marriage.[159] In 1753 by the *Hardwicke Act* all marriages except those of Quakers or Jews had to be celebrated by Banns or Licence. The law remained in force until by the *Marriage Act* of 1836 a marriage could be celebrated without either banns or licence in a building licenced for marriages,

---

[154] For a fuller discussion of the whole subject see *Parish Registers and the Genealogist* pp. 145–147. See also *Daily Telegraph* 29 April 1907 p.8. Col.6. and 30 April 1907 p.9. Col.1.

[155] *Glasgow Bulletin* 12 Feb 1924. Cited by C.L. Ewen *History of Surnames of the British Isles* p.419.

[156] See article on *Marriage Licences* p.228.

[157] *Memoirs of the Reign of King George II* p.338. (1846).

[158] For a discussion of this subject see *Marriage Licences.* pp.226–228.

[159] For a discussion of the subject see *Clandestine Marriages* pp. 292–293.

providing the Registrar was present.[160] Banns, however, are still necessary for marriages in churches belonging to the Church of England or Church of Scotland.

Espousal

In mediaeval times marriage was preceded by espousal and this still survives in the marriage service.[161] Espousal might be entered into by either sex at the age of seven years. Swinburn's *Treatise of Spousals* published in 1686 notes that the custom had largely gone out of use, and the *Hardwicke Act* of 1753 enacted that no suit or proceeding should be had in the Ecclesiastical Court in order to compel a celebration of any marriage *in facie Ecclesiae* by reason of any contract of matrimony.

Entries of espousals in the parish register are rare, but they are occasionally found:

Boughton Monchelsea, Kent.
" 1633. Sponsalia inter Gulielm' Maddox et Elizabeth' Grimestone in debitâ iuris formâ transacta 10 die Januarii."[162]

Restrictions on Marriage

Most of the restrictive rules as to marriage date from pre-Reformation times. As the nuptial mass formed part of the ceremonial, it could take place only in the forenoon. The register of *Soberton*, Hants, has several entries about the year 1580 of marriages "at iij ye cloke in ye morning" and one of "an oure before day breke by licence fro the chancelur." Canon lxxii of 1603 ordered that no minister, under pain of suspension for three years, "shall join any person in marriage at any unseasonable times, but only between the hours of eight and twelve in the forenoon."[163]

During the Commonwealth the restrictions seem to have lapsed in many places.

Great Staughton, Hunts.
Lucy Cosen widdow was married to Jo Cosen (brother to her former husband) the 15th daie of December 1659 at St. Neots by the mynister of the towne, and at seaven of the clocke in the nighte.[164]

---

[160] After 1899 the attendance of the registrar was not required where the marriage was celebrated by an *authorized person*.

[161] "Wilt thou have this woman to thy wedded wife?" "*I will*" constitutes the espousal or contract *de futuro.*

[162] J.S. Burn. *op.cit.* p.144. Espousal was customary in Leicestershire in the 16th Century — see *Marriage Contracts in the Reign of Queen Elizabeth:* Reports and Papers of Associated Architectural Societies Vol. xxx pt. 1. (1909) Cited and briefly discussed by P. Laslett. *The World We Have Lost* (1965) pp.141–2.

[163] Revd. R.W. Muncey *The Romance of Parish Registers.* p.71.

[164] Joseph Rix. *N & Q.* 2nd Ser. 5. p.139. (1858).

However they were largely reinforced at the Restoration and the Canon of 1603 was reiterated in the *Marriage Act* of 1753. The time was extended to three in the afternoon by the *Marriage Act* of 1886. Marriages on Sundays although not forbidden were discouraged.

The close seasons of the year, too, have very old canonical authority. There were anciently three of these: from Advent to S. Hilary's Day (January 13th), from Septuagesima to Low Sunday, and from Rogation Sunday to Trinity Sunday. The *Council of Trent* reduced these to two in the Roman Church, but they remained in the English Church after the Reformation. In 1575 unsuccessful attempts were made both in Parliament and Convocation to make marriage lawful at all seasons of the year. [165]

It seems that throughout the sixteenth century and a great part of the seventeenth these restrictions were generally observed. Archdeacon Cosin mentioned the rule in his visitation articles in 1627. It lapsed, of course, during the Commonwealth, and attempts to reimpose it after the Restoration were not entirely successful. It is now virtually obsolete, and probably any attempt to put it in force would be held by the Privy Council to be repugnant to common law. [166]

Information given in a Marriage Entry

Before 1753 normally only the names of the parties were given and sometimes (but by no means invariably) the name of the parish if one of the parties came from elsewhere. Sometimes it is noted whether the marriage was by banns or licence. In some early registers, however, only the bridegroom's surname is given.

St. Mary Minster, Kent.
Anno 1558 Maii 10. Nupt erant Johannes Andrewe et Agnes Uxor eius. [167]

Sometimes entries of this kind may have been due to the inadequacy of rough notes made at the time, [168] and the practice is occasionally encountered in later registers. The Hardwicke registers give much fuller information according to the prescribed form i.e. names and parishes of the parties: date and place of marriage, whether by banns or licence; whether with the consent of parents or guardians; and the name of the officating minister. There are also the signatures or marks of the parties, the minister and of the witnesses. Not infrequently, even after the passing of the Hardwicke Act, the marriage registers were improperly kept and all the details were not entered. [169]

---

[165] W.E. Tate *The Parish Chest* p.62.
[166] *ibid* p.63.
[167] Cited by Burn *op.cit.* p.166.
[168] See above pp.27–32.
[169] The classic example is *Feltham*, Middlesex, where almost incredibly, sometimes only the marks of the parties were recorded, without even their names. See *above* p.34.

Marks

The post-1753 marriage registers were signed by both the parties and by witnesses. This is therefore a useful test of minimal literacy and a statistical survey based on these registers is at present being conducted by Dr. Roger Schofield of the *Cambridge Group for the History of Population and Social Structure*. However, it must be borne in mind that a mark does not invariably indicate illiteracy. Not only might a person use a mark through old age or blindness[170] but there are numerous cases known of feigned illiteracy, It was considered unseemly for a literate bride to sign when her husband could not,[171] and even as late as 1903 a registrar wrote:[172]

> "I am a superintendent registrar in Cornwall and it is by no means un-common for all the parties to a wedding to deny before me the power of writing and to make their cross. Inquiry often shows that either bride or bridegroom cannot write, and that the others feign ignorance to spare the ignorant one's feelings – a little disturbing for statistical purposes, but showing real kindness."

The study of Marks, although of no genealogical significance is of considerable interest. Although the cross was the most common, many others are found in marriage registers and elsewhere. In the registers of *Betchworth*, Surrey is a memorandum dated 1697 to the effect that the vicar had assented to the 39 Articles of Religion in the presence of witnesses. Two of these made marks, these dividing the Christian name from the Surname. One mark is of the arrow-head type. The other consists of a circle, from the right of the circumference of which is drawn a horizontal line with two short vertical lines from its lower side near the end furthest from the circle.[173] Similar marks have been pointed out elsewhere.[174] Many marks represent attempts to write initials.

Post-1837 Marriage Registers

These were a further improvement on the Hardwicke Registers as there were columns for the ages of the parties and for the names and occupations of the fathers. However, one unfortunate aspect of these registers particularly in the first 30 years or so was the custom of entering *"full age"* or *"minor"* in the age column.

Following a complaint against this practice in *Notes and Queries*[175]

---

[170] I. Chalkley Gould. *N & Q.* 9th Ser. 11. p.237.
[171] W.C.B. *N & Q.* 9th Ser. 11. p.294. For more discussion on this subject see Maitland *"Dark Ages"*.
[172] *ibid*, p.294.
[173] Francis R. Rushton. *N & Q.* 9th Ser. 11. p.109 (1903).
[174] e.g. *West Hadden*, Northants. J.T. Page. *N & Q.* 9th Ser. 11. p.175.
[175] 4th Ser. 9 p.277 (1872).

a vicar wrote:

> "Having seen the registers of a large number of parishes both small and great, I believe the omission complained of will be far more generally in the latter than the former, much time being necessarily taken up in filling up the double registers of several married couples; and both parties to the contract shy of telling, perhaps for the first time to each other, their exact ages, both also, in country parishes often apparently wofully ignorant of their own ages. I have, from the first time I had to make an entry recognised the importance of giving the ages correctly; and I have sometimes been amused at a discussion between the man and wife and the clerk, who appeared to know better what was the husband's or wife's age than themselves. Frequently I could plainly see that the age stated was a mere guess, probably ten years from the truth, and in despair of even approximating to it have entered "full age."[176]

However, a further correspondent pointed out that only *full age* or *minor* was required in the specimen schedule attached to the 1836 Act and denounced the asking of exact ages as impertinent.[177]

Banns Registers

Under the Hardwicke Act marriages could be celebrated by banns or by licence. In the former case, banns had to be called in the parishes of both parties on three successive Sundays before the marriage. As is pointed out elsewhere[178] the name given for the banns to be valid should be the name by which the party is generally known, which need not necessarily be the name given at baptism. Where one or both of the parties have been misdescribed in the publication of banns, the court must prove an intent to deceive by *both* parties for the marriage to be invalid.[179]

Surviving Banns registers are of three kinds: (a) banns only, (b) banns in the first half of the volume and marriages in the second (c) entry of banns and marriage on the same form. Although some pre-1753 banns registers survive, in general these are found only from 1754 when the printed books were issued. Many banns registers were started when by the Marriage Act of 1824:[180]

> "the banns shall be published from the said register book of Banns by the officiating minister and not from loose papers, and after publication shall be signed by the officiating minister or by some person under his direction."

However this was not intended to prevent the entry of banns in the marriage register and the use of these composite registers continued until

[176] Francis J. Leachman. *ibid.* p.345.
[177] *ibid.* p.434.
[178] Appendix III *Surnames* pp.90—91 Appendix IV *Christian Names* p.127. *Divorce and Annulment* p.325.
[179] J.T. Hammick. *The Law of Marriage* p.72. See also *Divorce and Annulment* p.325.
[180] 4 Geo IV cap. 76. clause 6.

1837 when the use of duplicate marriage registers in accordance with the 1836 Act necessitated a different banns book, printed in small quarto.

It is extraordinary that many genealogists appear to show so little interest in banns registers. Often they give the sole indication of where a marriage not in the parish actually took place, and it is very unfortunate that many transcribers of parish registers have not included records of banns. The clergy also often regard these as of no importance as records and not infrequently in a parish where a perfect series of registers of baptisms, marriages and burials survives no banns registers at all are to be found. In the past many surveys of parish registers have not included banns registers and although the volumes of the *National Index* have included banns wherever possible, if no banns register is listed, it cannot be taken that none exists.

Civil War and Commonwealth Marriages

The Marriage registers, of course, suffered in common with other registers from the general chaos of the Civil War period. Additional factors, however, affected the marriage registers particularly. After the ejections of 1643 and 1645, it was not uncommon for Royalists in a parish having an intruded minister to resort for marriages to the nearest Anglican clergyman who had managed to keep his living.

The institution of civil *registers* in 1653 also had a considerable effect on marriage entries. Often more detail was given than hitherto. At *St. Benet Paul's Wharf,* London the trade of the groom was included:

> "Begone the 30 of September 1653. John Ridgway, bricklar, and Mary Chart, widdow, according to a act of parliament baringe date the 24 August 1653 was three several times publissed in the market-place and afterwarde maried by mee upon Tuesday the six of December 1653.
> Thomas Atkin."[181]

Sometimes the registers record *"publication"* of marriages (i.e. Banns) rather than the marriages themselves, but these often give very considerable information as in the following entry in the register of *Shepton Mallett,* Somerset;

> "Memorandum: That the intended marriage between Richard Mallett of Sutton Mallett, in the countie of Somersett, gentleman (now an officer in the standing army) the sonne of Francis Mallett, some tyme of Sutton Mallett, in the countie of Sommersett aforesaid, gentleman, deceased, and of Elizabeth his relict, now living in the parish and countie afore-said of the one part; and Susanna Newbery, spinster, daughter of Henry Newbery esquier, and of Frances his wife, both now living in the town of..... and countie of..... of the other part, was published on three several Lords days in the parish church; that is to say, on the 3d. 10th Decemb. no exception was made against the same."[182]

181 Cited by R. Bigland *op.cit.* p.9.
182 *ibid* pp.7-8.

Sometimes ambiguous entries of *"marriages"* do in fact record dates of *"publication"* as in the following examples of *St. Alphage, Canterbury* in 1657.

> Tho' Ady of Eastwell and Elizabeth Titterden of Kingsnoth wer married
> May – 8-15-18
> Joh' Hales of Dover and Elizabeth Skilet of of (*sic*) Burgate was maried
> March – 13-20-27.
> Steven Cort of Reculver and An Houson widdow of Hackingtun was maried
> Aprill – 24-28-May the 5. [183]

Often the marriage was performed by the *register* at the nearest town and therefore appears in that register rather than the parish of either of the parties. Thus in the register of *Arundel,* Sussex is the entry:

> 1653 March 9 "John Turner of Steyning, Sussex, and Sarah Campion of Sounting, in the said country, spinster, with consent of friends. Published in Steyning and Sounting."[184]

Sometimes the incumbent was elected *register.* However, he had no power to marry and could only register a civil marriage. Nevertheless, some clergy entirely ignored the new legislation. For example, at Maid's Moreton, Bucks:

> A.D.1653 By the act before mentioned in the year 1653 marriages were not to be performed by the Minister, but the Justices of the Peace, yet none in this parish were bedded before they were solemnly wedded in the Church and that according to the orders of the Church of England.[185]

On the other hand the new legislation gave more scope for non-religious (probably traditional) marriage ceremonies: For example at *Eastling,* Kent:

> 1654 Sept 4 James Gylman being carried to marying uppon ffoure mens backes to Joan Ottaway house (being both of Eastling) out of his ffather's house were maried uppone ye bedd, they carried him by a Justice in Achoritie choisen by com'ission namelie Maior Bealke according to an acte of p'lement.[186]

Mr. T.F. Allen has noted[187] that many marriages of the Commonwealth period were recorded in the registers of more than one parish, and there are many instances of information in one register being more complete than in the other. Thus the registers of *St. Andrews, Hertford* generally gives parishes of origin. In the following examples

---

[183] Cited by J.M. Cooper. *N & Q.* 7th Ser. 6 pp.257-8. An example from *Abingdon Pigotts,* Cambs is given in *ibid.* 5 p.367.

[184] R. Bigland *op.cit.* p.9. The Mayor of Durham seems to have acted as a Registrar for the whole county, See C. Newton *A County Civil Register.* Journ. Soc. Archiv. III No.4 Oct. 1966 p.194.

[185] Cited by W.E. Tate *op.cit.* p.63. See also *above* p.

[186] Cited by C.E.G. Dickinson. *N & Q.* 8th Ser. 2 p.246.

[187] *Gen. Mag.* Vol.12 No.12 Dec. 1957 p.418.

the data in brackets do not appear in the register named at side.

Jn Charles (Watton) My. Kimpton (L. Munden)   *Watton.*
Wm Andrews (Benington) Eliz Clark (Watton)   *Watton.*
Thos. Wabey (Watton) Eliz Clarke (Digswell)   *Watton.*
Nic. Draper (Shephall) My. Cann (Benington)   *Benington.*
Ed. Anthony (Bayford) Alice North (Yardley)   *Yardley.*

In the case of *St. Albans Abbey*, cases occur where the parishes differ from that where the alternative entry occurs, and in addition the ages of the parties appear. Three examples are:

Timy. Norris 23 (S. Step) My. Megrum 22 (Abbots. Lang^y)   *Aldenham*
Ric. Eallin 21 (Shenley) My. Rawnce 20 (Shenley)   *Aldenham*
Nic. Camfield 27 (Cheshunt) Ann Man 27 (Kimpton)   *Ayot S. Lawr.*

In the case of *Much Hadham*, the register notes the parentage of the parties, not given in the alternate entry. Two examples taken from many:

Jn. Willie (s Ed. of Thorley) Eliz Hampton (d. Jn.) *Ware*
Wm. Feast (s. Wm of L. Hadham) Jane Calvert (d. Felix)   *L. Hadham*

Doubtless this practice occurred in the registers of other counties during the Commonwealth.

Marriages of Dissenters

Up to 1753 practically all Roman Catholics, Quakers and Jews and a large minority of the other denominations married in their own places of worship without any second form of marriage in the parish church. Nevertheless, entries may be found in Anglican parish registers of marriages performed elsewhere. Thus, many Roman Catholic Marriages celebrated at *Old Hall*, Herts. and appearing in that Catholic register also appear in the Parish Register of *Braughing* four miles away. [188] However, marriages by dissenting ministers were severely checked by the *Hardwicke Act* of 1753. The Quakers and Jews were specifically exempted, but the other Nonconformist denominations seem to have complied with the law. From 1754, one should therefore expect to find the marriages of nearly all dissenters recorded in the Anglican registers. Many, – probably most – Roman Catholics henceforth went through a second form of marriage in the Anglican Church. [189]

Missing Marriages

Entries of marriages may be missing in the relevant parish register for a variety of reasons. Marriages were, of course, frequently in the bride's parish and marriages by licence were often in one of the churches of the city or town where the licence was obtained. Where the clergyman held several livings he might frequently marry couples from one

---

[188]   For further discussion of this subject see *Roman Catholics. The Three Denominations* and *Society of Friends* all in Volume II.
[189]   See *Roman Catholics* in Volume II.

parish at the church of another. An extension of this practice was the custom for Fellows of Oxford Colleges holding livings in Oxfordshire, North Berkshire or Buckinghamshire to marry couples in their college chapels. Sometimes the marriage was entered both in the parish register and that of the College Chapel, but sometimes in one or the other. There are thus numerous instances of marriages, missing in the parish register but entered elsewhere.[190] As has been pointed out, during the Civil War and Commonwealth period, it was quite usual for royalists in a parish having an 'intruded' minister to resort for marriages to the nearest Anglican clergyman who had managed to keep his living.[191]

Many marriages which have not been traced in a likely parish register may have been clandestine. Until the Hardwicke Act of 1753 these may have been celebrated by one of the *"marriage-mongers"* – clergy, often exercising peculiar jurisdictions who specialized in marrying without banns or licence. Macqueen alleges that the number of marriages without banns outnumbered the marriages *in facie ecclesiae*.[192] This is probably an over estimate and his implication that such marriages were irregular does not seem to take into account the large number of marriages by licence. However, every genealogist is familiar with pedigrees where for one generation after another the marriages have not been traced and the number of irregular marriages was certainly very high. It would seem that up till 1753 the majority of those contracting " clandestine" marriages did so to get married more cheaply they could in the parish church, rather than because there was parental opposition. This was probably also the case with the marriages at the *Fleet Prison* the vast majority of which one may assume not to have been genuinely clandestine. After 1753 when those wishing to contract clandestine marriages had to go to *Gretna Green* or elsewhere in Scotland or to the *Channel Islands* clearly the saving of expense could not have ever been the motive.[193] Until the invalidity of such marriages was finally decided by the Courts in 1843,[194] lawful marriages have also been proved from the fact of long co-habitation with common reputation of marriage. Thus a marriage may have been nowhere recorded until and unless it was challenged before the ecclesiastical courts, which occurred with only a minute fraction of such unions. In the

---

[190] Mrs. Gabrielle Lambricke, *Oxford Colleges and Some Country Parishes round Oxford in the Early 18th Century.* Oxoniensia Vol.25. (1960). More details on the colleges and parishes concerned are given in the *General Information* sections of *Oxfordshire* and *Berkshire.* For marriages in Cambridge chapels see J.F. Williams *"A Marriage Register at Queens' College, Cambridge "* Proc. Camb. Antiqu. Soc. 40. pp.13–23 (1944).
[191] See *Civil War and Commonwealth Marriages* above p.59.
[192] Macqueen. *On Divorce and Matrimonial Jurisdiction* (1858) p.2.
[193] For a full examination of the whole subject see *Clandestine Marriages.*
[194] *Reg v Millis.* See *Clandestine Marriages* p.315.

poorer areas of cities after the Industrial Revolution marriages in church were probably the exception rather than the rule. In his famous survey *London Labour and the London Poor* (1851) Henry Mayhew wrote:

> "Only one tenth – at the outside one-tenth – of the couples living together and carrying on the costermongering trade, are married. In Clerkenwell parish, however, where the number of married couples is about a fifth of the whole, this difference is easily accounted for, as in Advent and Easter the incumbent of that parish marries poor without a fee. Of the rights of "legitimate" or "illegitimate" children the costermongers understand nothing and account it a mere waste of money and time to go through the ceremony of wedlock when a pair can live together, and be quite as well regarded by their fellows, without it. The married women associate with the unmarried mothers of families without the slightest scruple. There is no honour attached to the marriage state, and no shame to concubinage. Neither are the unmarried women less faithful to their "partners" than the married; but I understand that, of the two classes, the unmarried betray the most jealousy."[195]

Another observation made by Mayhew is also of considerable interest to those concerned with the "genealogy of the submerged":

> "Unions take place when the lad is but 14. Two or three out of 100 have their female helpmates at that early age; but the female is generally a couple of years older than her partner. Nearly all the costermongers form such alliances as I have described, when both parties are under twenty."[196]

Child Marriages

If the "marriages" of costermongers at 14 were something of an oddity in 19th Century England, child marriages were certainly common in Mediaeval times. The children used the same words same vows as were made and used by adults, and a widow of 9 received her wifely dower as legally as a widow of 19. A child marriage held good for life unless it was denounced at or soon after the parties attained the ages of 14 and 12 respectively. In all probability most of the child marriages remained firm, while some were confirmed at ripe age in the Bishop's Court. Others, however, were broken by what was called a process of divorce, but was really a suit for nullity of marriage.[197]

By the commencement of Parish Registers child marriages were less frequent but still by no means exceptionally rare. They are

---

[195] p.459. Abridgment by Peter Quennell *Mayhew's London* p.57.
[196] *Mayhew's London* p.58. The reason given for these early unions is that in the event of a quarrel with the father, the boy and his wife can start trading on their own account.
[197] Rev. C. Moor. *The Mediaeval Marriage Market* Gen. Mag. Vol.12 No.8 Dec. 1956 p.258.

particularly difficult to identify except from other sources as ages were seldom given in Parish Registers. However, when the first child is born many years after the marriage, the possibility of child marriage should be borne in mind and the records of the relevant Consistory Court searched. Thus in the records of the Chester Consistory Court appear the following cases[198]

1561, December. John Bridge 13-4, and his wife Elizabeth. He cried, but his father compelled him to be married at Bury Church, having made a bargain to do so when he was 2. John would eat no meat at supper, but the priest persuaded him to sleep that night with his wife though he turned his back upon her all night.

1564, April 15. John Somerford, 3, and Jane Brereton, 2, were marriaed in Brereton Church by agreemant between Sir William Brereton and the boy's father. The boy was carried in a man's arms, who held him while the words of matrimony were in speaking. Another man carried the girl and spake all or most of the words for her.

Although the majority of child marriages were of the nobility and gentry and were of course marriages of convenience involving the descent of estates, this was by no means invariably the case. Sometimes it would appear the marriages were celebrated at the whim of one or other of the children without even the consent of the parents. Such a marriage was valid, but the minister was subject to ecclesiastical censure as the following case shows.[199]

1565, November 8. James Ballard and his wife Anne. She, when aged 10-11, enticed him with two apples to go to Colne Church and marry her. The Archbishop of York sternly reprimanded the curate for marrying this youthful couple at 10 p.m.

The Revd. C. Moor comments:
" We have no means of ascertaining the whole number of child marriages in this country in any year, nor the whole number of divorces, but eight suits were brought in 1565 in the single and comparatively small diocese of Chester. Considering the deterrent effects of publicity and the expense of ecclesiastical litigation it would certainly be safe to assume that marriages broken at ripe age were but a small proportion of the whole number, and that most child marriages were quietly acquiesced in when the parties came to years of discretion. Had it not been so the custom would before this have died a natural death."

The attitude of the Church all along, from the 12th Century at least, was simple acceptance of the custom, and the clergy performed the marriage rites. From this point of view an interesting case occurred in 1582, when Richard Brooke aged nearly 11 married Joan, aged 9, daughter of William Chaderton, Bishop of Chester. Their

---

[198] F.J. Furnivall *Records of Consistory Court of Chester* Surtees Soc. 1845 pp.54-8 cited with numerous other examples by Rev. C. Moor. *op.cit.* pp.260-1. P. Laslett in *The World We Have Lost* (1965) p.86 points out that only one half of one per cent of the marriages in the diocese of Chester between 1561 and 1566 could have been child marriages.

[199] Furnivall *op.cit.* cited by Rev. C. Moor *op.cit.*

marriage was ratified in the Bishop's Court in 1586. After this, child marriages still continued. In 1606 the Earl of Essex, aged scarcely 14, married Frances, aged 13, daughter of the Earl of Suffolk. In 1666-7 Elizabeth, heiress of the Percies, at 12 years 2 months married the son and heir of the Duke of Newcastle. On 20th May 1673 the Earl of Aylesbury wrote in his diary:

> "This morning about 10 of the clock, at Lambeth, the Archbishop of Canterbury married my grandson, John Power,[200] not 8 years old, to Mrs Catharine Fitzgerald, his cousin german, about 13 years of age. I gave her in the chapel there, and they answered as well as those of greater age. The wedding dinner and supper I gave them..... I did duties and commended them to God's blessing."

In Scotland, however, an Act of Assembly was passed in 1600 "to correct divers and great inconveniences arising from the untimeous marriage of young and tender persons" and it was ordered

> "that no minister presume to join in matrimony any persons in time coming except the man be 14 and the woman be 12 years of age complete."

It is uncertain at what period this obnoxious custom finally died out in England.

Re-Marriages

In cases of child marriage, a further ceremony was normally held when the parties had attained the ages of 14 and 12 respectively. In John Evelyn's diary appear the following entries:

> "1 Aug 1672. I was at the marriage of Lord Arlington's onely daughter (a sweet child of ever there was any) to the Duke of Grafton, the King's natural son by the Dutchesse of Cleaveland. The Abp of Canterbury officiated, the King and all the grandees being present. I had a favour given me by my Lady, but tooke no greate joy at the thing for many reasons."

> "6 Nov 1679. Was this evening at the remarriage of the Dutchesse of Grafton to the Duke (His Majesty's natural sonn) she being now 12 years old. The ceremonie was performed in my Lord Chamberlaine's (her father's) lodgings at Whitehall by the Bishop of Rochester, His Majesty being present. A sudden and unexpected thing, when everybody beleiv'd the first marriage would have come to nothing; but the measure being determin'd I was privately invited by my Lady, her mother to be present."

In later more scrupulous times the age of one of the parties could create doubt as to the validity of a marriage and result in a second ceremony. In the registers of *Wootton St. Laurence,* Hants. is recorded the marriage of George Wyatt of Lyss and Elizabeth Lavey, to

---

[200]   Afterwards 2nd Earl of Tyrone.

which the following note was appended:

> "It having appeared after 26 March that Geo Wyatt had not attained the age of twenty one years by two days, the officers of the parish of Preston Candover where he had gained a settlement, and to which he was removed, objected to the marriage and the ceremony was therefore performed again at the request of the said Geo Wyatt and Eliz. Lavey on 4 April 1792 by me D.B. Thain curate. "[201]

There could be other reasons for remarriage. In the register of *East Quantock's Head*, Somerset 7th August 1560 is recorded the remarriage of "Thomas Luttrell and Mrs Margaret Hadley." This is the last known instance of remarriage of two persons whose marriage had been annulled on the grounds of spiritual relationship. [202] At St. Mary, Bermondsey on 1 Aug 1604 is recorded the remarriage of Ralphe Goodchilde and his wife Elizabeth, who, on account of the former's long absence had taken another man to be her husband. [203] The most common reason for remarriage was, however, that the previous marriage had been a clandestine one. Thus at *West Haddon*, Northants on 1 May 1816 John Page was married by licence to Ann Dunkley "with consent of her father John Dunkley." An endorsement in pencil reads:

> "This couple had eloped and said to have been married in London, but the father of the woman wished to have them remarried."[204]

In the *Leeds Mercury* of 5th June 1802 appears the marriage notice:

> "On Monday last at Gretna Green, Mr. Blakelock to Miss Sturdy, daughter of Mr. Sturdy of this town, merchant. The lovers left Leeds on Sunday evening at 11 o'clock and arrived at the Temple of Hymen (a distance of 130 miles) before 3 o'clock on Monday afternoon."

On 19th June 1802 is the announcement:

> "On Monday last at our Parish Church, Mr. Ralph Blakelock to Miss Sturdy, daughter of Mr. Sturdy of this town."[205]

Perhaps the most famous example of remarriage is, however, that of the poet Shelley who eloped with Harriet Westbrook and married her at *St. Andrew's, Edinburgh*:

> "Aug 28 1811 Percy Bysshe Shelley, farmer, Sussex and Miss Harriet Westbrook, St. Andrew Church Parish daughter of Mr. John Westbrook, London."

The couple were remarried in London in March 1814.

---

201 Cited by C.S. Ward *N & Q*. 9th Ser. IV. p.135 (1899).
202 R.E. Chester Waters *op.cit*. p.28 See *Divorce and Annulment* p.323.
203 Cited by J.S. Burn *op.cit*. p.181 and R.E. Chester Waters *op.cit*. p.31 in both of which the text of the entry, recording the form of ceremony, is given in full.
204 Cited by John T. Page. *N & Q*. 9th Ser. 4. p.73.
205 Cited by G.D. Lumb. *N & Q*. 9th Ser. 4. p.73.

Frequently the cause of remarriage is not stated, but most probably a previous clandestine marriage is the explanation in the following instances:

> *St. George the Martyr Queen Square Middlesex.* 11 Dec 1799 John Richardson and Penelope Richardson, formerly Lucas both of this parish, they having already been married to each other.

> *St. James Picadilly 27 Apr 1802*
> The Rt. Hon. William Edwards, Lord Kensington and Rt. Hon. Dorothy Edwards, Lady Kensington formerly Dorothy Thomas, they having been already married to each other. Lic. Cant. Witnesses Robert Baxter, Furnival's Inn. Samuel Pride. N.B. The former marriage was on 2 Dec 1797 [signed] R.B. [presumably Robert Baxter above named][206]

D. BURIALS

In the country, until the early 18th century, burials were normally without coffins except for the wealthier classes, although most towns-folk were buried in coffins nearly a century earlier. In general, the local gentry were buried in the church and the remaining parishioners in the churchyard.[207] Burial registers bear witness to the virulance of the outbreaks of plague and other epidemics which were very frequent, particularly in urban areas.[208] In many years, therefore the number of burials greatly exceeded the numbers of baptisms and marriages combined. Very often, however in such troubled times the system of registration broke down completely. Quite apart from this, however in general, burial registers are far less complete than registers of marriages[209] and it is not uncommon to find monumental inscriptions with no equivalent entry in the registers. Thus in *West Haddon*, Northants churchyard are tombstones for the following unregistered persons:

> Rev. Gregory Palmer "Minister of West Haddon" died 11 June 1693.
> Elizabeth wife of Richard Lord died 10 April 1807.
> Elizabeth wife of James Adams died 19 November 1834.

Sometimes the omission is immediately explicable:

> *Stone:*
> In Memory of William and Ann Peck, son and daughter of Thomas and Elizabeth Peck who died Decemb[r] ye 3rd 1776. In the..... th year of their Age.

---

[206] Cited by G.E.C. *N & Q.* 9th Ser. 4 p.9.

[207] For more discussion on this subject see article on *Monumental Inscriptions* pp.246–247.

[208] For more information on this topic see J.S. Burn *op.cit.* pp.118-9.

[209] They are, of course, more complete than the registers of baptisms, in which the births of many, if not most, Catholics and Nonconformists were not entered.

Register:

26 Dec 1776. Burial of Ann D^r of Tho^S and Eliz Peck.

Sometimes the wrong name has clearly been put in the register.

Stone:

William Lucas, son of John and Jane died 22 December 1727

Register:

Thomas Lucas was buryd Decr 25 1727.

Stone:

Mark Lord died 11 December 1826.

Register:

John Lord buried 15 December 1826.

and sometimes discrepancies of date are probably due to rough notes being copied into the register long after the events.

Stone:

Mary wife of John Killworth died 20 July 1786.

Register:

Buried 14 July 1786.

Stone:

Elizabeth Barnett widow died 1 April 1788.

Register:

Buried 5 April 1789. [210]

Apart from omissions and errors due to carelessness, the principal omissions in the burial registers probably concern unbaptized persons, whether children or adults, and soldiers and sailors who died abroad. Moreover, from early times some Roman Catholics and other dissenters were buried privately, sometimes at night in the churchyard by the connivance of an exceptionally tolerant incumbent. [211] After the Toleratio Act numerous cemeteries were opened for the benefit of Nonconformists including Roman Catholics and Jews. A few, especially some belonging to the Society of Friends had been opened half a century earlier. [212] In London the position with regard to the registration of deaths was particularly unsatisfactory. Every parish had its *Searchers*, who were generally two aged female paupers. L. O. Henderson observes:

> When the searchers heard from the parish clerk that there had been a death in a house, they were expected to go and demand a sight of the body. And for that, they were entitled legally to a fee of 4d. But being needy

---

[210] All these examples are from *West Haddon*, Northants and are cited by J. T. Page. *N & Q*. 9th Ser. 4. p. 482 (1899).

[211] See *Roman Catholics. The Three Denominations* and *Society of Friends* all in Volume II.

[212] See *Monumential Inscriptions* pp. 250—251 and *The Three Denominations* and *Society of Friends* in Volume II.

people, they were open to any fee which might be offered to them to dispense with their office altogether. If they were given a 1/- or 2/6 they made no demur about verifying the report of the death without having had a sight of the body at all. They were easily made incapable with gin, and in every respect no reliance could be placed on them or their reports.[213]

Many of the 18th century private burial places kept no efficient registers themselves and vast numbers of interments took place.[214]

Information given in a Burial Entry

Before 1813, most frequently only the name of the deceased is given, sometimes with some short description such as *"widow"* *"wife of X"* or an occupation. Parentage is normally given only in the case of infants or children. Fortunately, however, longer entries are not by any means rare, and perhaps the most interesting of the burial entries are those in which the incumbent (or clerk) has recorded his opinion of the deceased as in the following examples:

> *Attleburgh,* Norfolk. 1625, Aug. 11. *"* Then was buried Mary, wife of Gilbert Greene, hoastesse of the Cock, who knew how to gain more by her trade than any other, and a woman free and kind for any in sickness or woman in her travail or childbed, and for answering for anyones child, and readie to give to anyones marriage.*"*

> *Ramsden Bellhouse,* Essex. 1772, Aug. 24. *"*Samuel Douset (Ebrius iracundus, inops, miserandus abivit) sepultus.*"*

or even a relative of the deceased:

> *St. Peter's in the East, Oxford.* *"*1568. There was buried Alyce, the wiff of (a naughtie fellow whose name is) Mathew Manne.*"*[215]

Sometimes the information is disappointingly meagre due to the not infrequent custom of recording a person's burial under his nickname, as in the following examples:

> *Croydon* 1596 Dec 7 Old Megg buried.
> *Hart,* Durham 1641 Feb 12 Old Mother Midnight of Elwick buried.
> *Cheshunt,* Herts 1600 Feb 7 Old Plod buried.[216]

Some registers are worse than others in this respect. In the registers of *Blackburn,* Lancs. between 1600 and 1660 are 49 of these entries, and at *Ribchester,* Lancs. between 1598 and 1695 thirteen.

---

[213] L. O. Henderson *Parish Registers* Amateur Historian, Vol. 4, No. 6, Winter 1959-60.

[214] For more information on private and public London cemeteries see *Monumental Inscriptions* p. 252-3 and Holme *London Burial Grounds.*

[215] These three examples are taken from Chester Waters. *op. cit.* pp. 46 & 84. Some interesting entries of this kind are found in W. J. Harvey *"Great Amwell Past and Present"* (1896).

[216] Many others are given in J. S. Burn *op. cit.* p. 121.

These include: *Thinke on, Numbd Hard, Chrunchon, Dicked Baculus, Thick Skin, My Lordes, Guyley, Frappo.* As late as 1772 in one entry in the parish register of *Esher,* Surrey there is a string of alternative nicknames:

Dec 1, Bacchus alias Hogtub alias Fat Jack alias John from Ld Clive at Claremont bur^d.[217]

The position of the grave in the churchyard is often given, the word *pit* normally being used for grave.

St. Peter Cornhill, London

1593 25 Jan John Randoll, Draper and Sexton of this church, his pit in the belfrie

1593 3 Sept Henry Drables, sonne of Robert Drables Fishmonger, his pit in the east yrd

1646 Mar 30 Our Reverent Pastor. Mr. Tho Colema' pitt in ye vpper end of ye chancele.[218]

Occasionally, as in the register of *Boxley,* Kent the disease from which the person died is given.[219] Notes of accidents are not uncommon and are often detailed.

After 1813 in the printed registers there are columns for *"name" "abode", "when buried", "age"* and by whom the ceremony was performed.

Mortuaries

Frequently in burial entries one finds a note that mortuaries had been paid, often with the amount.[220] The paying of mortuaries was derived from the mediaeval feudal right of heriot. When a tenant died the lord of the manor had the right to choose as heriot the best beast of the deceased. Often the priest of the parish had the right to choose the second best. The system lent itself to gross abuse, and it was regulated by an act of Henry VIII which enacted that strangers, non-residents and non-householders were not liable, and that such persons as were liable should pay at a fixed rate in cash on a sliding scale.[221] Nevertheless some clergy continued to extract mortuaries from strangers as in the following entry in the register of *Ripe,* Sussex.

---

[217] Cited by J.S. Burn *op.cit.* p.121 and C.L. Ewen. *History of Surnames of the British Isles* (1931) p.203.

[218] These examples are cited by Henry Fishwick *N & Q.* 10th Ser. 1 p.287.

[219] The practice of stating the disease was recommended by Dr. Burrows in his *Structures on the use and defects of Parish Registers* (1818).

[220] Thus in the parish register of *Manaton,* Devon are recorded mortuary receipts at 10/- each for members of the Nosworthy family in 1752, 1792 and 1797.

[221] 21 Hen VIII, c.6 (1529). W.E. Tate *op.cit* p.69.

1664 I buried Alice Whitesides Feb 22 who being but one weeke in the parish of Ripe, died as a stranger, for whose mortuary I John Goffe had a gowne of Elizabeth her Daughter price 10/-.[222]

Heriots remained, although in a highly vestigial form until they were abolished in 1852. The 1836 *Tithe Act* specifically excluded mortuaries, but they were already rare and they seem to have disappeared finally either by commutation, together with other minor ecclesiastical dues, or by simple lapse.

The Aristocracy and Gentry

If a person were armigerous the College of Arms was responsible for supervising the funeral. This duty was at various times taken very seriously and until the Civil War distinctions of rank were scrupulously observed. In the 18th century it fell into abeyance. The College of Arms has a large collection of funeral certificates such as the following:

> "Sir Francis Chaplin, Knt. late Lord Mayor of the city of London, and Alderman of Vintry Ward, one of the governors of Christ Hospital (to which said hospital he bequeathed two hundred pounds by his last will and testament) departed this life at his house in Bury-street on Sunday the 27th day of June 1680, and was privately interred in the parish church of St. Catharine Cree on Saturday the 3d day of July following. The said Sir Francis Chaplin was eldest son of Sir Robert Chaplin of Bury St. Edmond's, in the county of Suffolk, and Elizabeth his wife, daughter of Francis Asty of Bury St. Edmond's aforesaid; which said Robert Chaplin, and Elizabeth his wife left issue (besides the deceased) Robert Chaplin of the parish of St. Swithin, London, Merchant, his second son, who married Anne, eldest daughter of Sir Thomas Tomkins of Mornington, in the county of Hereford, Knight, and widow of Roger Vaughan of the county of Hereford aforesaid, Esq; The said Sir Francis Chaplin the defunct married Anne, the daughter of Daniel Huett of Essex, Esq; by whom he left issue John Chaplin, his eldest son; Charles, 2d son; Robert 3d son; and Anne his only daughter. John Chaplin, Esq; son and heir of the defunct, married Elizabeth, the daughter and sole heir of Sir John Hamby of Tathwel, in the county of Lincoln, Knt. by his wife Elizabeth, daughter and sole heir of Richard Porter of Lamberhurst in Kent, Esq; by whom he hath issue three sons and one daughter; viz. Porter, eldest son; Francis, 2d son; and John, 3d son, and Anne his daughter. This certificate was taken the 23d of July 1683, by Henry St. George, Knt. Clarenceux king of arms, and attested by the subscription of Robert Chaplin, brother to the defunct."[223]

Rob. Chaplin.

The Series of certificates begins in 1567 and continues until 1688. The Heralds' supervision of funerals died out finally in the early

---

[222] J. Radcliffe. *N & Q.* 9th Ser. Vol. 1 p.376 (1898).

[223] This example is taken from R. Bigland *op.cit.* pp.26-27 where numerous other examples are also reproduced in full.

18th century.

Chrisome Children

Entries of burials as follows are not uncommon: "Buried was a
chrisome daughter of N. and M." The chrisome was the white linen cloth
laid on a child at baptism and worn by it until the mother was
churched, when it was presented to the church and used for ablutions.
A child that died before the mother was churched was called a *chrisome
child*, and was buried in the chrisome cloth. It was the custom to
anoint a child at baptism with the chrism or holy oil in the form of
a cross on the breast and between the shoulders, and the cloth was
to protect the chrism marks. The custom was abandoned after 1552, but
the use of the cloth long continued and indeed in some parishes
survives in a highly vestigial form even today. It would seem, however,
that in many registers the term *Chrisome* is used synonymously with
unbaptised, and Dr. Johnson defines *Chrisom* to be a child that dies
within a month after its birth.

Burials in Woollen

Among the most interesting of the burial entries are those relating to burials in woollen under the act of 1666 and its more famous
successor of 1678, which provided that:

> "no corpse of any person (except those who shall die of the plague),
> shall be buried in any shirt, shift, sheet or shroud or anything what-
> soever made or mingled with flax, hemp, silk, hair, gold or silver or
> in any stuff or thing, other than what is made of sheep's wool only.. or be
> put into any coffin lined or faced with.. any other material but sheep's
> wool only."

The act was ordered to be given in charge at the sessions and the
assizes, and heavy penalties were ordered upon those neglecting to
comply with it. Not infrequently a new volume of the burial register
begins in 1678 and sometimes special books were provided for the affidavits. At *Cardington*, Beds two separate volumes of affidavits cover
the period 1678-1775. There is in the Lincolnshire Archives Office a
file of original affidavits, covering the eighteenth century, made at
St. Michael's, Stamford. In other parishes it was thought worth while
to lay in a stock of printed forms for use in making the affidavit,
and two such printed certificates, still survive at *Luton*, Beds. [224]

The act provided that within eight days of the funeral, affidavit
must be made that the law had been complied with. The 1678 act
authorised the making of this before a clergyman if no justice was
available. Penalties were ordered of £5 on the estate of every person

---

[224] W.E. Tate. *op.cit.* p.67.

not buried in woollen, on the householder in whose house he died, on the persons connected with the funeral, on ministers neglecting to certify the non-receipt of the affidavit, and on overseers neglecting to levy the penalty. The act was not repealed until 1814. In some parishes, it was observed to the last. Thus at *Great Oakley*, Essex, the vestry minutes contain notes of burial in woollen up to 1813. The wealthier classes had long regarded it as imposing a tax to be paid rather than containing an injunction to be observed, and to judge by the register entries, for some years before its repeal the act had been generally disregarded.[225] It is possible that the term *buried naked* need not necessarily be interpreted literally, but may merely indicate burial not in woollen.

Burial of the Heart in a separate Place

The term *partly buried* is sometimes encountered as in the following entry in the parish register of *Faccombe*, Hants.

"Edward Reade, Esq., dyed the 10th day of July and was partly buryed on the 11th day of July Anno Dni 1638."[226]

The term was used to describe the burial of the heart separately from the body,[227] a practice which, of course, occurred almost entirely among the upper classes, as is illustrated by the following entry from the register of *Norton*, Durham:

"1756. March 22 bur: the heart and bowells of the right honourable James Earl Wemyss. The remains was buried with his Ancestors at Wemyss Castle in Scotland, the 8th day of April."[228]

At the end of the second register of St. Thomas Portsmouth was an entry relating to the Duke of Buckingham.

"My lord duckes bowels wear burried the 24th Augt 1628."[229]

Usually in the case of the burial of the heart separately this is requested in the will of the deceased. Thus the will of Sir Nicholas Crispe (23 Feb 1665) requests:

"... cause my heart to be imbalmed and to be put into a small urne to be made of the hardest stone and ffastned in it placed upon a Pillar of the best and hardest Black Marble to be sett up in Hammersmith Chappell neare my Pew the place I soe dearely loved. And I appoint my body to be put into a Leeden Coffin and laid in a vault in St. Mildred's Church in Breadstreet in London....."[230]

225 *ibid* p.68.
226 Cited by A.J. Winsbury. *Gen. Mag.* Vol.11. No.9 March 1953.
227 *Amateur Historian* Vol. 1 No.4. (Feb./Mar. 1953) p.122.
228 J.S. Burn. *op.cit.* p.110.
229 The page with this entry has since been lost.
230 Rev. Adam Glendenning Nash. *N & Q.* 11th Ser. 9 p.38.

The will of Myles Salley, Bishop of Llandaff (29 Nov 1516)[231] directs
that his body is:

"To be buried in the North side of our lady chapell before the image
of St. Andrewe as the Gauntes of Bristoll; my hart and bowelles at the
high aulter in the church of Martharn before St. Theodoryk."[232].

The whole subject is one to which considerable attention has been
given.[233]

Burials without Christian Rites

As well as the unbaptised, the church forbade the ceremonial
burial of all excommunicated persons and suicides. Whenever a burial
was performed without Christian rites – for Catholics, excommunicates
or suicides – the word *interred* was normally used, which, thus more
often than not indicates recusancy. Excommunications were not infrequent and might be not only on religious grounds but for moral reasons
or for non-payment of tithes.[234] Excommunicated persons were often
buried in an orchard and suicides with a stake through the heart at
the crossroads although sometimes the burial was in the churchyard
without any ceremony.[235] This latter, more merciful practice was embodied in the Act of 1823,[236] which abolished the custom of burial at
the crossroads and provided that the body should be buried between
nine and twelve at night without any religious rites. This statute has
been repealed by the *"Interments (Felo de se) Act"* 1882,[237] which
provides that a body may be buried in any way authorized by the
Burial Laws Amendment Act, 1880,[238] i.e. either without any religious
service or with such Christian and orderly religious service at the
grave as the person having charge of the body thinks fit. Executed
criminals were usually buried in the consecrated ground of the parish
where the gaol stood. Normally, the burial service was used. There
are thus an abnormal number of burials in the parishes of Assize

---

[231] P.C.C. Holder 26.

[232] F.S. Hockaday. *N & Q.* 11 Ser. 9 p.92.

[233] There is a section on Heart burial in T.F. Thisleton Dyer, *Church Lane Gleanings* (1891) pp.130-135 and an article by the late Canon Benham ("Peter Lombard") *Church Times* 5th March 1897 p.272. See also *N & Q.* 1st Ser. VI 433; 2nd XI 70, 134, 240, 256, 379. 8th Ser. VI 364, 386. viii 241, 363, 483. 10th Ser. i 385, 470. 11th Ser. 8 p.289, 336, 352, 391, 432, 493. 8th Ser. iii 83, 138, 193, 276. vii 516. 9th Ser. ii 106. xii 307, 434. 15th Ser. Vol.188 pp.59, 127, 161, 169, 194, 219, 262.

[234] Cox *op.cit.* p.110-113.

[235] For examples see Cox *op.cit.* p.109 and 114.

[236] 4 George IV c 52.

[237] 45 & 46. Vict c 19.

[238] 43 & 44. Vict c 41. On the burial of suicides see also *below* p.247. Also R. Bartel *Suicide in 18th century England. The Myth of a Reputation.* Huntingdon Lib. Qwart XXII 2 (1960), C.E. Sprott *The English Debate on Suicide,* La Salle, Illinois (1961) and F. Burgess *English Churchyard Memorials* p.53.

towns.[239]

Records of burials of travellers are quite numerous in all registers and in coastal parishes of course, there are burials of drowned shipwrecked sailors or passengers.

Post-1837 Burials

Parish Burial registers may very occasionally contain burials of persons not recorded among the deaths at Somerset House. Among these allegedly unregistered deaths are *Frederick Cruickshank,* artist (died c.1860), *Sir G.E. Campbell, Bt.* (died 1899), *J. Watson Dalby* (died c.1879-1883) and *Thomas Dalmane* music publisher (died 1866).[240]

---

[239] The register of *Little Brickhill,* Bucks, formerly an assize town contains entries for the burials of 42 criminals executed there between 1561 and 1621. Cox *op.cit.* p.118.

[240] Ralph Thomas *N & Q.* 10th Ser. 12 p.96.

APPENDIX I   BIBLIOGRAPHY

Lists and Indexes

Pending the publication of all volumes of the National Index, the following books (all of which will eventually be to some extent superseded) may be useful.

Original Parish Registers

Great Britain Census of Population 1831 Parish Register Abstract (House of Commons Paper 149 of 1833). Much out of date and often inaccurate but gives a detailed breakdown of the registers of each parish volume by volume. Arranged by counties subdivided into hundreds.

Burke, Arthur M. *Key to the Ancient Parish Registers of England and Wales.* (Pub. 1908 Reprinted 1962 from 1908 edition.) Also much out of date, but lists all parishes in alphabetical order, giving starting dates of registers.

Glencross, J.R.M. 2 manuscript volumes in the Society of Genealogists' Library. These were compiled in the 1930's, and give starting dates of registers. Also very inaccurate, but less so than either of the two previous works.

Original Parish Registers in Record Offices and Libraries (Local Population Studies, c/o Tawney House, Matlock, Derbys. DE4 3BT, 1975). A new guide to the whereabouts of deposited parish registers, much the most up-to-date.

Copies

Parish Register Copies, Part One, Society of Genealogists Collection (1973
Parish Register Copies, Part Two, Other than the Society of Genealogists Collection (1974)
A List of Parishes in Boyd's Marriage Index (1974)

Nonconformist Registers

List of Non-Parochial Registers and Records in the Custody of the Registrar-General at Somerset House. (1859) Now in the P.R.O. Many errors in the previous 1841 list were corrected, but many still remain. *See Nonconformist articles in Volume II.*

Legislation, Access Fees, etc.

British Records Association: *English Parish Records.*
Church Information Office. Leaflet LF 7 [guidance to clergy on fees for searching Parish Registers].

Crowder, F. *Parish Registers and Other Records and the Local Government (Records) Act 1962.* Family History 4. No. 19. p. 31.

Higgins, C.A. *Fees for Searching Parish Registers.* Gen. Mag. Vol. 11. No. 4 (Dec 1951) p.144.

Humphery-Smith, C.R. in editorial. Family History Vol. 2. No. 11 (1964).

Humphery-Smith, C.R. *Parish Registers and Family History.* Family History, Vol. 3. No. 13 (1965).

Institute of Heraldic & Genealogical Studies. *Parish Register Searching in England & Wales* (1966).

Legal Board of National Assembly of the Church of England. [Opinion on fees for searches] Reproduced in Gen. Mag. Vol. 7. p. 248 (1936).

Report of Local Records Committee (1902). This gives a summary of legislation concerning Parish Registers.

Report from the Select Committee on Parochial Registration; with the minutes of evidence and an Appendix. House of Commons. Sessional Papers 1833 (669).

A pamphlet showing the necessity for Legislative Provision for the better Preservation of Parish Registers (Kendal 1878).

General

Bigland, Ralph. *Observations on Marriages, Baptisms and Burials as Preserved in Parochial Registers* (1764).

Bradbrook, William. *The Parish Register* (1910).

Burn, J.S. *Registrum Ecclesiae Parochialis: The History of Parish Registers in England.* (1st edition 1829. Revised edition 1862.)

Cox, Dr. J.C. *The Parish Registers of England* (1910).

Dickinson, D.R. *The Value of Bishop's Transcripts and Some Notes on Parish Registers.* Gen. Mag. IX. No. 6. June 1952. pp. 212-213.

Dyer, T.F. Thiselton. *Old English Social Life as told by Parish Registers* (1898).

Emmison, F.G. *Our Parish Registers: their interest to the village teacher, historian and student.* The Library List [Journal of Northamptonshire County Library] No. 10 (1931). Repr. as sep. pamphlet.

Henderson, L.O. *Parish Registers.* Amat. Hist. Vol. 4. No. 6 232-4 (1960).

Jones, I. Fitzroy. *The Reliability of Parish Registers.* Gen. Mag. Vol. 9. No. 4 (March 1941) p. 130.

Muncey, R. Waterville, *The Romance of Parish Registers* (1929).

O'Rourke, J.J. *Parish Registers: an Historical Synopsis and Commentary*. Washington D.C. Catholic Univ. of America (1934).

Tate, W.E. *The Parish Chest* (1960). New edition to be published 1967.

Walne, P. *Parish Registers and the Registration of Births, Marriages and Deaths in England and Wales* Archivum Vol. 8 (1958) p. 79.

Waters, R.E. Chester. *Parish Registers in England* (1883).

Local

Austin, F.W. *Ramsden Bellhouse Parish Registers*. Essex Rev. July 1945, 89-92.

Bayley, T.D.S. *Pebworth Parish Registers. How Two Rectors Kept them*. Essex Rev. Jan. 1945. 18-20.

Berry, Lloyd. E. *London Parish Registers*. N & Q 10. Feb. 1963. pp. 55-7.

Busby, J.H. *Wheathamstead Parish Registers. Extracts from lost Register books*. Trans. St. Albans and Herts Archit. Soc. 1937. pp. 152-9.

Byrchmore, J. *Parish Records*. Somerset Arch. Soc. Bath Branch. Proc. for 1939 (1940), 275-280.

Cater, F. *Robert Browne and the Achursh Parish Register*. Trans. Cong. Hist. Soc. Vol. 3. p. 127.

Chambers, L.H. *Berks. Parish Memorials*. N. & Q. CLXXXIV. 24 April 1943. 256.

Challen, W.H. *Bishop's Transcripts. Archdeaconries of Lewes and Hastings*. Sussex N & Q. X No. 1. (Feb. 1944), 9-13.

Challen, W.H. *Bishop's Transcripts. Archdeaconry of Chichester*. Sussex N & Q X 1944-45, 27-33, 56-57, 82-85, 100-01, 128-31.

Chapman, D. & Pamplin, M. *Parish Records Survey (Ipswich)* (1963).

Fawcett, J.W. *Northern Weddings from Distant Parishes*. N & Q. 20 Oct. 1936. p. 276.

Fearon, W.A. & Williams, W.E. *Parish Registers & Parochial Documents in the Archdeaconry of Winchester* (1909).

Goss, Charles W. *Parish Registers for London and Middlesex*. T. London & Middx. Arch. Soc. N.S. 8, 81-107.

Gough, C.E. *The Parish Books & Church Registers of Weobley* [Heref.] Trans. Woolhope Nat. Field Club 1939-41. Pt.3. 164-182.

Hodgkinson, H.R. *Parish Register of Morton Bagot, Warwickshire*. Trans. Birm. Arch. Soc. 63. 84-85, (1944.)

Leech, E.B. *The Parish Registers of Lancashire.* Trans. Lancs. & Ches. Antiqu. Soc. 57. pp. 138-157 (1946).

Ollard, S.L. *A recently Discovered Parish Register. Huggate, Yorks.* Yorks Arch. Journ. Vol. 26. pt 104. 1922. pp. 309-25.

Partridge, C. *Fragment from an Essex Parish Register found in Suffolk.* Essex R. Jan 1941, 41-44.

Pool, Anne. *Parish Registers.* Old Cornwall III. No. 9 (Summer 1941) 355-59.

Ramsey, Robert W. *Parish Records of Kingston St. Mary 1641-1852.* Proc. Somerset Arch. Soc. 87. 85-105 (1942).

Saunders, G.W. *Early Parochial Registers in the Diocese of Bath & Wells.* Som. & Dorset N & Q XXIII. pt. 207. Dec. 1940 172-75

Smith, A.R. Jabez. *An Interpolation in a Lamplugh Register.* Trans. Cumb. & Westm. Antiqn. & Arch. Soc. 61. 120-30 (1961).

Swift, F.B. *The Parish Registers of Cumberland, Westmorland and Lancashire North of the Sands.* Trans. Cumb. & Westm. Antiqn. Soc. Vol. 156. 144-154 (1957).

Whiting, C.E. *Parish Registers: with special reference to those of Yorkshire.* Yorks. Arch. Journal Pt. 146. 131-44 (?1947).

A Study of an Old Parish Register. Macmillan's Magazine 1880-1, p. 43.

Parish Registers of Hardwick, Northants. Journ. Northants Nat. Hist. Soc. June 1934, 109-134.

Specialised Subjects

Pre-1538 Registers.

Southam, Herbert. *Registration before 1538.* N & Q. 19th July 1941. pp. 37-8.

Alleged "Papal Registers" See Gen. Mag. Vol. 6. No. 10 (June 1934) p.453, No. 12 (Dec 1934) p. 565 and Vol. 7. No. 1 (March 1935) p. 21.

Commonwealth Registration

Allen, T.F. *Commonwealth Marriages.* Gen. Mag. Vol. 12. No. 12. Dec. 1957, p. 418.

Newton, C. *A County Civil Register* [St Nicholas, Durham City]. Journ. Soc. Archivists III, No. 4, Oct. 1966, p. 194

Smith, Harold. *Parish 'Registers' of 1654.* Essex Rev. Vol. 8, pp. 16, 157 (Jan & July 1929).

Baptisms

Hughes, J.S.D. *Babies at Washington* [Baptisms at Washington, Sussex] Sussex County Mag. Oct. 1953. pp. 494-6.

Marriages

Chambers, L.H. *Marriages of Hertfordshire People at St. George's Chapel, Mayfair.* N & Q. CLXXXVI (20 May 1944) 247. CLXXXVII (1944) 122-23, 145-6.

Chambers, L.H. *Marriages of Hertfordshire People at St. Paul's, Covent Garden.* N & Q. CLXXXIX (1945) 37-38, 60.

Fry, E.A. *Index to Marriages from Gentleman's Magazine . 1731-68.*

Lambricke, G. *Oxford Colleges and Some Country Parishes round Oxford in the Early 18th Century.* Oxoniensia Vol. 25 (1960).

Moor, Rev. C. *The Mediaeval Marriage Market.* Gen. Mag. Vol. 12. No. 8. Dec. 1956.

Williams, J.F. with suppl. note by J.H. Bullock. *A Marriage Register at Queen's College, Cambridge.* Proc. Camb. Antiqn. Soc. 40. 13-23 (1944).
Matrimonial Records in Birdbrook Church. Essex Rev. July 1934. 137-8.

Younger, G.W. Central Reference Lib. Walworth Road. List of 10 certificates at New Chapel Mayfair, by S. Keith 1746-53. Gen. Mag. VIII, No. 4 (Dec. 1938) p. 209. See also query from R. Stafford Gen. Mag. VIII, No. 2 (June 1939) p. 337.

Burials

Entries in Burial Registers. Practice of entering deaths in register of a Parish when burial elsewhere. Times Lit. Suppl. 12 May 1921. p. 308; 23 June 1921. p. 404; 30 June 1921. p. 421.

Funeral Certificates. Misc. Geneal. et Heraldica. 5th ser. VIII (1934) 282-83, 292-93, 350.

Transcription

Tillott, P.M. *Transcribing Parish Registers.* Amat. Hist. Vol. 7. No. 5 (1967) p. 138.

Microfilming

The Microfilming of Parish Registers. N & Q Oct. 1940 12, 26. Nov. 2, 23, Dec. 7, 28.

Indexing

Indexing of Parish Registers N & Q 1st ser. Vol. 2 pp. 1-3 (1850).
Vine R.E. *Printing and Indexing Parish Registers by Computer* Gen. Mag. Vol. 15. No. 12 (Dec. 1967) pp. 461–468.

Roman Registers

Schultz, Fritz. *Roman Registers of Births and Birth Certificates.* Journ, Roman Stud. 32. pp. 28-91. 33 pts. 1-2, 55-64 (1943).

Continental Registers

Articles on Parish Registers of Austria, Hungary, Roumania, Poland, Denmark, Norway, Finland, Switzerland, Portugal, Latin America and Yugoslavia in *Archivum*, Vol. 8 (1958).

Articles on Parish Registers of France, Spain and Belgium and German Jewish Registers. Archivum, Vol. 9 (1959).

Edge, P. Granville. *Vital Registration in Europe.* The Development of Official Statistics and some Differences in Practice. Journ. Roy. Statist. Soc. 91. 346-93.

Parish Registers and Historical Demography

Baker, W.P. *Parish Registers and Illiteracy in East Yorkshire.* E. Yorks Local Hist. Series No. 13 (1961).

Drake, M. *An Elementary Exercise in Parish Register Demography.* Ec. Hist. Rev. 14 Apl. 1962. pp. 427–45.

Laslett, P. *The World We Have Lost* (1965) [Describes some of the conclusions reached largely as a result of demographic studies on Parish Registers. Detailed criticism in *The Historical Journal.* Vol. 9 (1966) pp. 374–379].

Wrigley, E.H. (ed) *An Introduction to English Historical Demography.* (1966).

Wrigley, E.H. *Parish Registers & Population History* I & II. Amat. Hist. VI. Nos. 5 & 6 Autumn 1964, Spring 1965.

APPENDIX II   TITLES AND DESCRIPTIONS USED IN PARISH REGISTERS

The Gentry

Very frequently entries for the local gentry are written much larger and more boldly than the generality of entries, sometimes a special script being used. *Gent* was normally used only for persons who were armigerous. *Esquire* denoted status, but not gentility, although it was occasionally used for minor branches of a landowning family. It was applied to Justices of the Peace, Barristers, and all who held any Commission from the Crown, including all Army and Navy Officers.[1] In the 16th Century and before, other persons of social or educational standing were addressed as *Master*, abbreviated in time to M^r. As will be discussed more fully later, it was also the normal designation of the clergy.

The title *Mistress*, abbreviated to M^{ris} and later M^{rs} was also used as a sign of status. One finds frequent entries in Marriage Registers and marriage licences where the bride is described as M^{rs}, though previously unmarried, and normally this indicates high social standing.

> *Hawstead*, Suffolk 1710, Sir Dudley Cullum Bart. Widower, and Mrs Anne Wicks single woman, both of this parish, were married 12 June.[2]

The title could be used even of children.

Thus in the parish register of *Hackington*, Kent appears the entry:

> 1658. Mrs Esther Godfrey ye onely childe of Sir Thomas Godfrey. Kt. aged a yeare and three quarters was buried Jan. 3rd.[3]

Here it is probably used because the child was heiress of a knight. In the reign of Charles II M^{rs} tended to be largely displaced by *Madam*, which probably owed its introduction into England to Charles II's Mistress Louise de Querouelle, afterwards Duchess of Portsmouth. Though found frequently in manuscript material of all kinds, the clergy seem to have been conservative and its use in parish registers is rare befor

---

[1]   A.J. Camp *Wills and their Whereabouts* p.xv.
[2]   Cited by J.S. Burn *History of Parish Registers in England* p.163.
[3]   Gen. Mag. Vol.10 No 13. March 1950 p.493.

1690. With the accession of George III, and perhaps earlier, M^{rs} returned into fashion, though *Madam* was still used by many of the older generation and is occasionally found in registers as late as 1800.[4] When found in the 18th century registers, M^{rs} normally denoted status but it was sometimes applied to elderly spinsters, perhaps not necessarily of high status.[5] This may account for the following death announcement in the *Kentish Gazette* in 1777:

> "On Monday last died in an advanced age, Mrs Parker, a maiden lady, at Dover."

The abbreviation Mis or *Miss* is believed to have been first used after the Restoration.[6] However, it is seldom found in parish registers before the mid-18th century, and is then reserved for young unmarried ladies of quality as it seems to have been well into the 19th century.[7]

Widow

The term *Widow* was often used in the 18th century, not only in the modern sense but also to indicate a woman past middle age who lived alone and was either of independent means or maintained herself by her own efforts. Thus, Ann Soane was buried at Rogate, Sussex as *Widow* on 19th July 1808, while in the Letter of Administration of her estate dated Chichester, 8 August 1808, she is *spinster.* She was baptised in 1773.[8]

4
   Misc. Gen. et Her. May 1890.
5
   Housekeepers in the Royal Palaces were, and perhaps still are styled *"Mrs"* although unmarried. Also respectfully styled *"Mrs "* in the 18th century were ladies with a reputation for learning, such as *Mrs Elizabeth Carter* (1717-1806) friend of Dr. Johnson, and the famous author *Mrs Hannah More* (1745-1833) both of whom were unmarried.
6
   Samuel Pepys in his Diary does not use it except in the case of little Miss Tooker, but styles most women *"Mrs"*. Usually this title is prefixed to the Christian name in the case of young girls, but not invariably so. Thus Mrs Pepys' maid is always styled *Mrs Gosnell*, and we do not know her Christian name. C.H. Jeune. Gen. Mag. Vol.10. No.15. Sept. 1950 p.579.
7
   In the Memoir *Coelebs in Search of a Wife* by Mrs Hannah More, published in 1837, the author is called *Miss* Hannah More until she was about 40. After that it is always *Mrs* in the Memoir. But in Boswell's Life of Johnson *Miss* Hannah More is mentioned as having dined at Mrs Garrick's with, among others, *Mrs* Carter who was many years her senior in age and as a writer. Other examples of 18th century use many be found in fiction. Smollett wrote in *Peregrine Pickle* (1751) that "Mrs Grizzle was now in the thirtieth year of her maidenhood." C.H. Jeune *op.cit.* p.579.
8
   J.H. Longrigg. Gen. Mag. Vol.10. No.14 June 1950 p.538.

Relationships

The terms given to relationships, such as *Kinsman, Cousin, Nephew* etc. are common in Wills but seldom encountered in parish registers. [9]

Occupations

A great deal could be said on the subject of occupations or descriptions which are encountered particularly in burial entries, but often in those of baptism and marriage. *Pauper* normally indicates that the person was on parish relief, but as has been pointed out [10] it seems likely that between 1783 and 1794 charitable clergy described as such many persons who were not technically paupers, but for whom the payment of the duty would cause real hardship.

Some occupations which are frequently encountered and could be misinterpreted are *Yeoman* who was of course a freeholder cultivating his own land, *Husbandman,* which was often used to indicate a tenant farmer, although it was not infrequently used as synonymous with *Yeoman, Clerk* which before about 1800 always meant *Cleric,* and *Teacher* which was normally used for Nonconformist ministers, *Schoolmaster* or " *master at the school* " being the usual style for a teacher.

The Clergy

The last two on this list raise the larger question of description and titles of respect given to the clergy, which has been the subject of a thorough study by Ernest Axon. [11]

Sir

In mediaeval times the clergy were given the title of Sir, [12] but by the sixteenth century Sir was generally used only for the less educated clergy M^r or Magister being used for graduates. This use of Sir [13] had died out by the Civil War.

---

[9] Some of them are briefly explained in A.J. Camp *Wills and their Whereabouts* p. xvii. A few he does not mention are *father-in-law* to mean *stepfather; nephew* to mean *grandson, cousin* to indicate any degree of kinship by blood but, in contrast to the vaguer *kinsman*, not normally by marriage. For terms used for illegitimate children see *Form and Content,* p. 50.

[10] *Form and Content* p. 41.

[11] " *Reverend and some other styles of Nonconformist ministers* " Trans. Unit. Hist. Soc. Vol. VI 4 (Oct 1938) pp. 310-329 from which the greater part of the information in this sub-section is taken.

[12] e.g. Sir John, Chaucer's Nun's Priest.

[13] *Sir* preceding the surname without a christian name remained a University designation for a Bachelor of Arts.

Clerk

The word *Clerk* in the Middle Ages had been used for anyone tonsured, even if not ordained. After the Reformation it was (except for a few technical terms such as *parish clerk*) used exclusively for the clergy and was the most popular description in wills and parish registers of the sixteenth century. It was largely displaced by M^r in the seventeenth, though as has been pointed out, it is not infrequently found much later. Usually *clerk* occurs without any other title, but sometimes the name is preceded by *Sir* or *Mr* as in the following example:

> "*St Edmunds, Dudley*, Worcs.
>
> 1539 Samuell, son of Sir William Smithe Clarke, Vicare of Duddly, was born on Friday morninge, at 4 of the clock, beinge the xxviij day of February....."[14]

M^r

Except for clergy qualified to be discribed as D^r., M^r remained the usual designation until about 1700. In 1696 Thomas Gupps, Rector of Bury, Lancashire complained:

> "I do pretend to say that the Bishops are more excusable in accepting the title of Lord, than every Preacher is in assuming the Title of Master..... If men will deprive the bishops of their title of Lord, let 'em first begin to reform at home and strip themselves of that of Master.[15]

The Reverend

By the beginning of the eighteenth century *The Revd* was being used preceding the "M^r" or "D^r". The word is found as a title as early as 1620, but was normally used only preceding the first name in a list of clergy. Thus in the *Chester Marriage Licence Act Book* from about 1620 individual ministers are styled *magister* but where a licence is issued to several ministers, the first is styled *Reverend*, one reverend being used for them all. Similarly in the appointment of several ministers as triers during the Commonwealth, John Nye the clerk put *The Reverend* before the first name on the list.[16] In all cases when the style *The Reverend* appears in the 17th century applied to individuals it precedes the title M^r and probably another description and was used as a term of respect for deceased clergy, e.g. "that reverend divine Mr. Robert Collard" (1650), or

---

[14] J.S. Burn *op.cit.* p.80. For fuller text of the entry *see Form and Content* above pp. 42–43.

[15] *Testamen Novum* – Cited by E. Axon *op.cit.* p.313.

[16] Ernest Axon. *op.cit.* p.315.

"the reverend and pious Mr. Charles Adams" (1683) or "the Reverend
Mr. John Blackburn" (Roger Lowe's Diary 1666).

It was not until the end of the 17th century that *Reverend* was
applied to living clergymen or Nonconformist ministers. In Mill Hill
Chapel registers there are some early examples: the Reverend Mr. Sharp
(death 1693), the Rev. Doctor Manlove (baptism of a child 1698), the
Reverend Mr. Timothy Manlove (death 1699), but the next minister was
described as M^r. only. Generally, the Anglican clergy were ahead of
the Nonconformists in using the style *"The Revd M^r"*. Caleb Rotheram
was married in 1719. In the *Thornton-in-Lonsdale,* Yorks. parish register he is given the title of *Mr.* only, but the clergyman who had
granted the licence was *the Revd* Mr. Lancaster. Throughout most of the
18th century *The Rev. Mr.* was the normal style for both Anglicans and
Nonconformists. However, in Walker's *"Sufferings of the Clergy"*
(1714) and other books of the time *The Rev.* was used without the
"Mr." if degrees were given. e.g. *The Reverend Mr. Astley of
Whitehaven,* but *the Reverend John Allen M.D.*

Reverend first appears directly before the Christian name in the
case of Doctors. However, in *Goosnargh,* Lancs. parish register there
are other cases found as early as 1720, and by the mid- 18th century
the practice was common but not invariable. By 1800 it was universal
when the Christian name was known. If the Christian name was not known,
the *Rev. Mr.* was still used. Many Nonconformists were slow to adopt
the Anglican styles. In the register of Kendal Chapel, Westmorland,
ministers are described as *Mr.* in 1712, 1728 and 1752. The first
"Rev. Mr." appears in 1753 and the first *"Rev"* without the Mr. 1791.
Methodist ministers were exceptionally late in using *"The Rev."*[17]
However, curiously the first case in law of Reverend was decided in
favour of a Wesleyan minister. In 1874 the vicar of Owston Ferry,
Lincs. refused to allow a minister to describe himself as *Rev. H. Keet,
Wesleyan minister* on his child's gravestone. Two years later the
Privy Council decided that *"Rev"* was not confined to ministers of the
Established Church.

Minister

The word was sometimes used to mean *curate*. In the will of 1635
of Abdie Asheton, Rector of Prestwich, Lancs. one of the legatees is
"Cristofer Hudson, sometime my minister."

Priest

When this is used in parish registers it normally refers to a

---

[17] *"Rev"* without the *"The"* is a comparatively recent Americanism.

86

Roman Catholic:

"baptized by a Popish Priest"

It was used of Nonconformists only by the Anglican clergy, perhaps in ignorance. (e.g. in *Torver*, Lancs. parish register in 1703 there is a marriage "with a Nonconformist Priest.")

Teacher

As mentioned above, when encountered in parish registers this is normally used for a Nonconformist minister. In 1705 in *Newcastle-on-Tyne* registers, there is the marriage of Mr. Roger Anderton, teacher. In *Radcliffe*, Lancs. parish registers between 1716 and 1719 there are records of baptisms "by Mr. Heywood teacher of Dissenting meeting house at Stand", by "Dissenting teacher" and by "the Dissenting Teacher at Stand." In *Bispham*, Lancs. registers in 1723 and 1729 are baptisms "by a Presbiterian Teacher."[18]

Clergy entitled to Styles of Rank

Clergy who by rank or wealth were entitled to be described as *gent* or *esquire* sometimes used these terms in preference to *Mr.* or *clerk*. William Holland of Heaton (died 1682) was an *esquire* to his neighbours in Lancashire and *Rector of Malpas* to his Cheshire neighbours. In his will he is *clerk*, in Prestwich Lancs. parish register he is *esqr* and in *Dukinfield*, Cheshire register *Mr.*[19]

V.D.M.

This abbreviation, standing for *verbi Dei Minister*, was frequently used by Nonconformist ministers especially on tombstones:
e.g. English inscription to John Cooper of Gee Cross, Cheshire (1731)
Latin inscription to Joseph Molleshead's wife (1739)
English inscription to Samuel Waterhouse, minister at Risley, Lancs. (1762)
Sometimes they appear in Nonconformist registers. Thus Edward Gibson, minister at Stockport 1794-9 added them to his signature in Stockport Cheshire Chapel Register.

---

[18] The term was by no means used only in registers. In 1711 was published "*An Impartial Account of a Conference between Mr. Thomas Kirby, a Teacher of an Anabaptist Meeting and a Lay Member of the Church of England.*"

[19] Ernest Axon. *op.cit.*

APPENDIX III   SURNAMES

The origin and development of surnames is of course beyond the scope of this work and for information on this subject readers are referred to the standard works especially C.L. Ewen *"History of Surnames of the British Isles"* (1931), C.M. Matthews *"English Surnames"* and P.H. Reaney *"A Dictionary of Surnames."* However, there are several aspects of the subject which intimately concern the genealogist. Though surnames were adopted by the majority of the population in the 14th and 15th centuries, they were by no means fixed. Surnames might change from one generation to another, or indeed the same person might change his name or be known by several aliases. However by the start of the 16th century in the vast majority of cases one family was known consistently by one surname, recognizable in spite of the many forms in which it appeared. The institution of parish registers reinforced this trend towards stability. In 1538 many, perhaps most families were only four or five generations removed from the first ancestor to bear the surname, and this was probably the first occasion the family appeared consistently in official records. C.L. Ewen observes

> "Although these books seem to have been kept very irregularly, they must have had a great influence in fixing the surnames, which otherwise would rarely have been recorded officially or in a manner available for ready reference."[1]

However, even in parish registers, the *alias, changes of name* and other problems are not infrequently encountered.

Change of Surname

As has been pointed out, in mediaeval times when surnames were still in the process of emerging, change was frequent. In the thirteenth and fourteenth centuries it seems to have been quite usual for the surname of an apprentice to be replaced either temporarily or definitely by that of his master.[2] In most cases where sufficient

---

[1] *op.cit.* p.203.
[2] For full discussion see Ekwall *Variation and the Early London Subsidy Rolls.*

material is available the new surname displaced the old one altogether.
Dr. Reaney[3] cites various examples from the City of London records:

> "Sewald son of Sewald de Springefeld (1311 *Letter Book B*) is identical
> with Sewal son of Sewald de Sprengewell, apprentice of Richard de
> Godesname, paternostrer (1311 *Letter Book D*) and with Sewellus de
> Godesname (1319 *London Subsidy Roll*). Robert Podifat (1288 *Letter Book A*)
> was an apprentice of Roger Fuyster (1312 *Letter Book D*) who is also called
> Roger Podifat (1320 *Letter Book E*). Robert therefore assumed his master's
> nickname as his surname. Thomas de Cavendisshe son of William atte Watre
> de Ewelle, late apprentice of Walter de Caverndisshe mercer was admitted
> a freeman of the city in 1311-12 (*Letter Book D*). His original surname
> would have been atte Watre or de Ewelle. From 1319 to 1349 he is regularly
> called de Cavendish, and in the enrolment of his will Thomas de Caverdych,
> mercer or draper."

There is also evidence of this custom at York, where we have
William Payne serviens John Payne (1323).[4] Roger Storre, servant of
Johan Storre (1379),[5] Richard Redhode, draper serviens Willelmi
Redhode (1386),[6] Thomas Gauke, cocus filius Roberti Nyd servicentis
simonis Gauke (1424).[7] Here Thomas bore the surname of his father's master
which had probably been assumed earlier by his father.[8] However, it
is necessary to exercise caution as, of course, a boy might be
apprenticed to a relative.

Later changes of name were usually connected with the inheritance
of property, and though from the fourteenth to the seventeenth century
the alias was frequently used, thereafter there was usually a complete
change of name. Like the alias, however, a complete name change might
take place if there was a marriage into an important family, even if
there were no major inheritance of property. This was the reason for
the change of the name *Russell* to *Gorges* in the branch of the Kingston
Russell family of Russells to which Ferdinando Gorges belonged.

It has been held that a change of surname is within the prerogative
of the Crown:
Fox-Davies wrote in 1906:

> "Haphazedly, from time immemorial, but consistently since, at any rate,
> the reign of Charles II, the Crown has asserted the matter of names and
> changes of name to be within its prerogative, but it has, whilst
> definitely asserting this attitude through such of its ministers and
> officers as are concerned with the subject, as persistently avoided put-
> ting its prerogative to the test of legal action."[9]

---

[3] *Dictionary of British Surnames* (1958) p.xii. The references are mostly
to the Letter Books of the City of London.
[4] *Register of the Freemen of York* (Surtees Soc. 96, 102) 1897, 1900.
[5] *Yorkshire Poll Tax Returns* – Yorks. Arch. Journal 5-7, 9, 20.
[6] *Register of Freemen.*
[7] *ibid.*
[8] These examples have also been taken from Reaney *op.cit.* p.xii. On Mediaeval
apprenticeship see also *Proofs of Age* below p.363.
[9] *Treatise* p.2.

However, as C.L. Ewen pointed out,[10] Fox-Davies is mistaken. From the early 14th century onwards, the Crown expressed interest only in changes of surname of the tenants-in-chief, and recorded formally its approval. The first royal licence and authority to use a specific surname was a grant to Henry Cavendish, Earl of Ogle son of the Duke of Newcastle in 1679 to take the name of Percy on his marriage with the heiress of that family:

> "To assume and take the surname of Percie and to bear the arms of Percie quarterly with his own paternal arms neither of which may regularly be done, according to the law of armes, without the special dispensacon and licence of Us, as We are Our supream power and prerogative the onely Fountain of Honour."[11]

In later grants of authority, for a change of name, it is said the right belonged to the *College of Arms*. It is not known when they acquired it. The Earl Marshal's books, which contain *inter alia* entries relating to change of surnames, date from the time of Queen Elizabeth.[12] However, there certainly was a regulation in 1783 that all applications for permission to change names should be referred to the College of Arms.[13] Fox-Davies argues that the case of *Barlow v Bateman* "absolutely upsets the bold contention that any man may change his name as he pleases."[14] However, this was not so. George Barlow had made a bequest to his daughter Mary conditional on her marrying a person by the name of Barlow. On his marriage Robert Bateman took the name of Barlow. It was held that a man must not change his name to obtain a qualification essential to a beneficiary which he did not have at the time of the execution of the will.[15]

It seems clear that a change of surname does not have to be recorded in any way, and that a man's surname is the name by which he chooses to call himself and by which he is generally known. This is important with reference to the calling of banns:

> Joseph Price had been known for sixteen weeks prior to his marriage in 1815 as Joseph Grew, a name he had assumed in an attempt to conceal himself from the Army authorities, and had been married in that name. The marriage was upheld.[16]

> Abraham Langley married in 1814 had for three years been known in the village where the banns were published by the name of George Smith. It was held that the banns were properly published and that his original

[10]   *op.cit.p.* 408-9. The whole subject is discussed at greater length in A Linell *The Law of Names, Public, Private and Corporate* (1938) pp.19-45.
[11]   Phillimore. *Index to Changes of Name* p.xxvi. Cited by Ewen *op.cit.* pp.408-9.
[12]   Rev Mark Noble *History of the College of Arms* App. M. xlii.
[13]   *Phillimore* op.cit. p.xxiv.
[14]   *Treatise* p.48.
[15]   Barlow v Bateman. *Williams' Reports* Vol.iii p.65.
[16]   C.L. Ewen. *op.cit.* p.401.

name would not have been his true name within the meaning of the Statute 26 Geo II c 33.[17]

Marriage under a different surname is thus a possibility which the genealogist must always consider when other lines of research have failed. Similarly, when there is positive evidence of a date and place of birth and the parish register fails to reveal the relevant entry, evidence for a later change of name should be sought.

Description of Married Women

The custom of the wife assuming her husband's surname goes back to mediaeval times, though frequently in legal documents the maiden name was retained with the word *formerly*.

> e.g. Margaret Eynesford formerly Swylyngton (1418)
> Elizabeth Lynch formerly Curthopp (1550)[18]

Less commonly an alias was used instead.[19] However in Scotland the wife has always retained her maiden name, and this practice may have prevailed in some parts of England. C.L. Ewen cites the following burial entries in *Blackburn*, Lancs. parish registers:

> 16th Aug.1647 Vxor Thomas Sudell Peg Nance
> 26th Apl.1649 Vxor Thomas Livesey Nan Darby

However, as has been pointed out elsewhere[20] this register is notorious for its use of nicknames and unless further examination proved the contrary it may be assumed that these were nicknames and not maiden names.

A writer to *Notes and Queries* in 1865[21] alleged that in Dorset it was the custom for a married woman to retain her maiden name which also descended to her children and descendants! Unfortunately, no examples were cited.

It was the Elizabethan practice for a widow to retain the name of her first husband, even if she married again.

> e.g. Anne wife of George Baildon was buried at Leeds 1577 as ' Mastris Anne Standish (i.e. her 1st husband) doughtere to my Ladye Hassye' who in turn was buried (1597) in that name, being widow of Thomas Falkingham.[22]

Sometimes the name of her second husband was used with an alias.[23]

---

[17] Rex v Inhabitants of Billingshurst. *Maule and Selwyn's Reports*, K.13, Vol.iii p.250. See also, *Divorce and Annulment* p.325.
[18] *Index to Wills P.C.C.*
[19] *See below* p.93.
[20] *Form and Content* p.69.
[21] *N & Q.* 23. Dec 1865. p.518.
[22] W.P. Baildon *Baildon and the Baildons* Vol.3 (1927). p.3.
[23] *See below* pp.93—94.

As has been pointed out, in late mediaeval times the alias was very common. Sometimes an alias was added with a change of residence:

> e.g. Alice Caunterbury alias Alice de Bermundesey (Close Roll 1385).

The alias might be derived from a nickname:

> e.g. William Howbergh alias Blobbere (Close Roll 1409);

or from the person's trade:

> e.g. John ffremantell alias dictus Piper (Close Roll 1427)
> William Parchemenmaker alias Fisshere (Close Roll 1416)
> Gummerus Gerardson, alias Joyner (Pat. Roll 1473)[24]

This may also explain the following example:

> Ricardus White Plomer alias dictus Ricardus Plommer alias dictus
> Ricardus Chapman alias dictus Ricardus White Chapman. (Pardon Roll 1412)

Thus a territorial surname might be yoked with another territorial name, with a patronymic or a trade name. The Chaucer family appear to have used all three. Miss Lilian Redstone points out:[25]

> "In Ipswich they were styled *Malyn* (doubtless a patronymic or matronymic) or *Chaucer* (a trade name),[26] or (in some cases) *de London!*

The alias is not uncommonly encountered in parish registers particularly in the 16th and 17th centuries, and much research still needs to be done into the reasons for its use, which appear to be many and varied.[27] Sometimes the alias acts as the equivalent of the modern hyphenated surname, indicating the inheritance of land in the female line or the desire to perpetuate an ancestral surname on the female side. Thus Oliver Cromwell appears in some documents as *alias Williams* the Cromwells having sometimes used this form since Oliver's great-grandfather Richard Williams assumed the surname of Cromwell from his maternal uncle Thomas Cromwell the Vice-Gerent.[28] Similarly in his preface to *Coke upon Littleton*, Coke mentions Littleton as *alias Westcott*, the latter his paternal name which he had exchanged for his mother's. T.S. Leadham concludes:[29]

---

[24] There is a list of aliases in *N & Q*. 7th Ser. 12 pp. 450-1.
[25] *The Use of an Alias in English Surnames* American Gen. Vol. 17. p. 68.
[26] Old French *Chaucier*, (hosier or cordwainer) Lat. *calcearius*.
[27] There is a collection of aliases in A. Clark: *Register of University of Oxford* Vol. ii. pt iv. index iv sub-section D.
[28] Lilian J. Redstone *op. cit.* p. 68 cites this as an example of the use of an alias with a Welsh patronymic. However, clearly the importance of the Cromwell connection was the significant factor in this particular case. Dugdale says Sir Richard Williams "being preferred to the service of King Henry, afterwards affirmed the name of Cromwell." (Vol. ii p. 374.)
[29] *The Use of the Alias* N & Q. 7th Ser. 12. p. 401. (1891).

> "My view then is that the use of the 'alias' in England, like the addition of the maternal name in France is connected with the succession to real estate..... In England the mother's name was added with an alias to denote that the bearer of it was *mulieratus* or *mulier* in cases where an illegitimate family by the same parents existed, and thus to designate the heir to the real estate, and perhaps in Bracton's time to indicate that members of the family so distinguished were free. This would be more likely to occur in the lower ranks of society and it is there that the practice appears to have obtained. It would be continued long after its meaning had been forgotten, as is the case abroad at the present day."[30]

Thus, if a person was adopted, or inherited or was given property, or if he married an heiress, the alias might be used. Most frequently in such cases the first part of the alias was the paternal name; The following example is of particular interest as it illustrates not only this use of the alias, but that a surname used as a Christian name could serve the same function.

> The second son of Sir Thomas Dilke of Wootton and of Maxstoke Castle and of Anne Fisher of Packwood was christened *Fisher*. He married Sybil Wentworth and when the manor of Sir Peter Wentworth came to his grandson with the direction to take the name of *Wentworth* the latter was called *Fisher Wentworth Esq.* by his family, but shown in their pedigrees as *Fisher Dilke otherwise Wentworth.*

Thus in this family the descent of property was demonstrated in the case of the son by the Christian name, and in that of the grandson by an alternative surname. Though the paternal surname was not normally used, it was this retention of it in pedigrees and on legal documents which brought about its ultimate resumption by the family.[31] As has been pointed out an alias was sometimes used to indicate the maiden name of a married lady and this usage has survived in Scotland to the present day. In particular, it was the frequent practice in grants of administration in 16th and 17th century ecclesiastical courts to the son-in-law of the intestate, of describing the daughter of the intestate who was married to the administrator by her husband's surname alias the surname of her intestate father. There are instances where it is vice versa.[32] However, as has been pointed out, it was more common to indicate a maiden name by the use of the word *formerly*. When a widow remarried although as has been pointed out she normally retained the surname of her first husband, she is sometimes described on official documents (including perhaps parish registers) under the names of *both* her husbands.

---

[30] For example in Spain, the mother's name is added to the paternal. e.g. the father of Iago *Hernandez y Carrera* would be a *Hernandez* and his mother a *Carrera*.

[31] A.O. *N & Q.* 7th Ser. 12. p. 450.

[32] S. Allyn Peck. *Gen. Mag.* Vol. 10. p. 187.

Thomas Penny of Bridgewater (one of the Yeovil family) who died in 1730 married as his second wife Elizabeth Lockett, a widow. When she died intestate in 1731, she is described twice in the Commission granted to her next of kin as Elizabeth Penny alias Lockett.[33]

Apparently if a woman remarried and a son of the first marriage was brought up in her second family, he might unite his own surname by an alias with that of his step-father.

An alias is often found when the surname is a generally common one (e.g. Smith) or is common in a particular area. It is frequently found with Welsh patronymics.[34] The alias was certainly used to differentiate one branch of a family from another. The alternative surname was not infrequently a trade name as in the case of the form *Rivers alias Comber* which continued for well over a century.[35] Perhaps this is the explanation of the form *Gilbertsonne alias Derricke* 70 entries of which appear in the registers of *Holy Trinity Guildford,* Surrey between 1560 and 1685. The wills from 1563 to 1680 give the same form.[36] Miss Redstone notes that this is most likely to happen when two well-known families springing from a man who had two wives, remain in the same neighbourhood.[37] In the case of the family of *Warren alias Waller* of Bassingbourne, Cambridgeshire and Ashwell, Herts, *Warren* ceased, and *Waller* became the recognised surname. The alias here may have originated because of the family's successful claim to bear the Arms of the *de Warennes.*[38]

The alias was also sometimes used to unite the names of the parents of a child born out of wedlock. Thus the *Lodge* family were descended from the *Lyttletons,* and at first were styled *Lyttleton alias Lodge.*[39]

An alias may represent an alternative name used for business purposes, when for some reason it is inconvenient to use one's family name. For example, as Mr. Samuel points out[40] the Sephardic Jewish London merchants often used an alias to avoid embarrassing relatives still in Spain or Portugal. However, English merchants also frequently used a different surname and sometimes a seemingly inexplicable alias may have arisen from a business connection. Thus, in the 15th century Stephen Russell, the earliest certain ancestor of the Dukes of Bedford, and his son Henry both used the alias *"Gascoigne".* Gladys Scott

[33] *P.C.C. 1731-2 Admons.* Cited by Frank Penny. *N & Q.* 8th Ser. 1 p.74.
[34] Miss L. Redstone *op.cit.* p.68. Ewen *op.cit.* p.206. For more information on this subject see article on *Welsh Nomenclature* in Volume II.
[35] John Comber. *N & Q.* Vol.157. p.29.
[36] David Williamson. *N & Q.* 10th Ser. Vol.2. p.13.
[37] *op.cit.* p.69.
[38] *N & Q.* Vol.157. p.69 (1929). The Society of Genealogists has a large collection of notes on this family.
[39] Rev. Mark Noble *op.cit.* p.439.
[40] *Jewish Births Marriages and Deaths* in Volume II.

Thompson suggests: [41]

> " This may be a reference to Gascon ancestry; it is as likely to be
> merely an indication of their known business connections with Bordeaux."

The most obvious use of the alias is, however, where two or more
alternative spellings of the same name are used, one of them sometimes
being archaic. (e. g. Christofer Brunolvesheved alias Burneshead alias
Burnesyde). This could occasionally survive extraordinarily late as in
the following anecdote recorded in *Notes and Queries* in 1891:

> " About fourteen years ago a well-to-do merchant in the West Riding
> brought me the Will of his father to prove. The testator described him-
> self as *"Oldroyd otherwise Holroyd"* and the registrar asked why the
> testator gave himself an alias. The son, whose name was *Holroyd,* explained
> that his father had for the greater part of his life been known as
> *Oldroyd,* that being his father's name, but he had ordered a brass plate
> to be put on a house into which he was moving, and the name was by mis-
> take engraved Holroyd. As my informant put it *"Olroyd* and *'Olroyd,*
> there's very little difference between them in sound, and as the plate
> was all fixed up, it seemed a pity to change it, so my father and all us
> children changed our names."[42]

However, the use of the alias after the 18th century is relatively
rare in parish registers and those that appear sometimes defy obvious
explanation. Thus, as late as 1831, the following entry appears in
the marriage register of *Arlesey,* Bedfordshire:

> 24th October 1831. William Cooper, Bachelor to Sarah Kitchiner alias
> Fossey, spinster.
> Witnesses: Thomas Fletcher, Joseph Kitchiner and Ann Kitchiner alias
> Fossey.[43]

In general, the use of the alias tended to survive much later in
Scotland than in England, and is frequently encountered in parish
registers. As has been pointed out, many of such cases are easily
explained by the custom in Scotland of the wife never losing her

---

[41] *Some notes on the Ancestry of John Russell Lord Russell, First Earl
of Bedford.* Gen. Mag. Vol.9. No.2. June 1940. p.47. See the same author's
Two Centuries of Family History (1930) pp.78, 90, 315, 319.

[42] J.J.F. *N & Q.* 7th Ser. 12. p.451 (1891).

[43] The last named survived into the period of Civil Registration, and her
death certificate gives her name as Ann *Kitchener.* Joseph and Sarah were
two of her eight children, but none except Sarah appears to have ever
used the *"alias Fossey".* Ann's maiden name was Bailey and no Fossey
connections have been found. A possible clue is the fact that Ann's
husband, John Kitchiner died in 1813, leaving a young family. Perhaps
Ann was living with a man named Fossey, and was known as Fossey in the
village. Her daughter Sarah was the only unmarried child and therefore
was presumably living with her, which may account for the fact that she
signs with the alias, but her elder brother Joseph does not.

maiden name,[44] and others derive from the later survival of
patronymics as an alternative to the clan or family surname.[45] Thus,
whenever the alias is encountered each individual case must be studied
on its own merits. Miss Redstone warns:[46]

> "Such study might or might not solve the problem. It would be a matter
> of luck. Records might or might not produce what is wanted. If the reten-
> tion of the alias was due to sentiment, as one suspects in some cases, it
> would be even more difficult to discover."

The use of an alias remains therefore one of the more perplexing
problems which is likely to confront the genealogist.

Double Surnames

In Scotland the widespread use of a patronymic together with the
surname or clan name often produced the appearance of a double surname. In England, no evidence of a similar custom has been found as
late as the period of parish registers. However, it was not uncommon
in the North of England in the 14th and 15th centuries as is shown
by the following examples:

> In Yorkshire in 1381-2 William Johnson Wilkinson was a witness to two
> deeds.[47] He might have been called William son of John Wilkinson or
> William son of John son of Wilkin.
> In 1396 pardons were granted to Robert Johanson Dobson and John Dicson
> Robynson.[48]

In the 17th and 18th centuries ancestral surnames on the female side
were perpetuated by the use of these as Christian names.[49] These tended
to become hereditary, and in a few instances in the latter part of
the 18th century a hyphen was added, producing the modern double bar-
relled name. However, the practice only became widespread in the nineteenth century. Usually the descent of property was involved, but the
hyphenated surname was sometimes used in cases of illegitimacy. Persons
bearing very common surnames obviously have had a great incentive to
adopt a second one. This is not always another ancestral surname. In
some cases (e.g. the Abel-Smith family) it is a hereditary Christian
name.

Foundlings and Workhouse Children.

Often foundlings were given the name of the parish or that of some

---

[44] In such cases the first surname is normally the maiden name and the
second, her husband's name.
[45] See article on "Scottish Registers" and especially "Patronymics in
Caithness and Sutherland" in Volume 12, pp. 32-33.
[46] op.cit. p.69.
[47] Yorks Arch Journal 1879. Vol.V p.76.
[48] Cal Pat Rolls p.686. Other examples are given in Ewen op.cit. p.216.
[49] See Appendix IV. Christian Names pp. 113-115.

street in it as a surname and the christian name was derived from the
Saint's Day nearest to the date of their discovery. This is particularly noticeable in the case of the London parishes where foundlings
were extremely numerous. For example in the register of *St. Denis,
Backchurch*:

> "1567, Dec 14. A chylde that was found at the strangers dore in
> Lymstrete whych chylde was founde on Saynt petter day, and founde of the
> p'ishe coste. Wherefore they named the chylde by the day that he was
> founde, and surname by the p'ishe, so the chyldes name ys Petter
> Dennis."[50]

In the register of *St. Lawrence Jewry*, there are the baptisms of
a great many foundlings to whom the surname of *Lawrence* was invariably
given. In the registers of *St. Martin's Ludgate* are a number baptised
between 1735 and 1750 named *Martin*. A variation from this is "John
Lud" a foundling baptised on February 18th 1744. In *St. Anne's
Blackfriars*, a favourite name given during this period seems to have
been *Fryer*. In the *Temple* register between 1728 and 1755, 104 Foundlings were christened, all surnamed *Temple* or *Templer*.

Frequently foundlings were named from some circumstance connected
with their finding. Thus we find foundlings with surnames such as
Church, Style, Field or *Hedge*, or even more specific such as *Peartree*
at Wheathampstead, Herts. in 1712.

At *St. Dunstan's West*, London, a foundling of 1618 was named
"*Mary Porch*" doubtless from the porch where it was discovered; to
another foundling buried on 16th January 1629/30, the strange but not
inappropriate name of *Subpoena* was applied, whilst an infant found in
Chancery Lane in 1631 was styled Elizabeth *Middlesex*.[51] At *St. Anne's
Blackfriars* in 1306 is the baptism of "Thomas Bridge (a child dropt on
the bridge.)" and at Cranford, Middlesex on 31 March 1745 was buried
"Pick up Brown at Hide Park Corner."[52]

By an Act of 1761, a Register Book was directed to be kept by
every parish within the "*Bills of Mortality*" in which were to be
entered all infants under four years old who should be in any workhouse or place provided for the maintenance of the poor "with the

---

[50] J.C. Cox *The Parish Registers of England* (1910) p.63.
[51] *ibid*. p.64.
[52] Numerous other examples of foundlings are given in *N & Q*. 12th Ser. Vol.V.
pp.40, 71-72. The well known story that Dr. Thomas Magnus (died 1550)
Henry VIII's Ambassador to Scotland was a Newark-upon-Trent foundling
named.*Tom Among Us* – has been disproved. He was, in fact the son of John
and Alice Magnus. However the story, which appeared in Wood's *Fasti Oxon*.
(ed. Bliss i 53) had a wide currency and is stated as a fact by R. Bigland.
*Observations on Marriages, Baptisms and Burials as Preserved in Parochial
Registers* (1764).

times when they were received, their names, age and whatever description tion relates to them as far as can be traced." It contained the provision:

> " In case any infant be received into the Workhouse etc. before the said infant is baptised, due care should be taken to baptise the same, so that the Christian and true Surname, if known, and if not known, a Surname to be given by the Churchwardens and Overseers, be regularly entered in the said book, and the name and surname of such infant be also registered in the Parish Register of the Parish; and in case of a difficulty in distinguishing children, some proper mark should be affixed to the child's clothes or hung round his or her neck. A copy of this register to be annually deposited with the Company of Parish Clerks, and to contain the following particulars viz. name of child, whether foundling, bastard or casualty – age, when born or when admitted – by whom sent and what sum received with it – when died, or when discharged – if nursed by the mother – nurse's name, abode etc, etc.

Although a few such registers do survive, it would seem that the Act was widely ignored.

Undoubtedly, many descendents of foundlings are living totally unaware that an ancestor was given his surname by a vicar, parish clerk, Churchwarden or Overseer of the Poor.

BIBLIOGRAPHY

Bardsley, C.W.   *A Dictionary of English & Welsh Surnames* (1901).

Bardsley, C.W.   *Our English Surnames, their Sources and Significations* (1873).

Bernau, C.A.   *? County.* The first part of an index of surnames with their county of origin, compiled from the Chancery Depositions in the P.R.O. (1932).

Bowman, W.D.   *What is Your Surname?* (1932).

Bowman, W.D.   *The Story of Surnames* (1931).

Ekwall, Eilert. *Variations in Surnames in Mediaeval London.* Soc. Roy. des Lettres de Lund Bull. 1944–45 (1945) pp. 207–262.

Ewen, C.H.L'Estrange. *History of Surnames of the British Isles* (1931).

Ferguson R.   *Surnames as a Science* (1884).

Fransson, G.   *Middle English Surnames of Occupation 1100–1350* (1935).

Guppy H.B.   *Homes of Family Names in Great Britian* (1890).

Harrison, H.   *Surnames of the United Kingdom* 2 Vols. (1908).

Hitchings K and K. *References to English Surnames in 1601.*

Hughes, J.P.   *How you got your name: The Origin and Meaning of Surnames* (rev. edn. 1961).

Knapp O.G.   *Homes of Family Names.* Gen. Mag. Vol. 5. No. 7. Sep. 1930.

Leeson, F.L.   *The Study of Single Surnames and their Distribution* (Gen. Mag. Vol. 14. No. 12. Dec. 1964).

     Discussion of this article appears on pp. 78–80, 82–3 of Vol. 15 No. 2 (June 1965) and p. 150 of Vol. 15 No. 3 (Dec. 1965).

Leeson, F.L.   *The History and Technique of Surname Distribution Studies* (Family History Vol. 3. No. 14/15. May 1965).

Linell, A.   *The Law of Names, Public, Private and Corporate* (1938).

Maidbury, L.   *Family History in Surnames.* (Amateur Historian II p. 114 Feb/Mar 1955).

Maidbury, L.   *English Surnames in Latin* (Amat. Hist. I No. 12. June/July 1954).

Matthews, C.M.   *English Surnames* (1966).

Pine, L.G.   *The Story of Surnames* (1965).

Reaney, A.   *Dictionary of Surnames* (1958).

Stewart-Brown, R. *Name and Arms Conditions in Wills.* Gen. Mag. Vol. 5. No. 12. Dec. 1931. p. 391.

Vernon, H.V.   *Surnames and their Origin.* Australian Gen. I pt. 5. (Jan 1934) 80–94.

Wagner, Sir Anthony. *Genealogy and the Common Man* (1961) [The Jubilee Lecture to the Society of Genealogists, it suggests methods of investigating the areas of origin of surnames]

Weekley, E.   *Surnames* (3rd edn. 1936).

Weekley, E.   *The Romance of Names* (1914)

Change of Surname. For and Against. Discussion Meeting of Soc. of Genealogists. Gen. Mag. Vol. 7. No. 7. Sept. 1936. p.355.

APPENDIX IV — CHRISTIAN NAMES

Fashions in Christian Names

After the Norman Conquest the vast majority of the old Saxon names became extinct and were replaced by the Norman importations: - the Germanic names, *William, Richard, Robert, Henry, Ralph, Odo, Hugh* and *Walter* together with a few Celtic names from Brittany (*Ives, Sampson, Alan*). Biblical names are rare in Domesday Book, but in the 12th and 13th centuries they became increasingly common. At first these were mostly the names of apostles (*John, Matthew, Peter, Andrew, Bartholomew, Philip, James, Simon*) or Evangelists (*Luke, Mark*). Though these did not affect the popularity of the most common male Germanic names, Germanic female names almost disappeared, being replaced by *Joan* (first encountered in England 1189), *Agnes* (1189), *Catherine* (1196), *Mary* (1203), *Elizabeth* (1205) and *Anne* (1218).

During the 13th and 14th centuries, Old Testament names from the Mystery plays made their appearance (*Adam, Eve, Noah, Sarah, Abraham, Isaac, Jacob, Joseph, Daniel, David, Absolom, Susanna, Judith, Anna, Hester, Tobias, Jonah*). Nevertheless the number of names in common use actually declined. Names such as *Austin, Basil, Bennet, Blaise, Brise, Christopher, Clement, Crispin, Denis, Fabian, Gervase, Hilary, Martin, Quentin, Valentine* and *Viel* became rare or disappeared altogether. *Henry, John, Richard, Robert* and *William* accounted for 38% of names in the 12th century, 57% in the 13th and 64% in the 14th. The confusion resulting from such common names was undoubtedly one of the main factors in the development of surnames. [1]

With the Reformation a host of the obscurer Biblical names appeared. These were, of course, especially favoured by the Puritans and so will appear not only in Puritan families but also amongst the parishioners of Puritan clergy. Many Puritans started coining their own names, at first in Latin, (e.g. *Renovata, Donatus, Renatus*) and later in English (e.g. *Desire, Given, Love*) becoming more radical as time went on.

---

[1] All the above information on fashions in names has been taken from Miss E.G. Withycombe *Christian Names*. Gen. Mag. Vol.10. No.2 pp.42-48.

Between 1580 and 1640 Thomas Heley, minister of Warbleton
called his children (born between 1583 and 1589) *Much-Merceye,
Increased, Sin-denie,* and *Fear-not.* Camden in his *Remains* refers to
names such as *Freegift, Reformation, Earth, Dust, Ashes, The Lord is
near, Praise-God* and many others.[2] A fanatical minister had much'
influence on names. While Thomas Heley was minister of Warbleton
(1585-9) the parish registers show at least 100 eccentric names
including *Sorry-for-Sin* and *No-Merit.*[3] Edmund Snape, curate of St.
Peter's Northampton in 1590 refused to christen a child *Richard* (after
its grandfather) because it was not a scriptural name.[4]

Most, but not all of the unusual names appearing in Parish
Registers at this time were scriptural. St. Sepulchre's, Northampton,
contains *Abisha, Herodiah, Hortimias, Mehatabel, Peterlaine, Timmatha:*
North Luffenham, Rutland yields *Bezaliell, Esay, Repent, Patience,
Trephosa, Obedience* (all before 1600), *Anthrea* (1614), *Obediah* (1629),
Harboria (1632) etc and *Babolina* in 1717. Little Brickhill, Bucks.
gives, and not merely once each, *Sabine, Sampson, Hadria, Penelope,
ffayrefford, Duglas, Athanasius* (1575), *Embrey, Benedict* etc. Clyst
St. George, Devon records *Pentecost* (a girl), *Zedwill, Marhoodum,
Fitzchakum, Jechezkelem, Pascover* (a girl) etc.[5]

Twins were often named *Esau* and *Jacob, Moses* and *Aaron* or *Joseph*
and *Mary.* Bastards were sometimes given names indicative of contempt
or derision.

> *Stratford-on-Avon, Warwickshire* 1620. Rahab, filia Johanna West, bastard
> bap Dec 25.
> *Stoke Hammond, Bucks* 1594. Lazarus sonne of a begger woman, bap, 30th
> March.

This practice was of course much more widespread in the case of
foundlings who were freely given such names as *Helpless, Repentance,
Lament, Forsaken,* and *Flie-fornication.* In 1644, in the register of
Ballonsborough, Somerset, an unfortunate girl was baptised
Misericordia-adulterina.[6] Similarly *Peregrine* was often given to the
children of tramps and travellers.

The more extravagant of the Puritan names died out with the
Restoration leaving many Biblical names and a few moral qualities such
as *Faith, Hope, Charity, Prudence, Patience* etc. Of the Biblical names
Samuel, Benjamin, Joseph, Jacob, Sarah, Susan and *Hannah* were fully

---

[2] The quotation is given in full in E.G. Withycombe *Oxford Dictionary of
English Christian Names* p.xxxviii.
[3] Bardsley *"Curiosities of Puritan Nomenclature"* p.55.
[4] E.G. Withycombe *Ox. Dict.* p.xxxix.
[5] William Bradbrook. *The Parish Register* (1910) p.68.
[6] For more information on Puritan names see Bardsley *op.cit.*

acclimatized and others e.g. *Elijah, Amos, Zachary, Ebenezer* and *Caleb* were used by Nonconformists and later by the Wesleyans and Evangelicals. The permanent effect of Puritan nomenclature was greater in America than in England.[7]

The 16th century also saw the introduction of a number of classical names (e.g. *Julius, Horace*) though these were never as popular as on the continent. In the 18th century the Latin forms of women's names were preferred especially among the upper classes e.g. *Anna, Maria, Sophia, Olivia, Evelina, Cecilia, Juliana.* The late 18th century saw the revival of Old English or Mediaeval names (e.g. *Edgar, Edwin, Alfred, Emma, Matilda*). This accelerated with the Romantic Movement and with Tennyson and the Pre-Raphaelites (e.g. *Wilfred, Guy, Roland, Nigel, Quentin, Amy, Hugh, Walter, Roger, Ralph, Alice, Mabel, Edith*). The Oxford Movement revived names such as *Aiden, Augustine, Alban, Theodore, Benedict* and *Bernard.*[8]

Names Used by Both Sexes

The following names have been used indiscrimately for both sexes[9] – *Evelyn, Hilary, Leslie, Vivien.* To this list, since spelling was so variable, may be added *Francis/Frances,*[10] and *Jesse/Jessie.*

Men's Names used for Women

The custom of forming a feminine equivalent from a masculine name came in with the Norman Conquest, and they were often given to daughters because a son had been hoped for, to perpetuate a masculine hereditary Christian name or to place the girl under the patronage of a male saint. (e.g. *Joan* of *St. John.*). The Scots in the 18th century were fond of making feminine forms from masculine names (e.g. *Abrahamina, Adamina, Jamesina, Roberta, Robina*) most of which have since become extinct. However, often masculine names were given to girls without alteration. Miss Withycombe points out:[11]

"Latin records of the 13th to 15th centuries show that the custom of giving masculine names to girls was also common in England; they appear

---

[7] The famous *Preserved Fish* (1766-1846) would not have been given this name at that time in England. The commoner Biblical names *Benjamin, Samuel, Daniel* etc, now rare in England are in general use in America and many others are also found: e.g. *Seth, Ira, Jedediah, Elihu.*

[8] E.G. Withycombe. *Christian Names*, loc. cit. p.45.

[9] In Spain there were many more. e.g. *Trinidad, Encarnacion, Guadalupe, Refugio, Rosario, Luz, Paz, Cruz* etc.

[10] e.g. In West Hendred churchyard, Northants is buried a woman named *Francis Wilcox Gardner* who died as late as 15 Dec. 1899.

[11] *Ox. Dict.* p. xxv.

in Latin with feminine endings e.g. *Phillippa, Nicholaa, Alexandra, Jacoba,* but it is clear that girls so named were in fact baptized and called *Philip, Nicholas, Alexander, James* etc."

Thus one of the three daughters of Richard Emelden who died in 1333 often appears in records as *Jacoba,* but in a *Proof of Age* in 1339, a witness remembered the baptism because "it seemed to him wonderful that he called her by a boy's name when she was herself a girl." She is usually called *Joan* in later records, but after her marriage to Sir Alan Clavering, there is a reference to "Sir Alan and *James* his wife."[12] This practice continued right up to the 19th century. *Nicholas,* as a girl's name was particularly common at the end of the 17th century, and is sometimes found even later. Thus, there is a stone in Stepney churchyard to:

Nicholas Ann Aitken daughter of William and Mary Aitken of Blackwell died 5th April 1812 aged 26.

Other names which were commonly used for girls were *Aubrey, Basil, Bennett, Cecil, Douglas, Edmund, Eustace, Florence, Gilbert, Giles, Hildred, Julian,* [13] *Laurence, Reynold, Simon, Sydney,* [14] *Valentine, Vernon.*

Women's names for Men

The following, though normally given to girls were also used for boys. *Alison, Ann/Anne,* [15] *Caroline, Cassie, Christian, Clare, Comfort, Essex,* [16] *Grace,* [17] *Mary/Maria, Marion, Patience,* [18] *Radegund.*[19]

Interchangeable and Confused Names

Elizabeth and *Isobel*

In the Middle Ages the names *Isobel* and *Elizabeth* were inter-changeable, the best known case being that of Isobel or Elizabeth de Vermandois, the wife of Robert de Beaumont and William de Warenne. This survived occasionally into the Parish Register period. Thus a

---

12 Miss E.G. Withycombe *Christian Names* loc. cit. p.45.
13 e.g. *Julian Balfour* who married James 6th Earl of Radnor.
14 e.g. *Harriet Sydney Dobbs,* who married (1850) George 6th Duke of Manchester.
15 e.g. *William Anne van Keppel,* 2nd Earl of Albemarle (born 1702 died 1754).
16 The name was frequent among female descendants of Penelope daughter of Robert Devereux 1st Earl of Essex, who married Robert Lord Rich. It has been used as a male name in Pembrokeshire and also in the Pawlet family.
17 Sometimes found given to boys in the 17th century.
18 e.g. *Sir Patience Ward,* Lord Mayor of London 1680.
19 This is used for both sexes in the Parish Registers of Bengeworth, Worcs.

Berkshire yeoman in his will in 1542 named his wife *Isobel*. In her own will two years later she calls herself *Elizabeth*.[20]

Ann and *Agnes*

Ann and *Annis* (Agnes) were very frequently confused. In the case of *King v King* (42 Eliz) it was argued that they were "all one name." The court decided they were different names. [21]

Gillian and *Julian*

These too were used interchangeably. However in *Griffith v Middleton* (15 James I) it was held that they were different names.

Anne and *Hannah*

These are frequently used indiscriminately.

Hester and *Esther*

These are also used interchangeably.

Phyllis and *Felice*

In the 16th and 17th centuries the Renaissance importation *Phyllis* was confused with the mediaeval name *Felice*.

Marion and *Mary Ann*

The old diminutive *Marion* was in the 18th and early 19th centuries (when it was commonly spelt *Marian*) believed to be identical with *Mary Ann*. Thus the real name of the novelist *George Eliot* is commonly given both as *Mary Ann Evans* and as *Marian Evans*.

Joan and *Jane*

These were used interchangeably and in *Griffith v Middleton* (15 James I) it was held that they were one name.

Obsolete Names

Many Christian names once fairly common have become obsolete.. Some Mediaeval names which had become rare by the start of Parish registers have already been listed. Other old names died out during the parish register period. *Piers* or *Pierce* the most common mediaeval form of Peter survived into the seventeenth century, as did also the Mediaeval name *Ellis* (from *Helias*). *Amyas* and *Fulk* (*Fowk, Fawk*) were

---

[20] E.G. Withycombe *Ox. Dict.* p.157, *Christian Names* loc.cit. p.45.
[21] *N & Q* 10th Ser. viii. For a 17th Century Parish Register example of their indiscriminate use for the same person see D.E. Gardner and F. Smith *Genealogical Research in England & Wales* Vol.1 pp.270–271.

still common in the 16th century. Of female names, *Sence* (Sanchia) and *Dionys* (Dionysia) were current in the 16th century and *Tace* (Tayce), *Douce* and *Amphyllis* well into the seventeenth. *Wilmot,* a mediaeval diminutive of *William* was quite common as a woman's name into the 18th century. *Philpot* and *Emmot* died out about a century earlier.

Other names such as *Magdalen* (usually spelt *Maudlin*) now rare were once common, in addition of course to the host of Bible names brought in by the Puritans.

Spelling

In addition to these, the spelling of Christian names has often changed very considerably, making some old names almost unrecognizable. Some of the more important, with their modern equivalents are as follows:

Agace, Agas	Agatha
Aleyn	Alan
Annis, Annys, Annais	Agnes
Barnet, Barnard	Bernard
Deenes, Deenys	Denis
Deryk, Derrick	Derek
Dorat(e)	Dorothy
Etheldred (abbrev. to Theldred)	Audrey
Fithian	Vivian
Frauncis, Fraunce	Francis, Frances
Garret	Gerard
Grisel, Grissel, Grizzel	Griselda
Halbert (in N. of Eng.)	Albert
Hammond	Hamon
Jarvis	Gervase
Lewes	Louise
Maidline, Madlin, Maudlin	Magdalen
Meriel, Meryall	Muriel
Phythian	Vivian
Raff, Raphe, Rayfe	Ralph
Sence	Sanchia
Sisley	Cicely
Symond	Simon
Tibald	Theobald

One of the most interesting of these is *Audrey*. The name is derived from the Anglo-Saxon *Etheldred*. The same person is named in Market Rasen parish register as *Ethelia* in 1787 and *Theldred* in 1795.[22]

---

[22] E.G. Withycombe *Ox. Dict.* p.103.

Nicknames and Diminutives

Before the emergence of fixed surnames, nicknames and diminutives were an essential means of identifications. Miss E.G. Withycombe convincingly argues[23] that the majority of peasants from the 13th to. the 15th century went by nicknames and this is amply borne out by the vast number of surnames derived from these. A name such as *Bartholemew* produced a whole crop – *Bat, Bate, Batty, Bartle, Bartelot, Bartlett, Batcock, Batkin, Tolly* – all of which have given rise to one or more surnames. The custom of shortening names or forming nicknames by rhyming seems to have started earlier than the use of suffixes.[24] Both practices have continued to the present day and new variants were continually manufactured. Thus *Richard* became *Dick* or *Hick, Robert* – *Hob, Bob* or *Dob, Roger* – *Hodge* or *Dodge, Margaret* – *Peg, Mary* – *Polly*.

The Normans brought in the French diminutive suffixes *–ot, –et, –un, –in, –el* which combined with the shorter forms produced names such as *Philpot, Hewett* and *Dickin*. Sometimes, more than one would be used. Thus, *Hamo(n)* became not only *Hamel* but also *Hamelin, Hamelet* and *Hamonet*. *Hugh* became *Hewett, Hewlett, Howlett* and *Hewin*.

These diminutive forms were used for both men's and women's names but survived longer in the latter case. Thus as has been pointed out *Philpot, Wilmot, Marriot* and *Emmot* are found as women's names in the 16th and 17th centuries and even later in Cornwall.[25] The most tenacious was the suffix – *on,* which still survives in Alison and Marion.[26] The English suffixes *cock* and *kin* (*Perkin, Hawkin, Dawkin, Hancock, Hitchcock* etc) came in from the end of the 13th century. Most were masculine, but a few such as *Malkin* or *Mawkin* (*Mary*) were feminine. They were particularly common in the second half of the 14th century, but are rarely found after about 1450 though of course they survive in surnames.

By the beginning of Parish Registers a large number of nicknames had died out and there was a further reduction in the sixteenth and seventeenth centuries. Thus, all those beginning with H have disappeared (e.g. *Hob, Hodge, Hick, Hitch, Hudd* [Richard], *Hibb* [Isobel]). Others, (e.g. *Robin, Philpot, Marion, Alison*) had assumed a status as names in their own right. Nevertheless it is never safe to assume that the *Marion* in a marriage entry cannot be identical with the *Mary*

---

23 *ibid* p.xxxiii.
24 This custom seems to have been part of a wider practice which has survived in Cockney rhyming slang.
25 *Mariot* is found in Cornwall as late as 1725. E.G. Withycombe. *Ox. Dict.* p.201.
26 This suffix was always feminine in French, but in England was sometimes used for men e.g. Gibbon from Gib (Gilbert).

in a baptism, and pet Names are not infrequently found in baptisms, marriages and burials right throughout the period of parish registers, as in the following examples:

Potsgrove, Beds.
Baptisms
    19 Feb. 1764 Elizabeth daughter of William and *Nanny* Kitchener
    1 June 1770 Mary daughter of William and *Ann* Kitchen
    24 Dec. 1775 Sarah daughter of William and *Ann* Kitchiner

Burials
    17 Dec. 1782 Elizabeth daughter of William and *Ann* Kitchiner
    2 Aug. 1796 Sarah daughter of William and *Ann* Kitchener

Arlesey, Beds.
Baptisms
    5 Oct. 1822 Martha daughter of William and *Frances* Kitchener, Cordwainer
    13 May 1827 John son of William and *Frances* Kitchener, shoemaker
    5 Oct. 1835 Joseph son of William and *Fanny* Kitchener, shoemaker

In Census returns they are even more frequent:

Hinxworth, Herts.
Baptism
    20 Jan 1839 *Irene* daughter of Joseph and Mary Kitchener, Baker
    1841 Census (Household of Joseph Kitchener) *Rena*, daughter 2
    1851 Census – *Rena*, daughter 12

The following list contains some of the more common diminutives.[27] However, it must be borne in mind that frequently the diminutive form itself was given as a baptismal name, and sometimes one name was used as a pet name for another (e.g. *Elsie* for *Alice*)

Ada	Sometimes used as pet name for *Adelaide*
Addie	Adelaide
Aggie	Agnes
Annie	Sometimes used as pet name for *Ann*
Bab, Babbie	Barbara
Belle	Isobel, Isobella
Bess, Bessie, Beth, Betsy, Betty	Elizabeth
Biddy	Bridget
Bob, Bobbie	Robert
Caddie, Caro, Carrie	Caroline
Cassie	Cassandra
Celia	Sometimes used as pet name for Cecilia
Cherry	Charity
Ciss	Cecilia
Clara	Clarissa
Cuddie, Cuddy	Cuthbert

---

[27] Others encountered more commonly in America will be found in *American Genealogist* Vol.34, No.2 April 1958 p.97.

Debby	Deborah
Delia	Cordelia
Dick	Richard
Dob	Robert
Doll, Dolly	Dorothy
Dora	Sometimes used as a pet name for *Dorothy*
Dot, Dotty	Dorothy
Ede, Edie	Edith
Effim, Effum	Euphemia
Eliza	Sometimes used as pet name for *Elizabeth*
Ellen	Sometimes used as pet name for *Eleanor*
Elsie	Sometimes used as pet name for *Alice*
Emily	Sometimes used as pet name for *Amelia*
Epham	Euphemia
Essie	Esther, Hester
Etty	Henrietta
Fanny	Frances
Frank	Francis, Frances
Fraunce	Francis
Gertie	Gertrude
Ginnie	Virginia
Gussie	Augusta
Harriet	Sometimes used as pet name for *Henrietta*
Harry	Henry
Hessie	Hester, Esther
Hettie, Hetty	Henrietta, Esther
Hick	Richard
Hob	Robert
Hodge	Roger
Jack	John (also used as general nickname irrespective of Christian name)
Jenny	Jane
Kate	Catharine
Kit, Kester	Christopher
Lena	Eleanor, Helen, Magdalen
Libbie, Libby	Elizabeth
Lina	Caroline
Lisa	Melissa
Lizzie	Elizabeth
Lottie, Lotty	Charlotte
Lucy	Sometimes used as pet name for *Lucinda*
Madge	Margery
Maggie	Margaret
Mally, Mamie	Mary
Manda	Amanda
Massey, Mattie, Matty	Martha, Matilda
Mena	Almena
Millie	Mildred
Mina	Wilhelmina
Minnie	Mary, Wilhelmina
Molly	Mary
Nan, Nancy, Nanny	Ann
Nat	Nathaniel
Nell, Nellie	Eleanor, Helen, Ellen
Nettie	Antoinette

Nob	Robert
Nonie	Joan
Patty	Martha, Patience
Peg, Peggy	Margaret
Phyllis	Sometimes used as pet name for *Felicia*
Piers, Pierce	Peter
Polly	Mary
Pru	Prudence
Rena	Irene
Rita	Marguerite
Rob, Robbie	Robert
Sally	Sarah
Sander, Saunder	Alexander
Sissie	Cecilia
Sukie	Susan
Taggy, Taggett	Agnes
Tetsy, Tetty	Elizabeth
Thirza	Sometimes used as pet name for *Theresa*
Tibby	Elizabeth
Tilly	Matilda
Tom	Thomas
Tony	Anthony
Totty	Charlotte
Viney	Lavinia
Wat	Walter
Winnie	Winifred

Latin Equivalents of Personal Names

In early registers written in Latin, it was customary to Latinize Christian names, but not surnames. Many were formed merely by adding *-us* or *-a* to the English name. The following list gives the Latin forms normally encountered for most others.[28a] Latinized forms o Welsh Christian names will be found in Volume II.

Aegidius	Giles
Agatha	Agace, Agas
Agneta (Ana)	Agnes
Ailmaricus	Emery
Alberedus, Aluredus	Alfred
Alecia, Alicia	Alice
Alionora	Eleanor
Aloysius	Lewis
Ambrosius	Ambrose
Amfelisa	Amphyllis
Amicius	Amyas
Anabilia	Anable
Andreas	Andrew
Anna	Anne, Ann, Hannah
Antonius	Anthony
Bartholemaeus	Bartholomew
Benedictus	Benedict, Bennet

[28a] A more complete list will be found in D.E. Gardner and F. Smith *Genealogical Research in England and Wales* Vol. 3 pp. 87–92.

Carolus	Charles
Christophorus	Christopher
Clemens	Clement
Coleta	Nicholas (fem)
Constantia	Constance
Dionisia	Dionys, Denyse
Edvardus, Eduardus	Edward
Egidius	Giles
Emelina	Emily
Emmota	Emmott
Etheldreda	Audrey
Eugenius	Owen
Eustachius, Eustatius	Eustace
Francisca	Frances
Franciscus.	Francis
Galfridus, Gaufridus	Geoffrey
Georgius	George
Gilemota	Wilmot
Godefridus	Godfrey, Geoffrey
Goisfridus	Geoffrey
Gratia	Grace
Gregorius	Gregory
Gualterus	Walter
Guido	Guy
Gulielmus, Guilielmus	William
Hadrianus	Adrian
Helena	Eleanor, Helen
Helias, Helyas	Ellis
Henricus	Henry
Hieronymus	Jerome
Horatius	Horace
Hugo	Hugh, Hugo
Humfridus	Humphrey
Imania	Emma
Isacus	Isaac
Isabella	Isabella, Isobel
Jacobus	James or Jacob
Jocosa, Jodoca	Joyce
Johanna	Joan, Jane, Jean, Janet
Johannes	John
Laetitia	Lettice
Laurentius	Laurance
Lionhardus	Leonard
Lucas	Luke
Ludovicus	Lewis
Maggota	Margot
Marcus	Mark
Mariota	Marriot
Matthaeus	Matthew (Mawe in Yorks.)
Mauritius	Maurice
Misericordia	Mercy
Natalis	Noel
Nicholaus	Nicholas
Patricius	Patrick
Pero	Piers

Petrus	Peter
Philippus	Philip
Richardus	Richard
Seisillus	Cecil
Sescilia	Cecily
Sidneus	Sidney
Silvanus	Silas
Susanna	Susan
Umfridus	Humphrey
Villefridus	Wilfred
Vincens	Vincent
Williametta, Willelma	Wilmot

Influences on Choice of Name

In the 16th and 17th Centuries children were normally named after either relations or godparents. [28] Mr. E. Chitty suggests that

"In certain periods naming after godparents was the orthodox practice and only the fact that godparents were most often chosen from within the family produces the appearance that "family names" were deliberately perpetuated. Bequests to godchildren bearing the testator' name or to selected nephews and other kin similarly named support this contention, though we naturally find godchildren bearing other names, since a child bore only one name though it had more than one godparent- two of its own and one of the opposite sex being made the ecclesiastical rule in 1661.

Further evidence may be derived from such Family Bibles as record the godparents. In an 18th century example, of seven children, six were named after godparents – all members of the family – the exception being a son who was given the name borne by both his father and his deceased paternal grandfather. Parents were not acceptable as godparents, but the very usual practice of naming the eldest children after the grandparents, whether living or dead might surely have arisen from an earlier custom of honouring the living grandparents by inviting them to act as sponsors for the first grandchildren."[29]

The implication that family names were seldom "deliberately perpetuated" probably overstates the case. However, there is considerable evidence of Norman families naming the eldest son after the grandfather in the first centuries following the Norman Conquest and that Mr. Chitty's explanation of this custom is likely, is shown by the fact that the custom of the grandfather standing as godfather of his eldest grandson survived much later in the island of Jersey.

---

[28] For a detailed study of these and other influences see D. J. Steel *The Descent of Christian Names* Gen. Mag. Vol. 14 No. 2 June 1962.

[29] *Gen. Mag.* Vol. 14 No. 8 Dec. 1963. p. 268.

Madam A. Mersery points out[30] that in the 16th and 17th centuries this resulted in alternate generations with the same Christian name. Thus for seven generations the names Philippe and Thomas alternated in the ancestry of Philippe Falle, the historian.

The custom of naming after godparents seems clearly to be a legacy from pre-Reformation England when a spiritual relationship was at least as important as kinship by blood and marriages could be annulled and the parties punished on this ground alone. However, that it was more important than kinship as a naming influence is as yet unproven. The exception in Mr. Chitty's example rather than being named after his grandfather was more likely named after his father, a practice of which every genealogist must have found innumerable examples, and which accounts for the long consecutive series of persons bearing the same name which are frequently encountered in pedigrees. Clearly more research on this subject is needed before final conclusions can be drawn.

Surname as Christian Name

The first known example of this practice was Lord Guildford Dudley, son of the Duke of Northumberland and husband of Lady Jane Grey. His mother's name was Guildford.[31] The fashion became general among the landed gentry in Elizabeth's reign. Camden approved of the practice:

> "Whereas in late years surnames have been given for Christian names among us, and nowhere else in Christendome, although many dislike it; for that great inconvenience will ensue; nevertheless it seemeth to proceed from hearty good will, and affection of the god-fathers to show their love or from a desire to continue and propagate their own name to succeeding ages and is in no wise to be disliked, but rather approved in those, which matching with heirs generall of worshipfull antient families, have given these names to their heirs, with a mindful and thankful regard of them, as we have now *Pickering Wotton, Grevill Varney, Bassingburne Gawdy, Calthorp Parker, Pecsall Brocas Fitz-Raulf Chamberlaine,* who are the heirs of *Pickering, Bassingburne, Grevill, Calthorpe* etc."

He appears to refer obliquely to a suggestion that the practice had originated through fathers acknowledging children, illegitimately or perhaps even adulterously conceived:

> "Neither can I believe a wayward old man which would say that the giving of Surnames for Christian names first began in the time of King Edward the sixt, by such as would be god-fathers when they were more than half fathers, and thereupon would have persuaded same to change such names at the Confirmation."[32]

---

[30] *Bulletin de la Societe Jersiaise* 1922.
[31] A *James Lynch Fitzstephen* was Mayor of Galway in 1493, but see below p.121.
[32] Cited by E.G. Withycombe. *Ox. Dict.* p.xli.

Camden's emphasis on the role of the godfather is significant. In the 16th and 17th centuries the practice of giving surnames as Christian names was largely confined to the upper classes, and it seems likely that in the majority of cases where the maiden name of the mother is given, the maternal grandfather was a god-father, and his surname rather than his Christian name would most probably be given if his daughter were an heiress, or if it otherwise seemed likely that the male line would become extinct. G. Andrews Moriarty notes:

> "An entry in the Diary of Judge Samuel Sewell throws some light on this custom. His son Samuel married Rebecca, daughter of Governor Joseph Dudley, and the Judge records that when his daughter-in-law wished to name a son Dudley, old madam Dudley objected, saying that her son might still have a son."[33]

However, too much must not be made of this, for the editor of the *American Genealogist* cautioned:

> "I agree that there was a special inducement to give a child the family name of a mother or grandmother when her family had died out in the male line, but the custom seems to have been fairly common even when that was not the case. My ancestor, John Hall of Wallingford, Conn. named his first son *Street* and his second son *Lyman*, after his wife and his mother, although there were plenty of *Streets* and *Lymans* to carry on the family name."

Often, of course, the godfather was not a relative and on occasion the parents might wish to name the child after a deceased friend, particularly if the latter was well-known.

> *Stratford-on-Avon* 1616.
> Nov.23rd Shaksper fillias Thomas Quyny. gent. bapt.[34]

The use of surnames as Christian names was rare among the lower classes until the 18th century when entries such as the following become more frequent:

> *Olney, Bucks.*
> 27 Jan 1744/5 West son of John and Elizabeth Kitchiner
> 7 June 1745 Hooton son of Richard and Susanna Kitchiner

and even

> 18 May 1766 West Kitchiner Whitmey, son of James and Merena Kitchiner

He is presumably the *"West Whitmey"*, buried on 30 June 1767 for on 29 May 1768 the same persistent parents baptized another child *"West Kitchiner"*. Other baptisms in the same register are:

> 21 June 1769 Gilman son of William Kitchener aged 13 years
> 18 April 1772 Berwith son of Thomas and Ann Kitchener

---

[33] *Nomenclature* Amer. Gen. Vol.37 (April 1961) p.73.
[34] Cited by W. Bradbrook *The Parish Register* p.71.

and curiously

24 March 1776 West son of John and Sarah Green.[35]

Parents have been prepared to run the risk of ambiguity by giving children names such as *Lord, Lady, Sergeant* or *Major*. Surnames have been most frequently given to boys, though when two or more surnames became common, girls were increasingly given a surname as a second name. Clearly these surnames are of immense genealogical value and as long ago as 1929, Mr. F.H.M. Hugo proposed that when a parish register was copied, surnames used as Christian names should appear separately in the index.[36]

However, one must beware of assuming automatically that a surname used as a Christian name is necessarily ancestral. As the Editor of the *American Genealogist* observed:

> "No one expects that because [one has]..... ancestors with such given names as *Washington, Jefferson,* or *Franklin,* that he will discover an actual descent from these families."[37]

The same is of course equally true for the English genealogist.[38]

Brothers and Sisters with the Same Name

Throughout the period of parish registers brothers and sisters will be found baptized with the same Christian name. In the majority of cases of course, the first child died before the baptism of the other. This was most frequent where the older child died in infancy, and in the days of high infant mortality, even three or four children may have been successively given the same name. However, sometimes it was done when an older child grew up, married but died quite young. This can be a pitfall for the genealogist. John G. Hunt and D.L. Jacobus quote an example in New England:

> Ensign George Clark of Milford, Conn, named his second child by his first wife, *Abigail*; she was born 1 April 1680, married Joseph Talcott of Hartford (later Governor of Connecticut), gave him two sons and died 24 March 1704. Some years later. Ensign George Clark had an only child by his third wife, born 4 Jan 1713-14 and named her *Abigail* in commemoration of the daughter he had lost. Until the details have been worked out, the Will of Ensign George Clark is very confusing, for he names the two sons of *"my daughter Mrs. Abigail Talcot, decd."* and also his

---

[35] Entries such as these show that Miss Withycombe is mistaken when she states (*Ox. Dict.* p.xlii) that the practice was confined to the nobility and gentry until the 19th century when it was imitated by the middle classes. All the above belonged to the labouring class.

[36] *Notes & Queries* 156 p.31.

[37] *loc.cit.* p.76.

[38] For a fuller discussion of the whole subject see D.J. Steel *op.cit.*

"daughter Abigail Curtis wife of Ebenezer Curtis."[39]

However there was a once widespread curious custom of giving children the same names even though they were both living at the same time. There is some possibility that the custom might have been introduced before the Norman Conquest. Thus Cospatric, 11th century Earl of Northumberland had two sons named *Waltheof*.[40] However, almost all known mediaeval instances are from the Norman nobility and since many cases have been recorded in France, in spite of the Saxon names and connections of the Waltheof brothers, one must assume it was a Norman importation.[41] There were two brothers named *Fulk fitz Warin* (13th Century)[42] *Helias de Say* (13th century) had two brothers named *Robert*.[43] Occasionally additions were made to distinguish the brothers. Thus there were two brothers called *John Giffard le Hof* and *John Giffard le Box*.[44] (*le Boef* on *Fine Rolls* 1316). Sometimes the *"brothers"* were in fact only half brothers, as in the case of *John le Strange* 2nd Lord Strange of Knockin, Salop and his half brother *John le Strange*, King's yeoman,[45] or John Matravers (Baron 1351) who by two wives had two sons named *John*. The younger also had two sons named *John*.[46] However, it was not until the fifteenth century that more than isolated cases are found. Then many instances are encountered. Thus the two sons of John Paston were *Sir John Paston the elder* (1422-79) and *Sir John Paston the younger* (died 1503). John Vavasour in his Will 24 April 1461 names two sons *John*.[47] Thomas Mallory of Papworth, Hunts in his Will 1469 mentions John, his son and heir and *"my son John the younger"*.[48]

In the sixteenth century it was extremely common particularly among the gentry and aristocracy. Thus the Protector Somerset had no less than three sons named *Edward* who were all living at the same time viz: *Sir Edward Seymour*, his eldest son (born 1529, died 1593); *Edward, Earl of Hertford* (born 1539, died 1621); and *Sir Edward*, the King's godson (born 1548, died 1574). The 8th Duke of Beaufort had five sons named Henry, and the 7th Earl of Shaftesbury five sons

---

[39] *Brothers and Sisters of the Same Given Names.* American Gen. Vol. 36. No. 3 p. 159 (July 1960).

[40] *Vide* Peter de Blois, sub Anno 1112 "The Two Brothers Woldev."

[41] In France there was normally a distinguishing suffix added to each of the names: e.g. *Jehan* and *Jehannot*, *Guillaume* and *Guillot*, Michaelsson *"Les Rôles de Taille Parisiens 1292-1303."* Cited by Ewen *History of Surnames of the British Isles* p. 404.

[42] Eyton *Antiquities of Shropshire* vii p. 82.

[43] *ibid* viii p. 62.

[44] *Placita de Quo Warranto* p. 86.

[45] This has caused confusion in all peerages from Dugdale to the present day.

[46] *Coll. Top et Gen.* Vol. iii p. 78.

[47] *Baildon and the Baildons* Vol. i p. 526.

[48] *Athenaeum* 11 Sept 1897 p. 354.

named *Anthony*. John Dudley, Duke of Northumberland had two sons named *Henry*. The Will of Sir Anthony Hungerford, Knt of Down Ampney, Glos. 1558 mentions the eldest and youngest sons both called *John*, whilst his fourth and fifth sons were named *Edward*.[49] In the church of Beddington, Surrey there is a brass to Philippa Carew and her thirteen brothers and sisters, among whom were four named *John*. Thomas Pepys, the diarist's grandfather had a brother of the same name and in the late 16th century Serjeant Thomas Gawdy had two sons, both of whom were baptized Thomas.[50] Sir John Sharpe of Coggeshall, Essex, in his 1518 Will (P.C.C. 13 Ayloffe), leaves reversion to Robert Browne, eldest son of testator's sister Isabel, with reversion to Robert, younger brother of aforesaid Robert.[51]

Although most commong among the aristocracy and gentry, the practice was by no means confined to them as is shown by the following examples: Richard Aleyn of Thaxted, Essex, in his 1508 Will (P.C.C., 11 Bennet), lists *three* sons, all legitimate, named John Aleyn.[52] The Will of John Parnell of Gyrton (8 Mar. 1545) reads:

> "Alice my wife and old John my son to occupy my farm together, till Old John marries..... Young John my son shall have Brenlay's land plowed and sowed at Old John's cost."[53]

and the Will of Nicholas Brent of Stow on the Wold (22 Oct 1582)

> "To William Brente my eldest son if he live to accomplish his age of twenty years 30 1. To William Brent my second son 30 1 and to William Brent my third son 40 1 etc."[54]

John Writer, baker of All Saints' Worcester (Will 1601 "23 Montague") had a son baptized Thomas in 1590, and buried the following year. In 1592 another son was born and he too was baptized as Thomas, and known in later years as *"Thomas the elder"*. In the same year John's wife died and he married again; among other children born of this second marriage a son was baptized Thomas in 1594, and hereafter known as *"Thomas the younger."*[55] John Vivian of Trelowarren (died 1562) had two sons John Vivian of Arralas (died 1564) and John Vyvian of Trelowarren (died 1577) both of whom left issue.[56] John Baron of Bardharlocke (now Badharlick) in Egloskerry, yeoman died 1624. His younger brother, John Baron died in 1619, leaving a son John Baron

---

[49] *Coll Top & Gen.* Vol.7.
[50] Cox *op. cit.* p.69. The younger Thomas changed his name at Confirmation. *See below* p.125.
[51] Cited by J.G. Hunt and D.L. Jacobus. *op. cit.* p.158.
[52] *ibid.* p.158.
[53] J.S. Burn *History of Parish Registers in England.* p.69.
[54] P.C.C. Rowe 8.
[55] Cited by W.R. Buchanan-Dunlop. *Gen.Mag* Vol.11 No.6. June 1952. p.214.
[56] See *Vivian's Visit. of Cornwall* pp.528-9.

who died in 1654-5 pre-deceased by a brother, yet another John Baron,
who however died an infant, and John Rogers, the elder of Bruge
(born 1609, died 1673) names in his will his brother John Rogers the
younger (born 1612, died 1690).[57] Where there were two brothers of
the same name it is important to note that as in many of these
examples they may be distinguished by *"The Elder"* and *"The
Younger"*. In an Administration Bond in the Archdeaconry of Berkshire
of the deceased John Winkworth dated 11th May 1573 are mentioned the
ten children including John Winckworth the elder and John the younger.
Thus there were two sons living both with the same name as their father,
distinguished as *"Elder"* and *"Younger"* though the father has no
such designation.[58] More curiously G. Andrews Moriarty refers to a
case in which three brothers were described in their father's will as
"John the Elder, John the Middler and *John the Younger"*.[59]

As with the mediaeval example cited earlier, in some cases
brothers of the same name may have been in fact only half brothers:

> "Angell Smith died in 1626, Lord of the Manor of Stratton, Dorset, for
> 52 years. His daughter Joane had two sons named Angell: the first was
> born in 1602, son of her first husband, George Grey Esq., of Kingston
> Maureward, Dorset; the second Angell was by her second husband, Laurence
> Miller of Frome, Dorset."[60]

> "Thomas Wheeler "the elder" of Cranfield, co. Bedford, had two sons
> named Thomas by different mothers as suggested in *Families of Old
> Fairfield* and afterwards confirmed by the will of the father."[61]

In other cases they were twins, as in the following examples:

> *Beby, Leics.* 1559 Aug. 29 John and John Sicke, the children of Christopher
> and Anne Sicke were baptized. Item 31 Aug. the same John and John were
> buried.[62]

> Rothwell, Yorks. 1547 Decr. Joh' es et Joh' es fil' gemelli Joh' es Sayvell
> bapt.[63]

It has been suggested[64] that the practice of calling two sons John

---

57   J.P. Rogers. *Gen. Mag.* Vol.11. No.3 Sept. 1951. p.108. A number of similar
     examples concerning the names *Richard, William* and *Francis* occur in letter
     on this subject from A.J. Willis, and Walter G. Davis in *Gen. Mag.* Vol.11,
     No.6. June 1952, pp.213-214. Many other examples are given in *N & Q* 12th
     Ser. ix. pp.273, 312.

58   C.W. Winstanley. *Gen.Mag.* Vol.11 No.2. June 1951 p.65. Other examples of
     this practice are cited by A.J. Willis and W.R. Buchanan-Dunlop. *Gen.Mag.*
     Vol.11 No.6. June 1952. pp.213-214.

59   *Nomenclature.* Amer. Gen. Vol.37. p.72 (April 1961).

60   J.G. Hunt and L. Jacobus *op.cit.* p.158.

61   *ibid* 158. The elder son was Thomas, called *Senior* of Fairfield, Conn.; the
     younger was Lieut. (later Capt.) Thomas of Fairfield and Stratford and of
     Concord, Mass.

62   R.E. Chester Waters *History of Parish Registers in England* p.43.

63   G.D. Lumb *N & Q* 12th Ser. ix p.436 where other examples are also given.

64   J.H. Harvey. *Gen. Mag.* Vol.11 No.5 March 1952 p.182.

was in honour of the Baptist and Evangelist respectively and connected with the child's date of birth at or near their mid-summer and mid-winter festivals. This explanation is unlikely and of course cannot apply either in the cases where the name is other than John or even where more than two brothers are given the name John. Thus Abraham and John Truscott, married at Landulph in Sept. 1541 had eleven children, of whom no less than five were all christened John. Only one appears to have died in infancy,[65] and John Wode of Sanderstead, Surrey in his Will mentions four sons named John.[66]

The custom has also been explained as being the result of the practice of granting leases for three lives e.g. To John Doe and his sons John and William. If one son John died there would still be one of the same name left to hold the lease.[67] That this motive was not uncommon is shown by the following quotation from *The Most Profitable and Commendable Science of Surveying* by Valentyne Leigh, published in 1577:

> "And let the Surveiour, that hath to doe in the west parties, looke diligently to this one pointe, that the name of a young Infaunte crepe not into the place of an olde man, for the vse muche there (I will not saie for that intent) if the Father or Mother who have state for life in possession or reversion, bee named Ihon and Agnes, or suche like, then if they have ii or three boyes, or as many girles, their names shal be all christened as they or those who state in their holdinges are named. But now this is more narrowly looked to, than in tymes past."[68]

However, deliberately creating ambiguity as to who was the leaseholder might actually prove a disadvantage. The reversioner might contend that the demise ended at the death of the brother who died first.

Mr. Chitty suggests that the duplication of names arises from the custom of children being named after god-parents.

> "It is most probable that the circle of uncles, aunts and other suitable god-parents would have included two Johns, two Elizabeths and so on."[69]

C.E. Ewen makes a similar point though without emphasising the importance of the godparent:

> "Three sons, for instance might be named Robert after father grandfather and uncle respectively, without calling for critical comment."[70]

The most likely explanation is therefore the simplest – that the practice occurred as a result of the desire to perpetuate a family

[65] J.H. Adams. *Gen. Mag.* Vol. 11 No. 9 March 1953. p. 315.
[66] *N & Q* 12th Ser. ix p. 396.
[67] E.G. Withycombe. *Ox. Dict.* p. xxxi *Christian Names*, *loc. cit.* p. 43.
[68] p. 23 Cited by H. Thornton. *N & Q* 12th Ser. 11 p. 152.
[69] *Gen. Mag.* Vol. 14, No. 8, Dec. 1963 p. 268.
[70] *History of Surnames of the British Isles* p. 403.

Christian name or that of some revered relative or friend.[71]
G. Andrews Moriarty concludes:[72]

> "The custom evidently arose from the high mortality among children and the desire to perpetuate the name of a near relative, usually that of the grandfather."

This view is supported by the following extract from Gibbon's autobiography:

> "So feeble was my constitution, so precarious my life, that in the baptism of my brothers, my father's prudence successively repeated my Christian name of *Edward*, that in case of the departure of the eldest son this patronymic appellation might still be perpetuated in the family."[73]

A case as late as Gibbon's was exceptional, for, as Mr. Moriarty points out, the custom had already begun to decline by the commencement of the seventeenth century.[74]

The giving of two or more daughters the same name was less common, as there was, of course, in the case of girls less motivation to ensure the perpetuation of a family name. However, it was by no means exceptional:

> James Isaac of Patricksbourne, Kent who died in 1501 by enfeoffment provided £100 toward the marriages of each of his daughters "Elizabeth the elder" and "Elizabeth the younger."[75] Sir Richard Walden of Erith, Kent in his will, proved in 1539 left his estate to his two daughters Elizabeth Hawte and Elizabeth, Countess of Shrewsbury.[76] The Will of Thomas Reade of Calcott, Hunts in 1595 mentions "my daughter Katheryn the Younger" and "my eldest daughter Katheryn."[77]

The practice is also found in Scotland:

> 24 Nov 1551 Isabel Scot daughter of George Scot gave and ceded her right etc to her sister Isobella Scot, younger.[78]

---

[71] In the correspondence on this subject in the *Gen. Mag.* Vol. 11, No. 6 pp. 213-4. Mr. Willis suggests the former and Mr. R. Buchanan-Dunlop the latter. Both these views, which are complementary rather than contradictory are also of course compatible with that of Mr. Chitty, though it is a mistake to assume either that family names were not perpetuated *per se* or that the revered relative or friend was invariably a godparent.

[72] *op. cit.* p. 72.

[73] Cited by Paul de Castro, *N & Q* 12th Ser. IX p. 415.

[74] *op. cit.* p. 72.

[75] *Early Chancery Proceedings.* Bundle 411, No. 20.

[76] *P.C.C. 28 Dyngeley* These two examples have been taken from a letter of Walter G. Davis. *Gen. Mag.* Vol. 11, No. 6, June 1952, p. 214.

[77] *N & Q* 16 July 1898 p. 51.

[78] *Protocol Book of Sir Alex. Gow, notary, Strathinlo.* cited in *N & Q* 1st June 1901 p. 436.

18 May 1564 John Woddrop Senior, son of q. Thomas Woddrop junior in Dalmarnock, renounced all right..... in favour of John Woddrop junior his brother german.[79]

A curious case on the other side of the Atlantic, fully proved by Wills is found in Jacobus *"The Waterman Family"*.

" Sarah Waterman of Norwich, Conn., married first, Thomas Sluman and had five children including a daughter *Sarah*. She married second, Capt. John Wattles of Labanon, Conn., who by a first wife, Judith Fitch had six children including a daughter *Sarah*. The second marriage of Wattles to Mrs. Sluman produced seven children, and one of them was also named *Sarah*. All three Sarahs lived and all three married. Thus the second Sarah Wattles had a half sister *Sarah Wattles* on her father's side, and a half sister *Sarah Sluman* on her mother's side. Furthermore, her half sister Sarah Sluman married her half brother Samuel Wattles, the bride and groom being merely stepsister and stepbrother to each other.*"*[80]

Thus, although the genealogist is usually safe in pursuing his method of *"* elimination of possibilities *"* when he has provided a recorded husband for a daughter in a certain family, it is advisable not to lose sight of the chance that in one of these unusual cases there may have been *two* daughters of the same name in the family group he is considering.

More than one Christian Name

Very few cases in England are known before the sixteenth century. The earliest recorded examples in Britain appear to be *Roger Paye Loveday* of Yorkshire who appears in a Close Roll in 1288 and *Androe Ricar Adam*, the name of a moneyer on a coin of Alexander II of Scotland.[81] A Deed Poll dated 36 Edward III 1363 was executed by Stephen son of *John Fylip Curpet* of Fincham (Norfolk),[82] *John William Whytting* was vicar of Egdean 1389-1432, a *William Michael Stonhard* is recorded in 1421,[83] and a *Thomas Arnold Williamson* in 1471.[84]

However with regard to these early examples, C.E. Ewen cautions that they probably resulted from the dropping of the words *"* son of *"*. There may be a similar explanation for *James Lynch Fitzstephen* who was Mayor of Galway in 1493.[85] Certainly it was the mediaeval custom

---

[79] *Renwick Protocol of the Town Clerks of Glasgow.* Vol.V p.68 cited in *N & Q* 4th June 1898. p.446.

[80] Cited by J.G. Hunt and D.L. Jacobus *op.cit.* p.159.

[81] *N & Q* 23 Jan 1875 p.77.

[82] *N & Q* 6th Sept 1856 p.197. This example is cited by Miss E.G. Withycombe. *op.cit.* p.xliii but he is called John Philip *Capel* of *Fineham*!

[83] Brit. Mus. *Addl Ch.* 23 538-9, Complete Peerage (1913) Vol.iii p.621.

[84] Brit. Mus. *Harl. Ch.* 50 D 22.

[85] *N & Q* 1854 p.275. Possibly his father was Stephen Lynch.

in the North of England to combine a patronymic with the surname to produce double surnames.[86] The most famous of these early examples is *Henry Algernon Percy*, 5th Earl of Northumberland (1478-1527) but it is unlikely that he was christened *Algernon*.[87]

In 1547 John Dudley Viscount Lisle had a licence to alienate the house of the dissolved hospital of St. Giles in the Fields to *John Wymonde Carewe*[88] and Queen Mary gave her godsons her own name in addition to their Christian names, so that they were called *Anthony-Maria, Edward-Maria* etc.[89] Three early parish registers examples are:

> *Badingham, Suffolk.* Baptism 30th Dec. 1564
> Arthurus Rous Russhe filius Johnanis Russhe
> *Saffron Walden, Essex.* Marriage 9th July 1571
> Anne Agnes Parnell
> *Mexborough, Yorks.* Baptism 18th January 1592
> Robert Browne son of John Lillie [Browne was his mother's maiden name]

Other early examples are:
John James Sandilands (English Knight of Malta 1564,) *Thomas Pope Blount* (born c 1556), *Paulus Ambrosius Croke* (born c 1564), *Richard Clement Fisher* of Packington, Warw. (16th century),[90] *Mark Alexander Boyd*, (poet b.1563), *Thomas Posthumous Hoby* (b.1566), *Henry Doune Lee* (subscribed to the 39 Articles, 11th October 1588)[91] *Charles Maria Shute* (1610) *Gulielma Maria Postuma Springett* (born 1644).

In the majority of these early cases the second name was either chosen for religious or other obvious reasons, or else was a surname. In some cases the latter may have been the result of the dropping of an alias. The custom of naming after godparents was also certainly an important factor. Theodore Rowland Verstegan, who was born in the Duchy of Geldres and came to England about 1508 wrote;

> "It is often seen in Germany that either godfather at christening giveth his name to his godson, and therefore it cometh that many hath two proper names beside the surname."

Chester Waters[92] cites numerous examples to show this as originally a uniquely Italian custom brought into France by Catherine de Medicis.

---

[86] See *Double Surnames* in Appendix III *Surnames* p.96.
[87] He probably assumed this additional name in adult life in memory of his 11th century ancester William de Percy who was known as William *Alsgernons* or William *"with the moustache"*. Chester Waters *op.cit.* p.41.
[88] R. Dobie. *History of St. Giles and Bloomsbury* p.24.
[89] Fuller. *Church History* (ed Brewer) Vol.iv p.249.
[90] *N & Q* 3rd Oct. 1874 p.271.
[91] *N & Q* 10th May 1856 p.384.
[92] *Parish Registers in England* p.40.

However, he overlooks both the frequency of double names in the mediaeval Spanish ruling families and the Ramón Berengars of Provence. Camden provides a clue when he points out that it was common in Italy and Spain to add a saint's name as an additional Christian name. Clearly this was a custom which, originating in Southern Europe, spread later to Germany and then to England.

However, although isolated cases are found throughout the sixteenth century, they remained extremely rare. Camden states:

> " I only remember now his Majesty, who was named *Charles James*, and the prince his sonne *Henry Frederic*; and among private men, *Thomas Maria Wingfield* and *Sir Thomas Posthumus Hoby*. "[93]

In the early 17th century, the aristocracy occasionally gave a second name. The first Earl of Shaftesbury (born 1621) was baptized Anthony Ashley and Henry Frederick Stanley, son of James 7th Earl of Derby was born in 1635.[94] In *High Wycombe*, Bucks. register the first instance, *Katherine Mary* occurs in 1661. In *North Luffenham*, Rutland the first occurence is in 1686 when *Mallory John*, son of Samuel Wing was baptised (June 9th). In *Canon Frome* Herefordshire register from about 1700 onwards, several members of the Hopton family received double names, the surname Cope in each case being combined with another name.[95] However, in the register of *Westminster Abbey* there is only one example of two Christian names before 1705.

Miss Withycombe suggests that the spread of the fashion was probably due to the French influence of Henrietta Maria and later of the court of Charles II, and points out that Charles II's daughter by Lady Shannon, born in 1650 was named *Charlotte Jemima Henrietta Maria*. It is certainly true that after 1688 the double names *Mary Anne* and *Anna Maria* are found, probably in honour of the Queens Mary and Anne. However, these and other later combinations such as *Mary Jane* and *Sarah Jane* were treated as a single name and used in address well into the 19th century. They were gradually confined to the poorer classes and eventually died out. With these exceptions two Christian names still remained extremely rare until the reign of George II. In the Lincolnshire Poll Book for 1723 out of 4,990 freeholders only five had more than one Christian name.[96] From 1730 onwards a second name becomes more noticeable in the registers among the minor gentry. In

---

[93] *Remains* p. 44. There appear to have been two *Thomas Maria Wingfields*, one Rector of Warrington 1527-37, the other M.P. for Huntingdon in 1553.
[94] Further 17th century examples are given in *N & Q* 1854. pp. 275-6.
[95] W. Bradbrook. *The Parish Register* p. 70.
[96] *N & Q* 7th Nov. 1857 p. 376.

1738 the Court set the example with three.[97] More than one name was relatively rare among the lower classes right up to the beginning of Civil Registration but there were occasional aberrations as in the following baptism at Burbage, Wilts. in 1781.

> Charles Caractacus Ostorius Maximilian Gustavus Adolphus, son of Charles Stone, tailor, bapt. 29 April.[98]

However, the enterprising Mr. Stone had been forestalled more than a century earlier. In the registers of Old Swinford, Worcs. appears the following entry:

> Dancell Dallphebo Marke Anthony Dallery Gallery Cesar Williams Sonn of Dancall Dallphebo Marke Anthony Dallery Gallery Cesar Williams bapt Jan xviii 1676.[99]

Change of Name

Though authorities disagree as to the validity of changing the name given at Baptism all accept that the Western church from an early date reserved to itself the power of altering or adding to the Baptismal name at the time of Confirmation. However, this seems to have originally been possible only in the case of unsuitable names. Archbishop Peccham in 1281 advised:

> "Let the priests also take heed that they suffer not nyse and wanton names to be given to the youngles when they be baptised specially of the women kind which names spoken sound to wantons, and if the contrary be done let it be redressed by the Bishops that confirm them."[100]

After the Reformation it was a disputed point whether the civil law of England would recognise a revised Confirmation name.

Bishop Scambler of Peterborough commented in 1567:

> "I may not change usuall or comen names at the Confirmacion but onlie strange and not comen: and further if the name be changed at Confirmacion it taketh effect but from the Confirmacion."[101]

However, the Roman Catholic Church did not seem to confine the practic to strange names. The registers of Holme Hale, Norfolk, furnish an instance of a change of name being duly entered when Queen Mary was on the throne:

> "1554. Deci'o nono die Novembris. Baptizat' filius Richi Lorington et Cecilie consor sue et no'iat Samuell et mutat' nomen ejus ad confirmacionem at noiat' Willmus."[102]

---

97   George III was baptized *George William Frederick*.
98   *N & Q* 2nd May 1874 p. 271. Chester Waters *op. cit.* p. 42.
99   *N & Q* 2nd May 1874 p. 271.
100   1534 Translation. Lyndwood's *Provinciale* (Bullard & Bell 1929) p. 102. cited by Ewen *op. cit.* p. 415.
101   Landsdowne MS 50 f 127.
102   Cox *The Parish Registers of England* p. 69.

Though changes of Christian name at confirmation have never been frequent, an addition to the baptismal name has been very common in the Roman Catholic Church.[103] Coke gave the legal view:[104]

"If a man be baptized by the name of Thomas and after at his confirmation by the bishop he is named John, he may purchase by the name of his confirmation. And this was the case of Sir Francis Gawdie chief Justice of the Court of Common Pleas, whose name of baptism was Thomas,[105] and his name of confirmation Francis, and that name of Francis, by the advice of all the judges, in Anno 36 Hen.VIII [1544-5] he did bear, and after used it in all his purchases and grants."

In this case it is noteworthy that Sir Francis did not venture to use the name in purchases until the advice of all the judges had been taken. Coke also cited a further example:

"And the Court said that it may be that a woman was baptised by the name of *Anable*, and forty years after she was confirmed by the name of *Douce*, and then her name was changed, and after she was to be named *Douce*, and that all purchases etc, made by her by the name of baptism before her confirmation remain good; a matter not much in use, nor requisite to be put in ure, but yet necessary to be known."[106]

Coke's view on this, as on so many other subjects was used authoritatively:

"On Sunday Dec.21 1707, the Lord Bishop of Lincoln confirmed a young lad in Henry VII's Chapel; who upon that ceremony was to change his Christian name; and accordingly the sponsor who presented him delivered to the Bishop a certificate, which his Lordship signed, to notify that he had confirmed a person by such a name, and did order the parish minister then present to register the person in the parish book under that name. This was done by the opinion under the hand of Sir Edward Northey and the like opinion of Lord Chief Justice Holt, founded on the authority of Sir Edward Coke, who says it was the common law of England."[107]

Another 18th century case occurred in Ireland:

"1761 Sept.21 Robert St. George Caulfield, Lieutenant in His Majesties 93 Regiment of Foot, commanded by Colonel Samuel Bagshaw and eldest son of Robert Caulfield minister of, and residing in the parish of Finglass, near Dublin, was by me presented to the Rt. Revd. Father in God, Jemmett, Lord Bishop of Corke and Ross, in the Cathedral and Parish Church of St. Finbarry, Corke to be admitted to the holy rite of confirmation, and to be admitted to change his name of Robert St. George for that of William, and by the name of William I did then present him; and the bishop

---

[103] Phillimore & Fry. *Index to Changes of Name* (1905) p.xxi *N & Q* 10th July 1926 p.31.
[104] *Institutes* 1823 edn. Vol.1. 3a.
[105] His elder brother was also called Thomas. see above p.117. Both brothers went to the bar and rose to be judges. Sir Francis died in 1606.
[106] *ibid* Vol.1 3a.
[107] Bishop Kennett. MS notes to the Prayer Book (now in the British Museum) cited in Blunt. *Church Law.* p.60.

consenting to the changing of his name to William did then confirm him William."[108]

Changes of name at confirmation certainly occurred until the end of the 19th century.

11th June 1886 at St. John's Church, Tue Brook, near Liverpool, the Bishop of Liverpool confirmed a female candidate by her two baptismal names with an additional Christian name (being her mather's maiden surname) and signing a certificate to that effect which was afterwards noted in the candidate's baptismal register. It is said that the bishop nevertheless expressed an objection to the practice of changing a name once solemnly given in baptism.[109]

In the *Daily Journal* 22nd February 1923 appeared the following report:

" At an inquest in the Paddington Coroner's Court on Monday, a young man testified that his mother who died suddenly of heart failure, had been christened Mary Ann, but that when she grew up she took the name of Margaret Mary. Mr. Oswald, the Coroner, asking how she did this, was answered. "She asked the clergyman to allow her to make the change when she was confirmed." The Coroner is reported to have then said that he did not think the change was legal. People could take new surnames by deed poll, but he had never heard of them altering christian names only by such means. There are a good many church-people with imperfect knowledge on this point. The law seems clear. Lord Coke laid down that the name assumed at confirmation becomes a legal name, citing authorities, and he is supported against objectors by the late Sir Robert Phillimore and Lord Phillimore. The practice is not so uncommon as might be supposed though no case turning on it has arisen in the courts for many years."

Christian names have also been changed by deed poll – on 4th November 1879 George Jonathan Carley by Deed Poll renounced the name of *Jonathan* and assumed the Christian name of *Leyburn*[110] or even by Act of Parliament – In 1907 Raymond Hill Baines changed his Christian names to Henry Rodd. More frequently, it has been done by advertisement: In the *Times* of 1st April 1880 appeared a notice that Henry Wyley intended to assume the Christian name of *James* in addition to and before his name of *Henry*.[111] All these examples post-date the period for which parish registers are normally consulted. However, a Christian name can in fact be changed at any time without any formalities, and this must have affected hundreds, possibly even thousands of parish register entries. In 1912, Sir H.H. Shepherd commented:

" A man may at any time assume another name in addition to or in place of his baptismal name, and that for all practical purposes the name so assumed may become his first Christian name..... The name which a man

---

[108]   *N & Q* 2nd July 1870 p.17.
[109]   *N & Q* 24 July 1886 p.77.
[110]   *N & Q* 15th July 1882 p.50.
[111]   *N & Q* 15th May 1880 p.399.

himself adopts, and which is adopted by his friends and other persons
having dealings with him, becomes his name."

Thus the name given for the valid publication of banns must be
the name by which the person is generally known, not necessarily his
baptismal name.

> Abraham Langley married in 1814 had for three years been known in the
> village where banns were published by the name of *George Smith*. It was
> held that the banns were properly published and that his original name
> would not have been his true name within the meaning of the Statute
> 26 Geo II c 33.[112]

In this case, both Christian name and surname were different.[113]

It therefore. seems clear that William Bradbrook was in error in
supposing:

> "The Catholic Church only regards the name bestowed in baptism as the
> person's real, legal and undeniable name; and there is not, and never
> has been, any legal way of changing this name."[114]

The position has been aptly summed up by J. T. Hammick.[115]

> "Where a party has adopted a new Christian name it has been decided
> both in the ecclesiastical courts and in the courts of Common.Law that
> that such a name is his proper and true name."

and by C. L. Ewen:

> "It seems perfectly clear that a forename may be bestowed at baptism
> or assumed at later date; changed by the church, by Act of Parliament,
> or at the will of the bearer; added to or dropped entirely without
> formality. Provided that the modification is honestly made, and of common
> repute, the law would not uphold any objection..... registration of a
> forename does not in any way improve its status."[116]

---

[112] Rex v Inhabitants of Billingshurst. *Maule and Selwyn's Reports*, K.B.
Vol. iii p. 250.
[113] For a discussion of the legal position with regard to a change of surname,
see Appendix III *Surnames* pp. 89–90.
[114] *The Parish Register* (1910) pp. 63-64.
[115] *The Marriage Law of England* pp. 71-72.
[116] C.L. Ewen. *op. cit.* p. 418. A fuller discussion of the whole question will
be found in A. Linell *The Law of Names, Public, Private and Corporate*
(1938) pp. 9–11.

BIBLIOGRAPHY

Bardsley, C.W.   *Curiosities of Puritan Nomenclature* (1880).

D., T.C.   *Some Unusual Christian Names*. Gen. Mag. Vol. V. p. 144 (March 1930).

Gumbley, W.   *Unusual Baptismal Names* (1956).

Johnston, G.D.   *Eighteenth Century Christian Names*. Sussex N & Q. IX No. 5 (Feb 1943) 113-4.

Linell, A.   *The Law of Names, Public, Private and Corporate* (1938).

Moriarty, G. Andrews.*Nomenclature* Amer. Gen. Vol. 37 (April 1961) p.73

Smith, E.F.   *Baptismal and Confirmation Names* (1935).

Steel, D.J.   *The Descent of Christian Names* Gen. Mag. Vol. 14. p. 34, June 1962.

Withycombe, Miss E.G. *The Oxford Dictionary of English Christian Names* (1950).

Withycombe, Miss E.G. *Christian Names*. Gen. Mag. Vol. 10. No. 2, June 1947. p. 41.

III. PARISH REGISTERS and the GENEALOGIST

Some practical notes and suggestions.

Parish registers are one of the most important single sources of
genealogical information, and not only the beginner, but also the
more experienced genealogist is likely to come back to them time and
again as other source material suggests a lead to be followed up.
Many genealogists are, however, unfamiliar with the legal position
with regard to searches, and there are numerous other points often
overlooked but extremely important.

Custody and Access
Incumbents.

In spite of widespread deposits at recognised Record Repositories,
the majority of registers are still held by the clergy. Each incumbent
is responsible to his Archdeacon or Ordinary for the safe preservation
of all parish records in a suitable chest or safe either in the Church
or in the vicarage, and he should transfer a proper inventory to his
successor.[1] In addition, clergy have a legal obligation to see that
the Bishop's or Archdeacon's transcripts of their registers returned
to the Diocesan registry are as complete as possible.

An incumbent must by law permit a search to be made in parochial
registers at all reasonable times. This was clearly laid down by the
Registration Act of 1836 and by the *Ecclesiastical Fees Measure* of
1962. In January 1963, at the request of the Convocation of York
the Legal Board of the Church Assembly prepared explanatory notes on
the Act for the guidance of incumbents, clerks, sextons and parochial
church councils and these were published on a card by the Church
Commissioners.[2] They emphasized that reasonable access must be
granted and that the incumbent must supply certified copies of entries
in the registers upon personal application and payment of fees fixed
by law for searches and certified copies. The Commissioners pointed
out, however, that the incumbent is not legally bound (a) to permit
the photographing of registers, (b) to supply certificates on postal

---

[1] *Parish Register Searching in England and Wales* a leaflet published by the
Institute of Heraldic and Genealogical Studies, Canterbury, 1966.
[2] A revised pamphlet containing the same information was published by the
Church Commissioners in May, 1972, as "Parochial Fees Order, 1972:
Explanatory Notes".

application (though this normally is done on payment of the appropriate fee), (c) to make searches on behalf of an enquirer (though he may consent to do this for such remuneration as may be agreed).

The accepted legal view is that the incumbent retains the freehold of the registers and that no one may copy registers without his consent, even if they are deposited at County Record Offices. However, some have maintained that no individual incumbent may alienate the rights of his successors by allowing records to be copied, and that permission to copy can legally come only from the Bishop or, as has been seriously suggested,[3] from the Queen, the mandate of 1538 and subsequent acts etc. being statatory. Many Bishops certainly take the view that they can forbid the copying of registers, and this has, in fact, occurred in the Welsh dioceses.

Record Offices.

The *Parochial Registers and Records Measure* 1929 empowered the bishops to establish a diocesan record office at the diocesan registry or elsewhere. Since then, many county record offices or large libraries such as the Bodleian or Gloucester City Library have been recognised as diocesan repositories. In such cases the only interpretation of "reasonable times" is clearly the normal hours when the Record Office is open. A certain doubt existed until recently whether Local Authorities could legally permit Record Offices, set up for their own records, to be used as diocesan record offices, but a circular issued by the Ministry of Housing and Local Government made it clear that the 1962 Act did, in fact, confer this power.[4]

Fees for Personal Searches.

Incumbents.

The question of fees for searching parish registers was first laid down by Statute by the *Registration Act* of 1836 (*6 & 7 William IV c 86, Sec.35.*) However, this left open a number of doubtful points which were thereafter the subject of conflicting legal opinions. Firstly, the Act mentioned registers of *births and deaths* but not of *baptisms and burials*. As late as 1936, the Legal Board of the National Assembly of the Church of England gave as their opinion that "The

---

[3] e.g. by C.R. Humphrey-Smith, in *Family History*, Vol.2, p.129.
[4] Felix Crowder *"Parish Registers and other records and the Local Government (Records) Act, 1962.* Family History Vol.4, No.19, p.31. This article discusses in detail the relation of the act to the care, transcription and publication of parish registers.

Statutary provision of 6 & 7 William IV c 86 sec 35 as to searches
does not apply to registers of baptisms and burials.[5]" a view which
contradicted the assumption in the *Burial Act* of 1853 and the
Registration of Burial Act of 1864.[6] Secondly, although the fees laid
down in 1836 were not altered by Statute until 1962, they had been
previously raised by the Ecclesiastical Commissioners probably on
the strength of a rather doubtful interpretation of sec.1. of the
Ecclesiastical Commissioners (Powers) Measure of 1938 which referred
to "tables of fees for the solemnization and performance of Church
Offices, the erection of monuments in churchyards *and such other
services or matters as may by any law or custom be none included in
such tables* ".[7] Thirdly, fees for marriages were laid down by sec.
63 of the *Marriage Act* of 1949 and clearly, even if the Commissioners
were empowered by the 1938 Act to lay down fees for other registers,
they could not amend a statute.

The present situation is governed by the Parochial Fees Order, 1972,
made under the Ecclesiastical Fees Measure 1962, which laid down the
following scale of fees, still in force at the time of publication:-

Baptisms

Searching register (for the first year)	30p
Searching register (for every year after first year)	15p
Certificate	50p
Short Certificate	25p

Marriages

Searching register for period before 1837 [7] (for the first year)	30p
Searching register (for every year after the first)	15p
Certificate [8]	£2.50p

Burials

Searching register (for the first year)	30p
Searching register (for every year after the first)	15p
Certificate	50p

The 1962 Measure, though having statutory force, still left
several important points capable of diverse legal interpretations:-

(a) *Legal Custody of pre-1837 Registers*
      The keeping of parish registers has constantly been the
      subject of Acts of Parliament. Indeed, they have twice been
      used for taxation purposes. It has therefore been argued that

---

5   Quoted in Gen.Mag. Vol.7, p.248.
6   C.A. Higgins. *"Fees for Searching Parish Registers."* Gen.Mag. Vol.11,
     p.144.
7   Search fees in marriage registers after 1837 were abolished by the
     Registration of Births, Deaths and Marriages (Fees) Order 1968,
     S.I. 1968 No. 1242. Fees for pre-1837 searches were re-established
     by the Parochial Fees Order 1972, S.I.1972 No.177.
8   Under s.63, Marriage Act 1949, and S.I.1975 No.1291.

they are public records and that by analogy with other public
records, no fees whatsoever should be payable for access to
pre-1837 registers unless certified copies are required
although when incumbents are prepared to make searches they
should be remunerated as record searchers.

(b) *General Searches*

When the original charges were laid down in the Act of
1836, the framers clearly had in mind a person searching for
one entry of birth or baptism, normally his own. In fact, the
wording of both this Act and that of 1962 seems to suggest that
the intention of the fees is to remunerate the incumbent of the
benefice when he acts as registrar and is asked to provide a
certified copy of an entry. In any case, such charges are wholly
inappropriate for a searcher who, for historical or genealogical
reasons wishes to search the entire registers of a parish for
300 years. Mr. C.R. Humphery-Smith points out:

> "Applying the 1962 Fees Measure as it is usually described to
> incumbents, the rector of a small village ·with a population of
> 400 gets paid at the rate of £8 an hour, and the rector of a parish
> in London, Manchester or Birmingham at the rate of 5½d an hour; and
> each gets the equal sum of something like £56 every time he is
> asked to make a complete search of his registers for one name or a
> hundred names between 1540 and 1840. This makes the whole thing
> ridiculous, particularly when the fees are payable, not for the
> incumbent making a search, but for making the registers available
> for the applicant to make his own search; and when the Bishop's or
> Archdeacon's transcripts, although frequently incomplete – but
> for which under the Acts of 1597 and 1603 each incumbent is legally
> responsible for making complete – can be consulted free of charge
> as historical public documents."[9]

Most incumbents recognise the absurdity of applying the scale of
fees to general searches, and are prepared to settle for a
reasonable fee; some indeed allow bona fide students or amateur
genealogists to search the registers without any fee at all,
perhaps only suggesting that a small donation be given to the
funds of the church. Nevertheless, a few do insist on the payment
of the full fees, making a comprehensive search so expensive as
to be prohibitive. It is doubtful whether they are legally
entitled to do this. Not only is it ambiguous whether the Table
of Fees applies to general searches, but there is provision in
Section 11 3 (ii) of the 1929 Measure for fees to be waived
when the registers are deposited in a Diocesan Record Office and

---

9   Family History Vol.2.No.11. 1964.

when the search is for historical (including genealogical)
purposes. Thus, although incumbents agreeing a reasonable fee
are under the impression that they are voluntarily waiving
fees to which they are entitled, this would seem not to be the
case.

(c) *Mixed Registers*
It would appear that when entries of baptisms, marriages
and burials are in one volume, only one search fee is payable.
This, at any rate was the opinion of the Legal Board of the
National Assembly of the Church of England in 1936. [10]

Record Offices.

The Parochial Registers and Records Measure 1929, which
established diocesan record offices, provided that the fees for
searches and certificates shall continue to be payable and that one
half of any fees so paid shall be accounted for and paid to the incumbent who would have received the fee if the register books had
not been deposited.
However, as a result of local attempts to grapple with the problem
of the general search, the actual policy adopted varies from place
to place.
Some record offices continue to charge the full fees unless the searcher
has come to some prior alternative arrangement with the incumbent, but
most will not bother to collect the small amounts involved, incumbents
being persuaded to waive their rights when depositing their registers.
Some have only recently abandoned fees on the expectation that the
Measure now before the General Synod of the Church of England effective-
ly abolishing such search fees for deposited registers will soon come
into effect.

Recent Developments
Problems of access and fees are part of the wider problem of preservation, copying and indexing. A resolution of these vexed problems
was proposed in the report of the 1871 Commission and in the Bills for
the Better Preservation of the Ancient Parochial Registers promoted in
1882 and 1897. A new bill dealing with all aspects of parish registers
was drawn up in the early 1960's by the Institute of Heraldic and Genealogical Studies, Canterbury. *(Family History,* vol. 3, No. 13. pp. 1-4, 1965),

---

[10] Reproduced in Gen. Mag. Vol. 7. p. 248.

but it found little Parliamentary support because of the expense which
would have been involved in the recommended copying and indexing of
parish registers.

In 1968 by Statutory Instruments 1242 and 1309 it was generally considered that the Registrar General had abolished the fee for searching
in marriage registers. The House of Clergy in November 1969 indicated
its dissatisfaction with the removal of the fee and asked its standing
Committee "to make further enquiry in regard to fees for searches in
marriage and other registers". The report of the latter Committee, "Fees
for Searches in Church Registers" (GS 114/C), which contains a useful
summary of the Law, was accepted by the Church Assembly in November 1972
and the Church Commissioners were requested to frame a scale of fees
based on the time taken on a search rather than on the number of years
of the register searched. No such scale has yet been authorised but
meanwhile in May 1972 the Commissioners had issued the Parochial Fees
Order described above, this revised scale of charges still being based
on the number of years searched. The scales of fees suggested in the
report "Fees for Searches in Church Registers" and its other recommendations were strongly attacked in an editorial in *"Local Population
Studies "* (No. 10, 1973). Concern in historical circles that proper con-
sultations had been lacking in the preparation of the report voiced
itself at a meeting held on 13 September 1973 when many organisations
joined together to urge the Synod that all registers no longer in current use for pastoral purposes should be deposited in diocesan record
offices and freed from search fees. As a result of this and other rep-
resentations a new Parochial Registers and Records Measure has been
proposed to supersede the 1929 Measure. A Standing Committee of the
Synod has prepared a draft Measure (G.S. 274) which having been formally
received by the Synod is now with a Revision Committee. It would relieve Record Offices from the obligation to charge fees for searches in
deposited registers, provide for the inspection every five years of
those registers which remain in parochial keeping, and give the bishops
power to require the temporary deposit of records for extended historical research. There is considerable pressure from many quarters within
and without the church to have the draft Measure strengthened so that it
requires the deposit of all pre-1837 registers. Howsoever the draft is
revised it will again come before the Synod in July, 1976, but if
accepted could not receive the Royal Assent until well into 1977.
Meanwhile a private bill has been introduced in the House of Lords
which would require all documents in parochial custody (with certain
exceptions) to be stored in a fireproof safe of certain specification.
The intention is that registers be kept in adequate and secure conditions or that incumbents relieve themselves of that responsibility by
depositing them with diocesan archivists. Thus 1976 may see some of
these problems clarified and, may one hope, resolved.

Searches by the Incumbent

As noted above, an incumbent is not legally bound to make searches on behalf of enquirers, though he may consent to do so on financial terms and conditions as may be agreed. Whatever the position is with regard to fees for general searches, the incumbent is entitled to payment for his services as a record searcher *in addition to* the fees which are payable for making the registers accessible. When an application is made by post, an incumbent is not legally bound to supply certified copies of entries. If an applicant knows the date of baptism, marriage or burial, an incumbent will normally supply a certificate by post on receipt of the appropriate fee and a stamped addressed envelope. [11]

In the case of a request for a certified copy of a baptismal entry, unless a full certificate is especially requested the short certificate authorised by the *Baptismal Registers Measure*, 1961 is normally supplied. Genealogists requesting an incumbent to make a lengthy search would be wise to ignore the scale of fees and send with their request an advance based on a rate of at least ten shillings an hour. This is readily calculated from personal experience of searching, taking the population at the 1831 Census (which may be found in Lewis's *Topographical Dictionary*) as a guide to the size of pre-1837 registers. [12] Most clergy will readily accept this basis. However, those who request an incumbent to make searches should bear in mind that he cannot be expected to take much interest in the search when he has to attend to important and pressing matters associated with his parish. Furthermore, he, or the person to whom he delegates the search may be inexperienced in reading early handwriting, and is probably unaware of the many other pitfalls. Thus in 1934 an incumbent, in reply to a correspondent's request for the christening of John Bennet said to be born in that parish in 1802 sent the following: -
" Baptized 26 Sept. 1802 John son of James Bennet and Elizabeth his wife ". After considerable unsuccessful research the correspondent personally inspected the registers and found that the entry actually concerned John son of James Rennet. [13] Wherever possible, therefore, one should undertake the search oneself or employ a reliable searcher.

Parish Maps

A knowledge of the geography of the locality is essential before undertaking any search of parish registers. It does not follow that

---

[11] *" Parish Register Searching in England and Wales."* cit.
[12] Family History, Vol. 2. p. 129.
[13] D. E. Gardner, – Letter in Gen. Mag. Vol. 12. p. 169.

the nearest parish is the most likely to search as the location of hills, rivers and roads should be taken into consideration. The person sought might have lived right on the edge of one parish and near the church of one of the adjoining parishes, making a knowledge of the position of the church quite essential. Thus, in Sussex, the parish of Iping is less than one mile wide and over six miles long, and the parish church is within fifty yards of the southern end of it. Maps must therefore be used in conjunction with any search.

The standard 1 inch Ordnance Survey map is not a reliable guide to parish boundaries. Not only are these faint and at times almost indecipherable but they are the boundaries of the civil parishes which do not necessarily correspond to the ecclesiastical parishes; in fact, there are often gross discrepancies between the two. Furthermore, the parish boundaries may have changed since 1837.

The series of county maps produced by the Institute of Heraldic and Genealogical Studies, Northgate, Canterbury although on a smaller scale, and lacking the information on roads, country houses etc on the Ordnance maps are extremely useful as they include deanery and diocesan boundaries, peculiars and starting dates of registers, enabling the overall picture of the area to be mastered very quickly. A new edition is in course of preparation indicating the sites of the churches relative to the parish boundaries.

Nevertheless, the genealogist would be well advised to consult the earliest editions of the Ordnance Survey 6 inch maps, which show all farms etc in some detail and may well clarify difficulties.

The Location of Entries[14]

Irregular Order.

It is important to remember that entries may be recorded out of sequence. Incomplete pages may have been filled in at a later date with entries of a different period. Furthermore baptisms may be found among the burials or marriages or vice versa. Hard to detect are those entries which appear at odd places in the volume, such as inside the front or back cover, or written vertically in the margins. Sometimes the pages in parish registers have come away from the binding of the volume and are out of order. At least one parish register is reported to have been cut in half and re-bound as two volumes.

---

[14] The first four items treated in this sub-section have been adapted from D.E. Gardner and F. Smith " *Genealogical Research in England and Wales* " Vol.1. pp.175-6.

Blank Pages.

These are often very misleading. Entries may be found scattered throughout blank pages or in a separate group with blank pages on either side. It is wise to examine each page of the book, whether it is blank or not.

Misleading Titles.

On the front (or the back) of a volume may appear a title, for example " Baptisms 1776 to 1803 ", but there may be within the volume additional records as well, perhaps of baptisms of other years, or of marriages or burials. Registers entitled " *Banns of Marriage* " may also contain Marriages, and conversely, marriage registers may also contain banns.

Overlapping Registers.

Volumes do not usually end completely at a fixed date. If the pages allotted to baptisms were filled, a new book may have been started for them with the marriages and burials continuing in the old book. Occasionally the incumbent or clerk started a new book and then came across the old one which had been temporarily mislaid; thus a few entries from a period in the middle of one register appear at the beginning of another. Sometimes it may be found that similar or identical entries are found in two books of registers, entries having been copied from the old book, into the new one. Discrepancies in the entries often clearly show how mistakes can be made in reading, even by contempories. In such cases, it is essential to take down both versions and to use other sources to arrive at the correct interpretation. Occasionally the overlapping registers contain different sets of entries. Sometimes these defy explanation, but often on closer examination one set will prove to be a special group, such as births of Dissenters, although this may not be anywhere indicated. At St. Luke's Old Street, Finsbury, London, where a set of baptismal registers covers 1813-1841, there is a special register containing entirely different entries for 1822-1841 marked *"Supplementary Register of Baptisms"*. This actually records private baptisms.

Entries Recorded Elsewhere.

Baptisms, marriages and burials may have been entered in other church records such as churchwardens' accounts. This was perhaps done in error or because the register had been temporarily mislaid. Burial entries were sometimes, as at St. Bride's, Fleet Street entered in the actual accounts with a record of the burial fees paid.[15]

---

[15] For an examination of the entries of St. Bride's, Fleet Street, see *Burials* below, p. 150.

The Interpretation of Entries

Handwriting.

Though difficulties may arise with regard to handwriting even when searching 18th and 19th Century registers, these can normally be searched with little prior training or experience. However, sqme knowledge of palaeography is essential before a search of 16th or 17th Century registers is even contemplated. Courses in palaeography are organized by the Extra Mural Boards of several universities. The Society of Genealogists has published a concise handwriting guide and there are many excellent manuals, *"Examples of English Handwriting 1150–1750 "* by Hilda E.M. Grieve, B.E.M., B.A., (pub. Essex County Council 1954), *"Handwriting of English Documents "* by L.C. Hector, M.A. (pub. Edward Arnold, 1958) and the third volume of *"Genealogical Research in England and Wales"* by D.E. Gardner and F. Smith, (pub. Bookcraft Ltd., Salt Lake City).

When difficulties arise, it is wise to look in later parts of the register which can be read clearly, indentify the surname and follow it through. However, whatever one's degree of palaeographic skill, one must beware of hypotheses build on a doubtful reading, or of allowing wishful thinking to undermine one's judgment. When only four letters of a surname are legible, it is only too tempting to assume it is the entry sought.

Spelling.

Spelling varies enormously partly due to the fact that there was no recognised orthography and partly because the persons concerned were often illiterate and the clerk (sometimes only semi-literate himself) wrote the names phonetically. The more common names are usually easy to identify.[16] However, with regard to the rarer surname, Mr. Oldaker comments.[17]

> " If the name was new to him he might put down the nearest he could get to the sound of it; and if his record was made some time after the event and he relied on his memory, unrecognizable corruptions might appear. My own surname, rare as it is, has appeared in over 190 different forms, many so corrupt that they can be identified as Oldaker only by other evidence – Aken, Aldecr, Accers, Guldeger, Holdecar, Oldham, Oldshaw, Oldrink, Ouldace are but a few of them. It has long been my practice to look for the name under A,H, and W (Woldaker) as well as under O, in indexes prior to 1800. The same wide variation doubtless exists with other rare names; and the identification of such

---

[16] I have myself found 29 different spellings of Steel but they are easily recognisable e.g. Stiel, Steill, Stealle etc. The most interesting is where one imagines the person concerned had some speech impediment for the clerk wrote the name " Seteill ".

[17] A.E. Oldaker *Searching for the Rare Surname* Gen. Mag. Vol.11, No.9, March 1953, p.310.

variations is a study in itself, adding immensely to the interest of the search ".

In this connection Mr. D. E. Gardner mentions three children of a couple named Reynold, the spelling being given in the baptismal entries as Rennet (1802), Rynallt (1805) and Rynold (1805).[18] Other examples are:

Great Wymondley, Herts	Bonfield, Bonefield and Bonfill
Coventry, Warwickshire	Meacock and Maycock; also Deakin
	Daken, Daykin.
Swansea, Glamorgan	Peregrine and Perkins
Cardiff, Glamorgan	Avery and Every
Bristol	Wroe, Rowe and Roe
Pembrey, Carmarthenshire	Hennings and Hennys
Bromsgrove, Worcs.	Harbach, Harbridge, Arbig.
Rowinton, Warws.	Sparrow and Sparry
Harlech, Merioneth.	Ames and Eames[19]

Spellings are, however, normally phonetic and local dialect and pronunciation should therefore be borne in mind. Thus, in the registers of Chilham, Kent, *Wright* appears as *Wright, Wrait, Rate, Raith* and *Wraith*, of which *Wrait* is now the accepted spelling in that district.[20]

However, no one should ever assume that he may without discrimination accept any name that looks or sounds like the one he may be seeking. Evidence must be sought to confirm a particular spelling as being a variant of the same surname. The Rev. S. H. A. Hervey noted:[21]

" We must expect therefore, to find each name spelt in several different ways, not only when registers were kept by illiterate men, but also when they were kept by good scholars... Sometimes, at any rate... two names have been bracketed together though really they have got nothing whatever to do with each other.... The names are Tyley and Tilly. These are not two forms of the same name, but two distinct names ".

To assist the searcher to identify surname variants, the following classification was suggested by the late Mr. Percival Boyd.[22]

A. *Phonetic, due to similarity of sound.*
1. Consonents.
Examples: ph=f;   hard c=k or ck;   chr=cr;   soft c=s;   g=j; cks=x

[18] D. E. Gardner. Letter in Gen.Mag. Vol.12, p.169.
[19] The list is taken from D. E. Gardner and F. Smith *op.cit.* Vol. 1, p.179.
[20] This example has been supplied by C. R. Humphery-Smith who also once encountered, but not in a parish register a quite extraordinary case of idiosyncratic spelling, " *the elder Wood's lease* "becoming " *Old Wives Leas* ".
[21] *Preface to Wedmore (Somerset) Parish Registers Burials 1561-1860.*
Cited by D. E. Gardner and F. Smith.op.cit. Vol.1, p.180.
[22] Gen.Mag. Vol.7.p.114.

2. Vowels.
   Partly owing to the different sounds given to vowels
   (single and double) with a further variation due to
   dialects, almost any vowel may occur as a variant.
3. Aspirate, either added or dropped.
4. Fancy Spellings.
   Marjoribanks for *Marchbanks.*
5. Final Syllables in names of more than one syllable.
   Example: *Haywood* may be a variant of *Hayward,* but *Wood* is
   not likely to be a variant of *Ward.*

B. *Literal, arising from names when written.*
   1. Similar letters.
      Examples: u=v, u=n, R and K, c and t, I and J, Fl and Ll.
   2. Abbreviations.
      Examples: *Cart = Carter. Pker = Parker.*
   3. Silent Letters.
      Examples: Final e is often silent; h in *Thompson.*
   4. Other languages.
      Examples; French *de,* etc. Dutch *van.*
   5. Inversion of letters.
      Examples:. *Brid* for *Bird; Cirsp* for *Crisp.*
   6. Common names for rare names.
      Example: *Clark* for *Chuke.*

This classification was put forward by Mr. Boyd as a tentative
list, and he intended to compile a fuller list of the letters that
may cause variants, especially in Group B, and which would also give
some idea of the dates when different types of variants are likely
to occur. Unfortunately, it appears that such a complete list was
never published.

Entry of the wrong name.

The Clerk may not only have given a surname a curious spelling.
He may have misheard it or failed to remember it correctly when he
made the entry some days later. Mr. Oldaker points out[23]

> " That entry in the name of Cornland that has puzzled you for so
> long and which you cannot begin to fit in with your other data may
> really not concern you at all; it may have been written in error for
> Cornford or Wheatland ".

The error may be more serious even than this. The clerk may
have confused the names of parties of different marriages or the
parents of different infants baptized. A frequent error was for the

---

[23] op. cit.

child's name to be reproduced as the name of one of the parents, or vice versa; *William, son of William and Mary Smith* might therefore have been an error for either *William, son of John and Mary Smith*, or for *John, son of William and Mary Smith*. Alternatively, the clerk may have reversed the names. Thus, *William son of John and Mary Smith* instead of *John son of William and Mary Smith*. Such assumptions can only be made with confidence when the evidence from other sources is very strong, and simple slips like these may well be responsible for years of fruitless searching.

The Calendar - Old Style and New Style

The New Style Year.

In 1750, the Calendar New Style Act changed the beginning of the legal year from 25th March to 1st January with effect from 1st January 1752/3. This must be borne in mind when searching entries prior to that date. Thus 1st January to 24th March 1727 were *after* 25th March to 31st December 1727 and, to avoid confusion January, February and March dates before 1752 are usually referred to with both years given. e.g. 15th February 1727/8, or else with the abbreviations O.S. (Old Style) or N.S. (New Style) written after the year.

The Eleven Day's Difference.

At the same time as the commencement of the year was brought forward, the difference between the Old Style and the New Style, which amounted to 11 days was removed by ordering the day following 2nd September 1752 to be counted as 14th September. Although most genealogists are aware of the implications of the shift from 25th March to 1st January, few seem to appreciate that dates before 1752 may have been in subsequent documents " revised " according to the New Style. Thus, a Family Bible, which has been brought to my notice, and which belonged to a certain Jacob and Ann Ping, has the following birth entries at the front:-

Ann	Apl. 21 1734	Rachell	May.12 1741
John	Feb. 27 1735	Christian	Nov. 26 1743
George	Nov. 3 1738	Joseph	Apl. 4 1746

Between the Old and the New Testaments there is a heading " *Ping According to the New Stile* " with the following entries:-

Jacob	Mar. 16 1709	George	Nov. 14 1738
Ann	Dec. 20 1708	Rachel	May. 23 1741
Ann	May. 2 1734	Christian	Dec. 7 1743
John	Mar. 10 1736	Joseph	Apl. 15 1746

Clearly the Baptism of Jacob Ping should be sought shortly after *5th* March 1708 and that of his wife after *9th* December 1708.

How far this practice was general is uncertain and undoubtedly more
research is needed. [24] However, the implications are important. Dates
of births found in military, naval and insurance records may have
been revised, and it is possible that this might also apply to events
other than birth dates.

Figures.

Figures rarely appear for the month in dates in parish registers,
though they are not infrequent in other documents. As the year was
reckoned from March until 1752, 5.7.1697 would probably indicate 5th
September and not 5th July. [25] The Quakers avoided the use of the names
of the months as savouring of paganism, though they inserted them in
legal documents. For them, also the whole of March was always 1st
Month. Thus *5th September* would be written either *5 7mo 1697* or
7mo 5 1697. [26]

The Noting of Information

In noting information from Parish Registers the following points
should be borne in mind:
   (a) The page number and entry number should be included, as,
       particularly with a large City register, they are often
       helpful if a recheck is needed later.
   (b) Witnesses to marriages should always be included as well as
       whether the marriage is by Banns or Licence.
   (c) If an entire section of a register, or certain entries are
       illegible, or the writing is difficult to decipher, notes
       should be made of the dates and pages involved and the Bishop's
       Transcripts, if available, searched for that period.
   (d) Abbreviations should be used with caution.
   (e) Dates should be written in full, and on no account should a
       figure be used for the month, unless a figure appears in the
       original document, in which case it should be reproduced.
   (f) Detailed notes should be kept of all the families and periods
       for which the search has been made, whether information has
       been found or not. Only too often this is overlooked.

---

[24] A useful start could be made with the large collection of leaves from
   Family Bibles collected by the late Mr. C. Hall Crouch, and now in the
   Library of the Society of Genealogists. For further discussion see
   Form and Content pp. 39–40.
[25] George Sherwood, *Dates and Figures,* Gen. Mag. Vol. 5. 1929 p. 21.
[26] Harold W. Atkinson. Gen. Mag. Vol. 5 (1929) p. 45. For more clarification
   of Quaker dating see *Society of Friends* in Volume II.

Baptisms

Errors of Indentification and Misinterpretation.

When a Baptism has been tentatively identified as the one
sought, there is, of course, always the possibility of error. This
may arise either from confusion with a different family altogether,
or with another member of the same family.

(a) *Confusion of two or more similarly named families.*

While persons of the same surname in a locality are more often
than not related, even if distantly, particularly if the surname
is uncommon generally, this is not invariably so. In the same parish
and in several neighbouring parishes, three or four Johns and Marys
may be found having similarly named children more or less contemp-
oraneously, and it is easy to take the first one encountered as the
entry sought without searching any further. In such a case, there
are several possibilities of solution. The simplest is to trace copyhold tenure through the admissions in the manorial rolls and to compare a signature on a will with that in a Court Leet entry.[27] After 1754
the Hardwicke marriage registers may also provide signatures for
comparison.[28]

(b) *Christian Names Misinterpreted as Surnames.*

Although a second Christian name was not common before the 19th
Century, when it occurs it is often a surname used as a Christian
name and this may cause confusion. Thus, in seeking the baptism of
a Susanna Bennett born in London about 1786, the following entry was
traced in the registers of the parish of St. Martin Orgar, City of
London: -

Chr.19 April (1788) Susanna d.of John Bennett and Dinah Morris (born Mar.22).

This was accepted as the likely entry for Susanna Bennett.
However, the correct interpretation of the Christening entry would be
Susanna, daughter of John Bennett Morris and Dinah his wife, unless
some other evidence was found to discount such an interpretation.[29]

(c) *Confusion with a brother or sister.*

An error of identification sometimes arises from the fact that
a child of the same name (often a brother or sister) failed to survive.
A search should be made in the burials for a possible entry relating to
a child whose record of christening makes him a likely ancestor. At
best, however, this is a poor substitute for a comprehensive search
of all registers for every entry of the surname sought, which should
always be made wherever possible, and which will normally bring to
light errors of this kind. Of course, it must also be borne in mind

---

[27] See *Other Records: Some Brief Notes* pp.341–343.
[28] See under *Marriages* below, p.149.
[29] D.E. Gardner and F. Smith, *op.cit.* Vol.1. p.182.

that two brothers or sisters may have been baptized with the same name even though both survived. [30]

(d) *Second Marriage.*

Where brothers or sisters have been given the same name, the reason is sometimes that they are children of two different marriages. This is not infrequently a cause of other mistakes in pedigrees. A series of entries of children of *William and Elizabeth Richardson* may conceal two marriages, the wives being named Elizabeth in each case. Whilst this may, of course, occur with even two entries, it must be especially considered when the baptisms are very numerous and spread over a long period. In the comparatively rare cases where the order of a child in the family (*3rd child of...*) is given, this information is most valuable, but care must be exercised, as, occasionally the numbering may be continued into a second marriage, as in the following example from the Barony Parish of Glasgow.

John Conningburgh and his wife Margaret *Henderson* had 6 children baptized during the years 1735 and 1746. In May 1755 John Kinneburgh and Margaret *Richardson* had their *1st* child baptized and on the 11th October 1757 the same couple had an 8th child baptized and continued with their 9th, 10th, 11th and 12th and so on until their 16th child born in February 1774. [31]

(e) *The Elder.*

The use of the terms "*the elder*" and "*the younger*" was, of course only temporary, as is illustrated by the following series of extracts:-

1711 John son of John Hawkins the younger and Mary his wife baptized.
1713 Mary daughter of John Hawkins the Younger and Mary his wife baptized.
1714 Richard son of John Hawkins the Elder and Mary his wife baptized.
1715 William son of John and Mary Hawkins baptized.
1717 Elizabeth daughter of John and Mary Hawkins baptized.
1719 Susanna daughter of John and Mary Hawkins baptized.
1726 James son of John Hawkins the Elder and Mary his wife baptized.

Here the same John Hawkins was known as *the Younger* during the lifetime of his father, then as plain *John Hawkins* and finally when his son was 15 as *John Hawkins the Elder.* Furthermore, the unwary searcher might assume that *James* born in 1726 was a brother of *Richard* born in 1714. A closer examination of the register will show, however, that Richard was the youngest son of the *first* John Hawkins the Elder and therefore *uncle* of James, both John Hawkins having married a Mary. A search of the burial register may show that John Hawkins the Elder died in 1715, although probably the entry is given simply as "*John Hawkins*".

Another more insidious trap is the use of *The Elder* and *The Younger* in the case of brothers of the same name.

---

[30] For an examination of this curious custom *see above* pages 115–121.
[31] I am indebted to Mr. T.C. Kinniburgh for this example.

Late Baptisms.

Frequently the searcher rather than finding two or more entries, any of which may be the one sought, fails to find any possible entry at all. In this case, before assuming that the baptism took place in another parish, the possibility of a late baptism must be considered.

(a) *Children.*

Baptisms should be searched if possible for at least 20 years after the supposed year of birth. In some instances families may have been indifferent to religion, have lived somewhat remote from the Parish Church, or may have had leanings towards Nonconformity in which case the christening by a Church of England clergyman might have been delayed. Often, clergy would make a periodic effort to check up on unbaptized children, and one may find several children in one family baptized together. This may also occur at the time of Confirmation of one of them.

(b) *Adults.*

Adult baptisms are not necessarily so indicated. Thus Mr. A.B. Clarke cited the following example from the registers of Wanlip, Leics:

Samuel and Matthew, sons of John Woodcock by Elizabeth his wife, were baptized 3rd September, 1699.

However, there are also the following entries:

Samuel Woodcock and Mary Perkins, both of Wanlip were married 9th Nov. 1699. Matthew Woodcock and Mary Green both of Wanlip were married 25th Oct. 1711. Now John Woodcock of Thurmaston and Elizabeth Brooks of Wanlip, the parents, were married 26th May 1669, and the following Archdeaconry presentment (book Q.5) shows what happened in 1674.

"John Woodcock of Wanlip and Elizabeth his wife, for children unbaptized. He owns he hath 4 male children, three of whom are unbaptized, whom he calleth Samuel, Edward and Thomas, being above 1 year old."

It seems not unlikely that Edward (above) was the man of that name married at Thrussington 16 Nov. 1705, whose baptism might be sought in vain. Thomas Woodcock was buried in 1682, and Matthew would be a still younger brother. It will thus been seen that the casual reader would be very much mistaken in assuming that the Samuel and Matthew baptized in 1699, were either infants or twins.[32]

It is especially important to remember to scan post-1837 registers for late baptisms, as, of course the persons concerned may have been born before the introduction of Civil Registration.

Unregistered Post-1837 Births.

Post-1837 registers may contain, not only late baptisms, but those of some infants who, though born after 1837, were never registered.

---

[32] *'Misleading Baptisms'* Gen.Mag. Vol.11, (1951). p.103.

In 1936 the statement in the *Genealogist's Handbook* that registra-
was compulsory from its inception was contradicted by two articles
in *Notes and Queries*, in one of which an official leaflet was
quoted as stating that birth registration was not compulsory prior
to 1875.

This provoked an official reply from the General Register Office,
Somerset House,[33] which clarified the position.

" The first stage in the pre-1875 law consists of a provision
(Section 20 of the 1836 Act) that the father or mother of any child born
(or, in default, certain other persons) may within 42 days give notice
of the birth to the Registrar. The corresponding stage in the 1874 Act
consists of a provision that " it is the duty " of the father or mother
(and in default of certain other persons) to give information to the
Registrar of the particulars to be registered and to sign the register.
But for a breach of this " duty " the 1874 Act provides no penalty; and
in regard to the question at issue the position is thus substantially
the same in both the pre- and the post- 1874 Act law in this stage.

The second stage in the earlier law is the subject of a provision
that the father or mother (or, in default, certain other persons) *shall
upon being requested so to do* give information to the Registrar of the
particulars to be registered, etc. The corresponding stage in the 1874
Act is the subject of a provision that if registration has not been effected within 42 days in pursuance of the unenforceable " duty " of the
parents, etc, the Registrar shall require by notice in writing any of the
eligible persons to attend and give particulars for registration within
a specified period. But for the failure to comply with such a written
requisition the 1874 Act enacts a penalty enforced by legal proceedings.

The provision of this penalty is the main difference between the two
sets of provisions; and it is, indeed the only feature upon which the
description of post-1874 Act registration as " compulsory " can properly
be based.

The matter is largely one of terminology; and the official leaflet
was correct in stating that birth registration was not compulsory before
1875. But.... the fact that pre-1875 registration was " non-compulsory "
does not mean that it was not obligatory. Still less does it mean that it
was optional or voluntary; and the statement in the Society's Handbook
that birth registration was a universal requirement from its inception
and never optional or voluntary is, in the Registrar-General's opinion,
entirely correct. It was always the duty of the Registrar (as it is now)
to inform himself by all possible means of all births occurring in his
sub-District, and to call upon the parents, etc. to give information for
registration; and the persons so called upon were placed by the law under
an obligation entirely independent of their choice of preferences " .

The extent to which births escaped registration in the early days
is controversial. The Registrar-General took the view that it was
relatively small, and that there was no appreciable change after the
passing of the 1875 Act. With the latter statement few genealogists

---

[33] Published in Gen.Mag. Vol.7, pp.367-8.

would disagree, but the scanty statistical evidence available seems
to suggest that it was by no means rare for births to remain unregistered, particularly in the first ten years after 1837.

In tracing detailed pedigrees of all families in Bedfordshire
and Hertfordshire, bearing a common surname, [34] a study of the
Birth Indexes at Somerset House yielded between 1837 and 1851, 74
registrations from these counties. Parish Register searches and census
returns have, however, to date revealed a further 16 for whom there
is no trace of any registration even though registration of un-named
male and female children have also been taken into account. It would
seem likely that further searches of post-1837 Bedfordshire and
Hertfordshire parish registers may reveal other cases, bringing the
total of unregistered births up to 15% to 20% before 1851. Since the
majority of the 16 unregistered births were in the first three years,
the percentage was, of course, much greater and may even have amounted
to a quarter of the total in 1838 and 1839. While no firm conclusions
can be deduced from such a limited survey, the same view has been
arrived at independently by Mr. C.R. Humphery-Smith, who estimates that in
his professional work one search in seven in these early years fails
to produce a birth certificate. The evidence does therefore seem to
suggest that the proportion of unregistered children was far greater
than has hitherto been supposed. It would seem that research on this
question on a much wider and more systematic basis is imperative. [35]

Missing Baptisms.

Baptisms often for a variety of reasons took place outside the
parish in which the family normally resided. Of course, as mentioned
above, this may be simply because the church of another parish was
nearer or more accessible, [36] or else because the family disliked the
local vicar. In the Civil War period especially, parents might go some
distance to find a vicar with Anglican sympathies. Sometimes, however, the baptism took place many miles away or even in another
county. It is important to remember that it was customary for the
first child of a marriage to be born and baptized at the native
parish of the mother and this often applied to subsequent children
as well. The parents may, of course, have been staying with other
relatives. If the occupation of the father involved his travelling
far from home, his wife may have been with him.

More frequently, one wishes to trace, not a baptism of a child
of known parentage, but to establish the place of origin of a person
who appears to be the first member of a family to live in a certain
parish. Again, occupation may give a possible clue. A shoemaker in

---

[34] *Kitchener* and variant spellings.
[35] For a detailed study of the subject from a statistical point of view
see D.V. Glass *A Note on the Under Registration of Births in Britian in
the 19th Century.* Population Studies V Part 1 Jan. 1951 (p.70). See also
Form and Content pp.52-54.
[36] See under *Parish Maps* above, pp.135-6.

London or another city may have come from the Northampton area, a potter from Staffordshire or a hatter from Luton. Mr. A.J. Willis cites an example where the place of origin of a pipe maker was located with the aid of a geological map which showed the existence of a pipe clay deposit some miles distant.[37]

The place of birth of servants in the towns (especially London) might be located by searching registers in the locality of the Country Houses or places of origin of their masters. Similarly baptismal entries can often be located in registers of an entirely different part of the country by finding out as much as possible about the family owning the manor where the person first appears.

Mr. F.W. Masham points out:-[38]

> "The aim is to discover whether the Lord of the Manor held land or had business or family connections in other parts of the country than the one where my family was known to have been. In my own case I have been repeatedly surprised and gratified to discover how important a role the lord of the manor (or his steward) paid as an employer of his tenants. If jobs could not be found locally for all the members of a growing family, it seems to have been quite usual for some of them to be switched to other manors owned by the same, or a related family. "

Thus, in 1693, Thomas Kitchener (an ancestor of Lord Kitchener) went from Binsted, Hants to Lakenheath, Suffolk as agent to Sir Nicholas Steuart, Bart. It is interesting to note also that the only discovered source of information about this move was on a tombstone in Lakenheath Churchyard, which emphasized the importance of Monumental Inscriptions However, even without this assistance, it is possible that the move could have been inferred from a study of manorial ownership.

Marriages

Local Features and Occupations.

The importance of studying the geography of the district has already been stressed. It is especially important with regard to marriages, the most significant features being the roads, and the location of market towns and of the principal houses of the gentry in conjunction with the occupations or social status of the family. A young man visiting the market town on business or pleasure might meet his future wife there, although they came from villages far apart. A young woman might be employed many miles away from home as a servant, or might be visiting friends or relatives, and there meet her future husband, also employed many miles from his home.[39] As with baptisms,

---

[37] *"Genealogy for Beginners"* page 111,
[38] Gen.Mag. Vol.12 (1955) p.98.
[39] D.E. Gardner and F. Smith. *op.cit.* Vol.1 pp. 188-9.

the family trade may help to locate the place of marriage.

Marriage Licences.

Whenever a marriage is recorded as by Licence, the marriage bonds and allegations should be consulted for they often give the name of the father, if not otherwise known.

Signatures.

When a post-1754 Hardwicke Marriage has been located, it is wise to have a photostat made if possible, or failing that to use tracing paper to copy any signatures of parties or witnesses, as these can often be usefully compared with signatures from other sources.[40]

Delayed Marriages.

These are cases where the marriage took place after the birth of the first child, even though the christening record may imply that the child was legitimate. When no likely marriage entry is located by a search of an earlier period, it is important to search for a year or two after the birth year of the first child.[41]

Child Marriages.

In 16th and 17th Century registers when the first child is born long after the marriage, a child marriage is a possibility, and the records of the relevant Consistory Court should be searched.[42]

Commonwealth Marriages.

Marriages during the Commonwealth period may be recorded in two different parish registers and one may contain much more information than the other.[43]

Missing Marriages.

The majority of Missing Marriages will probably be located if the wife's native parish can be discovered. However, they may often be found in one of the churches of the nearest city or town where marriage licences could be obtained. Marriages from some parishes in Oxfordshire, North Berks and Bucks may have been celebrated in chapels of Oxford Colleges and not recorded in the parish registers.[44] Clandestine Marriages may have been celebrated by a local "marriage-monger",[45] at one of the "lawless" churches or chapels in London, by

---

[40] For examples of the ways in which signatures can be used see *"Errors of Identification & Misinterpretation* under *Baptisms* above p.143 and also *Society of Friends* in Volume II.

[41] D. E. Gardner and F. Smith *op.cit.* Vol. 1. page 191.

[42] For more details see *"Form and Content"* pp. 63–65.

[43] For examples see *Form and Content* pp. 60–61.

[44] See *"General Information"* sections of these counties in Volumes V, III and VII.

[45] Registers with a high percentage of "foreign" marriages are indicated in the General Information section of each county.

a "Flect parson," or even at Gretna Green or in the Channel Islands Islands. [46]

Burials

Names.

People may be buried (or even married) under other names they were "known by" and not by those with which they were baptized; and this is not always a "nick name". Thus, *John Henry* might be married and buried as *Henry* or *Harry* or as *Jack*. *Elizabeth Ann* might be married as *Ann* and buried as *Elizabeth*. [47]

Ages.

Ages given in parish registers may be grossly inaccurate the persons themselves often having little idea of their real age. In particular ages of old persons were often exaggerated, sometimes by as much as ten years. [48]

Churchwardens' Accounts.

The churchwardens were often handed the burial fees and these may be entered in the accounts with the name of the deceased. Thus, at St. Bride's Fleet Street, these entries are often better spelled and give fuller details than in the register. A few entries are missing in the register altogether. The extent of the variations is shown by the following examples, the churchwardens' version being given in brackets.

```
1641. April 3. Sara w of Wm. Woodward (Woodruffe L.G.)
           4. Jonathan s of Sackary Smith (in the church)
           4. Margaret w of Barth. Barcklet (Barnard U.G.)
          10. (Humphrey s of Allen Ellitt. L.G.)
          10. (Richard s of William Jacob. L.G.)
     May   1. John Wardenner (Warner. L.G. Pens.)
           4. Francis (& Edward) d of John White parishe childe.
           5. Andrew Wandrick (servant to Mr. Palmer. L.G.)
          31. Mr. Thos Baker   (Mr. Richard Barker to Sr. Will. Compton
              kt. L.G)
     June 19. Edward Aulworth Gentle man (Mr. Edward Aylworthe gent,
              in the church)
          27. (Sara d of John Green, L.G.) [49]
```

Monumental Inscriptions.

Whenever possible Burial entries should be checked against Monumental Inscriptions, which may give a great deal of supplementary

---

[46] For more details, see *Clandestine Marriages* pp. 292–318.
[47] On change of name see *Surnames* above pp. 89–91, *Christian Names* pp. 124–127
[48] On uncertainty as regards ages, see also *Form and Content* p. 50 and *Proofs of Age* pp. 365–366.
[49] J. Harvey Bloom. *St. Bride's Fleet St.* Gen. Mag. Vol. 8, p. 331. The abbreviations in the accounts presumably stand for Lower Ground and Upper Ground and *Pens* for *pensioner*.

information, even if they do not in fact provide the evidence the searcher has been seeking. Thus, if a baptism has been late in life, an age on the tombstone will provide a date of birth and perhaps suggest earlier years to be searched for the marriage. Place of residence, occupation, station in life, and relationships may also be given on one or a group of headstones or monuments. More and more graveyard monumental inscriptions are being copied and it is hoped that before long a list of those available will be published.[50]

Missing Burials.

A person who died at his usual residence in one parish may be buried elsewhere (e.g. his place of origin). He may have left express instructions to this effect in his Will or have owned a family grave lot. This may be of assistance from whichever end it is tackled. Not only may the Will provide the place of origin, but conversely, a note in the burial register may give a clue as to a move from the place of origin or the whereabouts of relatives. This may be of value even after 1837. Thus, Ann Kitchener, aged 86 was buried at Hinxworth, Herts, in 1844. A note in the register says *"died in London."* Her death certificate was therefore obtained, which gave the address. The 1841 Census return listed her with the household of a certain John *Slocombe*, whom subsequent research showed to have been her youngest son who had changed his name. This opened up a new line of investigation which might never have been explored if she had not been taken back to her village of origin for burial, or if the vital three words in the register had not been followed up.

Of course, many burials far away from the normal parish of residence are not so easily traceable. The death might have taken place while visiting friends or on a journey.

Use of Parish Registers in Conjunction with other Sources

Even the beginner appreciates that entries in the parish register should always be checked wherever possible against the Bishop's Transcripts, and the importance of Monumental Inscriptions has already been stressed. However, there is a tendency even for more experienced genealogists to treat Wills, Manorial Records etc as supplementary to parish register information, rather than their being used in strict conjunction, passing from one to the other and back. This may be illustrated by the following examples:

Wills.

Often a wife's christian name is known from baptisms, although the marriage has not been found. For example, if a wife's name is known to be Joan, it is often rewarding to note all Joans born in the locality within five years of the husband's birth, and then look

[50] For more information on this subject see article on *Monumental Inscriptions* pp. 245-269.

up the Wills of these surnames for any mention of *"my daughter Joan X"* or of grandchildren of the name sought. Even the nature of the bequest in Wills may provide clues leading back to registers. Mr. H.W. Atkinson cites the following example:

> Richard Dearman of Manchester, draper, in his Will of 1821, proved 1832, left everything to his wife except one small bequest of *"Claude's Essay on the Composition of a Sermon"*. He directed that he should be buried at Bethesda Chapel, Pendleton. The mention of this book suggested that possibly he had to compose sermons himself and was some sort of minister. Enquiry showed that this chapel belonged to the Methodist New Connexion. The register of births and baptisms 1806-1837 was found among the [surrendered] non-parochial registers, and among a number of persons who had administered baptism was Richard Dearman. Following this, further search was made in the like register of another chapel of the same denomination at Oldham Street, Manchester, and in that was found the birth and baptism of his son Richard, in 1822.[51]

Trade Directories and Rate Books.

There is a tendency to ignore sources which are not of direct genealogical value. However, in London and other cities, where the trade is known, Trade Directories may supply the address, and hence the most likely parish. Conversely, if an address is given in the register, the directories will often supply the person's trade. This may suggest a likely affliation.

Rate books, in supplying the successive holders of property will also suggest likely relationships, particularly in the case of a common name, where several affiliations are possible.

Manorial Rolls.

Mention has already been made that signatures in parish registers may be compared with those in Manorial Rolls which of course may also supply much other useful information.[52]

Other Documents in the Parish Chest.

Settlement certificates and other Parish Documents may be extremely important and might be completely overlooked if a *copy* of a parish register is used.[53]

The use of parish registers in conjunction with several other sources is well illustrated by the following example from the work of Charles F. Russell:[54]

---

[51] H.W. Atkinson – *Some Experiences in Genealogical Work.* Gen. Mag. Vol.3. p.35.

[52] See *Other Records: Some Brief Notes* pp.340–343.

[53] See *Other Records: Some Brief Notes* pp.343–351.

[54] *On the Statement of Evidence* Gen. Mag. Vol. 9 pp.382–3.

"I was interested in the family of a certain Thomas Bullock of Canterbury, who was the son of Edward Bullock and was baptized at St. Paul's in 1664. His father was a carpenter and a freeman of Canterbury, and "Thomas Bullock, the younger, carpenter" son of Edward Bullock, carpenter was admitted to the freedom by birth in 1687. He married Margaret Whitewood, the marriage licence (in which he is described as "carpenter") being dated 8 February 1700. Two children of "Thomas and Margaret Bullock " were baptized at St. Paul's – John in 1704 and Susannah in 1706-7. In October 1710 his wife died, So far, all is plain-sailing.

On 8 May 1711 a licence was issued for the marriage of "Thomas Bullock, carpenter, widower, with Mary Pettitt, both of St. Paul's. But when Margaret Bullock died in 1710 it was stated in the register that she was buried "by her husband" and the more usual interpretation of these words is "by the side of her husband". So the question arose whether her husband had predeceased her or not. Some evidence seemed necessary before the two Thomas Bullocks married in 1700 and 1711 could be regarded as the same man. The difficulty, it may be said, would not arise if we were to interpret the words " by her husband " to mean no more than that her husband made the arrangements for her funeral; but this interpretation, though possible, is not quite so likely, so the desirability of further evidence remained, especially in view of the fact that there were other families of the name of Bullock living in Canterbury at the time.

Thomas and Mary Bullock, the parties to the second marriage, had six children baptized at St. Paul's in 1713, 1714/15, 1716, 1718, 1721 and 1723. The first five are described as the children of Thomas Bullock and Mary, the last as the son of Thomas Bullock, Alderman, and Mary. In 1738/9, Thomas Bullock, Alderman, was buried, Evidently the husband of Mary was an Alderman during the latter part of his life, his election occurring probably between 1721 and 1723, and certainly not later than the latter year. Was there anything to show that Alderman Bullock had previously been the husband of Margaret.

We have already noted that Thomas Bullock and Margaret had a daughter Susannah, baptized in 1706/7, and the list of Freemen supplies the last link in the chain. In 1727, Stephen Moys, carpenter was admitted a Freeman in virtue of his marriage with "Susan ", daughter of Alderman Bullock of Canterbury, Carpenter ".

It is plain that in this case no single entry is sufficient to establish the identity of the two Thomas Bullocks. Without the baptismal entry of 1723, we should not know that the husband of Mary became an Alderman; without the list of Freemen by marriage we should not know that Susan was the Alderman's daughter; and without the baptismal entry of 1706-7 we should not know that Susan's mother was Margaret."

Only too frequently the genealogist has the material in his possession to solve a tricky problem, but fails to interpret it through consulting the value of each item rather than the cumulative effect.

Documentation of Pedigrees

Parish register entries are often given as evidence in pedigrees when they alone do not prove identification. Thus, an account of a family may state that Thomas Wilson was the son of James Wilson and was baptized 1634. It is usual to give, as if it were adequate authority for the statement, a baptismal entry from the parish register such as: *" 1634 April 26 Thomas son of James Wilson. "* This is expected to satisfy the reader, and indeed may do so; yet it is possible that there were several families of Wilson living in the same place, and that two or three Thomas Wilsons may have been baptized within the space of a few years, all of them at first sight equally well qualified to be the one dealt with in the history. Quoting only the one entry conceals this fact from the reader, but if he should take the trouble to examine the registers himself, he may be left wondering whether the alleged relationship can be accepted with confidence. Clearly, the reasons must be given why the compiler judged that this particular entry, and not another, is the one required, unless the reasons are straight-forward and easy to discover. [55]

Thus, in the above example concerning Thomas Bullock, all the sources used to establish the identity of the two Thomas Bullocks should be cited.

This article has attempted to point out only a few of the more obvious pitfalls and suggest possible ways of solving a few common difficulties. Every piece of genealogical research, however, has its own unique problems and only experience will help to solve them. Beginners should never be reticent in asking advice. Much fruitless searching may thus be avoided. However, many problems baffle even the most experienced professional genealogist and occasionally one hears of a chance discovery which may instantly provide an answer which has been patiently and systematically sought for years.

---

[55] Charles F. Russell loc.cit.p.381.

IV PARISH REGISTERS AND THE HISTORIAN
by Dr. E.A. Wrigley

*Dr. Wrigley is a Fellow of Peterhouse, Cambridge and is a founder-member of the Cambridge Group for the History of Population and Social Structure. For a much fuller treatment of material contained in this article readers are referred to "*An Introduction to English Historical Demography*" Ed. E.A. Wrigley (Pub. Weidenfeld and Nicolson 1966).*

History is helpless without sources: and of all the sources of knowledge about English society from Tudor times until Victoria's accession, few are more valuable than the parish registers. In sheer bulk they may well exceed any other single source, since there were some 11,000 parishes in this period and in some cases a single parish filled dozens of volumes with entries relating to the baptisms, burials and marriages of its inhabitants. And their value matches their bulk. Between their covers is to be found the source material from which the historical demography of England may be traced. The purpose of this brief article is to suggest some of the ways in which the information contained in parish registers may be used to enrich our knowledge of English social and economic history at all levels and, more generally, to further the understanding of social function and change.

Parish registers have, of course, been consulted frequently by local historians for many years and are of major importance to those engaged in genealogical studies. But until recently they were comparatively little used for general historical purposes. The failure to use them more extensively has been due to three main circumstances, which may be considered in turn.

I

Parish registers have long been rather inaccessible to any but the local historian: and in two senses. In the first place they were inaccessible simply because until recently the great majority of registers were kept in the parish chests of their several parishes. To consult more than a very small number was therefore a slow and costly undertaking. And even if both time and money were available there were sometimes difficulties in securing the goodwill of the incumbents and churchwardens without which no examination could be

made. If their goodwill was forthcoming there were still often
practical problems in finding good working conditions in cold and
cramped church vestries. On occasion all these difficulties might
be absent, but anyone wishing to work upon a large number of
registers was sure to encounter them from time to time. Secondly,
the registers were also inaccessible in that no full inventory or
calendar of parish registers could be consulted. Without such a
guide a great deal of time had to be spent in preliminary surveys
to determine the characteristics of individual registers. As a
result much effort might go unrewarded because the registers themselves were so scattered and so variable in quality and completeness[1].

The problem of the peppering of the registers across the face of
England in thousands of parish chests is now becoming less acute
since more and more registers are now housed in County Record Offices
The counties differ greatly in this respect but the trend is clear.
The removal of registers to the County Record Offices has sometimes
caused bitter comment among local historians obliged to travel many
miles to see volumes which were once on their own doorsteps. But
registers in County Record Offices are much more safely housed than
those in parish chests. Too often even within the last twenty years
registers have been stolen, destroyed by fire, mice or mildew, or
simply mislaid. For most historians the concentration of registers
in the County Record Offices has meant a clear gain in accessibility.
Moreover, working conditions in them are usually much better than
in church vestries.

Even if there had been no problem of accessibility, however, it
is doubtful whether parish registers would have been used as
extensively in the past as they seem likely to be in the future,

---

[1] Rickman published in the 1831 Census information about the registers
extant in each parish at that time. This he had assembled by addressing
a circular letter of inquiry to each incumbent. The 1831 returns are a
useful guide but contain little detail (typically just an indication of
years in which the registers were defective or deficient). In many
cases registers then in the parish chests have subsequently been lost,
and occasionally some then missing have been recovered. In some areas
fuller, recent inventories are available. For example, the invaluable
*Inventory of Parochial Documents in the Diocese of Bath and Wells and
the County of Somerset*, edited by J. E. King was published in 1938, but
even in works of this type the description of register contents given
is too condensed to be satisfactory for many purposes.

It is of interest to note that in Scotland all registers are housed in
the General Register Office in Edinburgh which greatly alleviates all
these problems.

for both the incentive to make use of them and the techniques for exploiting them were much weaker years ago than they have recently become. The question of incentive and that of technique are, of course, closely bound up with each other, but it is convenient, if rather artificial, to separate them for the purpose of exposition.

II

The incentive to search grows more intense as the importance of that which is sought increases in the eyes of the seeker. Local historians were always clear about the importance of parish registers because from them they could glean a great deal of information about events and individuals in the history of the parish which could not be found elsewhere. The close interconnection between the registers and other sources of information about the local community was evident. It is no accident that in a number of cases the history of a parish contains a complete transcription of the registers. But in the larger framework of national history there might seem little connection between the life histories of poor and illiterate men and women and the events recorded in the main national archives. In virtue of this it was sometimes thought appropriate to transcribe from the parish registers only the baptisms, burials and marriages of the most important local families. And for the same reason when parish registers were consulted, it was often only to obtain or verify the date of burial of a man who had made his mark upon the national scene, or to investigate the ancestry of a woman who had contracted an advantageous match. To use parish registers extensively was to invite the danger of being judged to be just on the wrong side of that fine line sometimes drawn between historical scholarship and antiquarianism.

A change of heart has come about partly through the development of social and economic history which have their roots in the lives of the masses, and more generally because of the perception of a sociological truth of the greatest importance. This last is the crucial point and deserves emphasis. Once it is accepted the immense value of the parish registers necessarily follows.

Of all social institutions the family is the most nearly universal[2]. When sociologists and social anthropologists study a contemporary society they invariably devote much effort to the analysis

---

[2] Indeed it has been argued not merely that the family is found in all societies but that it is necessary to the very existence of society. See M.J. Levy, *'Aspects of the Analysis of Family Structure '* in the book bearing the same title by A.J. Coale and others (Princeton, 1965), esp. pp. 13-26.

of its family system. The family occupies a central place within the social structure. It is interlinked with every other institution and type of social activity, so that changes elsewhere will be reflected within it, and vice-versa. Almost all men and women are members of a family at some time during their lives: many are members from the moment of birth until death. The process of socialization takes place very largely within the family, and it is within the family that the personality traits of each individual are shaped during the first few years of life[3]. Even today this is true, and in pre-industrial England the family was perhaps relatively still more important since it was then the scene of many economic and other activities which have latterly been hived off into specialist organisations outside the home[4].

The parish registers cannot, of course, be made to yield the entire range of information about family life in the past which can be obtained today from the investigation of families of living men and women who can be questioned and observed in ways for which the historian can find no equivalent. Nevertheless they will provide a very detailed picture of many aspects of the family in England between the sixteenth and nineteenth centuries. Half a loaf is here certainly much better than no bread at all, especially as the half which can be had provides important clues about the shape of that other half which is beyond reach. If it is possible to discover the average age at which men and women married, the average size of their families, the average intervals between births of different ranks (and, of course, the standard deviations of these statistics); if expectation of life can be calculated, and infant, child and adult mortality rates derived; if the frequency of illegitimate births can be discovered and the proportion of first births which were pre-nuptially conceived; if the likelihood of widowhood at different ages can be estimated and the frequency of remarriage known; if differences in all these respects between different occupational groups and classes within the whole population can be elucidated; if regional variations and changes over time can be defined and the correlation between these in turn and other measures of social and economic change be laid bare; if all this can be done, then the historian will have at his disposal data which will allow him to attempt many of the forms of sociological analysis which until recently had seemed beyond reach. And, given suitable registers and appropriate techniques,

---

[3]   An excellent discussion of family structures and their associated characteristics in societies in different parts of the world is to be found in W.J. Goode, *World revolution and family patterns* (New York, 1963).

[4]   See P. Laslett, *The world we have lost* (London, 1965) for a vivid discussion of this question.

information under all the heads listed, and many more, can be produced from the long columns of baptism, burial and marriage entries.

Because the family occupies a central place within the total network of social activity and institutions, it changes in sympathy with changes elsewhere in the system. It is possible to gain some insight into these changes and into the normal functioning of social institutions by studying demographic indices, since these are quantifications of various aspects of family experience. For example, the study of ages at marriage in different social groups may throw much light upon the effect of prevailing systems of inheritance and upon other social pressures which governed decisions to marry. Sometimes these statistics may permit an interesting commentary upon the beliefs of those then living. A knowledge of ages at marriage of first sons and others in areas in which primogeniture prevailed, for example, may serve either to confirm or dispel assumptions made by contemporaries about what was normal (the contrast between these areas and those in which partible inheritance or Borough English was customary might also prove illuminating). Or again, it is often possible to give quantitative expression to the gap between norms of behaviour and the behaviour itself. Illegitimacy rates, for instance, can reveal surprising differences between what a society prescribes as an ideal and what it may tolerate in practice (and the rates may also underline how different the gap between the ideal and the actual was in, say, Catholic and Protestant areas).

Similarly, the sensitivity of demographic indices to economic and other stresses in pre-industrial communities can also be illustrated in many ways. The sudden surges of mortality which sometimes killed one person in five in parishes from one side of Europe to the other provide an example of this. The effects of the periodic outbursts of epidemic disease or runs of poor harvests which occurred sooner or later in the lives of many, perhaps most men and women are immediately visible in the registers. But the registers can show much more than the crude total of those who died. They can show whether the scourge acted indifferently over the whole population or whether it killed selectively in certain age-groups, certain areas, or certain occupational groups. Further the effect of the heavy mortality on marriage and on fertility levels can be measured (it was often quite different when the mortality was due to epidemic outbreaks from those occasions when the basic cause of death was lack of food). And the remarkable resilience of many populations even in the face of losses which might at first sight seem crippling is faithfully recorded in a good register. The social mechanism of recovery can be investigated. For example, in an area where the death of the occupant of any holding created the opportunity for his successor in the holding to marry, a heavy mortality might be followed almost at once by a steep rise in the number of marriages, and within a year by a sudden rush of entries in the columns of the baptism register. And examples like these of the strategic importance of a knowledge of family structure and demographic behaviour to a very wide range of questions about social function and social change in the past could be multiplied many times over[5].

One further point must be stressed. Historical demography based on parish registers is vital to work on many scales of history, as it were. It is important on the grand scale. For example, a clear understanding of population changes in England during the seventeenth and eighteenth centuries would be of immense value to those interested in the genesis of the Industrial Revolution, the event which opened the gateway to the modern world[6]. But all measures of population change, even though they relate to millions of families, are only shorthand expressions of the events in the histories of individual families, repeated with variations many times over. The greatest of demographic events is inevitably the history of individual family units writ large. There is an unbroken continuum between the suffering of the panic-stricken weaver in the brief hours between the first onset of pneumonic plague and his last agony and the cataclysmic impact of the Black Death on the society and economy of Europe in the mid-fourteenth century. There is a similar continuum between the anxious discussions and decisions of couples into whose hands the works of Place or Knowlton fell, and the steady fall in European fertility which has made a family of five or more children a rarity in most of Europe today.

Work on all historical scales can be firmly based on parish registers. They can be used simply to trace back the ancestry of individual men and women. It is perhaps true to say that they have been used more frequently for this purpose than for any other over the last hundred years. But this has usually been a private act of piety or pride, or an aspect of a biographical study. Much more is possible. Between the dusty covers of the bound volumes of parish registers lie the keys to many historical puzzles, both those which have teased local historians and the larger issues which preoccupy general economic and social historians. When the demographic

[5] A fuller discussion of this question may be found in the chapters by Eversley and Wrigley in E.A. Wrigley (ed.), *Introduction to English historical demography* (London, 1966).

[6] See, for example, J.T. Krause, 'Some neglected factors in the English industrial revolution', *Journal of Economic History*, xix (1959), 528-40; H.J. Habakkuk, 'English population in the eighteenth century', *Economic History Review*, 2nd ser., vi (1953), 117-33; E.A. Wrigley, 'Family limitation in pre-industrial England', *Economic History Review*, 2nd ser., xix (1966), 82-109.

characteristics of communities are more fully understood they can be used as barometers, sensitive to economic and social pressures of many types, at once a way of appreciating the nature of such pressures more accurately and of measuring their intensity.

III

I turn finally to the question of technique, the third of the obstacles to a fuller use of the registers for historical purposes which has proved frustrating in the past.

The most serious general problem which plagued historical demographers in the past when using parish registers was the difficulty of calculating rates to express fertility and mortality. Totals of baptisms, burials and marriages were comparatively easy to obtain but reliable rates seemed in many cases beyond reach. The distinction between the two is important. If all that is known about the population history of a parish in, say, the 1670's is that on an average 50 baptisms, 45 burials and 15 marriages occurred annually, the value of this knowledge is limited. It is impossible to be sure whether fertility and mortality were high or low. It is not even possible to be sure whether, if existing fertility and mortality levels were to continue, the long-term trend in population numbers would be up or down. To gain a clear insight into the demography of the parish it is essential to know not only the totals of events but also the totals of people at risk so that by relating one to the other a rate can be calculated. If, for example, the population of the parish were known to be 1,250 then the crude birth (baptism) rate would be 40 per 1,000. This is a much more valuable statistic than the simple number of baptisms for most purposes. But for a more searching analysis breakdowns both of the number of events and the totals of people at risk are necessary. For example, any full study of fertility requires rates which express the fertility of married women by five-year age-groups (for instance, by relating the number of legitimate children born to married women aged 25-9 to the total of married women in that age-group).

Only when dependable rates for each aspect of the fertility and mortality of the community can be calculated, is it possible to put the contents of the parish register to their best use and to exploit to the full their sensitivity to the social and economic environment of the events which they record. Yet frequently there is little or no reliable evidence even of the crude totals of parish populations, far less of the totals by age-group and marital status. Occasionally detailed listings of inhabitants exist for individual parishes but

161

these are rare[7]. And even where a listing which names each inhabit-
ant, gives his age, and makes clear his occupation and his position
in the family, is found, it is usually available only for a single
point in time (successive listings for a number of years are extremely
rare) and cannot therefore be of help for more than a short span of
years. Returns of inhabitants having a wider coverage, such as the
Hearth Tax returns, the Protestation returns of 1641-2, or the Compton
census of 1676, are a useful guide to approximate totals but each
requires multiplication by a conversion factor to give a total of
population. Conversion factors are a fertile source of disagreement
and any error imported by this operation may be magnified further if
the original count was itself deficient or if the totals were rounded
up or down for convenience. In general only rough estimates of total
population are attainable from these sources.

In spite of these difficulties some remarkably penetrating and
stimulating studies have been carried out using straightforward aggregative methods in summing the baptisms, burials, and marriages
recorded in the registers and relating them to approximate totals of
population[8]. Using only the totals of baptisms and marriages, for
example, it is a simple matter to calculate baptism/marriage ratios.
Both the absolute level of these ratios and their changes over time
can be very helpful in studying fertility, especially if a group of
neighbouring parishes is taken together to minimise the danger that
changes in the popularity of the local church for weddings in any
one parish might distort a ratio calculated for that parish alone.
Or again, the fluctuations in burial totals when related to other
information about local economic, social or medical conditions are
often very suggestive. So too are any correlations, whether positive
or negative, between baptism and burial totals. Where estimates of
total population are also available and crude rates can therefore be
calculated a wider range of opportunities is opened up.

All aggregative work based on parish registers, however, suffers
from certain limitations. Some of these have been touched on already.
Others, such as the relative distortions which may occur in the totals
of baptisms, burials and marriages with the local spread of

---

[7] They are less rare than was once thought and are of the utmost value. See
P. Laslett, 'The study of social structure from listings of inhabitants',
in Wrigley (ed.), *Introduction to English historical demography*. See also
Other Records: Some Brief Notes below pp.333–336.

[8] See, for example, the exemplary study by J.D. Chambers, 'The Vale of Trent
1670-1800', *Economic History Review*, supplement no.3 (undated); also
D.E.C. Eversley, 'A survey of population in an area of Worcestershire
from 1660-1850 on the basis of parish registers', *Population Studies*,
x(1957), 253-79; and S. Sogner, 'Aspects of the demographic situation in
17 parishes in Shropshire 1711-60' *Population Studies*, xvii (1963), 126-46.

Nonconformity have frequently been discussed and are widely familiar[9]. Two further related points must be stressed in this context. Purely aggregative work does not reveal anything of the demography of individual families and it does not produce measures of fertility and mortality sufficiently precise to give a keen cutting edge to the tools of demographic analysis. One end of the continuum of demographic experience is missing; one scale of operation is neglected. The interplay between social and economic conditions on the one hand and the demography of individual families on the other, therefore, cannot be satisfactorily examined. If, for example, aggregative methods suggest a significant lowering in fertility, it may well prove very difficult using these methods alone to decide between a number of possible reasons for the fall – a rise in the age at marriage of women, an increase in the average spacing between births, a sharp increase in adult mortality bringing with it more frequent interruptions of unions while child-bearing was still incomplete, a spread of the practice of family limitation, and so on. With this further knowledge other aspects of local history may fall into place and a pattern of interrelationships emerge. Without it analysis tends to remain much clumsier. It may sometimes be essential to know about changes in age-specific mortality rates, or the range of age differences between grooms and brides, or the average interval between widowhood and remarriage, in order to test a hypothesis about social structure or to measure the pressure exerted by a changing aspect of community life upon the families which composed it. For example, if it were argued that a change in the attitude of parents to the nurture of their offspring significantly enhanced their chances of reaching adult years[10], a knowledge of age-specific mortality rates would go far towards settling the question. Indeed if there were no fall in infant and child mortality rates the thesis would immediately fall to the ground (much of the value of detailed demographic studies lies in their *disproof* of supposed relationships: such apparently negative virtues often give rise to very fruitful alternative hypotheses).

Recently a new method of analysing parish registers has been developed which appears likely to overcome some of the difficulties just described. This technique is known as family reconstitution. As the name suggests, it places the individual family firmly in the centre of the stage, and produces that fineness of detail so valuable in attempting to unravel the complexities of stability and

---

[9]   There is an interesting discussion of this question in J.T. Krause, 'Changes in English fertility and mortality, 1781-1850', *Economic History Review*, 2nd ser., xi (1958), 52-70. Krause takes a pessimistic view of the completeness of registration after 1780. Further work may modify this.
[10] See P. Ariès, *Centuries of childhood*.

change within pre-industrial communities. Family reconstitution means the consolidation upon a single sheet of paper (called a Family Reconstitution Form, FRF for short) of all the information which can be gleaned from the registers about birth, death and marriage within a particular family. Each separate family about which anything is known is described on a separate FRF[11]. By the further analysis of the information on the FRFs, detailed fertility and mortality rates can be calculated since both the totals of events and the numbers at risk in the sample of reconstituted families can be discovered. The family reconstitution method was first fully developed in France for historical and demographic purposes and has only recently been adapted for application to English parish registers[12], though a pioneering study of British ducal families using a slightly different form of analysis was carried out some time ago[13]. If done manually family recontitution is a laborious undertaking[14] and involves heavy expenditure on printing (a separate slip must be made out for each baptism and burial and two slips for each marriage recorded in the registers, and at a later stage of analysis an FRF is created for each marriage about which anything is known). It is normally also necessary to make a xerographic copy of the register which increases the cost of the work still further.

The game, however, is well worth the candle, for from the material in the pile of FRFs produced the changing demography of the parish

[11] The technique of family reconstitution is described in detail in Wrigley, *Introduction to English historical demography*, chapter 4. The type of registers to which this technique of analysis can be applied with success is discussed in E.A. Wrigley, *Some problems of family reconstitution using English parish register material*, mimeographed paper for Section VII, Third International Economic History Conference, München 1965. This paper is to be published in the collected papers on historical demography given at the conference.

[12] The first monograph applying family reconstitution to a French register was published almost a decade ago: E, Gautier and L. Henry, *La population de Crulai*, I.N.E.D., Cahier 33 (1958). The latest full statement of the technique used by French scholars will be found in M. Fleury and L. Henry, *Nouveau manuel de dépouillement et d'exploitation de l'état civil ancien*, I.N.E.D. (Paris, 1965). The potential importance of work in historical demography for many branches of history is well exemplified in P. Goubert, *Beauvais et le Beauvaisis de 1606 à 1730*, S.E.V.P.E.N. (1960).

[13] See T.H. Hollingsworth, 'A demographic study of the British ducal families *Population Studies*, xi (1957), 4-26. Hollingsworth has recently extended his survey to cover a much larger section of the aristocracy. See his 'The demography of the British peerage', supplement to *Population Studies*, xviii, no.2(1964).

[14] The Cambridge Group for the History of Population and Social Structure and the Computing Laboratory of the University of Newcastle upon Tyne are at present jointly engaged in an attempt to devise computer programs which will greatly reduce the labour involved in family reconstitution.

over two or three centuries can be examined and the way is cleared for the study of communities in the past with a new precision and subtlety. Individual families can be grouped by occupation, by tenurial status, by size, by the period in which the marriage took place, and so on. When results for several different parishes are available further cross tabulations by region, or by a division into urban and rural parishes are possible. Each tabulation and cross tabulation helps cumulatively to establish what was distinctive about each group, time period, or area in the past, and how long it survived.

Work of this type is essentially both comparative and cumulative. The shape of the demography of England in the three centuries preceding the beginning of civil registration in 1837 will not emerge abruptly with all its contours crisply clear. It will take shape slowly, the shadowy outline gradually growing firm and a wealth of detail becoming visible as time passes. Aggregative work and family reconstitution are complementary rather than mutually exclusive[15]. Indeed the former at its most developed shades off into the latter since there are elaborations of the aggregative method which will yield approximate infant mortality rates and ages at marriage[16]. Aggregative work of great value can be carried out on registers too lacking in detail or too defective in other respects to be suitable for reconstitution. But the advent of family reconstitution has notably enhanced the importance of parish registers to historical scholarship. The strictly demographic results of family reconstitution are much fuller and more precise than any which can be obtained with traditional methods and much of interest follows from this[17]. More generally, concepts familiar to sociologists and social anthropologists can be used much more freely and successfully because the material necessary to sustain analyses of this type is made more readily available.

IV

If common methods are used when working on parish registers so

---

[15] This is particularly well illustrated by the invaluable group of papers brought together in D. V. Glass and D. E. C. Eversley (eds.), *Population in history* (London, 1965).

[16] See D. E. C. Eversley, 'Exploitation of Anglican parish registers by aggregative analysis ' in Wrigley (ed.), *Introduction to English historical demography*.

[17] See, for example, L. Henry, *Anciennes familles genevoises*, I.N.E.D., Cahier 26 (1956), 93-110. In this passage Henry demonstrates most elegantly the appearance of the practice of family limitation among the Genevan *bourgeoisie*, a change of great significance, from purely demographic material.

that results from any one analysis can be compared directly with those from any other, then the isolation of the local historian, the sense that what he writes can be of interest only to those who live locally, is largely dispersed. Just as there is a continuum of demographic experience from the individual family to the populations of countries and continents, so too there is a continuum between the effort to understand the history of the remotest parish and the attempt to grapple with the general nature of change in societies as large as the nation state[18]. The parish registers are microscopes in which the fundamental detail of life in the past can be inspected. By peering into them we see not trivial details blown up so large that matters of moment can find no place, but rather the functioning of society on a scale which permits the relationships between its constituent parts to be examined with precision.

E. A. Wrigley,
Peterhouse,
Cambridge

The Cambridge Group for the History of Population and Social Structure can always make available the necessary slips and Family Reconstitution Forms at cost to anyone wishing to undertake independent work on Family Reconstitution. The understanding will be that if at any stage the Group wishes to make use of material produced in this way, it will refund the cost of materials used. The Group can also usually give advice about the suitability of a particular register for reconstitution purposes and provide details of a pilot study method for establishing the suitability of the register before embarking on full reconstitution which is a laborious undertaking.

Volunteers to assist in the work of the Group are still required. In particular Gloucestershire, Worcestershire, Wiltshire, Devon, Cornwall and Northamptonshire are still not well represented, either by completed work or work in progress.

All enquiries or offers of help should be addressed to Dr. E.A. Wrigley, Cambridge Group for the History of Population and Social Structure, 20 Silver Street, Cambridge.

Works on Historical Demography are listed in the General Bibliography, pages 420–424.

---

[18] Goubert, *Beauvais et le Beauvaisis*, illustrates this point excellently.

V BISHOP'S TRANSCRIPTS

A Bishop's Transcript is the return made (usually annually) by
the incumbent of a parish, recording baptisms, marriages and burials
during that year.

For convenience the term *Bishop's Transcripts* is used in this
article (and the abbreviation BT throughout the index) for any
transcripts of registers sent in to the proper authority, though in
many cases such as the Diocese of Norwich or the majority of
Peculiars in all dioceses they were in fact often sent not to the
Bishop, but to an archdeacon or a clergyman exercising Peculiar
jurisdiction.

Origin of Bishop's Transcripts.

It is normally assumed that Bishop's Transcripts date from the
Provincial Constitution of Canterbury of 1597, which, in addition to
ordering the old paper registers[1] to be transcribed on to parchment,
also provided that the churchwardens of each parish should, within a
month after Easter each year transmit to the Diocesan Registry a
transcript of the register entries for the preceding year. It is
certainly true that in most dioceses the Bishop's Transcripts start
in 1598. However, there are in existence in certain dioceses Bishop's
transcripts of earlier dates than 1598. How many of these were made
at the time, and how many were later copies is difficult to determine.
Thus, in 1693 it is probable that the Bishop of Lichfield instructed
incumbents to fill in all the gaps in the transcripts. Many lists
were made covering the years 1660-1693 except for years where
separate transcripts existed and a few incumbents completed the
transcripts back to the beginning of their registers.[2]

On the other hand, a number of dioceses have transcripts beginning
in 1558, 1560 or 1561. Henry Hartop, writing in 1909 noted[3]

"Although the first mandate for sending in these yearly transcripts was
issued to the clergy in 1597, for reasons which cannot clearly be explained, there exist at Leicester a good number of transcripts of
earlier date: the earliest being those for the year 1561."

---

[1] See *"History"* pp.9-10.
[2] See *"Bishop's Transcripts"* in the General Information sections of
    Shropshire, Warwickshire, Staffordshire and Derbyshire.
[3] *Leicestershire Parish Registers,* Leicester (1909).

In fact Leicester was not the only archdeaconry in the diocese of Lincoln with early transcripts; nearly all parishes for the Lincoln Archdeaconry begin in 1561. At Leicester, many parishes have transcripts from 1561 or 1562, though the number is not proportionately so great as in Lincoln, and they lack the almost continuous series between 1587 and 1600, which is characteristic of the latter archdeaconry. In Stow archdeaconry there are none earlier than 1598 and for the most part they begin in 1599. However, while there is no Stow transcript in the episcopal archives earlier than 1598, there is a note by Canon Foster in the Index to the Stow transcripts that he had seen among the Haxey parish records the transcript of 1561 for the parish. [4] It therefore seems likely that transcripts were sent in from all parishes in the diocese, but that those for Stow archdeaconry have failed to survive. The situation is analagous in the diocese of Norwich, where the transcripts for the Archdeaconry of Sudbury start shortly after 1560, but few pre-1597 transcripts survive for the Archdeaconry of Suffolk. [5]

The most complete series in the country is, however, that of the Diocese of Canterbury. Not only do the earliest transcripts begin in 1558 and extend to 1870, but up to 1812, separate transcripts were prepared each year for the Archdeacon's Court and for the Consistory Court of the Archbishop. Thus the odd year missing in one series can normally be made up from the other.

It would seem that in the Diocese of Canterbury there were two visitations in the year, at each of which a transcript of the register for the whole of the preceding year was sent in, so that there were two transcripts of the same entries during that period.[6] Each is usually for a year, but some are only for six months, though the other half of these transcripts may be missing. It is only the Archdeacon's transcripts which begin in 1558, those for the Consistory Court rarely beginning before 1600. That the latter were clearly the outcome of the injunction of 1597 is shown, not merely by the starting date, but by the fact that unlike the Archdeacon's set which run from Michaelmas, they run from Easter and after 1603 from Lady Day.

Thus in at least three dioceses, transcripts were sent in at least 36 years before the 1597 Injunction, and the fact that these dioceses are so dispersed points to an earlier general, rather than a local injunction. With regard to the Canterbury transcripts,

---

[4] Miss Kathleen Major, *Lincoln Diocesan Records as Sources for the Genealogist.* Gen. Mag. Vol.9, No.5, p164.

[5] See *Bishop's Transcripts* in the General Information sections of Norfolk and Suffolk.

[6] Burn. *History of Parish Registers* in England – footnote p.207.

J. Meadows Cowper pointed out[7]

"I have gone somewhat minutely into the matter, and have come to the conclusion that the earliest transcripts were made in 1559. A Headcorn transcript purports to have been sent to the Archdeacon "a Cording to the qvenis magesties Iniuncion" and this must, I think, refer to the "Articles to be Inquired" issued in 1559, one of which reads as follows: "Item, That you make a true presentment of the number of all persons, which died within your parishes sithence the feast of St. John the Baptist, which was in the year of our Lord God one thousand five hundred fifty and eight, unto the feast last past; making therein a plain distinct declaration how many men, women, and men children the same were, and the names of the men". (Cardwell:Doc.Ann.i.215.)

Whether or not Mr. Cowper was correct in attributing the sending in of transcripts to this particular injunction, that the instruction was a central one is confirmed by the earliest transcript of Pinchbeck in Lincoln Archdeaconry, which has the following heading

"This ys a true registre of ye names and surnames of all them which have been baptized married and buried within the parish of Pinchbeck in Holland in the diocese and countie of Lincoln showing what daye of everye moneth the sayd persons have been baptised married or buried from the third day of October in the yere of Our Lord m.ccccclxi unto the xth day of the same moneth in the yere of Our Lord God m.ccccclxii that ys during one whoale yere noted out of the originall subscribed and exhibited unto the Register by the vicar and churchwardens of the same parish accordyng to the order for that purpose sette forth by ye Quene's hyhnesse Commissioners for Causes Ecclesiasticall,"[8]

The early Lincoln transcripts are on paper and in most cases beautifully written, sometimes as at Pinchbeck divided into Baptisms, Marriages and burials, sometimes as at Long Sutton, where Thomas Aleyn the curate signs himself as the writer of the transcripts, with the baptisms, marriages and burials in three columns divided horizontally by the months written in ornamental capitals. In 1588 came a notable change: in the previous year, paper was still in use, but all the transcripts for 1588 are on parchment and this material was henceforward used except in a few instances in some parishes where apparently the order was occasionally ignored. In 1592 at Market Deeping 11d was paid "for a skinn for making the register": it seems likely that this is the parchment for the transcript ("register indented") as the register itself was still kept on paper and 16d had been expended in 1588 for four quires of paper for the register book.[9] In 1563, a bill confirming the making and transmissions of the transcripts to the registries was introduced into the House of Commons but, with its failure to pass, nothing more seems to have been done apart from an abortive attempt by Lord Burghley in 1590 to establish county

[7] Foreword to "Canterbury Marriage Licences, 1st series (1892)"
[8] cited by Miss Kathleen Major op cit. p.165
[9] Miss Kathleen Major op cit. p.166.

registries, until the orders of 1597 which made the keeping of such records general.

Methods of Returning the Transcripts

It was in 1603 that the 70th Canon of the Convocation of Canterbur regulated the method of returning the Transcripts

> "And the Churchwardens shall once every year, within one month after the five-and-twentieth day of March, transmit unto the Bishop of the Diocese or his Chancellor a true copy of the names of all persons christened, married, or buried in their parish in the year before (ended the five-and-twentieth day of March), and the certain days and months in which every such christening marriage, and burial was had, to be subscribed with the hands of the said Minister and Churchwardens, to the end the same may faithfully be preserved in the Registry of the said Bishop; which certificates shall be received without fee. And if the Minister or Churchwardens shall be negligent in performance of anything herein contained, it shall be lawful for the Bishop, or his Chancellor, to convert them, and proceed against every of them as contemners of this our constitution[10]".

The principal amendment from the 1597 injunctions was the provision that the transcripts were to run from Lady Day to Lady Day, rather than the rather vague 1597 wording that the transcripts for the preceding year were to be sent in written a month after Easter. In the diocese of Lichfield, the returns were made every two years rather than annually as in most other dioceses. Consequently, many of the transcripts are very bulky, particularly with the large industrial parishes, where three years of Baptisms, Marriages and Burials might cover up to a dozen skins each about three feet square. Normally one transcript was sent from each parish, even if the parish included a number of chapelries which kept separate registers. This does not apply, however, to Lancashire and Yorkshire, where the parishes were often very large and chapelries numerous. Sometimes we find entries from the chapelries on the transcripts of the mother church, but often they sent in individual returns. In all dioceses in cases of plurality, entries from two different parishes might appear for a limited period on the same transcript.

In the Diocese of Norwich, it was clearly the practice before 1597 to send in the transcripts to the archdeacons rather than the Bishop, although they were sent to the latter during Visitation years. No alteration was made to this practice after 1597 and there are thus two series in each Archdeaconry, those sent in to the archdeacons being termed *"Register Bills"* and those sent to the Bishop being called *"Bishop's Transcripts"*. Mr. Tate suggests that in some

---

[10]   *Gibson's Codex Juris Ecclesiastici Vol.1, p. 229.*

dioceses the transcripts

"were handed in to the archdeacon at the Visitation, *presumably with the intention that he should transmit them to the registry*. Often they never found their way, but remained till late years with the records of the archdeaconry, perhaps because the same person held the offices of commissary to the Bishop and official to the archdeacon. This may explain why the Leicestershire transcripts are, and the bulk of them always have been, at Leicester, how the archdeaconry of Richmond transcripts came to Leeds, and so on".[11]

However, it seems more likely that, as in the Diocese of Norwich the Bishop specifically delegated his powers to the archdeacons, and this would clearly seem to be the case as regards Leicester and the other Lincoln archdeaconries. However, these were exceptions to the general system laid down in 1597, by which most parishes sent their transcripts direct to the diocesan registry and which remained unchanged until the 19th Century.

Diocesan Boundaries

An important point to bear in mind is that the boundaries of the present dioceses have been subject to a great deal of alteration. In the 16th Century there were, excluding Sodor and Man but including Henry VIII's five new foundations of 1541 (Bristol, Chester, Gloucester, Oxford, and Peterborough), twenty-two Dioceses in England and four in Wales. There are now forty three (including Sodor and Man), forty-nine including the six Welsh dioceses.[12] Many of the dioceses bore little relation to the areas now covered by the same title. Lincoln included half the Midlands. Lichfield covered Derbyshire and Cheshire as well as Staffordshire, North Shropshire and North Warwickshire, and so on. Consequently, the old transcripts of Derbyshire are at Lichfield, not at Derby; those of Nottinghamshire were until a short time ago at York and so on. The position is further complicated by the fact that, apart from peculiars, parishes might often be geographically in one diocese, but ecclesiastically in another, and therefore their records are most likely to be found amongst those of the latter. Thus, Rossington, in the West Riding of Yorkshire, was an outlying parish in the Archdeaconry of Nottingham, so that its ecclesiastical records, including parish register transcripts, are with those of that archdeaconry. The archdeaconries were in as confused a state as the dioceses. Thus, the county of Huntingdon lay in four different archdeaconries although mainly in that of Huntingdon.[13]

---

[11] W. E. Tate "*The Parish Chest*" p. 42.
[12] *ibid* p. 53.
[13] *ibid* p. 53.

171

Peculiars.

Until comparatively recent years, parishes in *Peculiars* were not, like their neighbours, subject to the jurisdiction of the Ordinary. The peculiars had arisen in various ways. Some were liberties within which a royal castle was situated. Others were possessions of an Archbishop (e. g. Bocking, Essex) estates of a Bishop in another diocese, or parishes under the Dean, Dean and Chapter or individual prebendaries of a Cathedral (e. g. Banbury, Oxon, a Peculiar of the Dean and Chapter of Lincoln). Other parishes, including most that had been properties of the Knights Templar or the Hospitallers, and those such as Winkburn and Ossington, Notts., and Kirkstead, Lincs, which were the sites of Religious Houses, were donatives, and were chaplaincies of the squire, quite exempt from diocesan jurisdiction, yet possessing registers. The Peculiars for each county are normally listed under *Bishop's Transcripts* in the *General Information* section of each county. The incumbents of Peculiars (at least in theory) transmitted to their ecclesiastical superior the same records which a normal parish sent forward to its Bishop, so both probates of will and parish register transcripts for such parishes will normally be found, not in the Diocesan Registry, but among the records of the Peculiars,[14] which may have ended up in a most unexpected place or have been destroyed altogether. Thus of the four Shropshire Peculiars within the boundaries of the Diocese of Lichfield, the transcripts of one, Shrewsbury St. Mary, which included four other parishes are now found (but only incomplete) with the deposited registers of St. Mary at the Shropshire Record Office; the transcripts from 1636 to 1812 of the five parishes of the Bridgnorth Peculiar were purchased by the British Museum in 1871 from a private individual and are now with the Additional Manuscripts. A third Peculiar, Buildwas was formerly under the jurisdiction of Buildwas Abbey and no transcripts are known; the fourth, Prees, returned to the Dean and Chapter of Lichfield Cathedral, transcripts (each for three years) at the time of the Bishop's triennial visitations. There are transcripts at Lichfield for all four after 1813. The complete absence of transcripts from Buildwas illustrates the fact that in most of the donatives transcripts were never made at all as the incumbents had, in fact, no ecclesiastical superior. Where transcripts from the peculiars and donatives were sent in to the Registrar it was often under protest. This can be seen in a note at the bottom of the Bishop's Transcript for the parish of Bishop's

---

[14] *ibid* pp. 52-3.

Cleeve, Gloucestershire for the year 1674/1675 which runs as follows:-

> We ye Church Wardens of Bishop's Cleeve whose names are under written do declare yt hath alwayes been o'r custom to give in ye Transcript to ye Rector of B'ps Cleeve or his Officiall at his Court holden at Cleave for ye exercise of ye peculiar Jurisdiction of ye sd parrish: but being now cited to ye Court of Glocester and comanded by ye sd Court to bring in ye Transcript thither, we have accordingly yielded Obedience to ye sd Court in this Case but desire yt this Act of o'rs may not tend any wayes to ye prejudice of ye Rector of Cleave or to ye betraying ye Rights of his peculiar.
>
> John Cooke   Curate of Bishop's Cleeve
> Toby Sturmy, Richard Hobbes, John Hollbroock,   Churchwardens.

In the case of the Peculiars of the Diocese of Norwich, the situation was somewhat curious. The Bishop of Norwich, having apparently as we have seen delegated his powers throughout the diocese at large to the archdeacons, the transcripts of his own Peculiar were nevertheless sent to him. They were sent only in Visitation years, but each of these transcripts included all the years since the previous visitation, so there was the extraordinary position that the only consecutive series of Bishop's Transcripts, properly so called were sent in from a peculiar, although as has been pointed out, transcripts were also sent in to him from the various archdeaconries in Visitation years.

Post-1813 Transcripts.

In 1812 Rose's Act[15] made new regulations governing the returning of transcripts.

In future, within two months after the end of every year the transcripts were to be made by the incumbent on parchment, verified and signed. Copies were to be sent before June 1st each year to the registrar of the diocese, who must, before July 1st every year report to the Bishop whether such copies had been sent. The Registrars were to cause the copies to be securely deposited and preserved from damage by fire or otherwise, and to be carefully arranged. Furthermore, correct alphabetical lists were to be made of all persons and places mentioned in such copies for public use. There seems to have been little effort to enforce this latter provision, but nevertheless the Act had the effect that henceforth all peculiars normally sent transcripts to the Registrar. Thus the transcripts for the Lichfield Peculiars held at Lichfield Diocesan Registry nearly all start in 1813. Also, after 1813 the transcripts were normally entered on proper forms, and in some dioceses such as Gloucester they were bound up into volumes.

---

[15] For the other clauses in the Act see *"History"* p.14.

Information given in the Transcripts.

For the most part the Bishop's Transcripts are copies of the Parish Register although some details may be omitted as is shown by the following examples:

Truro, Cornwall

Parish Register;	9 June 1756 Richard Surgent, mariner, and Mary Williams, widow, married by licence. Witnesses, William Startridge, Edw. Terrill
Bishop's Transcript:	9 June 1756 Richard Surgent and Mary Williams married by licence.

Dalston, Cumberland

Parish Register;	25 Sept. 1769 Henry Graham, widower and Jane Bulman, spinster married by banns
Bishop's Transcript:	25 Sept. 1769 Henry Graham and Jane Bulman married. [16]

Sometimes entire entries may be omitted, such as those of illegitimate children, perhaps on the principle that the less said, the better. Nevertheless, at other times these transcripts betray unmistakable signs that they, and the register are both copies of some earlier text, probably the clerk's rough notebook. Thus, the transcript may have entries not in the register, and what are actually telescoped entries in the register are given correctly.[17]

Sometimes extraordinary discrepancies occur between the two texts, such as the interchange of bride and bridegroom's surnames in a marriage entry or the interchange of the brides' surnames in two separate entries. Some examples from the register of Walton, near Liverpool[18] are given with the corresponding B. T. entry below in parentheses.

1729 Aug. 9 Ellin and Anne Bridge of Walton, buried.
(Ellin Bridge Sp. and Ann w. of Jo: Bridge husb)

1730 June 5 Mercer's wife of Everton, buried
(Alice w. of Tho: Mercer of Everton agrico:)

1744 Nov. 10 Richard Whitehead and Jennet Voce of Formby
(Richard Voce and Jennet Whitehead of Formby)[19]

---

[16] These examples are taken from D. E. Gardner and F. Smith "Genealogical Research in England and Wales" page 202-3.

[17] For a detailed discussion of the question of Parish Registers as secondary texts, see *Form and Content* pp. 27–32.

[18] Lancashire Parish Register Society, volume 91.

[19] These examples and observations have been taken from Dr. D. R. Dickinson "The Value of Bishop's Transcripts and some notes on Parish Registers" Gen. Mag. Vol. 9. No. 6 p. 212.

There is also evidence to suggest that in some cases the Bishop's Transcripts were copied from neither the register nor the rough notebook. Not infrequently one finds that a considerable number of entries are in the Bishop's Transcripts which are not in the register at all. Thus, the register of St. Nicholas, Gloucester has no marriages at all for 1687 and yet the transcript shows 18 entries. Other marriages missing in the registers but in the Bishop's Transcripts are one for 1690, 1719, 1724, and 1725 and two for 1695 and 1718. These were probably copied from loose slips that were never written up in the register.[20]

This also leads to the interesting possibility that however neglected the transcripts were in most parishes, in the eyes of some vicars or clerks they were more important than the registers. The registers were after all normally seen only by priest or clerk who would supply certificates for their parishioners when required. In country districts they may seldom have been used at all. The transcripts, however, were in theory at least going to an ecclesiastical superior. Many country clergy, whose knowledge of central administration was limited, may have erroneously assumed that the transcripts were used for Civil (especially fiscal) purposes. This view is supported by the fact that in some dioceses information of a fiscal kind is given on the transcripts. Thus, in the Huntingdon Archdeaconry of Lincoln, the burial entries have been annotated with a reference to the value of the estate of the deceased and in the St. Albans Archdeaconry many transcripts were found bundled up with the inventories of estates. If this supposition regarding the standing of Bishop's Transcripts is correct one might infer that, in such parishes, existing gaps in Bishop's Transcripts are more frequently the result of diocesan rather than parochial negligence.

Whatever the reasons for the discrepancies between parish registers and Bishop's Transcripts and omissions in the former, the transcripts may even when the register appears to be perfect, provide additional information and should not be overlooked.

Completeness of the Transcripts.

Few series of Bishop's Transcripts are anywhere near complete. As Dr. Cox points out,[21] the great defect of the Canon of 1603 was the neglect to attach any fees for the transcript, either to the parish officials in making the copy, or to the Bishop's officials for its safe storage. Thus, their present number and condition varies widely, document by document as well as accumulation by accumulation, and

---

[20] For a fuller discussion of this question see *Form and Content* pp. 29–30.
[21] Cox. *The Parish Registers of England* p. 240.

they were described by Mr. Chester Waters in 1883 as "a lamentable picture of episcopal negligence, parochial parsimony and official rapacity". Many parishes failed to send in any returns at all. By 1800, when the Committee on Public Records issued its report, the Diocese of Salisbury with 434 parishes was in the habit of receiving only 9 or 10 a year, and no action had been taken by the Bishop or Registrar. In Rochester Diocese, at that date only seven parishes out of 95 were sending in their transcripts. Very few transcripts exist for the Diocese of Winchester before 1780, and transcripts for London, Middlesex and Essex are almost non-existent. The Registrar of London Diocese had the impertinence to send the following certificate to the Commissioners: "I hereby certify that it is not the custom within the Diocese of London for any returns to be made to the Bishop's Registry of either Burials or Baptisms."[22]

However, fortunately the situation was better in some dioceses. In Hereford, all 323 parishes were at that time making their annual returns, though there are only a few transcripts older than 1660. Mention has already been made of the two series of Canterbury and of the transcripts in some dioceses which antedate 1597. Furthermore, as has been observed it is possible that in some parishes the Bishop's Transcripts were more highly regarded than were the parish registers. Nevertheless, the overall picture was singularly depressing, and as we have seen in the case of some peculiars, transcripts were seldom made at all. Understandably, there is an almost universal gap for the Commonwealth period, and in most cases back to about 1645. However, in a few dioceses, such as Lincoln, an effort was made to fill in the missing transcripts, although even then the results were patchy. Thus, the Bishop of Lincoln issued instructions to incumbents and churchwardens to transmit copies of all entries from 1645 to 1660. Miss K. Major points out[23]

> "This order was more universally carried out in the Archdeaconry of Stow where forty-seven out of eighty-seven parishes have returns either for all, or a substantial number, of those years, while many others have returns for odd years; of these 47 the higher percentage comes from the two northern deaneries of Manlake and Corringham. In Lincoln Archdeaconry only 18 parishes out of over 500 show any series of years covered: two Lincoln churches, St. Mark and St. Martin, and eight parishes in the two neighbouring deaneries of Graffoe and Longoboby have copies mainly from 1653 to 1660: but two parishes in North Holland, Quadring and Swineshead, and six in South Holland have transcripts either from 1653 to 1660, or, as at Lutton, Long Sutton and Crowland, from 1645 to 1660. Pinchbeck has an even more

---

22 Cox. op. cit. p. 241.
23 op. cit. page 167.

complete and finely written set to which was attached a slip of parchment inscribed

Christinings, Marriages and Burialls
Taken out of the Register of Pinchbeck from the 25th day of March 1643m unto the 25th day of March 1660 as followeth
Nicholas East ibidem vicarius
Edmund Calthrope)
George Carr   ) Churchwardens.

It is, I think, of some significance that the parishes fall into two groups representing well-recognized association of certain deaneries for purposes of visitation. Christianity, Graffoe and Longoboby were visited together at Lincoln and North and South Holland at Boston from the Restoration onwards. "

Where the "filling in" of missing transcripts occurs it is not invariably of the Civil War period. As mentioned above, in 1693 the Bishop of Lichfield probably instructed incumbents to fill in the gaps in the transcripts, and many lists were made covering the years 1660-1693 except for years where separate transcripts existed, and, as we have seen[24] a few incumbents completed the transcripts back to the beginning of their registers. However, few dioceses even made the gesture of filling in missing transcripts and seemed to find it difficult enough to obtain returns in normal years.

As well as obvious gaps in the transcripts, it must be remembered that transcripts may be misplaced in the bundles or might be inconsistent as to dates. Although up to 1752 most transcripts went from March 26th to March 25th in accordance with Canon LXX of 1603; sometimes they went from January to December or different months altogether. This applies to a lesser extent even after 1752, so if the transcript for one year ends in December and the following one does not start until May, some entries in the register were probably never copied. Thus the transcript for Hirnant, Montgomeryshire for January to December 1795 is followed by the transcript for May 1796 to May 1797. The transcript ending December 1810 is followed by the transcript commencing 2nd July 1811.[25]

D.E. Gardner and F. Smith comment "Some clergymen used the various events of the year as dates to conclude their transcripts, such as 31st December, Easter (a different date each year) or the Visitation of the archdeacon or Bishop (which dates vary)."

Also, after 1754 when the marriages were in a separate volume, they may have been omitted in the Bishop's Transcript. In some small parishes there may have been no marriages during the year, but this

---

[24] See above, p.167.
[25] D.E. Gardner and F. Smith *Genealogical Research in England and Wales,* Vol.1 p.200.

was often, as in the case of Loveston, Pembrokeshire noted on the transcripts. [26]

The general situation improved after Rose's Act of 1812. As has been already pointed out, the peculiars now sent in transcripts. However, in 1831 a Parliamentary Return was made by the several dioceses in answer to enquiries whether the directions of the Act of 1812 had been complied with in various particulars, more especially as to what transcripts had been sent in since 1813 and whether they were kept in security from fire. In London Diocese there were 192 defaulting parishes. J.S. Burn had referred to some of these in 1829:

" It is believed to be a fact, that the populous parish of St. Luke has not sent any transcript since 1815; the parish of St. Leonard, Shoreditch, since 1821; and the parish of St. Matthew, Bethnal Green, has never sent any transcript whatsoever; and the Bishop's Registrar has not the means of compelling it or of punishing the neglect. The churchwardens of St. Luke's provided parchment for the transcripts for the years 1813, 1814 and 1815, and the parish clerk transcribed the register, but as he could not obtain any remuneration for his trouble (although he only required five guineas per annum) he has discontinued to transcribe, and the consequence has just been stated. It should be observed that the entries of baptisms, marriages and burials, in the parish of St. Luke amount together to nearly 2000 annually. Those at St. Leonard, Shoreditch must be still more numerous. "[27]

The situation was little better in the diocese of Bath and Wells (139 defaulting parishes) and Lincoln (103 defaulters). In twelve dioceses it was admitted that the returns were " subject to fire", Only one Bishop (Lichfield) had complied with the direction of the Act and made a survey and report.[28]

Some transcripts were made but never found their way into the diocesan registries. By the Act of 1812 transcripts which were posted in accordance with its directions could be sent postage free. However, in many cases these directions were ignored and the transcripts thus became chargeable. In these cases they were almost invariably refused by the registrars and taken back to the General Post Office. There was thus a large accumulation of transcripts there, which were eventually burnt. This privilege of sending transcripts post free was cancelled by the Postage Act of 1840. [29]

Condition of the Transcripts.

Even when fairly regular transcripts were returned, their quality

---

[26] D.E. Gardner and F. Smith. op. cit. p. 200-201.
[27] History of Parish Registers in England p. 208 (1862 edn).
[28] Cox. op. cit. p. 241.
[29] Burn op. cit. p. 207 (footnote).

varies enormously. Though the Act of 1597 directed that they should be made on parchment, many are on paper. The size of the parchments varies enormously from small pieces a few inches square to large sheets big enough to cover the top of a large desk, and instances have been noted where the larger parchments have been used as wrappers for a bundle of other parchments.[30] Some are written lengthways and others, crossways. All these varieties make listing and preservation difficult.

The transcripts were scarcely valued very highly at the Bishop's registries. The vast accumulation of documents in some registries created a storage problem, and the records were bundled into some out-of-the-way place and consequently neglected.

Revd. A.R. Maddison in 1882 read a paper to the Lincolnshire Architectural Society[31] describing the state of the Lincoln Transcripts:-

> "But the condition of these manuscripts: it almost beggars description. The dirt is such as only exists in documents which have lain undisturbed for years, it is dirt which even soap itself can hardly cope with. The writing in many cases is so encrusted with grime that it is necessary to soak the parchment in water before it can be deciphered. Damp also has played its part with a vengeance. Bundles of transcripts are literally glued together and seem often nothing but pulp. If you separate them too roughly the strips of parchment get torn or crumble into dust."[32]

This description could equally well have applied to most other diocesan registries. Mr. Maddison could count himself fortunate to find the transcripts at all. With reference to the Lincoln transcripts J.S. Burn quotes from *Household Words*:

> "The Duplicate Parish Registers are tied up in the parcels in which they were sent, bundled into boxes, and those which had been written on parchment were regularly cut up for binding modern wills."[33]

The transcripts for Pembrokeshire were used in book-binding, so that very few remain for that county prior to 1799. In other diocese they have suffered from fire – those for the county of Dorset were so destroyed in 1731.

In the case of peculiars, not only were the transcripts seldom returned from many parishes, but even when they were made they fared even worse than the Bishop's Transcripts. This was partly because they were comparatively small in number in any single repository and partly because there was normally no official comparable with the

---

[30] The large Old Swinford transcripts were so used in Worcester Diocese, and as a result have been separated from their natural position in the yearly bundles.

[31] The Transcripts in the Bishop of Lincoln's Registry AASR, Vol.XVI, pt.2. pp 159-66.

[32] Cited by Miss. K. Major, op.cit.

[33] J.S. Burn op.cit. p.204 Footnote 4.

Diocesan Chancellor who was responsible for them. Thus, a complete series from a peculiar must be regarded as exceptional.

Present Custody and Arrangement of the Transcripts.

Because of their incompleteness, their relative inaccessibility and the fear that further losses might occur, numerous proposals were made from time to time that the Bishop's Transcripts should be collected in the Public Record Office, the Lambeth Library, Somerset House or elsewhere. More recently, however, they have been increasing deposited in County Record Offices, or at other recognised repositories, such as Gloucester City Library or the Bodleian Library Oxford. Nevertheless the transcripts from the peculiars are, of cours often in a different repository from the main series and furthermore, as transcripts were moved in the past from place to place, some becam separated from the main series and were left behind. Thus, the National Library of Wales still holds some transcripts for the deanery of Oswestry, the others having been moved to Lichfield when the Deanery was transferred to that Diocese on the Establishment of the Church of Wales.

These are perhaps cases where the archivist's guiding principle of the sanctity of archive groups might be slightly modified. If the existing holders of such transcripts are reluctant to part with them, this is however, quite understandable. Perhaps more than any other genealogical source material, except perhaps the surrendered Nonconformist Registers, the Bishop's Transcripts have suffered from archive groups being torn asunder. Thus the Norfolk Bishop's Transcripts now in the custody of the Norfolk County Archivist were disarranged some time before the last war by a person who obviously had scant knowledge either of Genealogy or Archives. Similarly, the original order of the Worcester Bishop's Transcripts by year and then Deanery was thoroughly disrupted in 1878 and the transcripts were rearranged by parish with no regard for date order.[34]

Of course it must be remembered that in many dioceses the transcripts were kept from the start with a "parish" rather than a "year" arrangement, and in many cases it is now impossible to tell whether the parish bundles reflect the original filing or a later rearrangement. However, the fact remains that in most dioceses the transcripts are now kept in parish order.

From the genealogist's rather than the archivist's point of view, there are advantages and disadvantages in both the parish and yearly

---

[34] The modern archivist's insistence on the sanctity of archive groups and the irritation felt by E.H. Sargeant, Worcestershire County Archivist with regard to the work done in 1878 provides an interesting contrast to the view of Dr. Cox in 1910. "In a few dioceses the extant transcripts have of late years been well arranged notably those of Worcester, and to a considerable extent of Lincoln." Cox op.cit. p.241-2.

arrangement. The rearrangement at Worcester and elsewhere had the
effect of destroying the year/deanery arrangement and thus making
the consultation of transcripts of the whole diocese or a whole
deanery for a particular year virtually impossible; it is therefore
particularly difficult for users to check information unless they
have the names of the actual parishes concerned. It also left certain
transcripts with no clear place names virtually unidentifiable. The
transcripts in a miscellaneous bundle at Hertford County Record
Office were identified finally by reference to T.F. Allen's Card
Index of Hertfordshire Marriages, but few counties are so fortunate.
However, on the other hand, the parish arrangement does make a check
of the parish register with the Bishop's Transcripts a simple matter,
such a check as we have seen, not infrequently revealing variations
or even entirely new entries. Thus, searchers can "fill in"
missing years from the parish register or even years when the whole
register is missing.

Above all, a parish rather than a yearly arrangement of the
transcripts is almost a necessity for the thorough transcriber of
a parish register, an enormous amount of labour in locating each
year's transcript otherwise being involved. It is, perhaps because
in some dioceses the transcripts are arranged annually that there
are so many inadequate parish register copies, where obviously
there has been no attempt to check doubtful readings against the
transcripts.

The Value of Bishop's Transcripts.

Emphasis has already been placed on the value of Bishop's
Transcripts in "filling in" entries missing in the parish register
or in clarifying doubtful readings. It is, of course, by no means
unusual for the transcripts to go back to an earlier period than the
existing originals. In some cases transcripts are preserved where
churches and registers have disappeared altogether. Thus, there are
a number of very early transcripts for some of the Gloucester City
parishes whose churches were destroyed or taken down at the time of
the siege in 1643. Invariably, no parish registers remain but the
transcripts enable us to learn about the families of Gloucester
before the Siege. Nor is it only the genealogist who finds such
transcripts useful. These Gloucester transcripts have been particularly
helpful to the local historian in the information given about the
earliest pin-makers, who commenced the trade in Gloucester in 1626
in those parishes now no longer in existence. Of course, whenever a
register is missing the Bishop's Transcripts can also supply useful
raw material for the historical demographer.

As well as the genealogist and the historian, lawyers have had
frequent recourse to Bishop's Transcripts to check suspected forgeries
in parish registers, and various cases are described at length by

J. S. Burn. [35]

Copies of Bishop's Transcripts are extremely useful if used with caution. Only too often the unwary searcher assumes that in searching a copy of the Bishop's Transcripts he avoids the necessity of examining the original registers. Unfortunately, this is seldom the case, as most dioceses have at least the odd year here and there missing in a series. Thus, although copies of Bishop's Transcripts are invaluable for checking register entries and filling in gaps, except in the case of a few dioceses they are only of limited value on their own.

Information on Bishop's Transcripts listed in the Index.

The amount of information on Bishop's Transcripts given in this index varies considerably from Diocese to Diocese. It depends on two factors – the degree of completeness of the transcripts and the extent to which they have been sorted and listed. Sometimes, as in the case of the Diocese of Bristol, where there is normally a fairly complete series for each parish except for a few odd missing years, it has been possible to list each individual year missing. Elsewhere, as in the case of the Diocese of Worcester, all gaps of four years or more are given, but minor gaps ignored. Occasionally, where there are a very large number of gaps, only missing periods of ten years or more have been noted. Some Bishop's Transcripts are, at the time of going to press still in the process of being sorted and listed and in some, the process of sorting and listing has hardly begun. Thus, in the case of the Diocese of Gloucester, only the starting years have been given and for the Diocese of Lichfield starting and terminal dates only. Occasionally, the amount of information given varies within one Diocese. In the Diocese of Hereford, most of the Herefordshire transcripts have been listed and all missing years have been noted. For the majority of the Shropshire parishes in the Diocese, however, it has been possible to list only overall dates. The exact amount of information given is explained in each County Preface, and it is important that readers using more than one county should be familiar with the procedure adopted in each.

---

[35]   op. cit. pp. 205-206.

VI   MODERN COPIES AND INDEXES OF PARISH REGISTERS AND BISHOP'S TRANSCRIPTS

The continual loss of original parish registers makes their transcription a matter of extreme urgency. Even when a reasonably connected series of Bishop's Transcripts exists, almost invariably some years are missing and in any case the Bishop's Transcripts may not contain all the data in the original. Not infrequently, a register is lost of which no copy of any kind is in existence. Thus, the compilation of the *National Index* has been in many respects depressing. In every county fresh losses have continually come to light and it is imperative that some copy whether printed, typescript, manuscript or microfilm should be made of every register. That this is by no means an impossible objective has been shown by the extensive work already done in many counties; it merely needs a co-ordinated effort by a number of people.

Transcription and Printing - A Historical Summary

The transcription of registers to ensure a security duplicate is of course nothing new and can be dated back to the Injunctions of 1597 and 1603 which inaugurated the general keeping of Bishop's Transcripts. However, as has been pointed out elsewhere these were very irregularly kept and preserved even after the 1812 act ordered their proper return.[1] Apart from these, until the 19th century copies of registers were exceedingly rare, though there are a few copies of extracts dating back to the 18th century. In 1791 a Mr. Lucas, a surgeon at Leeds possessed "a very neat and correct transcript of the registers of *Leeds* from the year 1572"[2] but this must have been almost unique.

In the 1820's Sir Thomas Phillips had a few partial registers printed at Middle Hall[3] and in 1833 recommended to the

---

See article on *Bishop's Transcripts* pp.175–180.
An Impartial Enquiry into the Present State of Parochial Registers (Leeds 1791) p.129.
Durnford, Wilts 1574-1650 (1823) *Bretforton*, Glos. M1538-1752, *Tref Eglwys*, Montgomeryshire 1695-6, *Leek Wotton*, Warwickshire 1685-1742 and *God's Hospital Chapel, Hull*, Yorks from 1695.

Chairman of the Parliamentary Select Committee that all registers previous to 1700 should be transferred to the British Museum and a modern transcript made at the expense of the parish. [4] Nothing came of this suggestion and by 1850 only one further partial register had been printed. [5]

In 1850 in a paper read before the statistical society Rev. E. Wyatt Edgell proposed that *all* registers should be transcribed and printed, but as James T. Hammack pointed out[6]

> "The want of funds to defray the cost of copying and printing is the one great difficulty of the plan."

There was some scepticism as to whether Parliament might be persuaded to provide these. Another correspondent wrote[7]

> "Parliament might perhaps be induced to vote an annual grant for so important a work till it was accomplished; albeit when we think of their niggardly denial of anything to the printing or even the conservation of the public records, sanguine hopes from that quarter can hardly be indulged."

However, he thought that complete transcription in manuscript was well within the bounds of possibility:

> "To insure correctness, without which the scheme would be utterly valueless, I would propose that a certain number of competent transcribe: be appointed for each county, either at a given salary or at a remuneration of so much per entry, to copy the registers of those parishes the ministers of which are unwilling to do it, or feel themselves unequal to the task. The option, however, should always in the first instance be given to the minister, as the natural custos of the registers, and as one, from local knowledge likely to do the work correctly. To each count: there should also be appointed one or more competent persons as collator: to correct the errors of the transcribers."

Six years later, however, the possibility of persuading the gover ment to print all parish registers was still being seriously urged:

> "The necessity of having all the parish registers transcribed and printed is universally admitted..... an undertaking too gigantic for private enterprise; and from its national importance, should be done at government expense. If some of your readers were to bring the matter before Parliament, there is no doubt it would be sanctioned at once. The affair must not again be allowed to sleep, as from the state of many of the registers, every week is of importance..... I only wish to urge the *immediate necessity* of having it done some way."[8]

This letter provoked a certain amount of correspondence. The magnitud

---

[4] J.S. Burn. *History of Parish Registers of England* (1862) p. 267.
[5] *Denton,* Durham 1586-1662 (1842).
[6] *N & Q.* 1st Ser. Vol. 1. p. 443 (1850).
[7] L.B.L. *N & Q.* 1st Ser. Vol. 2. pp. 1-3 (1850).
[8] *N & Q.* 2nd Ser. Vol. 2. p. 66 (1856).

of the problem was shown by J.S. Burn's correct claim:

> "I believe the only entire register printed verbatim is that printed by me – the "*Livre des Anglois à Genève*".

He pointed out the difficulties of printing every parish register and concluded:

> "I suggest therefore that only registers prior to 1700 should be printed and that they should be printed verbatim"[9]

Edward Peacock wrote;

> "The best course to pursue would be..... to have them all printed, but the expense would be so very great that I despair of ever seeing the project put into execution. If manuscript copies were taken and deposited in the General Register Office a great point would be gained, but really some immediate provision should be made for the safe custody of the originals."[10]

The following year a bill was prepared and printed proposing that particulars of all baptisms, marriages and burials from 1750 to 1837 should be copied on paper to be furnished by the Registrar-General and sent to the General Registry Office in London. The clergyman was to be paid a certain sum per thousand entries, and the amount when audited by the Registrar-General to be paid out of the poor rates of the parish.[11] This was criticised by J.S. Burn:

> "It is the ancient registers which want copying, not those since Lord Hardwicke's Marriage Act 1753 and which are in tolerably good preservation."[12]

He now supported the proposal that copies should be made up to 1754 and deposited at the Bishop's registry with the proviso that

> "The Bishop might have power to limit the extent of the copy to the year 1650 or 1700, if it should be shown that all the subsequent Register Books were in good state and condition and that a transcript thereof exists in the Bishop's Registry."[13]

The proposed bill was dropped and nothing came of any of the alternative suggestions, some of which were quite ambitious such as the proposal of 1857 that after the registers had all been centralised the pages should all be numbered and separate consolidated indexes should be prepared for the periods 1538-1600, 1601-1700, 1701-1800, 1801-1837 with the following columns: *Surname, Christian Name(s), Parish, County, Year, Number of Book, Page.*[14] Today after another

---

[9] *N & Q.* 2nd Ser. Vol.2. p.118 (1856).
[10] *N & Q.* 2nd Ser. Vol.2. p.151.
[11] J.S. Burn *op.cit.* p.267.
[12] *ibid.* p.268.
[13] *ibid.* p.269.
[14] *N & Q.* 2nd Ser. Vol.3. p.324.

century's indifference to the problem, this proposal may seem naïve, but it must be remembered that the 1812 Act had directed Diocesan Registrars to make proper indexes of the Bishop's Transcripts, so the principle was hardly revolutionary. At the same time agitation for the printing of registers continued. In 1868, F. FitzHenry proposed the formation of a *Parish Register Society*,[15] but J.S. Burn finally came out against any general printing.

> "The printing of a vast number of uninteresting registers..... would be an enormous expense without a corresponding benefit to the public."[16]

For the time being the whole question of transcription was subordinated to the more urgent problem of ensuring the safe custody of registers, and a committee was in fact appointed to draw up another bill.[17]

By 1878 there were still only a handful of manuscript copies at the *College of Arms*, the *British Museum* and in private hands, and only two further registers had been printed – that of *Somerset House Chapel* 1714-1776 (1862) and, curiously, *Wisbech*, Cambridgeshire General Baptist Church (1860). The year 1878 was a turning point. In that year the *Harleian Society* formed a register section which published the entire registers of *Canterbury Cathedral* 1564-1878, and followed this with the registers of the *City of London* churches. Many other registers were privately printed in the 1880's by F.A. Crisp and others. Finally, in 1889 the *Congress of Archaeological Societies* in union with the *Society of Antiquaries* appointed a Committee to consider the best means of assisting transcription and publication. This caused a great acceleration in the work but unfortunately in their *"Suggestions as to Transcriptions"* printed as an appendix to their first report (1892)[18] the committee suggested 1812 as a suitable point to which registers should be copied, and this resulted in a large number of copies being made and many printed with a gap of 25 years untranscribed before the beginning of Civil Registration. This precedent has, regrettably been followed since by many other excellent series such as that produced by the Bedfordshire County Council. In 1895, E.A. Fry revived the idea of a *Parish Register Society*,[19] and a vigorous correspondence followed in the columns of *"Notes and Queries."* W.P.W. Phillimore suggested that the *Harleian Society register section* should be re-organized to become a book publishing society open to all. He supported the idea of 1812 as a terminal date and felt strongly that only marriages should be printed

---

[15] *N & Q.* 4th Ser. Vol.2. p.118.
[16] *N & Q.* 4th Ser. Vol.2. p.142.
[17] *ibid* p.262.
[18] *Report on the Transcription and Publication of Parish Registers* (1892).
[19] *N & Q.* 8th Ser. Vol.8. p.13.

s these formed only one thirteenth or fourteenth of the average
arish register. Indexing also should not be regarded as urgent.[20]
rnest Brand considered that the best way of securing the printing
f registers on a large scale was to try to persuade incumbents to
rint them in the parish magazine, as had been done in the case of
arrow.[21] However, in spite of these dissentient voices,largely
hrough the efforts of G.W. Marshall the Rouge Croix Pursuivant of
,rms and a member of the Parish Register Committee, the *Parish
Register Society* was formed that year, and decided in favour of print-
ng complete registers. Mr. Phillimore therefore continued independ-
ntly with his own scheme for printing marriages only. In 1896 the
arish Register Committee optimistically reported[22]

> "The Committee..,.. have great pleasure in calling attention to the
> large increase in the number of transcripts made; many of these, there
> is reason to believe, owe their existence to the help and stimulous
> given by the former Report..... It appears to the Committee that the
> evidence supplied by this Supplemental List shows the supposed impos-
> sibility of ever transcribing the whole of the Parish Registers of the
> Kingdom is imaginary, and that by enlisting and encouraging local effort,
> the very desirable object may be obtained at no great distance of
> time."

There was some cause for this optimism. In addition to the five
olumes which the *Parish Register Society* had already printed
hillimore's *Gloucestershire Marriages* was in process of being
rinted, and volumes for Hants, Kent, Northants, Notts and Somerset
ere in active preparation. Numerous manuscript copies had been made,
he work of J. Harvey Bloom and A.S. Scott Gatty being pre-eminent.

In 1900 G.W. Marshall produced the first comprehensive list of
arish Register Copies[23] which was fairly substantial, though the
ajority of references were in fact to extracts.

The twentieth century saw the formation of county Parish Register
ocieties in Durham and Northumberland, Buckinghamshire, Shropshire,
taffordshire and Lancashire and local archaeological societies took
n active part in transcription work. More recently, county archivists
ave also given active encouragement, Bedfordshire showing the way
ith Emmison's series covering two-thirds of the registers of the
ounty up to 1812. Thus, since 1878 the devoted work of genealogists,
lergymen, antiquarians, local historians and archivists who have
pent countless hours transcribing and indexing registers, has not

20 *N & Q.* 8th Ser. Vol.8. p.173.
21 *N & Q.* 8th Ser. 8. p.373.
22 2nd Report.
23 *Parish Registers – A List of those Printed or of which Ms Copies exist in
Public Collections* (Parish Register Society, London 1900).

only provided copies of many registers no longer in existence but has made the pursuit of genealogy incomparably easier. However, unfortunately rising printing costs in this century have reduced the printing of registers to a mere trickle, most of the Parish Register Societies have ceased to exist and few archaeological societies and local historical societies now engage in transcription work. [24] However the *Staffordshire Parish Register Society* and the *Shropshire Archaeological Society* are still very active. The latter has now almost completed the work of supplementing the printed volumes of the *Shropshire Parish Register Society* with manuscript, typescript, and in more recent years microfilm copies of the remaining registers up to 1837. This fine collection is kept at the Shrewsbury Borough Library and other libraries also have good collections, among the best being those of the *Guildhall Library*, the *Shakespeare Birthplace Trust, Stratford-upon-Avon* and the *Bodleian Library, Oxford*. The *College of Arms* has a fine collection both of extracts and complete transcripts. Among them are the 87 volumes of extracts made by Colonel Chester. However these are not of course available to the public. Nevertheless increasingly since the Second World War the main burden of copying has fallen on the *Society of Genealogists*, and in recent years, the *Church of Jesus Christ of Latter Day Saints*.

The Society of Genealogists

Since its inception in 1911 the *Society of Genealogists* has placed considerable emphasis on transcription work. Many of the members have needed little prompting and have worked indefatigubly. Some transcribers have taken on a whole county or diocese almost single-handed, such as the work of the late Sir T. Collyer Ferguson on registers of the diocese of Rochester, of E. Roe on Gloucestershire marriages, of T.F. Allen on Hertfordshire marriages and of J.S.W. Gibson on Oxfordshire registers. Some, such as the late W.H. Challen have extended their activities more thinly over several counties and others have laboured for years on whatever work was most urgent at the time. Thus H.N. Peyton, C.V. Appleton and the late K.V. Elphinsto have transcribed registers from all over the country whether they hav had a particular interest in the area or not. However, enormous thoug the contribution of these dedicated individuals has been, much of the transcription work has been done by a large number of persons with only a limited amount of time available.

As a result of all this voluntary work, the Society now has copie

---

[24] An encouraging exception is the *Banbury Historical Society* which is publishing Banbury registers.

of parts of several thousand registers.

Photostating

The mass photographing of registers was proposed as long ago as 1887. In *Notes and Queries*, J.W. Watson wrote:[25]

"It is hopeless to expect that some 10,000 volumes will ever be printed at the public expense. But a process of photo-zincography or photography has been suggested as practicable for their re-production, and more recently it has been stated that the collotype process secures an absolute facsimile and that the cost of copying would be infinitely less than the cost of a mere transcription – something under sixpence a folio."

Since then photostats of a number of registers have been made and of parts of many more. However, it has proved too expensive to be undertaken on any scale.

Microfilming

This has tended to replace photostating as a means of securing an exact copy of the original. Surprisingly, this too was suggested for parish registers in 1887. Following the publication of Mr. Watson's proposal an anonymous correspondent to *Notes and Queries* wrote:

"It appears that the Americans are now preparing a dictionary to eclipse even Dr. Murray's labours and being cumbered with much "copy" have had the whole 40,000 sheets, not slips copied and reduced by photographic process. The whole mass lies quietly in one drawer. Could not our registers be so reduced?"[26]

However, relatively little microfilming was done until the Second World War, when large scale work was undertaken by the *Committee for Microfilming Parish Registers*. This independent body envolved almost by accident from a Committee originally set up by the Society of Genealogists in 1939 to compile a *National Index of Parish Register Copies*.

Following the publication of this work with the aid of a grant from the *Pilgrim Trust* it was the intention to form an association to deal exclusively with Parish Registers, their preservation, duplication, printing etc., the Council of which was to be composed of people in touch with the various Parish Register and Record Societies having an interest in this subject. Unfortunately the war began before the association could be formed, and although many distinguished people had expressed their willingness to serve on the Council of such a body, the general opinion was that the moment was not propitious

---

[25] *7th Ser.* III p.343.
[26] A.H. *N & Q.* 7th Ser. III p.521.

to launch a new enterprise. The position then was that parish registers might be destroyed by enemy action without any copy having been taken unless members of the Committee originally concerned with the production of the *National Index of Parish Register Copies* undertook the work of getting parish registers micro-filmed and the informa tion they contain thus safeguarded. Thus the *Committee for Micro-filming Parish Registers* was set up under the Chairmanship of Viscount Mersey. This was supported by the *Society of Genealogists,* but the money to carry on the work was principally given by the *Pilgrim Trust* and it was emphasized that the films were made solely with the purpose of ensuring that a copy of hitherto unique parish registers survived the war.[27] The Society therefore had no interest whatsoever in the films and members were not allowed access to them. Where possible, the films were kept in a place approved by the Bishop of the Diocese.

Up to September 1940, the photography was done at a studio in London. Thereafter, local centres were set up and an operator sent to work on the spot. The Archbishops of Canterbury and York agreed to be patrons of the Committee, and Messrs Lever Brothers and Unilevers Ltd, placed their apparatus and operator at Unilever House, Blackfriars at the disposal of the Committee for the purpose of micro-filming the registers of London Churches. However, only a small percentage of London Parishes took advantage of this. Nevertheless, by March 1943 registers of 1500 parishes had been micro-filmed.

After a long period of uncertainty the *British Records Association* into whose hands many of these microfilms eventually passed, have distributed them to county archivists though not all those originally made are at present fully accounted for.

The Church of Jesus Christ of Latter Day Saints

The work of the *Committee for Microfilming Parish Registers* extensive though it was pales into insignificance beside the work of the *Church of Jesus Christ of Latter Day Saints*. In the last ten years they have been engaged in microfilming on an unprecendented scale parish registers and Bishop's Transcripts as well as much other genealogical source material, about 4000 reels of film being taken in England every year. The *Genealogical Society, Salt Lake City* thus has the largest genealogical collection in the world, consisting of about 600 million pages of microfilm.[27a]

---

[27]   In spite of this, there was some suspicion concerning the Committee's motives as was shown by a letter in *N & Q.* Vol.179 p.316 (1940) to which Mrs. Blomfield made a vigorous reply.

[27a] See J & R Cunningham *The Genealogical Work of the Latter-Day Saints* Gen. Mag. Vol. 14. No.11 (Sept. 1964) and A.F. Bennett *The Microfilming Activities of the Genealogical Society of the Church of Jesus Christ of Latter-Day Saints* Archivum Vol.9 (1959) pp.121-123.

The Institute of Heraldic and Genealogical Studies, Canterbury

This non-profit making organisation has launched the ambitious project of compiling a *British Vital Records Index* of all Baptisms, Marriages and Burials before 1837. Transcription and indexing is initially being organised using the Deanery as a unit, and the Society of Genealogists will receive a copy of all transcripts and indexes made.

Pitfalls in the Use of Copies

If the strongest reason for the making of copies is the possibility of loss or damage to the original, the question of convenience is none the less extremely important. Instead of having to travel to distant parishes one can inspect the copy in a library and in the case of a microfilm this should, in theory, be as satisfactory as searching the original, although the difficulties of interpreting handwriting are still present. In the case of printed, typescript and manuscript copies. this problem is overcome and in many cases there are reliable indexes, thus reducing searching time to a minimum. However, all copies and especially indexes must be used with caution, for the pitfalls are numerous and serious. Some of the more important of these are as follows:

1. *Mistranscription of Surnames*

Not infrequently the transcriber has misinterpreted surnames. *Turk* may appear as *Lurk, Tennison* as *Fennison, Boud* as *Bond* or *Cock* as *Cook*.[28] Sometimes the errors are even more serious, *Sussex* has been found as *Lupez, Hawkins* as *Harrokins* and *Felbridge* as *Selfridge*. In the printed register of *Madron,* Cornwall twice the surname *Heex* appears and it is indexed as a variant of *Hicks*. From the Bishop's Transcripts it is apparent that it is a misreading for *Hooper*.[29] Although such errors are most commonly found in copies of 16th and 17th century registers, they are not infrequent even in copies of 19th century entries.[30] In particular the printed volumes published by Phillimore vary a great deal in reliability. These transcriptions were undertaken by volunteers (often the vicar or his wife) who not infrequently had more goodwill than palaeographic skill. The printed marriage register of Eversley, Hants, not only leaves out two marriages

---

[28] D.E. Gardner & F. Smith. *Genealogical Research in England and Wales.* Vol.1. p.176.
[29] *Gen. Mag.* Vol.1. No.4. p.121 (Dec.1925).
[30] A classification of surname variants, several of which arise through faulty reading is given in *Parish Registers and the Genealogist* pp.139–140.

completely, but has a truly imposing list of errors, among them the following:

Ezitt for *Hill* 1639	*Merry* for *Mercy*
Alfredus for *Humphredus* 1619	*Backe* for *Bathe* 1671
Setlar for *Sellon* 1630	*Coss* for *Cox* 1673
Lovewye for *Lovejoye* 1592	*Sawer* for *Saucer* 1676
Claverton for *Staverton* 1563	*Saber* for *Saser* 1695
Pither for *Rither* 1597	*Parran* for *Parrant* 1706
Payer for *Payce* or *Payte* 1626	*Eager* for *Caser* 1715
Trigg for *Crigg*	*Laws* for *Tewse* 1716
Annerley for *Annesley* 1636	*Patkild* for *Patfield* 1727
Gilbert for *Gibbon* 1637	*Cauteret* for *Carteret*[31]

Nor are transcriptions undertaken by local Societies often any more reliable. The Marriages of *Norton*, Hertfordshire, were published in the *Proceedings of the East Hertfordshire Archaeological Society*. In comparing this copy with the original register, Mr. T.F. Allen found no less than 48 cases of incorrect renderings of surnames, as well as 5 marriages entirely omitted.

Some of the renderings are quite extraordinary, as is shown by the following examples

March for *Crouch*	*Cocke* for *Kerke*
Hart for *Start*	*Sacbut* for *Tarbut*
Reinold for Searle	*Hursberry* for *Trusteram*
Wages for *Negus*	*Kitchiner* for *Fitzjohn*[32]

Even the *Harleian Society* registers though undertaken by more experienced palaeographers contain transcription errors. For example in *Christ Church, Newgate Street, London*[33] is recorded the burial on 18th August 1579 of

"Richard Ingge, paynter to the Queen's Majesty at St. Faith's Church under Powle's"

This should be Richard *Jugge*, the Queen's *printer*. When his widow was buried, the profession was given correctly but the name incorrectly. 28 August 1588

Mrs Inges in the parish of St. Faith's under St. Pauls whose husband

---

[31] This list is taken from *N & Q*. 155 pp. 386-7.
[32] Letter of T.F. Allen. *Gen. Mag.* Vol. 12 p. 101.
[33] *Harl. Soc.* **xxi** p. 274.

was sometime printer to our sovereign Lady Queen Elizabeth.[34]

Mr. W.P. Fletcher points out[35] some of the most likely errors concern the initial Z[36] and the letter " c " which in the court hand of the latter 16th century are easily mistaken for " S " and t. Thus the name *Zouche* and variant spellings has been transcribed not only as *Souche* and variants such as *Such, Sooch, Sutch* or *Soach* but also as *South*. The omission of a cross stroke on the Z also has led to the name being transcribed and indexed as *Louch, Lowth* etc. Thus a Marriage Allegation at the Consistory Court of Bath and Wells reads:

> 1676 July 27, Mr. William Wadden clerk, Rector of Marksbury and Mary Zouch of Littlecott parish of Ramsbury, Wilts spinster 30. Marriage to take place at Tiverton, Corston or St. Peter and St. Paul, Bath.

The typescript copy of the register of *Tiverton,* Devon reads:

> 1676 July 27, William Wadden of Marsbury (sic) and Mary Louth of Rainsbury (sic) Wilts.

In the Index Library *Calendar of Marriage Licences* issued in London appears:

> 1668 June 13 John Louch and Hannah Boyse.

The transcript of the *Knightsbridge,* Middlesex register reads:

> John Souch and Hannah Boil.

It is interesting to note that it is not only transcribers of registers who have misread these letters. The families themselves have sometimes adopted spellings such as *Such*.

2. *Copy made from Another's Copy or a Rough Draft*

The transcription may in fact be a retranscription from a copy and not correlated with the original register. Thus the first transcriber's errors have been perpetuated and perhaps fresh ones added. Many direct transcriptions have in any case probably gone through two stages – the original rough draft made perhaps in a rough notebook in the vestry and the neatly written or typed finished copy. Thus there have been at least two chances of errors being made.

---

[34] p. 282 *Paynter* for *printer* was a not infrequent error. cf. *Smyth's Obituary* (Camd. Soc. 1849) ed. Sir Henry Ellis p. 77. where is recorded the death on 5th Oct. 1667 of Roger Daniell, " paynter in London and sometime heretofore at Cambridge " etc. He was University printer at Cambridge. Cited in *N & Q.* 9th Ser. 11. pp. 326-7 (1903). Other errors in Harleian Society registers are *Landtoft* instead of *Sandtoft* (xviii p. 9) and *Sararia* instead of *Saravia* (xxv p. 90).

[35] *Some Hazards of Palaeography* Gen. Mag. Vol. 12 No. 14 June 1958.

[36] Initial " T " and " F " have also been confused. *See below* under *Indexes* p. 199.

3. *Misinterpretation of Entries*

A surname may be misinterpreted as the person's trade or vice versa. Thus, *William Saunders Nailor* was transcribed as *William Saunders, nailor,* and indexed under the surname of *Saunders* instead of under Nailor.[37]

The misinterpretation of course may be by the searcher rather than the transcriber.[38]

4. *Incomplete Copy*

This may be coupled with a misleading title which gives the impression that the copy is more comprehensive than in fact it is.

(a) *Some Years Omitted*

The Lancashire Parish Register Society published in 1910 *The Registers of the Parish of Walton-le-dale in the County of Lancaster, Baptisms, Burials and Marriages 1609-1812* with the note that "this volume contains an exhaustive index to the names of all persons mentioned in it."

However, the index in the printed volume covering 1609-1812 includes no reference to Ellen Southworth, born in Walton-le-dale, 20th August 1809. It would be reasonable to assume either that she was baptized after 1812, or else in another parish. However, despite the title page stating the book contains baptisms, marriages and burials, 1609-1812 it actually contains: baptisms and burials *from the Bishop's Transcripts* from 1609-1641 and from the *original parish register* from 1653 to December 1808, marriages from the *Bishop's Transcripts* 1609-1641 and from the *original parish registers* from 1654 to December 1812. The years that are missing in the baptisms include the year 1809 in which Ellen Southworth was born. When the original parish registers for 1809-1812 were searched, the baptism was discovered.[39]

In compiling the *National Index of Parish Registers*, all printed, typescript and manuscript copies held by the *Society of Genealogists* (though not in all other repositories) have been carefully checked. The years covered by baptisms, marriages and burials have been noted and if necessary broken down between the part covered by the parish registers and that covered by the Bishop's Transcripts. Often, however,

---

[37] D.E. Gardner and F. Smith *op.cit.* p.179.
[38] See *"Parish Registers and the Genealogist"* p.143.
[39] This example has been taken from D.E. Gardner and F. Smith *op.cit.* Vol.1.pp.177-178.

the reader must refer to the description of the original registers
to discover gaps in the original and hence in the copy, though of
course other gaps left by the transcriber have been noted. However,
some misleading descriptions, such as the example quoted may have
escaped notice and it would be wise for the searcher to check.

(b) *Misplaced entries overlooked*

Mr. Willis observes:

" In examining the registers of a parish from which the marriages
had been printed, I found a marriage in amongst the burials which had
not been found by the editor of the printed volume."[40]

The transcriber of the *Devon and Cornwall Record Society* copy of
Slapton, Devon overlooked a number of years in the mid-18th century
which were misplaced in the register.

(c) *Extracts*

Some 19th century copies may in fact be only extracts even if
they appear fairly voluminous. In such cases the preface may well
have a note to the effect that "all entries have been copied with
the exception only of persons obviously of the very humblest station."[41]

(d) *Details omitted*

Most parish register copies are not verbatim copies, but list
all entries in an abbreviated form. In some cases information may
have been omitted. For example, the printed marriage register for the
parish of *Mansfield*, Nottinghamshire, lists the following entries:

11th July 1782 Edward Marshall married Ann Simes
6th May 1788 Thomas Humphrey married Sarah Webster

However, the entries in the original parish register read:

11th July 1782 Edward Marshall of Mansfield, framework knitter, aged
26 years, a bachellor and Ann Simes of Mansfield, aged 40 years,
a spinster.

6th May 1788 Thomas Humphrey of Mansfield aged 51 years a bachelor and
Sarah Webster of Mansfield, aged 34 years a spinster.

The printed marriage register of *Lanlivery*, Cornwall gives

11th June 1774 William Udy,y. and Isabella Varcoe, Lic.

---

40 A.J. Willis. *Genealogy for Beginners* p.30.
41 This also applies to published volumes of Marriage Licences. See p.237.

The original parish register shows:

> June 11th 1774 William Udy, Yeoman of this parish and **Isabella Varcoe**, Widow of this parish were married by licence.
> They signed *William Udy, Isabella Varcoe*
> Witnesses signed *Walter Hill, Joseph Lukey*.

Prior to obtaining the certified copy of the entry of marriage various unseccessful attempts had been made to trace the christening of an Isabella *Varcoe*. She was actually born Isabella *Pearse*, under which name she had married a George Varcoe in 1769.[42] The omission of the status of *widow* is unfortunately not uncommon in printed copies and if the copy does not give the full entry of marriage as recorded in the original parish register, it is always wise to obtain a certified copy of the entry.

A large number of otherwise extremely reliable transcriptions of marriages omit the names of witnesses although very frequently at least one was a relative whose name may provide a vital clue.[43]

5. *Failure to Correlate Register with Bishop's Transcripts*

The majority of copies are probably of the Parish Register only or at best the Bishop's Transcripts may have been used only for some period before the start of the registers. In using the copy the searcher may assume he has adequately covered the parish and period concerned. This may be far from the case.

(a) *Illegible parts of the register not copied*

The title page for a typescript copy of the parish registers of *Llanglydwen,* Caermarthenshire, indicates it is a copy of baptisms and burials from 1765 to 1909 and of marriages from 1755 to 1840. It does not state that portions of the baptism and burial registers were unreadable to the transcriber. The copy has been indexed and if one should check the index for *John Blethin* (born in 1787) no mention of his name appears. However, a check of the text of the typescript copy shows that much of the parish register prior to 1793 was lost or illegible. The entry was in fact found in the Bishop's Transcripts.[44]

(b) *Gaps in the Parish Register*

The Phillimore printed copy of the marriages of *Thornbury*

---

[42] These examples have been taken from D.E. Gardner and F. Smith *op.cit.* Vol.I. pp.182-183.
[43] C.R. Humphery-Smith has encountered one case in which the printed register gave the "marriage" of the groom to one of the witnesses – also male!
[44] D.E. Gardner and F. Smith *op.cit.* Vol.I. p.178.

Gloucestershire, states that there were no marriages between 15th February 1663/4 and 2nd March 1669,'70. Mr. E.A. Roe, however, using the Bishop's Transcripts copied 81 marriages for this period. For two later gaps of 5¾ years and 9¼ years, Mr. Roe copied 39 and 71 marriages respectively in spite of one year's transcripts in each period being missing. [45]

(c) *More complete information in the Bishop's Transcripts overlooked*

As is pointed out elsewhere, [46] the Parish Register and the so-called "Transcripts" may be in fact both copies of some earlier text. Thus the transcript may not only have entries not in the register or additional information, but incorrect entries in the register may be given correctly. [47]

6. *Copy is from Bishop's Transcripts only*

This is the reverse side of the coin and even more insidious if not used with care.

(a) *Illegible parts of the Bishop's Transcripts*

Illegibility is probably more widespread among Bishop's Transcripts than Parish Registers. The latter have at least normally been protected by a cover and binding and been kept flat. Bishop's Transcripts have usually been folded and tied up in bundles, probably with string cutting the top and bottom few transcripts. The edges have frayed. This is normal wear and tear. In addition, they have often been rescued from the most extraordinary places. Where only the Bishop's Transcripts have been copied, one can assume many entries have been lost or multilated.

(b) *Gaps in Bishop's Transcripts*

Only too often the unwary searcher assumes that in searching a copy of the Bishop's Transcripts he avoids the necessity of examining the original registers. Unfortunately this is seldom true as even in the best series there are usually at least a few years missing and in many dioceses the missing years are numerous. However, the copy is often misleadingly described as *Baptisms, Marriages and Burials*

---

[45] Printed in *Gen. Mag.* Vol.13 p.246 Dec. 1960.
[46] See *Bishop's Transcripts* p.174 *Form and Content* pp.27–32.
[47] An example of this from the printed register of *Walton* near Liverpool (Lancashire Parish Register Society Vol.91) is given on p.174.

1660-1812 taken from the Bishop's Transcripts with little indication
on the title page of the degree of completeness of the transcripts.
Although the missing years will doubtless be noted in the text, if the
searcher used only the index he will have scant idea of how complete
the copy actually is.

(c) *Inaccuracy of Bishop's Transcripts*

The Bishop's Transcripts may have been hurriedly copied by an
inefficient clerk. Numerous entries may have been mistranscribed or
omitted.

(d) *Information is less than in Register*

This is more frequent than the reverse. There was often
"editorial" suppression of some details and sometimes of entire
entries, such as the baptisms of illegitimate children.

(e) *Witnesses omitted*

As with parish register copies the transcriber may have ignored
names of witnesses.

Although copies of Bishop's Transcripts are invaluable for checking register entries and filling in gaps, except in the case of a
few dioceses they are only of limited value on their own, although
they may of course give an indication that a family of the surname
sought was resident in the parish.

Indexes

Obviously an adequate index is a great time saver and indexes
of trades and parishes can also prove extremely useful. [48] Some parish
registers have been indexed with exceptional thoroughness sometimes by
the incumbent as an aid to searching the original register, and more
frequently as the complement of a copy of the registers. An excellent
example of the former is an index to the registers of *Rochdale*, Lancs.
1582-1801. Baptisms are indexed under the *child's name*, *father's name*,
and the *mother's name*, the marriages under both *husband* and *wife* and
the burials under the *person buried* and the *parent* or *husband* of the
deceased. [49]

---

[48] These were normally included in printed copies made by the *Parish Register Society* and most of the County Parish Register Societies. The *Harleian Society* included them in their later volumes.
[49] Henry Brierley. *N & Q.* 9th Ser. 2 p. 90 (1898).

However, such indexes are exceptional and many printed and manu-script registers are also unindexed. In 1928 this deficiency evoked a proposal in *Notes and Queries* for the formation of a *Parish Index Society*[50] which was supported by Mr. C.A. Higgins.[51] Although nothing came of this, the phenomenal work of Mr. Percival Boyd in compiling a general index of parish registers for the *Society of Genealogists* made such a society to some extent redundent, and his work has been continued by others.[52]

The task of indexing a parish register is an extremely thankless one and on the whole the average standard of indexing is higher than that of transcription. This is because it is a task requiring immense patience and common sense rather than palaeographic knowledge. How-ever, the following points should be borne in mind.

    (a) Entries may have been accidentally overlooked in making the index.

    (b) There may be more than one entry of the name on the page.

    (c) Names of Witnesses, though given in the copy, may not be in the index.

    (d) *Mistranscription of Surnames intensified by indexing.* The searcher of a register copy may well suspect that *Lurk* may have been a transcription error for *Turk* but the person who searches only an index is unlikely even to find the entry.

Thus for years Ellen Terry was unable to trace her birth certifi-cate at Somerset House, but it was finally located under *Ferry*. Con-versely, a Lady Jane *Ferry* appeared in the obituary columns of the *Gentleman's Magazine* of Sept. 1802 as Lady Jane *Terry*.[53]

(e) *Trade indexed as a Surname*

The transcription error quoted previously[54] was made much more serious by being indexed under *Nailor* instead of *Saunders*.

(f) *Additional Christian name indexed as a Surname*

The baptism of Margaret, daughter of John Hassell and Dorothy Gardner, was indexed incorrectly as Margaret *Hassall* instead of as Margaret *Gardner*, she being the daughter of *John Hassall Gardner* by his wife Dorothy.[55]

---

[50] Vol.155 p.386.
[51] *ibid* p.425.
[52] See below pp.201–205.
[53] Patrick Montague Smith. *Gen. Mag.* Vol.11. No.16. Dec.1954 pp.549–50. cf the transcription of *Zouche* as *South, Louth* etc. above p.193.
[54] *See above* page 194.
[55] This example is taken from D.E. Gardner and F. Smith *op.cit.* Vol.1, p.179.

(g) *Variant spellings not adequately cross indexed*

In the indexes the surname may have a variety of spellings. If they are checked under only one spelling, the correct index reference may be overlooked. If a thorough check under variants is not success- ful a careful search of the text of the register may reveal any unusual rendering of the surname of the family which was not evident when checking the index. [56]

(h) *Index to Bridegrooms only*

There are old indexes to original parish registers (often at the back of the register) that are misleading. Care must be taken to determine whether the index refers to all entries in the register. Thus the index to the parish register of *St. Peter's Liverpool* for 1821 does not refer to any marriage for a Margaret Wilson, but the marriage register contains the record of her marriage. A careful check of the index shows that it is an index for all the names of the males, with no mention of any females. As each marriage was registere the name and surname of the bridegroom was placed in the index under the initial letter of his surname. [57]

Indexing by Computer

Recently, the *Church of Jesus Christ of Latter Day Saints* has begun the indexing of registers by computer. The method used is of some interest. The register copies are typed by two different persons on to two punched tapes. These are then converted to two magnetic tapes which are matched by computer and a *print-out* made. Where the two do not match a third person checks the entry and gives both versions if necessary. Only baptisms and burials are being covered at present. The first *print-out* is chronological and then this is re- arranged alphabetically. An attempt to match baptism and burial entri has been made where the parents are given in both cases and about 11% success achieved; family groups are also being constructed from baptismal entries. About 2000 registers have so far been included, most being taken from printed copies.

'Interesting work in this field has also been carried out by R.E. Vine, a member of the Society of Genealogists. His prototype studies have been concerned not only with indexing, but also with the "printing" of registers, and an account of his work appears in the *Genealogists 'Magazine,* December 1967.

---

[56] For examples of variant spellings see *Parish Registers and the Genealogist.* pp. 139–140.
[57] D.E. Gardner and F. Smith *op. cit.* Vol. I. p. 180.

Boyd's Marriage Index[58]

This is a typewritten index of marriages from the Parish Registers, Bishop's Transcripts and Marriage Licences of the country, limited to the period 1538-1837. The index was almost totally compiled by the late Mr. Percival Boyd, M.A., F.S.A., F.S.G. (1866-1955) at his own expense, primarily for use of the Members of the Society of Genealogists, but also to aid the science of Genealogy as much as possible. With this latter aim in view copies of certain sections of the Index were given to various local repositories, e.g. the Devon and Cornwall sections to the Devon and Cornwall Record Society, the Durham section to Newcastle Public Library, the Middlesex section to the Guildhall Library, the Essex section to the Essex Record Office, and a complete copy to the College of Arms. A further complete copy of the Index is at the Genealogical Society, Salt Lake City. It is not known how many marriages are included, but it has been estimated at over seven millions. The Index gives only the year, the Surnames and Christian names of both parties and the parish where the marriage took place.

It should be remembered that the volumes are only *indexes* and that the parish register should always be referred to for full particulars of the entry. For example, in the Derbyshire Marriage Index for 1810 appears the following:-

1810   Wysall Robert   Mary Stanley   Pentrich

There is a corresponding entry under STANLEY because all names of brides as well as grooms have been indexed except in the case of Yorkshire and some periods of the two Miscellaneous Series (see below). The full entry appearing in the printed marriage registers for Pentrich reads:- *12 Apl.1810   Robert Whysall age 18 years to Mary Stanley age 21.*

Surname Variants

Boyd's Marriage Index is invaluable if used correctly. Only too frequently, however, a searcher fails to find references of interest because he has not fully grasped the system by which in his original index Mr. Boyd grouped surname variants under one spelling. Only the slips left untyped at Mr. Boyd's death, and subsequently typed by the library staff of the Genealogical Society, Salt Lake City, were arranged strictly alphabetically.

---

[58]   The sources used for this section have since formed the basis of the booklet *A List of Parishes in Boyd's Marriage Index* (1974).

Variations of the spelling of Surnames were generally treated under the following rules:

A. *Initial Letters*

Gh	see	G	Ku	see	Cu
Gn	"	N	Ll	"	l
Ka	"	Ca	Ph	"	F
Kl	"	Cl	Sc	"	Sk
Kn	"	N	Th (h silent) see T
Ko	"	Co	Wh	see	W
Kr	"	Cr	Wr	"	R

B. 1. Silent final e is ignored.
   2. Double letters as single, e.g. *Willson* see *Wilson*.
   3. For "cks", "x" is used e.g. *Hix* for *Hicks*.
   4. For "tch", "ch" is used, e.g. *Huchinson* for *Hutchinson*.
   5. "Y" is sorted as "i" and is written "y" at the end of a name "i" elsewhere, e.g. *Lily*.

C. The last syllable of names of more than one syllable is treated with some freedon:
   1. an, en, in, on, un.
   2. ar, er, or.
   3. field, feild, feld.
   4. bourn, born, burn.
   5. wood, wode, ward.
   6. bridge, brig.
   7. ey, ye, y, ie.
   8. el, al, ell, all, ale, le.
   9. ford, forth.
   10. son, sonn, sone, sonne. and so on.

The variations of a Surname should be studied with great care when using the Index.

Abbreviations of Christian Names

The abbreviations used are listed in Appendix II. Note especially the following: *Elnr* is used for both Eleanor and Helena; *Esth* for

Esther and Hester; *Sue* for Susan and Susanna(h); *Math* for Matthew and Matthias.

First Series (Counties)

The index is divided by Counties, the Counties covered with the number of parishes included in each, being as follows:

Cambridgeshire	170	Lancashire	101
Cornwall	202	London & Middlesex	160
Cumberland	34	Norfolk	146
Derbyshire	80	Northumberland	84
Devonshire	169	Shropshire	125
Durham	72	Somerset	120
Essex	374	Suffolk	489
Gloucestershire	121	Yorkshire	206

Each County is divided into ten. periods: 1500-1600, 1601-1625, 1626-1650, 1651-1675, 1676-1700, 1701-1725, 1726-1750, 1751-1775, 1776-1800, 1801-1837. In most cases the Counties are indexed under the names of the men and women separately (the two sections thus formed may be bound together, however, in one volume), but in some cases the men and women are indexed together.

Volumes indexing men only are marked   M
    "   "   women "   "   "   W
    "   "   men and women mixed are marked   –
    "   "   "   "   " separately marked   MW

Each volume of marriages should be carefully examined as there are in the first and second series sometimes two divisions within each volume.

Second Series (Miscellaneous)

Mr. Boyd commenced a Miscellaneous Section taken from other printed and manuscript transcripts then available including most of the printed calendars of Marriage Licences and the marriages in the *Gentleman's Magazine* and including many marriages from Counties not already partially covered by the main series. This ended with the volumes covering the period 1751-1775, the period 1701-1725 having covered men only, and that for 1726-1750 having covered men only A-M. The First Miscellaneous Series was bound in red to differentiate from the main series, which had been bound in green.

Third Series (Miscellaneous)

At the time of Mr. Boyd's death in 1955, over a million slips remained untyped. These were typed by the Library Staff of the

Genealogical Society, Salt Lake City, where they are now shelved as
the second part of England 131. At the Society of Genealogists'
Library they are with the main index. As has been pointed out, before
typing the Library Staff arranged them *strictly Alphabetically* an
arrangement different from that adopted by Mr. Boyd in typing the
first two series, and it is important that all surname variants
should be looked up.

Parishes Covered by all Three Series

It has been estimated that contained in all three series is the
following number of parishes;

Bedfordshire	8	Herefordshire	6	Shropshire	125
Berkshire	13	Hertfordshire	48	Somerset	123
Buckinghamshire	64	Huntingdonshire	16	Staffordshire	4
Cambridgeshire	170	Kent	129	Suffolk	492
Cheshire	18	Lancashire	103	Surrey	69
Cornwall	204	Leicestershire	140	Sussex	56
Cumberland	35	Lincolnshire	99	Warwickshire	30
Derbyshire	86	London & Middlesex	202	Westmorland	13
Devonshire	170	Norfolk	278	Wight, Isle of	28
Dorset	79	Northamptonshire	43	Worcestershire	40
Durham	73	Northumberland	82	Yorkshire	212
Essex	381	Nottinghamshire	161	Wiltshire	73
Gloucestershire	182	Oxfordshire	36		
Hampshire	107	Rutland	23	Total	4211

It must be borne in mind, however, that the marriage registers
of many of these parishes have been covered only in part, and that
copies of Extracts unreliable copies or defective Bishop's Transcript
may have been used as the source from which Index slips were made.

The periods covered by the Index are entered on the County lists
under the parishes in italics after the copies. With the exception of
Gloucestershire (see "Supplementary Indexes" below), the dates have
been taken from *"A Key to the Parishes included in Boyd's Marriage
Index"*, prepared by the Church of Jesus Christ of Latter Day Saints,
a copy of which is kept at the Society of Genealogists Library on the
shelves with the Boyd volumes. This is a somewhat fuller catalogue
than the Society's own 1963 Edition of *"A Key to Boyd's Marriage
Index"* and includes the dates of the parishes in the Miscellaneous
volumes not included in the latter. *Boyd Misc.* indicates that entries
from the parish are included in one of the two miscellaneous series.
The following symbols may be found after the dates:

(∗) indicates that the periods covered disagree with those listed in
    A Key to Boyd's Marriage Index, and that the dates shown are
those taken from Mr. Boyd's original note books.

(X) indicates that the parish is listed in the original note books, but not in *A Key to Boyd's Marriage Index*. This usually means that the entries for that parish will appear in either the second or third series.

(0) indicates that the parish is listed in *A Key to Boyd's Marriage Index* but does not appear in Mr. Boyd's original notes.

Supplementary Indexes.

1. *Gloucestershire Marriage Index.* The figure given for Gloucestershire on the above list is actually for the Gloucestershire Index compiled by E.A. Roe, which continues the work begun by Mr. Boyd. Only part of this Index is at present on the shelves of the Society of Genealogists with the main Boyd series, the remainder being with the Gloucestershire collection. It is important to note, however, that *"A Key to Boyd's Marriage Index"* lists overall dates for the complete index. The full details are explained in considerable detail in the preface to the Gloucestershire Section.[59]

2. *Index to Stray Registrations.* There are several volumes compiled by H.N. Peyton of stray registrations (i.e. persons married in parishes different from their places of origin). These may be extremely valuable in locating long sought after marriages.

3. *Oxfordshire Marriage Index.* Covering 142 parishes for all or part of the period 1538–1837, in one alphabetical sequence, and not split into 25-year periods as Boyd does. The copy at the Society of Genealogists is on microfilm, but the Bodleian Library also has a computer print-out.

4. *Hertfordshire Marriage Index.* This is a complete card index compiled by Mr. T.F. Allen from his own copies of Hertfordshire Marriages. It includes almost all known pre-1837 marriages in the county, and is deposited at the Hertford County Record Office.

Printed Marriage Indexes.

An index to Marriages in the *Gentleman's Magazine* 1731-68 was published in 1922.

C. Bernau's *16th Century Marriages* published in 1911 lists 25,000 names from 94 parishes.

---

[59] See Volume V pp.9–10.

Microfilms

Before making an intensive search, it is wise to make a quick check of the entire record on the roll of microfilm, and thus obtain an idea of how extensive the register may be and whether the baptisms marriages and burials are recorded together or separately. Such a pre-check will show whether an index is included or if the material is in logical sequence and easy to read. The following are the main pitfalls to look for:-

(a) *Errors in Filming*

Ideally microfilm copies are an exact copy of the register book, but in reality they are an exact copy only of the pages that are filmed. The completeness of the filming and the quality of the reproduction depends largely on the skill of the photographer and the condition of the page surfaces. When a search was made of a microfilm register it was discovered that an error had been made resulting in the omission of all marriages from April 1832 to May 1834 and from August 1835 to June 1837 involving the records of over one hundred marriages.

(b) *Gaps in Original Register*

It is important to watch for continuity. As the search of one page is completed, watch carefully that the next page follows in numerical and logical sequence. A mere search for the entries of a particular surname is not sufficient. The record may not be complete even if it is an accurate microfilm and one should look for gaps in the original which might be filled from the Bishop's Transcripts.[60]

---

[60] These points on microfilms are adapted from D.E. Gardner and F. Smith *op.cit.* Vol.I. pp.183-184.

APPENDIX I RECOMMENDATIONS FOR COPYING AND INDEXING PARISH REGISTERS.

As has been pointed out elsewhere, the Society of Genealogists lays considerable emphasis on the transcription of Parish Registers. Whilst experienced transcribers and indexers have developed their own particular techniques and preferences, not only may the beginner well feel that he needs some guidance, but it is clearly desirable that a consistent policy be pursued with regard to the many problems which arise.

Ideally, whenever a transcript is made, an index should also be prepared. In practice it may often be more convenient for it to be indexed later by another volunteer who lacks the opportunity or expertise to engage in transcription work.

Copying

The following recommendations are based on those which the Society of Genealogists has for some years been sending to transcribers. The general aim of these recommendations is to produce a typescript or manuscript "copy" that includes all the information in the original whilst using typographical arrangement, abbreviations and word omission to reduce the reproduction of repetitive material to a minimum. The basic format was devised by the late Percival Boyd, but considerable modifications have been made over the years by J.S.W. Gibson, D.J. Steel, C.R. Humphery-Smith, and more recently by a detailed consideration of each item by the Parish Register Sub-Committee.

In Spring 1967 an article by P.M. Tillott appeared in the Amateur Historian[1] entitled *Transcribing Parish Registers*. This included a discussion of the main problems involved and a list of specific recommendations for transcription work. Whilst these agree in the main with the recommendations which the Society has been sending to transcribers, there are several differences on points of detail. In the main these spring from a difference of approach. Mr. Tillott is primarily concerned with the preparation of transcripts for printing by local

---

[1]   Vol.7 No.5.

societies and he therefore advocates what might be called a calendared edition of each register. The Society of Genealogists, while it does not exclude such a purpose, aims rather at easy reference transcripts for the use of genealogists. The differences have been noted as they appear. On some points, Mr. Tillott's observations have been quoted and the Parish Register sub-committee have incorporated some additional matter from his recommendations, which had hitherto been overlooked. The sub-committee is grateful to him and to the Editor of the *Amateur Historian* for permission to quote extracts from the article.

* * * * * * *

1. If the transcription is in typescript, quarto paper is to be used, (top copy medium thickness, carbon copies thin paper.) If the transcription is in manuscript, special lined paper can be obtained from the Society of Genealogists. *Please do as many copies as possible.*

2. If you are copying an original register in your own locality, make your own arrangements with the incumbent. Please make a copy for the incumbent; this is often a help in getting permission. Emphasise that the Society's membership is mostly amateur, and that the main purpose of transcription is to ensure the preservation of a copy. A letter of recommendation will be supplied if necessary.

3. The title page or following page should include the name and county of the parish, the size, composition and condition of the volumes and a note of any gaps, the name of the transcriber and the date of the transcription and whether or not the Bishop's transcripts have been examined. [2]

4. Use one side of the paper only. [3]

5. Do not write in the margin; it would be hidden by the binding. A margin of at least an inch is essential.

---

[2] A fuller introduction is useful, though not essential. P.M. Tillott advises "The Editor should locate the parish and describe the townships or chapelries within it. The physical nature of the register (material, legibility, lacunae, size, binding) and its whereabouts should be discussed. Commentary on the contents of the register will depend upon the space available but might include such topics as unusual registrations, remarkable non-registration entries, the incumbents mentioned in the register, rare Christian names etc. *ibid* p.145.

[3] Tillott recommends the foliation or pagination of the original register and that the folio or page number, enclosed in square brackets, should appear in the top left hand corner of each page of transcript above the date column. While not essential this could be useful as it would enable any doubtful entry to be immediately checked against the original.

6. Baptisms, marriages and burials to be copied separately – all baptisms for the whole period covered, then all marriages, then all burials.[4] These should be copied to 1840 if possible, and certainly to the end of 1837. Civil registration started in July 1837, but many persons were not registered in the early days. It is advisable to search the baptisms to about 1880 noting down the baptisms of any adults born before 1840.

7. Head each page with the name of the parish (in capitals) and level with it the word baptisms, marriages or burials as the case may be.

8. Banns should be copied on a separate list where the marriage did not take place in the parish.

9. Each year should be headed. Details should be entered as follows:

(a) *Baptisms*

July 11   WATKINS John s of John & Mary
Include dates of birth and baptism if given. After a birth date write *born* in full.
or the columns may be headed:

	Surname	Chr. name		Father	Mother
July 11	WATKINS	John	s	John	Mary

After 1813, the columns in the original register may be kept:

	Surname	Chr. name	Father	Mother	Fath's occ	Abode
Aug 15	WATKINS	John	John	Mary	Lab	otp

If the date of birth is given, a separate column headed *born* should be added after the column for date of baptism.

(b) *Marriages*

Sept 3   WATKINS John otp   SMITH Mary of Ludlow

After 1753 more details are given, and it will be necessary to use two lines for each entry. Miss a line between entries.

Sept 3	WATKINS John otp Bach	Lic	Charles WATKINS
	SMITH Mary of Ludlow Spr (X)		Mary SIMKIN (X)

Indicate date, names of parties; parishes; state (*bachelor, spinster, widow* etc); Banns or licence; Names of witnesses in last column as above. Indicate a mark with an (X) as above. If the spelling of a surname differs in the signature write (sig WATTKIN) immediately after the surname. Only record the officiating minister if he is not the incumbent or curate.

---

[4] Tillott recommends retaining the original arrangement.

(c) *Burials*

These are straightforward

July 17   WATKINS John

Further information is sometimes given: e.g. "*aged above 60 years.*"
After 1813 more information is given.

Aug 15   WATKINS John   Farmer   Mill End   67

N.B. *This lay-out applies whether originals or copies are being
transcribed.* Do not follow the existing lay-out. A borrowed transcrip
being re-copied may not have a lay-out suitable for easy reference.

Wherever the name of the parish appears it should be indicated by
otp. (of this parish) All other places to be given in full.

In every entry all available detail should be included.

10. *Old Style Calendar.* Until 1752 the year commenced not on 1st Jan,
but on 25th March. Thus 11th February 1642 was *after* 31st Decembe
1642. Please leave dates exactly as they are, but state clearly
that you have done this at the start of the transcript.

11. *Entries out of date order.* These should be put in their correct
position but with a note "*misplaced in register*" and the neares
date to the place they appear noted. e.g. "beneath entry for
11 Dec. 1697."[5]

12. *Abbreviations.* s = son, d = daughter, C = baptized, M = married,
wd = widow, wdr = widower, ob = died, n = born, Bn = banns; *bach,
spr, lab* (labourer), *husb* (husbandman), *Lic* licence, *otp* (of this
parish), *sig* (signs). Full stops after these abbreviations are no
necessary.

Months should be abbreviated as follows:

Jany[6]	Apr	July	Oct
Feb	May	Aug	Nov
Mch[6]	June	Sept	Dec

Everything else in full. Do *not* abbreviate names.

13. *Spelling.* Reproduce spelling of surnames exactly. If two differen
spellings are used in one entry, give both. Christian names are

---

[5] Tillott recommends that they be transcribed in the order they appear.
[6] Tillott recommends *Jan* and *Mar*, but these are not recommended by the
Society on the grounds of possible misreading in manuscript for *Jun* and
May.

also best left as they are (e g. *Margreat* for *Margaret*),[7] as are
also abbreviated Christian names.[8] It should be remembered that
some names now wholly given to one sex were formerly given to
both.[9] All names should begin with an initial capital. *ff* should
be transcribed as *"F"*. Place names should be reproduced exactly.
Trades and descriptions may be abbreviated (*husb* = husbandman,
lab = labourer, *wd* = widow).

14. *Latin.* Dates should be translated but not Christian names,[10]
Surnames[11] or places. Descriptions may be abbreviated – (*vid* =
vidua, *gen* = generosus, *arm* = armiger.)

15. *Omissions* in the register may be shown by the form [blank] and
illegible entries by [illegible].

16. *Historical notes* (e.g. fires, floods, storms, political events)
to be copied separately, unless it is of immediate relevance to a
particular entry. (e.g. *"who was drowned in the flood"* in a
burial entry.)[12]

---

[7] P.M. Tillott comments:

> *"Edwarde son of Edward* is a common enough example of those hundreds of
> cases where it is hard to see that any meaning whatsoever should be
> read into the spelling variation. It is no doubt from the experience of
> such cases that transcribers and the printing societies evolved the rule
> that 'common Christian names should be given in modern form' – a practice
> perhaps adapted from the Public Record Office calendars. It is an
> impossible rule to follow consistently. Recent experiments with a
> register [Braithwell, Yorks] for the sixteenth, seventeenth and eighteenth
> centuries produced a list of fifty or so names that might be thought to
> fall within the rule; but quite apart from the difficulty that modern
> spelling is not standardized for all names, further consideration of our
> list in conjunction with *The Oxford Dictionary of English Christian
> Names* very soon reduced the number to no more than half a dozen about
> which there could be any degree of certainty that the modern form truly
> represented that found in the register. Even amongst those, who is
> prepared to say that an entry for *Edwurd* in 1603 may not have something
> to say to the historian of language?" op.cit.* p.140.

[8] Tillott recommends the extension of abbreviated names under certain
circumstances, but points out that it is impossible to set down really
comprehensive rules to be followed; in almost every case it must be left
to judgment born of experience.

[9] For a list of these see pp.103–104.

[10] The risk of translation is greatest with contractions. Thus *Fraunc' fil*
could stand for *Francis son of,* or *Frances daughter of,* and *John' fil
John'* could mean *John son of John* or *Joan daughter of John.* However, even
Johanna in full, though most probably *Joan* might possibly be *Jane* or *Jean.*
Anna could stand for *Ann(e),* *Hannah* or possibly even *Agnes.* A list of
Latin equivalents of English Christian names will be found on pp.110–112.

[11] These are very rarely Latinized anyway. See *Form and Content* pp.36–37.

[12] Tillott recommends they should be transcribed as they appear. *ibid.* p.144.

17. *Do not transcribe any period where you find the writing difficult,* but make it clear which years are covered by the transcript. A handwriting guide will be provided by the Society of Genealogists. If you are doubtful about a particular entry, put a question mark after your conjecture.

18. Lists of Vicars, churchwardens, clerks etc may be compiled and added at the end. These are often useful in deciding whether witnesses to marriages are genealogically significant or not.

19. A comparison with the Bishop's Transcripts is always desirable. These may include entries not in the register or with important differences.[13] Illegible entries in the register may also be filled in from the B.Ts.

    However such a comparison may not be possible, in which case the title page should include the note *not collated with Bishop's Transcripts.*

Do not hesitate to ask if you have any queries.

* * * * * * *

It will be seen that the chief differences between the recommendations of the Society of Genealogists and those put forward by Mr. Tillott lie in the arrangement of material in the transcript. Mr. Tillott advocates retaining the original order in which the material is found; the Society prefers to re-arrange it in such a way that it will be more accessible for enquiring genealogists. The Society, however, is in complete agreement with the basic principle of transcription to which Mr. Tillott gives considerable emphasis, namely

> "The transcriber must never amend or interpret the text unless he is sure that every informed reader would have interpreted it in exactly the same way. Whenever there is the slightest element of doubt the transcriber must render the original in as exact a way as print will allow and notice the difficulty in a footnote."[14]

Indexing

The standard of accuracy in indexing has, on the whole, been higher than that of transcription. However, the inconsistency has been even greater. Various recommendations for indexing parish registers have been put forward from time to time, probably the earli‹

---

[13] See *Bishop's Transcripts* pp.174–175, *Form and Content* p.30.
[14] *op.cit.* p.143.

being those of an anonymous correspondent to *Notes and Queries* in 1850.[15]

The current recommendations of the Parish Register sub-committee are as follows:

1. It is most important that *each volume* when bound should have its own Index. The number of pages to be indexed as one volume will be indicated by the Society's organizer of transcription.

2. The index should be constructed on 5 × 3 slips which will be supplied by the Society.

3. Use paper the same size as the transcript and leave a margin of about one and a half inches for binding.

4. Head first page with name of Parish, County and periods of Baptisms, Marriages and Burials covered by the index, with a note of any periods of deficiency.

5. Head every subsequent page with the name of the parish.

6. Either (a)
Index by surnames only, grouping variants together, but making cross-references where necessary.[16] The Surname should be written in block capitals in the left hand corner of the slip and subsequent entries made on the same slip. New variants of the surname should be added after the surname and separate cross reference slips made out (WATTKIN — see WATKINS). It is helpful to put a pencil mark against each entry as a slip is made. These can be subsequently erased.

or (b)
Index by surnames and Christian names, using the standard abbreviations for the Christian names, and grouping variants of the surname together (but making cross references where necessary) as above. If this form of index is made, the lay-out in the specimen below is recommended. In marriage entries, the bride's name should be

---

[15] *N & Q* 1st ser. Vol.2 pp.1-3 (1850). For its probability of accuracy and its general thoroughness the plan has much to commend it, but the writer appears to recommend separate indexes for each type of entry, thus requiring the reader to check three lists instead of one.

[16] Opinion on the Parish Register Sub-Committee is divided as to whether or not this is preferable to an index under Surname and then Christian name. Although professional genealogists are more frequently seeking a particular entry, many (perhaps most) searchers are interested in all entries of one surname. There is certainly no doubt that a surname only index saves the indexer considerable labour. When surnames have been used as Christian names, these should however also appear in the index.

indexed under both her maiden name and married name. Use the following abbreviations:-

Baptisms

C	Person baptized only
Ca	Adult Baptism
Cp	A parent in a baptismal entry
Cs	A sponsor (or godparent) in a baptismal entry

Marriages

M	Bride or Groom only
Mp	A parent in a marriage entry
W	A witness to a marriage (excluding the Parish Clerk etc)

Burials

B	Person buried only
Bp	Parent of child buried
Bx	Any other person named in a burial entry, including witnesses to a burial in woollen

7. *If a small register* index the Baptisms, Marriages and Burials together, according to year[17] (e.g. C 1727,[18] M 1747, B 1811 W 1783, the latter indicating a witness to a marriage. An adult baptism can be indicated by an (A) after the year. e.g. C 1727 (A).[19] *If a large register* (i.e. one in which the average number of baptismal entries in a year covers more than one page of transcript) index the Baptisms, Marriages and Burials together, and according to *page.*[20]

8. If there is more than one entry under each name on any one page, or in any one year, indicate the number of entries by placing that number in brackets after the index reference. e.g. C 1727, 1729 (2), 1731, 1736 (3) 1738.

9. *Place and Trade Indexes* should be made whenever possible. The place index should exclude the Parish itself, its townships and hamlets, and other parishes in the same town. The trade index should include Clergy, Churchwardens, Parish Clerks, and other officials.

Do not hesitate to ask if you have any queries.

---

[17] With a small register this is preferable to a page index, as the latter is not equally valid for the original or for another transcript.

[18] For convenience, a birth (e.g. of a Roman Catholic or Nonconformist) may be indexed under C.

[19] Surnames used as Christian names can appear in the same list, but in square brackets. e.g. Watkins, C 1727, 1731, [1737], 1753. Here the entry for 1737 refers to *Watkins* used as a Christian name.

[20] With a large register one year of baptisms may occupy several pages and entries might prove difficult to locate with a year index.

Abbot, Abbott			**Alford**			
Mary	M	1798	Ann		Cp	1798
Abell			Elizabeth		Cp	1823
Edward	M	1822			Cp	1827
Lucia Eliz	M	1822	Marianne		C	1823
Ackers			Peter		C	1827
Elizabeth	M	1696	Samuel		C	1798
Adame, Adams					Cp	1823
Agnes	M	1742			Cp	1827
Mary	B	1563	William		B	1825
Addiscott			Dr		Cp	1798
John Thos	B	1827	**Allaton — see Talaton**			
Mary	W	1816	**Allen, Alline, Alling,**			
William	W	1816 (3)	**Allinge, Allyn**			
	B	1814	Ann		B	1810
Adglen — see Hadgeland			Elleanor		M	1660
After			Elizabeth		C	1570
Joan	Bx	1683			C	1611/2
	Bx	1684 (2)			B	1570/1
					B	1603
Agget, Aggett, Aggitt					B	1611/2
Dorothy	M	1614			Bx	1695
Grace	C	1622	Joan		C	1613
	M	1616			M	1569
John	B	1616			M	1572/3
Judith	C	1617			B	1613
	B	1627	Mary		M	1638
Julian	C	1615	Nicholas		M	1638
	B	1615	Sarah		B	1832
Richard	Cp	1617	Susan		C	1607
	Cp	1622			M	1599
	M	1614			M	1614/5
	B	1622	Temperance		C	1602
	Bp	1615	Thomasin		C	1610
Mr	Cp	1615			B	1610/1
Air, Ayre			William		C	1572
Betty	M	1777			C	1600
Mary	M	1749			Cp	1570
Susanna	B	1756			Cp	1572
Thomas	M	1777			Cp	1600
	W	1791			Cp	1602
— see also Eyre					Cp	1604
					Cp	1607

	Cp	1610
	Cp	1611/2
	Cp	1613
	M	1569
	M	1599
	B	1612
	B	1613
	B	1738
	Bp	1610/1
	Bp	1611/2
	Bp	1612
Wilmot	C	1604
	M	1624
Mrs	Bp	1613
Widow	B	1620

Allere
(blank)	B	1567

Allerhede
Dorothy	C	1574/5
John	Cp	1574/5

Alley
William	B	1571/2

Alline, Alling, Allinge,
Allyn
   – see Allen

Alsap
Mary	M	1681
William	M	1681

APPENDIX II ABBREVIATIONS FOR CHRISTIAN NAMES
USED IN BOYD'S MARRIAGE INDEX

The current policy of the Parish Register Sub-Committee of the Society of Genealogists is to recommend that Christian names be transcribed in full. However, in *Boyd's Marriage Index* and in many past transcripts the following list has been used:

Abigail	Abig	Eleanor Helena		Elnr
Abraham Abram	Abr	Emmanuel		Eman
Agnes Annis	Agn	Esther Hester		Esth
Alexander	Alex	Ezekiel		Ezek
Alfred	Alf	Ferdinand		Ferd
Ambrose	Amb	Frederick		Fred
Andrew	And	Gabriel		Gab
Anne Anna Ann	An	Geoffrey Jeffery		Geof
Anthony	Ant	George		Geo
Arthur	Art	Gertrude		Gert
Augustus	Aug	Gilbert		Gilb
Augustine	Austin	Godfrey		Godf
Barbara	Barb	Gregory		Greg
Bartholomew	Bart	Griffith		Grif
Benjamin	Ben	Hannah		Han
Catherine Katherine		Henry		Hen
etc.	Cath	Herbert		Herb
Charles	Chas	Hester		Esth
Christian	Xtian	Hubert		Hub
Christopher	Chris	Humphrey		Hum
Clement	Clem	Isabel		Isb
Cornelius	Corn	James		Jas
Cuthbert	Cuth	Jeffery		Geof
Daniel	Dan	John		Jn
David	Dav	Joseph		Jos
Deborah	Deb	Katherine		Cath
Dorothy	Dy	Lancelot		Lan
Edmund	Edm	Lawrence		Laur
Edward	Edw	Leonard		Leon
Elizabeth	Eliz	Lucretia		Lucr

Lydia	Lyd	William	Wm
Magdalen	Mgd	Winifred	Win
Margaret	Mgt	Zachariah	Zach
Margery Marjory	Mgy		
Marmaduke	Marm		
Mary	My		
Matthew Matthias	Math		
Maurice	Maur		
Michael	Mich		
Nathaniel	Nath		
Nicholas	Nic		
Patrick	Pat		
Penelope	Pen		
Peter	Pet		
Philadelphia	Philad		
Philip	Phil		
Phineas	Phin		
Priscilla	Prisc		
Prudence	Prud		
Rachel	Rach		
Raymond	Ray		
Rebecca	Reb		
Reginald	Reg		
Richard	Ric		
Robert	Rob		
Roger	Rog		
Roland Rowland	Rol		
Samuel	Sam		
Sarah	Sar		
Silvester	Silv		
Simon	Sim		
Solomon	Sol		
Stephen Steven	Ste		
Susan Susanna	Sus		
Theodore	Theo		
Theophilus	Theoph		
Thomas	Tho		
Tomsin Thomasine	Tomsin		
Timothy	Tim		
Ursula	Urs		
Valentine	Val		
Vincent	Vinc		
Walter	Walt		
Wilfred	Wilf		

PREFACE

In England, in contrast with the intensive use made of Parish Registers, many of the other sources of Births, Marriages and Deaths are strangely neglected.

The most valuable source treated in detail in this section is undoubtedly Monumental Inscriptions. Yet of all records this is the least durable, and as is emphasized in the article, little is being done to prevent the wholesale destruction of tombstones, and efforts to transcribe M.I.'s before it is too late have been local, spasmodic and un-coordinated. That more has not been done is a sad reflection on the inertia of genealogists, and with every year that passes genealogy is becoming increasingly difficult.

Marriage Licences have been given more publicity in recent years, and a beginning has been made of transcribing and publishing them. There are still a great many amateur genealogists however who fail to follow up a marriage recorded in the parish register as by licence and are quite happy to ignore the evidence of affiliation which a marriage allegation will afford. It is to be hoped that the publication in the volumes of the National Index of what allegations and bonds exist for each county will stimulate more interest in this important source.

In England work on newspapers has scarcely begun. Perhaps this is as it should be for the splendid series of files of newspapers in the British Museum and provincial libraries are not likely to disappear overnight and other tasks are more pressing. Nevertheless, English genealogists show up in a very poor light when one considers what has been done in Ireland under the stimulus of the loss of so much other material in 1922, and undoubtedly the belief that only those working on well-to-do families can gain assistance from newspapers is still widespread.

Even more than parish registers, these sources underline the sad truth that although there are many ready to profit from the work of a few devoted enthusiasts, the vast majority of those interested in genealogy are not prepared to take the trouble themselves to copy the M.I's in their local churchyard or index a few years of the newspapers in their local library. They will travel a hundred miles to look at one tombstone and leave the rest of the churchyard unrecorded. Genealogy in England can only be furthered by every person interested in the subject doing all he can to record data available locally whether or not the families in which he is interested come from that area. Only then will genealogy in this country rest on a sound and systematic basis.

The following two articles in this section are in the main concerned with those who married or divorced without the blessing of Church or State. Inevitably, there is some overlap with the Parish Register Section for many of the marriage mongers were clergy of the Established Church and entered the marriages in their registers in the normal way. However, the greater part of the article on *Clandestine Marriages* is concerned, not with these but with the marriages in and around the Fleet Prison and other clandestine centres in London and with the marriages at Gretna Green and elsewhere in Scotland. Although the scandal of the Fleet marriages is well known, even many quite experienced genealogists do not realise how vast were the numbers of clandestine marriages and how extensive the records are.

The article on *Divorce and Annulment* is included in this section as being complementary to that on clandestine marriages. Before 1753, the majority of persons "divorced" in this way probably remarried at the Fleet or another clandestine marriage centre, but it seems likely that after the Hardwicke Act many bigamous marriages may have been performed in churches.

In addition to clandestine marriages and divorces, the principal other records of births, marriages and deaths are the registers and other records of the various religious denominations. These are given detailed treatment in volume II of this work, as is also the *General Registry of Births* started by the Heralds' College in 1747, for the greater number of the entries refer to Roman Catholics, Moravians or Jews. Of course, almost any genealogical record may prove evidence of birth, marriage or death, but, due to exigencies of space, it has not been possible to include complete articles either on other classes of record (such as *Census Returns* or *Wills*) very thoroughly dealt with in the standard genealogical manuals, on those (such as *Family Bibles, letters* and *diaries*) which are individualistic in form and normally easy to interpret, or on those such as *marriage settlements* which affect only a relatively small group of people. However, some of these are briefly treated under the heading *Other Records: Some Brief Notes.*

I MARRIAGE LICENCES

In this article, use has been made of chapter XIV of *Genealogical Research in England and Wales*, by D.E. Gardner and F. Smith (published by Bookcraft Ltd., Salt Lake City, Utah, U.S.A.) and the *Introduction* by B. Frith and *Notes on the History of Marriage Licences* by Patrick McGrath, both from *Gloucestershire Marriage Allegations 1637-1680*, (published by the Records Section of the Bristol and Gloucestershire Archaeological Society.) The writer wishes to thank the authors and publishers concerned for permission to use their work, and B. Frith, A.J. Willis, T.F. Allen, C.R. Humphery-Smith and M. Heenan for reading through the manuscript and offering useful comments and suggestions.

The use of the phrase *Marriage Licences* to describe a class of documents increasingly used by genealogists is misleading, as any collection is mainly composed of the *allegations* and *bonds* which were drawn up preceding the grant of a licence; the actual *licences*, which were presented by the parties to the vicar of the parish where the marriage took place, have for the most part failed to survive.

Location

In general Marriage Allegations and Bonds are to be found in the same repositories as the Bishop's Transcripts. Thus many still remain in the hands of diocesan registrars, often uncalendared and occasionally in disorder. Sometimes access is difficult and considerable fees may be charged. However, increasingly they are being deposited at county record offices or other repositories recognized as diocesan record offices, where they are almost invariably available for consultation free of charge.

History

Before Hardwicke's Marriage Act of 1753 a marriage was valid if performed by a priest even without either banns or licence. [1]

---

[1] Indeed in Mediaeval times a marriage was valid if it was performed before witnesses without a priest being present, though the court was bound to compel the parties to renew their marriage vows at the parish church door. Marriages "by repute" where long co-habitation has been proved have also been recognised by the courts. For more details on this question, see *Clandestine Marriages* below pp.292-295 and *Roman Catholics* in Volume II.

In such a case the parties concerned were subject to legal penalties and the minister was likely to lose his benefice. As is pointed out elsewhere[2] a considerable number of such technically valid marriages did take place at local " Gretna Greens ", the Fleet Prison and other "peculiars" or extra-parochial places and the scandal the provoked was the main reason for the passing of the 1753 Act. In effect, if banns were not published, to avoid legal complications a licence was necessary.

Although Marriage Licences were granted in the later Middle Ages, they seem to have been relatively few in number. They increased considerably after the Reformation, and in the late sixteenth and early seventeenth centuries not only were marriages by licence common, but the increasing abuses in the system received considerable attention both from the ecclesiastical authorities and from Parliament. Special Licences from the Archbishop of Canterbury were particularly criticis It was possibly because the Archbishop, Matthew Parker, was sensitive to these criticisms that in Canterbury Diocese the granting of licences seems to have been discontinued altogether between 1569 and 1574. J.M. Cowper comments:

> "From January 17 1569 to January 12 1574 there is no record to be found of marriage licences issued in Canterbury. It is not that a volume has got lost or mislaid, for the volume in which they ought to appear is perfect, the entries relating to matters not matrimonial being continued regularly. I have no explanation to offer. I simply record the fact." [3]

It would appear that in 1579 the Bishops took steps to meet parliamentary criticism of marriage licences by requiring bonds that certain conditions had been fulfilled and that this practice was established in most dioceses. These conditions were elaborated in 1583 by Archbishop Whitgift in *Articles* he sent to the bishops, and finally in 1597 after further criticism from Parliament they were embodied with additional safeguards in a canon. [4]

In spite of all these precautions the frequent granting of marria licences remained a grievance to the Puritans, and in the so-called Millenary Petition presented to James I on his way to London in 1603 there was tacked on to the end of a clause listing the abuses in chur discipline a request ' that licences for marriages without banns asked, be more cautiously granted.'[5]

---

[2] See *Clandestine Marriages* below pp. 292-315.
[3] Foreword to *Canterbury Marriage Licences 1568-1618* (Canterbury 1892) p. ii
[4] A detailed account of the criticisms and of the attempts to remedy the abuses is given in Patrick McGrath. *Notes on the History of Marriage Licences* in *Gloucestershire Marriage Allegations 1637-1680* pp **xxi-xxvi**.
[5] Henry Gee and William John Hardy. *Documents Illustrative of English Churc History* p. 510. cited by Patrick McGrath *op. cit.* p. xxvi.

In 1604, the Canon Law was thoughly overhauled and the new canons laid down that licences could be granted only by episcopal authority and not by holders of peculiar jurisdictions and that bonds should be entered into, binding the sureties under certain strict conditions. If all the injunctions had not been complied with, the licence was void and the commissary who granted it was to be suspended for six months.[6] Nevertheless, licences continued to be issued by the clergy of peculiars, and the bishops frequently infringed the prerogative of the Archbishop of Canterbury to issue special licences.[7] Thus, the Puritans still continued to claim that the licence system was abused and the subject was included in the Root and Branch Petition of 1640. By now, however, it was a question not of abolishing bishops' licences but of abolishing bishops, and from the Civil War to the Restoration of 1660 there is naturally a gap in the records of marriage licences. The system was revived at the Restoration and continued to enjoy great popularity.

In 1694 the Government imposed a tax of 5/- on licences, and further attempts at regulation were made by the King, Parliament, the Archbishop of Canterbury, the Bishops and Convocation.[8] The Hardwicke Act of 1753 cleared up many of the worst abuses and henceforth licences were granted only for churches or chapels where one of the parties had resided for four weeks before the granting of the licence. This did not put an end to the problem, however, and further acts dealing with marriage by licence continued to be passed. In 1824 the period of residence was reduced to 15 days. (4 Geo. 4 c 76 sect. 10).

Reasons for Marriage by Licence

Some of the reasons for the popularity of licences were given by Convocation in answer to Parliamentary criticism in 1597.[9] It was said that it facilitated marriage of persons of full age against parental opposition and the marriage of persons of different social stations. Such reasons must, however, have been exceptional. A more widespread motive particularly among the gentry was that of avoiding the publicity of announcements from the pulpit. Gerald Hamilton-Edwards comments:[10]

> " They [the upper classes] did not enjoy having their names called out in church for all and sundry to hear. They felt this revelation of their intentions in such a personal matter as marriage was rather vulgar and they had no wish to see the village yokels gaping with curiosity at hearing about their squire's daughter's matrimonial future. Such things were

---

[6] The relevant Canons are reproduced in full in Patrick McGrath *op. cit.* pp xxvii-xxviii

[7] Patrick McGrath *op. cit.* p. xxviii.

[8] On an attempt of the Bishop of Norwich, *see below* p. 314.

[9] The text of this document is reproduced in full in Patrick McGrath *op. cit* pp xxiv-xxvi

[10] *In Search of Ancestry* (1966) p. 65.

considered private family affairs and not the concern of the villagers."

Sometimes, no doubt, the marriage was one of real urgency. Thus sailors might wish to marry in haste before their ships sailed. [11] The calling of banns would not lead to great delay but marriage by licence could certainly be a little quicker. Another important reason quoted in 1729 by Giles Jacob in his *A New Law Dictionary*[12] was that "Marriages are prohibited in Lent and on Fasting-Days because the mirth attending them is not suitable to the Humiliation and Devotion to those Times; yet Parsons may marry with Licences in Lent, although the banns of marriage may not then be published." [13]

Extent of Marriage by Licence

Although it was the gentry that had the most interest in privacy, the practice of Marriage by Licence was not limited to any particular social class, and people of many occupations, from labourers upwards, are found making allegations. The idea that most licences were issued to the better-class families may have arisen because marriage by licence became *proportionately* more frequent the higher the social standing of the families. Moreover, the Canons of 1604 included the direction that licences should be granted "unto such persons only, as be of good state and quality", but this regulation must have been interpreted very widely, if indeed it was not completely ignored. [14] It is possible that in some dioceses middle and upper-class families figure prominently merely because the officials charged fees that ended to exclude the poorer people. [15] In 1597 after there had been many complaints of exactions in ecclesiastical courts, Archbishop Whitgift issued a table of fees which was supposed to be displayed in every ecclesiastical court. It would appear that in the diocese of Gloucester 6/8d was payable to the Chancellor and 3/4d to the Registrar. These were the official fees, and one may well doubt whether in the seventeenth Century applicants in practice found their costs limited to what was officially required. Nevertheless, they may well have found in many cases that a quiet wedding by licence actually saved expense. [16]

The whole question of the extent to which the poorer classes were married by licence can be resolved only by a comparison of the number of marriages by licence to marriages by banns at different

---

[11] In Rochester, however, sailors seem to have been generally married by banns. See below p.227.
[12] Published London 1729. Article on *Marriage*.
[13] Cited by Patrick McGrath *op.cit.* p.xxx.
[14] B. Frith, Introduction to *Gloucestershire Marriage Allegations 1635-1680* p.xviii.
[15] D.E. Gardner and F. Smith *Genealogical Research in England and Wales.* Vol.1. p.211.
[16] B. Frith, *op.cit.* p.xvi-xvii.

periods of history. The number of allegations in Gloucestershire during the period 1637-1680 covered by the published *Gloucester Marriage Allegations* was about 200 a year. The number of parishes in the diocese was in the neighbourhood of three hundred. No figures have been compiled for the total number of marriages in the diocese, but in 1670, for example, in 86 parishes there appear to have been only 166 marriages. This gives an average of 1.93 marriages per parish, and although this average is almost certainly too low if we consider the diocese as a whole, yet it is clear that marriage by licence formed a considerable proportion of the total marriages, and that the licence system was very popular. [17] There is no reason to suppose that if detailed statistics were worked out for other dioceses they would be very different, and a study of almost any published list of Marriage Licences shows that it was by no means exceptional for even the poorest to be married by licence. Nevertheless the belief that labourers were invariably married by banns still persists and is found even in the most reliable genealogical manuals. Thus Gerald Hamilton-Edwards rightly emphasizes: [18]

> " It was not merely the upper classes as is sometimes thought who were married by licence, but most farmers, yeomen, merchants and clerks in city offices did so."

Yet even he believes that:

> " The ordinary workman.....would perhaps.....have been thought presumptuous at marrying by licence and laughed at by his fellow workers as having ideas above his station."

Of course it is obviously true that the majority of the lowest class were married by banns, but it certainly appears that marriages by licence occurred amongst this class often enough not to arouse excessive attention.

Some parishes have an abnormally high incidence of marriages by licence. Thus, at St. Nicholas, Rochester, Kent, between 1727 and 1754 there were 554 marriages by licence as against 197 by banns. It is significant that out the latter, 137 were marriages where both parties came from the parish. Curiously, soldiers and sailors seem to have been mostly married by banns, which tends to eliminate the otherwise plausible explanations that urgency was the main reason or that frequently the bridegroom's parish was far distant and it was difficult to arrange for banns to be called. Perhaps the most likely explanation is the simplest. As Rochester was the seat of a bishop, no travelling was necessary in order to obtain a licence, and if either party came from elsewhere, it may well have been less trouble to obtain a licence than to arrange the calling of banns in a parish church even

---

[17]   B. Frith *op.cit.* p.xvi.
[18]   *op.cit* p.66.

a few miles distant. Once the custom was established, it would be recognised as the normal procedure and banns as the abnormal. However, before such an explanation can be accepted, it would seem essential to get statistical information on the relative proportion of marriages by banns and by licence in the churches of other cathedral cities.

In the case of Holy Trinity at Stratford-upon-Avon, Warwickshire, of the 2978 marriages celebrated there between 1703 and 1812, no less than 1103 or 37% of the total were by licence. The percentage over ten year periods varied from 19% to 54%, but, except for a few such periods, the general variation was only between 35% and 45%. Where the trade or profession of the bridegroom is given, there is a high incidence of lowly trades e.g. shoemaker, soap-boiler, labourer, butcher and weaver, even when both parties were of the parish. In a typical 10 year period, in 60 cases of marriage by licence both parties came from the same parish and only in 45 was one party from another parish. The popularity of marriage by licence in Stratford can be explained by the fact that the vicar was also surrogate for the Bishop of Worcester, where the marriage bonds and allegations were deposited. (They are now in Worcester Archivist's Office)[19]

Authorities empowered to issue Licences.

Licences might be issued by the authority of any of the following officials:-

i.   The Archbishop of Canterbury,
ii   The Archbishop of York,
iii The bishop of the diocese in which one of the parties resided.
iv   Certain archdeacons,
v   Clergy appointed as surrogates,
vi   Clergy exercising Peculiar jurisdiction.

The Archbishops

When neither of the persons considering marriage was resident within the diocese where the intended marriage was to take place then a *Special Licence* had to be obtained from one of the Archbishops. When the parties lived in two ecclesiastical provinces (i.e. Canterbury and York) or lived in one province and wished to marry in another, the licence had to be obtained from the *Faculty Office* of the Archbishop of Canterbury which could authorize a marriage at any parish in England and Wales. The *Vicar-General* of the Archbishop of Canterbury issued licences to marry in any parish within the Province of Canterbury.

---

[19]   I am indebted to Mrs B.E.R. Hall and Mr. T.F. Allen for the statistics for Rochester and Stratford-upon-Avon respectively.

oth these offices were in London. A licence from the Archbishop of
ork permitted a marriage within that province. [20]

Bishops and Archdeacons

If one of the persons was a resident of the diocese and the
marriage was to take place in a parish within that diocese, then the
licence was obtainable from the Chancellor at the Diocesan Registry.
In many large dioceses, archdeacons were empowered to grant licences.

Elsewhere, it was not always possible or convenient for the
parties or their representatives to appear personally before the
Diocesan Registrar in which case a licence might be obtained through
a local surrogate.

Surrogates

A surrogate was usually a clergyman in some part of the diocese
who acted for the Chancellor, took down details of the allegations,
and sent them to the Chancellor at a later date. Often he would wait
some considerable time before sending the information to the Registry,
and thus a group of surrogate allegations ranging over a period of
time might be entered in the Allegation Book on a particular date.
These entries are often disappointing, for the surrogate frequently
obtained only the briefest information, sometimes recording only the
names of the parties without their parishes. [21] Not infrequently the
surrogates failed to send in any information at all. This may explain
some of the many cases where a marriage is stated in a parish register
to be by licence, but where no allegation or bond can be discovered
at the Diocesan Registry. Another possible explanation is that allegations were sometimes entered on loose sheets of paper and subsequently
lost.

Peculiars

Licences were issued either by the incumbent or by the *official*
of a peculiar, although as we have seen, this was expressly forbidden
by the Canon of 1604. The vicar and churchwardens of Bishop's Cleeve,
Glos., were especially jealous of what they considered to be their
rights and protested, for example, against the request to send in
Bishop's transcripts of their registers. [22]

It is not therefore surprising to find that on 23rd June 1674
there is a reference in the Bishop's Cleeve parish register to a

---

[20] Licences issued by the Faculty Office, the Vicar-General and the
      Archbishop of York are listed in Appendix I to this article, p.237.
[21] B. Frith *op.cit.* p.xv.
[22] See *Bishop's Transcripts* above p.173.

marriage performed "by vertue of a licence granted by ye Rectour of Bishops Cleeve " and on 10 October 1677 to a marriage 'by vertue of a licence granted by ye official of ye Peculiar of Bps Cleeve '.[23] Such practices no doubt occurred in peculiars all over the country, though often it is probable that no such indication was made in the parish register. Many of the smaller peculiars such as Banbury, Cropredy and others in Oxfordshire shared an *official* with another court, so that the records of several may be entered in one sequence in one book, and it may now be impossible to determine with what authority a licence was issued.[24]

Types of Document

Although the granting of licences in all parts of the country was governed by one uniform law, the authorities employed various methods of recording the details. As mentioned above, there are three documents connected with marriage by licence – the *allegation*, the *bond* and the *licence*. Rarely are all three still in existence. Sometimes only two and often only one is traceable. In many cases none of the actual documents have survived but some of the details may be found entered in *act books*.

The Allegation (or Affidavit)

When a couple wished to marry without the publication of banns one of them had to visit the registry of the appropriate authority and make an allegation or sworn statement ensuring that the Canon Law (of the Church of England) had been complied with and that there was no known lawful impediment to the marriage. An example of what was involved when an allegation was made may be seen from a typical entry in the Marriage Allegation Books of the diocese of Gloucester:-[25]

> "Decimo Octavo die Aprilis 1637
> On wch day appeared personally John Barra of Newnton in the county of Wilts husbandman aged 30tie yeares or thereabouts before the right Worll.ffrancis Baber doctor of the Civill Lawes and Chancellor of the dioces of Glouc'r and alleadged that he intendeth to marry with one Mary Wight of Kingcott in the said dioces of Gloucr single-woman aged 22tie yeares or thereabouts And sayeth that the consent of parents is had and obteyned on either side to be lawfully married together And further sayeth that there is noe lett or impediment by reason of any precontract, consanquinity, affinity or any other lawfull meanes whatsoever that may barr or hinder the said intended marriage ffor the trueth of all wch premises he the said John Barra maketh faith
> Jurat die pred'   John Barra
>   coram me
> ffran : Baber "

[23] B. Frith *op.cit.* p.xv.
[24] On Clandestine Marriages in peculiars see *Clandestine Marriages* pp.295-296, 313-314.
[25] This example is reproduced from B. Frith *op.cit.* pp.xi-xii.

Although the consent of parents had been laid down in 1579 as a
condition for granting a licence, in most dioceses this rapidly
became a dead letter except in the case of minors. In Canterbury
Diocese the formula used was "at his own government" or "at his
own disposing." Elsewhere, as in the example above, the parties had
to swear that the consent of parents had been obtained, but there was
no attempt to verify this, and it is unlikely that any action would be
taken even if a parent complained. However, if one or both persons
were minors (under 21 years of age) written consent of the parents or
guardians had to be furnished at the time of the allegation. With
regard to the ages given in the allegations, a word of warning is
necessary. Little reliance can be placed on some of the early figures.
Often the age is given correctly, but sometimes it is only an
approximation normally due, no doubt, to ignorance, but occasionally
because the bride or groom wished to conceal his or her real age,
perhaps even from the other party. Ages are frequently given as so many
years *and upwards*, and although it has been suggested that the *upwards*
refers only to the odd months, this does not seem to be the case. The
important point was whether or not the parties were minors. Thus *21
years and upwards* can clearly refer to any age, but so also may *21* or
the formulae *21 and a day* and *both aged 21½*.[26]

In some dioceses the allegation included more information. Thus,
in the Archdeaconry of Chichester the allegations not only give the
parish of each of the parties but how long they have resided there.[27]

Sometimes the applicant obtained a letter of introduction from the
parson before going off to make his allegation. Although the allegation was frequently made by the prospective bridegroom, there were
many occasions when it was inconvenient for him to appear personally.
and he called on the services of a friend or relation. Occasionally
the prospective bride made the allegation.[28]

The allegations have seldom survived with the completeness of those of
the diocese of Gloucester. The earliest records of those issued by
the Dean and Chapter of Westminster are in a series of Act Books
of the Dean and Chapter and as Col. J.L. Chester pointed out were
"mere records of licences issued, the original allegations, which
had long been in the custody of the solicitors of the Dean and
Chapter, having been only a few years earlier sold to a paper-maker
and converted into pulp."[29] The earliest Licence book in the

---

[26] J.M. Cowper, *op.cit.* p.iv.
[27] *Calendar of Sussex Marriage Licences* (Archdeaconry of Chichester)
1575-1730 (London, Sussex Record Society 1909).
[28] B. Frith *op.cit* p.xiii.
[29] *Allegations for Marriage Licences issued by the Dean and Chapter of
Westminster,* (*1558-1699*) Edit. G.J. Arymtage, Harleian Society, vol.23
(1886) p.1.

Lincolnshire diocesan records, covering the years 1598-1601, makes
no mention of an appearance and an allegation by the person concerned,
and is a record of licences issued to school-masters and curates as
well as a record of marriage licences. [30] At Ely, there are five volumes
containing registrations of administrations, sequestrations, curates'
licences and other licences, intermingled with the records of marriage
licences. [31] At Bristol, there are no surviving records of marriage
allegations before 1746, and then the allegations are recorded, not in
volumes but on separate printed forms. [32] The procedure for recording
allegations no doubt varied from diocese to diocese and from one period
to another, and it is likely that the variations now appear even
greater because many records have not survived. In 1823 the use of the
marriage allegation was abolished.

The Marriage Bond.

In general the practice of requiring marriage bonds seems to have
been insisted on from at least as early as 1579. The licence was not
to be issued unless the party was bound with sureties under the following conditions: that consent of parents or guardians had been
obtained; that there was no impediment to the marriage; and that no
suit was depending touching any impediment. The Canons of 1604
required also security that the marriage would take place in the
parish church or chapel where one of the parties dwelt and between the
canonical hours. Two sufficient witnesses, one of them known to the
judge or to some person of good reputation then present, had to swear
that the consent of parents or guardians had been obtained (except in
the case of widows and widowers), and one of the parties had also to
swear that there was no impediment to the marriage. [33] In a bond, the
first part, known as the *obligation* is the declaration by two bondsmen
(or sureties), one of whom is normally the bridegroom, and the sum in
which they are bound. In the second part, known as the *condition*,
appear the names of the parties together with the name of the church
(or choice of churches) where the marriage ceremony was to be performe
At various times and places more information was given. Thus for a few
years after 1697 in the Archdeaconry of Richmond a very full form was
in use, requiring among other details the ages and conditions of the

---

[30] The second Lincolnshire Allegation Book begins in 1612 and, unlike the
first, contains nothing but allegations. It gives full details of appearance and allegation, as at Gloucester.

[31] A. Gibbons, *Ely Episcopal Records*, (Lincoln, 1896), p.154 ff. These
cover the period 1562-1693. The later volumes contain only Marriage
licences.

[32] B. Frith *op.cit* p.xii.

[33] B. Frith op.cit p.xiv.

parties.[34] Usually the *obligation* is in Latin and the *condition* is in English.[35] Thus the names of trades may appear in Latin. [36] However, sometimes the trade was given in English even though the rest of the obligation is in Latin. [37] After 1731 when an act of Parliament[38] enacted that all proceedings in *Courts of Justice* should be in English, the use of Latin for legal documents was generally abandoned[39] and the obligation is henceforth also normally in English.

The following is a typical example of a Bond. [40] Although entirely in English the wording of the obligation follows closely the Latin used in earlier bonds.

> " Know all men by these presents that we John Lucas of Over Kellett in the parish of Bolton by the Sands Taylor and Richard Poole of Lancaster taylor, both in the county of Lancaster are held and firmly bound unto the Right Reverend Father in God, Samuel by Divine permission, Lord Bishop of Chester in Two Hundred Pounds of good and Lawful Money of Great Britain.... dated the twenty-seventh day of July 1751.
> The Condition of this Obligation is such, that if there shall not hereafter appear any lawful Let or Impediment.... that the above bounden John Lucas and Margaret Threlfall of Over Kellett aforesaid spinster, both in the Archdeaconry of Richmond may lawfully marry together... in... (the) Parish Church or Chapel of Over Kellett aforesaid.
> Sealed and Delivered
> in the Presence of
> Chas Lambert   John Lucas
> Notary Publick   Richard Poole

There are bonds where the bridegroom is not a bondsman. In these, the name of the bridegroom will appear with that of the bride in the *condition*. It was of course intended that the " bondsmen " or sureties (one of whom was, normally the bridegroom) would as has been pointed out, ensure that there was no impediment to the marriage. However, from the beginning the second bondsman became a formality. J.M. Cowper observes

"Vintners; Victuallers, innholders and men of lower standing were always

---

[34] J. Brownbill Introduction to *Lancaster Marriage Bonds* Record Society of Lancs. and Cheshire Vol 74 (1920) p.vii.

[35] An example of a bond with the obligation in Latin is given in J. Brownbill *op.cit* p.vii.

[36] A glossary of Latin trade names and descriptions is given in Appendix II.

[37] E.H.W. Dunkin Preface to *Calendar of Sussex Marriage Licences.* Sussex Record Society Vol.1. (1901) p.xv.

[38] 4 Geo 2 cap 26.

[39] This act appears to have been generally misunderstood and thought to apply to all legal documents. Thus in the Parish Register of Clyst St George, Devon is the entry: " 9° Georgii 2^{di}, 1735,6. The Law now forbids ye keeping any records in Latin " J.S. Burn *History of Parish Registers in England* (1862) p.61.

[40] This example is taken from D.E. Gardner and F. Smith *op.cit.* p.215.

on hand, and ready to give a bond for £40, £100 or £200 according to the period.... They had degraded what was intended to be a security into a trade. " [41]

Of Surrey bonds, A. R. Bax observes: - [42]

"About 1770 the farce was enacted of substituting the names of John Doe and John Roe, ficticious persons as second sureties, and their suppo signatures were actually appended in the hand of the person who filled up the Allegation."

That this practice was widespread is shown by the following similar quotation from J. Brownbill's Introduction to *Lancaster Marriage Bonds* [43]

" There are normally two bondsmen, the first being the bridegroom....In many cases his is the only bona fide bond, the other name being ficti- tious, (such as) John Doe, Richard Roe, or the like, the humourous surrogate or other official sometimes adding 'esq' or 'gent' to these names and even providing them with a signature. "

John Doe also frequently appears in the Gloucester Bonds.

Bonds, like allegations do not always survive. Thus, for example, no bonds before 1729 have been found in the Gloucester Diocesan Registry; from 1729 there are bonds for some, but by no means all, of the marriages for which licences were issued; and it is a curious and interesting fact that the procedure used in the Gloucester Regist differed in the case of an allegation accompanied by a bond from what it was when there was an allegation without a bond. The latter was entered in the Marriage Allegation Book as before; the former were not so entered. Instead details of the allegation were entered, not in the Allegation Book, but on a special form which was attached to the bond, and these were collected together in bundles. One might assume that Gloucester did not require the completion of a bond until 1729 and until then regarded the sworn allegation as sufficient, but this would have been clearly contrary to the Canon Law, and in any case, it is known that at least some bonds did exist in the seventeen century. [44]

The Marriage Licence

When all the formalities had been completed, a marriage licence was issued. This was taken to the clergyman performing the ceremony and he presumably retained it as his authority for dispensing with the

---

[41] *op.cit.* iii - iv.

[42] Introduction to *Allegations for Marriage Licences issued in the Commissar Court of Surrey between 1673 and 1773* (Norwich 1907).

[43] The Record Society of Lancs and Cheshire Vol. 24 (1920) p. vii.

[44] B. Frith op.cit p. xiv.

banns required by the rubrics. A number of marriage licences survive among the parish records. The licence was not necessarily in the lengthy form suggested in the Canons of 1597. A licence for the early seventeenth century which has been preserved, attached to a bond, in the Lincolnshire Diocesan Archives[45] runs as follows:

Fiat licentia curato de Alvingham arch' Lincoln' ad solempnizandum matrimonium inter William Mansert de Alvingham predicto generosum et Annam Goge de eadem ancellam.

Obligetur Humfridus Ashton de eadem in centum marcis
Thomas Rands commissarius
Archdiaconus hinc.

Some licences may have been returned to the Diocesan Registry, for now and again one may find such a licence attached to the original allegation or bond.

Copies

Genealogists are fortunate in that for many counties Marriage Bonds and Allegations have been transcribed and in a number of cases they have been printed by a local society. Of these, the publications of the Record Society of Lancashire and Cheshire, the Bristol and Gloucestershire Archaeological Society and the Sussex Record Society have already been cited. The 17th century special licences issued by the Faculty Office and Vicar General have been printed by the Harleian Society[48] who have also published others such as those of the Dean of Westminster. It is fortunate that although some of the earlier volumes printed extracts only, the gaps were later filled in. Collections of Marriage Allegations have also been printed by other individuals, publishers or societies, one of the more recent being the Hampshire Allegations transcribed by A.J. Willis. In addition, the Society of Genealogists possesses typescript copies of many more, including a continuation of the Vicar General's licences to 1709. In the course of its large-scale microfilming activities, the Church of Jesus Christ of Latter Day Saints has filmed immense numbers.

Although there are many dioceses such as Lichfield or Hereford virtually untouched, and others such as York where little more has been done than to scratch the surface, nevertheless the prospect of all Allegations and Bonds being transcribed and indexed in the forseeable future is considerably brighter than is the case with almost any other class of genealogical document.

In using copies of allegations care must be taken to ensure that the bonds have been examined, as not infrequently these reveal variant spellings and other details. Moreover, many abstracts of bonds have been made which do not record the names of bondsmen, although often

---

[45]   *Lincolnshire Diocesan Records* M.B. 1601/3-4. The licence is undated, but the accompanying bond is dated 6th April 1601. This example is taken from B. Frith *op.cit* p.xv.

[48]   For details see Appendix I, below p.237.

when the second bondsman was taken seriously he was a relative or other connection of the groom (or less frequently, the bride) and his name may therefore provide a valuable clue. Sometimes, alas, the omissions in copies are much more serious. In the Harleian Society volume of London Marriage Licences[47] appears the following "copy" of an allegation:

"1610 June 25 Anthony Phillips of the City of London, draper and Anne Packer of St. Gabriel Fenchurch Street, City widow of William Packer late of same, merchant taylor: at St. Mary's Islington, Middlesex."

The original, however, gives the following information

"Anthony Phillips of *St. Margaret Pattens*, draper, *widower, age 43* and Anne *Parker* (*sic*) of St. Gabriel Fenchurch Street *widow* aged 30 relict of William *Parker* of same merchant taylor dec. at *Shrovetide last*; consent of her father *Nicholas Collier of London, pewterer*: at Islington.

It can be seen that all the information in italics was omitted, or incorrectly rendered, in the copy.[48] This throws grave doubt on the value of the Harleian Society volumes and the searcher would be wise to make a practice of studying the original documents. This is to be recommended even when the transcript is known to be of a high standard as signatures can be compared with those from other sources.

However, the importance even of poor copies or copies of entries from Act books cannot be overstressed. Often these give the searcher the first indication that a marriage recorded in the parish register without comment was in fact by licence.

* * * * * * * * * *

Allegations, bonds and licences must be cautiously used. They are not evidence that a marriage took place, but merely prove that there was an *intention* to marry. When an allegation gives the name of the parish or parishes in which the marriage may be solemnized and a search of the registers fails to trace it, the persons may have been married at some other parish church or parochial chapelry. It is also possible that there was a change of mind and that the marriage never took place.

---

[47] Harl. Soc. Vol. 25. *Allegations for Marriage Licences issued by the Bishop of London 1520-1610 and 1611-1828.* Extracted by J. Chester and edited by G.J. Armytage.

[48] *Gen. Mag.* Vol. 6. No. 9, March 1934, p.396

APPENDIX I CANTERBURY AND YORK MARRIAGE LICENCES

Archbishop of Canterbury

Faculty Office.

Originals. *Allegations* 1543-1549, 1567-1575, 1632-1869 at Lambeth
Palace Library, London, S.E.1.
Act Books (Calendars) 1632 onwards at the Faculty Office,
1, The Sanctuary, Westminster, London, S.W.1.

Copies

Allegations. Harleian Society Vol.XXIV (1886) *"Allegations for
Marriage Licences issued from the Faculty Office of the
Archbishop of Canterbury at London, 1543-1869"* extracted
by Col. J.L. Chester and edited by G.J. Armytage.
Contains all Licences 22 Nov 1543-25 Apl 1549 and 4 Apl
1567-16 Sep 1575 and extracts only from 1632-1869.
Introduction states *"I* extracted only the more
important of these *":-* fairly full 1632-1703; three or
four each year 1703-1800; less than one a year 1800-1829
then a gap and one in 1869.
All details given in the originals are included.

Act Books Index Library Vol.33 (1905) *"Calendar of Marriage
Licences issued by the Faculty Office 1632-1714"*
edited by G.E. Cokayne and E.A. Fry.
Contains all entries from Calendars for period 1632-1714;
these have not been collated with the originals.
Those covered by Chester above are marked with an
asterisk.

Vicar-General

Originals. *Allegations* 1660 onwards (missing 2 Jan 1663/4 – 13
Feb 1664/5 and 2 Sept – 22 Sept 1666 supposed to have
been burnt in the Great Fire).

Act Books 1660 onwards.

Copies

Harleian Society Vol.23 (1886) *Allegations* 25 July
1660 – 15 July 1679. *Extracts only.* Colonel J.L. Chester

states: "I have taken all, except those persons evidently of the humblest rank."

Harleian Society Vol. 33 (1892). *Allegations* 25 July 1660 – 24 March 1668/9 omitted in Vol. 23.

Harleian Society Vol. 34 (1892) *Allegations* 26 March 1669 – 15 July 1679 omitted from Vol. 23.

Harleian Society Vol. 31 (1890) *Allegations* 1 July 1687 – 30 June 1694.

Typescript continuation at Society of Genealogists.

Vol. 1 (1932) July 1694 – Dec 1699
Vol. 2 (1935) Jany 1699/1700 – Dec 1705
Vol. 3 (1946) Jany 1705/6 – Dec 1709.

These are an alphabetised calendar only. Licences issued by the Faculty Office and Vicar-General are also included in Col. Chester's *"London Marriage Licences 1521-1869"* ed. J. Forster (1887). However these are extracts only. The Introduction states " I extracted the most important of them "

Archbishop of York

Originals These are at Borthwick Institute, St. Anthony's Hall, York.
Allegations 1567 – 1723
Bonds 1660 – 1723 (Separate)
Bonds and Allegations 1723 onwards.

These have not been listed or indexed and are arranged only in a very rough chronological order. The class as a whole is extremely bulky and a considerable proportion of them requires attention before any attempt at indexing can be made. As there are many other classes also waiting attention, it is likely to be a considerable time before the staff of the Institute will be able to spend any time on the bonds and allegations.

Copies

Allegations 1567 – 1630 Yorks. Arch. Journal Vols 7, 9, 10-14, 16, 17, 20.
1630-1714 Yorks. Arch. Society Vols. 40, 43, 46.
Some extracts in *Northern Genealogist* (1886) Vol. 2.

APPENDIX II GLOSSARY OF LATIN TRADE NAMES, TITLES AND DESCRIPTIONS

Latin	Description	Latin	Description
abbrocator	broker	auctionarius	retailer, broker
abra	maidservant	aurifex	goldsmith
abrocarius	broker	balius, balivus	bailiff
acicularius	comb-maker, pin maker	barbitonsor	barber
acupictor	embroiderer	barrastorius, barrista	barrister
admirilis	admiril	baronettus	baronet
aegyptiacus	gypsy	bersarius	forester, park-keeper
agillarius	hayward	bibliopola	bookseller
agricola	husbandman	bladarius	corn chandler
altiharius	fattener, capon maker	boscarius	woodman
alutarius, aulutarius	cordwainer	bostarius	grave-digger
androchia, androgia	dairymaid	bostio	cattle driver
antigraphus	scribe	botescarlus	boatman
apothecarius	apothecary, shopkeeper	brasiator	maltster
architector	thatcher	burriarius	dairyman
architectus	master builder, architect	buticularius	butler
arconarius	person concerned in the wool trade	caementarius	mason
		calcarius	spurrier
arcularius	chest maker	calcearius, calciarius	shoemaker
armurarius	armourer	caligarius	bootmaker
armiger	esquire	campanarius	bell-founder
aromatarius	grocer	campsor	banker
aromatopola	grocer	candelarius, chandelarius	chandler
attornatus	attorney	candidarius	whitster
aubobulcus	oxherd	capistrius	maker of halters

239

carectarius	carter	colonellus	colonel
carnarius	butcher	colonus	husbandman
carnifex	butcher	comes	earl
carpentarius	carpenter	comptista	accountant
carpetor, carpetrix	wool-carder	confectionarius	confectioner
carseatrix	cheese maker	constabularius	constable
catellarius	pedlar	cophinius, cophinarius	basket-maker
cauponarius	inn holder	coquarius, coquus	cook
causidicus	attorney, advocate	coralius, corarius,	currier
cellarius, cellerarius	cellarer	corbio	basket maker
cementarius	mason	cordebanarius,	cordwainer
censarius	farmer	corduanerius	
cericus	wax chandler	corderius	rope-maker
cervisiarius, cervisior	brewer	corerius	courier
cheirothecarius	glover	coriarius, coriator	currier
chirurgus	surgeon	corralius	currier
cipharius	cup-maker	correctarius	broker
circa	watchman	corrigiarius	girdler
circulator	cooper, turner	cortinarius	curtain maker
cissor	tailor, shearman	corversarius,	cordwainer
cives	burgess	corvisarius, corvisor	
clavigarius	lorriner, bit-maker	cotmannus	cottager
clericus	clerk in holy orders	coupiator	woodman
clericus parochialis	parish clerk	cultrarius	upholsterer
cocarius	cook	curagulus	caretaker
coctiliarius	charcoal burner, sometimes baker	cursor	courier, crier
		curvarius	cooper
cocus	cook	daia, deia	dairymaid, dairyman
coelebs	bachelor	dapifer	steward

daya	dairymaid, dairyman
discifer	steward
disgerbigator	haymaker
dispensarius, dispensator	steward
doliarius	cooper
domifex	carpenter
ductor	carrier
dux	captain
ephippiarius	saddler
equitator	forest officer
faber	smith
faber aererium	coppersmith
faber ferrarius	blacksmith
faber horologicum	clockmaker
faber lignarium	carpenter
fabricus sericarius	locksmith
fabrifer	blacksmith
famulum	servant
ferrarius	ironmonger, smith
ferrator	smith
ferrifaber	blacksmith
figulus	potter
firmarius	farmer
fistulator	piper
flecharius, flexarius	fletcher
formulus	attorney
frumentarius	corn-dealer
frunes, frunio	tanner
fugator	drover
funerius	rope maker
furnarius	baker
galerius	? silk weaver
gardinarius	gardener
geburus	villager
generosus	gentleman
grocerus, grocerius	grocer
guardianus	guardian
helwardus	hayward
herbergiator	innkeeper
horologiarius	clockmaker
hortarius, hortulanus, hortulanius, hortulanius	gardener
hospitator	innkeeper
hostellarius	innkeeper
hostiarius	usher
hostillarius	ostler
husbandus	husbandman
inewardus	watchman
informator	tutor
ingenuus	yeoman
jurista	lawyer
laborarius	labourer
laborator	labourer
lanarius	wollen draper
laniator	butcher
lanius	butcher
lapidarius	stonemason
laterarius	? brickmaker

lecuarius — grasier
librarius — librarian
lignarius — carpenter
ludi-magister — schoolmaster
macellarius, macerarius — victualler
mansionarius — sexton
marinarius, marinellus — sailor
medicus, medicinis doctor, in medicina professor — physician
menestrallus — artisan
mercator — merchant
mercator pecu — cattle jobber
mercearius, mercerius, merciarius, merciarius — mercer
miles — soldier, knight
molarius — mill-wright
molendarius, molendinarius, molendinator — miller
molitor — mill-wright
musicus — musician
nauta — sailor
navigator — boatman
numacius — tollman
nuncius — sergeant, beadle
officiator — officer
olator — oilman, ? purfumer
operarius — day labourer
opilio — shepherd
opifex — ? joiner

orarius — clockmaker
ostiarius — usher
ovium pastor — shepherd
paedagogus — schoolmaster
panicius — baker
pannarius — clothier
pannitonsor — shearman, cloth-cutter
papiropalus — paper maker
parmentarius — tailor
passarius, passiagiarius — ferryman
pecuarius — grazier
peletarius — pelterer
pellicarius, pelliparius, pellius — skinner
pesarius — weigher
pharmacopola — apothecary
pheliparius — fripperer
pictaciarius — cobbler
pictor — painter
pileo — hatter
pinsor — ? baker
piscator — fisherman
piscenarius — fishmonger
pistor — baker
piteo — feltmaker
plebeius — villager, labourer
poletarius — poulterer
polimitarius — stainer
pomarius — fruiterer

porcarius, porcator	swineherd	serifaber	locksmith
porcorum emptor	pig jobber	serviens ad legem	sergeant at law
portarius	carrier	servus	servant
promarius	waiter	solutus	bachelor
propola	huckster	speciarius	spicer
provisor	purveyor	sportarius	basket maker
puletarius	poulterer	stabularius	ostler
quarrerius	stone-cutter	stagnator	tin-miner
quassillarius	pedlar	stallarius	groom
rebroccator	cobbler	stannarius	pewterer
restionius	ropemaker	structor	builder
revelus, revolus	pedlar	sutor	shoemaker, cobbler
ripator	reaper	sutor pannarius	tailor, cloth cutter
rogatorius	beggar	sutor vestiarium	tailor
rotarius	wheelwright	syndicus	advocate, burgess
rotularius	notary	tabellio	notary
ruptarius	mercenary soldier	tabernarius	innkeeper
salarius	salter	tabularius	innkeeper, notary
saponarius	soap maker	tanator	tanner
sarrator	sawyer	tannarius, tannator	tanner
sartor	tailor	tannerius	tanner
scindifaber	bladesmith	tapetiarius	carpet maker, upholsterer
scissor	tailor	tector	plasterer, pargeter
scriba	scrivener	tegularius, tegulator	tiler, bricklayer
scriptor	scrivener	textor	weaver
scurio	stableman	tibialis confector,	stockiner, framework-
sellarius	salter	tibialis factor	knitter
senescallus	steward	tignarius	carpenter
septessarius	merchant, grocer	tinctor	dyer

tolonarius	tollkeeper
tonellarius	cooper
tonsor	barber
turnarius	turner
urigenator	furbisher
vaccarius	cowherd
valettus	groom, yeoman, journeyman
vestiarius	clothier
victor	? cooper
victualarius	victualler
vidulator	fiddler
virgiferens, virgator	verger
viridarius	hayward
viro	boatman
vitellarius, vitillarius	victualler
vitrarius	glazier
xylopola	dealer in wood
zigarus	gypsy

II MONUMENTAL INSCRIPTIONS.

The author acknowledges with gratitude the assistance of the following in writing this article:- H.L. White, the late F. Burgess and Mrs P. Burgess, J.F. Mitchell and C.R. Humphery-Smith. Thanks are particularly due to Mr. Burgess for permission to reproduce material from 'English Churchyard Memorials' (published Lutterworth Press 1963) and other works and to J.F. Mitchell and the Scottish Genealogy Society for permission to quote from "Burial Ground Inscriptions" (The Scottish Genealogist Vol. X1 No.1 p.8 (1964).

The term *Monumental Inscriptions* has been retained in this article because of its wide currency, although the less popular *Memorial Inscriptions* is perhaps preferable, for this covers everything from inscriptions on church furniture representing gifts *inter vivos* to those on stained glass windows. Nevertheless it is certainly true that monuments in the church and headstones in the churchyard supply the greater part of the information of genealogical value. Unlike parish registers and marriage licences, the value of monumental inscriptions does not decrease sharply after 1837. Even 20th century inscriptions may contain information extremely difficult to obtain from other sources.

Monumental inscriptions in churches have always been given a great deal of attention, and there have been many excellent works on the subject, particularly those of Mrs K. Esdaile. However, the situation with regard to stones in churyards is lamentable. At a time when increasing efforts are being made to preserve parish registers it seems likely that more deliberate destruction has been wrought in churchyards in recent years than at any time during the past three centuries[1]. The greatest study of churchyard monuments in this country has been undertaken by the late Mr. Frederick Burgess and his masterwork *English Churchyard Memorials* is essential reading for anyone interested in the subject. Although Mr. Burgess's interest in it was artistic rather than genealogical, all genealogists must acutely feel the loss occasioned by his untimely death in December 1966.[2]

---

[1] For a detailed discussion of this subject, see below pp. 261–264.
[2] So frequently have Mr. Burgess's works been cited in this article that the following abbreviations are used throughout.

ECM *English Churchyard Memorials* (Lutterworth Press, 1963)
ST *Spoils of Time - Churchyards and Education*, Amateur Historian, Spring 1965.
EG *English Gravestones of the Post Reformation and their Masons*. Gen. Mag. vol. 10 p. 310 (1949)

Monuments to the dead have, of course, for thousands of years been considered of extreme importance both among primitive tribes and in highly sophisticated civilizations such as that of Classical Greece. In Britain numerous inscriptions have been found dating from Roman times, and Saxon stones, though rare, have survived in various places. The main importance of Mediaeval monumental brasses and effigies is, of course, artistic. Naturally they are of interest to the genealogist as well, but in general surviving inscriptions dating before the Reformation are entirely of the nobility and gentry or of ecclesiastical dignitories and even the genealogist interested in these families is unlikely to obtain much information not found in other records. It is not known to what extent in Mediaeval times churchyard tombstones were erected to the memory of merchants or craftsmen, but clearly the poorest could not afford any form of monument to their deceased relatives except, perhaps, a simple wooden cross. Surviving mediaeval churchyard tombstones tend to contain little or no information of genealogical value, often not even the name of the deceased, an incised or relief cross being deemed sufficient.

After the Reformation the number and value of inscriptions both inside the church and in the churchyard increased enormously.

Church Inscriptions

The custom of burial in the church was at first limited to ecclesiastics and those of royal birth, and later to church founders and benefactors. Although frowned upon by the ecclesiastical authorities it developed rapidly, and by the mid-18th century inscriptions on the church walls to even minor gentry became normal. As Frederick Burgess points out

"It was certainly apparent to the Georgian *hoi polloi* that only in the act of death was mankind united in a temporary commonalty. Burial quickly restored them to their proper station – for them the churchyard, whilst their betters paid for the privilege of lying snug within the church. The custom is cynically acknowledged in an epitaph at Kingsbridge, Devon (1795):

Here I lie at the chapel door
Here lie I because I'm poor,
The farther in the more you'll pay,
Here lie I as warm as they.[3]

---

[3] *ST* p. 229. The epitaph is also cited in *ECM* p. 20. In 1521 at Banwell (Somerset) Robert Cabull and Robert Blundon buried their wives, the first in the porch for a fee of 3/4, the latter in the church at double the sum. *Churchwardens' Accounts ECM* p. 50.

Many of the higher clergy, including several Archbishops of Canterbury, such as Archbishop Sancroft and Archbishop Secker, objected to this practice and were themselves buried in churchyards. Many incumbents followed this lead and refused to bury in the church and some gentry had conscientious scruples.[4] The presence of family vaults in churchyards tended against the practice, so it is by no means infrequent to find in the churchyard memorials to distinguished local families. However, even when burial in the church was not customary, memorial tablets may have been erected in the interior.

The form of church memorials differs considerably. 'Sepulchres should be made according to the quality and degree of the person deceased that by the tombe everyone mighte be discerned of what rank hee was living' said Weever in 1631.[5]

Mediaeval monuments normally required the semblance of the tomb with or without an elaborate architectural canopy, and were generally designed to receive a recumbent effigy. Even the simple brasses let into marble floor slabs were engraved with a full length figure of the deceased. However, a more practical form of memorial was the wall tablet. Although a few examples are found in the late Mediaeval period, this type belongs essentially to the Renaissance and has remained the commonest form of church memorial ever since.[6]

Officially, the College of Arms is responsible for the supervision of heraldry in connection with funerals and in the use of arms and epitaphs on monuments,[7] and up to the seventeenth century they took their responsibilities seriously. The heralds were still influential well into the 18th and 19th centuries though by then, as more and more local masons and painters took over from the heralds, quality of design and taste as well as accuracy both in heraldry and inscriptions had deteriorated.

Churchyard Inscriptions

The position of a stone in the churchyard to some extent may be taken as an indication of status. In particular, the Northern part of the churchyard was often appropriated to paupers, the unbaptised, the excommunicated and suicides.[8]

---

[4] For example John Evelyn's father-in-law see *ECM* p. 50.

[5] *Funeral Monuments.* Cited in *ECM* p. 219.

[6] For more information on the design of church memorials see Walter H. Godfrey's Introduction to Batsford's *English Mural Monuments and Tombstones* (1916), R. Gunnis *Dictionary of British Sculptors* (1953) and Mrs K. Esdaile *English Church Monuments* (1946)

[7] See A.R. Wagner *Heralds and Heraldry in the Middle Ages,* (1939), and *Records and Collections of the College of Arms;* G.D. Squibb *The High Court of Chivalry.* (1959). See also above p.71.

[8] On the burial of suicides see *above* p.74, *ECM* p.53, C.E. Sprott *The English Debate on Suicide,* La Salle, Illinois (1961) and R. Bartel *Suicide in 18th Century England: The Myth of a Reputation,* Huntingdon Lib. Quart XXII 2 (1960).

Sometimes position in the churchyard indicates, not status but the precise locality from which the deceased came. Thus the North-west part of the churchyard of Christchurch Priory, Hampshire was allocated to the tithing of Holdenhurst. The Holdenhurst church-wardens paid 2/- a year for the privilege of these burials in Christ-church church-yard from at least as early as the middle of the 17th century until 1834, when the Holdenhurst Chapel was unfortunately demolished and a new church (that included a churchyard) was built on an adjacent site.

As in the interior of the church, the style of monuments varied and, in general, this too reflected the status of the deceased. Mr. Burgess points out:

> "The headstone persisted as the most economical memorial, its surface reliefs often imitating the shapes and patterns of wall-tablets, while the larger chest and pedestal tombs were derived from the architectural supports and surrounds used to embellish interior effigies. Country stone-masons thus devised by a certain snobbery of imitation monumental status-symbols to satisfy the nouveaux-riches among their patrons. A case in point are those monuments set up to the rich wool-merchants of the Cotswolds, popularly known as bale-tombs, which were derivitive from the mediaeval effigy covered with its hearse"[9]

Each part of the country developed its own form of monument. Apart from the bale-tombs of the Cotswolds, table tombs[10] distinguish the West Riding, and brick box-tombs, Kent. There are varieties of material, such as the terracotta memorials of the Potteries or the iron slabs of the Weald, Herefordshire and Coalbrookdale.[11] In the London area some early 19th century headstones have cast-iron insets.[12]

Many, if not most, early churchyard memorials were however of wood. These were usually *grave-boards* consisting of an inscribed plank between two uprights, which at first sight seems part of a broken fence. Frederick Burges observes

---

[9] *ST* p. 229. See *ECM* Chap. 2, esp pp 112-140. A *bale-tomb* is a type of chest-tomb with a semi-cylindrical or grooved top.

[10] Inscribed slabs or ledgers raised from the ground by supporting slabs or columns.

[11] The earliest known iron slab is at Burwash (14th Century) and the earliest dated one (1570) at East Grinstead. Wadhurst has the largest number, 31 interior and one cast iron ledger and one iron headstone in the churchyard. *ECM* pp, 146-7. The Wadhurst slabs were copied by Mr. H.L. White in 1963. Some comprise only the initials and date. He comments "In one case I found it impossible to distinguish between the original initials and those made in later periods by visitors to the church."

[12] *EG* p. 310.

" In Surrey at least during the 17th century these were the sole means of commemoration[13] and it is evident that throughout the Weald and in other wooded areas of the Home Counties where the heavy clay lands made transport of the stone difficult, wooden memorials were once numerous, for in spite of their vulnerable nature, many still exist, albeit decrepit and illegible". [14]

These interesting monuments are no more highly regarded than the tombstones. Mr. H.L. White laments:

" I found one in August of this year still legible from 1811. This was on a long plank used as a tombstone at Charing, Kent and supported between feet that have decayed. The original in position in the churchyard is shown in a painting of 1826 (of the old church) hung inside the present church. Unfortunately, this survival that should be in a museum is now lying by the church as thrown out rubbish"[15]

Not surprisingly, few churchyard inscriptions survive from the 16th and early 17th century and probably in any case relatively few were erected. The increasing use of churchyard monuments from the 17th century onwards is particularly noticeable in districts where stone was abundant, such as the area between the Severn and the Wash. The majority of the stones were carved by local craftsmen or in many cases by the local schoolmaster. With the development of the writing schools in the 18th century, Mr. Burgess comments:

"The gravestone-cutters of the Midlands set themselves to rival the penmen, as the hard Swithland slate they used for headstones encouraged a technique similar to that of the metal-engraver. Their calligraphic luxuriance is thus imperishably preserved on thousands of slate tablets, which the makers, in competitive spirit invariably signed"[16]

It is of interest to note that up to the middle of the nineteenth century headstones and footstones faced outwards. From the mid-nineteenth century there was a fairly dramatic and widespread change in this practice and inscriptions will be found facing inwards.

Not infrequently tombstones have been adorned with the representation of the tools of trade or profession of the deceased, and this may occur in cases where the trade is not mentioned in the inscription. Thus, there are stone-mason's tools on a stone at Gatcombe, Isle

---

[13] Aubrey noted in 1673 " They use no tombstones in churchyards but rayles of wood over the grave on which are printed or engraved theinscriptions". *ECM* p. 28.

[14] For more details on this subject see *ECM* pp28, 117-119, 148.

[15] *Letter to the author* 19th November 1966.

[16] *ST* p. 230.

of Wight. [17]

Documentary evidence as to the price of memorials is scanty.
Mr. Burgess notes:

> "A comparison of burials recorded in parish registers checked with
> existing 18th century gravestones reveals them as confined even in
> country districts to the wealthier members of its community, the farmers
> and craftsmen, and on the whole it was not until the growth of canals
> and railways reduced both the cost and transport of stone that monuments
> came within the purchasing power of the lower classes. [18]

Owing to poverty it is not uncommon to find older monuments doing
double duty with an added inscription for a more recent interment. [19]
However, he also suggests that often there may have been a payment in
kind rather than cash, or payment over a period similar to our hire-
purchase system. [20]

Nonconformist Churches

Although memorials in the church are not as common as in Anglican
churches, tablets are not infrequent on the walls of the older Free
Churches. Occasionally these have been copied, and articles relating
to the memorial tablets and tombstones of individual churches have
appeared in the magazines of the denominational historical societies:
However, in general, Nonconformist memorial tablets present unexplored
genealogical territory.

Nonconformist Burial Grounds.

Burial Grounds were started by the Nonconformists in the 17th
century, some of the earliest being those of the Quakers. They considerably increased in number throughout the 18th century when some
were also started by the Jews. As with those of the Anglican church
many of these burial grounds have been allowed to get into a bad
state, and in some cases the stones have been taken down by the Local
Council and used for paving. Of all the denominations The Society of
Friends shows the most concern for its burial places and they also
have good records of the tombstones. The other denominations, however
seem sadly uninterested.

---

[17]   In Mediaeval times trade or profession symbols on tombstones are frequently found, as on some of the fine collection dating from 1100/1300
at Bakewell, Derbyshire which include a key, shears, a bow and arrow, a
sword, an axe, a bugle and a chalice. However, here of course there is
no clue as to the indentity of the deceased. See R.W.P. Cockerton. *Some
Interesting and Unusual Inscriptions in All Saints Church and Churchyard,
Bakewell* (1957). Considerable detail on the decoration of tombstones,
including the use of symbolism and allegorical scenes will be found in
ECM pp 154-216, and a briefer summary in *EG* pp 310-314.

[18]   *ECM p.* 27
[19]   See *ECM* p. 53
[20]   *ST* p. 230.

The chief public Nonconformist burial ground for the London district for two centuries was that of *Bunhill Fields*. It is estimated that in the period from the enclosing of the ground in 1605 to the stopping of interments in 1852, upwards of 120,000 were buried there. Valuable transcription work on these inscriptions has been done from time to time. In the closing years of the 18th Century, the Rev. Dr. John Rippon of Carter Lane church, a Baptist historian, undertook to transcribe all such inscriptions as were then legible. He spent several years on this enormous task, but never completed it. What he did accomplish is contained in manuscript volumes, preserved in the libraries of the College of Arms and the British Museum. In 1849, J.A. Jones published his *Bunhill Memorials* giving particulars of 300 of the better known worthies. This volume is now very scarce. In 1868 the City Lands Committee prepared an accurate copy of every inscription which was legible then, and this list is preserved in the Guildhall Library. More recently, in 1913 and 1933 Alfred W. Light has issued two invaluable volumes on Bunhill Fields containing much biographical information and photographs both of individuals and of tombstones.

Important Nonconformist burial grounds existed in other parts of the country, both adjacent to and also apart from the church buildings. In some instances when these have been closed and the site possibly put to other public uses, careful records were made by the local council. For example in 1938 the disused Baptist Burial ground at Mount Street, Nottingham (earlier known as Bearwood Lane Burying Ground) was cleared by the Nottingham Corporation in connection with the construction of a new street from Park Row to Friar Lane. The City Engineer compiled a schedule of the 128 headstones and vaults, giving the sizes and descriptions, and complete copies of the inscriptions except in a very few instances where they were quite illegible. But in general little has been done to preserve the information contained on Nonconformist tombstones. There are exceptions; one of the best is the *History of Friar Lane, Nottingham,* which not only contains a complete copy of the register of births and burials but also includes the inscriptions on 80 tombstones which were legible at the time of publication in 1903. [21]

There is urgent need for an examination of Nonconformist burial grounds and for the copying of the tombstones, before the stones become quite illegible or are removed by the local council.

---

[1] This book is made the more valuable by the inclusion of the pedigrees of 14 leading Nottingham families. For more information on Bunhill Fields and other Nonconformist Burial grounds see article on *The Three Denominations* in Volume II.

Cemeteries.

Between 1741 and 1765 the official figures record 588,523 burials
in London and a further 605,832 between 1766 and 1792. [22] Thus, by the
end of the 18th century London churchyards and their additional paris
burial grounds had become so over-crowded that private speculators
often bought up land and opened up private cemeteries. To attract
custom, their burial fees were lower than those of the churchyards.
They were grossly overcrowded and highly insanitary. [23] In Enon's
Chapel in Clement's Lane 20,000 were buried in a very small space.

In 1842 a very strongly worded Report was presented to Parliament
by a Select Committee appointed to examine the question of London
burials. However, long before this, public cemeteries had been starte
The first was Kensal Green in 1827 which was eminently respectable an
even fashionable being the "leading cemetery for what is called art
and intellect". [24] Here is displayed, says Mr. Burgess "the best and
worst of sepulcrimagery" during the last 130 years. Kensal Green was
followed in quick succession by Norwood, Highgate, Abney Park,
Brompton, Nunhead and Mile End.

Some of the more important early provincial cemeteries were
St. James's Cemetery, Liverpool (1829), Leeds (1835), Sheffield (1836
Reading (1843), Bath (1844), Lewes (1845) and Leamington (1852). The
practice of public cemeteries was reinforced by the Act of 1850 *To
make better provision for the interment of the Dead in and near the
Metropolis.* This conferred powers upon the General Board of Health to
establish cemeteries or enlarge burial grounds, and also to close any
of the old churchyards. In 1852 a more stringent act was passed and
this was in the following session extended to the whole of England
and Wales, the General Board of Health having reported strongly in
favour of a scheme for "Extra-mural Sepulture" in the country towns,
declaring that the graveyards there were in no better condition than
those of London.

Alongside the work of public authorities, private enterprise stil
continued. In 1852 the London Necropolis Company was formed which
bought up a tract of 2000 acres at Woking and established its own
private railway for the conveyance of funerals, monuments and
mourners. [25] In the last century, therefore, the majority of burials
have taken place in cemeteries rather than churchyards. Many
cemeteries maintain indexed registers of grave plots making the
location of inscriptions relatively simple, although the cemetery

---

[22] Between 1741 and 1837 a total of 2,105,112 burials were recorded.
[23] For an examination of this gruesome subject see Holme *London Burial
      Grounds* and *ECM* p. 39.
[24] *ECM* p. 40.
[25] *ECM* p. 40

might be very large. Information on which cemetery in a town or city is the most likely for any given address will normally be supplied by the Town Clerk, who will often also arrange for a search of the indexes to be made. However, it must be borne in mind that headstones are by no means invariably erected, particularly if, as often occurs, six or seven unnamed persons are buried in one grave. Burials were, of course, often far away from the place of death, but a search of deaths recorded in the local newspapers will often supply the place of burial.[26]

Extent of Information

Information from M.Is may be of considerable genealogical value in supplementing that of the parish register. H.L. White once attemped a comprehensive comparison of an 1851 census return with the parish register, finding the latter to be about 33% deficient a discrepancy that it is to be hoped is exceptional. Not infrequently the burial register is lost altogether. C. Partridge points out:

> "Nearly 10% of Suffolk's parish registers proper are missing before 1700 and about 2½% are missing before 1740. The churchyards of such parishes often have gravestones earlier than the earliest book-register, which are unique records of departed parishioners, and, subtracting age from year of death, they tell the approximate year of the deceased's birth, a fact that, owing to the pre-1700 or pre-1740 book-registers having been lost, cannot be elsewhere obtained.[27]

It would be a mistake, however, to assume that monumental inscriptions are chiefly valuable in that they supply deficiencies in the parish registers. Not only is there considerably more information of genealogical importance, but the long epitaphs often found may give vital biographical information and interesting side lights on the social history of the time. Weever declared that an epitaph should consist of "the name, the age, the deserts, the dignities, the state, the praises both of body and minde, the good or bad fortunes in the life and the manner and time of the death and of the person interred."[28]

Church

Church inscriptions tend, on the whole, to supply much more information than those in the churchyard. Many of the 17th and 18th Century

---

[26] See *Births, Marriages and Deaths from Newspapers* below p. 282.
[27] C. Partridge *Suffolk's Stone Parish Registers*. Gen Mag Vol. V p. 409.
[28] op. cit. Cited in *ECM* pp 219-220.

inscriptions are in Latin. The information given may include birth-place, thus:

> " To the memory of Mrs Sarah Scott and of her two Brothers the Revd Dr. John and Mr. George Scott Natives of the City of Norwich . . . . . (St. Lawrence Jewry 1750)

Sometimes the information given is very considerable and may include ancestry, wife's parentage, children and former parish of residence.

> "Here lyeth buried the body of John Davenport, late of Datchet in the County of Buck. Gent who lineally descended from that antient family of Davenport de Davenport in ye County Palentine of Chester and also Katharine his wife who was the daughter of John Miles of Cuddington in the County of Huntington Gent. They lived most vertuously together 53 years and had issue 3 sons and 2 daughters John the eldest son Ambrose and Katherine living at his death he departed this life 27 Decemb 1683 aged 89 years she died ye 20 August 1679 aged 72 years he was a benefactor to the poor of St Michael Le Quern where he had formerly lived 44 years. "
> (St. Vedast, Foster Lane, London 1679)

Sometimes the wife's ancestry may be given in more detail and the husbands and wives of children are often recorded.

> "Here lie the Bodies of Harry Constantine late of Merly in the County of Dorset Esq who died Decr 30 1712 And of Mary his wife (Daughter of Robert Dillington Esq deceased eldest son of Sr Robert Dillington late of Knighton in the Isle of Wight Baronett) who died Feb 7th 1704. Here also lieth the Body of the Revd Mr. Harry Constantine Son of the above Harry Constantine He married Williamsa Daughter of John Leigh of North Court in the Isle of Wight Esq He died April 12th 1744 She 21st September 1748 And is here also buried. His age 73. Hers 64." (Wimborne Minster, Hants (1748)

Where the deceased had married more than once this is usually recorded.

> "Sir Francis Dashwood Kt. Bart. Third son of Francis Dashwood of Nallow Wood in the County of Somerset Esq Turky Merchant . . . Departed this life November 4th MDCCXXIV aged LXXV years. He married 4 wives -Mary Jennings, Lady Mary Fane, Mary King and Lady Elizabeth Windsor and left seven children Susanna Mary Rachael Francis Mary John and Charles. The three last wives lie in the family vault. Also Dame Susanna Bridgman his first daughter and Mary her daughter and also Charles Dashwood King the said Sir Francis Dashwood's third son. (West Wycombe, Bucks 1724).

It must be remembered that memorial tablets may be erected to persons not buried in the church or churchyard, and this may provide information very difficult to obtain elsewhere.

> "Sacred to the Memory of Marianne Scrivener who lies buried in the Protestant Cemetary, at Aix la Chapelle in Germany. . . . . on the 11th of Aug^st 1781, at the Age of twenty three, taken from her

Parents, her Sister and her Friends, ... Also in Memory of
DOROTHEA, sister to the above and Heir of J.F. SCRIVENER Esqr. She was
married to DR JOHN FISHER Bishop of Salisbury and died Septr 5th 1831,
aged 69 and was buried by the side of her husband in ST GEORGE'S CHAPEL
WINDSOR.' (Sibton, Suffolk 1781)

An interesting sequence of M.I's occurs in the church of Bakewell,
Derbyshire. An altar tomb, just East of the chancel records:

> John Denman, Apothecary of Bakewell, Father of Joseph and
> Thomas Denman M.D.D. Died 25th September 1752

It is not often that a father is identified by reference to his sons,
and still rarer to find a record of the same person having been buried
in two places, for in the chancel immediately to the left of the altar
on the North Wall is a large mural tablet:

> "Within this Chancel were interred the remains of John Denman; a very
> able and honest apothecary in this town who died 25th September 1752. By
> his wife Elizabeth, daughter of Anthony Buxton, Esq, of this place, he
> had five children, Joseph, Thomas, Sarah, Hannah and Mary. Joseph became
> an eminent physician and was for many years an active and intelligent
> magistrate in the neighbourhood; Thomas, a Physician in London, caused
> this tablet to be erected in the year 1815."

Evidently Thomas, a pioneer in obstetrics, who had established a
great reputation for himself in London, had his father's body re-
interred in the Chancel, but modestly omitted a reference to the distinction of his own career. This omission was remedied on the bi-
centenary of his birth, by British Obstetricians who placed a tablet
immediately below:

> To commemorate the bi-centenary of the birth at Bakewell of
> Thomas Denman M.D. This tablet was placed here by British Obstetricians
> 27th June 1933.

It is in accordance with the best traditions of their profession
that they recorded a birth rather than a death, which is quite
exceptional for a church inscription. [29]

Churchyard

In the churchyard, although the information given on older stones
tended to be limited, with the spread of literacy the biographical
data on churchyard monuments increased. The deceased's habitat is
usually given and sometimes, as at the Huguenot Burial Ground in
Wandsworth, the actual address. His trade, manner of death and
genealogy may also be included. Thus, it is not uncommon to find
several generations on one stone as in the following examples from a

---

[29] W.P. Cockerton *op.cit* p 5-6 It is of interest to note that Thomas Denman's
son Thomas became Lord Chief Justice of England in 1832.

ledger stone[30] in the churchyard of Christchurch Hants:

> Martin Stokes died 20 Oct. 1712
> Aged 63 Years
> Jane his Widow died 20 April 1715
> Aged 63 Years
> Martin their son died 20 July 1728
> Aged 48 Years
> Martin his sone died 14 Oct. 1730
> Aged 23 Years
> Sarah his Mother died 15 May 1744
> Aged 63 Years
> Francis her Son died 1 June 1763
> Aged 54 Years
> Mary his Widow died 6 March 1789
> Aged 75 Years
> Martin son of Francis and Mary
> died 6 March 1815
> Aged 68 Years

Clearly such a "document in stone" is of the same genealogical interest as a lawsuit "document in parchment". As with inscriptions in the church, one great advantage of finding a whole family recorded together is that it may include members of the family who died elsewhere and who may have been even buried elsewhere. D.E. Gardner and F. Smith[31] cite an example from Cartmel Lancs recording a couple who died in 1784 and 1789 and their children who included:

> William Spencer Barrow, mariner, died upon the Coast of Guinea in his 23rd year.
>
> Robert Barrow died in Norway 1795 in his 34th year
> Richard Barrow, mariner died at Lorraine in France in 1796 in his 28th year

The last of the children recorded died in 1835 aged 60.

It is wise to try to trace all monumental inscriptions of collateral branches of the family as they may supply clues to family origins not easily discoverable elsewhere. For example, the earliest known ancestor of a family might be a Charles Richardson *clerk at the dockyard* who died in Portsmouth in 1821. Neither the parish register nor his tombstone throw any light on his origins and there are no further relevant tombstones in the churchyard or other Portsmouth churchyards. It would be natural to assume that no further information can be obtained from monumental inscriptions. However, his will mentions a nephew, Stephen Richardson, baker of London. A search of trade directories reveals his address and hence the most likely parish where a monumental inscription might be found. After a long search a headstone is found of Stephen Richardson who died in 1829, aged 36 and who is described as *formerly of the parish of Medstead in the County o*

---

30 *ledger:* horizontal memorial slab, incised or in low relief.
31 *Genealogical Research in England and Wales* Vol. 1 p. 44.

Southampton, which proves to be the place where the family had resided for several generations. Needless to say the relevant parish register entry would not give this information.

It is by no means infrequent to find not only a reference to a former abode which may or may not prove to be the birthplace, but a specific statement of where the deceased was born. [32] Furthermore a tombstone may also give an indication of a change of name.

As with a tablet in the church, a headstone to a wife may include her father's name as in the following example from the churchyard of Silkstone, Yorks:-[33]

Mary, wife of Joseph Couldwell of Cheesebottom and daughter of John Womersley of Coates died 7 Feb 1797 aged 33. John Womersley died 27 June 1801 aged 66 Ann wife of John Womersley died 22 April 1807 aged 69. John Womersley their son died 16 December 1815 aged 54.

This may be compared with the paucity of information in the relevant burial entries in the parish register:

11 Feb. 1797 Mary wife of Joseph Caldwell of Cheesebottom
30 June 1801 John Womersley of Coates
22 Apr 1807 Ann wife of John Womersley
16 Dec 1815 John Womersley aged 54

This example also shows how members of two related families may be buried in the same grave. Even more frequently the position of the grave in the churchyard may provide a clue, as related families bearing a different surname may be buried nearby.

The amount of miscellaneous information given on monumental inscriptions tended to diminish in Victorian times. Mr Burgess observes

"Certain clergy, inspired by the prevailing Gothic ideals of the Camden Society, printed slender tracts intended to show that the erection of a tombstone could be made 'A Christian act and one that shall benefit the living'. Georgian monuments were condemned for their pagan imagery, and stonemasons for their taste and business methods. It was suggested that parishioners should no longer seek their advice as heretofore, but rather consult the parson, particularly with regard to the framing of the inscription. In brief it was mainly *by suppressing personal details,* avoiding prayers for the dead, and introducing more sacred texts into epitaphs, that the church thought it could make tombstones 'an effective and popular medium of conveying religious instruction and improvement' [34]

Nevertheless, although on the whole one does not often get from the mid-19th Century the flowery epitaphs, biographical detail and wealth of genealogical data sometimes found earlier, the inscriptions are still of enormous value. Not only will post-1837 inscriptions give dates and places of death enabling civil registration certificates

---

[32] For example see D.E. Gardner and F. Smith *op.cit.* p.44.
[33] Cited by D.E. Gardner and F. Smith *op.cit.* p.43.
[34] ST p 232 The whole subject is discussed at length in *ECM* pp 31-38

to be obtained, and often addresses which can be used in searching census returns, but as we have seen they may still throw light on family origins, moves and relationships even back into the eighteenth Century. The custom of recording numerous members of the same family on the one stone increased and, as before, not infrequently these included persons not actually buried in the grave.

Footstones

Footstones should not be ignored. Not only are these sometimes inscribed with the epitaph but they may be of great assistance in deciphering headstones. Mr. Partridge warns:-

> In innumerable cases the footstone is the key to the deciphering of the more worn headstone. Example: You partly decipher the headstone, *John P   , late of Walton, yeoman, died 4 May 17   , aged 80.* To search through the book-register for a John P   buried in May between 1700 and 1799, would be a hopeless task. Turning to the footstone, you read: *J.B. 1735* On the headstone you had mistaken the B for a P. Consulting the book-register under 1735, you read: *John Bond buried 7 May 1735.* The footstone gave you the clue. The headstone supplements the book-register by telling you the deceased's place of abode, rank and age at death. Had the foot-stone been missing, you would have had no key to tell you to whom these three additional facts refer. You know, too, that John Bond was born about 1655, and can now search for his baptism about 1654-56 in baptismal registers of that district.
>
> We antiquaries object to the removal of these "key" footstones. If, however, they must be removed, each footstone should be carefully set up behind its own headstone, back to back with the footstone's inscribed side facing outwards. [35]

Monumental Inscriptions and the Historian

The suppression of personal details in the 19th century was unfortunate not only for the genealogist, but for the local historian as well, for monumental inscriptions reveal the minutae of life which show the changing pattern of social conditions. Some of these are indicated by Mr Burgess: [36]

> "High infant mortality, the periodic epidemics of small-pox and Cholera, and widespread tuberculosis emerge from these sad statistics. When the circumstances of violent or accidental death are given, gravestone texts may remain the only records of such crimes and fatalities. The prevalence of smuggling is shown by the many coastal monuments to warring smugglers and excisemen. Inland we have those other inveterate enemies, poachers and gamekeepers, together with a host of unfortunates who suffered from contemporary occupational hazards: labourers' falls fro horses, carts, trees and buildings; trapped quarrymen and miners; scalded railway engineers. The record of mishap is sometimes concluded with advic A stone at Marton, Yorks of 1812, to three men who lost their lives in a well, remarks 'From this unhappy accident let others take warning, not to

---

[35] C. Partridge *op.cit.* p.410
[36] ST p 231 Epitaphs are dealt with in great detail in *ECM* pp 216-241

Venture in Wells without first trying whether a candle will burn in them.
If the candle burns to the bottom they may be entered with safety: if it
goes out human life cannot be supported'. Such monuments which give the
physical reasons for death and imply remedies, e.g. asphyxiation through
fire in close-shut bedrooms, or clothes catching fire, showed that gravestones served a useful as well as pious purpose. Murders too are recorded
such as Sarah Smith's at Wolstanton, Staffs in 1763 written in the vein
of purple melodrama. [37]

Condition

As has been pointed out, the speed with which Monumental Inscriptions are disappearing is alarming. Even without the help of man, time
itself is an efficient destroyer. Frederick Burgess emphasizes:

" Any memorial once set up in the ground and left undisturbed has a
natural life expectancy before sinking beneath the turf and being lost
to sight and to memory"[38]

W.T. Vincent made an estimate of this life expectancy:

" The period required for total disappearance may more accurately be
regarded as from 200 to 250 years. It has been found by careful observation in
a few random cases that the stones subside at the rate of about one foot
in forty or fifty years, and, as their ordinary height is from 5 feet to
5 feet 6 inches, we can readily tell providing the rate rules evenly, the
date when any particular stone may be expected to vanish. In confirmation
of this theory is the fact that scarcely any headstones are discoverable
of a date earlier than 1650, and whenever they have been left to their
fate the veterans of 150 years have scarcely more than their heads above
ground. Wherever we find otherwise, it may be assumed that conscientious
church officers or pious parishioners have bethought them of the burial-
ground, lifted up the old stones and set them once more on their feet. [39]

Fortunately, it is likely that Mr. Vincent slightly underestimated
the period before total disappearance, which of course in any case
varies according to the type of soil and drainage.

An even greater natural force of destruction than subsidence is
erosion of the surface. The rate varies with the nature of the stone,
the amount of acid deposit from the atmosphere and the exposure to
frost damage. Marble deteriorates rapidly in the open air and many
other types of stone are equally perishable. On the other hand
Portland Stone, much used in London Churchyards, weathers well in any
atmosphere. So long as headstones remain in vertical position or
incline forward their inscriptions often remain legible, but once
ground settlement brings them down their survival is limited unless
they fall face downwards so as to preserve the inscriptions and then

---

[37] The epitaph is given in full in *ST* p. 231 and *ECM* p. 225. Other examples
of murders recorded on tombstones occur at Tandridge, Surrey and Wareham,
Dorset.
[38] *ECM* p. 28.
[39] W.T. Vincent. *In Search of Gravestones Old and Curious*, pp 65-66

get turfed over before removal out of the way of mowing. There is a photograph in the possession of Mr. H.L. White taken in 1897 of a recently fallen headstone dated 1709 with an extremely good and legible inscription. When it was transcribed in 1930 the remaining inscription was largely illegible. Nearly 200 years of vertical stance had made little difference, but 30 years face upwards virtual destroyed the inscription.

There have been periods of preference for churchyard vaults, the most significant being the 50 years from about 1780 to 1830. These were covered by large ledger stones at ground level and like the large raised flat stones covering table tombs, have much more space for engraving than the usual headstones, and usually contain far mor genealogical information. Unfortunately, as these stones are exposed upwards they also suffer most from weathering with illegibility spreading outwards from the centre where water tends to collect. It is unfortunate that in recent years there has been an increase in th deplorable practice of deliberately laying headstones flat to make the upkeep of the churchyard easier. The late Mr. C. Partridge lamented:

"We do not fear time, for he treats them gently; but we do fear the vandal who removes them and lays them flat"[40]

In point of fact man has always proved a more efficent destroyer than nature. H.J. Stone pointed out[41] that at St. John's church, Glastonbury in a century the headstones had been reduced from about seventy to something under a dozen. It is likely that now there are even fewer. This pattern is repeated all over the country, and as W.T. Vincent observed.

"From one cause or another it is pretty certain that for every old gravestone now to be seen twenty or more have disappeared"[42]

Gravestones have always been easy prey for re-use as building material. Numerous old stones are frequently found embedded in churc walls and the preservation of many mediaeval stones is due to their discovery during restorations.[43]

The deliberate clearing of churchyards is also nothing new. Examples quoted in Gough's "*Sepulchral Monuments of Great Britain*" were summarised by W.T. Vincent as follows:

---

[40]   C. Partridge. *op.cit.* p 410.
[41]   *A Comprehensive Plan for copying Churchyard Inscriptions.* Gen. Mag. vol.12, p. 54 (1955)
[42]   W.T. Vincent *op.cit.* p 55.
[43]   For example the magnificent collection at Bakewell, Derbyshire. See *ECM* pp 28-29.

"In some cases the church officers, ... gave public notice
prior to removal of the gravestones, in order that persons claiming an
interest in the remains might repair and restore them; but more
frequently the stones were cleared away and destroyed, or put somewhere
out of sight without observation. Sometimes this was the act of the
Rector; at other times individuals, exercising rights of ownership,
having done the disgraceful work, and occasionally the whole of the
parishioners have been implicated. Gough says that the inhabitants
of Letheringham in Suffolk, being under the necessity of putting
their church into decent order, chose to rebuild it, and sold the
whole fabric, monuments and all, to the building contractor, who
beat the stones to powder, and sold as much at three shillings a
pound for terrace as came to eighty guineas". [44]

owever it is doubtful if the scale of destruction has ever approached
hat of today.

The reason for this is, of course, obvious. The rise in manpower
osts of the present century makes it increasingly expensive to keep
hurchyards mown and tidy. Since the obstacles of tombstones add to
he costs there is increasing pressure to find it inexpedient to
reserve them. Local authorities tend to adopt a policy of 'grassing
own' after removal of tombstones, and incumbents follow suit. These
azards of today are far more formidable than the normal processes
f erosion and decay have been in the past. And there are others;
hurchyards are built on or ploughed over and sometimes suffer from
oad widening schemes. Tombstones with their memorial inscriptions
re as much a part of local history as the parish church and the
arish registers. With every year that passes, there are enormous
osses and the need for the preservation and transcription of the
emainder becomes more urgent.

In London, under the open spaces act, the old graveyards have
een gradually made into public gardens. However, Mr. Burgess
omments:

"The many hundreds of tombstones destroyed in the process involved
little irreparable loss in this particular case, for even those remaining in the Metropolitan Area are often little more than blackened shards
owing to soot pollution"[45]

In many churchyards it may be impossible to be certain where M.I's
ere originally sited. At Great Chart, Kent a stone with an indent
riginally carrying a brass that almost certainly came from inside
he church is now used as part paving of a churchyard path, and nave
isles may, as at Christchurch Priory, Hants be paved with M.I's that
ertainly were brought inside from the churchyard. In many churchyards
articularly in urban areas the stones have been moved and placed round
he periphery of the churchyard. This practice is almost as disastrous
s laying the stones flat. Not only can one no longer infer relation-

4   W. T. Vincent. *op.cit.* p. 55.
5   *ECM* p 40.

ships from the close proximity of the stones to those of other families, but they are sometimes two or more in depth and in some cases shrubs have been planted in front of them as if deliberately to hide them. Sometimes, as at Corfe, Dorset they suffer a more direct exposure than before, When they are not cared for in their new positions they soon become hidden by ivy and brambles. Ivy particularly wreaks havoc with some types of stone especially the soft sandstones found in the Forest of Dean and Herefordshire. As at Bodenham, Herefordshire it frequently pulls away the top surface of the stone together with the carving and the inscription. When in their "natural positions stones are protected from wind and rain not only by the close proximity to the church but by each other, and therefore even completely illegible stones should be allowed to remain.

Mr. and Mrs. Burgess who have done enormous work on photographing stones have frequently revisited churchyards to re-photograph particular stones and on arrival have found them broken up as paving, or gone completely. That such vandalism is not necessary is shown by the many churchyards, such as that at Ledbury, Herefordshire which are beautifully kept. At Ledbury the turf has been cut away for a depth of 6 inches around each stone, including those that are broken or illegible, thus making the yard easy to maintain, and maybe even more important, the stones are not damaged by the machines used to cut the grass. In 1930 the Central Council for the care of churches published an important pamphlet *"The Care of Churchyards"* [46] for the guidance of incumbents and Members of Parochial Church Councils. It strongly urges the conservation of the character of the traditional graveyard, ensuring the retention of all monuments of antiquarian merit, and the accurate recording of gravestone inscriptions for the purpose of genealogy.

In a more recent memorandum, the Central Council made more specific proposals relating to the growing tendency towards drastic clearance and replanning of closed churchyards, drawn up after consultation with several learned societies interested in the preservation of antiquities. While agreeing that a case for removal was legitimate for illegible or broken monuments, or those whose huddled condition endangered the safety of the church fabric, it suggested that in all cases where legible gravestones were removed, or alterations made in a churchyard of architectural, historical or general scenic value, the following tasks should be made a condition of granting the necessary faculty:

(a) That arrangements should be made with the County Archivist through the Society of Genealogists for recording inscriptions, and that copies be deposited in the County Record Office and with the Society

---

[46] Reprinted 1962 as *The Churchyards Handbook.*

itself.

(b) That arrangements be made with the National Buildings Record for a photographic survey, and prints to be deposited in the Record's archives. [47]

This was a step in the right direction, but Mr. Burgess cautions:

"Unfortunately these proposed safeguards depend to a large extent upon goodwill, for it is virtually impossible to ensure authoritative supervision during all stages of an alteration or clearance, so that in practice these objectives can be defeated through carelessness or indifference. In some cases suitable protest has been made, and the matter righted,– but these are exceptional, for once a clearance has been made, restoration is seldom feasible because of the litigation, bad feeling and the expense involved. If it is decided after most careful thought that removal of monuments is imperative, some tighter degree of control or inspection is necessary, and here a liaison between diocesan officials and a specially appointed sub-committee of the local archaeological society might be effected as a check."[48]

As matters stand at the moment, almost every day monuments are still being wantonly destroyed, often without due record being made of inscriptions and carvings. Even after a transcription has been made, the stones are still of value both as works of art, with a wealth of lettering, and as a media by which local children can carry out their own personal researches. [49] Genealogists may wish to photograph stones of their ancestors, and also many people interested neither in monumental art nor in genealogy feel that once a churchyard is reduced to a "lawn", the atmosphere of the church is impaired. It is therefore to be regretted that many incumbents make the recording of inscriptions an excuse to clear the churchyard.

It is the duty of every student of local history or genealogy to do what he can to combat the wilful destruction of unique stone documents but at present a general air of ineffectiveness seems to prevail and it is time that there was much greater co-operation between the learned societies concerned with a view to doing something positive. In 1963, Mr. Burgess emphasized:

Owing to the increasing tempo of iconoclasm, future investigation needs to be both co-operative and co-ordinated: presumably the immediate solution would be the election by county learned societies of working committees to investigate the available material in their own localities."[50]

---

[47] *ECM* p. 46.
[48] *ECM* p. 47.
[49] See Pamela Burgess in *New Education* Aug. 1966 and the *Surrey Teacher*, March 1965.
[50] *ECM* p. 13.

However, the problem is so urgent that it must be tackled on the largest possible scale. A joint committee should be formed with representatives from the Society of Genealogists, the Society of Antiquaries and local archaeological Societies. This could circularise all local authorities and church authorities with a request (a) to notify if any copies of inscriptions are held and (b) to notify when a churchyard is to be cleared. On information being received that a churchyard is in danger, if attempts to dissuade the authorities failed, a full-time paid employee could be sent to copy the inscriptions and photograph those most important on artistic grounds. If the work was too great for one person a local appeal could be made for assistance. This scheme would involve at least two full time employees (one for administration) but the expense should not be prohibitive if spread between the different organizations that ought to be interested, for the appalling losses are artistic well as documentary.

Transcription

As has already been emphasised, even without the help of man, time itself is so efficient at completely effacing monuments that their transcription is a matter of extreme urgency. As long ago as 1830, J.S. Burn and others proposed a Parish Register Bill, one of the provisions of which should be:

> "that a copy of every inscription on any monument, tombstone or tablet affixed in any church or churchyard, shall be entered by the clergyman in a book to be kept for that purpose with the registers of his parish, and the copy attested to be true by his signature, for which a fee of 5/- shall be paid if in the church, and 2/6 if in the churchyard. [51]

Nothing came of this or of subsequent proposals for large scale official copies of monumental inscriptions, and such copying as has been done has been undertaken by genealogists or antiquarians. However, many substantial collections of monumental inscriptions have been made, some, like the remarkable Gloucestershire work of John Bigland, as long ago as the 18th century. Sadly many old collections include only inscriptions in the churches, which may still remain intact. Nevertheless early printed books may well include inscriptions which have since disappeared. Thus E. Hatton's *A New View of London* published in 1708 includes several hundred epitaphs, a great many now no longer in existance, particularly those in City churches rebuilt after the Great Fire which had disappeared before the list of inscriptions in City churches was made by A.J. Jewers. [52]

---

[51] J.S. Burn *Parish Registers of England* p. 211.
[52] Jewers' manuscript list is in the Guildhall Library.

The College of Arms has many copies of inscriptions, some going back to the 18th and early 19th centuries. J. S. Burn cites a case in which such a copy was used:

> "An Ejectment Case was tried at Guildford in 1847; it was of great importance to prove the identity of a lady who was buried at St. Christopher-le-Stocks in the City, but the register only gave her name and date of burial, and the church itself has been pulled down. This was mentioned to Sir Charles Young at the Heralds College, who at once recollected that when the church of St. Christopher was taken down to enlarge the Bank of England, one of the Heralds had copied the monuments and deposited the copy at the Heralds' College. It was at once produced, and there was found the Inscription in question, giving the particulars required, 'Mrs Mary le Keux, wife of Mr. Wm le Keux, Merchant, died etc (1724).[53]

The Society of Antiquaries also has a substantial collection of inscriptions begun in the middle of the 19th century and intended to form a General Index of Monumental Inscriptions.[54]

Since its inception, the Society of Genealogists has encouraged the copying of M. Is and now has a substantial collection, although this tends to be rather scattered throughout the Society's Library. Many copies are bound and on the county shelves, some are bound in with the parish register copy and others are in the Manuscript Collection normally boxed under the place name.

Good local collections have been made, such as the Suffolk transcriptions started by Revd Francis Haslewood (died 1900) and organised with enthusiasm by the late C. Partridge. Almost all churchyards in Suffolk -nearly 500 in all- were transcribed. Mr. Partridge optimistically hoped that:

> "some day when funds permit, these tens of thousands of inscriptions will be printed and fully indexed. Meanwhile we have collected them before Time altogether obliterates them."[55]

This is an exceptional collection. With many others, however, a word of warning is necessary. Just as one does not expect genealogy to be faithfully served by an incomplete transcription of a parish register, so are incomplete transcriptions of M. Is equally unsatisfactory. As has been pointed out, in the past, transcribers have frequently confined themselves to the church only, neglecting the churchyard where there is no protection from weathering, or to limited objectives, such as mediaeval brasses or inscriptions that accompany armorial shields. In his preface to *The Monumental Inscriptions of the Cathedral, Parish Churches and Cemeteries of the City of Durham* (1880), C. M. Carlton wrote:

---

[53] *op.cit.* p. 255
[54] *Notes and Queries* July 1858 pp 60, 86, 108, 171.
[55] C. Partridge *op.cit.*

"Besides possessing other merits this collection has a claim to being the first complete one of the kind printed in this country. It is true that other works of a somewhat similar nature have been published, but they are all little more than selections, comprising such inscriptions only as seemed to the compilers important, curious or otherwise worthy of preservation. This collection, on the contrary, contains every monumental inscription in the City of Durham, however humble it may be."

As C.M. Carlton realised, in order to obviate the uncertainty arising from omission, it is essential to record all M.I's both from the church and the churchyard.

As with parish registers, the transcription of Monumental Inscriptions has many pitfalls. Inscriptions that appear illegible in poor light or with strong sunlight directly upon them may well become perfectly legible in strong sunlight from the side. Headstones face East or West and the sun at some time in a summer's day is suitable for the reading of practically all churchyard M.I's, (except those on the panels of table tombs that may face North or South) but it may be necessary to follow the sun round as it slants in turn across the M.I's that are marginally legible. In a dry summer a buried stone shows up by a change in the turf above it in the same way as a mediaeval village on an aerial photograph. Incrustation on stones can be removed most easily by rubbing with a small piece of sandstone. [56]

The three errors that are usually to be found in transcriptions of M.I's are the confusion of 4 and 1, the confusion of 6 or 9 with 0 and the transposition of 3 and 5. 4 is usually engraved with a deep down stroke while the other two strokes are so light that in time they are completely removed by weathering. Consequently a 4 literally becomes a 1 with passage of time though the original 4 may in some cases still be inferred from the spacing. All transcriptions of M.I's should be compared wherever possible with the burials of the parish register, a procedure that is a check on the effects of weathering and also discloses the occasional lapses of both the transcriber and the original engraver. Because of the many pitfalls, ideally the most suitable transcribers of M.I.s are those who have already transcribed the registers. However, the transcription of monumental inscriptions is even more urgent than that of parish registers and the only likelihood of ensuring that surviving M.I.s are rapidly transcribed is to tackle the problem on a large scale using school-children under the direction of the History teacher. Obviously, many more errors are likely than if the work is tackled by an expert, but it is clearly preferable to waiting until many of the inscriptions are completely illegible or have disappeared altogether. The late H.J.W. Stone, while a headmaster of Brentwood School was a pioneer in this work. [57] He described the methods he used to try and eliminate errors.

---

[56] Charles Rogers *N & Q* 4th Ser. Vol. 2 (1868) p. 20.

[57] The employment of school children on transcribing MI's was suggested as long ago as 1858 (*N & Q* 2nd Ser. 4 p. 136) but to no effect.

"After permission has been obtained to copy up a burial ground, the size of the party must be considered. Ten boys will copy about four hundred inscriptions a day. It is best to have two boys working together; each pair should be given a small, but clearly defined group of stones to copy so that as soon as they have finished the particular work they can be moved on to another area, if possible in a different part of the burial ground to give them variety. All work should be recorded in an exercise book with names in block capitals. Whoever is in charge should move about among the groups to sort out difficulties. The type of boy to whom this work appeals most is not necessarily one from the most academic form. It calls for plenty of drive, a sense of improvisation and above all a little humour. After the copying has been finished, all the work should be checked off against the burial register. There will have been mistakes, but usually these can be corrected at once. When checking with the burial register time is saved if two boys are available to go out to the burial ground, perhaps dozens of times, to have another look at a stone that does not appear in the register under the date recorded."[58]

Efforts have also been made by Mrs. Pamela Burgess to encourage an interest among children and teachers. An exhibition of churchyards and their monuments arranged by her is available to primary and secondary schools in Surrey through the county museum loan service at Guildford and she is at present engaged in writing a school textbook for the local history in country churchyards idea. Mr. S. Cramer who has transcribed many Scottish stones has urged that the B.B.C., the Press and the Educational Authorities should co-operate with voluntary labour from learned societies to organise instruction to teenage schoolchildren and adults on how to transcribe local church-yards during school holidays. The Institute of Heraldic and Genealogical studies has promoted a scheme for school children to copy M.I's and has the co-operation of Educational Authorities throughout the country. In one summer holiday M.I's in more than 200 churchyards have been copied and the work goes on. These will be included in a comprehensive list of collections of memorial inscrip-tions which is in course of preparation.

Methods of Recording Inscriptions

The ideal method of recording is to copy out each inscription in full and for those who can find the time and opportunity of doing so this method is to be recommended. A full copy gives a stronger impression of authenticity and reproduces sentiments and modes of expression which can be of great interest to the reader. At the same time it must be recognised that a full transcript is a cumbrous way of reproducing the essential genealogical facts enshrined in an inscription, and that with the vast majority of inscriptions still

---

[58] *A Comprehensive Plan for Copying Churchyard Inscriptions.* **Gen.Mag.** vol. 12 p. 54. (1955).

unrecorded there is something to be said for a summary method, the use of which would not be such a deterrent to compilation as the more detailed method.

J.F. Mitchell who has used such a summary method in the transcription of over two thousand Scottish inscriptions argues:

> If I had had to copy out the inscriptions in full, I would not have done half the number. To indicate the saving in clerical work (and printing costs perhaps, where printing is undertaken) I find after careful calculations that The Scottish Record Society publication about inscriptions in St. Cuthbert's, Edinburgh, would, using the same type, style, spacing etc require only one third of the number of pages actually taken up. [59]

Mr. Mitchell's system is shown in the following example from Greyfriars Churchyard, Edinburgh:

> JAMES NEWTON Esq.
> Sacred to the memory of Christian Brown, his wife, who died 28th June 1816, aged 46 years.
> Abram Newton, their third son, who died 21st August 1815, aged 14 years.
> John Newton, their second son, died 17th Sept 1826, aged 27 years.
> Isabella Newton, their daughter, died 8th Decr. 1831, aged 26 years.
> Also James Newton above mentioned, who died 14th December 1844, aged 76 years. Also James Newton of Castlandhill, Writer to the Signet, son of the above James Newton, who died 18th June, 1861, aged 64 years.
> Sacred to the memory of Abram Newton, merchant in Edinburgh, who died 25th April 1828, aged 64 years.

This could be put in the summarised form:

> Jas. Newton Esq 14 Dec 1844 76, w Christian Brown 28 Jun 1816 46, 3s Abram 21 Aug 1815 14, 2s John 17 Sep 1826 27, da Isabella 8 Dec 1831 26, s Jas of Castlandhill WS 18 Jun 1861 64; Abram N.mert 25. 4. 1828 64.

Mr. Mitchell points out:

> The more significant features of this method of transcription are—date is date of death and is followed by age in years or otherwise (two dates after a name would signify date of birth and of death respectively); suppression of surname where the expressed relationship leaves no doubt as to the surname; repetition of surname represented by initial letter where relationship is not indicated and no ambiguity is involved; starting with head of household and showing relationships to him; use of abbreviations for the commoner christian mames, relationships (eldest son being 1s, second son 2s etc), occupations the periods of time (m,w,d); restriction of punctuation to absolute necessity, the comma being used between related persons and the semi-colon between persons whose inter-relationship is not mentioned; non-repetition of name of the same person; omission of name of place in which the burial ground is situated (in above instance "Edinburgh" for Jas the merchant); in the "capital letter" and other abbreviatior

---
[59] *Burial Ground Inscriptions.* Scottish Genealogist xi, No. 1, May 1964.

such as "WS" above for "Writer to the Signet" omission of the periods
or full stops (thus one would put "HEICS" for H. E. I. C. S. or "Honorable
East India Company Service"); omission of expressions like "Here lies
the body of" and In (loving) memory of" and of biblical quotations
    Generally, however, if it is thought that summarising may lead to
ambiguities in particular cases, a fuller transcript is given. It has
generally been assumed in summary recording that the mother is the wife
of the father when only parentage is mentioned.

One small criticism of Mr. Mitchell's system is the omission of
the place name. Thus, there is nothing in his summary to show that
Abram Newton was a merchant *in Edinburgh.* The original inscription
could equally well have said "Abram Newton, merchant" and he could
have been a merchant anywhere. However, whilst the adoption of such
a summary system is bound to be a subject of much controversy, it
clearly has considerable advantages, even more in England than in
Scotland owing to the much greater number of inscriptions to be copied.

There are few more pleasant occupations on a fine summer's day for
those who are genealogically inclined than the transcription of churchyard M. I's. However, considerable care must be taken with regard to
equipment before embarking on a transcription expedition, or some
simple but necessary tool will be lacking half way through the task.
Mr. Mitchell suggests the following list:- an old mackintosh to lie
on, a garden fork to raise turf encroaching on flat stones, a trowel
to dig up a few inches just in front of the headstone where a line or
two of the inscription has been buried, a piece of dry stick for
scraping off moss, and worn to a point for probing incised items and
a pair of secateurs for dealing with the ivy and shrubs. If mutual
confidence has been established with the incumbent, the searcher can
experience something of the excitement of an archaeological dig in
the recovery of the past and the relatively insignificant labour of
the removal of about three inches of turf instead of the tons of soil
that the archaeologist may be faced with. Anyone who has experienced
the satisfaction of putting together the inscriptions from broken
headstones, completely buried and apparently lost for ever, must be
surprised that genealogists in general seem to do so little work in
transcribing churchyard M. I's when so much yet remains to be done in
this field. And the increasing hazards of wholesale destruction leave
us so little time in which to do it.

BIBLIOGRAPHY.

Periodicals

The Monumental Journal (now called *Commemorative Art*) 1934–date

General

K. Esdaile. *English Monumental Sculpture since the Renaissance*
(S.P.C.K.) (1927)

R. Gunnis. *Dictionary of British Sculptors 1660-1851* (Odham's
1952)

L. Weaver. *Memorials and Monuments* (1915)

D. Knoop & G.P. Jones. *The London Mason in the 17th Century* (1935)

Henriette S' Jacob. *Idealism and Realism, a Study in Sepulchral
Symbolism* (Leiden 1954)

Richard Gough. *Sepulchral Monuments of Great Britain.* 2 Vols
(1786-96)

W. Brindley & W.S. Weatherley. *Ancient Sepulchral Monuments* (1887

Church Memorials

K. Esdaile. *Monuments in English Churches* (1937)

K. Esdaile. *English Church Monuments 1510-1840* (O.U.P. 1946)

J Le Neve. *Monumenta Anglicana* (covers M.I's of notables 1600-171
5 vols (1715-1719)

E. Blore. *Monumental Remains of Noble and Eminent Persons* (1826)

C.A. Stothard & A.J. Kemp. *The Monumental Effigies of Great Brita*
(Chatto & Windus, London 1876)

A. Batsford & W.H. Godfrey. *English Mural Monuments and Tombstone*
(London 1916)

Churchyard Memorials

F. Burgess. *English Churchyard Memorials* (Lutterworth Press 1963)

F. Burgess. *English Gravestones of the post-Reformation and their
Masons.* Gen. Mag. vol 10. p 310 (1949)

F. Burgess. *Spoils of Time.* Amateur Historian Spring 1965

F. Burgess. *English Churchyard Carving.* The Connoisseur Year Book
1956.

A. Stapleton. *The Churchyard Scribe* (1908)

W.T. Vincent. *In Search of Gravestones Old and Curious* (Mitchell
and Hughes 1896)

Cemeteries etc.

A. Whittick. *History of Cemetery Sculpture* (1938)

A. Whittick. *War Memorials* (1946)

Lists of M.I's

*A Bibliography of Monumental Inscriptions in the City and County
of London.* (Gen.Mag. vol.5, pp 363, 406. vol.6, pp 22, 68, 107,
213, 285, 439, 503)

A.J. Jewers. *List of Inscriptions in the Churches of the City of
London.* Indexed. Manuscript Guildhall Library

III BIRTHS, MARRIAGES AND DEATHS FROM NEWSPAPERS

The author gratefully acknowledges the assistance of B. Frith[1]
F.L. Leeson, H.G.H. Singleton and H.D.W. Lees in writing this article.
Thanks are particularly due to Miss Rosemary ffolliott and the Irish
Genealogical Society for permitting the use of extracts from her
article "Matched and Dispatched" *(Irish Genealogist vol.III, No.7)*

Although records available in English Newspapers over a given
period of years cover only a small fraction of the total number of
births, marriages and deaths, these records are a source which should
not be neglected – they may bring to light useful genealogical
material not available in the more formal entries in parish registers.
All too often, however, the searcher overlooks them, usually deterred
by the apparent immensity of the task, the smallness of the print, and
the time taken to find his way around. The more he uses them, however,
the easier becomes the task. If the person about whom particulars are
sought was wealthy or took a prominent part in local or national
affairs there may well be fairly substantial accounts in the London
papers and in the body of the local paper as well as in the lists of
births, marriages and deaths. Indeed, some of the information given
cannot be found elsewhere and even early newspapers which do not
contain many death or marriage entries, often give such information
in other ways, such as advertisements, businesses changing hands through
death, legal notices, and various other occurrences which they noted.

Early Newspapers

The first English Newspapers were the *Corantos* or news sheets
(later small books) which appeared from 1620 and contained only
foreign news. From 1642 onwards, newspapers appeared in increasing
profusion. The following year Parliament set up a Board of Licences,
and newspaper titles were recognised and registered. The freedom of
the press was curbed by Cromwell's ordinance of 1655 and except for
a brief period from 1658-9 the period of government control lasted
until 1695. The *London Gazette* (formerly the *Oxford Gazette*) is the
only survivor today from this long "licenced" period.

Interesting though these papers are for the historian, their
genealogical value is small, though towards the end of this period
some information of interest can be gleaned from advertisements. From
1695 onwards the mostly short-lived licenced papers tended to be
replaced by newer and freer publications, many short-lived but some
surviving a considerable time, though changes of title were frequent.
In 1701 the first Provincial paper appeared.

---

[1] All the examples from the "*Gloucester Journal*" have been supplied by
Mr. Frith.

Three important papers were started in 1695, all appearing three times a week – the *Post Boy*, the *Flying Post* and the *Postman*. The first Daily paper, the *Daily Courant* was started in 1702 and survived until 1735. Four of the London daily papers started between 1719 and 1730 lasted over twenty years. These were the *Daily Post* (1719-1746), the *Daily Journal* (1720-1742), the *London Journal* (1720-1744) and the *Daily Advertiser* (1730-1807). Two evening papers started in the early 18th century – the *Evening Post* (1709-1740) and the *London Evening Post* (1727-1806) were also long-lived. A number of weekly papers were also started, but the only one to last any considerable time was *The Weekly Journal or The British Gazetteer* (afterwards *Read's Weekly Journal*) which appeared from 1716 to 1761. Thus, by the year 1731, when the *Gentleman's Magazine* was started, there were 9 London weekly papers, 7 issued three times a week, three issued twice a week and five issued daily. Most of these papers reported intended marriages: "We are informed that a marriage is on foot between......." and often the marriages themselves. Announcements of birth are rarer, though from about 1710 onwards reports sometimes appear concerning the births and baptisms of the children of the aristocracy. The news items in the *Gentleman's Magazine* summarised the news contained in the London papers. However, only a small proportion of the births, marriages and deaths which appeared in these were re-produced and considerable detail was omitted. Nevertheless, the *Gentleman's Magazine* is indexed and may be of assistance in locating an entry in the daily newspapers.

The remainder of the 18th century saw ten other long-lived London papers founded. Of these, the *London Daily Post and General Advertiser* (afterwards the *Public Advertiser*) (1734-1794) was the outstanding daily paper of the mid-18th Century and published the famous *Letters of Junius*. Between 1764 and 1771 its monthly circulation increased from 47,500 to 84,000. In 1769 William Woodfall started the *Morning Chronicle* whose daily circulation in 1819 reached 4,000 and in 1843 (when Dickins was a contributor), 6000. Another long-lived daily paper whose top circulation was about 6,000 was the *Morning Herald* (1781-1869). In 1785, *The Times* was founded as *The Daily Universal Register*. The circulation reached 5,000 by 1815 and in 1854 reached 50,000 when its most circulated rival the *Morning Advertiser* (founded 1794) had a sale of less than 8,000 copies. The other famous survivor of the 18th century dailies was the *Morning Post* (1772-1937). In addition to the dailies a fair number of 18th century London evening papers survived well into the 19th century and also

---

[2] A list of the longer lived London papers up to 1837 is given in Appendix II to this article, pp. 288–291.

two Sunday papers of which the *Observer* (founded 1791) still exists.

The abolition of the Stamp Tax in 1855 began a new era. The number of newspapers established from the early part of 1855 when the repeal of the duty had become a certainty and continuing in existence at the beginning of 1857 amounted to 107, of which 26 were London papers. Furthermore, there were such reductions in the prices of newspapers, that they speedily began to reach the many rather than the few.

Provincial Newspapers[3]

It is impossible to be certain of the dates many early newspapers started, as the first surviving issue often dates from many years later. The number on this issue is an imperfect guide as earlier the paper might have appeared more or less frequently than it did at that time. Thus calculations may be one, two or even three years out. However, authorities are generally agreed that the first provincial paper was the *Norwich Post*, which was probably started in 1701 and that this was followed by the *Bristol Post Boy* probably started in 1702. *Berrow's Worcester Journal* claims descent from a 17th century news-sheet, but if this is doubtful there can be no doubt that this paper, started as the *Worcester Post-Man* in 1709, is, after the official *London Gazette* the oldest surviving paper in England.

The cradle of the Provincial Press was the rural South and South-west, and it was only with the Industrial Revolution and the shifting of population to the North that the majority of Northern papers appeared. If a line is drawn from the Severn to the Humber, by 1715 there were 16 country papers South of it and only 8 North. The 16 Southern papers were in six towns only[4] and the Northern papers in five.[5] Between 1716 and 1725 there were 17 new newspapers in the South[6] and eight in the North.[7]

Between 1726 and 1740 the trend towards the Midlands and North began. Only 10 new papers were started in the South[8] (Colchester and Sherborne being the only new towns represented) whereas 22

---

3 See also *Welsh Newspapers* in Volume II.
4 Norwich (6) Bristol (3) Exeter (2) Stamford (2) Salisbury (1) Yarmouth (Local editions of 2 Norwich papers)
5 Newcastle (2), Nottingham (3) Shrewsbury, Worcester, Liverpool (1 each)
6 Norwich (1 more), Exeter (2 more) Bury St Edmunds, Canterbury, Cirencester, Gloucester, Ipswich, Maidstone, Northampton (2) Plymouth, Reading, St. Ives (3) Taunton
7 Newcastle (1 more), Chester, Derby, Leeds, Ludlow, Manchester, York (2)
8 Colchester, Sherborne, Cirencester, Exeter, Ipswich, Maidstone, Reading, Salisbury (2), Stamford

were started in the North,[9] and between 1741 and 1760 there were 27 new papers in the North[10] and 23 in the South, the latter due to an outburst of activity in the South-West, Bristol producing 6 newspapers and Bath 4.[11] In all, before 1760 newspapers appeared in 55 towns. In Bristol there were 9 attempts to establish a paper, in Manchester there were 8, in Exeter, Newcastle and Norwich 7, in Nottingham 5 and in Bath, Derby and York 4 each.[12]

It is curious that in some large towns newspapers appeared surprisingly late. Thus there was no paper in Birmingham until 1732, and the first successful one, the *Birmingham Gazette* was started in 1741. Other late starters were Hull (1739), Coventry (1741), Leicester (1753), Oxford (1746) and Cambridge (1744). Portsmouth and Gosport long had to be satisfied with a local edition of the *Salisbury Journal*. Though there was a short-lived Liverpool paper from 1710 to 1712, there was no other paper until Williamson's *Liverpool Advertiser* was started in 1756. After 1760 newspapers emerged almost everywhere and it is interesting to note that by 1825 Liverpool was the source of 11 newspapers of which one appeared daily. Nevertheless, at the beginning of the 19th century the provincial Press consisted of less than a hundred papers, as compared with the considerable number at the present day. They were at that time practically without influence and expressed no political views. Under the control of Edward Baines (1801) the *Leeds Mercury* became the most important and influential of the North Country papers in the first half of the 19th century. After the Reform Act of 1830 and the contemporaneous spread of self-education, the country newspapers developed in importance, but it was not until after the removal of the Stamp Duty in 1855 that the provincial press really came into its own, and in that year alone 81 Provincial papers were founded.

---

[9] Manchester (4 more), Newcastle (2 more), Chester, Derby, Nottingham (1 more each). New towns represented Birmingham (2), Boston, Durham, Hereford, Hull, Kendal (2), Lincoln, Preston, Whitehaven. Also one paper printed in London for distribution in Shropshire.

[10] Further activity in Hull, Leeds, Lincoln, Manchester (3), Newcastle (3), Nottingham, Preston, Worcester, York. Liverpool 2 papers reappeared for the first time since 1712. 8 new towns represented for the first time, Coventry (2), Doncaster, Halifax, Leicester, Middlewick, Sheffield (2) Stratford, Warrington.

[11] The remainder were Exeter (2 more), Northampton, Reading, New towns represented: Cambridge, Eton, Gosport, Lewes, Oxford (3) Winchester, Yeovil.

[12] All these statistics on early Provincial papers have been taken from G. A. Cranfield " *The Provincial Newspaper 1700-1760* pp 25-7

Lists of Newspapers

Full details of the dates when newspapers began, ended or were taken over will be found in the *British Union Catalogue of Periodicals* and in *The Times Tercentenary Handlist of English and Welsh Newspapers, Magazines and Reviews* published in 1920. Willing's *Press Guide* gives similar information for papers still in existence. Good lists of early newspapers are to be found in R.S. Craze and F.B. Kaye *Census of British Newspapers and Periodicals 1620-1800*[13] and the *Cambridge Bibliography of English Literature.*[14] Perhaps the best list for early Provincial newspapers is G.A. Cranfield's "*A Handlist of English Provincial Newspapers and Periodicals 1700-1760.* There is also the *Catalogue of English Newspapers and Periodicals in the Bodleian Library 1622-1800,* for those who may have access to the magnificent collection at Oxford. Details of the regional coverage of newspapers is given in the *Newspaper Press Directory,* published annually from 1846 onwards. A list of some of the pre-1837 London Newspapers for which reasonably long runs are available is appended to this article and the General Information Section of each county contains a similar list of Provincial Newspapers.

With regard to the shorter-lived papers, the compilers of all the works referred to above found great difficulty in keeping up with the frequent changes of name of newspapers and where only a few isolated issues survive, their identification is often difficult. Another cause of difficulty concerns the calendar.[15] Some newspapers adopted the New Style long before 1752. In some cases they put O.S. or N.S. after the dates, but in many cases they did not, and it is now often difficult to be certain in which year they were issued.

Availability of Newspapers.

The British Museum's collection of pre-19th Century London Newspapers is available in the Reading Room in London, as are also an incomplete file of "*The Times*" and the complete series of the *London Gazette.* All 19th and 20th century newspapers and Provincial and foreign papers before 1800 are at the special newspaper Library at Colindale.

Thanks to the enterprise of librarians who in many cases have acquired bound files following the dispersal of privately owned collections, many libraries now contain useful runs of national and regional newspapers. For example in Northampton Public Library there is a complete set running from 1720 to the present day of the

---

[13] *Studies in Philology* xxiv 1927 pp 1-205
[14] Vol 1 pp 736-763, Vol 2 pp 656-739
[15] See *Parish Registers - Form and Content* pp. 39–40. *Parish Registers and the Genealogist* pp. 141-2

Northampton Mercury, one of the oldest newspapers in England, and Gloucester City Library holds a similar set of *The Gloucester Journal* running from 1722. Many 18th century volumes of the latter have been microfilmed as well. The nature and type of library holdings can be seen by referring to the invaluable *Yorkshire Newspapers*, a bibliography with locations compiled for the Yorkshire Branch of the Library Association (1960) by G.E. Laughton and L.R. Stephen. County Record Offices also have often long runs of certain papers. Furthermore, newspaper offices often have considerable collections of past issues, maintain indexed references to matter of importance and are usually prepared to accord facilities to bona fide students.

As might be expected, entries of English people sometimes occur in Irish Newspapers and if residence in Ireland is suspected, the searcher would do well to consult one of the excellent Irish indexes particularly that for the county of Cork compiled by Miss Rosemary ffolliott. [16] For example in the Cork Evening Post for Thursday 18th June 1795 appears the entry:

> Married last Friday 12th inst. Philip John Miles Esq., son of William Miles of Clifton, Co.Glos to Miss Whetham daughter of Revd Dean of Lismore[17]

Early Colonial and American papers too many reveal unsuspected information about persons born in Britain. A number of these papers are kept at the British Museum, and some at the Public Record Office For others, it may be necessary to institute enquiries at overseas public libraries.

Extent of Information of Genealogical Value

It is often assumed that newspapers contain entries only for the well-to-do. While this is, broadly speaking, true of entries of marriages or deaths (though even here there are exceptions) it is certainly not true of newspapers as a whole, which of course contain a whole range of other material. Miss Rosemary ffolliott points out[1]

> " The diversity of persons who may be traced in newspapers could well amaze the unwary. Not only nobility, gentry, farmers and professional people (church, law, medicine, army and navy) but traders and craftsmen of all kinds, printers, grocers, butchers, clothiers, cabinet-makers, clockmakers, silversmiths, publicans, shoemakers and inn-keepers (inevitably inn-keepers) turn up in great profusion"

---

[16] For more details on these indexes see *Irish Newspapers* in Volume II.
[17] Cited by Miss Rosemary ffolliott *Matched and Dispatched*, Irish Genealog vol.III No.7, p. 273.
[18] op.cit. p. 273

Miss ffolliott was of course referring to Irish Newspapers, but this applies equally to the English ones.

In general, purely local news, including births, marriages and deaths of local rather than national interest appeared in newspapers only in the latter half of the 18th century, though there were often local advertisements much ealier. When such local news began to appear, the papers tended to concentrate on items in their place of origin. Coincident with improvements in communications, transport and literacy their coverage and sphere of influence widened and progressively they became more informative about the region as a whole, and often included items of genealogical importance from a wide area. Just how wide the coverage was can be seen from the list of names prepared by the late George Sherwood from one edition of *Jackson's Oxford Journal* (21st April 1810).[19] The list includes nearly 300 persons, many of them appearing in advertisements. The 23 marriages recorded were as follows: -[19a]

Danvers, Derbyshire Rev. James Henry Cotton to Mary Ann, 3rd daughter of the Bishop of Bangor.

Linton Kent Sir Matthew Blakiston to Lucy, eldest daughter of James Mann Esq. of Linton Place.

Banbury Mr Thomas Bartlett, mercer and draper to Miss Wheel of Rowington, Warwickshire.

West Hendred Mr Thomas Ansell of Burford to Miss Ann Brooks of Ginge.

P. Wood Esq., of Cotes to only daughter of W. Button of Sowdley, Salop.

Mr John Routh of Lawrence Lane to Miss Cain, niece of Thomas Cain Esq., Thoyden Place, Epping.

Maidstone, Kent Ely Crump, Surgeon H.M. Forces to Maria Louisa, eldest daughter of the late Hint Stacey Esq.

Abingdon, St Helen's James Sherwood, Surgeon, to Miss Mary Fortiscue

Clapham, Surrey. William Albin Garrett Esq of Lincoln's Inn to eldest daughter of James Stephen Esq., M.P.

Mr. J.C. Morris of Willey, Salop to eldest daughter of Mr. Gilpin of Wedges Mills near Cannock.

John Gorle Esq., of Napleton, Worcs. to Ann youngest daughter of W. Tatler Esq of Kenilworth.

Mr. J.T. Rutter of Mark Lane to Harriet, youngest daughter of late Perrot Hanger Esq., of Norwich.

St Martin in the Fields J. Ireson of Spring Gardens to Sarah, eldest daughter of the late Mr Swayne of Chertsey.

W.J. Kendall of Wakefield to Miss Jane Campbell Kettle of Cradley.

George William Newton Esq., of Stockport to Louise Maria Warre of Rugby.

Eugenius Roche Esq., to Miss M.J. Oliver.

---

[19] The list is printed in full in Gen.Mag. Vol.9 pp. 229-234 and 274-277.
[19a] The place of marriage when given has been put in italics but note that this applies to one entry only and not to those which follow where no place of marriage is stated.

Dunnekler House Col. Smith of Methvin Castle, Perth to Mary, 2nd
Daughter to J. Townsend Oswald Esq..

Marylebone Edward Jervis Ricketts to Mary Ann Parker, 2nd daughter of
the late T. Parker Esq., of Park Hall, Stafford

Milverton, Somerset. Rev. S. Reeve to Eliza Gratiana, daughter of
W. A. Webber Esq.

Bath Col. C.N. Cookson, R.A., to daughter of Joseph Russell Esq., of
Kenton, Devon.

Reading Thomas Allen Shuter Esq., of St. John's, Southwark to Fanny,
3rd daughter of Revd. Dr. Valpy.

Oxford, St Giles Mr. Richard Castle Toner of Ensham to Miss Frances
Honour of St. Giles.

Mr. John Watts of Aynho to Miss Ann Wadham of Steeple Aston.

It can be seen that in the majority of cases, one or both of the
parties resided far from Oxford and frequently the marriage took
place outside the county. Even the scantiest entry, that of Eugenius
Roche might be useful as the groom's unusual Christian name would help
to indentify him. [20]

Of the 21 deaths recorded, 10 were: -

the infant daughter of a Canon of Wells Cathedral,
the 33 year old daughter of a Norwich gentleman who died at Deptford.
a deputy Naval Officer of Barbadoes who died on passage from Trinidad
to St. Kitts.
the widow of John Goodrich *of Virginia* who died at Topsham, Devon.
a Trinity College Undergraduate who died "at his brother's house" in
Pall Mall.
Flora Macdonald who died in the island of Lewis aged 120.
a graduate of Pembroke college
a Bristol Woollen draper, killed in a duel.
the widow of a picture frame maker at St Aldate's
the wife of a Mr. Williams of London and elder daughter of Thomas Carden
of Worcester, who died at Brompton.

The remaining deaths recorded took place in Paris, Barton-on-the-Heath
Woodstock, Ludlow, (Salop) Ensham, Bloxham, Hatton (Warwickshire)
Northleigh, Bridgnorth (Salop) and Darlaston (Staffs).

In strange contrast to the marriages and deaths, no births at all
were recorded.

As can be seen from these entries, the extent of the information
in newspapers varies considerably. Sometimes, of course, it may be
meagre but useful, such as the marriage of Eugenius Roche mentioned
above or the following death in Doncaster, recorded in the "*Doncaster
Nottingham and Lincoln Gazette*" for 5th September 1828:

" "On Wednesday last, of a rapid decline, much and deservedly respected
Mrs Morrill, wife of Mr. William Morrill of York, printer"

---

[20] It would seem likely that he was an Irishman. Roche is an Irish surname
and Eugene was much used in the South of Ireland (particularly in the
Roman Catholic Registers which were entered in Latin) as a version of
Owen.

In considering in more detail the extent and quality of informaion obtainable the examples will be taken mainly from one typical rovincial paper – the *Gloucester Journal.*

irths

Announcements of births do not appear until a much later date han those of marriages or deaths. The earlier entries relate to irths of the aristocracy, but by the mid-18th century, one finds a ention of the births of children of lower status, though all the ntries are still of "persons of quality". Sometimes there is an nnouncement of the baptism of the child, which may include the place f baptism and the names of god-parents and proxies. However, births – r more precisely birthplaces– can often be found in news items or bituaries. The birthplace of Charles Mason, the surveyor and stronomer, best remembered for the "Mason and Pixon line" was ccidentally discovered from the *Gloucester Journal,* at a time when search was being independently made for his baptism, without success. n 1777 an item concerning his career appeared which stated that he was native of Sapperton, Gloucestershire, and much information was sub-equently found as a result of this entry. In the *Gloucester Journal* f Monday, 30th September 1793 is an item concerning a patent machine ' for expediting the formation of Canals. By this admirable contrivance, he labour of removing the earth, which used to require a great number f hands with wheelbarrows, is performed with much more expedition by man and a horse" The inventor was one Mr. Carne who, we are told ' is a native of St. Austle, in Cornwall". There are many other nstances of this type of entry, which help to throw light on the irthplace of people who were far from their native country, and this s information not always easy otherwise to find. Not infrequently fter searching parish registers in vain, one may discover from ewspapers that the person sought was a Dissenter, and in all robability no record of his birth survives.

arriages

A considerable number of marriages are recorded, and occupations nd ages are often given, particularly in the nineteenth century, hen some entries tend to be very extensive and descriptive, and ometimes state that a person being married was, say, the third son, r youngest daughter, of the parents, who are also named. Marriage nnouncements usually include a reference to the Bride's portion which ives an idea as to her social position. Thus in the *Gloucester Journal* f Monday 17th May 1725:

"..........Cockerell, Esq., of Gloucester, a Gentleman of 2000 l. per Ann. was married to a pretended West India Lady of 40,000 l.Fortune".

Unfortunately subsequent evidence indicated that the marriage was no quite such a success as their fortunes might have suggested, and it may well have been that her fortune was by no means as handsome as s claimed. Such estimates must therefore be taken with a certain degre of caution.

Newspaper men were not entirely without a sense of fun, as the following will show, in the *Gloucester Journal* of Saturday 26th September 1829:

> " At Timsbury, J. Dudden, Esq. m of Temple Cloud, to Mrs Edgell, mother of Dr. Edgell, of Chew, There were present at the wedding 2 fathers, 1 mother, 1 mother-in-law, 1 father-in-law, 1 son, 1 daught 1 daughter-in-law, 1 son-in-law, 1 grandfather, 1 grand-daughter, 2 nieces, 2 nephews, 2 uncles, 3 first cousins and 1 second cousin; yet there were only *six* persons present; and the bride and bridegroom no kin before marriage."

Even more curiously the *Derby Mercury* for 9 May 1799 contains the following:

> Married Friday, at Aymestrey in Herefordshire, Mr John Palmer. second son of Mr Wm. Palmer of Yatton Marsh, to Mrs. Mary Palmer, relict of the late Mr. John Palmer of Leinthall Earls, who was grandfather to her present husband. The bride, though she may properly be called grandmother to the bridegroom, is not more than thirty years of age, and should the present union produce a family (of which there is every flattering appearance) the son will be uncle to his father an great grandson to his mother, and it will involve in no small intricac the different degrees of propinquity in which the parents and children will stand to each other. [21]

Since the marriage to a grandfather's widow was within the prohibited degrees[22] one may well wonder whether this newspaper report attracted ecclesiastical or civil attention to the case. [23]

As has been seen in the case of *Jackson's Oxford Journal* newspapers can be extremely useful in tracing marriages which took place outside the county. Though this was the newspaper of a University ci it was not exceptional in that respect, as is shown by the following examples from the *Gloucester Journal*:

Monday 29th May 1775
> "A few days ago, Mr. John Jefferies one of the Sheriffs of this cit was married to Miss Ann Atkinson, of Macclesfield, in Cheshire",

Monday 17th November 1783
> "Lately was married at St.James's Church, Bristol, Mr. Edward Aldri of Bisley to Miss Clissold, of Duke Street in that city".

---

[21] Cited by T.M. Blagg. Gen. Mag. Vol.8 p. 96.
[22] In fact it is only the second item on the Table of Kindred and Affinity.
[23] For a discussion of the legal position with regard to such marriages and the legitimacy of the children see *Divorce and Annulment*, below pp.324–5.

Monday 17th May 1813

"On Tuesday the 4th inst. at Horsham, Sussex, Charles Greenaway Esq., son of Giles Greenaway, Esq., of this city, to Charlotte, youngest daughter of Robert Hurst, Esq., M.P. of Horsham Park."

In addition to the marriage entries themselves, one finds announcements of engagements. There are also advertisements of husbands whose wives have eloped. In some of these details are given such as a wife's maiden mame, her father or mother's name and place of abode, her Birthplace and the names of any former husbands. Of less direct genealogical value, but of great personal value are the descriptions of the wives and their paramours.

Thus in the *Gloucester Journal* of Tuesday 10th February 1746/7:-

"Whereas Sarah, wife of William Gyde, the Elder, of the parish of Painswick, in the county of Gloucester, Innholder, did on Saturday, the 7th instant, Elope from her said Husband, and their family, together with one Thomas Holder, of the same place, Butcher, and hath took with her Money, and other Things, to a very considerable value; This is therefore to desire all Constables, Officers and so forth, to apprehend the said Sarah Gyde and Thomas Holder, or either of them, so that he, or she, or both, may be brought to Justice and they shall be amply rewarded for the same. Witness my hand, the 8th day of February 1746.   Wm. Gyde. N.B. The said Thomas Holder is a well-built man, aged near 36, about five Foot eight Inches high, pitted in the Face with the Small-Pox, with short curl'd Hair, but sometimes he wears a Wig: she is near the same Age, about five Foot six Inches high, and pitted likewise with the Small-Pox. They are supposed to be gone towards London.

Deaths.

Both London and provincial papers often give considerable detail concerning the career of the deceased, as is shown by the following entries from the *Gloucester Journal.*

27 Jan. 1848, after a short illness, at Rouen, aged 77, much respected and esteemed, Mr Cargill, of Newcastle-upon-Tyne, and formerly of Barton Street, in this city. Mr. Cargill was for many years the intimate friend of the late Mr. Telford, and under the directions and plans of that celebrated engineer, he erected that admirable structure, the Over Bridge, near this city ...."

or again

"March 20, 1856, at his residence, Spa, Gloucester, highly respected in this and the counties of Hereford and Monmouth, Louis Charles Quintin Esq., Vice Consul of France, an ancient Naval Officer of his Imperial Majesty Napoleon I. He was taken prisoner by Admiral Sir John Duckworth, at the battle of St. Domingo, 6th February 1806, on board the Diamede, commanded by his uncle, Commodore Henri. He was one of 45 saved out of 700 when the action commenced"

Deaths taking place outside the county are often noted. Thus in the *Gloucester Journal* for 23rd August 1790, we read:

"A few days ago died, at Daulish, in the County of Devon, Mrs Nayler wife of Mr. Nayler, surgeon of this city"

As the years went by, the value of the notices in the papers increased, and even as late as the end of the 19th century, the obituaries (often very extensive) may frequently give birth-places, family connections and burial places, not to be found elsewhere. The *Gloucester Journal* commenced to give its obituaries etc., in alphabetical order, and with capital letters, in 1872, so that the searcher, from then on, need not be so overawed by the task of search ing, whilst at this period the last number of the year tended to incl a resumé of the principal marriages and deaths for the past year, thu helping the searcher who may otherwise have little time to spare.

Indexes.

One of the difficulties in using newspapers as a source is the lack of indexes to them. In the case of *The Times* there is *Palmer's Index*, running from 1st October 1790 to 30th June 1941, with the *Official Index to The Times* overlapping it from 1907 onwards. Palmer' was published in quarterly sections usually now found bound in annual volumes, and surnames do not appear in the normal alphabetical run of the index but under such section-headings as Bankruptcies, Births, Civil Actions, Criminal Trials, Deaths, Marriages (males first), Meetings of Creditors, and Parliamentary Speeches. It is preferable, therefore to use the Official Index whenever it is available, as surnames appear in the normal run.

With regard to the provincial newspapers, only enthusiasm will make up for the deficiency of indexes. However, some do exist. Thus, on the open shelves of the British Museum Newspaper Library at Colindale are indexes to births, marriages and deaths in the *Bury and Norwich Post* from 1794 to 1830. Four manuscript volumes list strictly alphabetically references in the Court and News columns of that paper under these three classifications on both a local and a national basis. Only a few births are recorded, but there are many thousands o marriages (both surnames given, but listed under the male only) and deaths, though the lack of Christian names or initials reduces the immediate identification value of the indexes. In the same hand are two other indexes, one to the *Yarmouth Herald* of 1804-15, and one to the *Suffolk Chronicle* of 1817. A later note in the former mentions that the newspaper files themselves are not in the British Museum Newspaper Library.[24]

---

[24] F. Leeson. Gen. Mag. vol. 14, No. 9, March 1964, p. 302. Further details on these indexes will be found in the *General Information* sections of Norfolk and Suffolk.

A number of provincial newspapers have been indexed by local public libraries. *The Hull Advertiser and Exchange Gazette* has been indexed from its beginning in July 1794 to December 1825 by a local History Group in the University of Hull and the York City Library has a card index to considerable portions of the *York Courant* which was established as early as 1725. It is worth enquiring locally whether a manuscript index exists, before tackling a long run of any provincial newspaper. [25]

On the whole, however, probably because there is so much other genealogical source material available, England has nothing to compare with the fine indexes of Irish newspapers, particularly that of Miss Rosemary ffolliott. Her index of Cork newspapers could well be taken as a pattern for anyone contemplating indexing English newspapers. Her major innovation has been the creation of an area index rather than indexes to individual papers. As she points out, the traditional newspaper index, though good in theory, has great disadvantages.

> "It makes it difficult to handle papers of which only a few issues for each year are extant, or of which only fragments remain; it also takes small account of geography, which is all important in genealogy. [26]

Although she was writing of Irish Newspapers, her second criticism would be valid if, for example, an index was compiled of *Jackson's Oxford Journal* and included the geographically widespread entries listed earlier and must apply to all or nearly all English indexes compiled to date. It would be especially applicable to indexes of London papers. Miss ffolliott continued:

> "Instead, I suggest that the indices be compiled by area rather than by paper; this enables one to include fragmentary papers or ones in which serious gaps occur, but which are not in themselves extensive enough to warrant a separate index, and also has the notable advantage that the local paper (if existent) generally chronicles local events in much fuller detail than the [national] paper".

Of course because of the greater population of England the problems would be much greater than in Ireland. However, if central county indexes were started (or perhaps even area indexes within counties) and indexers of all newspapers were to sift cards into these, duplicate entries would soon become apparent in widely separated newspapers and others recorded in newspapers far from their place of origin would be located. What is clearly needed is a newspaper sub-committee of the Society of Genealogists with a devoted band of workers, many of whom, because of lack of palaegraphic skill or difficulty of access might not be able to undertake Parish Register transcription.

---

[25] Details of newspaper indexes are included in the National Index volumes.
[26] Miss Rosemary ffolliott. op.cit. p. 270.

English newspaper indexers can probably also learn much from Miss ffolliott's technique.

(a) entries copied from the newspaper into a notebook, usually a full year at a time, taking care to note any missing issues.

(b) each entry typed on to an unruled card 5½ inches by 2½ inches a convenient size for this type of work, the card headed with the subject's name – HARRIS Mrs Joseph, beneath which comes the name and full date of the paper, "Cork Evening Post, Thursday 17 February 1791" and beneath the verbatim entry "died in an advanced age Mrs HARRIS, relict of Mr. Joseph HARRIS, book binder."

(c) As a final exercise the entire series of entries for the year are typed in chronological order as originally transcribed, on to loose leaf sheets. Miss ffolliott explains:

> "The object of this is partly to preserve a chronological record of each paper, so as to know later whether it carries many or few entries at a particular time and partly to avoid duplication: thus when transcribing the Cork Hibernian Chronicle for 1791 I would have before me the typed sheets of the Cork Evening Post already done and thereby save doubling entries. If, of course, the CHC announcement added any extra information, both versions would be entered in the index, e.g.
> Corke Journal, Thursday 3 August 1769: married this morning at Lower Shandon, Captain Brooks to Miss Westin with £1000.
> Cork Evening Post, same date: this morning Captain Thomas Brooks to Miss Weston, daughter of Mr. Harmon Weston of Cork. [27]

In some marriages, the Christian name of the bride is omitted (..... "to Mrs Webb of said place"). With extraordinary thoroughness Miss ffolliott checked these marriages against the diocesan marriage licence indexes available in Ireland, thus cutting down the number of cards not properly able to be indexed because of the absence of Christian names. In England, where such comprehensive indexes do not exist, more work would be involved, but it would not be impossible.

Other Information of Genealogical Value

Newspapers provide a rich and virtually untapped source for genealogical information of all kinds. From advertisements for missing relatives, or even such an unlikely source as advertisements for runaway and kidnapped children and apprentices, newspapers can certainly fill in a number of the blanks that genealogists often meet up with, and they help to give a truly local flavour to many of their families and their doings.

Mention has already been made of advertisements. Their possible

---

[27] Miss Rosemary ffolliott op.cit p. 271.

genealogical value is illustrated by the following, which appears in the *Gloucester Journal* of Tuesday, 11th March 1728/9.

> "The Bell Inn and Tavern in the Southgate Street, Gloucester; Which hath been lately in the Possession of Capell Longden, and formerly kept by Elizabeth his Wife, Relict of Thomas Whitefield, is now held by Richard Whitefield, his son; who hath always been in the Business, and will continue the same.........."[28]

Even advertisements inserted by "quack" doctors can be useful, as they often include statements of "cures" signed by local people. Such a one is in the *Gloucester Journal* of the 13th April 1778:

> "I Susannah Coleman, of the parish of Longhope, 80 years of Age, do hereby most solemnly return my real and sincere Thanks to Doctor De Compty...... at Mr. Francis Lett's in St Aldate's Square, for having perfectly restored my Sight which I had unfortunately lost for many Years".

Newspapers are, of course, of even more value to the local historian than to the genealogist. Thus, the bulk of the history of the stage in Gloucester has been acquired by diligent searching in the *Gloucester Journal* which often gives information about the actors and actresses, while information concerning local music and musicians is also to be found.

Often newspapers are the only source of information for movements. Such items as finding that the local eminent clockmaker, Richardson Peyton, had moved from Gloucester to Shepton Mallet in Somerset where he died in 1782, are invaluable. One can also often gain insight into the characters of local people as in the notice of the forthcoming sale of the effects of the Revd. William Smith of Church Street, Tewkesbury in 1797. This revealed him to be a man of some surprising interests, for the sale included "Philosophical, Astronomical, Geographical, Mathematical machines and instruments, Mechanical Apparatus and Library of Books". The items also included a reflecting telescope and other telescopes, with micrometers, microscopes, globes, ring dials, etc. This information throws an unexpected light on the man, who might otherwise be remembered merely by a name.

It is often surprising what one *can* find in local papers, and one such item is to be seen in the *Gloucester Journal* of Monday 3rd October, 1768:

> "On Monday last Mr. Robert Chambers, late of Minchin-Hampton, in this county, waited upon his Danish Majesty at St. James's with some specimens of his art of staining marble, with which His Majesty expressed himself highly pleased. This Mr. Chambers erected the Earl of Stafford's Monument in Westminster Abbey.

---

[28] This entry is of particular interest in that the famous Methodist preacher, the Rev. George Whitefield, was a brother of the younger Richard Whitefield, and was himself born at the Bell in Gloucester.

Perhaps the most interesting, if sinister entries in local newspapers are the detailed accounts of trials which are every bit as sensational as the reports in the modern popular press. Only too frequently a report of a trial for theft is terminated by the laconic phrase "Found Guilty, Death Recorded".

Far more even than the modern tabloids, the newspapers exercised freedom of expression regardless of feelings, as is shown by the following extract from the *Gloucester Journal* of the 23rd February 1747/8:

> "On Friday last a *certain young Woman*, not exceeding 17 years, was brought to bed of a *pretty Daughter* in the House of a famous Stay-Maker near this city."

Sometimes their near-libellous statements were covered up by merely putting the capital letters to the names of such parties, thereby only faintly disguising the identities. Today the Press Council does at least spare us this type of innuendo.

The reader is referred also to the section on Scottish Newspapers in Volume 12, pp. 127-32, and to other regional volumes as they appear.

ists of Newspapers

ritish Union Catalogue of Periodicals

.S. Craze and F.B. Kaye. *Census of British Newspapers and Periodicals 1620-1800*. Studies in Philology xxiv 1927 pp 1-205.
This lists all British papers before 1800 and the American Libraries which hold copies.

ambridge Bibliography of English Literature vol 1 pp 736-763, ii 656-739.

.A. Cranfield. *A Handlist of English Provincial Newspapers and Periodicals 1700-1760* (Cambridge, 1952)

imes Tercentenary Handlist of English and Welsh Newspapers, Magazines and Reviews (1920)

illing's Press Guide

ewspaper Press Directory

atalogue of English Newspapers and Periodicals in the Bodleian Library 1622-1800

eneral Works

.A. Cranfield: *The Development of the Provincial Newspaper 1700-1760* (Oxford 1962)

. Morison: *The English Newspaper 1622-1932*

.M. Salmon: *The Newspaper and the Historian* (Oxford 1923)

.K. Weed and R.P. Bond: *Studies of British Newspapers and Periodicals from their beginning to 1800* (University of North Carolina; Studies in Philosophy, Extra Series No.2, Dec.1946)

raham Dukes: *Newspapers and History* (History Today 1954, p. 421).

.R. Mellor: *History from Newspapers* (Amateur Historian, vol.2, No.4. (1955)

onald Read: *North of England Newspapers (1700-1900) and their Value to Historians* (Proc of the Leeds Philosophical Soc. Vol VIII, pt iii 1957)

regoe D.P. Nicholson: *The Genealogical Value of the Early English Newspapers.* (Gen.Mag. Vol.5 Nos.1-4)

iss Rosemary ffolliott. *Matched and Despatched.* Irish Genealogist Vol.3 No.7 Oct 1962.

LIST OF THE LONGER-LIVED
LONDON NEWSPAPERS BEFORE 1837

These have been listed under the names by which they were known for the longrst period.

17th Century

Weekly

Oxford Gazette 1665-6 contd as the *London Gazette* 1666 onwards.

18th Century

Weekly

The *Weekly Packet* 1714-1721

The *Weekly Journal or the British Gazetteer* (various titles-
Read's *Weekly Journal* 1733-61) 1716-1761

The *Weekly Journal or Saturday's Post* (afterwards *Mist's Journal*
1718-1728

New Weekly Miscellany (contd as *The Westminster Journal* and othe
titles) 1741-1825

Adams Weekly Courant 1772-1782

The *British Gazette and Sunday Monitor* 1780-1829

Ayre's Sunday London Gazette and Weekly Monitor 1783-1800

The *Observer* 1791-date

Bell's Weekly Messenger 1796-1896 (contd as *Country Sport*)

3 Times a Week

The *Post Boy. Foreign and Domestic* 1695-1728 contd as *The Daily
Post Boy* until 1736.

The *Flying Post or The Post Master* 1695-1731

The *Postman and The Historical Account* 1695-1730

Daily

The *Daily Courant* 1702-1735

The *Daily Post* 1719-1746

The *Daily Journal* 1720-1742

The *London Journal* 1720-1744

The *British Journal* 1722-1727

Parker's Penny Post 1725-1727

The *Daily Advertiser* 1730-1807

The *Daily Post Boy* 1732-1736

The *London Daily Post and General Advertiser* (afterwards *The
Public Advertiser*) 1734-1794

The Daily Gazetteer 1735-1744

The London Courant (started as three times a week- various titles
   esp. *London Courant and Daily Advertiser*) 1745-1782

Penny London Post (afterwards *London Morning Penny Post*) 1745-51

The General Advertiser 1746-1787

The London Gazetteer (afds *The Gazetteer and London Daily
   Advertiser*) 1748-1797

The Universal Chronicle 1758-60

The Morning Chronicle and London Advertiser 1769-1862

The Morning Post 1772-1937

The Morning Herald 1781-1869

The London Recorder 1783-1795

The Times (*Daily Universal Register* 1785-8) 1785 onwards

The World, Fashionable Advertiser 1787-1794

The Diary or Woodfall's Register 1789-1793

The Oracle, Bell's New World (afterwards *The Oracle and The Daily
   Advertiser* and various other titles) 1789-1809

The Courier 1792-1842

The True Briton 1793-1803 (incorporated with *Daily Advertiser and
   Oracle*)

The Morning Advertiser 1794-date

The Telegraph 1794-1797

Mirror of the Times 1798-1823

Evening Papers

The Evening Post 1709-1740

The London Evening Post 1727-1806

The General Evening Post 1735-1813

St.James' Chronicle or British Evening Post 1761-1866

Whitehall Evening Post (afds *English Chronicle & Whitehall Evening
   Post*) 1747-1843

Lloyd's Evening Post and British Chronicle 1757-?1815

The London Chronicle 1757-1823 (united with *The London Packet*)

The London Packet 1770-1836 (incorporated with *St.James' Chronicle*)

The English Chronicle 1779-1843

The Star and Evening Advertiser 1788-1831 (contd as Albion and
   Star)

The Evening Mail (issued by "*The Times*") 1789-1868 (title altered
   to *The Mail*)

The Courier (afds *The Courier and Evening Gazette*) 1792-1842

The Sun 1792-1876.

Magazines

The Gentleman's Magazine or Monthly Intelligencer (1731-1883)

The British Magazine (1746-1750)

The Monthly Magazine and British Register (1796-1843)
The Commercial and Agricultural Magazine 1799-1802, contd as
   The Argicultural Magazine 1802-7 or *Farmer's Monthly* 1807-16
    •

19th Century

Weekly

  Cobbett's Annual Register (*Cobbett's Weekly Political Register*)
    1802-1835
  Baldwin's London Weekly Journal 1803-1836
  Sunday Review 1804-9
  London Recorder and Sunday Reformer 1806-9
  Imperial Weekly Gazette (contd as *Imperial Gazette*) 1804-1810
  Sunday Monitor 1814-29
  Philanthropic Gazette 1817-23 (incorp. with *Baldwin's Weekly
    London Journal*)
  Weekly Advertiser (afds *Weekly Register*) 1818-1827
  Weekly Intelligencer 1818-21 (contd as *British Luminary and
    Weekly Intelligencer*)
  London and Provincial Sunday Gazette 1818-23
  Independent Observer (afds *The Sunday Times*) 1821 onwards
  Weekly Times 1826-33
  Weekly True Sun 1833-9 (contd as *The Statesman*)
  Weekly Chronicle 1836-51

Daily and Evening

  British Press or Morning Literary Advertiser 1803-26
  The Globe (afds *The Globe and Traveller*) 1803-1921
  British Neptune 1805-23
  Independent Whig 1806-21
  The National Register 1808-1823
  Alfred and Westminster Gazette 1810-1833
  Anti Gallican Monitor and Anti Corsican Chronicle 1811-1818
    (contd as *British Monitor*)
  Commercial Chronicle 1815-1823 (incorp. with *London Chronicle*)
  London Moderator and National Advisor 1818-23
  British Mercury 1818-1825
  British Luminary 1818-1823
  The Guardian 1819-1824
  John Bull 1820-1892
  New Times 1818-1828 (contd as *Morning Journal* 1828-30)
  Albion (afds *Albion and Star*) 1830-35

New Monthly Magazine and Universal Register 1814-1884
The Theatrical Observer 1821-76
London Medical Gazette 1827-51 (incorp. with the *Medical Times*)
New Sailors Magazine 1830-32 (contd as *Mariners Church Sailor's Magazine*. 1833-61)
Legal Observer 1831-56
Legal Examiner 1831-33
Naval and Military Gazette 1833-1886

See also lists of religious magazines in articles on *The Three Denominations* and *The Methodists* in Volume II.

IV CLANDESTINE MARRIAGES

The author is grateful to R.L. Brown for supplying the greater part of the information on Fleet Marriages and Registers, most of it derived from his personal research on manuscript sources, especially the Fleet Registers and Fleet Prison Records. Unpublished material in his possession has also been used occasionally elsewhere.

Marriage Law

The ecclesiastical canons of 1603 ordered all marriages to be performed after due publication of banns or the dispensation from such a requirement which a licence gave; to be celebrated within certain hours at the parish church of one of the parties[1] and in the case of minors to have the consent of a parent or guardian. Statute Law reiterated the requirement that all marriages should be celebrated only after banns had been read or a licence obtained. Nevertheless both Canon Law and the Ancient Common Law of England were agreed not only that it was not essential to the validity of a marriage that a priest should be present,[2] but that the marriage was still valid without any formal ceremony, secular or ecclesiastical. The consent of the parties alone mattered. So a contract made *per verba de presenti* or *per verba de futuro* followed by co-habitation between persons able to contract, was deemed a valid marriage and as binding as a marriage *in facie ecclesiae* (i.e. in the presence of the parish priest and two other

---

[1] Innocent III (4th Lateran Council 1215) appears to have been the first to ordain the celebration of marriage at the church; previously the man came to the woman's home and led her to his own house, which was all the ceremony used. J.T. Hammick. *The Marriage Law of England* p.4.

[2] This was a subject of much controversy in the courts. Blackstone (*1 Com c 15*) refers to various writers in its support and cases are cited (e.g. Bunting's Case, *Moor's Rep* 169) which seem to establish it in the clearest manner. J.T. Hammick. *op.cit.* See also Reeves *Hist. Eng. Law* Vol.4 p.52 2 Kent's Com 5.26 p.74. Burn's Eccl. Law *tit. Marriage.* Nevertheless, it was decided by the House of Lords in 1843 in the case of *Reg. v Millis* 10 Cl & F 534 that there could not have been a valid marriage in England before the Reformation without the presence of a priest ecclesiastically ordained, or afterwards without the presence of a priest or a deacon. J.T. Hammick. *op.cit.* p.5. *See below* p.315.

witnesses).[3] Thus in England in the 17th century and before, marriages were occasionally celebrated by laymen. As late as 1710 Gabriell Rose, a dairyman, was brought before the bishop for marrying a couple in a Public House at Shrivenham, Berks.[4] However the King's Courts were inclined more and more in their casual jurisprudence to refuse to recognise a marriage as valid unless contracted with the assistance of a priest. If one of the parties denied that such a clandestine marriage had ever taken place, could he or she be convicted of bigamy for contracting a subsequent formal marriage? Countless questions of property and of legitimacy would also arise, and it was difficult then, as it was until very recently in Scotland, to prove a clandestine marriage to the satisfaction of the Court. But there was normally less difficulty in securing the recognition of the validity of a marriage if a priest was present,[5] though the minister was subject to heavy legal penalties. In practice this applied whether the priest was recognised by episcopal authority or not, although in the case of Roman Catholics the position was never fully clarified.[6]

The marriages of Quakers and Jews were regarded as valid though irregular, and as early as 1661 a jury at Nottingham found a verdict for the legitimacy of a child of Quaker parents. Nevertheless, it has been suggested that many clergy put children down as illegitimate if the parents had gone through a form of marriage of which they dis-approved.

There were thus three distinct modes of contracting valid matrimony under the Ancient Law of England. (1) by public celebration *in facie ecclesiae* (2) by clandestine celebration covertly conducted by a priest episcopally ordained and (3) by the mere consent of the parties before witnesses. However, although in general all three types of marriage were regarded as valid and the children as fully legitimate, the wife could not claim her dower, i.e. the one third for life of the income of her husband's lands if she survived him.[7] When such marriages came to the ears of the higher clergy they were invariably the subject of ecclesiastical censure which in the 16th and earlier part of the

---

[3] In 1563 the Council of Trent declared that a marriage not contracted *in facie ecclesiae*, should be regarded as invalid. Hitherto such marriages had been regarded as illicit, but valid. But of course, the Council of Trent had no power to bind the Church of England.

[4] E. R. C. Brinkworth. *Records of Bishops' and Archbishops' Visitations.* Amateur Historian Aug-Sept 1954 p. 20.

[5] This did not however apply to Fleet Marriages, where even in cases when the parson himself testified, the marriage was not regarded as proven. *See below* pp. 305–306.

[6] See *Roman Catholics* in Volume II.

[7] T. C. Dale. *Marriage in England.* Gen. Mag. Vol. 5. No. 7. Sept 1930 p. 213.

17th centuries was a real and unpleasant experience. In 1598 Sir Edward Coke, Solicitor-General was put to penance for marrying without the publication of banns. In the case of marriages by consent, either party might in the spiritual court compel the other to solemnize the marriage *in facie ecclesiae*, and the church could insist on this even if both parties were unwilling.[8] However, Clandestine marriages were always very numerous. As early as 1347 the *Constitution of William la Zouch* No.7 notes that

> "Some contriving unlawful marriages and affecting the dark, lest their deeds should be reproved, procure every day, in a damnable manner, marriages to be celebrated without publication of banns duly and lawfully made, by means of chaplains that have no regard to the fear of God and the prohibition of the laws."[9]

In the Parish Register period most genealogists are familiar with pedigrees on which there is generation after generation of unlocated marriages and few must be unaware of the popularity of Fleet marriages in the 18th century. In 1868, the Report of the Commission into Marriage Law estimated that over one third of all the marriages performed in the United Kingdom during the first half of the eighteenth century were clandestine. Though this is probably an exaggerated estimate, and in any case it included, of course, marriages celebrated by Roman Catholic priests and Nonconformist ministers, it is almost certainly accurate as regards many parts of London, and in many country parishes as many as a quarter of the marriages may be missing. On the other hand it must be remembered that marriage licences were easy to obtain and the qualifications of the parties rarely checked. Thus a great many marriages which did not take place in the parish of either of the parties were not clandestine in the strict sense of the word.[10]

Although clandestine marriages afforded an opportunity to transgress the rigorous family control of marriage then customary, and enabled abuses to be perpetrated that would be detected if the Canons of the Church were enforced, it would be a mistake to suppose that in most cases one of the parties was under age or that the marriage was against the wishes of the parents of one of them. The "Marriage Mongers" would seem to have offered a saleable commodity at a lower rate than most of the parochial clergy and certainly in most cases when the couples came from parishes which were fairly near, it seems likely that economy was the only motive.[11] The saving came not only on the marriage fee; since such marriages were performed with some

---

[8] e.g. in the case of Recusants. See *Roman Catholics* in Volume II.
[9] Cited by J.S. Burn. *History of the Fleet Marriages.* p.3.
[10] See *Marriage Licences* pp.226–228.
[11] See J. Ashton *Old Times* (1885) p.26 and *below* pp.301–302.

ount of secrecy, they were not attended by the customary elaborate
ntertainment and feast and the noisy display of the "marrow-bones
d cleavers."

ondon Lawless Churches

In and around London, in the first half of the seventeenth century
everal centres arose to meet the popular demand for clandestine mariages, among the earliest being the Tower of London. This was suppres-
ed by Archbishop Laud, but others remained, such as Harfield. Thus on
th October 1644 there was a Presentation at the Visitation of
Illingdon:

"As likewise a marriage fee due from the same John Allen, who, his
banns being published here, and he, neglecting to be married in due tyme,
when marriage was out, went to Harfield, a Lawless Church as it is called,
and was there married in a prohibited tyme, and upon that grounde refused
to pay me, as some others have done."[12]

By the end of the Commonwealth period there were other centres
uch as *St. James, Duke's Place*; *Trinity, Minories*; *St. Martin's
Ironmonger Lane*; and *Lamb's Chapel*, Monkwell Street.[13] Each of these
awless churches had probably some ground for considering itself exempt
rom ecclesiastical control. Thus, with regard to *St. James' Duke's
Place*, the Mayor and citizens of London claimed exemption as Lords of
he Manor and patrons of the Church. *Trinity, Minories* was in the gift
f the crown, and was neither Rectory nor Vicarage institutive.

The number of clandestine marriages at these churches was very
onsiderable. At *St. James' Duke's Place*, there were sometimes thirty
r forty per day, and in the first register book (1664–1691) are entered
ome 40,000 matches. They continue very numerous in the second book
1692-1700). *Trinity, Minories* appears to have become a clandestine
arriage centre in the 1640's. Whereas one register covered the whole
eriod 1579 to 1644, most subsequent registers covered only a few years
ach.[14]

In the registers of both St. James Duke's Place and Trinity,
inories, in and after March 1678/9 for about 20 years, a third name
always that of a man followed in almost every case by the abbreviation

---

[2] Bps. Reg. Cited by J.S. Burn. *History of Parish Registers in England.*
(1862 edn) p.146 footnote.

[3] A list of the lawless churches and chapels of London and Middlesex will
be found in Appendix I pp.319–320.

[4] The second register ran from 1644 to 1648. No register survives for 1648
to 1657, but the next register lasted for only two years and the following one for three. The only other surviving proper registers are from
1676-1683 with 6000 entries and 1692-1754 with 9000 entries. However there
is a rough register from 1686-1692 with between 5000 and 6000 entries.

Fr occurs after that of the bride. The third name in a marriage register is very unusual and possibly even unique. [15] The abbreviation *Fr* stood for *father or friend* and derived from the rubric in the marriage service requiring the minister to receive "the woman at her father's or friend's hands." "Obviously this third name may assist identification or even be of direct genealogical importance as the "friend" may sometimes have been a relative.

During the reign of James II the *Commissioners for Ecclesiastical Causes* made an effort to tackle the problem of clandestine marriages. In 1686, Adam Elliott the Rector of St. James, Duke's Place was suspended for three years for having married without banns or licence However the suspension was relaxed on 28th May 1687; the Rector resum his practice and married at the rate of 16 couples a day. [16] After the Revolution of 1688 clandestine marriages continued on the same scale, until finally the Marriage Act of 1696 laid down a penalty of £100 on any clergyman who performed a marriage ceremony without banns or licence. This had an immediate impact; the number of clandestine marriages in London dropped considerably and there was a correspondin increase in the number of marriages performed in parish churches. Thu the average number of marriages at *St. Giles, Cripplegate*, during the period 1680-86 was 33 per annum, but in 1687, when the effect of the work of the Commissioners for Ecclesiastical Causes was beginning to have its effect, the number of marriages rose to 104. Similarly during the period 1688-95 the average number of marriages at the same church was 34 per year, but the annual average from 1696-1700 was 140. [17] However, though the 1696 Marriage Act had the effect of checking the practice by beneficed clergymen, it increased the number celebrated in private chapels, such as *Lincoln's Inn Chapel*. Much more significant, however was the near monopoly it gave to the Fleet parsons most of whom had nothing to lose, not even their liberty. [18]

Fleet Marriages

The Fleet Prison in Farringdon Street, on whose site the Congregational Memorial Hall now stands became prominent from being used as a place of reception for persons committed by the Star Chamber, and from the time of Charles II onwards was used for debtors and persons imprisoned for contempt of court by the Court of Chancery.

---

[15] *London Parish Registers* Vol.1 *Marriages at St. James, Duke's Place.* ed. W.P.W. Phillimore and G.E. Cokayne. 1900 *Preface* p.vi.
[16] J.S. Burn *Fleet Marriages* p.4.
[17] W. Denton. *The Records of Cripplegate Without* (London 1883) p.200 ff.
[18] This was not true after about 1720 when few of the Fleet parsons were prisoners. *See below* p.299.

It was burned down in the Great Fire of 1666, but subsequently rebuilt.[19] The head of the prison was termed the *Warden* and was appointed by letters patent. It became a frequent practice of the holder of the patent to 'farm out' the prison to the highest bidder, a custom which made the prison long notorious for its cruelties.

The first recorded marriage in the Fleet Chapel was in 1613,[20] but it is not known whether it was clandestine or regular in its celebration. The development of the Fleet as a clandestine marriage centre came about during the 1670's and the first surviving register commences in 1674. However, business was very slow until after the passing of the 1696 Marriage Act which, as has been pointed out, not only allowed the Fleet parsons to carry on as before, but almost gave them a monopoly. The earlier marriages took place within the Fleet Prison itself, some perhaps in the Prison Chapel, but more probably in one of the Prison Chambers. Thus the marriage of Phoebe Morris in 1694 took place in a "darkish room" which "had two candles alight in it."[21]

Robert Ellborrow, the aged Chaplain of the Prison acquiesced in the performance of these marriages, and even celebrated a few himself. In 1702 the Bishop of London held a Visitation at the Fleet and a Mr. Alley was forbidden to marry or perform any divine office in the Chapel until he had presented his orders. A note adds:

"Mr. Alley soon afterwards fled from ye sd Prison and never exhibited his orders."[22]

In 1711 Parliament attempted to deal with the problem and an Act was passed[23] which prescribed a heavy fine for any prison Keeper who permitted any such marriage to be performed in his prison. While this meant that the parsons were prohibited from performing their function within the Prison House, it did not mean that the marriages were ended. Due to overcrowding of the Prison House debtors were, on payment of substantial security, permitted to reside in an area outside the Prison known as the *Rules* or *Liberties* of the Fleet. This congested area, bounded by Farringdon Street, Ludgate Hill, the Old Bailey and

---

[19] It was destroyed in the Gordon Riots of 1780, again rebuilt in 1781-2 and closed in 1842 by Act of Parliament which consolidated the Marshalsea, Fleet and Queen's Bench prisons as the Queen's Prison. In 1844 it was sold to the corporation of the City and pulled down.

[20] This was referred to in a letter from Alderman Lowe to Lady Hickes. Sept. 1613. *Lansd. Mss* 93-17. The letter is quoted in full in Burn *Fleet Marriages* p.5.

[21] Bodleian Library, Oxford, Rawlinson MS B 382 fol. 445.

[22] Paper in the Registry of the Consistory Court. Quoted in full by Burn. *Fleet Marriages* pp.9-10.

[23] *10 Anne c 19*, clause CLXXVI.

Fleet Lane, consisted largely of courts, alleyways and passages and throughout the eighteenth century was one of the most notorious parts of London. Even before 1711 several parsons appear to have been marrying couples within the *Rules*. An anonymous letter in the Bishop's Registry written between 1702 and 1714, after mentioning marriages in the Fleet chapel, continues:

> "There is also one Mr James Colton a clergyman, he lives in Leather Lane next door to ye Coach and horses, he hath bin there these four year to marry, but no Prisoner, he marries in Coffee-houses, in his own house and in and about ye Fleet gate and all ye rules over not excepting any part of city and Suburbs."[24]

In 1711, after a slight check, the remainder of the parsons re-established themselves in these new, and much more prominent surroundings. Not all the marriages, however, took place within the *Rules*. Indeed, several of the Marriage Houses were outside it altogether; th Crown Tavern was in Turnagain Lane, the Swan Alehouse in Salisbury Court, the home of Dr. Wyatt was in Seacoal Lane,[25] while Doctor Ashw dwelt in St. Bride's Lane. Many of the parsons were summoned to perfo marriages in private houses all over London and sometimes one finds i the registers directions for reaching them. One parson, Barrett, went as far as Up-Park in Sussex to marry a couple and for this he receive a fee of one hundred guineas, although both the distance and the fee must be regarded as exceptional.[26] Doubtless such customers either disliked the idea of marrying in the unsavoury neighbourhood of the Fleet or wished to preserve complete secrecy.

The Fleet Marriages together with clandestine marriages all over the country ended abruptly on Lady Day, (March 25th) 1754 as a direct result of the Marriage Act of 1753 promoted and forced through Parliament by Lord Hardwicke. This act made all marriages that were not contracted in the parish church of one of the parties, by a duly ordained priest, after banns or by licence, "null and void to all intents and purposes whatsoever." A priest solemnizing matrimony, except under these conditions was guilty of felony.

It is extremely difficult to estimate the number of couples marrie at the Fleet, but it is so high that probably a large proportion of British people alive today have some ancestors who were married there. In the year 1700 over 2000 couples were married, in 1710 the number

---

[24] Burn *Fleet Marriages* p.10. where the letter is reproduced at length.
[25] Then in a different position from the present lane of that name.
[26] This marriage led to a celebrated case in Chancery, *Edes v Brereton*, Edes being a ward of court and married without the permission of the Court of Chancery: M.J. West. *Chancery Cases* (London 1827) p.348f. The marriage is recorded in the notebooks of Barrett, although in the trial the parson's name is stated to be Barry.

had risen to 3000, and by 1740 it was well over 5000 couples. *Reed's Weekly Journal* on June 25th 1737 claimed that Parson Gaynam, the most notorious of all the Fleet Parsons "by his own books as it appeared at Christmas last had married 36,000 persons," and on the last day before the Hardwicke Act came into operation there were no less than 217 marriages. In all, perhaps, 150,000 to 200,000 couples were married, and this fact is sufficient to make the Fleet registers one of the most important genealogical sources of the eighteenth century.

From 1711 until the marriages ceased in 1754, there were five main categories of persons concerned with this lucrative business – the *parsons*, the *marriage-house keepers*, the *register-keepers* the *plyers* and, most important of all, the *customers*.

The Parsons

An act of 1712 ordered that prisoners who solemnized marriages should be removed to the county gaol, but after 1720 few of the parsons were prisoners in the Fleet; most of them were sheltering in the Rules in the hope that their capacity might go disguised and unpunished. This is borne out by a petition by some Fleet prisoners for an extension of the limits of the *Rules* in 1745-1746:

> "Your petitioners humbly beg leave to assure your Lordships that not one of the parsons who marries Uncanonically in or about the rules of the Fleet or of the pretended clerks who assist these persons at such marriages, or of the plyers for weddings that infest the streets as setters for these parsons and clerks are prisoners, but on the contrary these parsons, clerks and plyers live and marry at houses out of the Rules as well as in several of the Rules not occupied by prisoners which evil neither the Warden nor the prisoners can prevent."[27]

The majority of the parsons came from the ranks of the poorer class of clergymen who, having no influence to obtain preferment were destined either to remain curates all their lives or at best to obtain only very poor livings. Many of them had received a university education, several had held colonial livings and some others had served as Naval chaplains or as schoolmasters. Several of them had come to the Rules of the Fleet after having been deprived of their benefices for matrimonial offences, and probably others arrived attracted by the reputed profits.[28] No doubt by the early 18th century marriages at the Fleet had become so popular that none of its rivals could offer a comparable income.

---

[27] *Guildhall Library* MS 84.21 fol.5f.
[28] A list of all the Fleet parsons and more detailed consideration of the more important will be found in Burn *Fleet Marriages* Chapter III pp.25-36.

Marriage-House Keepers

Although one was a barber and another kept a coffee house, these were mainly innkeepers or alehouse proprietors, [29] who provided a room generally termed a *chapel* where marriages could be performed, and either maintained a parson at a fixed salary or obtained one as required. Though their matrimonial sideline could prove very lucrative, their main concern was to obtain the profits that would accrue from the wedding reception. On numerous occasions wedding guests overstayed their welcome, so that the constable or the night watch was forced to remove them from the Marriage-House in the early hours of the morning. Competition between the Marriage-House proprietors was intense, partly because there were too many marriage houses and too few parsons and partly because many parsons such as Dr. Ashwell, dissatisfied with their share of the matrimonial fee, attempted to make themselves independent of the marriage-house keepers.

The Register Keepers

These were often already established as marriage-house proprietors and drew a fee in both capacities. Sometimes they did duty also as the bride's *'father or friend'* and gave her away in the marriage ceremony. Many entries indicate that a marriage might be performed at one establishment, but its particulars registered at another, mainly the houses owned by Lilly or by Burnford. This was because many of the Fleet parsons who conducted marriages in private houses did not keep their own registers and many small establishments in and around the Fleet with only a few weddings per month found it uneconomic to provide their own register and have their own certificates printed; it was much cheaper and more satisfactory to register the marriages elsewhere or to request the attendance of the register keeper. Some register keepers made exaggerated claims. Lilly claimed that he had paid the Lord Chancellor one thousand pounds for his appointment as "Clerk of the Fleet" (a self appointed office), and Burnford asserted that he kept the *original* register of the Fleet.

The Plyers

These persuaded couples to be married at the Fleet and conducted them to the marriage-houses. By the 1740's there must have been many hundreds, each having a small share in the fee received by the proprietor. Some brought only one or two couples a year, but others were able to maintain a living from their practice. Many were watermen, coachmen, or chairmen; others (especially before 1700) had been

---

[29] A list of the Marriage-House Keepers is given in Burn. *Fleet Marriages* pp. 37-38.

themselves married at the Fleet, and persuaded their friends to follow their example. Sometimes the work of the plyers was done by the parochial officers in order to remove unwelcome claims on their funds.

"Patrick Fitzgerald, a Carter, of St. George's Hanover Square, and Grace Bennit, of St. Giles's in the Fields. B & Sp. pr Jno Floud. Marr: five shillings, certif. one do.; brought by Mr. Clark, overseer of St. Giles's."[30]

In the *Daily Post*, 4th July 1741 appears the following report:

"On Saturday last, the Churchwardens for a certain parish in the City in order to remove a load from their own shoulders, gave 40s. and paid the expense of a Fleet marriage, to a miserable blind youth, known by the name of Ambrose Tally, who plays on the violin in Moorfields, in order to make a settlement on the wife and future family in Shoreditch Parish. To secure their point they sent a parish officer to see the ceremony performed. One cannot but admire the ungenerous proceeding of this City parish, as well as their unjustifiable abetting and encouraging an irregularity so much and so justly complained of, as these Fleet matches. Invited and uninvited, were a great number of poor wretches, in order to spend the bride's parish fortune."[31]

The Customers

Though "Parish" weddings account for only a minute proportion of Fleet marriages, consistently throughout its history, the majority of persons married at the Fleet were similar to those married at the earlier centres for clandestine marriage in London. Clients from the upper or middle classes were rare, as those merely wanting a quiet ceremony could easily afford the fee for marriage by licence.[32] Few of the customers resided within the City of London. They normally came from one of the poorer parishes of London, such as *St. Martin-in-the-Fields, St. Giles-in-the-Fields, Shoreditch, Aldgate, Bishopsgate, Clerkenwell, Cripplegate* or *Stepney* and other riverside parishes. Many especially from the parishes of *St. James* and *St. Margaret's, Westminster* were servants; the bulk of the remainder were artisans or labourers – weavers, shoemakers, men in the building trade and those concerned in the purveyance of foodstuffs. Of interest is the great number of Chelsea pensioners; in 1712 for example there were 39, but how many were In Pensioners is not recorded. Thus as with clandestine marriages in rural parishes, it seems likely that the main reason for marriage at the Fleet or one of the lawless London chapels was the saving of the marriage fee. For example in 1675, to be married by banns at Clerkenwell cost 7/-d, which fee was still demanded (in theory at least) if the bride married away from her parish church. In

---

[30]   Cited by Burn *Fleet Marriages* p.84.
[31]   *ibid* p.85. footnote. On Settlement, see below pp.343-347.
[32]   See *Marriage Licences* pp.225-8.

301

1694 the tax on marriages and the stamp duty on marriage certificates added to this cost. Though there was no fixed charge for a Fleet marriage, each parson extracting as much as he could obtain, one could be married at the Fleet for as little as 2/6 and it was also possible to do without a wedding reception which was expected if a bride was married from her home. One suspects that getting married at the Fleet later became a social habit because with the abolition of th tax on marriage and the increase in the charges demanded by the Fleet parsons it was almost as cheap, although less convenient to be married with the established form. Nevertheless Keith, the marriage monger of the Savoy Chapel, in his pamphlet *Observations on the Act for Prevent ing Clandestine Marriages* written in the Fleet Prison in 1753 claimed

> "Another inconveniency which will arise from this act will be that the expence of being married will be so great that few of the lower class of people can afford; for I have often heard a Flete parson say that many have come to be married when they have but half-a-crown in their pockets, and sixpence to buy a pot of beer, and for which they have pawned some of their cloaths."[33]

Though the greater proportion of the register entries as a whole appear to concern the urban labouring masses, in every year seamen formed the largest single group. The number of soldiers was also grea though much below that of sailors. The reasons are obvious; such men often had no fixed parish of residence for the calling of banns or no time for banns to be published, and lacked the finance or inclination to obtain a licence. The number of sailors married at the Fleet is commented on again and again in every contemporary report of these marriages. In his pamphlet Keith told an anecdote how when he was visiting a Public House in Radcliffe, a sailor decided to get married and within a few moments many of his companions found themselves wive and the party left for the Fleet. When Keith, visiting the Public Hou again some time later, mentioned the incident to the landlord, the latter could not call it to mind and commented that it was a common thing when the fleet came home to have among the sailors two or three hundred marriages in a week.[34]

Many couples are described as *travellers*. Some of these may have been soldiers or sailors who had no place of settlement where they could legally be married in London. Others may have come from country parishes. Where the names of parishes outside London are given, these tend to be villages on the outskirts of London, most of the males in such cases being engaged in agriculture. Some of the Fleet customers

---

[33] Cited by J. Ashton, *The Fleet, its River, Prison and Marriages* (*London 1889*) p.359.
[34] Cited by Ashton *op.cit.* p.359.

came from further afield. There was a sprinkling from Wales and
Scotland and a few even from abroad. However, it is probable that in
many such cases the people concerned gave the place of their origin
or of their legal settlement rather than the parish in which they then
resided in London.

Although the marriage business proved extremely lucrative for
everybody concerned, it was not without its hazards. There was often
considerable trouble over the price demanded:

> "This 31st of May came a man and a wooman to be married at Mrs Levi's
> Gave Mr. Ashwell 2s6d he would have 5s0d all, but they abused him, and
> all persons there went to..... Bates or Mr. Dare's and gave 6s6d and was
> married, which was nine shillings when they might have been done
> cheaper."[35]

Some couples went away 'half married' rather than pay what was
demanded of them. As has been pointed out, a further charge was made
for the registration of the marriage. This explains why so many of
the entries contain only Christian names; for while some refused to
give any further particulars besides the names which were used in the
service, others declined to pay to have such particulars entered. On
many occasions the couples married, or their guests are described as
'rude', 'abusive', or 'saucy'. It was commonplace for wedding parties
to leave the reception without paying, and incidents are recorded when
blows were exchanged or money and goods were stolen. Small wonder many
of the parsons tried hard to leave their occupation.

Abuses

Throughout the 18th century the reputation of Fleet marriages was
very low. London clergy such as Gally, Rector of St. Giles in the
Fields, who published a pamphlet on the subject[36] were outspoken in
their contempt, perhaps because of a sense of outraged decency, but
more probably because the activities of the Fleet parsons deprived
them of a considerable part of their surplice fees. There were, of
course, many very real abuses. Questions were seldom asked about the
qualifications of the parties. Marriages of minors without the parents'
consent were common and there were at least two occasions when the
parties were both women!

> "1 Oct 1747 John Ferren Gent Ser of St. Andrew's Holborn B^r and Deborah
> Nolan D^o Sp^n. The supposed John Ferren was discovered after ye ceremonies
> were over to be in person a woman."[37]

---

[35] Cited by Burn. *Fleet Marriages* p.46.
[36] *Some Considerations upon Clandestine Marriages* (1750).
[37] Cited by Burn. *Fleet Marriages* p.90.

Sometimes bigamy was openly connived at:

> Xmas 1714. John Caterwood in White Lyon Cort Cornhill married to Mad[m] Wattgraves att Mr. Lilleys – and her former husband is Liveing. Married by Mr. John Mottram. Shee lodging att Charles Street in Westminster. [38]

Complaints of the abduction of gentlewomen by adventurers were not infrequent and a French observer, M. l'Abbé le Blanc, noted that the converse was also not unknown – common prostitutes making their visitors drunk and having a parson conveniently at hand. [39]

Another abuse frequently practiced was for the parson or marriage-house keeper to find a husband for an unmarried woman, either to provide coverture for any action for debt or to legitimize an expected child:

> Oct. 14 1732. John Blewington, of Rippon, in Yorkshire, Bricklayer, B, & Sarah Barington of Colchester, wid[w]. N.B. This Barrington s[d] she had £40 pr annum, had been confined for debt, and married Blewington to skreen her. [40]

Though doubtless most of such grooms were found for the occasion, there were also professionals who did duty on numerous occasions. One such was married four times in fourteen months by Parson Floud: on 8th May 1727 (entry untraced), on 11 Dec. 1727 as Walter Janes, on 23rd Dec. 1727 as Richard Armstrong and on 22 July 1728 as Josiah Welsh. [41] If one parson ever had any scruples there was never any difficulty in finding another:

> *Whitehall Evening Post July 24 1739*
> "On Tuesday last a woman indifferently well dress'd came to the Sign of the Bull and Garter, next Door to the Fleet Prison, and was there married to a Soldier; in the afternoon she came again and would have been married to a Butcher, but that Parson who had married her in the Morning, refused to marry her again which put her to the trouble of going a few Doors further to another Parson, who had no scruple!"[42]

It was not uncommon for register keepers to agree, no doubt for a substantial fee, to antedate entries and certificates:

> November 5th 1742 was married Benjamin Richards of the Parish of St. Martin in the Fields B[t] and Judith Lance D[o] Sp – at the Bull and Garter and gave g and for an antedate to March y[e] 11th in the same year, which Lilly comply'd wth and put 'em in his Book accordingly, there being a vacancy in the Book sutable to the time. [43]

Sometimes this was due to the pregnancy of the bride, but more often

---

[38] *ibid.* p.78. On *Madam* see pp. 82–83.
[39] Cited in full by Burn *Fleet Marriages* p.81.
[40] Cited by Burn *Fleet Marriages* p.83. footnote.
[41] *ibid.* pp.82-3.
[42] J. Ashton. *op.cit.* p.372.
[43] Cited by Burn *Fleet Marriages* p.45.

than not it constituted an attempt to make *de jure* a *de facto* situation:

> June 10 1729. John Nelson of y[e] Pa of St George Hanover Batchelor and Gardener and Mary Barns of y[e] same Sp married Jn[o] Floud Min[r]. Cer: dated 5 November 1727 to please their parents. [44]

A stock part of the evidence for the defence in bigamy trials in which a Fleet marriage was involved, was said to be that the Registrars would grant certificates of marriage without there being a marriage performed at all. If this is doubtful, certainly erasure of an entry at the urgent request of one of the parties was not unknown. Several marriages are specifically described in the registers as to be kept secret, but in any event the relative secrecy of the ceremony facilitated runaway marriages with heiresses or marriages between persons of widely differing social status. These provided the material for many 18th century scandals. Thus at the trial of Beau Fielding in 1706 for marrying the Duchess of Cleveland, a Fleet register was produced to prove the person Fielding had first married was a married woman, and had been married at the Fleet. In 1744 Charles Henry Fox (afterwards Baron Holland of Foxley, Wilts) was married at the Fleet to Georgiana Caroline, daughter of Charles, 2nd Duke of Richmond. [45]

Such marriages, though only a minute fraction of the total number performed, attracted considerable attention and caused Lord Hardwicke's temper to rise on numerous occasions when he encountered them in Chancery proceedings. The abhorrence of the middle and upper classes was intensified by the shameful manner in which the plyers went about their business, and the open way in which they advertised their function. Nevertheless, the parsons tried to give their marriages the best possible appearance, carefully avoiding mentioning the Fleet in their certificates and registers. They styled themselves *doctors* and in the London Press advertised their previous occupations as undergraduates or as domestic or naval chaplains. Yet this was not enough, and even as early as 1710 when Matrimonial Insurance was at its height, the policies excluded marriages performed in the Fleet.

The Legal Position

Although some judges such as Mr. Justice Willes in 1780 and Mr. Justice Heath in 1794 were prepared to admit evidence of a Fleet marriage the consensus of legal opinion was against their reception as evidence. In 1732, although the relevant register was produced and

---

[44] *ibid.* p. 45.
[45] He was subsequently one of the leaders of parliamentary opposition to the Hardwicke Act.

the parson swore to the marriage, a party was decreed to have died
a Bachelor. In 1740 in a bigamy case the register was not admitted.
However in 1792 in the case of *Lawrence v Dixon*, Lord Kenyon ruled
them admissible in a Pedigree Case. Finally in 1840 on their transfer
to the Registrar-General, these registers were declared to be
inadmissible as evidence to prove a marriage. [46]

Fleet Baptisms

The parsons did not confine their attention only to marriages;
many of them also performed the sacrament of baptism, and broke the
Canons of the Church yet again in charging a fee for so doing. However,
the number of baptisms compared with the number of marriages is very
few. Of special note is the unusual fact that a substantial portion of
those baptized are described as *negro*, *black* or as *Indian*. Such were
all of adult age, mainly males born in India, Jamaica or 'Guinea' and
usually described as servants. There seems no obvious explanation as
to why these people were baptized at the Fleet. There are also some
marriages in which one of the partners is described as a negro.

The Registers, Notebooks and Indexes

The registers of the Fleet marriages, which also contain the *Mint*,
the *King's Bench* and some of the *May-Fair* marriages within them, [47]
are kept in the Public Record Office under the serial number of R.G.7.
Another register is contained in the *Rawlinson Manuscripts* at the
Bodleian Library, Oxford. [48]

The bulk of the registers were in private hands until in 1821
about 200 or 300 large registers and 1000 or more rough notebooks were
bought by the government from the then owner Mr. William Cox. They
were deposited in the Registry of the Consistory Court of London
whence they were transferred in 1840 to the Registrar-General and are
now at the Public Record Office. This collection has been added to fro
time to time by other collections and single registers. However, these
by no means account for all the Fleet registers. Undoubtedly many have
been lost or destroyed: indeed there was a tradition at one time in
Westminster Hall that Lord Hardwicke had on one occasion torn up a
Fleet register which had been presented to him in order to prove a

---

[46] The whole subject is discussed at length in Burn *Fleet Marriages*
pp. 127-136.

[47] *See below* p. 312.

[48] *Rawlinson Ms* B.360. The register runs from March 1725 to January 1731;
the number of marriages recorded in it are few. The ministers concerned
are Crawford, Evans, Houd, Jones, Wagstaffe, Gaynam, Cuthbert, Starkey
and Wigmore. Various notes refer to the fact that it was transcribed
into a register owned by one Walter James.

arriage. As a very rough estimate, about two-thirds of the probable otal number of the registers seem to have survived, but this stimate must be treated with great caution. As many of them, like he Bodleian example mentioned above were presented to law courts as vidence of a marriage having taken place and were retained amongst he papers of that court, it is not improbable that a few registers re still hidden away in the dark recesses of legal archives. Others ay be still in private hands, their owners not being aware of their ignificance.

The *Rolls Room* of the Public Record Office holds a catalogue of ts own collection: Whilst this is useful, in several cases amendments re required: the dating of the registers as given is often between the irst and the last dates mentioned in the register, irrespective of he fact that the main chronological sequence accounts for only a raction of this period, and the noting of duplicated registers is ften incorrect and on the whole fragmentary.

There is a great deal of duplication, an entry being sometimes ecorded in four or more different registers. This occurred because oth parson and marriage-house keeper or register-keeper took down he couples' particulars into their own notebooks and then copied them nto their own registers. Transcription errors were frequent, the rincipal variations being in the spelling of surnames and places, hough there might be differences of several days in the dates of the arriages. The duplication of course makes it much easier for the enealogist to discover an entry.

Entries in the majority of the registers are in chronological rder, although this is not the case with some of the rough books. here was an almost universal practice of writing some entries on the nside of the covers and the fly leaves, and often they were not re-ntered in their correct position in the register. In some cases, aptisms are separated from the marriage entries and appear on the last ages of the book.

The registers may be divided into three distinct groups. The first nd most important group consists of the *actual registers* (nos. 1-273). he second is a small group of *indexes* to the first group. The third roup is a collection of *register note-books* (nos. 291-833).

he Registers

This group may be sub-divided into three: the registers that elonged to the parsons, those that were kept by the register keepers, nd lastly various registers that appear to have been compiled later rom both. They range from rough books to neatly compiled entries, and ome of the parsons and register keepers even employed professional cribes.

Most of the registers give the full names of both parties, their marital status, (*bachelor, spinster* etc), the parishes in which they resided, (and in some of the earlier registers the actual place of residence), and the occupation of the groom. In the case of sailors, sometimes the name of the ship was given. In some cases additional information may be given, often of a sordid kind. However, as has bee pointed out, many entries are of Christian names only, the parties either refusing to give their names or else refusing to pay the register keeper's fee. Several of the registers, mainly those belongi to 'Doctor' Wyatt are compiled on a rough alphabetical principle: the first letter of the male surname forms the key and the entries for each letter are listed in chronological order.

The Indexes

The indexes, either contained in the separate group mentioned earlier, or bound into the actual register to which they refer use the same system as these alphabetical registers. Here too, though the indexing is based on the male surname, the name of the bride is also given. However, these indexes refer to only a few of the registers and there are none for the notebooks. The amalgamation of thes indexes into one large one was urged by J.S. Burn. [49]

Notebooks

The notebooks are all of pocket size, and probably represent only a small fraction of those originally kept. Most of those surviving ar from the period 1710-1750, and the collection for the period 1727-48 is the most comprehensive. Several were all purpose notebooks and contain inventories, accounts, recipes, medical remedies, drinking songs and family circumstances, besides the usual marriage entries and comments. The notebooks are important as they often contain additional material to that given in the register into which their entrie have been transcribed. In other cases the register transcription has not survived at all. Most of the surviving notebooks were owned by th parsons, and a considerable section of the P.R.O. collection is devot to a near complete set of notebook entries of the marriages performed by the parsons Wyatt, Gaynam and Ashwell. The only important marriage house collection belonged to Burnford's establishment.

Certificates

Most of the persons married at the Fleet obtained certificates of their marriage, but as this was an additional expense many did not

---

[49] *Fleet Marriages* p.136.

do so, while many others had the date of marriage antedated on the certificate. As it appears that the couple had to obtain their own 'stamp' in order to comply with the demands of the Stamp Duty legislation, it seems that few of the certificates issued were completed in accordance with legal demands. Two types of certificate were issued: one handwritten on paper, and a rather more expensive one which was printed (normally on parchment, but sometimes on paper) and on which the particulars were filled in by hand. Though some of the earlier certificates, such as those of Mottram in 1716 contain the words *married at the Fleet*, as has been pointed out[50] few of the certificates issued after 1720 have any mention of the Fleet in them, and instead they give the name of the parish in which the marriage was celebrated or registered – *St. Bride*, *St. Martin Ludgate*, or *St. Sepulchre*. Most of the certificates were given added but illegal dignity by having printed on them the arms of the monarch or of the Lord Mayor. At the bottom of the certificate is normally the signature of the parson who married that couple, and many of them indicate in whose register the entry of the marriage will be found. As the name of the parish was often written in ink and not printed it appears that certificates were issued that were common to many marriage houses and to many of the parsons.

In spite of the very considerable bulk of the Fleet registers, providing that the names of the parties and the approximate date of the marriage are known, that there is definite evidence to suggest that the marriage took place at the Fleet and that the relevant register has survived, it should not be too difficult to locate the entry. If an inspection of the indexes proves unsuccessful, the searcher should examine first the registers compiled by the parsons, as these have many more entries than the Marriage-House Registers. If the entry is found it is often rewarding to examine the notebooks and registers of the marriage-houses in the hope that further (or perhaps more correct) information might be found. It is to be hoped that some time the Fleet registers will be transcribed, edited and fully indexed although the difficulties and expense will prove considerable.

Other London Centres

The Fleet seems to have been initially only one of a number of marriage centres, though for the last 30 years or so before the Hardwicke Act, it enjoyed by far the largest share of the trade and

---

[50]   *Above* p.305.

had squeezed out most of its rivals. Thus there seem to have been few clandestine marriages in *Lincoln's Inn Chapel* after about 1710 and Marriage-Houses in the *Mint* in Southwark appear to have been closed down in the 1730' s. There was a certain interchange of parsons in the early years. Fleet parsons certainly married in *Lincoln's Inn Chapel, Newgate* and the *King's Bench* Prisons and the *Mint*. Doubtless as time went on the Fleet parsons found it unnecessary to go far afield, and those hitherto resident elsewhere moved to the *Rules* of the Fleet. The only one of these chapels that continued to do well was *May Fair Chapel* that specialised in a higher class clientèle than the Fleet. Marriages at practically all the chapels in and about London ceased in 1754, because by the Hardwicke Act of 1753, marriages could henceforth be celebrated only in a church or chapel where banns *"had been theretofore usually published."* The *Savoy* Chapel was a conspicuous exception, for clandestine marriages seem to have commenced there *after* the Hardwicke Act came into operation. However, this effort to defy the Act soon ended with the transportation of all concerned.

Lincoln's Inn Chapel

There are a number of entries of marriages by Fleet parsons, such as the following:

> "Then Sunday the 6 Novemb[r] 1698, were marr. by Mr. Taylor, Minister of y[e] Fleete, James Ruthwen from y[e] parr. St. Bartholomew Great Gentle[n] and Eliz. Bladen, of parr. St. Clem Danes."

Many of the entries are almost indistinguishable from those in the Fleet registers:

> "Then Wednes: Feb[r]y[e] 2[d] 1703-4 were marr Balthazar Sommer & Mary Smith but yey refused to pay y[e] dues for yer marriage, or to give any account where yey lived, yey were known to M[r] Sandars a Concellor in Devereux Court."

Sometimes only Christian names were given:

> "Jany. 1, 1709, were mar by M[r] Haliday one William and Rebecca, etc."

and sometimes no names at all:

> "Then Thurs. y[e] 4 of August. 1709, were marri first a couple brought by one that keeps a chandlers shop backside Clem: Yai came from y[e] City & went to Oxford."

> "Then Thurs Octob[r] y[e] 6, 1709, were marri Mr. Dampneys two friends, the one from Southgate I think, in y[e] Countrey, & y[e] other from a Combmakers Holb: bridge."

In all, there were between two and three thousand marriages in th register. The social status of the parties was in general similar to that of the Fleet customers.

> "21 July, 1700, Benj[n] Barodale from y[e] Pallace Yard of y[e] parr of

St. Margar Westmin[r] pot painter, and Mary Milcox of y[e] same par."[51]

The number declined sharply after about 1710 and this seems to coincide with the increase in marriages in the Rules of the Fleet after 1711. [52]

Newgate Prison Chapel

No register survives, but a few marriages are known from other sources. Floud, one of the most notorious of the Fleet parsons celebrated marriages there:

"John Thomas Briquett, of the pa of St. Giles's Attorney at Law, and Sara Jarman of the pa of St. Anns Westm[r] W & Sp, mar by me in Newgate some years since, Jno Floud, Cler, in Major Barnardy's room."[53]

A satirical newspaper account of a Newgate marriage appeared in the *Daily Post* of 14th April 1738:

"We are surprised our Collectors of News should miss so considerable a marriage as was solemnized last Sunday in Newgate; when the famous Mr. Warwick who stood in the Pillory some time since, was married to Mrs. Barton who keeps the tap on the common side in that gaol, relict of Mr. Barton a watchmaker, who died about two months since, & niece to Mrs. Cruda's who keeps the grand Tap in that prison."[54]

King's Bench Prison and the Mint

Relatively few marriages were performed in the King's Bench Prison, in Southwark but its neighbourhood, known as *The Mint* and notorious as a resort of thieves and malefactors, was very similar to the *Rules* of the Fleet. As well as locally resident parsons it was also served by Fleet parsons who often entered their marriages into the Fleet registers. These centres seem to have died out in the 1730's and by 1740 many couples are noted as having been sent to the Fleet by the landlords of several of the former Marriage-Houses of these places. As with *Lincoln's Inn Chapel*, in general the customers of these establishments differed little, if at all, from those of the Fleet. Not surprisingly a fair proportion of couples in the *Mint* and *King's Bench* Registers came from Kent and Surrey, and entries such as the following are frequent.

1725 Sept 27 Wm Bayley, Hawkhurst and Ann Compion Croydon.
1724 March 22 R[d] Pierce, Tunbridge and Sarah Cooper Ditto.

---

[51] All these examples have been taken from J.S. Burn. *History of Parish Registers in England.* p.149.
[52] *See above* p.297.
[53] J.S. Burn. *History of Parish Registers in England* p.149. No Source or date is given. Presumably this entry is taken from a Fleet register.
[54] *Ibid.* p.150 where the report is reproduced in full.

All surviving registers of the Mint and King's Bench are with the Fleet Registers at the Public Record Office.

May Fair Chapel

Clandestine Marriages at the more famous chapel at May Fair which catered for a more aristocratic clientèle began in the late 1720's. The first surviving register, which covers the period 1729 to 1731, has 1300 entries. The peak was reached in the five or six years preceeding the Hardwicke Act. The register 1747-1749 has 2,403 entries and that from 1749 to 1753 6,258 entries. The chaplain, Alexander Keith was sent to the Fleet Prison[55] on a writ of excommunication for his matrimonial offences, but the marriages were continued by Fleet parsons acting on his behalf. On 25th March, 1754 the day before the Hardwicke Act came into operation, 61 couples were married at Mayfair. Although the bulk of the registers are at the Public Record Office with those of the Fleet, three are at St. George's, Hanover Square. [56]

The Savoy Chapel

Until the passing of the Hardwicke Act there were only a normal number of marriages at the Savoy Chapel – in 1752 there were 15 and in 1753, 19. However, in 1754 there were 342 and in 1755, 1190. The chaplain, Wilkinson who had served an apprenticeship in the clandestine marriage business within the Fleet, claimed the privilege of granting marriage licences as the chapel was extra-parochial, and because Dr. Killigrew and others of his predecessors had granted them. When an effort was made to arrest him, he fled but continued to grant licences the ceremonies being conducted by his curate, Mr. Grierson. Grierson was tried and sentenced to transportation for 14 years. Undeterred, Wilkinson appointed another curate, Brooks and continued to derive a considerable income from the marriages, until he was finally apprehended and sentenced. During its short life as a clandestine centre, the Savoy seems to have attracted its clientèle from a wide area around London. At Wilkinson's trial the clerk said that 900 out of the 1190 married

---

[55] In spite of many assertions to the contrary, Keith never solemnized any marriages while a prisoner in the Fleet. As a non-debtor prisoner he was unable to obtain access to the Rules, and no marriages were permitted to take place in the Prison House. The idea that he did so probably arose from the fact that Keith signed all the marriage licences for the couples that were married at May-Fair, but these were brought for him to be signed and then taken back so as to be ready for the ceremony.

[56] The 3 volumes of Mayfair marriages at St. George's cover the period 1735 to 1754. Between October 1753 and 25th March 1754 there were 1136 entries The Mayfair registers at the Public Record Office are (1) 1729-1731, (2) 1747-1749, (3) 1749-1753, (4) 1748 (86 entries), (5) 1748 (includes many Fleet Marriages), (6) 1750-1754, (7) 1753-1754. Several of the latter groups are duplicates.

in 1755 came from the country.[57] The Savoy clandestine marriages ceased as abruptly as they had begun. In 1756 there were 63, in 1757, 13 and in 1758, 17.

Rural Clandestine Marriages

Clandestine marriage was by no means an urban phenomenon. In searching the registers of a country parish it is not unusual to find a quarter of the marriages missing, and before the Hardwicke Marriage Act of 1753, one cannot expect with any degree of confidence to find a marriage celebrated in the parish of either of the parties. In 1794 in the case of *Reed v Passer* in the King's Bench it was observed:

> "By the 26th Geo II, the evidence of the fact of marriage is more easily obtained than it was before when people wandered up and down the country marrying wherever they pleased."[58]

Thus every county had its *marriage mongers* – clergy who were willing to marry without banns or enquiry, parties neither of whom resided in their parish. At *Rowner,* Hants, there were 390 marriages between 1655 and 1754 of which 225 were irregular. Between 1743 and 1753 there were 83 marriages of which 47 were irregular, but from 1753 to 1773 there were only 28 marriages altogether.[59] At *Old Warden,* Beds. between 1658 and 1666 out of 115 marriages only 12 had children baptized in the Parish Church.

Peculiars[60] were frequently local marriage centres, as the vicar had the right of granting marriage licences.

The title of the Minister of the Chapel of *Peak Forest,* Derbyshire was *Principal Official and Judge in Spiritualities in the Peculiar Court of Peak Forest.* He held a seal of office, dated 1665 which is still extant. Dr. J.C. Cox points out:

> "In consequence of this undoubted and exceptional privilege, the chapel in this wild moorland district gradually became the resort of runaway couples and of those seeking clandestine marriage from various parts of the kingdom. There are numerous proofs of this in the earlier registers, which begin in 1665 but are in a fragmentary condition. So much did this practice increase that in 1728 a new register book was purchased and endorsed *Foreign Marriages.* It simply contains the names of the contracting parties without any other particulars. It concludes with the year 1754, when Lord Hardwicke's Act put an end to this use of the chapel.

---

[57] For more detail on Wilkinson's activities see *History of the Mint, Savoy and May Fair Marriages,* Chambers Book of Days Vol. 2, and J.S. Burn, *Fleet Marriages* pp. 139-141.

[58] *The Times* Dec. 3 1794. Cited by J.S. Burn. *Fleet Marriages* p. 85.

[59] W.A. Fearon and W.E. Williams *Parish Registers and Parochial Documents in the Archdeaconry of Winchester* (1909).

[60] i.e. parishes outside the jurisdiction of the Bishop. See *Bishop's Transcripts* pp. 172-3 and *Marriage Licences* pp. 229-230.

The minister stated at that time that he lost thereby £100 per annum. These foreign marriages averaged about sixty a year."[61]

In the early part of the 17th century, even in the parish church of *Banbury*, Oxon, a Peculiar of the Diocese of Lincoln, banns, canonical hours and registers were lightly dispensed with.[62]

Sometimes a marriage-monger was not the Vicar of a peculiar but a surrogate of a bishop who misused his powers to grant licences. Thus at Holy Trinity, *Stratford-upon-Avon*, of the 2978 marriages celebrated there between 1703 and 1812, no less than 1103 or 37% of the total were by licence and there is a high incidence of lowly trades.[63] Similarly Rev. W. Sweetapple, vicar of *Fledborough*, Notts. from 1721-1751 married couples from far and near. Some surrogates even held weekly markets for the purpose. Dean Prideaux[64] considered that part of the fault lay in the appointment of poor clergy to be surrogates. However, some of the bishops made strenuous efforts to combat abuses in the granting of licences and Prideaux notes that the bishop of Norwich issued a series of regulations. However, it was impossible to enforce them. The Bishop discovered that the Master of Faculties and Vicar-General of the Province of Canterbury sent into the diocese their own licences over which he had no control. Thus he thought it better "to suffer the corruption to be still continued by his own officers, over whom he had some awe, than by those interlopers with whom he had nothing to do", and he relaxed his former orders.[65]

Other registers which should not be overlooked in trying to trace a missing marriage are those of chapelries attached to a parish, but often in the care of a curate whose meagre stipend made the temptation to engage in such malpractices very great. In the case of *Dale Abbey* Chapel, Derbyshire, the marriages were not even performed by an ordained clergyman, but by the Clerk who, Dr. Burn stated, until a few years previous to the Marriage Act of 1753, solemnised them at one shilling each, there being no minister.[66] In the volumes of the National Index the *General Information* section of each county indicate parishes known to have a high incidence of "foreign" marriages.

61 J.C. Cox. *The Parish Registers of England.* pp.94-95.
62 E.R.C. Brinkworth *Records of Bishops and Archbishops' Visitations.* Amateur Historian Aug-Sept 1954 p.20. See also *Marriage Licences* pp.227-8 229-300.
63 See *Marriage Licences* p.228.
64 Humphrey Prideaux. *The Case of Clandestine Marriages Stated* (1691). Harl Misc. Vol.1. (1743) p.369.
65 *ibid* p.369. For a fuller discussion of the whole problem of marriage by licence see *Marriage Licences* pp.224-225.
66 J.S. Burn *History of Parish Registers in England* pp.159-160.

Common Law Marriages

Although the Hardwicke Act ended the celebration of clandestine marriages in England there was a loophole both in this act, and that of 1823 which superseded it. Both acts spoke of marriages which had been *solemnized* with some attempt at formality such as the Fleet marriages. What of marriages of the old Common Law or Scottish Type, which were not *solemnized* at all? Consequently it was argued that purely secular marriages were not affected at all by either act. The matter was not finally settled till 1843, when George Millis appealed from Ireland to the House of Lords, against a conviction for bigamy.[67] It was then decided that "by the ecclesiastical and the common law of England the presence of an ordained clergyman was, from the remotest period onward essential to the formation of a valid marriage.[68] Nevertheless, since by the Rule of Law a marriage is valid if contracted according to the law of the place where the parties entered into the contract, the possibility of such a marriage by English people in Scotland still existed until abolished by Statute in 1856.[69]

Gretna Green Marriages

After 1753, those wishing to make clandestine marriages (usually with heiresses or when one or both of the parties was below age) had to cross the border into Scotland, where until 1949 Scottish Law required only a mutual declaration of consent by the parties before witnesses and no formality of any kind was necessary.[70] Any place in Scotland would serve the purpose of eloping couples, and in fact near the border, *Halidon Hill*, *Coldstream* and *Lambton Toll Bar* were popular. The reason why the obscure hamlet of Gretna Green rapidly outstripped its rivals is a question of considerable interest and has been the subject of thorough study by W. T. McIntyre.[71] He quotes three reasons for the "success" of Gretna. Firstly, Gretna had been from time immemorial a meeting place well known to the dwellers on both sides of the Border. Secondly, in the wild country around Gretna and the Debatable Land a curious system of temporary marriages had developed. Mr. McIntyre explains its origin:

"The religious needs of a vast area of country were administered to by the remote abbeys of Jedburgh and Kelso, and it was only at long intervals that this remote district could be visited by a priest, who,

---

7 T. C. Dale. *op. cit.* p.213.
8 Pollock & Maitland. *History of English Law* II pp.372 ff. This contradicted previous decisions. *See above* pp.292–3.
9 T. C. Dale *op. cit.* p.213.
0 This was recognised in *Courtier v Elder* 1930.
1 *Gretna Green Marriages*. Gen. Mag. Vol.9. No.3 p.77 ff.

known as a *book-a-bosom* man from the service book he carried with him in his cloak, performed the marriages as he made his circuit of the country. Hence sprang up the custom among the people of the district of *hand fasting*. A man and woman would join hands in public and agree to live as husband and wife for a year. If at the end of that period one of the parties was dissatisfied with the arrangement, he or she might withdraw from the contract, the dissatisfied party remaining responsible for the maintenance of any child or children resulting from the union."

This curious system of temporary marriages was not confined to the poorer classes.[72] In 1577 for example, John Lord Maxwell thus espoused a sister of the Earl of Angus. Even after the Reformation, th the practice survived amid the local population and the records of Gretna Kirk Sessions contain denunciations of it. Gretna therefore wa associated from an early date with irregular marriage contracts. Thir with the union of the Crowns of England and Scotland and the gradual cessation of Border warfare, the inhabitants of this part of the Bord were slow to settle down to the new order of things.

"The old "Graitney thieves" found their occupation gone, and experienced difficulty in settling down to regular work. What was more, there were now abundant opportunities for earning money by the smuggling of whiskey and other contraband goods round the head of the Solway and over its fords. Many evil characters from elsewhere settled at Gretna. There was thus at Gretna, at the time when the celebration of irregular marriages became popular, no lack of men who, tempted by "easy money" were only too willing to act as "priests."

Mr. McIntyre offers convincing evidence to demolish the "blacksmith" legend and gives a detailed account of many of the "priests." Robert Elliot, the Gretna priest, in his curious memoirs published in 1842, claimed to have performed upwards of 3,000 such ceremonies. Most of his records were destroyed, and none at all survived of those of Joseph Paisley who operated between 1791 and 1814. However, surviving registers include those of John Linton, who in 1825 turned the Old Gretna Hall into a hotel and marriage centre, and performed more than 1000 marriages before his death in 1851. These are kept at Gretna Hal Other surviving registers may be consulted at Carlisle through a loca firm of solicitors. However, these records include but a fraction of the marriages celebrated at Gretna. It is estimated that in the cours of the years which followed the Hardwicke Act there were over 50,000 them. Many families in Carlisle and the neighbouring Border country preserve certificates of their ancestors' marriages at Gretna, but much still needs to be done to collect and render available informati

---

[72] Nor perhaps to Scotland. H.L. Hicks in *A Mountain Chapelry* (1934) records a tradition that at Ulpha, Cumberland in 1730 the parson married seventeen couples 'living together and not yet legally united'. In citing this in *The World We Have Lost* (1965) p.143 P. Laslett assumes that this was a survival of the practice of cohabitation following espousal. Whilst this is possible it seems equally likely that the Border custom was also prevalent in the Lake District.

upon this important subject.[73]

A disastrous blow was struck at the system by Lord Brougham's Marriage Act of 1856. By this act it became illegal to perform a marriage at Gretna if one of the parties had not been in residence in that parish for at least 21 days immediately preceding the marriage. This act did not, of course, put an end to marriages at Gretna, but it made it impossible to solemnize hurried run-away unions and to some extent stripped marriage at Gretna Green of its romantic associations. However, it is important to remember that Brougham's Act left intact the Old Canonical Marriage simply by the consent of the parties concerned. As has been pointed out, the act did, however, abolish the possibility of such a marriage by English people in Scotland.

Subsequent acts made clandestine marriages in Scotland still more difficult. After 1878 a marriage had to be celebrated in a duly licensed building and in 1939 the old marriage by consent was finally abolished: marriage could be contracted only in the office of an authorized registrar on production of a certificate of the publication of banns or a notice of intended marriage. Section 5 of the act stated specifically:

"No irregular marriage by declaration *de presenti* or by promise *Subsequente copula* contracted after the commencement of the Act shall be valid."

Thus today only one form of irregular marriage is recognised in Scotland – by cohabitation and habit and repute. Before such a marriage can be registered a decree of Declaration of Marriage must be obtained from the Court of Session. In May 1967 a Commission was set up to examine the Scottish Law of Marriage. It seems possible that this may recommend the abolition of marriage by repute and highly probable that it will recommend that Scotland is brought into line with England with regard to the age to which the consent of parents or guardians is necessary. It seems likely therefore that the marriages of runaway English minors will before long be finally abolished.

Channel Islands and Isle of Man

Other possibilities for those wishing to make clandestine marriages were the Channel Islands and the Isle of Man. The *Gentleman's Magazine* in 1760 reported that sailing vessels were always kept ready at

---

[73] Much information on the history of Gretna marriages is to be gleaned from a book of cuttings and letters preserved in the *Bibliotheca Jacksoniana* at Tullic House, Carlisle, while perhaps the most satisfactory book among many upon the subject is *Gretna Green and its Traditions* by "Claverhouse" (Miss Fowle Smith), 1905.

Southampton which, for a fee of five guineas would carry runaway couples to Jersey or Guernsey. [74]

* * * * * * * * * *

Records of Clandestine marriages are among the most important for the genealogist, and anyone wishing to avoid the long succession of untraced marriages so common in pedigrees of the poorer classes should turn his attention firstly to the registers of the peculiars and other marriage centres in the county, secondly[75] to the registers of the Fleet and other London centres and as a last resort to those of Gretna Green, the Channel Islands and the Isle of Man. Until these invaluable records are properly indexed, the searches are likely to be long and perhaps unrewarding, but unfortunate indeed is the searcher unable to fill at least one of his "blanks" from these sources.

---

[74] Lecky. *A History of England in the 18th century* (1892) p.126. Rev. R.W. Muncey *The Romance of Parish Registers* p.81.

[75] For marriages of the London poor, these are, of course, the first place to search.

LIST OF **LONDON** CHURCHES AND CHAPELS AT WHICH MARRIAGES WERE PERFORMED BEFORE 1754 WITHOUT BANNS
Registers survive for those marked with a x

x Archbishop's Chapel
Ashford Chapel, Middlesex
x Ask's Hospital Chapel, Hoxton
Bancroft's Chapel, Mile End
Beaufort Chapel
x Berwick St. Chapel
Brentwood Chapel
x Bridewell Hospital Chapel
Broadway, Westminster
Burlington House Chapel
Cannons, Chapel of
Carnarvon's Chapel
x Charterhouse Chapel
Chelsea College Chapel
x Chelsea Hospital
Chelsea Park
Compter Chapel, Wood St.
Conduit St. Chapel (Trinity)
Copthall Chapel, Essex
x Devonshire Square Meeting
x Duke St. Westminster
Dulwich College Chapel
Durham House Chapel
Ely House Chapel
Exeter Chapel, Clerkenwell
Fleet Prison Chapel
x Foundling Hospital
Fulham Palace
x Gray's Inn
Great Queen St.
x Greenwich Hospital
Grosvenor Square Chapel, Audley St.
Guildhall Chapel
Hammersmith
Hampstead, Zion Chapel
Hampton Court Chapel
Harfield
x Henry VII's Chapel, Westminster
Abbey
x Highgate
Homerton (Ram's Chapel)

Hounslow
Ilford
Kensington Palace
Kentish Town
King St, St. James's
x King's Bench Prison
Kingsland
x Knightsbridge Chapel
Lamb's Chapel, Monkwell St.
Leadenhall
x Lincoln's Inn Chapel
Long Acre Chapel
London House Chapel
Maddock Street
x May Fair
x Mercer's Chapel
x Mint
x Morden College Chapel
New Chapel, Westminster
New Street Chapel, St. Giles
Newgate Prison Chapel
Noble St. Chapel
Northall, Middx.
Norwood (Hayes, Middx)
Oxendon Chapel
Oxford Chapel, Marylebone
Poplar
Queen Square, Westminster
x Queen Square, Bloomsbury
Ram's Chapel, Homerton
x Rolls' Chapel
Romford Chapel
Russell Court Chapel, Drury
Lane
x St. James's Chapel Royal
x St. James's Duke's Place
x St. James's Dutch Chapel
x St. James's French Chapel
St. James's German Chapel
St. James's King Street
St. John's Ailesbury Chapel

St. John's Chapel, Bedford Row
St. John's, Clerkenwell
x St. Martin's Ironmonger Lane
Salisbury Chapel
Serjeants' Inn Chapel
x Somerset House Chapel
x Southgate, Arnold's or Weld Chapel
x Spitalfields – Wheeler's Chapel
Spring Gardens Chapel
Staple Inn Chapel
x Temple Church
Tower of London Chapel
Trinity Alms House
Trinity Chapel, Conduit St.
Trinity Chapel, Mile End
x Trinity, Minories
Wanstead Chapel
Wapping Chapel
Warwick St. Chapel
x Weld Chapel, Southgate
x Wheeler's Chapel, Spitalfields
x Whitehall Chapel
Wood St, Compter Chapel
Zion Chapel, Hampstead

APPENDIX II   BIBLIOGRAPHY

General

J. T. Hammick. *The Marriage Law of England*
T. C. Dale. *Marriage in England.* Gen. Mag. Vol. 5 No. 7. Sept 1930
Reginald Haw. *The State of Matrimony* (London 1952)
Humphrey Prideaux. *The Case of Clandestine Marriages Stated* (1691)
S. Gally (Rector of St. Giles in the Fields). *Some Considerations Upon Clandestine Marriages* (1750)
Rev. Dr. A. Keith. *Observations on the Act for Preventing Clandestine Marriages* (1758)

London Lawless Churches

Phillimore & Cokayne. *London Parish Registers. Marriages at St. James' Duke's Place, London.* (London 1900) 4 vols.
E. M. Tomlinson. *A History of the Minories, London.* (London 1907)

Fleet Marriages

J. S. Burn. *The Fleet Marriages* (London) 1833)
J. Ashton. *The Fleet, its River, Prison and Marriages* (London 1889)
E. Whitaker. *The Fleet Parsons and the Fleet Marriages.* Cornhill Magazine 1867 p. 555 ff.
London Sessions Papers c 1720-60 containing many bigamy trials in which Fleet Marriages were concerned.

Other London Centres

May Fair Registers. The Harleian Society. Vol. 15 (1889)
History of the Mint, Savoy and May Fair Marriages. Chambers Book of Days, Vol. 2.
J. S. Burn. *History of Parish Registers in England* (1862 edn) pp. 148-152.

Gretna Green

W. T. McIntyre. *Gretna Green Marriages.* Gen. Mag. Vol. 9 No. 3 pp. 77 et seq.
Miss Fowle Smith. ("Claverhouse") *Gretna Green and its Traditions* (1905)
J. M. Barrie. *Gretna Green Revisited*
P. O. Hutchinson. *Chronicle of Gretna Green* (1844)
R. Elliott. *The Gretna Green Register* (1842)

V DIVORCE AND ANNULMENT

Until the Reformation divorces could be granted by the Pope. After
the Reformation although divorces could be granted in Scotland by the
Court of Session on the grounds of adultery and desertion, in England
a divorce *a vinculo matromonii*[1] was impossible until Parliament later
assumed the sole jurisdiction over it. When in the 18th century divorc
were obtainable by Act of Parliament, these were very few in number,
ruinously expensive, and entirely confined to the aristocracy. Another
minority for whom divorce was possible was the Jews, who after their
re-admission into England were specifically exempted from the jurisdiction of the ecclesiastical courts. For a short time during the
Civil War and Commonwealth period some Presbyterian, Congregational
and Baptist ministers were prepared to grant divorces on the grounds
of gross immorality on the part of one of the partners, though this
practice was never recognised by the courts. With these exceptions,
however, between 1538 and 1837, the only possible method of securing
a divorce was to obtain from the ecclesiastical courts an *annulment*
or a *declaration of nullity* or alternatively a divorce *a mensa et
thoro*. The latter was merely a legal separation, and neither party
could re-marry during the lifetime of the other. This could be obtaine
on the grounds of adultery, cruelty, or unnatural practices, but the
fees charged made it available only to the middle classes. For the poo
therefore the only possibility was to ignore the law and separate by
mutual consent or else to obtain from the ecclesiastical courts a
declaration that the marriage was null and void.

Declarations of Nullity and Annulments

There was a technical difference between a *declaration of nullity*
and an *annulment*. Whereas the former could be asserted by any person
having an interest; the latter could be sought only by the aggrieved
party and during the lifetime of both spouses. In general, a *declaration of nullity* was granted in cases where marriages were void, and an

---

[1] i.e. where both the marriage is recognised as having been valid and the
    parties are free to marry again.

annulment where they were voidable – i.e. unless sentence was not pronounced by the competent ecclesiastical tribunals during the lives of both parties, the validity could not be questioned, nor the legitimacy of the children be impeached.

The grounds on which a declaration of nullity or an annulment could be granted were numerous and were classified into two groups – the *canonical disabilities* and *civil disabilities*. The former included *consanguinity, affinity, impotence, force* and *error* (i.e. marriage to the wrong person by mistake – always a possibility in the days of arranged marriages). The latter included *prior marriage, want of age, idiocy, lunacy and mental disability* and violation of the provisions in the statutes relating to the formalities of marriage.[2] In general the canonical disabilities made a marriage *void* and the civil disabilities *voidable*. However, the line was not clearly drawn and some catagories passed from one classification to the other. The marriage Act of 1849 clearly laid down the respective grounds which made a marriage voidable or void. A marriage was void on the grounds of a *former marriage, lunacy, insanity or weakness of the mind, force and fear,* and *error de persona, consanguinity* and *affinity*. A marriage was voidable on the grounds of *error in the banns,* a *defective licence,* the *celebration of the marriage without either, impotence,* or if one of the parties was a minor.

In the case of voidable marriages, the courts did not hesitate to grant annulments even when the parties had been married for twenty years.[3]

Spiritual Relationship

Until the death of Mary in 1558, the most frequent ground for a declaration of nullity was the spiritual relationship of the parties. By acting as god-parent, relationships were contracted with the kin of the god-child and with those of the other god-parents. Clearly, this made a vast number of marriages capable of being invalidated, and on occasion the courts annulled marriages on these grounds in spite of the protests of the two parties.[4]

Minors without consent of Parent or Guardian

Parties to a marriage were not normally required to produce

---

2   Shelford. *The Law of Marriage and Divorce* (1814) p.138.

3   Several examples are given in Gerhard O.W. Mueller *"Inquiry into the State of a Divorceless Society"*, University of Pittsburgh Law Review. Vol.18. 1957.

4   In 1560 at East Quantock's Head, Somerset, a couple whose marriage had been annulled for spiritual relationship were re-married. See *Form and Content* p.66.

documentary evidence that they were of age, or if minors that the
consent of parents had been obtained. A verbal statement was all that
was required. By the Hardwicke Act of 1753, if minors had been married
by banns and dissent had not been expressed, the marriage was lawful.
In the case of marriage by licence, where one of the parties was a
minor without the consent of the parent or guardian, the marriage was
null and void. [5] The *Marriage Act* of 1823 laid down that though the
lack of consent did not invalidate marriage, in the event of fraud the
guilty party should forfeit all property accruing from the marriage.

Marriage within Prohibited Degrees

Until the reign of James I, the regulations as to marriage within
the specified degrees of consanguinity and affinity were scrupulously
insisted upon and marriages within the prohibited degrees were null
and void. However, from the reign of James I such marriages were only
voidable. [6] Every effort was made therefore to bring offenders to
account, and in tiny close-knit communities, cases of marriages within
the prohibited degrees were not infrequent. Thus in 1707 John Burnham
of Thame (Oxon) was presented before the Bishop's Court "for marrying
with Ann Clarke spinster, his wife's halfe sister's daughter by the
father's side." [7] At *Great Stoughton,* Hants. a marriage within the
prohibited degrees is entered in the parish register with no attempt
at concealment.

> "1659. Lucy Cosen, widdow, was married to Jn Cosen (brother of her former
> husband) the 15th day of December at St. Neots, by the Mynister of the
> Towne, and at seaven of the clocke in the night." [8]

This was, however, during the Commonwealth period when since the
ecclesiastical courts did not meet, there was considerable uncertainty
about censure and many intruded ministers may have had no qualms of
conscience about this particular degree of affinity.

In 1835, by Lord Lyndhurst's Act [9] all marriages within the
prohibited degrees celebrated before the passing of the Act were
incapable of being annulled by the Ecclesiastical Courts, but all such
marriages after August 31st 1835 would be absolutely void. It is
important to remember, however that the status or legitimacy is
governed by the *lex domicilii* of the person concerned, any person
legitimate according to the law of the domicil of his father at his
birth is legitimate everywhere. So in a case in which a man was born

---

5   This section was repealed in 1822.
6   J.T. Hammick *The Marriage Law of England* pp.32-33.
7   E.R.C. Brinkworth *Records of Bishops' and Archbishops' Visitations.*
    Amateur Historian Aug-Sept 1954 p.20.
8   Revd. R.W. Muncey *The Romance of Parish Registers* p.71.
9   *5 & 6 William IV c 54.*

in New York of a woman who married there to her deceased husband's brother, being a marriage valid in the State of New York, it was held that, that notwithstanding such a marriage was invalid according to the law of England, being contrary to Lord Lyndhurst's Marriage Act, he was legitimate because at the date of his birth he acquired the the status of legitimacy from the law of his domicil of origin. [10]

Error of Name in the Banns or Marriage

Normally an error of name in the banns or marriage would not result in annulment unless there was an intention to deceive. C.L. Ewen observes:

> "Misnomer will not annul marriage unless one of the parties shows that he has been imposed upon; on the other hand, if fraud is the object, a wrong name in whole or in part, the addition or dropping of a name or even the use of an original baptismal or family name where an assumed name is the better known, would invalidate a marriage."[11]

Thus in the case of *William Peter* Pougett, who was generally known as *Peter* Pougett but was married in 1814 as *William* Pougett, the marriage was annulled as there was an attempt to deceive the parents.

On the other hand Joseph *Price* had been known for sixteen weeks prior to his marriage in 1815 as Joseph *Grew*, a name he had assumed in an attempt to conceal himself from the Army authorities, and had been married in that name. The marriage was upheld. [12]

Divorce in Scotland

Although divorce, as distinct from annulment has always been possible in Scotland, the number never seems to have been very high. [13] Curiously, in stark contrast to the English divorces by Act of Parliament, divorces seem to have been sought by and granted almost exclusively to lower class people. In any case, English people could not avail themselves of this possibility. The Court of Session would grant a divorce only if the marriage had taken place in Scotland, and the suitor had been a *bona fide* resident in Scotland for at least 40 days. Also, English Law was explicit that no sentence or act of any foreign country could dissolve a marriage contracted in England on

---

[10] The validity of the Jacobite claim of Prince Albrecht of Bavaria to the British Throne depends on this point. See Philip M. Thomas. *The Jacobite Heir – A doubt Allayed.* Gen. Mag. Vol.12. Dec. 1956. p.273.

[11] *History of Surnames in the British Isles* p.401.

[12] *ibid* p.401.

[13] Between 1836 and 1841 the Court of Sessions at Edinburgh granted only 95 divorces *a vinculo matrimonii* (66 for adultery, 19 for desertion). Mueller *op.cit.*

grounds for which it was not liable to be dissolved in England. [14]

Self Divorce

Since Divorce, although advocated from time to time by both clergy and laity, [15] was not possible for commoners until the *Matrimonial Causes Act* of 1857, if there were no grounds for the annulment of the marriage, the only solution was for the couple to separate by mutual consent and then re-marry. Although this was illegal and laid the parties open to a charge of bigamy, the courts seem to have been singularly unconcerned about it. [16] and though such cases certainly were not infrequent, prosecutions for bigamy were rare. It is not therefore unlikely that the genealogist may find entries in parish registers of marriages where a previous partner was still living and where no annulment seems to have even been decreed. [17] Understandably the Fleet seems to have been the favourits place for bigamous marriages and entries such as the following are not infrequent:

> Xmas 1714. John Caterwood in White Lyon Cort Cornhill married to Mad^m Wattgraves att Mr. Lilleys — and her former husband is Liveing. Married by Mr. John Mottram. Shee lodging att Charles Street in Westminster. [18]

Gerhard O.W. Mueller comments:

> "The practice of walking out on each other was prevalent — and the chances were practically nil that anybody would bother; and the practice of re-marrying after such a walk-out likewise was prevalent and again the chances were practically nil that anybody would bother."[19]

Wife Selling

This practice, so familiar to readers of Hardy's *Mayor of Casterbridge* was accepted among the poor all over the country in the 18th and early 19th centuries, as is shown by the following newspaper report.

> *Morning Post Oct.10 1807.*
> "One of those disgraceful scenes which have of late become too common took place of Friday se'nnight at Knaresborough. Owing to some jealousy or other family difference, a man brought his wife equipped in the usual style, and sold her at the market cross for 6d and a quid of tobacco."

---

[14] *Conway v Beezley*. 3 Hagg 639 (1831).

[15] For example — In 1702 Thomas Morer, Rector of St. Ann's, Aldersgate wrote a pamphlet recommending divorcing a wife for adultery or immorality.

[16] See Parry. *The Law and the Poor* (1914) p.131.

[17] I shall be interested to hear of any proven examples of the second marri᧐ being celebrated after banns or licence.

[18] Cited by J.S. Burn *History of the Fleet Marriages* p.78.

[19] *op. cit.* p.564.

What the usual style was and that the practice was not regarded as illegal are shown by the following report, where it appears that a market toll was exacted in the same way as for any other form of merchandise:

The Times March 30 1796.

"On Saturday last, John Lees stellburner, sold his wife for the small sum of 6d to Samuel Hall, fellmonger both of Sheffield. Lees gave Hall one guinea immediately to have her taken off to Manchester the day following by the coach: she was delivered up with a halter round her neck, and the clerk of the market received 4d for toll. It would be well if some law was inforced to put a stop to such degrading traffic."[20]

The custom seems to have survived almost until the twentieth century. J. Ashton comments:

"I could quote numerous instances of it from time to time, down to our own days. *Vide* the *South Wales Daily News*, May 2 1882, where at Alfreton, a woman was sold by her husband in a public house for a glass of ale; and again in the *Pall Mall Gazette*, October 20 1882, where it is recorded that at Belfast a certain George Drennan sold his wife to one O'Neill for one penny and a dinner."[21]

In the eyes of the poor, wife selling clearly constituted a legal divorce. At Maidstone on 3rd January 1815 even a quasi-legal document was drawn up:

"I, John Osborne, doth agree to part with my wife, Mary Osborne and child, to William Serjeant, for the sum of one pound, in consideration of giving up all claim whatever. Whereunto I have made my mark as an acknowledgment."[22]

Ashton comments:

"This degrading custom seems to be generally received by the low classes as of equal obligation with the most serious legal forms."[23]

Exchange of Wives

The law normally connived not only at wife sales, but even the exchange of wives.

Daily Post 5 Jan. 1742.

"On Tuesday last two persons, one of Skinner Street and the other of Webb's Square Spittle Fields exchang'd wives to whom they had been

---

[20] These examples are taken from Mueller *op. cit.* where other examples are given. pp. 568-70. Numerous examples are also given in J. Ashton. *The Dawn of the XIX Century in England.* p. 33.

[21] J. Ashton *op. cit.* p. 33.

[22] Mueller *op. cit.* p. 570.

[23] J. Ashton. *Social England Under the Regency.* p. 373-5. For further discussion of wife-selling see *N & Q* 1st Ser II, p. 217 (1850), VII pp. 429, 602 (1853), VIII p. 43, 209 (1853), and E. R. Yarham. *Wives to Market* Amat. Hist. Vol. 6 No. 6 (Winter 1965) pp. 188-191.

married upwards of twelve years, and the Same Day, to the Content of all Parties, the Marriages were consummated at the Fleet. Each husband gave his wife away to the other and in the Evening had an Entertainment together."[24]

It would thus seem that the absence of any legal divorce system until 1857 was a serious hardship only to the middle and upper classes of society. The vast majority of the labouring masses seem to have accepted divorce and re-marriage throughout the entire parish register period.

[24] J. Ashton. *The Fleet, its River, Prison and Marriages* p. 375.

VI OTHER RECORDS: SOME BRIEF NOTES

As has been pointed out in the preface to this section, almost any genealogical record may provide evidence of birth, marriage or death. Many of these have been given adequate treatment in general genealogical works, and here only the barest outline is given of a few of the more significant.

A. BASIC SOURCES
Bibles and Other Family Documents

Entries in Family Bibles vary considerably. Sometimes the first owner of the Bible would enter data retrospectively[1] such as the dates of births of himself, his wife and children. The possible existence of a family bible makes it extremely important to trace families laterally as well as vertically (i.e. as far as possible to locate every living relative). A large collection of Family Bible fly-leaves was made by the late C. Hall Crouch and is now in the document collection of the Society of Genealogists. Other important family documents include letters, diaries, memorial cards, wedding cards and certificates of baptism, birth, marriage or death.

Wills

Wills are, of course, one of the genealogist's principal sources and the 1974 edition of A.J. Camp's *Wills and their Whereabouts* has been described as "factual, detailed and essentially a definitive book of reference with a most scholarly introduction", an established work in which the information has been thoroughly overhauled and up-dated. It is arranged according to "repositories and their contents: thus the searcher looking for Berkshire wills will find only those of the Court of the Dean of Windsor listed under that County, the remainder appear by cross-reference to the repositories where they reside", in this case Oxford and Trowbridge (Wilts. R.O.). As an alternative, designed specifically for the less-experienced genealogist, there is J.S.W. Gibson's *Wills and Where to Find Them* (1974), "a book for the amateur providing all the essential information in a pleasing and approachable fashion"; "arranged essentially on a topographical basis and all the appropriate jurisdictions described in a narrative section under each county heading with a due note of the repository involved", with maps of each county showing the different probate jurisdictions. Between the two the genealogist is well served.[2]

---

[1] As in the example in the article on *Parish Registers and the Genealogist.* See p.141.

[2] Quotations are from Felix Hull's comparative review of the two books in the *Genealogists' Magazine*, vol.17, no.11, pp.595-97.

Census Returns have also been given considerable attention in the Genealogical text books, especially chapters 6, 7 and 8 in Volume I o. Smith and Gardner's work. A useful point which merits emphasis here is the possibility of obtaining, with the consent of persons mentione< or their next of kin, information from censuses not yet released unde1 the 100 year rule. Another important use of census returns is to provide the names of younger brothers or sisters of persons born shortly before Civil Registration started in 1837 enabling birth certificates to be obtained which reveal the maiden name of the mother. Two articles on Census Returns have appeared in the *"Amateur Historian"* and are listed in the general bibliography.

B. EARLIER CENSUSES

Although the first complete official census was not held until 1801 there exist for most centuries from the Domesday Book (1086) onwards records which supply at least a certain proportion of the names of individuals, either of the whole country or of particular counties The first attempt after Domesday to make a survey of the whole country was in 1279, though in fact *Hundred Rolls* were compiled (or still exist) only for the counties of Bedfordshire, Buckinghamshire, Cambridgeshire, Huntingdonshire, Leicestershire, Oxfordshire and Suffolk.[3] Nevertheless, these are of great value as they list the names of all tenants from the lord of the manor to the humblest cottage tenant.

Tax Returns

More extensive, though still incomplete are the *lay subsidies* which purport to list all householders though in fact evasion was widespread. They extend up to the reign of Charles I, but for the most part after 1334 supply only total quotas for each village and do not include lists of inhabitants. For 1377 and 1381 there are, however, the *Poll Tax Returns*, those surviving though still defective appearing to be rather more complete than the lay subsidies. The assessments for the *Great Subsidy* of 1524-5 are of particular importance as they are almost completely comprehensive in rural parishes and include names. The Public Record Office holds a detailed

---

[3] See J.B. Harley *The Hundred Rolls of* 1279. Amat. Hist. V No. 1. (1961) p. 9.

typewritten list of all surviving lay subsidies.[4] In 1660 there was
an assessment tax partly on rank, partly on wealth and partly a Poll
Tax. Many detailed assessments survive in the Public Record Office or
in local archives.

Most valuable of all are, however, the *Hearth Tax* returns 1662-
1689. The original returns are to be found in County Record Offices
amongst the Quarter Sessions papers and duplicates of the local assessments (i.e. giving full names) were sent to the Exchequer from
Michaelmas 1662 to Lady Day 1666 and from Michaelmas 1669 to Lady Day
1674. Not all of these survive with the exchequer records at the
Public Record Office. The returns for Lady Day 1664 are the most comprehensive for the names include persons both chargeable and non-
chargeable.[5]

Muster Rolls

These are also of considerable interest and normally list adult
males between 16 and 60. The earliest surviving Muster Rolls appear
to be those of 1522. This was a 'Census' ordered by Cardinal Wolsey
ostensibly to discover the state of preparedness of the kingdom for
the French War, but "the real reason which the Commissioners were
directed to take care to conceal was to obtain a true valuation of
property as a basis for a forced loan to be levied on an unprecendented
scale."[6] The completed survey books were to be returned to the

[4] See W.G. Hoskins *Local History in England* pp. 102-4, 142-9, W.G. Hoskins
    The Genealogical Value of the Subsidies of 1327 and 1332 Devon & Cornwall
    N & Q xxii Part 7 (July 1943), pp. 169-172. M.W. Beresford *The Lay
    Subsidies.* Amat. Hist. III. No. 8 and IV No. 3 (1958, 1959) and *The Poll
    Taxes of 1377, 1379 and 1381.* Amat. Hist. III. No. 7 (1958). These were
    reprinted by Phillimore 1963 as "*The Lay Subsidies and Poll Taxes.*"
    There are many excellent introductions to returns which have been printed
    by local societies and the best of these are listed in the general
    bibliography. On deductions with regard to populations and especially
    population movement see S.A. Peyton *Village Population in Tudor Lay
    Subsidy Rolls.* Eng. Hist. Rev. XXX (1915), pp. 234-250.

[5] See J. West *Village Records* pp. 131-135. An extremely useful list is in-
    cluded of published returns and the location of many originals.
    Appendix III of C.A.F. Meekings' *Dorset Hearth Tax Assessments 1662-1664*
    gives summaries of the 1662 Assessment for all counties of England and
    Wales. See also R. Howell. *The Hearth Tax Returns.* Short Guides to
    Records 7. History XLIX. No. 165 (Feb. 1964), *The History of the Hearth
    Tax 1662-88.* Journ. of Merioneth Hist. & Rec. Socy. (1953) and P. Styles
    Introduction to Warwickshire Hearth Tax Returns in *Warwick County Records*
    Vol. 1 (1957).

[6] J. Cornwall. *A Tudor Domesday: The Musters of 1522.* Journ. Soc.
    Archivists III No. 1 (Apl 1965). A full list is given of surviving rolls
    held centrally.

Star Chamber. None, however, of the surviving books are with the Star Chamber Records at the Public Record Office and only those of five counties are at the Public Record Office at all. The survival of othe returns is due to the fact that they were duplicated with one copy re tained locally or else only the loan books were forwarded.

Some Muster lists for c 1539-1542 appear in the *Letters and Paper* of Henry VIII but these are of little interest to the genealogist. In 1544 the whole manhood of the country was ordered to arm itself accor ing to its wealth, and instructions were issued to select residents to return the number of "able men" in each hundred. In 1558 instruc tions were sent to Lords Lieutenants and to Commissioners of the Musters in each shire. They were to divide the shire up among themselves into divisions and then to render their returns, in three classes: of all men between the ages of sixteen and sixty, those "unmeet to serve", those able and those chosen, the last class to be denominated with its weapons.

At the Public Record Office returns are extant for the years 1558 1559, 1560, 1569, 1570, 1573, 1577, 1580, 1583, 1587 and 1588 though all are defective in some way.[7] The first three give totals only, bu from 1569 onwards they give what is virtually a house to house enumeration of the male population of their areas. However, they are not entirely reliable. For example, the 1569 Warwickshire return list no member of the Shakespeare family in the town of Stratford.[8]

The seventeenth century returns are for the most part to be found in local repositories. For example, the Reading Borough Archives contain a fine series of 29 rolls, the earliest dating from 1614, but covering almost every year from 1629 to 1642. A number of Muster returns have been published. The finest is probably the Somerset Return for 1569 published in 1904 by the Somerset Record Society.[9] This is described as one which "could not have been more complete and as such is quite unique".

The Muster Rolls for the Surrey Hundreds of Godalming, Farnham an Godley for 1575 and 1583, preserved in the Losely manuscripts were published by the Surrey Record Society in 1901.[10] A collection of muster returns for Northamptonshire from 1586 to 1623 was edited by

---

[7] They will be found in *State Papers Domestic*. For the period up to 1588 there are about 450 returns in addition to the following complete volumes SP 12/55 Somerset July 1569: SP 12/91 Instructions SP 12/94. Returns 1573 SP 12/134.

[8] E.E. Rich. *The Population of Elizabethan England*. Ec. Hist. Rev. 2nd Ser. II No. 3 (1950) p. 247.

[9] ed. by E. Green. Somerset Record Society Vol. XX (1904). See also E. Gree Preparations in Somerset against the Armada (London 1888).

[10] A.R. Bax. *Preparations by the County of Surrey to Resist the Spanish Armada*. Surrey Archaelog. Collections Vol. XVI (1901) pp. 137-168.

Miss Joan Wake and was published by the Northamptonshire Record
Society (Vol. III). The Suffolk returns for 1638 edited by C.E. Banks
were published as long ago as 1831 under the title of
"Able Men of Suffolk" and the finest published 17th century return
is J. Smith's *"Men and Armour in Gloucestershire in 1608*" (1902) which
was analysed in detail by Prof. R.H. Tawney.[11] Other references to
local musters may be found in the publications of the Shropshire
Archaeological and Natural History Society, 3rd Ser. Vol. VIII and the
East Anglian Miscellany 1937-9 (Suffolk Returns, 1577).

Protestation Oath Rolls

In 1641 the House of Commons made a declaration of Abhorrence of
the designs of "priests and Jesuits ..... to subvert the fundamental
laws of the kingdom and to introduce Arbitrarie and Tyrannicall
government" and took an oath to oppose them. All males over eighteen
years old in every parish in England were invited to subscribe to the
declaration. The surviving original returns are in the Victoria Tower
of the House of Lords and a printed list has been published by the
Historical Manuscripts Commission.[12] A number of copies exist in
parish registers, and sometimes these are the only lists extant. Thus,
the returns for Derbyshire, Leicestershire and Norfolk are lacking in
the House of Lords lists, but lists appear in the registers of
Kedleston, South Wingfield, Pentrich and Ashover (Derbyshire)
Appleby Magna, Aylestone, Bitteswell, Frolesworth and Gaddesby (Leics)
and at East Rudham (Norfolk).[13]

Parish Censuses

Though the "census" records so far described are most useful for
supplying names and details of individuals, they are not of course a
source for births, marriages and deaths or for specifically genealogical information. From time to time ecclesiastical censuses were taken
of numbers of communicants and the like, but though the returns are
valuable for Population Studies they are of little interest to the
genealogist. However in the case of Bishop Compton's Census of 1676
enquiring into the number of persons in each parish, and the numbers
of Recusants and Dissenters, a few incumbents such as those of
Clayworth, Notts and Goodnestone, Kent, made detailed lists of

---

[11] A.J. Tawney and R.H. Tawney *"An Occupational Census of the Seventeenth
Century"*. Ec. Hist. Rev. 1st Ser. V No. 1. (Oct 1934) p. 25.

[12] *5th Report* (1876) pp. 120-134.

[13] W.E. Tate. *"The Parish Chest"* p. 72. Others mentioned by Mr. Tate are
Winsham (Somerset), Hawton (Notts.) and Swineshead (Beds). The full text
of the Protestation, from the Appleby Magna, Leics register is given in
J.C. Cox *The Parish Registers of England* p. 199.

inhabitants.[14] It was believed until recently that very few documents existed giving such information. However, about 200 full lists of inhabitants for particular parishes are now known, the earliest being that made at Ealing, Middlesex in 1599.

This is perhaps the sole survivor of a large number of similar censuses probably compiled to obtain statistics for the administration of the Poor Law. The arrangement is by households and it includes ages, relationships and occupations.[15]

The majority of surviving parish censuses derive, however, from the *Marriage Duties Act* of 1694, which with subsequent modifications and renewals remained in force until 1706. As has been pointed out elsewhere[16] this imposed duties on births, marriages and burials and a sliding scale of surcharges on the more prosperous, but there were also taxes of 1/- a year on bachelors over 25 and widowers without children. The execution of the act therefore involved not only the accurate recording of births, marriages and burials but the drawing up of an annual assessment, i.e. a list of all inhabitants. One copy of this was retained by the parson and the other copy went to the Exchequer. There should therefore in theory exist a complete census of the country for 11 years showing the sizes of parishes. In practice, all the Exchequer returns have disappeared and parochial copies are rare, though not quite as rare as was once thought, and they account for a large proportion of the 200 parish lists of inhabitants at present known. Some give ages, relationships, occupations and incomes. In 1885 R.E. Chester Waters printed the Melbourne, Derbyshire Assessment of 1695 with an introduction[17] and the 1698 assessment for Fenny Compton, Warwickshire has been the subject for a more recent study by Philip Styles.[18] This was ruled in six columns. The first was

---

14 The former made a second list in 1688. See P. Laslett: *The Study of Social Structure from Listings of Inhabitants* in E. A. Wrigley (ed) *An Introduction to English Historical Demography* (1966) p.160 ff. The principal other ecclesiastical statistical surveys were (1) the *Chantry Certificates of Communicants* for 1545 giving numbers of inhabitants aged 15 and over, (2) the *1563 General Census* when the Privy Council called on all bishops to survey thei[r] dioceses. The returns survive at the British Museum for eight dioceses (Harl. MSS. 594, 595 and 618. See J. Cornwall *An Elizabethan Census Records of Buckinghamshire* XVI Part 4 (1959) p. 258) and (3) *Registers of Communicants, recusants and other Nonconformists* compiled in 1603. (Returns for dioceses of Gloucester, Norwich and Winchester only. Harl. MSS. 594 and 595), (4) *Returns for diocese of Lincoln* 1705 (estimated population of each parish), (5) *Returns for diocese of Exeter* 1744. (number of families in each parish). (6) Returns for dio. of York 1764 (ditt[o]

15 K.J. Allison. *An Elizabethan Village Census.* Bull. Inst. Hist. Res. XXXV (1963).

16 See *Parish Registers: History*, above p.12 and P. Laslett *op.cit.* pp.174—

17 *Journ. of Derbyshire Arch. & Nat. Hist. Soc.* VII (1885) pp.1-30.

18 P. Styles. *A Census of a Warwickshire Village in 1698.* Univ. of Birmingham Hist. Journ. Vol. III (1951-2).

for the names and the others are headed "tytles", "burials",
"marriages", "births", "bachelors" and "widowers".

Very few parish censuses are known for the eighteenth century. Thus
Berkshire, for example, has only one – a "list of souls" in
Brightwalton in 1790 perhaps compiled for Poor Law purposes. The
majority of the other surviving pre-1841 censuses are rough drafts for
the statistical information required in the censuses of 1801, 1811,
1821 and 1831. Most commonly these give for 1801 and 1811 householders'
names, the number of families in each house, a breakdown of these into
males, females and totals, and the numbers employed in agriculture,
trade and otherwise. In Berkshire lists of this kind survive for
Brightwell (1801 and 1811) and Cumnor (1811). The 1821 census lists
give householders' names and a breakdown of each household into age
groups. In Berkshire they survive for Caversham and Earley. The latter
also gives occupations.[19] Surviving 1831 drafts rarely give ages as
these were not asked for. However, the Shellingford, Berks return is
broken down like those of 1821 into sex and age groups.

Sometimes one is fortunate enough to encounter drafts for the
census in which information was obtained far beyond the official requirements. Doubtless in such cases the overseers took the opportunity
to obtain information which might be useful to them. Thus for Berkshire
there are two magnificent lists. That for Binfield[20] compiled in 1801
lists under initial letter of surname not only every parishioner, but
deceased members of families and those who have left the parish
(indicated by 'out' on the list, or a more precise comment such as
at Ceylon'). John Jackman, a soldier, is recorded as "*supposed to be
dead*". Another notable feature is the inclusion of the wife's maiden
name, and if from another parish, her place of origin. Relationships
of one household to another are frequently given and sometimes
valuable negative information. Thus against 'John Butler, Labourer' is
the note "*This family is not related to Robert Butler's family*". A
number of couples are described as "*not married*". There are also
asterisks to indicate "that birth, death or change of whatsoever
nature it may be has happened between March and November the 25th
1801." A wide column is left for notes and these have been added in
profusion: "ran away for stealing Cooper's geese" "his wife dead:
and he and his family removed to his mother's" "her husband died in
St. Luke's Hospital". Richard Yeates, widower has the description:
"Once a Farmer at No. 1. He has burdened the Parish by a number of
illegitimate children, and at length is obliged to seek relief from it
himself." A number of persons are described as "blind" "a cripple"
or "deaf". The record was clearly kept up to date as far as possible

---

[19] Berks R.O. D/P 113/18/2. In fact this appears to be not a rough draft but
      a schedule returned for correction and never sent back.
[20] Berks R.O. D/P 18/18/3.

for many years. There are frequent notes of subsequent burials and sometimes others such as "married again in July to Ann Picket". There are two copies of this invaluable document. One, presumably the finished draft includes an accurately drawn map with the numbers for every dwelling which are used in the schedule. There are a number of differences between the two copies, some households appearing in one and not in the other.

The other remarkable Berkshire list is that for Hungerford[21] compiled, not in a census year but on January 1st 1825. It gives the names of householders, the ages of the householder and his wife and the names and ages of all children, though curiously not the names of wives. It appears to have been brought up to date on 4th December 1826, 12th April 1833 and in 1834 and 1835 (exact dates not given). However, further children were added from time to time in the intervening years. Clearly, though the previous censuses doubtless supplied the idea, this list was compiled to check outdoor relief claimed under the Speenhamland system on the basis of the size of the family. A revised list was complied on 14th May 1828, and new births were added in 1829, 1830 and 1831. Into this volume has been slipped a further schedule which appears on superficial inspection to date from c. 1820 and lists 218 persons (mostly children) for whom relief was claimed.

If Berkshire can be taken as being representative of the country as a whole the number and value of pre-1841 census lists which have survived is by no means negligible, and the Hungerford example would appear to suggest that other hitherto unnoticed lists may exist among the records of the Parish Overseers. [22]

C. RECORDS OF THE PROPERTIED CLASSES

Marriage Settlements

18th century marriage settlements have been the subject of a thorough study by H. J. Habbakkuk. [23] He examines the gradual inflation of marriage portions, the increase of the practice of marrying into mercantile wealth and the development of strict entails. Though principally concerned with their contribution to an understanding of the social conditions of the time (e. g. the increase in the practice of younger sons going into the professions) his article contains much to interest the genealogist working on a landed or mercantile family. Many marriage settlements, largely from the collection in the British Museum were edited by G. W. Watson and published in the *Genealogist,* New Series Vols. 33-37.

---

21   Berks R. O. D/P71/28/7.
22   For a detailed study of the whole subject see P. Laslett *op.cit* p.160 f
23   *Marriage Settlements in the 18th Century.* Trans. Royal Hist. Soc. xxxii (1950).

For an illustration of the amount of genealogical data that may be found in marriage settlements one cannot have a better example than the 1665 Kentish Settlement printed in *Family History* in 1963.[24]

"Betweene Edmund Stede of Biddenden in the County of Kent gent of the one part And John Cripps the younger of the Towne of Maidstone in the County aforesaid gent and one of the Juratts of the Towne and parrish of Maidstone aforesaid And Jane ffletcher of Maidstone aforesaid spinster sister in law of the said John Cripps and one of the Daughters of Richard ffletcher heretofore of Boxley in the said Countie of Kent yeoman deceased of the other part."

Then follows a detailed description of the land purchased from

"Robert Curteis of Tenterden aforesayd gent one of the Sonnes of George Curteis late of Tenterden aforesayd gent deseased, ffranceis Curteis of Maidstone aforesayd gent (one other of the Sonnes of the sayd George Curteis) Ann the wife of the said ffranceis Curteis and Richard Haffenden of Tenterden aforesaid gent and Mary his wife (late wife of the sayd George Curteis and mother of the sayd Robert Curteis and ffranceis Curteis) As by deede Indented beareing date the six and twentith day of December last past."

There is also a description of further lands which

"were by the last will and Tessament of Edmund Stede his late deceased father of the sayd Edmund Stede (party to these p^r sents) given and bequeathed into the sayd Edmund Stede (party to these p^{r}sents) and his heires for ever (As by the last will and Testament aforesayd of the said Edmund Stede the father bearing date the first day of Aprill which was in the yeare of our Lord one Thousand six hundred sixty one may more at large appeare."

The editor appends to the Settlement a tabular pedigree derived solely from information given.

Funeral Certificates at the College of Arms

These are extremely useful for armigerous families and have been treated elsewhere.[25]

Tontines[26]

Tontines are a useful and until fairly recently neglected source of deaths, and occasionally of marriages and births. A Tontine is a kind of Life Annuity increasing as subscribers die, the first organized by the British Government being in 1693. Although the original ledgers of this do not, as far as is known, survive, an

---

24 Vol. 1, No. 5 (June 1963).
25 See above, pages 71-72 Lancashire Funeral Certificates were printed by the Chetham Society, Vol. LXXV (1869) ed. by T.W. King and Rev. R. Raines.
26 All information on Tontines and Annuities has been kindly supplied by Mr. F.L. Leeson.

alphabetical list of the thousand-odd nominees, was printed, giving
the name of the nominee (usually a child), the name, address and
status or occupation of his or her father, the age of the nominee, the
sum subscribed and nominee's residence.[27] A list of 514 survivors was
published in 1730, giving their current status, and abode of the
husband in the case of female nominees who had married.[28]

The Second English Tontine was held in 1766, and three Irish
Tontines in 1773, 1775 and 1777. The third, or Great English Tontine
of 1789 had 8,349 subscribers holding 9,952 shares. The huge master
ledgers of these tontines are with the National Debt Office Records
at the Ashridge depository of the Public Record Office. When
Mr. F.L. Leeson first examined them in 1963 the ledgers had whole wads
of pages still roughly knotted together with string at their outer
corners, presumably to indicate closed entries and to ease the task of
turning the pages preceding the open sections. It was obvious that
these knots had never been undone.

Nominees were invariably children or minors, some subscribers
holding several debentures, sometimes on the lives of several related
children. A number of debentures were taken out on their children by
foreigners resident abroad, but most of the subscribers seem to have
been English, a number of them, in the case of Irish Tontines being
resident in Ireland. The following is a specimen entry from one of
the master ledgers.[29]

1. No. of the Debenture: Dead Acct. Christ[S] 1838, 767.
2. Subscriber: Teavil Appleton, of the parish of St. Mary, Beverley, in
   the Co. of Yorks, Esq.
3. Sum Subscribed: (a) Irish Currency (b) British Currency: [always
   blank].
4. Nominee: Thomas Leason of the parish of St. Mary, Beverley, in the
   Co. of Yorks, 2nd son of Ann Leason of the said parish, spinster.
   [where married, spouse's names are given.]
5. Age of the Nominee in 177(6): 2. [The final figure of the year, which
   is usually the year after the tontine concerned, is filled in ink.]
6. When the nominee died or was buried: Buried 9 June 1837.
7. Date of Assignment- [Left blank in this case, but often completed.]
8. Executors, Administrators and Assignees: Revd. Robert Rigby and
   Thomas Duesbury, Exors.
9. Volume of Wills or Assignments: 1.
10. Folio: 330.
11. Attornies: Cancelled/W. Currie, H.R. Raikes, G.R. & S. Lawford.
12. Volume of Powers of Attorney: 5/12.
13. Folio: 208 9/119.

---

27 A copy of this list is in the British Museum Library. Ref. 514,K2 (23).
28 British Museum Library. Ref. 8285 ee. 48.
29 'Register of Subscribers and Nominees, Executors and Administrators,
    Attorneys and Assignees, 2 and 3 Classes of 1773 and 1775 (Irish)
    Sessions' (NDO 3/5). The ledger is ruled both ways and contains printed
    headings across every two pages.

Alphabetical lists of nominees were printed for all save the 1766 tontine and the P.R.O. copies have been very usefully annotated so that they give almost as much information as the ledgers.[30]

The supporting documents to these ledgers include certificates of deaths and marriages, declarations of identity etc., but these are only occasionally cross referenced from the ledgers and the great bulk await listing and comprehensive indexing. The 1789 tontine alone has six volumes with an average of 400 certificates of baptism, marriage and death or burial pasted into each, though there is an index at the end of each volume.

Annuities

In addition to the tontines, normal life annuities were granted: the first series in 1745, 1746 and 1757; the second series in 1778 and 1779. There being less public interest in the longevity of the nominees, lists of survivors were not printed and we are dependent on the master ledgers in the Public Record Office. Mr. Leeson made an analysis of the 1745 ledger when he indexed the tontine and annuity records for the *Surname Archive*; 979 names are listed of which 522 are nominees. A breakdown of the status, occupation and origin, where given of the whole 979 shows that 65% of them derived from London and Middlesex, 21% from other counties, 13% from Holland and 1% elsewhere. Although many of the nominees were minors, they were fairly evenly divided between the sexes. Of the adults appearing among the 979 names, 33% were female (27% spinsters and 6% widows); of the males 22% were esquires, 11% gentlemen and 5% noblemen. In addition the following occupations are given: tradesmen (12%); merchants (10%); clergymen (3%); Service officers (3%) physicians and surgeons (1%).

Altogether there are more than 15,000 nominees in the tontines and life annuities between 1693 and 1789 with probably an equal number of other names of people who are often related to the nominees. Clearly tontines and life annuities constitute one of the most important sources for the genealogy of the 18th century middle classes. A Guide to the Tontine and Annuity records was published in 1967 by Pinhorns, Shalfleet Manor, near Newport, Isle of Wight. The *Surname Archive* of Channel Sound, Sea Lane, Ferring, Sussex, holds indexes giving all the genealogical information from the ledgers and printed lists, as well as microfilms and photocopies of the latter. Searches will be made in these at a nominal fee pending their eventual publication.

---

[30] The P.R.O. references to these printed lists are: 1773 and 1775: NDO 3/32; 1777: NDO 3/33; 1789: NDO 2/15. Copies have not yet been traced at the British Museum.

D. MANORIAL RECORDS[31]

Manorial Records are probably the most valuable class of genealo
cal records after Parish Registers and wills. Indeed some claim that
they are of even greater importance than either, for not only may a
single entry provide a three generation pedigree, but a great many
court rolls long antedate either Parish Registers or wills, some goi▸
back to the thirteenth century[32] and many to the fourteenth. For the
bulk of the population they are almost the only source of genealogic
information during the mediaeval period.

The Manorial Court of Norman times often acquired certain
'franchises' to hear cases more usually tried in the shire or royal
courts. The most common of these was the right to take the local
View of Frankpledge, an ancient Saxon presentment by *tithings* for
the maintenance of law and order. However, for the genealogist the
greatest point of interest is not so much the legal functions of the
court, but the references to the manumission of villeins who became
copyhold tenants, holding a copy of the relevant entry in the manori▴
roll.

The Manorial Court became in the fifteenth century divided into
two: the *court leet* or court customary for customary tenants and the
court baron for free tenants. These terms were, however, very loosel
applied. Frequently the two jurisdictions were combined on the same
court day. Even when they were held separately it is not unusual in
the sixteenth century to find a so-called court baron exercising all
the functions of a customary court. In fact, by the sixteenth centur,
the functions themselves had changed. The *Court Leet and View of
Frankpledge* elected the manorial officers, such as constable and hay
wards and dealt with the enforcement of the laws and customs of the
manor and the punishment of petty misdemenours and offences. The
Court Baron was mainly concerned with changes in tenancy in copyhold▴
with minor infringements of property rights and with the organizatio▸
of the open fields, meadows and commons. By the end of the 17th cent▾
the increasing power of County Justices and Parish Vestries made the
Court Leet redundant and in most cases in the eighteenth century the
was once again only a single court. By the 19th century periodical
courts were largely abandoned, the business hitherto dealt with bein▸
transacted in the office of the steward of the manor, invariably a
lawyer.

---

[31] The standard works on the subject are N.J. Hone: *The Manor and Manorial
Records* (1925), and E.M. Pollock: *Manors, their History and Records* (19

[32] e.g. Bridgewater & Haygrove, Somerset (c.1200), Alweras, Staffs (1259),
Hales, Worcs (1272), Wakefield, Yorks (1274), Wellington, Somerset (127▾
Chalgrave, Beds (1278), Isleworth, Middlesex (1279).

Early court rolls are normally made up of membranes of vellum about nine inches wide and two feet long stitched together. However, the stitching does not necessarily indicate that the roll is complete. Not infrequently surviving portions of earlier rolls were stitched together later for greater convenience. The entry for each court is usually clearly headed, and may take up only a few inches or run to several feet. Most early rolls are in poor condition and the writing tends to be considerably more difficult to read than that of the royal or ecclesiastical scribes. Up to 1653 court rolls were written in Latin with a complicated system of abbreviations. English was used during the Commonwealth period, but in 1660 Latin was restored and was used until 1732. Though most rolls end in the first half of the 19th century or earlier, some rolls continue until the abolition of copyhold tenure and manorial jurisdictions by the *Law of Property Acts* in 1922. At the beginning of each court the *Homage*, or jury, together with the *Essoins*, or absentees fined for "default of suit of court", provide a useful list of landholders in the manor.

In the Parish Register period, although the Manor Court was in decline both as a legal and a social institution, the Court rolls are still of immense value to the genealogist. Used in conjunction with Parish registers and wills they can clarify many ambiguities for they frequently recite the land held by customary tenants appearing before the court. C.R. Humphery-Smith points out:[33]

"John son of William and Mary Wilson may occur in the registers of a hundred churches for 1640. John son of William Wilson and Mary his wife being admitted to the holding of the North Shot of Salmonsfield abutting on X and Y to the North and South and P and Q to the East and West and so on according to the custom of the manor of Chertsey, can only be one."

Furthermore, identification may be assisted by comparing signatures with those in Hardwicke marriage registers. However, the value of manorial records is by no means limited to questions of identification The roll of the Court Baron records the death of a tenant and the admission of the new holder of his lands. In the case of freehold property a substantial relief – often a year's quit rent – was paid to the lord on alienation or inheritance. Copies or abstracts of wills (together with the date of granting probate) were frequently included and sometimes (e.g. the diocese of Exeter) these are the only copies extant. Particularly valuable are the admission of widows and minors or their guardians:

"Walter Burrel of Cuckfield in Sussex presented himself before the Seneschal or Steward of the Manor of Isleworth Sion at a Court held October 8th 1639 and was admitted as guardian during the minority of one

---

[33] *Genealogy from Manorial Records,* Gen. Mag. Vol. 14. No. 1 (March 1962) p. 2.

Francis Wyatt, gentleman, a customary tenant of the manor being then under age and eleven years old who had been admitted heir to his mother Tymethiea Wyat. Walter Burrell was then permitted to let the property of which Francis Wyatt had inherited the copyhold."[34]

To illustrate the value of Court Rolls, Mr. Humphery-Smith cited the following entries from the roll of the manor of Beeding, Sussex, part of the major manor of Cowfold:

22nd July 1735, Court of the Hon. Richard Edgcumbe. Thomas Butcher, only son and heir of Thomas Butcher of Hurstpierpoint, yeoman, deceased, assigns Ridges of Rudgeland in Cowfold, 50 acres, to Benjamin Richardson of Cowfold Clerk, and Katherine his wife or to the longest liver.

On October 19th, 1736, the following year, we find the surrender of the land by Thomas and the admission by the Rod of Benjamin, the Clerk and his wife Ketherine.[35]

October 13th, 1756 (the last Court having been held on July 22nd in that year) Benjamin Richardson is sworn to be dead and his widow Ketherine claims to be admitted to Ridgeland – fealty is respited.

On January 9th, 1760 Ketherine Richardson is dead (the previous court having been held in January of the year before), she is shown to have held Ridgelands 50 acres as did her father, and Mary the wife of Richard Tidy, daughter of Katherine Richardson is admitted.

He emphasizes the quantity of genealogical information which these entries give:

Thomas Butcher is the only son of a yeoman from Hurstpierpoint, a parish 6 miles away, who had died before 1735. He has a daughter Ketherine married before 1735 to one Benjamin Richardson, a Clerk who dies between July and October 1756. Ketherine also dies sometime during the year before the court of January 1760. Her only daughter is then already married to Richard Tidy.[36]

In addition to information of specifically genealogical interest Manorial Rolls are invaluable for the light they throw on the economic and social environment of our ancestors: on rural customs and institutions – the stocks, the lock-up or the cucking-stool, on enclosures, on archaic legal practices[37] or on the history of houses or inns.[38]

---

34 Abstract from the Latin. *ibid.* p. 6.
35 A transfer of land from one tenant to another was performed by surrendering lands to the lord by handing him or his steward a stick or rod as the symbol of his holding. On payment of an entrance fine, the land was then granted to the new tenant who was handed the rod by the lord or steward.
36 *ibid.* pp. 4-5
37 For an entertaining account of the legal fictions resorted to in disentailing lands held by copyhold tenure see H.W. Knocker, *Manorial Records.* Gen. Mag. Vol. 6. No. 3 (Sept. 1932) p. 92.
38 For more discussion of some of these topics see W. Branch Johnson. *Notes before reading Court Rolls.* Amat. Hist. Vol. 4. No. 3. (Spring 1959) p. 98 ff.

Other Manorial Records

As well as the Manorial Rolls, the records of a manor may include rent books, leases, surveys, maps, valuations and Chancery suits, all of which may be of the greatest significance to the genealogist and the local historian. It is important to remember that manorial records are frequently found among Borough Archives. Those of Guildford include sixteenth century books catalogued as *"Three weekly courts of the Lord, the annual Legal Court of View of Frankpledge, and three Gilds Merchant"*. Some manors had the status of seigneurial boroughs, conferred by grant of the lord, and not by royal charter.[39]

Lists of Records

A register of original manorial records held in repositories throughout the country is held by the National Register of Archives, Quality Court, Chancery Lane, London, W.C.2. N.J. Hone's *"The Manor and Manorial Records"* (1925) gives a list of those to be found (at the time of publication) at the Public Record Office, the British Museum, Lambeth Palace Library and the Bodleian Library. A list of printed rolls, rentals, surveys and account books is given in Robert Somerville's *Handlist of Record Publications* (British Records Association, 1951). A list arranged by counties of the more interesting published rolls appears in J. West's *"Village Records"* (1962) pp. 37-42.

E. THE POOR

The administration of the Poor Law occupied a greater share of the attention of the Parish Officers than any other parochial matter. Moreover, half the business of every Quarter Sessions consisted in deciding appeals on orders of removal under the Settlement Acts.[40] Poor Law documents are therefore indispensable in tracing what Charles A. Bernau described as the "Genealogy of the Submerged."

The various acts concerned with poor relief have been summarized by W.E. Tate.[41] Of particular importance to the genealogist are the 1662 Act of Settlement by which any stranger settling in a parish might be removed forthwith by the justices, unless he rented a tenement of £10 or found security to discharge the parish of his adoption from all expense it might incur to relieve him. A temporary stay (e.g. at harvest) necessitated a certificate from his own parish agreeing to take him back. The act of 1691 laid down other ways in

---

39 F.G. Emmison. *Archives and Local History* (1966) p. 36.
40 W.E. Tate. *The Parish Chest.* p. 199.
41 *ibid.* pp. 188-194.

which a legal settlement could be obtained: by serving a parish office, paying a parish rate, being apprenticed by indenture to a parishioner or by serving a year in service. The 1696-7 Act introduced the issue of Settlement Certificates for a permanent stay by which the parish of legal settlement agreed to receive a person back if he became chargeable. By the act of 1743-4 a bastard child of a vagrant woman did not gain a settlement in the parish of his birth and until 1794-5, those without a legal settlement could be removed whether or not they were chargeable. From 1795 the overseers, with the approval of the vestry could give out-relief to the able bodied, and the scale drawn up by the magistrates at Speenhamland, Berks. soon became followed throughout the country, until the system was abolished by the Act of 1834, which took the administration away from the parish, grouped parishes into Unions and forbade out-relief for the able bodied.

Although overseers' accounts, Constable's accounts, inventories of paupers' goods and various other documents may provide clues or data necessary for building up a complete picture, the most valuable sources are the documents connected with settlement and removal, with bastardy and with apprenticeship.

Settlement Papers

Until about 1740 certificates and other documents were handwritten. Increasingly from then onwards printed forms were used. A typical settlement certificate reads as follows:

> "Bucks, S.S. We, John Webb, Thomas Morris, John Bavin and Thomas Moodey Churchwardens and Overseers of the Poor for the Parish of Upton cum Chalvey in the said County, Doe hereby acknowledge Thomas Applebee and Mary his Wife to be Inhabitants legally settled in our said Parish of Upton cum Chalvey, In Witness whereof we have hereunto sett our hands and Seales the 8th day of Aprill In the Eleventh Year of her Majties Reigne Queen Ann of great Brittaine & c Anno Dom 1712. [42]

Important though Settlement certificates are in providing places of origin, records of examinations made before the magistrates after the parish officers had requested a removal order are of even greater genealogical value since they are virtually autobiographies of the persons concerned. A pauper in his sixties may give his history from boyhood when at the age of five years he hired himself as a stable lad and thereby gained a settlement. [43]

---

42 This example is taken from D.E. Gardner & F. Smith. *Genealogical Research in England & Wales*. pp. 125 and 126 where it is reproduced in facsimile.

43 M.F. Lloyd Prichard. *The Genealogy of the Poor*. Gen. Mag. Vol. 11. No. 3. (Sept 1951) p.100.

Full details of any marriages are invariably given, and sometimes marriage certificate is attached to the declaration.[44] Sometimes he names and ages of the children are given,[45] and sometimes the ather's name, as in the following example:-

BERKS: The Examination of Joseph Stride taken upon oath the eighth day of November in the Year 1791.
This EXAMINANT on his Oath saith that he is the Son of Joseph Stride who is a parishioner legally settled in the parish of ELING in the County of SOUTHAMPTON where the Examinant was born, And that he has never done any Act in his own right to gain a Settlement elsewhere. And that he was this day married in the Parish Church of Saint Lawrence in Reading in the said County of Berks to Ann his now wife.
Sworn Before Me
Henry Deane   Joseph Stride[46]

Examination was normally prior to the granting of a removal order y the magistrates. However, having been removed to the parish where e presumed he had a legal settlement, the pauper might be re-xamined on arrival. In an example quoted at length by W.E. Tate.[47] umphrey Foulds was removed from Boston, Lincs in 1809, the removal rder beginning:-

" The Borough and Parish of Boston
     In the County of Lincoln
     Upon the Complaint of the Churchwardens and Overseers of the Poor of the Parish of Boston aforesaid....in the said County of Lincoln unto us....that Humphrey Foulds and Frances his Wife and their three children namely Humphrey aged about six years, Mary Ann aged about five years and Sarah aged about two years have come to inhabit in the said Parish of Boston, not having gained a legal settlement there....; we the said Justices....do therefore require you....to convey the said Humphrey Foulds and Frances his Wife and their said three children..... to the said Parish of Shelford....

This was followed by a suspension on the grounds of sickness, ated 20th January 1809 and a confirmation dated 30th March 1809. On is arrival in Shelford, Foulds was examined before a Nottinghamshire ustice as follows:-

County of Nottingham
     (To Wit).
     The Examination of Humphrey Foulds taken upon Oath before me one of his Majesty's Justices of the Peace in and for the said County, this seventh day of April 1809 touching the place of his Settlement. This

---

4 For example a declaration in Southwark in 1765 has appended a certificate of a marriage celebrated at Frome, Somerset in 1754. A facsimile of the latter is reproduced in D.E. Gardner and F. Smith. *op.cit.* p. 131 and a transcript with an abstract of the declaration on p. 129.
5 For an example, see D.E. Gardner and F. Smith. *op.cit.* pp. 129, 133.
6 *ibid.* pp. 128-9.
7 *op cit.* pp. 202-203.

Examinant, upon Oath saith, That he is about the Age of Thirty Eight
Years, and that he was born, as he hath been informed, and verily
believes, in the Parish of Old Daulby in the County of Leicester of
parents legally settled at Shelford in the County of Nottingham, That
when about seventeen years of age he was hired to Mr. Simpson of Saxelby
in the County of Leicester aforesaid for one year and served him Two
years, That at Martinmas following he was hired to Henry Ellis of
Shelford in the County of Nottingham for one year and served him accordingly. That at Martinmas following was hired to Mr. John Cooper of
Shelford aforesaid and served him Eighteen Months. That in the Month of
December following he went to Work at Grantham Canal. That in the year
1800 he went to Great Grimsby in Lincolnshire and Married Fanny his now
Wife which gave him a Vote for Great Grimsby aforexaid, and there Rented
a House, at one Pound ten shillings a year and paid Rates or Assessments
about five Shillings a year, and lived there about five or six years.
That he afterwards went to live at Boston, and Rented a Room and Paid
Three Shillings a week for Thirty Nine Weeks, and remainder of the year
Paid 2s. 6d. per week, and was then Removed by a Warrant of Removal to
the Parish of Shelford aforesaid ...."

It is not clear from this whether Foulds had previously been
examined by the Boston Magistrates before the removal order was
executed, but it is apparent that a pauper might be examined twice –
at the instance of the parish seeking to remove him and that
reluctantly receiving him. [48] This was clearly necessary in this case
as it is apparent from his examination that his last place of legal
settlement was not Shelford but Great Grimsby, where he had paid
rates. There is sometimes therefore a double chance of these very
important examination records surviving. The various documents connected with removal are clearly complementary to each other. In the
above example the examination gives the father's biography, but it is
the removal order which supplies the names and ages of the children.

Examinations and removal orders for vagrancy may prove equally
valuable: - [49]

City of London to wit

Order for the removal of a
vagrant May 20 1709

Whereas Phebe Hood, widow, and her two children (seven and six years
old respectively) were on the day of the date of these presents brought
before me, one of her Majesty's Justices of the Peace of the City aforesaid next residing to the Parish of St. Sepulchre, where the said
Phebe Hood and her children were taken and in pursuance of a late act of
Parliament....I have carefully examined her, the said Phebe Hood: and it

---

48 Curiously, Tate fails to draw attention to this aspect of the case, and
    by printing the documents in reverse chronological order, he gives the
    impression that this was the examination preceding the removal. If Fould
    was examined by the Boston magistrates before removal, a copy of the
    record may have survived in the Boston chest.
49 In the 17th century the execution of the Vagrancy Laws is often recorded
    in Parish Registers. For some interesting examples, see Tate *op.cit.*
    pp. 211-212.

appears to me That her late Husband, William Hood had served his apprenticeship to his father John Hood of Attenborough in the County of Nottingham about twelve years ago, and I did not find that since that time he obtained any legall settlement elsewhere. And I have excused the correction of the Aforesaid Phebe for good reasons to me appearing.

These are therefore in her Majesty's name to Will and require you upon sight hereof to Remove the said Phebe Hood and her two children from the said Parish of St. Sepulchre, London, and to conduct her out of the said City of the Parish of St. Sepulchre in the County of Middlesex which I think the most direct and proper way to the said Parish of Attenborough.....to be from thence conveyed thither as the law directs.

Given under my hand and seal the 20th day of May Ano Dni 1709. To the Constable of St. Sepulchre, London, and to the Constable of St. Sepulchre in the County of Middlesex and to each of them and all others whom it may concern.

With endorsements instructing the Constable of St. Sepulchre's, Mx. to convey the persons to Barnet, Herts.

. . . .

St. Albans, Herts, to Studham, Beds.,
Studham, Beds., to Little Brickhill, Bucks.,
Little Brickhill, Bucks., to Passenham, Northants.[50]

. . . .

Bastardy

In cases of bastardy the responsibility of the father as well as the mother was clearly laid down by the Vagrant Act of 1575-6. Two justices were empowered to make an order against the mother or father. If it was not performed, the offender was to be goaled until the next sessions unless he gave security to appear, when a fresh order would be made or the old one confirmed. Later acts dealt with punishment of unmarried mothers, with infanticide and with the absconding of the parents.[51] The Act of 1732-3 laid down that a woman pregnant with a bastard child was to declare herself so, and to name the father. Until the act of 1743-4 bastards had a legal settlement in their birthplace. This act, in addition to prescribing a public whipping for the mother, ordained that the child was to have its mother's settlement.

Despite difficulties in obtaining evidence, for parish registers record only bastards who were baptized,[52] all the evidence seems to

---

50 This example is taken from W.E. Tate. *op.cit.* pp. 212-213. On 27th June Phoebe was reconveyed from Attenborough to Nottingham and the order for her removal there was confirmed July 1709

51 A brief summary of these is given by Tate. *op.cit.* p. 215.

52 There is evidence that bastards were not infrequently refused baptism. See *Parish Registers - Form and Content*, above p. 51-52.

suggest that the illegitimacy rate was relatively low in the 16th and
17th centuries, though somewhat higher it would appear than in France.[53]
W. E. Tate, basing his conclusions on tables for Letheringham, Suffolk
drawn up by J.C. Cox and for Nottinghamshire parishes drawn up by
J. Meeds, concludes:

> "In the sixteenth and seventeenth centuries the birth of an illegitimate
> child in the average country parish seems to have been an unusual event,
> such an occurrence perhaps becoming rather commoner with the seventeenth
> century, still more common with the eighteenth and so common as to create
> little surprise, though a great deal of consternation, in the years from
> 1750 onwards." [54]

P. Laslett reached a slightly different conclusion:

> "The tendency seems to be for figures to be higher in the late 16th and
> middle 18th centuries."[55]

Whatever the results of more thorough research on this subject,
illegitimacy was common enough at all periods for many genealogists to
discover they have a bastard ancestor. From the 18th century onwards
the parish registers normally give only the mother's name and for the
name of the putative father, one has to have recourse to other records.
These are of three kinds: the records of Quarter Sessions, the records
of Ecclesiastical Courts and the Bastardy papers in the Parish chests.

Punishment and Maintenance orders were sometimes prescribed at
the Quarter Sessions even in the 16th and 17th centuries. At Manchester
in 1604:

> "Jane Byrom widow, now dead, was mother of a bastard daughter Alice, of
> which Thomas Byrom of Salford, gent, is reputed father; it is ordered
> that he shall maintain Alice till she be 12 years of age and shall be
> whipped in Manchester market-place. Sureties for him: Adam Pilkington of
> Salford, gent, and John Mosse of Brughton, yeoman."[56]

Up to the mid-18th century, records of Ecclesiastical Courts are
also useful as the parents were often brought before them for in-
continence, and penance was laid down. Thus the Churchwardens'
presentments for the parish of St. Giles, Reading at the visitation
of the Archddacon of Berkshire, 26th April 1737[57] include:

---

53 On the evidence for this see P. Laslett *"The World We Have Lost"*.
    pp. 134-135.
54 *op.cit.* p. 213. Statistics from my own researches, though from too small
    a sample to be of much value, seems to support this view, the graph con-
    tinuing to rise steeply until it reached its peak in the mid-19th century
55 *op.cit.* p. 136.
56 *Lancashire Quarter Sessions.* Vol. 1. *Quarter Sessions Rolls 1590-1606*
    ed. J. Tait. Chetham Soc. Vol. 77 (1917) p. 228. Cited with an example
    from 1601 by P. Laslett. *op.cit.* p. 138.
57 Bodleian Library. Ms Oxf. Archd. papers — Berks c.130.

"Sarah Willats of our parish for being lately delivered of a Bastard Child.......William Thomas for being the reputed father of the said Bastard Child.......Elizabeth Palmoor for being lately delivered of a Bastard Child.......John Hall for being the Reputed father of the said Bastard Child.

Until about 1750 the most general method of dealing with bastardy was to make the father or his father responsible by bond for the maintenance of the child. Thus:

"July 21st 1747. Know all men by these presents that I Abraham Atkinson of Cambridge in the County of Cambridge apothecary am held and firmly bound unto William Smith and Francis Tipping Churchwardens of the Parish of Littlebury in the County of Essex and William Kent and George Buck Overseers of the Poor of the said Parish in the Sum of fifty Pounds of good and lawfull money of Great Britain.......

The condition of this Obligation is such that Whereas Mary Russell of the parish of Littlebury aforesaid Singlewoman was lately gotton with Child by John Atkinson Son of the above bounden Abraham Atkinson as she the said Mary Russell hath upon her Oath affirmed which Child when Born will be a Bastard and Likely to become Chargeable to the said Parish of Littlebury. If Therefore the above bounden Abraham Atkinson his heirs Executors or Administrators Do and shall from time to time and at all Times hereafter fully and clearly acquit Discharge.......the above named.......Churchwardens.......and......Overseers of the Poor of the said Parish.......of and from all and all manner of costs Charges and Expences.......for or by reason or means of the Birth Maintenance or bringing up of the said Bastard Child.......Then this Obligation to be void.[58]

Sometimes instead of a bond a lump sum was paid instead to discharge all responsibility.

After 1750 though presentments before the ecclesiastical courts are rare, Court Orders became increasingly frequent. For example:

"BERKS, to wit; The Order of George Mitford, Esquire and the Revd. Edward Cove, Clerk, Two of His Majesty's Justices of the Peace in and for the said County......made the 24th July 1824 concerning a female bastard child, lately born in the Parish aforesaid [Tilehurst] of the Body of Margaret Knibbs, single Woman.

Whereas it hath been duly made appear unto us, the said Justices as well upon the Complaint of the Churchwardens and Overseers of the Poor of the Parish of Tilehurst as upon the oath of the said Margaret Knibbs that she was delivered of a female Bastard Child at and in the said Parish on the nineteenth day of June last and that the said Bastard Child is now chargeable to the same, and likely to continue; and further that Moses Slade of Tilehurst in the said county labourer did beget the said Bastard Child on the body of her the said Margaret Knibbs, and Whereas the said Moses Slade hath appeared before us pursuant to our summons for that purpose but shown to us no sufficient cause why he should not be adjudged the reputed father of the said Bastard Child We, therefore, upon

---

[58]   This example is taken from W.E. Tate. *op.cit.* pp. 219-220 where it is quoted in full.

the Examination of the Cause and Circumstances of the Premises, as well upon the Oath of the said Margaret Knibbs as otherwise, do hereby adjudge him the said Moses Slade to be the reputed Father of the Bastard Child."[59]

With the increase of illegitimacy from about 1750 parishes differed in their policy. W.E. Tate notes:

" The problem to decide was whether it would be better to force the putative father to marry the woman before the child's birth, leaving it to the father to provide for his offspring, or whether to force the father to pay for the child's keep under an order from justices or quarter sessions."[60]

When the father came from a different parish, the parish officers often brought considerable pressure to bear to persuade the couple to marry. This would secure the legitimacy of the child and the settlement of child and mother in the father's parish. Removal could then follow. Sometimes indeed the churchwardens and overseers were prepared to seek out and bribe a poor man with a settlement in another parish to marry the girl and legitimize the child.[61] This is a fearsome pitfall for the genealogist and in cases where the first child is born soon after the marriage, there is always the possibility that the marriage was one of convenience only, or else a man had sufficient affection for the mother to marry her and legitimize another man's child. Also, since the putative father had to spend a month or so in goal waiting for quarter sessions there was a strong incentive for the man named as the father to obligingly marry the girl and bring proceedings to a halt. Not infrequently, girls must have named as father the men they wished to marry rather than the real father. Sometimes they may not have been sure themselves.

Parish Apprenticeship

Apprenticeship was recognised by the Act of 1691 as giving a legal settlement. Until 1757 apprentices had to be bound by indenture, but in 1757-8 binding by any deed properly stamped was recognised as legally binding.[63]

By the 18th century " apprenticeship " often consisted solely of a fiction convenient in disposing of a pauper child, generally in another parish. A girl could be bound apprentice to a day labourer " to learn the art and mystery of a housewife " or a boy to a clergyman " to learn the art and science of husbandry."[64]

---

[59] This example is taken from D.E. Gardner & F. Smith. *op.cit.* pp. 133-134.
[60] *ibid.* p. 216.
[61] For examples of marriages arranged by the overseers (though not necessarily to legitimize unborn children) see *Clandestine Marriages,* above p.301.
[62] A typical indenture of 1712 is given by M.E. Lloyd Prichard " *The Genealogy of the Poor.*" Gen. Mag. Vol. 11. No. 3. (Sept. 1951) pp.97-98.
[63] W.E. Tate. *op.cit.* p. 220.
[64] *ibid.* p. 220.

Clearly these were euphemisms for "farm labourer" and "domestic service". At Gnosall, Staffs, of 178 children apprenticed within the parish between 1691 and 1816, seven were to tailors, three to shoe-makers, two to cordwainers, one each to masters of nine other trades and 157 to 'husbandry' and 'housewifery'. Similarly from 1817 to 1835, 240 children were apprenticed, but only ten to trades properly so called.[65] When the parish wanted to bind a poor child within its own bounds the master could be compelled to receive him, irrespective of his own wishes, though he sometimes compounded with a fine. Lists of apprentices are sometimes found in Vestry Minute books and occasionally there are registers of apprentices.[66] At the beginning of the 19th century the apprenticeship of pauper children from the Southern counties to Lancashire mill-owners was by no means uncommon.

Free Apprentices

Until the 18th century, parish apprenticeships accounted for only a small fraction of apprenticeships, the vast majority being freely entered into. A considerable number of indentures survive, but although these are of considerable genealogical importance since they normally give the father's name and address, ages are rarely, if ever, given. From 1710 following the imposition of a tax on apprentice-ship indentures (except for parish apprentices and those where the apprentice paid less than a shilling fee) comprehensive registers were kept until 1802. These are at the Public Record Office[67] and a type-script index from 1710 to 1774 made by the late Percival Boyd is at the Society of Genealogists.[68] In London, valuable sources to be used in conjunction with the register of apprentices are the Records of Freemen held by the City Chamberlain, Gresham Street and the records kept by the Livery Companies.[69]

---

[65] S. A. Cutlack. *Gnossall, (Staffs) Records 1678-1837.* Staffs Record Soc. Collections (1936) pp. 53-62. Cited by W. E. Tate. *op.cit.* p. 220. An analysis of the apprenticeship records of Doveridge, Derbyshire conducted by W. E. Tate and H. E. Poole is given on page 221. Most children apprenticed within the parish were indentured for husbandry or housewifery, but those apprenticed elsewhere were mostly indentured for skilled trades.

[66] For examples see W. E. Tate. *op.cit.* p. 225.

[67] Two pages from one of the volumes are reproduced in A. J. Willis' *Genealogy for Beginners.* p. 96-97.

[68] With it there is an Index of Apprentice Masters up to 1762.

[69] For more information on these records see Gerald Hamilton-Edwards "*In Search of Ancestry*" pp.161–164. On Mediaeval apprenticeship see *Proofs of Age* p. 363 and *Surnames* pp.88–89.

F. ARMY AND NAVY RECORDS

Army and Navy Records, among which are many which may supply details of Births, Marriages and Deaths are thoroughly described in Gerald Hamilton-Edwards's *"In Search of Ancestry"* pp. 87-106 and D.E. Gardner and F. Smith's *"Genealogical Research in England and Wales"*, Vol. 2, pp. 144-182. Only a brief synopsis need therefore be given here. There is a possibility that records at present at St. Catherine's House may eventually be transferred to the Public Record Office

Army Records

Muster Rolls (Public Record Office)

The Muster Rolls of each regiment give place of birth, age on enlistment and often trade on enlistment. The earliest rolls are 1719 (Royal Artillery), 1732 (Cavalry and Infantry) and 1816 (Royal Engineers).

Description Books. approx. 1795 onwards (P.R.O)

These give details of each recruit including age and trade on enlistment and place of birth.

Chaplains Returns 1796-1880 (St. Catherine's House)

Registers of Births, Baptisms, Marriages and Deaths kept by Army Chaplains (normally abroad). There is a comprehensive index for which it is not necessary to know the regiment.

Regimental Registers 1790-1924 (St. Catherine's House)

These are the original registers of Births, Baptisms, Marriages and Deaths kept by the regiments at home and abroad. The Births and Baptisms are indexed.

Artillery Records of Service 1756-1917 (Public Record Office)

These record places of birth, marriages and discharges or deaths. For some regiments there are baptism and marriage registers 1817-1883

Pensions Records (Public Record Office)

Widows' Pensions 1735-1912. These normally include proof of marriage and often affidavits of date and place of birth.

Chelsea Hospital (St. Catherine's House)

Registers of Baptisms 1691-1812, Marriages 1691-1765, Burials 1692-1856.

Casualty Returns 1809-1857 (P.R.O)

Give name, rank, place of birth, trade on enlistment, details of casualty, next of kin.

Garrison Registers (St. Catherine's House)

The earliest register is that of Landguard Fort, Suffolk. The births are included in the index to births and baptisms of the Regimental Registers.

Returns of Retired Officers

The 1829 Army Returns of Officers retired on half pay supply ages and dates and places of marriage. The 1829 returns of those retired on full pay give in addition the place and date of birth.

Naval Records (P.R.O unless otherwise stated)

Lieutenant's Passing Certificates (1691-1832)

The Navy Board copies of Lieutenants' Passing Certificates have from 1789 onwards filed with them the baptismal certificate which the candidate had to produce to prove he was at least 20 years of age. Two manuscript indexes to these certificates are at the Public Record Office.[70]

Ships' Musters (earliest 1680. Fairly regular from 1696. Almost complete from 1740).

Ships' Musters list all the officers and ratings on board and in the case of Ratings (including midshipmen) give ages and places of birth. However, Gerald Hamilton-Edwards cautions:-

"It must be mentioned, however, that many of these places of birth are inaccurate and also that there are examples of forged baptismal certificates among the passing certificates. There are stories of how men sat outside the dockyards when the midshipmen were taking their examinations for Lieutenant, prepared for a small fee to issue bogus baptismal certificates to show that the midshipman was over 20 years of age, as required by the regulations. Ages as stated on returns are also often wrong. Both Nelson and Collingwood provide examples of false ages in their records."[71]

Description Books (from 1790)

These include date and place of birth.

---

[70] For further details *see above* p. 42.
[71] *In Search of Ancestry* (1966) pp. 92-93.

Certificates of Service 1802-1894

Give records of service of ratings, enabling a search to be made of the Ship's Muster of a particular ship.

Bounty Papers 1675-1822

Give names and addresses of the recipients of Bounty. If a relative, baptism and marriage certificates are often found.

Pensions Records 1734-1885

Applications and approvals of pensions include details of service and place of birth. Marriage certificates are included for widows' pensions.

Greenwich Hospital Registers (St. Catherine's House)

Baptisms 1720-1856, Marriages 1724-1754, Burials 1705-1857. Cover pensioners, their children and close relatives and perhaps families o Hospital Staff.

Other Greenwich Hospital Records

Entry Book of Pensioners 1704-1869 gives date of entry into hospital, date of discharge, date of death, place of birth, where las resided, name of last ship, years of service and if married. Register 1825-1865 include births, marriages, number of children, ages of children and parish of marriage of children.

Widows' Marriage Register

Gives details of widows whose pensions ceased on remarriage.

Seamen's Wills 1786-1882.

* * * * * * * * * * *

In these notes it has, of course been impossible to comment on more than some of the most important sources likely to yield information on births, marriages or deaths. Dates of birth, marriage or death may appear in many other classes of document such as Insurance or Medical records, and exact or approximate ages and parentage may b given in school registers, Chancery depositions, Borough records or elsewhere.

Although failure to trace entries of baptisms or marriages in Parish Registers is always disappointing, it is extremely probable th the required information is available somewhere. It may, however, tak many years of patience to find it.

MEDIAEVAL SOURCES

PREFACE

In general, sources of births and deaths (especially parish registers) tend to take a pre-eminent position among records of genealogical importance. Proofs of Age and Inquisitions *Post Mortem* differ however from most of the records examined in this volume, in that their genealogical value, though considerable, is no greater than that of many other sources, such as Visitation Pedigrees, Manorial Records, Deeds, Wills and above all, Lawsuits. Not infrequently, a long pedigree can be deduced from the evidence cited in rival claims to land or, in the case of a seven generation pedigree studied by Mr. N.H. MacMichael[1] to the advowson of a church. It could reasonably be argued that even among the Chancery records, the Proceedings, the Charter Rolls, Patent Rolls, Close Rolls and Fine Rolls[2] are all likely to be as valuable as the Inquisitions *Post Mortem* and Proofs of Age which possibly may be used more frequently to supply dates for an existing pedigree than to establish a new one. Furthermore their value to the genealogist is clearly limited by the fact that they relate exclusively to the landowning classes of society, though it is a mistake to assume that tenants in chief were necessarily large landowners.

Nevertheless, Inquisitions *Post Mortem* are important as they not only record the date of death and the property held, but also give the name, age and relationship of the next heir. Proofs of Age are the only large class of Mediaeval documents which set out, however imperfectly to establish dates of birth. Of course these normally concern only heirs who were minors at the time of the death of a tenant in chief and who were therefore wards of the King. Moreover they became highly formalized at a very early date,[3] though this does not necessarily invalidate the essential information they purport to convey.

The title given to this section may be misleading in that it must be remembered that since these records extend to the reign of Charles II, they may also be of value in establishing age and relationships long after the start of parish registers.

---

[1] *A Fourteenth Century Pedigree.* Gen.Mag.Vol.12, p.535.
[2] The genealogical value of each of these is touched upon by L.C. Hector *"Genealogy in the Public Records"*. Gen.Mag. Vol.8 pp57 et seq.
[3] E.H.R.xxix ('1914) pp323-4. The proofs there compared belong to the year 1350.

The two articles with very slight alterations are reproduced from the *Amateur Historian*, Spring 1963 and Spring 1965 (published by the National Council of Social Service for the Standing Conference for Local History), by kind permission of the authors, the editor and the publishers.

A few other sources for the Mediaeval period are dealt with elsewhere in this volume[4] and a short bibliography on Mediaeval genealogy appears on page 388[5]. The articles on *Surnames* and *Christian Names* include a few notes on Mediaeval naming customs.[6]

---

[4] *Taxes* pp. 330–331, *Manorial Records* pp. 340–343.
[5] See also *Public Record office* pp. 393-395 (esp. *Taxes*), *Local Records – General* p. 401, *Manorial and Estate Records* p. 403, *Historical Demography* p. 422 and *Place – Names* pp. 425-6.
[6] *Change of Surname* pp. 88–89 *Fashions in Christian Names* p. 101.

I PROOFS OF AGE
by E. Gillett

To genealogists, as to students of local history, the inquisitions known as proofs of age are perhaps the most rewarding of the various classes of documents printed in the *Calendars of Inquisitions*. Although the *Calendars* contain references to a great variety of places and people, these are often concerned mainly with technical details of feudal tenure. In the proofs of age however, the student will find not only information to date accurately persons whom he may have found on Visitation pedigrees or elsewhere, but also vivid details which enliven the history of the family and the locality.

From time to time it was necessary to find out whether a minor — usually a ward — had reached full age. An heiress who was fourteen could be disposed of, with her inheritance, in marriage: and an heir could at long last come into full possession of his estate. But to show the actual age of anyone, without reliable documentation, was difficult. The king would not be satisfied that a wardship should be terminated until he had the verdict of a jury, summoned by the sheriff of the county. The jury consisted of persons in a position to give credible testimony of the actual date of birth from their personal recollection of people and events. Often enough jurors merely said that the birth happened at about the same time as a birth, death, or marriage in their own family. However, they very often mentioned some other circumstance, a fire, a flood, a lawsuit, a pilgrimage, which had left a vivid impression on them. For this reason proofs of age can be accepted as giving us some clue to the mental furniture of our remote ancestors.

For example, in 1359, Robert de Cracroft, heir to a mere six acres at Hogsthorpe, Lincolnshire, had reached the age of twenty-four.[1] How was this proved? The date of his baptism had been written in the priest's missal. Robert de Alford said that he himself had a brother who celebrated his first mass a month later. Another said that ten weeks after the birth, the father joined him on a pilgrimage to Canterbury which they had vowed to make when they were caught in a thunderstorm on their way home from the assizes. To us, medieval church fabrics seem solid and enduring, but they were not always so, and there were two witnesses who said that the belfry of Huttoft church fell two months before Robert de Cracroft was born. Three more spoke of a high

---

[1] X 378-9. (All references are to the page and volume numbers of the *Calendars of Inquisitions*)

tide which broke the sea banks so that the fields were flooded for several days. One man remembered the year because in May his sister had taken her vows as a nun at Greenfield.

It will be noticed that there was some written evidence in the form of an entry in a missal, and frequently the first item of evidence does refer to something of this kind. But the written evidence does not seem to have been produced. Witnesses simply said that the priest wrote in the book and left it at that. To forify the written evidence, parents occasionally made some special effort to impress the date of the birth upon the minds of those who would probably be available to testify twenty-one years later. Sir Thomas Cary, a Dorset knight, when his son was born in 1336, summoned various people to his house and presented each of them with a bow.[2] John Radestone had three ash trees from the wood at Corston, Somerset, given to him by John Inge so that he should remember that his daughter Joan, was born on September the 30th, 1335.[3] When John de Foxoles[4] was being carried from the church of Foxholes, Yorkshire, after his baptism, his mother gave Richard Thorny a gold ring. When Hugh Cokheved[5] was born at Barton, Lincolnshire, and baptised on the same day, in December 1348, various people drank with the godfather, and at the feast to celebrate the churching of the mother, each yeoman was given a pair of black hose and the minstrels forty shillings. The father was a wool merchant and could well afford such useful ostentation. At Orlestone, Kent, John de Orlaston sent for Moses Egengam to come and fish with him in his pond on the day his son and heir was born, no doubt because this was an invitation which Moses would never have received in the ordinary course of things.[6]

The people actually present at the birth were women and not acceptable as jurors. A man might have been present at the birth of Sir Roger de Huntingfield's son, since he sent William le Kev to bring a doctor from Norwich, but when they arrived at Huntingfield the child was already born.[10] Doctors very rarely appear in this connection. Since actual eye-witnesses were pretty well excluded from any inquisition to prove age, the authorities were forced as an alternative to look to their male relatives. Alice Knot[7] was present when John Cordeboef was born at Buxlow, Suffolk, but it was not her evidence which was taken but that of her own son who said that she

2 X 327
3 XIII 45-6
4 VI 124-5
5 XII No. 382
6 XIII 207
10 VI 203
7 III 332-3

had often recited to him the years which had elapsed since John was born. Similarly, the male relatives of a wet-nurse might appear as jurors. Thomas del Ile[8] said that Millicent, his sister, had been suckling her son, John, now twenty-two, when she became nurse to John Nevill of Faldingworth. William Devias[9] knew that Nicholas Bonboucher was twenty-one in 1363, because he himself had a godson born at Swinhope on the same day and the mother of this godson nursed Nicholas.

Pilgrimages were common enough to be mentioned frequently by jurors as circumstances which fixed a date in their memory. At about the time when Joan Gower was born at Brabourne, Kent, Philip Pikehare, whose wife had just given birth to a daughter, set out for Rome.[11] Joan was actually born on the 25th of November, 1340, and on that day Robert Westbeck set off for Santiago, and as he then went to the Holy Land he was not back in Kent until the summer of 1342. Henry Clerk began his pilgrimage to Santiago[12] on the day the son of Sir John de Norwich was born. Marmaduke de Garton, one of those who showed that Robert de Foxoles was of full age, said that he was able to remember the year because he had been abroad for three years and returned with the pilgrims coming from Rome in the year of the Jubilee. Robert de Alford, besides remembering that his brother became a priest in the year when Robert de Cracroft was born, also said that about the same time he went on a pilgrimage to Santiago because he had been delivered from danger in crossing the Humber.[16] Two pilgrims were able to give their testimony as to the date of the birth of Thomas de Loudham at Kirton, Suffolk. Roger Martin went to the Holy Land about a month, and Robert alte Grene to Santiago about ten weeks, after Thomas was born.[14] John Curteys was able to recollect the February of 1351 because it was when he went barefoot as a pilgrim from Bedfordshire to Beverley.[13]

If pilgrimages attest medieval piety, the more frequent mention of robbery and other crimes is eloquent testimony to medieval violence. Of the jurors who declared that John de Lynford was born at Sherrington, Buckinghamshire, in 1351, there was one who mentioned that this was when his father went to the Holy Land, but another was robbed of his horse in the woods of Woburn as he was going to London, another had a brother who was slain in the wood at Olney, yet another had his smithy burned, and a fifth juror said that in that year his daughter was drowned in a pond at Tyringham.[15] Death by accidental drowning is mentioned so often that this would appear to have been a serious

---

[8] XI 297-8.
[9] XI 470-1.
[11] X 323.
[12] XIII 213.
[16] X 375-6.
[14] XIII 212.
[13] XIII 214.
[15] XIII 210-1.

hazard in village life, especially in the darkness of winter. The Tyringham girl was probably drowned in January. The brother of William Whyting was drowned at Stagsden, Bedfordshire, in January 1351,[13] the brother of Thomas de Farlesthorpe, Lincolnshire, on 6th March, 1359,[16] the son of Robert Rolvesson, Suffolk, in his pond about January 1351,[17] the son of John de Plessys in the river Blyth, Northumberland, in March 1308.[18] This was the day after John de Bakworth's brother was killed in the field of Tynemouth and on the day when John de Kynton departed for Rome.

In an inquisition as to the age of Emma Burdoun of Desborough, Northamptonshire, the jurors spoke of little but violence and disaster.[19] A felon who had taken sanctuary in the church abjured the realm on the day she was brought there to be christened. The parishioners kept a copy of his abjuration. The south aisle had collapsed, and, since it was not expected to be repaired before the winter, everyone said how cold it was going to be in church. John de Cotynghar had made an assart from his waste ground and there had been a riot because this involved an encroachment on Desborough wood. There was also a dispute going on about the benefice which caused such strong feeling that some were in favour of trying to hold the church by force. They barricaded the gaps caused by the collapse of the aisle.

Richard Heriz was born in the large stone chamber in the hall of the manor house at Stapleford, Nottinghamshire, on November the 7th, 1307. John de Strelle was able to recall the date very clearly, because on the night of the 16th he was wounded in defending the manor of Shipley against a band of armed robbers. His arm was pierced by an arrow. He was bailiff of the manor, which was within ten miles of Stapleford. The birth of Nicholas de Cheigny in 1307 preceded violence of a quite different order – the murder of the Prior of Otterton, Devon, by robbers attacking the Priory.[21]

Significantly, actual war seems to have made a much less deep impression that the violence of domestic enemies. Thomas Rakestrau, however, did mention that William le Archer was born at Dover three weeks before Edward I came with his ships from Winchelsea and two years after the burning of Dover by the French.[22] For the feast at the churching of the mother of John de Grey of Rotherfield Greys, Oxfordshire, Henry de Ardern, a merchant, paid out £6, and later in the same year, 1300 he crossed the sea and was one of the ten English

---

[13] XIII 214.
[16] X 375-6.
[17] XIII 212-3.
[18] VII 132-3.
[19] X 326.
[21] VII 135.
[22] VI 123.

merchants whose goods were seized by the Flemings.[23] As evidence of the age of John Paynel of Rampisham, Dorset, Richard de Crokeston said that in August of that year, 1296, he went with Sir William Russell in the army to Flanders.[24] Sir Roger le Nonaunt, a Wiltshire knight, remembered 1280 because for him it was the year of the war of David, brother of Llewelin.[25] References to matters of public concern other than war are infrequent, though John de Oxonia, who was acting as surveyor for the Abbot of Westminster, knew that Edmund de Benstede's birth was in 1307 because later in the year the future Edward III was born and all the London workmen took a week's holiday to celebrate the joyful event.[26]

Jurors were much more likely to speak as it were autobiographically rather than historically. William Ward remembered making his son apprentice to a Lincoln goldsmith.[16] Three Kentish jurors remembered 1340 as the year when they were apprenticed and also when they bought land.[11] One was apprenticed to a baker at Hythe, another to a baker at Wye and another to a tailor at Canterbury. Oddly enough, this last witness married his wife Joan in the same year. Clearly apprenticeship could begin quite late. Thomas le Barber was twenty-three when he brought the news of Edmund de Benstede's birth to the King's sister.[26] She rewarded him with thirty shillings, and in the following year he used the money to apprentice himself to a barber. John Swalowe said that he was butler and spencer to William de Helying in 1359 when William's son was born, and for another three and a half years after.[27] Thomas Cokheved was in the wardship of Sir Ralph de Bulmer at Castlethorpe, Lincolnshire, when Sir Ralph's son was born.[28] William de Stratton, a servant of Thomas de Loudham, married about the time his master's son was born. But there was more than this to stimulate his memory. He had married the maid of his master's wife, with permission, so in his anger Thomas struck him and wounded him in the hand.[17] Three jurors said they knew that William del Ile was born at Pulborough, Sussex, in 1352, because they were together in the retinue of the Countess of Ormond who had just come to England. One of their fellow jurors said that this was the year when his mother sued Richard Pyjon in the consistory court and so compelled him to marry her.[29]

23   VI 204.
24   VI 122.
25   III 329.
26   VII 382-4. On mediaeval apprenticeship see also *Surnames* pp.88–89.
16   X 375-6.
11   X 323.
27   X 427-8
28   XI No. 376.
17   XIII 212-3.
29   XIII 208.

Education is mentioned occasionally. Roger Longe said that 1351 was the year when he first sent his son to school at Bedford, and that he was now twenty-eight.[13] Jolland de Newton knew that John de Verdon's son was born at Whiston, Yorkshire, in 1276 because he himself, though apparently married, had been at school in Lincoln and came home for the vacation, at which time his own son was born.[30] The day after Nicholas de Cheigny was born at Upottery, Devon, Philip de Cranlysworthy returned from Montpellier where he may have been studying medicine.

Documentary evidence of the date of birth is mentioned in a great many cases. The date was entered in a service-book; or a kinsman had a psalter in which he caused the date to be entered before giving it to the church. Other written evidence appears more rarely. We have already noticed that at Desborough the villagers kept a copy of a felon's abjuration, no doubt to cover themselves if they were later charged with allowing him to escape. When John the son and heir of Walter Clerkbek was christened at Acton, Suffolk,[32] the church had been desecrated by bloodshed, probably on the same day. Within a week the Bishop of Norwich came to reconsecrate the church, and the date was written on the church wall for future parishioners to see. This was no doubt an expensive matter for the villagers, but a piece of good luck for the father, since it helped everyone to know when his son had been born. Indeed he was able to profit from another mishap. He sent his servant Richard to bring a godfather, and Richard broke his arm by falling from his horse into a pit.

In most proofs of age evidence had to be sought from men who might remember a variety of things which had happened round about the time when the person in question was born. Their recollections of what happened twenty-one years previously were not necessarily very convincing for the purpose for which they were produced. One has the impression that sometimes the birth of an heir prompted the parent to search among their neighbours for someone whose house had been burned, or who had taken the vows of religion, or suffered at the hand of robbers,[33] so that he could be informed of the birth and asked to remember that it was contemporary with such and such an event in his own life. Occasionally there were circumstances which made any such artificial contrivance unnecessary. In 1355, as Sir Hugh de Louther was riding to Scotland he noticed that a child was being baptised at the door of the church of Castle Carrock, Cumberland. He asked who it was, and was told it was the daughter of John de Eglesfield.[34]

---

13 XIII 214.
30 III 335-6.
32 XIII 47.
33 VII 129; X 378-9; XIII 47.
34 XIII 50-1.

At the same time William Vaux was hunting hares. He too noticed the people at the church door and asked who was being christened. On the night when she was born Richard de Laton had got lost in a wood on his way home from the market at Penrith. He came to a house and asked to be allowed to stay the night there, and this was the time and place of her birth.

Sometimes the verdict of the jury gives us a clue to how long it took to do various things in the thirteenth and fourteenth centuries. Four men from Gedney were with Philip le Despenser at Newsham Abbey when his son was born at Gedney. A letter with the news reached him on the same day, although the distance was at least seventy miles, and on the next day they were all back at Gedney. A day's journey of seventy miles was therefore feasible even when half the distance lay in the fens.[35] Again, after the birth of John de Helyng,[27] Roger de Toynton began on the 29th of June, 1335 to build his ship, the *Maudelayn*. The ship was finished on the 21st of September, and launched in Grimsby haven on the 9th of October.

It will be realised that this article surveys only part of the material. This is a source available for all genealogists and students of local history. Proofs of Age exist for most English Counties and for several in Wales and Ireland. They are not separately indexed in the *Calendars* but are easy to find in the text. In so far as they draw on men's memories of what happened to impress them they contain random material of much the same kind as that which in a later age would have been printed by a county newspaper. And they do incidentally, demonstrate a real difference between the mediaeval and the modern mind. In a society which used written communication so little, people had a mentality largely independent of literacy. A little introspection will make this apparent. Any reader who cares to try the experiment will probably find that he cannot recollect at all clearly anything which happened to him twenty-one years ago unless he uses some written or printed reminder. But this is just what the jurors summoned to make a proof of age could do, not because they were in any way superior to us, but because the conditions in which they lived compelled them to stuff their minds with details which we relegate to forms and registers.

Witnesses may sometimes have had only a very uncertain idea of their own age. In two Cambridgeshire cases[36] seven of the witnesses appear in both. One, who was sixty in 1308, in 1311 is simply said to be forty-eight and more. Wm. Morel, who was above fifty in 1308, had become more than eighty in 1311. There are discrepancies in

---

[35] XI 37.
[27] X 427-8.
[36] V 67; 357.

the ages of all witnesses. They can be accounted for on the assumption that the names are the same in both cases but belong to differer persons. This is unlikely, however, to be true of all seven, and it seems much more probable that when parents took no special steps to record the age of their children there could be great uncertainty about their actual age. [37]

---

[37] Uncertainty as to ages persisted until the 19th Century. See *Parish Registers - Form and Content* above p. 58, *Parish Registers and the Genealogist* p. 150.

II INQUISITIONS POST MORTEM

by Mary McGuinness

Inquisitions *post mortem* are, in general, the results of enquiries made in response to a royal writ issuing from Chancery upon the annoucement of the death of any tenant supposed to hold lands of the king in chief. Their purpose was to ensure that none of the king's rights as overlord were ignored and that Chancery might be informed of any escheats and wardships accruing to the king. An important source of royal revenue from the Norman Conquest until 1660 when feudal tenures were abolished was based on the legal theory that all land was held either by the king or of the king. Those lands that were not simply royal desmesne were held by tenants either directly (in chief) or indirectly, through a mesne tenant; and either by the payment of a money rent, or by the rendering of services, or by both. The tenant also owed the lord obedience. After his death, lawful possession (*seisin*) of his estate could be taken by the rightful heir or heirs only on payment to the lord of a sum of money known as a *relief*. If a tenant died without heir his lands escheated to the lord; while the heir remained a minor the lord claimed the revenues of the lands, the right of wardship and the disposal of the heir in marriage.

Writs ordering the inquisition were directed to the *escheators* of the counties in which the lands in question were held: these officials were ordered to certify into Chancery information on the tenancy and the heir. Initially two escheators were appointed by Henry III, one north and one south of the Trent; later, more were appointed to deal either with small groups of counties or with individual counties or cities. The Palatine counties had their own escheators who made returns into the Palatine chanceries, and these returns form separate series of inquisitions *post mortem*. The inquisition was made (theoretically) on the oath of a jury summoned by the sheriff, and the information required from it depended to some extent on the nature of the governing writ. The simplest and most common writ used was that of *diem clausit extremum* which was based on the information that the tenant had died; where a delay had occurred between the date of death and the ordering of the inquisition a writ of *mandamus* was used (as in our example) to discover, in addition, who had taken the issues and profits of the property from the time of the tenant's death. Other writs were framed to meet particular situations: an inquisition held to traverse a previous inquisition was ordered by a writ *ad melius inquirendum*; and one held upon the death of an heir while a minor, where the lands were already in the king's hands by virtue of wardship, was instituted by a writ of *devenerunt*, from the phrase *ad manus nostras devenerunt*.

There were circumstances other than death which gave rise to these inquisitions and other means than Chancery writs for initiating them. Enquiries were made into the lands of lunatics and of attainted persons, and the escheators on occasion returned inquisitions that were taken by virtue of office (*virtute officii*), with no Chancery writ Where the enquiry was to be made by persons not escheators or by others in association with escheators a Commission was issued by Letters Patent.

In general, it is assumed, a draft of the information to be returned would be supplied to the escheator by lawyers acting for the family of the tenant who had died. First, notification of death was made: in 1425 the lawyer William Paston 'was occupied about the due service of wryttes of *diem clausit extremum*' after the death of the mother of his master, the Duke of Norfolk (Paston Letters, Gairdner, i. 16). The date of death was then established; the lands, their tenure, value, and services were described. Feudal services were very varied, throwing light on local customs ('making wine calle Clar' for the king's coming to Clarendon' in Wiltshire), royal ceremonial ('serving the king with wafers at his coronations'), the finding and victualling of armies, and many other aspects of a feudal society. Some were of the nature of annual quit-rents, requiring the provision of a horse's curry-comb, for example, or a pair of gilt spurs, or bushels of wheat for church-scot. Finally, the heir was nam and his age given, and any relevant relationships were traced. The lawyers would have recourse to family documents – wills, surveys and title deeds – to enable them to make the return, and the Chancery officials would usually have, as a means of checking on the information, the files of earlier inquisitions on the same estate: they could, if the escheator's return seemed unsatisfactory, order a fulle enquiry by making use of the writ *ad melius inquirendum*, or the more categorical writ *que plura* used in cases where it was known that the tenant had undisclosed lands. The inquisition took the form of a two part indenture. The escheator returned one part into Chancery, attach ing it to the writ, if one had been issued, accordingly endorsed. If the heir was of age livery of seisin would follow on the payment of the *relief*. The admission of the heir can normally be traced in the orders to escheators enrolled on the Fine Rolls.

Circumstances revealed in the inquisition might lead to further writs and returns. Where the lands remained in the king's hands becau of the minority of the heir a writ *de aetate probanda* would in due course be issued and the heir's coming of age testified and where widows had claim to dower the writ *de dote assignanda* was used. When the descent of the property was to or through more than one female partitions were made under special writ.

As inquisitions were taken largely for the purposes of safeguarding the king's interests and sources of revenue the information they contain usually concerned the Exchequer. In accounting to the Exchequer for the revenues of escheated lands the escheators frequently returned, in their pouches of accounts, copies of the inquisitions as vouchers; later, from the reign of Henry VII, it was common for transcripts of the documents to be made in Chancery and sent to the Exchequer. Where this was done the original remaining in Chancery was noted accordingly. There is also, among Exchequer records, a small series of Enrolments of Inquisitions – abstracts presumably made in the Department. After the Court of Wards and Liveries was established in 1540 for the supervision of the royal wards and their lands, transcripts of relevant inquisitions were sent from Chancery into that Court also. The stages following an inquisition *post mortem* can usually be traced in the enrolments on the Fine and Close Rolls of orders to escheators in connection with wardships, livery of seisin and assignments of dower, and sometimes in the files of Escheators'Accounts where the issues of escheated lands appear. In our example the escheator when rendering his account for John Kitto's property rehearses the greater part of the inquisition in order to amplify and correct it. [1]

The starting point for a student making use of inquisitions *post mortem* is the account given in Volume I of the *Guide to the Contents of the Public Record Office* (1963) of the various Chancery series (C.133-142), the two Exchequer series (E.149 and 150), the Exchequer Enrolments of Inquisitions (E.152), and Escheators' Accounts (E.136). The printed *Calendars of Inquisitions post mortem* cover the period Henry III to Edward III, and the reign of Henry VII; two of the volumes for Richard II's reign are in the course of preparation and the text of the first (1-7 Richard II) is available in the Search Room of the Public Record Office. The Calendars make use of the Chancery and Exchequer series, as described in the introduction to the first volume. They give the main gist of the inquisition; where 'extents' occur these are not calendared but their existence is noted; the file number on which the document is ordered appears at the end of each calendar entry. For the intervening period there is the Record Commissioners' *Calendarium* which simply lists lands under tenants' names; and for the years Henry VIII to Charles I there are printed Lists of tenants arranged alphabetically within reigns, giving the counties involved, and the document-references for the Chancery,

---

[1] Escheator's Accounts for Surrey (6 Edw VI-I Mary, E.136/217/2).

Exchequer and Court of Wards series. The separate Palatinate series
are included in the last of these printed Lists, No. XXXIII; they
are also covered by various calendars published by the Record
Commissioners and by indexes which appeared as Appendices to the
Deputy Keeper's Reports.

In addition to these official publications there are calendars an
lists covering particular counties published by local Record Societie
Most of these appear in the Royal Historical Society publication *Text*
and Calendars: An Analytical Guide (edited by E. L. C. Mullins, 1958),
and many are noted in the Public Record Office Card Index of printed
records. A synopsis of all printed lists and calendars is given in
Appendix II.

Inquisitions *post mortem* are among the many sources in the Publi
Records for studies in social and economic history: they are used in
tracing land-owning families, the descent of property and the evolution of place names; J. C. Russell has applied them in a demographic
survey *British Mediaeval Population* (1948). To some extent it should
perhaps be assumed that the documents do not always accurately refle
all the facts: doubts have been expressed of the corroborative
evidence produced in 'proofs of age', and of 'extents' which, in
cases, remain unaltered throughout a century or more. These and othe
aspects of the value of inquisitions have been considered in article
in the *English Historical Review* and elsewhere in print.

APPENDIX I

The following Calendar entry gives some indication of the type o
information to be found in Inquisitions *Post Mortem*. The original
Inquisition summarized survives in the Chancery series (C142/98/73)
and transcripts are found in the Exchequer (E 150/1099/2) and Court
of Wards (Wards 7/6/96). It is reproduced in full with a facsimile
in the *Amateur Historian* Vol.6.No.7. Spring 1965.

JOHN KITTO, YEOMAN, SON OF JOHN KITTO

Writ of *precipimus*, 7 Feb. 7 Edward VI to Barnard Randolfe, Escheator
Surrey Inquisition (indented) taken at Southwark 11 Feb. 7 Edward VI
before the escheator and by the oath of jurors (named). At the time
of his death John Kytto senior, father of John named in the writ, was
thus seised in his desmesne as of fee:
Bermondsey.   10 acres of land and 18 acres of meadow with appurtenances in the parish of St. Mary Magdalen.
Croydon.   A messuage or dwelling house with cottage and adjoining
garden called Le Bell, and 4 acres and appurtenances leased together
with the said messuage; held of Thomas, Archbishop of Canterbury as

of the manor of Croydon by fealty and rent of 8/- p. a. for all
services, the annual clear value being 30/-.
Mitcham. A messuage and 15 acres of land with appurtenances; held
of the king as of the manor of Bigging by fealty and rent of 6d. p. a.
for all services, the annual clear value being 40/-. Three cottages
held of John Scott esquire as of his manor of Camberwell, services
unknown, the annual clear value being 30/-. A further cottage with
adjoining gardens formerly in the tenure of Richard Glover; held of
William Dymmoke esquire as of his manor of Tooting by fealty and rent
of 6d. p. a. for all services, the annual clear value being 6/8d.
John Kitto senior married, successively, Joan, by whom he had issue
John, and Elizabeth, by whom he had issue Agnes and Joan. On his
death the property descended to John his son and heir who, being
seised of it in his desmesne as of fee, died without heir. Agnes and
Joan are next heirs as regards the third part of the property of John
their father which was assigned by right as dower to their mother
Elizabeth; they are also coheirs of John their father. Agnes is aged
eight years and Joan seven. The will of John Kitto junior is produced
in evidence. He died without heir on 15 July 5 Edward VI. Since his
death his former wife Elizabeth now the wife of William Adlington
has taken the profits of the property; Elizabeth formerly wife of
John Kitto senior also survives and is living in Southwark.

A BRIEF GUIDE TO OFFICIAL AND RECORD SOCIETY PUBLICATIONS: CALENDARS, ABSTRACTS AND COUNTY LISTS*

A. Record Commissioners

Calendarium inquisitionum post mortem sive escaetarum, Hen. III — Chas. I. *Ducatus Lancastriae* Vol. 1 Part 1. *Calendarium Inquisitionum post Mortem*, Edw. I — Chas. I.

B. Public Record Office
Printed Calendars

Calendars of inquisitions *post mortem* and other analogous documents preserved in the Public Record Office, Henry III to 51 Edw. III. In progress.

Calendars of inquisitions *post mortem* etc. [as above] 1-24 Henry VI

Ms. Indexes — "Palmer's Indexes" — preserved at the Public Record Office:

Ind. 17357	Palmer's No. 82		York entries	Hen. III-Ric. II
Ind. 17358	"	" 83	*Ind. loc.* to 32	"
Ind. 17366	"	" 91	Cambridge	Hen. VII-5 Chas
Ind. 17367	"	" 92	York	Hen. VIII-Phil. and Mary
Ind. 17369	"	" 94	Berks., Bucks., Cambridge with *Ind. loc.* for Berks. and Bucks.	Hen. III-Ric. II
Ind. 17370	"	" 95	*Ind. loc.* for Cheshire, Derby, Devon	"
Ind. 17371	"	" 96	Calendar with *Ind. loc.* for Essex	"
Ind. 17372	"	" 97	Calendar for Kent, Leicester and Middlesex	"

---

* Editorial and publication details are given in E. L. C. Mullins *Texts and Calendars: An Analytical Guide* (1958).

Ind.	17373	Palmer's No. 98	Calendar for Northumberland, Oxford and Suffolk	Hen. III-Ric. III
Ind.	17374	" " 99	Calendar for Sussex, Warwick and Wilts., with *Ind. loc.* for Sussex and Wilts.	"
Ind.	17375	" " 100	Suffolk	Hen. VII-Jas. I
Ind.	17376	" " 101	Northampton with *Ind. loc.*	Hen. VII-Chas. I
Ind.	17379	" " 104	*Index nominum,* Miscellaneous Books of Court of Wards	Hen. VIII-Chas. I
Ind.	17388	" " 113	Leicester	Hen. VII-Chas. I
Ind.	17395	" " 120	*Index nominum,* A – L	Hen. VII-Hen. VIII
Ind.	17400	" " 125	Abstracts London	Hen. VIII-Eliz. I
Ind.	17401	" " 126	Abstracts, Middlesex	Hen. VIII-Eliz. I
Ind.	17417	" " 142	Essex	Hen. III-Ric. III

Lists and Indexes Nos. XXIII, XXVI, XXXI and XXXIII (1907-9).
Inquisitions *post mortem,* Henry VIII-Charles I, with references to transcripts in the Exchequer and Court of Wards. *Alphabetical Catalogue.*

Palatinates

Palatinate of Chester (Chester & Flint)
Persons and Places: *Deputy Keeper's 25th Report* App. pp. 32-60.
Persons Hen. VIII – Chas. I. *Lists and Indexes* No. XXXIII (1909) pp. 381-395.

Palatinate of Durham
Calendar. *Deputy Keeper's 44th Report* App. pp. 310-342
Index Hen. VIII – Chas. I. *Lists and Indexes* No. XXXIII (1909) App. II. pp. 397-413.
Index to Nos. 182-193. *Lists and Indexes* No. XL (1914) pp. 32-35.

C. Local Record Societies, etc.

Bedford
: *Bedfordshire Historical Record Society*
  Vol. 5 Calendar of Inquisitions *post mortem*, 1250-1271
  Vol.19 " 1272-1286

Cheshire
: *Lancashire and Cheshire Record Society*
  Vol.84 Cheshire inquisitions *post mortem*, 1603-1660 A-D
  Vol.86 " E-O
  Vol.90 " P-Y

Cornwall
and Devon
: *Devon and Cornwall Record Society*
  Vol. 1 Calendar of *inquisitiones post mortem* for Cornwall and Devon for Henry III to
  Charles I, 1216-1649.

Gloucester
: *British Record Society: Index Library*
  Vol. 9 Abstracts of Gloucester *inquisitiones post mortem* Part i 1-11 Charles I
  Vol.13 " Part ii 12-18 Charles I
  Vol.21 " Part iii Miscellaneous, 1-18 Charles I
  Vol.30 " Part iv 20 Hen.III-29 Edw.I
  Vol.40 " Part v 30 Edw.I-32 Edw.III
  Vol.47 " Part vi 1359-1413

374

Lancashire

Chetham Society Old Series

Vol.95 Abstracts of Inquisitions *post mortem*   Vol. i   1297-1422
Vol.99   "   Vol.ii   1423-1637

Lancashire and Cheshire Record Series

Vol. 3 Lancashire Inquisitions Stuart Period   Part 1   1-11   James I
Vol.16   "   "   "   Part 2   12-19 James I
Vol.17   "   "   "   Part 3   20-23 James I

Record Commissioners – Duchy of Lancaster Inquisitions
2. See list A (Record Commissioners) above.

Leicester

Transactions of the Leicestershire Archaeological Society
Vol. 6 Lists of inquisitions   1 Hen.VII-20 Chas.I.

London

British Record Society: Index Library
Vol.15 Abstracts of *inquisitiones post mortem*   1 Hen.VII-3 Eliz.
Vol.26 Abstracts of Inquisitions   4-19 Eliz.
Vol.36   "   "   19-45 Eliz.

Middlesex

Middlesex County Record Society
Vol. 1 Inquests *post mortem*   3 Edw.VI-45 Eliz.

Norfolk

Norfolk Records Vol.1 and 2, published by Norfolk and Norwich Archaeological Society.
Inquisitions *post mortem* Edward I-Charles I.

Nottinghamshire

Thoroton Society, Record Series

Vol. 3 Abstracts of *Inquisitiones post mortem* 1485-1546

Vol. 6 " 1321-1350

Vol.12 " 1350-1436

Vol.17 *Inquisitiones post mortem* relating to Nottinghamshire 1437-1485

Staffordshire

William Salt Archaeological Society

Vol. for 1911 Inquisitions *post mortem* etc. (From transcripts in the William Salt Library) 1223-1327.

Vol. for 1913 " Edward III

Sussex

Sussex Record Society

Vol. 3 A Calendar of *post mortem* inquisitions 1-25 Eliz.

Vol.14 Notes of *post mortem* inquisitions 1 Hen. VII-1649 and after

Vol.33 Sussex inquisitions, 1541-1616; Extracts from Rawlinson MS.B.433, Bodleian Library, Oxford.

Vol.44 Rape of Lewes: inquisitions and extents of manors in the rape, 1265-1300.

Westmoreland

Cumberland and Westmoreland Antiquarian and Archaeological Society, Record Series.

Vols.4-6 Records relating to the Barony of Kendale, including abstracts of inquisitions *post mortem*, Hen.III-Chas.I.

Wiltshire

British Record Society: Index Library

Vol.23 Abstracts of Wiltshire Inquisitions *post mortem*, Chas.I.

Vol.37 " 1242-1326.

Vol. 18 Abstracts of Inquisitions *post mortem*, ...
3 and 5 of *The Journal of the Wiltshire Archaeological and Natural History Society*].

Worcestershire   *Worcestershire Historical Society*

Vol. 2   The *inquisitiones post mortem* for the county of Worcester, 1242 to the end of the 13th century; bound with:

Vol. 24   "   1300-1326

Yorkshire   *Yorkshire Archaeological Society Journal*

Vol. 1   A catalogue of the inquisitions *post mortem* of the reigns of James I and Charles I.

Vol. 59   Inquisitions *post mortem*, of the reigns of Henry IV and Henry V.

BIBLIOGRAPHY

PREFACE

As is emphasized in the General Preface to this volume, this
Bibliography is designed principally for the use of the amateur family
historian. The section on *Genealogy and Archives* is intended to be
fairly comprehensive though a number of works on specialised subjects
(such as the *Army and Navy, Clergy, Lawyers*) together with many older
publications now to some extent (but not entirely) superseded have
been omitted for reasons of space. These will all be found in other
genealogical bibliographies.

In general, works of purely local interest have not been included.
Those that do find a place in these lists have been selected (1) as
typical of a class of documents, many of which have been printed –
e. g. the *Warwickshire County Records* Series or the *Kentish Sources*;
(2) representing a class of documents very few of which have been
printed. (e. g. *Men and Armour in Gloucestershire in 1608*); (3) because
the introduction or some other section is of considerable general
interest (e. g. *Guide to the Essex Record Office*).

The section on *Related Subjects* has inevitably had to be much more
selective. The *Economic and Social History* Section has been slanted
towards the needs of the average genealogist or family historian whose
family in all probability comes ultimately from a rural background.
Thus considerable attention has been given to works on the operation
of the Poor Law, Wage Rates, Population Movement and related subjects.
Although some general histories have been included whose content is
largely political, books specifically on political subjects have been
rigidly excluded, though of course economic discontent has frequently
found political expression. Similarly, works on Ecclesiastical History
on charities, and on the History of Education have also been almost
completely excluded (except for a few specifically on the clergy or
other parish officers) although these may throw considerable light on
the life and thought of the time. However, a fairly comprehensive
bibliography for Nonconformity will be found in Volume II.

In most subsections few if any works have been included before the
16th Century. The exception is that on *"Historical Demography"* where
genealogists may be interested in population movements or other
demographic studies of a period normally earlier than that to which
they have succeeded in tracing their own families. Another important
point to note is that very few contemporary sources have been listed.
It was felt that since the family historian would use primary material

concerned with his own family, he would be most interested in knowing what secondary or interpretative material was available to place the fruits of his own researches in a wider setting and as a guide on where to seek further primary material. Nevertheless, all Family Historians would do well to consult the larger historical bibliographies for surviving books, pamphlets, tracts and letters of the time.

Inevitably there is much overlapping between the *Economic and Social History* Section and the *Local History* Section, and the allocation of works to one or the other has at times been rather arbitrary. Inevitably, also there have been many works that one could classify equally under one of these headings or under *"Genealogy and Archives"*. Complete consistency has proved impossible, but works of outstanding importance (e.g. Hoskins's *"Local History in England"*) have been included in both. The same problem has arisen throughout with regard to sub-section classification. In the *Economic and Social History* Section, for example, the sub-sections on *"Agriculture"* and *"Yeomen and Farmers"* must be taken in conjunction.

Very few books on *Industry* have been included and scarcely any at all on particular industries. Obviously, in tracing any family connected with a particular industry, it will be necessary for the genealogist to consult one of the comprehensive historical bibliographies. *Transport* also has been another casualty and the bibliography includes only a few of the most basic works on roads, railways and canals which may help to suggest possible direction of migration or places of origin. The sub-sections on *Biography, Heraldry, Genetics, Law* and *Technical Aids* are sketchy in the extreme and have aimed to do no more than to list a few books or articles which the genealogist may find of value.

Normally, for reasons of space, no comments have been made on works, but where the title gives little indication of content, where the work is of quite exceptional value or where attention is drawn to a particular part of the work, a short note has been added. It is worth drawing special attention here to a few works which are basic to the needs of the family historian. They are D.E. Gardner and F. Smith: *Genealogical Research in England and Wales* (3 volumes) A.J. Camp: *Wills and their Whereabouts*, W.E. Tate: *The Parish Chest*, W.G. Hoskins: *Local History in England* and J. West: *Village Records*. The last three contain useful bibliographies. Of all the works on social history one is of outstanding importance for the genealogist: Peter Laslett's *The World We Have Lost*, in which are summarized the conclusions of recent research into the nature of pre-industrial society. *Maps* are indispensable, and the genealogist's needs are well served by D.E. Gardner, D. Harland and F. Smith *A Genealogical Atlas of England and Wales* or the relevant county maps produced by the *Institute of Heraldic and Genealogical Studies*.

I GENEALOGY AND ARCHIVES

See also Bibliographies on pages 76-81, *(Parish Registers)*, 99-100 *(Surnames)*, 128 *(Christian Names)*, 269-270 *(Monumental Inscriptions)*, 287 *(Newspapers)* and 321 *(Clandestine Marriages)*. Bibliographies for the Nonconformist Denominations will be found in Volume 2, for Roman Catholics and Jews in Volume 3, and for Scotland in Volume 12.

A. BIBLIOGRAPHY

General

> Gatfield, G. *Guide to Printed Books and Manuscripts relating to English and Foreign Heraldry and Genealogy* (1892).
>
> Hamilton-Edwards, G.K.S., *In Search of Ancestry* (1974) pp. 233–83. [Includes full Christian names of authors. Especially useful for *Army & Navy, Scotland, India* and *Heraldry*].
>
> Harrison, H.G. *Select Bibliography of English Genealogy* (1937).
>
> Humphreys, A.L. *Handbook to County Bibliography* (1917). A Bibliography of bibliographies.
>
> Kaminkow, Marion J. *A New Bibliography of British Genealogy* (1965). Largely replaces Harrison.
>
> Nichols, J. *Bibliotheca Topographia Britannica*, 8 vols. (1780-90). Contd. in *Misc. Antiquities*, 2 vols. (1791-1800).
>
> Nichols, J.G. *Collectanea Topographia et Genealogica*, 8 vols. (1834-43). Contd. in *The Topographer and Genealogist*, 3 vols. (1846-58).
>
> Willis, A.J., *Genealogy for Beginners* (1976), pp. 103–11. [A short bibliography 'for beginners' but includes useful comments on each book.]

Antiquarian Societies' Papers

> Gomme, G.L. *Index of Archaeological Papers 1665-1890.* Continued annually to 1900.
>
> Mullins, E.L.C. *Guide to the Historical Publications of the Societies of England and Wales, 1901-1933.*

Historical Manuscripts Commission

A Guide to the Reports on the Collection of Manuscripts of Privat *Families, Corporations and Institutions in Great Britain and Ireland 1870-1911.* Part I Topographical (1914); Part II Persor ed by Francis Bickley (1935-8).

Guide to Reports of Royal Commission on Historical Manuscripts 1911-1957. Part I. Index of Places [in preparation]. Part II. Index of Persons. ed by A.C.S. Hall. 3 vols (H.M.S.O. 1966).

General Analytical Survey and Key 1870-1957 [in preparation].

Published Texts

Government Publications: *Sectional List No. 24* Record Publication H.M.S.O.

Kellaway, W. *Record Publications of Societies* Archives VII 46 (1965).

Mullins, E.L.C. *Texts and Calendars: An analytical guide to seria publications.* Royal Historical Society, 1958.

Somerville, R. *Handlist of Record Publications.* British Records Association 1951.

Pedigrees

Bridger, C. *An Index to Printed Pedigrees contained in County and Local Histories, the Heralds' Vistations, etc.* (1867).

Coleman, J. *General Index to Printed Pedigrees* (1866).

Fane, A.G.C. *Complete Index to Family Names appearing in Burke's Royal Families* (1932).

Marshall, G.W. *The Genealogist's Guide* (1903). [A list of pedigre in printed sources].

Whitmore, J.B. *A Genealogical Guide* (1953). [Continuation of the above].

Family Histories

Thomson, T.R., *A Catalogue of British Family Histories,* (3rd ed. 1976).

Thomson, T.R. *Addenda to Catalogue of British Family Histories* Gen. Mag. Vol. 7 p. 645 (Dec. 1937).

Directories

Royal Historical Society. *Guide to the National and Provincial Directories of England and Wales* [excluding London] *published before 1856* (1950).

Goss, C.W.F. *The London Directories 1677-1855* (1932).

Sims, J.M. *A Catalogue of Directories and Poll Books in the Library of the Society of Genealogists.*

Newspapers. See bibliography on page 287.

Gentleman's Magazine

Farrar, R.H. *Index to the Biographical and Obituary Notices in the Gentleman's Magazine 1731-1780* (1891).

Fry, E.A. *An Index to the Marriages in the Gentleman's Magazine 1731-1768* (1922).

Gomme, G.L. *The Gentleman's Magazine Library.* Classified collection of the chief contents of the Gentleman's Magazine 1731-1868 29 vols. (1883-1905).

B. GENERAL WORKS

Genealogical Manuals

Burns, Nancie. *Family Tree. An Adventure in Genealogy* (1962).

Camp, A.J. and Spufford, P. *The Genealogists' Handbook* (1967).

Camp, A.J. *Tracing Your Ancestors* (1964).

Crofton, Helen A. *How to Trace a Pedigree* (1911).

Gardner, D.E. and Smith, F. *Genealogical Research in England and Wales.* 3 vols. (1957, 1959, 1964).

Hamilton-Edwards, G.K.S. *In Search of Ancestry* (1974).

Lea, J.H. *Genealogical Research in England, Scotland and Ireland* (1906).

Phillimore, W.P.W. *How to Write the History of a Family* (1887. suppl. vol. 1896).

Phillimore, W.P.W. *Pedigree Work: A Handbook for the Genealogist* (1936).

Pine, L.G. *Trace Your Ancestors* (1954).

Pine, L.G. *Your Family Tree* (1962).

Unett, J. *Making a Pedigree* (1961).

Willis, A.J. *Genealogy for Beginners* (1976)

Other Works of General Interest

Atkinson, C. *Some experiences of Genealogical Work.* Gen. Mag. III pp. 12 & 34 (March and June 1927).

Bennett, A.F. *The Microfilming Activities of the Genealogical Society of the Church of Jesus Christ of Latter-Day Saints.* Archivum Vol. 9 (1959) pp. 121-123.

Burke, Sir J.B. *Vicissitudes of Families* (2nd edn 1859).

Cunningham, J.R. *The Genealogical Work of the Latter Day Saints.* Gen. Mag. Vol. 14. No. 11. Sept. 1964.

de Battaglia, Prof. Forst. *Traité de Généalogie* (1949).

Durtnell, C.S. *The Fun of the Chase,* Amat. Hist. Vol. 3. No. 7. pp. 279-282. Vol. 4. No. 2. pp. 56-61 (1959).

Neale, E.F.W. *Amateur Genealogy - A Cruel Sport.* Lincolnshire Historian 2 (1964). pp. 17-21.

Pine, L.G. *Truth in Genealogy. The work of genealogical reference books* (Quart. Rev. Apr 1960. pp. 170-177).

Pine, L.G. *Royal Blood in the People of Britain.* Amat. Hist. Vol. No. 6 (June-July, 1953).

Pine, L.G. *Genealogy since Horace Round.* Gen. Mag. XIII 10 (1961)

Raglan, Lord. *Fiction in Pedigree.* National Review Dec. 1933. pp. 747-752.

Rost, Mrs. Miles E. *Utilizing Genealogical Interest* (Libr. Journ. July 1936. pp. 519-522).

Russell, Charles F. *On the Statement of Evidence.* Gen. Mag. Vol. No. 10. March 1944.

Spufford, P. *How I Did It, or Four Centuries of Spuffords.* Amat. Hist. V. No. 6 (Winter 1963) p. 173.

Spufford, P. *Recent Developments in Genealogy.* Amat. Hist. Vol. 7 No. 6 (1967) p. 178.

Steele, A.J. *Family History: some likely sources of information.* Essex Rev. Jan 1933. pp. 38-40.

Strickland, Lord. *Truth in Pedigrees.* Nat. Rev. Feb 1934. pp. 203

Wagner, Sir A.R. *English Genealogy* (1960).

Wagner, Sir A.R. *English Ancestry* (1961) [A condensed version of the above.]

Little Known Sources of Genealogy. Report of a Discussion meeting Gen. Mag. Vol. 7. p. 111 (Sept 1935).

Notable Ancestors and Elizabethan Ancestors. N & Q 12. 102-3. 6th July, 10th Aug. 1940.

Statistical and Scientific Aspects of Genealogy

Bramwell, B.S. *Frequency of Cousin Marriages*. Gen. Mag. Vol. 8. No. 6 (June 1939) p. 305.

de Battaglia, Prof. Forst. *Traité de Généalogie* (1949).

Pine, L.G. *Royal Blood in the People of Great Britain*. Amat. Hist. Vol. I. No. 6 (June/July 1956).

Ridge, C.H. *How Many Ancestors Have We?* Amat. Hist. Vol. 1. No. 1 (Aug/Sept 1952).

Ridge, C.H. *Scientific Genealogy*. Gen. Mag. Vol. 11. No. 4 (Dec 1951).

Vivian, S.P. *Some Statistical Aspects of Genealogy*. Gen. Mag. Vol. 6. No. 10. June 1934. p. 448.

White, H.C. *More Scientific Genealogy*. Gen. Mag. Vol. 11. No. 5 (March 1952).

Recording of Information

Dragsted, Ove. *The Marstrand System of Filing Genealogical Material* (Gen. Mag. Vol. 11. No. 2. June 1951).

Holmstrom, J.E. *How to Take, Keep and Use Notes* (1947).

Iredale, D.A. *Organization of Biographical Material for Use in Village Histories*. Amat. Hist. Vol. 6. No. 5. Autumn 1964.

Russell, C.F. *On the Statement of Evidence*. Gen. Mag. Vol. 9. No. 10. March 1944. pp. 381-4.

Thornhill, R. *Family Pedigree*. Amat. Hist. Vol. 2. No. 12. June-July 1956.

Pedigree Layout. Gen. Mag. Vol. 14. No. 11 (Sept 1964) p. 391.

Mediaeval Genealogy

Benson, J. *Feudal Age Pedigrees*. Gen. Mag. Vol. 10. No. 1. Mar. 1947. p. 10.

Bloom, J. Harvey. *Genealogical Data Before the Black Death*. Gen. Mag. Vol. VI. No. 10. p. 471. June 1934.

Cam, Miss Helen. *Pedigrees of Villeins and Freemen in the 13th Century*. Gen. Mag. Vol. 6. No. 7. Sept. 1933. p. 299.

Campling, A. *Sources of Genealogical Research before 1349*. Gen. Mag. Vol. 7. p. 61 (June 1935).

Hoskins, W.G. *The Genealogical Value of the Subsidies of 1327 and 1332*. Devon & Cornwall N & Q. XXII pt. 7 (July 1943) 169-172.

McMichael, N.H. *A Fourteenth Century Pedigree.* Gen. Mag. Vol. 12. No. 16 (Dec. 1958) p. 535.

White, G.H. *Notes on Anglo-Norman Genealogy.* Gen. Mag. IX. p. 463 (March 1945).

C. SOCIAL CLASSES AND OCCUPATIONS

Aristocracy and Gentry

Burke's *Peerage.* 103rd edn. 1963.

Burke's *Landed Gentry.* 17th edn. 1952.

Burke's *Extinct Peerage* (1841).

Burke, J. and Sir J.B. *The Royal Families of England, Scotland and Wales* (1847).

Cokayne, G.C. *The Complete Peerage.* 15 vols. 1910-1964.

Colby, R. *The Bryant Index* [of country houses] Gen. Mag. Vol. 10. No. 13. March 1950.

Fane, A.G.C. *Complete Index of Family Names appearing in Burke's Royal Families* (1932).

Howard, J.J. and Crisp, F.A. *Visitation of England and Wales* (1893 ff).

Ruvigny et Raineval, Melville de Massive de Ruvigny, Marquis de. *The Plantaganet Roll of the Blood Royal.* 4 vols. (1908).

Squibb, G. *Visitation Pedigrees and the Genealogist* (1964).

Trinick, M. *A Country House Index* [The Bryant Index] Gen. Mag. Vol. 11. No. 3. Sept. 1951.

Walford, E. *County Families of the United Kingdom 1860-1920.*

Yeomen and Farmers

Cannon, J. *Poll Books.* Short Guides to Records 2 History XLVII. No. 160. Available as sep. pamphlet.

Collins, E.J.T. *Historical Farm Records.* Archives Vol. 7. No. 35. Apl. 1966. p. 143.

Hoskins, W.G. *Yeoman Families and their Pedigrees* Trans. Leics. Arch. Soc. 1946.

The Poor (See also Other Parish Records, pp.402-3 and The Poor pp.414-4

Bernau, C.A. *The Genealogy of the Submerged* (1908). Vol. III of *Some Special Studies in Genealogy.*

Ketchley, C.P. *Settlement and its Legal Definition.* Amat. Hist. Vol. 2. No. 9. Dec-Jan 1956.

Ketchley, C.P. *Removal Orders.* Amat. Hist. V. No. 4 (1962) p. 111.

Ketchley, C.P. *Vagrancy*. Amat. Hist. Vol. 2. No. 10. Feb-Mar 1956.

Melling, Elizabeth. *Kentish Sources*. IV. The Poor (1964).

Oldham, C.R. *Oxfordshire Poor Law Papers*. Ec. Hist. Rev. 4. No. 4. p. 470 (Apr. 1934) [Includes Parish records, but emphasizes value of Quarter Sessions].

Prichard, M.E.L. *The Genealogy of the Poor*. Gen. Mag. Vol. 11. No. 3. Sept. 1951.

Army and Navy

Appleby, Lt. Col. C.E. *The National Army Museum and Genealogy*. Gen. Mag. Vol. 15. No. 1. Mar 1965.

Gardner, D.E. and Smith, F. *Genealogical Research in England and Wales*. Vol. 2. pp. 144-182.

Godfrey, M. *Personal Records of Officers of the British Army*. Amat. Hist. VI. p. 192 (Winter 1965).

Hamilton-Edwards, G.K.S. *Naval Ancestry*. Amat. Hist. I. p. 325 (Apr/May 1954).

Hamilton-Edwards, G.K.S. *In Search of Ancestry* (1966). pp. 87-106, 223-225.

Little, R.H. *Military History from Local History Sources*. Amat. Hist. VII No. 4 (1966) p. 112.

Merriman, R.D. *Naval Records*. Gen. Mag. X. No. 4. p. 95 (Dec 1947).

Trade and Commerce

Barker, T.C. & others. *Business History*. Helps for Students of History 59 Historical Association 1960.

Sources of Business History in the Reports of the National Register of Archives (Hist. Mss Comm. 1964).

Davies, Mair. *Business Archives as a Source of Family History*. Gen. Mag. Vol. 14. No. 10 (June 1964) p. 332.

Jones, I. FitzRoy. *Apprenticeship Books of Bristol*. Gen. Mag. vol. 8. No. 1. Mar 1938. p. 10.

Ketchley, C.P. *Apprentices – Trade & Poor*. Amat. Hist. II. p. 357 (June/July 1956).

Muir, A. *The Business Historian*. Amat. Hist. Vol. 6. No. 4 (Summer 1964).

Merchant Navy

Trinity House Petitions. Gen. Mag. Vol. 6. No. 11. Sept. 1934. p. 490.

Davis, R. *Shipping Records*. Archives Vol. 7. No. 35. Apr. 1966. p. 135.

Education

Bland, D.S. *The Records of the Inns of Court: A Bibliographical Aid.* Amat. Hist. V. No. 2 (1962) p. 77.

Foster, J. *Alumni Oxonienses.* 8 vols (1887-92).

Jacobs, Phyllis M. *Registers of the Universities, Colleges and Schools of Great Britain.* Bull. Inst. Hist. Res. XXXVII (1964) p. 165.

Stone, H.J.W. and Whitmore, J.B. *The Making of a School Register.* Gen. Mag. Vol. 10. No. 10 (June 1949).

Venn, J. and J.A. *Alumni Cantabrigienses.* 10 vols (1922-54).

Wicks, A.T. *School Registers.* Amat. Hist. Vol. 4. No. 1. Autumn 1958.

Medicine

Medical Records. Archives Vol. IV. No. 21. Lady Day 1959. p. 1.

Transport

Johnson, L.C. *Historical Records of the British Transport Commission.* Journ. Soc. Archivists I. No. 4. Oct. 1956. p. 94.

Theatre

Bullock, Dr. J.M. *Theatrical Families.* Gen. Mag. Vol. 6. No. 8. p. 339 (Dec 1933).

Gypies

Hawkes, C.P. *Gypsy Blood.* Gen. Mag. Vol. 6. No. 9 (March 1934) p. 386.

Immigrants

Cunningham, W. *Alien Immigrants to England* (1897).

Horton-Smith, L.G.H. *Naturalisation and Where to Look I.* Gen. Mag. Vol. 10. No. 12. Dec. 1949.

Kerling, N.J.M. Aliens in the County of Norfolk 1430-1485. Norfolk Archaeology. XXXIII. No. 2 (1963).

Wulcko, L.M. *Naturalisation and Where to Look II.* Gen. Mag. Vol. 1 No. 13. March 1950.

Wyatt, T. *Aliens in England before the Huguenots.* Proc. Hug. Soc. London XIX 1.

D. THE USE AND INTERPRETATION OF RECORDS

General

Emmison, F.G. *Archives and Local History* (1965).

Emmison, F.G. *Introduction to Archives* (1964).

Hanworth, E.M. Pollock, 1st Viscount. *The Preservation and Interpretation of Ancient Records* (1929).

Martin, C.T. *The Record Interpreter* (1910).

Newton, K.C. *Reading Mediaeval Local Records*. Amat. Hist. Vol. 3. p. 81 (Winter 1956/7).

Redstone, L.J. and Steer, F.W. (eds) *Local Records and their Care* (1953).

Rye, Walter. *Records and Record Searching. A Guide to the Genealogist and Topographer* (1897).

Thoyts, (afds Cope) Emma E. *How to Decipher and Study Old Documents* (1893. 3rd edn. 1909).

Palaeography

Denholm-Young, N. *Handwriting in England and Wales* (1954).

Gardner, D.E. and Smith, F. *Genealogical Research in England and Wales*. Vol. 3 (1964).

Grieve, Hilda E.P. *Examples of English Handwriting 1150-1750* (1959).

Hector, L.C. *The Handwriting of English Documents* (1958).

Jenkinson, H. *Later Court Hands in England from 15th to 17th Century* (1927).

Johnson, C. and Jenkinson, H. *English Court Hand 1066-1500 illustrated from the Public Records*. 2 vols 1915.

Judge, C.B. *Specimens of 16th Century English Handwriting* (1935).

Le Hardy, W. *How to Read 16th and 17th Century Handwriting*. Amat. Hist. Vol. 1. No. 5 (Apr/May 1953).

Le Hardy, W., and Evans, Claire, G.M. *The 16th and 17th Century Written Alphabet*. Amat. Hist. Vol. 1. No. 5 (Apr/May 1953).

Newton, K.C. *Reading Mediaeval Local Records*. Amat. Hist. Vol. 3. No. 2 (Winter 1956/7).

Tschichold, J. *An Illustrated History of Writing and Lettering* (1947).

Latin

Baxter, J.H. and Johnson, C. *Mediaeval Latin Word List from British and Irish Sources* (1934. revd. R.E. Latham, 1965).

Gooder, E.M. *Latin for Local History* (1961).

Latham, R.E. *Coping with Mediaeval Latin.* Amat. Hist. I. p. 331 (Apr/May 1954).

Legal, Technical and Ecclesiastical Terms

Collis, Ivor P. *Leases for a Term of Years Determinable with Lives.* Journ. Soc. Archivists I. No. 6 (Oct 1957) p. 168.

Cornwall, J. *How to Read Old Title Deeds XVI-XIX Centuries.* Dept. of Extra-Mural Studies. Univ of Birmingham (1964).

Du Boulay, Prof. *Handlist of Mediaeval Ecclesiastical Terms* (Standing Confer. for Loc. History).

Harris, P.V. *Glossary of Terms from Parochial Records.* Amat. Hist. Vol. 1. No. 4 (1953) pp. 122–124.

Johnson, G.D. *Legal Terms and Phrases.* Amat. Hist. III. p. 249 (1957-8).

Purvis, J.S. *Dictionary of Ecclesiastical Terms* (1962).

Rudden, B. *The Terminology of Title.* Law Qtrly. Rev. LXXX (Jan 196 p. 63.

Tate, W.E. *The Parish Chest* (1946. new edn. 1967). Glossary pp. 303-314.

Other works which may help to elucidate legal points are listed under '*Law*', below pages 432-434.

Dates

Cheney, C.R. *Handbook of Dates for Students of English History* (Royal Hist. Soc. 1945. Revd. ed 1955).

Hector, L.C. *The Beginning of the 'Natural Day' in the late 14th Century.* Journ. Soc. Archivists II. No. 3 (Apr. 1961) p. 8

House, W.H. *The Dating of Old Records.* Trans. Radnorshire Soc. XXXII (1962).

McKay, D.A. *The Dating of Records.* Amat. Hist. Vol. 2. No. 6 June/July 1955.

Powicke, F.M. and Fryde, E.B. (eds). *Handbook of British Chronology* (Royal Hist. Soc. 1939. 2nd edn. 1961).

Wallis, J.E.W. *English Regnal Years and Titles, Handlists, Easter Dates etc.* S.P.C.K. Helps to Students of History No. 40 (1921).

E. RECORD REPOSITORIES, LIBRARIES AND CENTRAL RECORDS

General

Record Repositories of Great Britain (H.M.S.O. 1964).

Phillimore's *Directory for Genealogists and Local Historians* (1963).

Archives and Manuscripts in Libraries. The Library Association Record 59 (1957) 7. pp. 238-239.

International Directory of Archives. Archivum Vol. 5 (1955) Lists all Record Repositories in 50 Countries.

Hall, Hubert (ed) *A Repertory of British Archives.* Part 1. England (1920).

Hepworth, P. *Archives and Manuscripts in Libraries, 1961* (1962).

Sims, R. *Manual for the Genealogist, Topographer, Antiquary and Legal Professor* (2nd edn. 1861).

Barwick, G.F. (ed) *The Aslib Directory. A Guide to Sources of Specialized Information in Great Britain and Ireland* (1928 and subsequent editions).

Kaminkow, Marion J. *Genealogical Manuscripts in British Libraries: A Descriptive Guide* (1967).

London Libraries

Harrod, L.M. *Libraries of Greater London* (1951).

Irwin, R. and Staveley, R. (ed) *The Libraries of London* (1964).

Public Record Office

General

Guide to the Contents of the Public Record Office. 2 vols. H.M.S.O. 2nd edn. 1963. Vol. I Legal Records etc. Vol. 2 State Papers.

Galbraith, V.H. *An Introduction to the Use of Public Records* (1934).

Hector, L.C. *Guide to the Contents of the Public Record Office.* (Amat. Hist. Vol. 6. No. 2. Winter 1964).

Hector, L.C. *Genealogy in the Public Records.* Gen. Mag. Vol. 8. No. 2. p. 57 (June 1938).

Johnson, Charles. *The Public Record Office* (S.P.C.K. Helps to Students of History No. 4, 1918).

Latham, R.E. *Hints on Interpreting the Public Records*: 1. Feet of Fines, 2. Letters Patent, 3. Inquisitions Post Mortem, 4. Ministers' Accounts, 5. Plea Rolls. Amat. Hist. I. Nos 1-5 (1952-3).

Census Returns

Beresford, M. *The Unprinted Census Returns of 1841, 1851, 1861 for England and Wales*. Amat. Hist. V. No. 8 (Summer 1963) p. 260.

Gardner, D.E. and Smith, F. *Genealogical Research in England and Wales*. Vol. 1. pp. 84-117.

Hector, L.C. *The Census Returns of 1841 and 1851*. Amat. Hist. I 274 (June – July 1953).

Taylor, A.J. *The Taking of the Census 1801-1951*. Brit. Medical Journ. I (1951).

Chancery Proceedings

Fines, J. Documents in the Public Record Office 3. *The Early Chancery Proceedings*. Amat. Hist. VI. No. 8 (Summer 1965).

Garrett, R.E.F. *Chancery and other Proceedings*. Gen. Mag. XV Nos 3 & 4 (Sept. & Dec. 1965).

Taxes, etc.

Beresford, M.W. *The Lay Subsidies*. Amat. Hist. III. No. 8 and IV. No. 3 (1958, 1959).

Beresford, M.W. *The Poll Taxes of 1377, 1379 and 1381*. Amat. Hist. III. No. 7 (1958).

Beresford, M.W. *Lay Subsidies and Poll Taxes*. Reprint of above (Phillimore, 1963).

Bradshaw, F. *The Lay Subsidy of 1296*. Archaeologia Aeliana. 3rd Ser. XIII (1916) 186-302.

Carter, W.F. and Wellstood, F.C. *Lay Subsidy Rolls for Warwickshire 1332*. Dugdale Soc. Publications VI (1926).

Cornwall, J. *Lay Subsidy Rolls 1524-5*. Sussex Rec. Soc. Vol. LVI (1956).

Dickenson, F.H. *Lay Subsidy Roll for 1327*. Somerset Rec. Soc. (1889).

Dietz, F.C. *English Government Finance 1485-1588*. Illinois Social Studies IX (1920).

Dowell, S. *A History of Taxation and Taxes in England from the Earliest Times to the Present Day*. 4 vols (1884).

Grigg, D.B. *The Land Tax Returns*. Agric. Hist. Rev. XI No. 2 (1963)

Grigg, D.B. *A Source of Landownership – The Land Tax Returns*. Amat. Hist. VI. No. 5 (Autumn 1964).

Harley, J.B. *The Hundred Rolls of 1279*. Amat. Hist. V No. 1 (1961) p. 9.

Hervey, S.H.A. Preface to *Suffolk in 1674, being the Hearth Tax Returns* (1905).

Hoskins, W.G. *The Genealogical Value of the Subsidies of 1327 and 1332.* Devon & Cornwall N & Q. XXII part 7 (July 1943) 169-172.

Hoskins, W.G. [Lay Subsidies, etc] *Local History in England* (1959). pp. 102-4, 142-9.

Howell, R. *Hearth Tax Returns.* Short Guides to Records 7. History XLIX No. 165 (Feb 1964).

Hudson, W. *The Three Earliest Subsidies in 1296, 1327 and 1332.* Sussex Rec. Soc. X (1910).

Jarvis, R.C. *Records of Customs and Excise Services.* Gen. Mag. Vol. 10. No. 7 (Sept. 1948) p. 219.

Meekings, C.A.F. *Dorset Hearth Tax Assessments 1662-1664.* [Appendix III gives summaries of the 1662 assessment for all counties of England and Wales].

Peyton, S.A. *Village Population in the Tudor Lay Subsidy Rolls.* Eng. Hist. Rev. XXX (1915) pp. 234-250.

Styles, P. Introduction to the Warwickshire Hearth Tax Records in *Warwick County Records: Hearth Tax Returns.* Vol. 1 (1957).

Ward, W.R. *The English Land Tax in the 18th Century* (1953).

Ward, W.R. *The Administration of the Window and Assessed Taxes 1696-1798.* Eng. Hist. Rev. LXVII No. 265 (Oct. 1952. repr. as sep booklet 1963).

West, J. *Village Records.* pp. 42-49 (Lay Subsidy Rolls), pp. 131-135 (Hearth Tax Returns), pp. 144-157 (Land Tax and Tithe Records) [All three include lists of published records].

Willard, J.F. *Parliamentary Taxes on Personal Property 1290-1334.* Mediaeval Academy of America. No. 9 (1934).

Willard, J.F. and Johnson, H.C. *Surrey Taxation Returns 1332-1623.* Surrey Rec. Soc. 1923.

Muster Returns. See under *Local Records,* below p.404.

Army and Navy. See under *Social Classes and Occupations,* above p.389.

Tontines

Leeson, F.L. *Tontines.* Letter in Gen. Mag. Vol. 14. No. 10 (June 1964) p. 344.

Leeson, F.L. *Tontines.* Letter in Gen. Mag. Vol. 15. No. 1 (March 1965) p. 30.

General Register Office, St. Catherine's House, Kingsway, London WC2B 6•

Buer, Mabel C. *The Reformed Parliament and the Civil Registration of Births and Deaths.* Public Admin. July 1930. pp. 323-4.

Gardner, D.E. and Smith, F. *Genealogical Research in England and Wales.* Vol. 1. pp. 46-83.

General Register Office. *Abstracts of Arrangements respecting Registration of Births, Marriages and Deaths in the U.K. and other countries of the British Commonwealth.........and in th•* *Irish Republic* (1952) [Includes a list of registers of British Births, Marriages and Deaths abroad].

General Register Office. *Story of the General Register Office* (1937).

Glass, D.V. *A Note on the Under-Registration of Births in Britain in the 19th Century.* Pop. Studies V pt. 1. (Jan 1951) p. 70.

Maidbury, L. *The General Register of Births, Deaths and Marriages* Amat. Hist. III No. 3 (Spring 1957).

Mallet, Sir Bernard. *Reform of Vital Statistics: Outline of a System of National Registration.* Eugenics Rev. July 1929. pp. 87-94.

Smith, G.T.B. *Vital Registration* (1907). Deals with law and practice concerning registration.

Compulsory Registration of Births. N & Q. 11. pp. 262, 299-300, 336-7 (25 April 1936, 9th May 1936).

Coroners' Law and the Registration of Births and Deaths. Brit. Med. Journ. 27 Mar 1927. pp. 582-3.

House of Lords Record Office

Bond, M.F. *The Archives of Parliament.* Gen. Mag. XI. No. 10 (June 1953).

Bond, M.F. *The Records of Parliament: A Guide for Genealogists an•* *Local Historians* (1964).

Bond, M.F. *The Records of Parliament.* 4 articles in Amat. Hist. I Nos 6, 7 and 8 (1959-60).

Bond, M.F. *Estate Acts of Parliament.* Short Guides to Records 9 History XLIX. No. 167. (Oct 1964). Repr. as sep. booklet.

Bond, M.F. *The Formation of the Archives of Parliament 1497-1691.* Journ. Soc. Archivists I. No. 6 (Oct. 1957) p. 151.

Cobb, H.S. *Sources for Economic History amongst the Parliamentary Records in the House of Lords Record Office.* Ec. Hist. Rev. 2nd Ser. XIX. No. 1 (Apr 1966) p. 154.

Historical Manuscripts Commission. *5th Report* (1876) pp. 120-134.
[List of surviving Protestation Oath Rolls.]

Society of Genealogists

Guide to the Library of the Society of Genealogists (1965).

Buck, W.S. *A List of Names in the Document Collection of the Society of Genealogists.*

Camp, A.J. *Collections and Indexes of the Society of Genealogists.* Gen. Mag. Vol. 13. No. 10 (June 1961).

Sims, J.M. *A Catalogue of Directories and Poll Books in the Library of the Society of Genealogists.*

Key Descents from the Manuscript Collections of the Society of Genealogists. Gen. Mag. Vol. 9. pp. 173, 224, 266, 302, 357, 389, 440, 471, 499 (Sept. 1941 — Sept. 1945).

British Museum

Esdaile, A.J.K. *The British Museum Library. A Short History and Survey* (1946).

Gilson, J.P. *A Students' Guide to the MSS of the British Museum* (S.P.C.K. Helps for Students of History No. 31. 1920).

Skeat, T.C. (ed) *Catalogue of Manuscript Collections* (B.M. 1951).

College of Arms

Wagner, Sir A.R. *The Records and Collections of the College of Arms* (1952).

Corporation of London & Guildhall Library

Beever, R.J. *City of London Rate Books* (Gen. Mag. Vol. 5. p. 115. Dec. 1929).

Challen, W.H. *The Records of the City of London.* Gen. Mag. VI. p. 503. Sept. 1934.

Hollaender, A.E.J. *Local Archives of Great Britain XII. Guildhall Library.* Archives Vol. II. No. 14. Michaelmas 1955. p. 312.

Hollaender, A.E.J. *Ecclesiastical Records transferred to Guildhall Library from Somerset House.* Trans. London and Middlesex. Arch. Soc. xxi (1959).

Jones, P.E.H. and Smith, R. *A Guide to the Records in the Corporation of London Records Office and the Guildhall Library Muniment Room* (1951).

Jones, P.E.H. *Genealogy and the City of London Records*. Gen. Mag. Vol. 11. pp. 134, 167 (Dec. 1951, March 1952).

Thomas, A.H. *Genealogical Material in the Guildhall Records*. Gen. Mag. Vol. 2. p. 45 (June 1926).

Unwin, C. *The Guilds and Companies of London* (2nd edn. 1962).

Bodleian Library, Oxford

Craster, H.H.E. *Western Manuscripts of the Bodleian Library* (S.P.C.K. 1921).

Hassall, W.O. *Local History Sources in the Bodleian Library*. Amat. Hist. II. p. 130 (Apl.-May, 1955).

Philip, I.G. *Diocesan Records in the Bodleian Library, Oxford*. Gen. Mag. VIII. No. 1 (Mar. 1938). p. 7-9.

F. DIOCESAN AND ARCHIDIACONAL RECORDS

General

Davies, J.C. *Ecclesiastical and Palatinate Archives at the Prior's Kitchen, Durham*. Journ. Soc. Archivists I. No. 7 (Apr. 1958) p. 185.

Gibbons, A. *Ely Episcopal Records* (1891).

Hill, G. *English Dioceses: a history of their limits from the earliest times to the present day* (1900).

Holworthy, R. *Discoveries in the Diocesan Registry, Wells, Somerset*. Gen. Mag. Vol. 2. Nos. 1 & 2 (March and June 1926) pp. 2, 34.

Jenkins, Revd. Claude. *Ecclesiastical Records*. S.P.C.K. Helps to Students of History, No. 17 (1920).

Major, Miss Kathleen. *Diocesan Records as Sources for the Genealogist*. Gen. Mag. Vol. 9. No. 5 (Sept. 1941) p. 158.

Major, Miss Kathleen. *The Nature of Diocesan Records*. Lincoln Archit. & Archaeolog. Soc. Reports. Papers New Ser. II pt. 2 (1945) 129-140.

Major, Miss Kathleen. *Parish History from Diocesan Records*. Lincs. Mag. III (1938) 331-4, 374-79.

Owen, Dorothy M. *The Use of Ecclesiastical Records for Secular Subjects*. Amat. Hist. V. No. 2 (Winter 1962) p. 44.

Owen, Dorothy M. *Lambeth Palace Archives*. Journ. Soc. Archivists I No. 4 (Oct. 1961).

Owen, Dorothy M. *Why and How? Some Thoughts on the cataloguing of Ecclesiastical Archives.* Journ. Soc. Archivists II. No. 10 (Oct. 1964).

Philip, I. G. *Diocesan Records in the Bodleian Library, Oxford.* Gen. Mag. VIII. No. 1 (March 1938) pp. 7-9.

Pilgrim Trust. *Survey of Ecclesiastical Archives of the Church of England* (1952) 45 duplicated pamphlets.

Purvis, J. S. *Ecclesiastical Records.* Journ. Soc. Archivists I. No. 1. Apr. 1955. p. 2.

Purvis, J. S. *Introduction to Ecclesiastical Records* (1953).

Purvis, J. S. *Dictionary of Ecclesiastical Terms* (1962).

Purvis, J. S. *The Archives of the York Diocesan Registry* (1952).

Sayers, J. *Estate Documents at Lambeth Palace Library* (1965).

Welch, C. E. *The Preservation of Ecclesiastical Records.* Archives IV. No. 22 (Michaelmas 1959) p. 75.

Willis, A. J. *Diocesan Records as Sources for the Genealogist.* Gen. Mag. Vol. 15. No. 5 (March 1966).

Woodcock, A. M. *Guide to the Leicester Archdeaconry Records* (1954).

Episcopal Registers

Fowler, R. C. *Episcopal Registers of England and Wales* (1918).

Church Courts

Brinkworth, E. R. C. *Records of Church Courts.* Amat. Hist. II. No. 2 (Oct-Nov 1954).

Brinkworth, E. R. C. *Archdeacon's Court, 1584.* Oxford Rec. Soc. Vols 22-23, (1942-6).

Brinkworth, E. R. C. *Study and Use of Archdeacon's Court Records.* Trans. Royal Hist. Soc. 4th ser. vol. 25 (1943).

Carson, I. A. Ritchie. *The Ecclesiastical Courts of York* (1956).

Furnivall, F. S. *Records of Consistory Court of Chester.* Surtees Soc. (1845).

Willis, A. J. *Winchester Consistory Court Depositions 1561-1602* (1960).

Willis, A. J. *Winchester Guardianship Records after 1700.* Gen. Mag. Vol. 14. Nos 7-12, (Sept. 1963 – Dec. 1964) and Vol. 15. No. 1 (March 1965).

Visitations

Brinkworth, E.R.C. *Records of Bishops' and Archbishops' Visitatio* Amat. Hist. II. No. 1 (Aug.-Sept 1954).

Owen, Dorothy M. *Episcopal Visitation Books.* History Vol. XLIX. No. 166 (June 1964).

Licences

Willis, A.J. *Bishops' Licences to Laymen in the 18th and 19th Centuries.* Amat. Hist. V. No. 1 (1961) p. 2.

Wills

Bloom, J. Harvey, *A Slip-Index to Stray Wills* (Gen. Mag. Vol. 5. No. 10. June 1931. p. 325.

Camp, A.J. *Wills and their Whereabouts* (1974).

Cirket, A.F. *English Wills 1498-1526.* (Beds. Hist. Rec. Soc. Vol. 37).

Gardner, D.E. and Smith, F. *Genealogical Research in England and Wales.* Vol. II. pp. 22-143.

Gibson, J.S.W. *Wills and Where to Find Them* (1974)

Marshall, G.W. *A Handbook to the Ancient Courts of Probate and Depositories of Wills* (1895).

Sharpe-France, R. *Wills.* Short Guides to Records 10. History Vol.L. 168 (Feb. 1965).

Sheehan, M.M. *A List of 13th Century English Wills.* Gen. Mag. Vol. 9. p. 259 (March 1961).

Skeel, C. *Mediaeval Wills.* History Vol. X (1926).

Stewart-Brown. *Name and Arms Conditions in Wills.* Gen. Mag. Vol. 5 No. 12 (Dec. 1931).

Thacker, Miss H. *Wills and Other Probate Records.* Amat. Hist. Vol. 1. No. 9 (Dec. 1953 – Jan. 1954).

Walne, P. *English Wills* (1964).

Wills. Trans. Devon Assoc. 53 (1921) pp. 48-83.

Inventories

Ashmore, O. and Bagley, J.J. *Inventories as a Source of Local History.* 4 Articles in Amat. Hist. Vol. 4 1959.

Emmison, F.G. (ed) *Jacobean Household Inventories* (Bedf. Hist. Rec. Soc. 1938).

Freeman, C.E. *Elizabethan Inventories.* Publ. Beds. Hist. Rec. Soc. XXXII (1952).

Gardiner, E.M. *East Sussex Inventories*. Sussex Notes & Queries XV. p. 124 (1939).

Havinden, M.A. *Household and Farm Inventories in Oxfordshire 1550-1590* (H.M.S.O. 1965).

Jones, B.C. *Inventories of Goods & Chattels*. Amat. Hist. Vol. 2. No. 3. 1954-5

Steer, F.W. *Farm & Cottage Inventories of Mid Essex 1635-1749* (Essex R.O. 1950).

Steer, F.W. *Probate Inventories*. Short Guides to Records 3. History XLVII No. 161 (Oct 1962. Available as sep. pamphlet).

West, J. *Village Records*. pp. 92-131. [This includes a glossary of unusual words found in inventories.]

G. LOCAL RECORDS

General (See also *Methods, Sources* etc. under *Local History* on pages 427-8).

Emmison, F.G. *Archives and Local History* (1965).

Hoskins, W.G. *Local History in England* (1959).

Jarvis, R.C. *The Records of the Deserted Village*. Journ. Soc. Arch. I. No. 4 (Oct. 1956) p. 100.

Kennedy, P.A. *Nottinghamshire Historical Documents in Facsimile*. (Notts Local History Council, 1962).

Meads, Dorothy M. *Searching Local Records*. Rev. of Eng. Studies 4 (1928) 173-90, 301-2.

Redstone, L.J. and Steer, F.W. *Local Records and their Care* (1953).

West, J. *Village Records* (1962).

Newspapers. See Bibliography on page 287.

Parish Registers. See Bibliography on pp. 76-81.

Monumental Inscriptions. See Bibliography on pp. 269-270.

Parish Censuses

Allison, K.J. *An Elizabethan Village "Census"*. Bull. Inst. Hist. Res. XXXVI (1963) [Ealing, Middlesex 1599. Arranged by Households and includes ages, relationships and occupations.]

Cornwall, J. *An Elizabethan Census*. Records of Bucks XVI. iv (1959) [Ecclesiastical Census 1563. Statistics only.]

Styles, P. *A Census of a Warwickshire Village in 1698.* [Fenny Compton]. Univ. of Birmingham Hist. Journ. Vol. III (1951) p.3

Waters, R. E. Chester. *The Melbourne Assessment of 1695.* Journ. Derbyshire Arch. & Nat. Hist. Soc. VII (1885) pp. 1–30.

Other Parish Records (See also *The Poor* pp.388-9 and 414-416. *Clergy and Parish Officers* pp.419-420, *Agriculture* pp.416-418 and *The Parish, Village and Manor* pp.428-429.

Barratt, D.M. *Glebe Terriers.* Short Guides to Records 13. History Vol. I. No. 171 (Feb. 1966).

Beck, Joan. *Church Briefs.* Amat. Hist. Vol. 2. No. 6 (June-July 1955).

Bewes, W.A. *Church Briefs* (1896).

Blain, J. *A List of Churchwardens' Accounts* (1939).

Brown, Eileen M. *Parish Records.* Lincs Mag. IV (April 1939) 73-83

Brychmore, J. *Parish Records.* (Somerset Arch. Soc. Bath Branch. Proc. for 1939 (1940). 275-280.

Cannan, G. *History of Local Rates in England* (1927).

Cox, Revd. J.C. *Churchwardens' Accounts* (1913).

Darlington, Ida. *Rate Books.* Short Guides to Records I. History Vol. XLVII No. 159 (Feb. 1962). Reprinted as sep. leaflet.

Drew, C. *Lambeth Churchwardens' Accounts* (1941-50) [Useful Introduction].

Erith, E.J. (& others). *Essex Parish Records 1240-1894* (1950).

Hutchins, B.L. *Parish and Other Accounts.* N & Q 9th Ser. iv 1899. pp. 301-2, 414-5, 452-3.

Major, Miss Kathleen. *Survey of Parochial Documents in the Dioces and County of Lincoln.* (Local Historian Nos 16 & 17 (1937-8).

Nichols, John. *Illustrations of the Manners and Expences of Antient Times in England....from the Accompts of Churchwardens* (London, 1797.)

Purvis, J.S. *Tudor Parish Documents of the Diocese of York* (1948)

Tate, W.E. *The Parish Chest* (1946 & edns. New edition 1968).
[An extremely thorough survey of all types of Parish Records]

Tate, W.E. *Parish Records and the English Village Community.* Amat Hist. 6. No. 4 (Summer 1964).

Tate, W.E. *Enclosure Awards and Acts.* Short Guides to Records 14. History LI, No. 172 (June 1966).

Thompson, A. Hamilton. *Parish History and Records.* S.P.C.K. Helps for Students of History, No. 15 (1919) Hist. Assoc. pamphlet, 1926.

Tupling, G.H. *Searching the Parish Records.* 1. Parish Registers;
2. Vestry Minutes and Churchwardens' Accounts; 3. Overseers'
Acts; 4. Highway Surveyor's Accounts; 5. Constable's Accounts;
6. Terriers, Tithe and Enclosure Records. (Amat. Hist. Vol. 1.
Nos 7-12 (1953).

Tupling, G.H. *Parish Books, Their Value to the Historian.* Trans.
Lancs & Ches Antiqn. Soc. LXII (1950-1).

Walford, C. *King's Briefs: their Purpose and History.* Trans.
Royal Hist. Soc. X (1882).

Wyatt, Sir Stanley. *Old Rate Books of a Hampshire Parish.* Gen. Mag.
Vol. 11. No. 13 (March 1954.

Parish Chests and their Contents. Gen. Mag. Vol. 4. p. 38
(June 1928).

Manorial and Estate Records

Emmison, F.G. *Estate Maps and Surveys.* Short Guides to Records 4.
History XLVIII No. 162 (Feb. 1963). Reprinted as sep. pamphlet.

Gardner, E.M. *Midhurst Court Rolls.* Sussex N & Q XIII (1951-3).

Havinden, M.A. *Estate Villages: A Study of the Berkshire Villages
of Ardington and Lockinge.* (1966).

Hone, N.J. *The Manor and Manorial Records* (1925).

Humphrey-Smith, C.R. *Genealogy from Manorial Records.* Gen. Mag.
Vol. 14. No. 1. (March 1962).

Johnson, W. Branch. *Notes before Reading Court Rolls.* Amat. Hist.
Vol. 4, No. 3 (Spring 1959).

Knocker, Herbert W. *Manorial Records.* Gen. Mag. Vol. 6, No. 3.
p. 92. (Sept 1932).

Latham, L.C. *The Manor.* Hist. Assoc. Pamphlet. No. 83 (1931).

Latham, L.C. *The Manor and the Village* in *Social Life in Early
England,* Historical Association Essays, ed. C. Barraclough
(1960).

Levett, A.E. (ed. H.M. Cam, M. Coate and L.S. Sutherland) *Studies
in Manorial History* (1938).

Maitland, F.W. *Select Pleas in Manorial and other Seigneurial
Courts,* Seldon Soc. (1889).

Pollock, E.M. *Manors, their History and their Records* (1933).

Sherwood, L. *The Court Baron.* Amat. Hist. Vol. 2. No. 12 (1956).

West, J. *Village Records.* pp. 30-42. [This includes a valuable
list of printed Court Rolls and other Manorial Records and
there is a glossary of words commonly used in manorial records
on pp. 182-186.]

Municipal Records

Darlington, Ida. *Rate Books*. Short Guides to Records I. History XLVII No. 159 (Feb. 1962). Repr. as sep. pamphlet.

Gross, C. *A Bibliography of British Municipal History*. Harvard Hist. Studies V (1897).

Hearnshaw, F.J.C. *Municipal Records*. S.P.C.K. Helps for Students of History 2 (1918).

Martin, G.H. *The Origin of Borough Records*. Journ. of Soc. Archivists II. No. 4 (Oct. 1961) p. 147.

Muster Returns

Banks, C.E. *Able Men of Suffolk 1638* (1831).

Bax, A.R. *Preparations by the County of Surrey to resist the Spanish Armada*. Surrey Arch. Collections XVI (1901) pp. 137-1

Cornwall, J. *A Tudor Domesday: The Musters of 1522*. Journ. Soc. Archivists III. No. 1 (Apl. 1965).

Green, E. *Somerset Muster Returns of 1569*. Somerset Record Soc. XX (1904).

Green, E. *Preparations in Somerset against the Armada* (1888).

Rich, E.E. *The Population of Elizabethan England*. Ec. Hist. Rev. 2nd Ser. II No. 3 (1950) p. 247.

Smith, J. *Men and Armour in Gloucestershire in 1608* (1902). [analysed by A.J. Tawney and R.H. Tawney in *"An Occupational Census of the Seventeenth Century*. Ec. Hist. Rev. 1st Ser. V No. 1. (Oct. 1934) p. 25.]

Wake, J. and Morris, J.E. *Musters, Subsidies etc. 1586-1623*. Northants Rec. Soc. pub. Vol. III (1926).

Shropshire Archaeological and Natural History Society. 3rd Ser. Vol. VIII.

East Anglian Miscellany 1937-9 [Suffolk Returns, 1577].

Hearth Tax See *Taxes*, under *Record Repositories*, above p.395.

Other County Records

Baker, K.H. *General Ledgers of Boards of Guardians*. Journ. Soc. Arch. II. No. 8 (1962) p. 367.

Cameron, Miss J. *The Middlesex Quarter Sessions Records*. Gen. Mag. Vol. 10. No. 1 (March 1947).

Coleman, Jane M. *Guardians' Minute Books*. Short Guides to Record 5. History XLVIII No. 163 (June 1963. Available as sep. pamphlet).

Coleman, Jane M. *Sussex Poor Law Records* (1960).

Dowdell, E.G. *A Hundred Years of Quarter Sessions. The Government of Middlesex from 1660 to 1760* (1932).

Emmison, F.G. and Gray Irvine. *County Records* (1948 repr. 1961). [includes list of Quarter Session Records in print.]

Emmison, F.G. *Guide to the Essex Record Office* (1947-8). Intro. on Quarter Sessions esp. useful).

Stanley-Morgan, R. *The Poor Law Unions and their Records.* Amat. Hist. II. No. 1 (1954) p. 11.

Marriage Settlements

A Kentish Marriage Settlement. Family History Vol. 1. No. 5. p. 155.

Dow, L. *Two Sixteenth Century Marriage Settlements.* Proc. Suffolk Inst. Arch. Nat. Hist. xxvi 2 (1953).

Habbakuk, H.J. *Marriage Settlements in the Eighteenth Century.* Trans. Royal Hist. Soc. xxxii (1950).

Richards, M. *The Marriage Settlement of Ellen, daughter of Ellis Wynne of Lasynys 1724.* Journ. of Merioneth Hist. & Rec. Soc. III iii 1959.

Watson, G.W. *Marriage Settlements from Collections in the British Museum and Record Offices.* Genealogist, New. Ser. 33-37 (1917-1921).

Deeds

Carr, A.D. *Deeds of Title.* Short Guides to Records 12. History Vol. L No. 174 (Oct. 1965). Available as sep. pamphlet.

Cornwall, J. *How to Read Old Title Deeds XVI-XIX Centuries* (1964).

Dibben, A.D. *Deeds* (Hist. Assoc. 1965).

Legg, E. *Title Deeds.* Amat. Hist. Vol. 6. No. 3 (Spring 1964) p. 86. [See also W. Branch Johnson's Letter vol. 6. No. 5 (Autumn 1964) p. 151.]

British Records Association Reports from Committees, 1938. No. 4. *Cataloguing of Deeds* Part 3 pp. 20-26.

II RELATED SUBJECTS

A. ECONOMIC AND SOCIAL HISTORY

Bibliography

Ashton, T.S. *The Industrial Revolution – A Study in Bibliography* (1937).

Ashton, T.S. *The Industrial Revolution.* Ec. Hist. Rev. Vol. 5 (1934-5).

Davies, Godfrey (ed) *Bibliography of British History – Stuart Period, 1603-1714.*

Economic History Review. Includes annual list of works on Economic and Social history published in Britain.

Frewer, L.B. *Bibliography of Historical Writings published in Great Britain and the Empire 1940-45* (1947).

Gross, Charles. *The Sources and Literature of English History fro the Earliest Times to about 1485* (1915).

Historical Association. *Annual Bulletin of Historical Literature* (1912-*date*).

Lancaster, J.C. & Kellaway, W. *Bibliography of Historical Works issued in the U.K. 1946-56* (1957) and *1957-60* (1962).

Milne, A.T. *Writings in British History.* Annually, 1934-9; 1940-4 (2 vols).

Moore, M.F. *A Classified List of Works Relating to English Manorial and Agrarian History.....to.....1660* (1912).

Mullins, E.L.C. *Guide to the Historical Publications of the Societies of England and Wales, 1901-1933.*

Pargellis, J. & Medley, D.J. (eds) *Bibliography of British History – 18th Century 1714-1789.*

Read, Conyers (ed). *Bibliography of British History – Tudor Period 1485-1603* (1959).

Williams, Judith, B. *Guide to Printed Materials for English Socia and Economic History* 1750-1850. 2 vols 1926.

Zagorin, P. *English History 1558-1640.* A Bibliographical Survey. Amer. Hist. Rev. LXVIII (1963).

Ashley, Sir W. *The Economic Organization of England.* 3rd edn (1949).

Baring-Gould, S. *Old Country Life* (1913). [Covers all rural figures from squire to village musician, but deals especially with country clergy].

Batsford, H. & Fry, C. *The English Cottage* (1938).

Birnie, A. *Economic History of the British Isles.* 8th edn. (1955).

Briggs, M. & Jordan, P. *Economic History of England.* 6th edn. (1954).

Clapham, Sir J.H. *Economic History of England.* 3 vols. (1926).

Clapham, Sir J.H. *Concise Economic History of Britain from the Earliest Times to 1750* (1930, 1932).

Drummond, J.C. and Wilbraham, Anne. *The Englishman's Food. A History of Five Centuries of English Diet* (1939-40).

Flinn, M.W. *An Economic and Social History of Britain 1066-1939* (1962).

Hamilton, H. *History of the Homeland* (1947).

Harding, D.P. *Domestic Everyday Life. Manners & Customs in this country.....to the end of the 18th Century.* Trans. Royal Hist. Soc. ix (1881) pp. 224-253.

Hartley, D. *Countryman's England* (1935).

Laslett, P. *The World We Have Lost* (1965). [This important pioneer work shows how new demographic techniques have modified or changed many accepted beliefs in social history].

Lipson, E. *The Economic History of England* (1931).

Lovejoy, A.O. *The Great Chain of Being* (1936).

McDonnel, K.G.T and others. *A Survey of English Economic History* (1960).

Meredith, H.O. *Economic History of England* (1949).

Mitchell, R.J. & Leys, M.D.R. *A History of the English People* (1950).

Morgan, E.V. *The Study of Prices and the Value of Money* (1950).

Notestein, W. *English Folk* (1938).

Quennell, M. & C.H.B. *A History of Everyday Things in England.* 4 vols (1950-52).

Traill, H.D. (ed) *Social England.* 6 vols (1901-4).

Trevelyan, G.M. *Illustrated English Social History* (1950).

Williams, Ellis A. & Fisher, F.J. *History of English Life, Political & Social* (1953).

Yarwood, D. *The English Home* (1956).

16th Century

Bindoff, S.T. *Tudor England* (Pelican History of England IV) (1950

Black, J.B. *The Reign of Elizabeth* (1936).

Brenner, Y.S. *Prices and Wages in England 1450-1550.* Bull. Inst. Hist. Res. XXXIV (1961).

Byrne, M. St. Clare. *Elizabethan Life in Town and Country* (1925. 8th edn. 1961).

Camden, Carroll. *The Elizabethan Woman* (1952).

Cheyney, E.P. *Social Changes in England in the 16th Century* (1895

Clarendon Press. (Various Authors) *Shakespeare's England.* 2 vols (1917).

Elton, G.R. *England Under the Tudors* (1955).

Furnivall, F.J. *Manners and Meals in Olden Times.* Early Eng. Text Soc. xxxii (1868).

Hall, Hubert. *Society in the Elizabethan Age* (1901).

Hoskins, W.G. *The Rebuilding of Rural England* (see 17th Century, below).

Rowse, A.L. *The England of Elizabeth* (1950).

Stratton, C.R. *The English Manor in the time of Elizabeth.* Wilts Arch. & Nat. Hist. Mag. xxxii 1902. pp. 288-310.

Were, S.L. *The Elizabethan Parish* (1882).

Williamson, J.A. *The Tudor Age* (1953).

17th Century

Ashley, M. *England in the 17th Century* (Pelican History of England V) (1952).

Barley, M.W. *Farmhouses and Cottages 1550-1725.* Ec. Hist. Rev. VII p. 291 (1955).

Bryant, A. *The England of Charles II* (1934).

Clark, G.N. *The Later Stuarts* (1934).

Clark, Alice. *The Working Life of Women in the 17th Century* (1919

Davis, G. *The Early Stuarts* (1937).

Hole, Christina. *The English Housewife in the 17th Century* (1953)

Hoskins, W.G. *The Rebuilding of Rural England 1570-1640.* Past and Present iv (1953). pp. 44-56.

Morpurgo, J.E. *Life Under the Stuarts* (1950).

Notestein, W. *The English People on the Eve of Colonization 1603-1630* (1954).

Notestein, W. *The English Woman, 1580-1625* in *Studies in Social History* by J.H. Plumb (1955) pp. 69-107.

Ogg, D. *England in the Reigns of James II and William III* (1955).

Sydney, W.C. *Social Life in England from the Restoration to the Revolution (1660-1690)* (1892).

Trevor-Roper, H.R. *The General Crisis of the 17th Century.* Past and Present XVI (1959).

Trotter, E. *17th Century Life in a Country Parish* (1919).

18th Century

Ashton, T.S. *Economic History of England – the 18th Century* (1955).

Bayne-Powell, Rosamund. *Housekeeping in the 18th Century* (1956).

Bayne-Powell, Rosamund. *English Country Life in the 18th Century* (1935).

Cole, G.D.H. & Postgate, R. *The Common People 1746-1946* (1962).

Fussell, G.E. *Village Life in the 18th Century* (1947).

Gaunt, W. *English Rural Life in the 18th Century* (1925).

George, M.D. *England in Transition: Life and Work in the 18th Century* (1953).

George, M.D. *London Life in the 18th Century* (1925).

Gilboy, M. *Wages in England in the 18th Century* (1934).

Harris, R.W. *England in the 18th Century 1689-1793* (1963).

Hughes, E. *North Country Life in the 18th Century. The North-East 1700-1750* (1952). *The North West* (1965).

Marshall, D. *English People in the 18th Century* (1956).

Martin, G.W. *The Secret People: English Village Life after 1750* (1954).

Mills, D. *English Villages in the 18th & 19th Centuries.* Amat. Hist. Vol. 6. No. 8. p. 271 (Summer 1965). Vol.7 No.1 (1966) p.7.

Moffitt, W.L. *England on the Eve of the Industrial Revolution* (1963).

Plumb, J.H. *England in the 18th Century.* Pelican History of England VI (1950).

Spalding, E.H. *England: A Social and Economic History 1760-1830* (1956).

Turberville, A.S. *Johnson's England* (1933).

Turberville, A.S. *English Men and Manners in the 18th Century* (1925).

19th Century

Bovill, E.W. *English Country Life 1780-1830* (1962).

Bowley, A.L. *Wages in the 19th Century* (1900).

Cobbett, W. *Rural Rides* (ed. Pitt Cobbett, 1893).

Cole, G.D.H. & Postgate, R. *The Common People, 1746-1946* (1962).

Cornish, F.W. *History of the English Church in the 19th Century.* Pts. 1 & 2 (1910).

Court, W.H.B. *A Concise Economic History of Britain from 1750 to Recent Times* (1954).

Derry, T.K. and Jarman, T.L. *The Making of Modern Britain: Life and Work from George III to Elizabeth II* (1956).

Dodds, J.W. *The Age of Paradox 1841-1851* (1953).

Fay, C.R. *Great Britain from Adam Smith to the Present Day* (1928 revd. 1950).

Fay, C.R. *Life and Labour in the 19th Century* (1920).

Fay, C.R. *The Corn Laws and Social England* (1932).

Finer, S.E. *The Life and Times of Edward Chadwick* (1952).

Gregg, Pauline. *A Social and Economic History of Britain 1760-1960* (1962).

Halévy, E. *History of the English People* [from 1815] (1925) repr. in Penguin.

Hammond, J.L. and Barbara. *The Age of the Chartists 1832-1854* (1930).

Hartwell, R.M. *The Rising Standard of Living in England 1800-1850.* Ec. Hist. Rev. 2nd Ser. 13. No. 3 (Apr. 1961).

Hobsbawm, E.J. *Economic Fluctuations and Social Movements since 1800.* Ec. Hist. Rev. 2nd Ser. Vol. 5. No. 1 (1952).

Hobsbawm, E.J. and Hartwell, R.M. *The Standard of Living during the Industrial Revolution. A Discussion.* Ec. Hist. Rev. 2nd Ser. XVI 1 (1963).

Howitt, W. *The Rural Life of England* (1838) 2 vols.

Lochead, Marion. *The Victorian Household* (1964).

Neale, R.S. *The Standard of Living 1780-1844. A Regional and Class Study.* Ec. Hist. Rev. 2nd Ser. XIX. No. 3. Dec. 1966. p. 590.

Porter, G.R. & Hurst, F.W. *The Progress of the Nation* (1912).

Reader, W.J. *Life in Victorian England* (1964).

Redford, A. *The Economic History of England 1760-1860* (1931 new edn. 1960).

Taylor, A.J. *Progress and Poverty in Britain, 1780-1850.* History XLV. No. 153 (Feb. 1960) p. 16.

Thomson, D. *England in the 19th Century.* Pelican History of England VII (1950).

White, R.J. *Life in Regency England* (1963).

Williams, J. E. *The British Standard of Living 1750-1850.* Ec. Hist. Rev. 2nd Ser. XIX. No. 3. Dec. 1966. p. 581.

Woodward, Sir E. Ll. *The Age of Reform.* 1815-1870 (1938).

Young, G. M. (ed) *Early Victorian England 1830-1865* (1934).

Young, G. M. *Victorian England – Portrait of an Age* (Repr. 1936).

Aristocracy and Gentry

General

Buckatzch, E. J. *The Geographical Distribution of Wealth in England, 1086-1843.* Ec. Hist. Rev. 2nd Ser. III (1950-1) p. 180.

Garnier, R. M. *History of the English Landed Interest.* 2 vols. (1892).

Hollingsworth, T. H. *A Demographic Study of British Ducal Families, 1330-1954.* Population Studies, July 1956. pp. 4-26.

Hollingsworth, T. H. *The Demography of the British Peerage.* Suppl. to Population Studies XVIII. No. 2 (1965).

Thompson, F. M. L. *The Social Distribution of Landed Property in England since the 16th Century.* Ec. Hist. Rev. 2nd Ser. XIX. No. 3 (Dec. 1966) p. 505.

Wingfield, Stratford, E. *The Squire and his Relations* (1956).

16th and 17th Centuries

Batho, G. R. *The Finances of an Elizabethan Nobleman: Henry Percy, Ninth Earl of Northumberland.* Ec. Hist. Rev. 2nd Ser. IX (1956-7). p. 433.

Coleman, D. C. *The Gentry Controversy and the Aristocracy in Crisis 1558-1641.* History LI. No. 172 (June 1960).

Cornwall, J. *The Early Tudor Gentry.* Ec. Hist. Rev. 2nd Ser. XVII No. 3 (Apr. 1965) p. 456.

Cooper, J. P. *The Counting of Manors.* Ec. Hist. Rev. 2nd Ser. VIII (1955-6) p. 377. [Questions statistical methods of Tawney and Stone].

Ditchfield, P. H. *The Errors of Lord Macaulay in his estimation of the squires and parsons of the 17th Century.* Trans. Royal Hist. Soc. 3rd Ser. IX (1915).

Goode, W. J. *Marriage among the English Nobility in the 16th & 17th Centuries: A Comment.* Comparative Studies in Society and History III. 1960-1.

Grant, Jennifer. *The Gentry of London in the Reign of Charles I.*
Univ. of Birmingham Hist. Journ. VIII. No. 2 (1962) p. 197.
[Based on Heralds' Visitations].

Kerridge, E. *The Movement of Rent 1540-1640.* Ec. Hist. Rev. 2nd
Ser. VI. No. 1 (1953).

Mercer, E. *The Houses of the Gentry.* Past and Present V (May 1954).
p. 11.

Mousley, J.E. *The Fortunes of Some Gentry Families of Elizabethan
Sussex.* Ec. Hist. Rev. 2nd Ser. XI No. 3. 467-483 (1960).

Simpson, A. *The Wealth of the Gentry 1540-1660.* East Anglian
Studies (1961).

Stone, L. *Anatomy of the Elizabethan Aristocracy.* Ec. Hist. Rev.
1st Ser. XVIII (1948) 1-53.

Stone, L. *The Elizabethan Aristocracy – a Restatement.* Ec. Hist.
Rev. 2nd Ser. IV (1952) 301-21.

Stone, L. *Crisis of the Aristocracy 1558-1641* (1965).

Stone, L. *Marriage among the English Nobility in the 16th and 17th
Centuries.* Comp. Studies in Society and History III. 1960-1.

Tawney, R.H. *The Rise of the Gentry 1558-1640.* Ec. Hist. Rev. 1st
Ser. XI (1941) 1-38.

Tawney, R.H. *The Rise of the Gentry: a Postscript.* Ec. Hist. Rev.
2nd Ser. VII (1954) 91-98.

Trevor-Roper, H.R. *The Elizabethan Aristocracy – an Anatomy
Anatomised.* Ec. Hist. Rev. 2nd Ser. III (1951) 279.

Trevor-Roper, H.R. *The Gentry 1540-1640.* Ec. Hist. Rev. Supplement
(1953).

Trevor-Roper, H.R. *The General Crisis of the 17th Century.* Past &
Present XVI (1959). [Detailed discussion of this in Past &
Present XVIII (1960)].

Welch, C.E. *Sussex Gentry in 1630.* Sussex N & Q. XV. No. 2 (1963).

Woodward, W.A. *The Countryman's Jewel: Days in the Life of a 16th
Century Squire* (1934).

Zagorin, P. *The Social Interpretation of the English Revolution.*
Journ. Econ. Hist. XIX Sept. 1959. No. 3. p. 376.

18th and 19th Centuries

Habbakuk, H.J. *English Landownership 1680-1740.* Ec. Hist. Rev. 2nd
Ser. X (1940).

Mingay, G.E. *English Landed Society in the 18th Century* (1963).

Plumb, J.H. *Nobility and Gentry in the Early 18th Century.* History
Today V (1955).

Spring, D. *English Landed Society in the 18th and 19th Centuries.*
Ec. Hist. Rev. 2nd Ser. XVII No. 1 (Aug. 1964) p. 146.

Spring, D. *The English Landed Estate in the 19th Century: its
Administration* (1963).

Thompson, F.M.L. *English Landed Society in the 19th Century* (1963).

Thompson, F.M.L. *English Great Estates in the 19th Century 1790-
1914.* In *First International Conference of Economic History:
Contributions and Communications* (1960).

Yeomen and Farmers

General

Barley, M.W. *The English Farmhouse and Cottage* (1961).

Fussell, G.E. and K.R. *The English Countryman: His Life and Work
1500-1900* (1955).

Fussell, G.E. and K.R. *The English Countrywoman: A Farmhouse
Social History 1500-1900* (1953).

Hoskins, W.G. *The Midland Peasant: The Economic and Social History
of a Leicestershire Village* (1957).

Hoskins, W.G. *Farmhouses and History.* History Today X (1960).

Massingham, H.J. *The English Countryman* (1942).

Slater, Dr. G. *English Peasantry and the Enclosures* (1908).

Tate, W.E. *The English Village Community and the Enclosure
Movements* (1967).

16th and 17th Centuries

Barley, M.W. *Farmhouses and Cottages 1550-1725.* Ec. Hist. Rev. 2nd
Ser. VII (1954-5) p. 291.

Campbell, M.C. *The English Yeoman under Elizabeth and the early
Stuarts* (1942 reprint. 1960.) [A very comprehensive work. For
the few sources not covered see its review by W.G. Hoskins.
Ec. Hist. Rev. 1st series Vol. 14. p. 193 (1944)].

Kerridge, E. *The Movement of Rent 1540-1640.* Ec. Hist. Rev. 2nd
Ser. VI. No. 1 (1953).

Savine, A. *English Customary Tenure in the Tudor Period.* Quart.
Journ. Econ. XIX (1904-5) pp. 33-80.

18th and 19th Centuries

Chambers, J.D. *Enclosure and the Small Landowner.* Ec. Hist. Rev.
1st Ser. X. No. 2 (Nov. 1940) p. 118.

Davies, E. *The Small Landowner 1780-1832 in the light of the Land Tax Assessments*. Ec. Hist. Rev. I. No. I (1927) 87-113.

Johnson, A.H. *The Disappearance of the Small Landowner* (1964).

Lavrovsky, V.M. *Tithe Commutation as a Factor in the Gradual Decrease of Land Ownership by the English Peasantry*. Ec. Hist. Rev. 1st Ser. IV. No. 3 (Oct. 1933) p. 273.

Lavrovsky, V.M. *Expropriation of the Peasantry in the 18th Century*. Ec. Hist. Rev. 2nd Ser. Vol. IX No. 2 (Dec 1956) p.271.

Mingay, G.E. *The Land Tax Assessments and the Small Landowner* [1780-1815]. Ec. Hist Rev. 2nd Ser. XVII. No. 2 (Dec. 1964) p.381.

The Poor

General

Ashcroft, P.F. & Thomas, A. Preston. *The English Poor Law System* (1888).

Burrows, Sir G. *Settlement Cases* (1768).

Davey, H. *Poor Law Settlement and Removal* (1925).

Fussell, G.E. *The English Rural Labourer* (1949).

Garnier, R.M. *Annals of the British Peasantry* (1895).

Gash, N. *Rural Unemployment 1815-34*. Ec. Hist. Rev. VI. No. 1 (Oct. 1935) pp. 90-93.

Hampson, E.M. *The Treatment of Poverty in Cambridgeshire 1597-1834* (1934).

Hampson, E.M. *Settlement and Removal in Cambridgeshire 1602-1834*. Camb. Hist. Journ. Vol. II. pp. 273-7 (1928).

Hasbach, W. (transl. by R. Kenyon). *History of the English Agricultural Labourer* (1908).

Hobsbawm, E.J. *Labouring Men* (1964).

Ketchley, C.P. *Vagrancy*. Amat. Hist. Vol. 2, No. 10 (Feb.-Mar. 1956).

Ketchley, C.P. *Settlement and its Legal Definition*. Amat. Hist. Vol. 2. No. 9 (Dec-Jan 1956).

Leonard, E.M. *History of English Poor Relief* (1900).

Melling, Elizabeth. *Kentish Sources IV. The Poor* (1964).

Nicholls, Sir. G. *History of English Poor Law*. 2 vols (1854) new ed. 1898/9).

Ribton-Turner, C.J. *History of Vagrants and Vagrancy* (1887).

Rodgers, J.T. *Six Centuries of Work and Wages* (1890).

Webb, S. & B. *English Poor Law History*. 3 vols (1927-9. reprinted 1963).

16th and 17th Centuries

Aydelotte, F. *Elizabethan Rogues and Vagabonds* (1913).

Elton, G. R. *An Early Tudor Poor Law.* Ec. Hist. Rev. 2nd Ser. 6 (1953-4) p. 55.

Emmison, F. G. *Poor Relief in Two Rural Parishes in Bedfordshire 1563-98.* Ec. Hist. Rev. Vol. III (1931).

Emmison, F. G. *The Care of the Poor in Elizabethan Essex.* Essex Rev. LXII.

Pound, J. F. *An Elizabethan Census of the Poor* [treatment of the poor in Norwich. Contains useful statistics] Univ. of Birmingham Hist. Journ. VIII No. 2 (1962) p. 155.

Styles, P. *The Evolution of the Law of Settlement.* Univ. of Birmingham Hist. Journ. IX No. 1 (1963) p. 33.

18th and 19th Centuries

Ashton, Thomas S. *The Standard of Life of the Workers in England 1790-1830.* Journ. Econ. Hist. IX (1949) Suppl. pp. 19-38.

Blaug, M. *The Myth of the Old Poor Law and the Making of the New.* Journ. Econ. Hist. XXIII (1963).

Blaug, M. *The Poor Law Report Re-examined.* Journ. Econ. Hist. XXIV (June 1964) p. 229.

Briggs, A. *Chartist Studies* (1959).

Burrows, Sir G. *Settlement Cases* (1768).

Cole, G. D. H. *A Short History of the British Working-Class Movement 1789-1947* (1948).

Cole, G. D. H. & Postgate, R. *The Common People 1746-1938* (1938).

Cuttle, G. *The Legacy of the Rural Guardians* (1934).

Davey, H. *Poor Law Settlement and Removal* (3rd edn. 1925).

Emmison, F. G. *Relief of the Poor at Eaton Socon, Beds. 1706-1834.* Beds. Hist. Rec. Soc. Pubs. (1933).

Gilboy, M. *Wages in England in the 18th Century* (1934).

Hammond, J. L. *The Industrial Revolution and Discontent.* Ec. Hist. Rev. II. No. 2 (1930) pp. 215-28.

Hammond, J. L. & B. *The Town Labourer 1760-1832* (1925).

Hammond, J. L. & B. *The Age of the Chartists 1832-1854* (1930).

Hammond, J. L. & B. *The Village Labourer 1760-1832.* 4 vols (4th edn. 1948).

Hammond, J. L. & B. *The Skilled Labourer 1760-1832* (1920).

Hobsbawm, E. J. *The British Standard of Living 1790-1850.* Ec. Hist. Rev. 2nd Ser. X (1957) pp. 46-61.

Hovell, Mark. *The Chartist Movement* (1918).

Inglis, K. S. *Churches and the Working Classes in Victorian England* (1963).

Jones, E. L. *The Agricultural Labour Market in England 1793-1872.* Ec. Hist. Rev. 2nd Ser. XVII. No. 2 (Dec. 1964) p. 322.

Kerr, B. *The Dorset Agricultural Labourer 1750-1850.* Proc. Dorset. Nat. Hist. & Arch. Soc. 84 (1963).

Ketchley, C. P. *Settlement and its Legal Definition.* Amat. Hist. Vol. 2. No. 9 (Dec-Jan 1956).

Leone, Levi. *Wages and Earnings of the Working Classes* (1867).

Lewis, R. A. *Edwin Chadwick and the Railway Labourers.* Ec. Hist. Rev. 2nd Ser. 2 (1950-1) p. 107.

Marshall, D. *The Old Poor Law.* Ec. Hist. Rev. 1st. Ser. Vol. III. No. 1 (Nov. 1937) p. 38.

Marshall, D. *English Poor in the 18th Century* (1926).

Marshall, J.D. *The Lancashire Rural Labourer in the Early 19th Century.* Trans. Lancs. & Ches. Antiqn. Soc. LXXI (1963).

Mayhew, H. *London Labour and the London Poor* (1850) abridged by P. Quennell in 3 vols. *'Mayhew's Characters', 'Mayhew's London' 'London's Underworld'* (1951).

Pelling, H. *Religion and the 19th Century British Working Class,* Past and Present 27 (1964).

Redford, A. *Labour Migration in England 1800-1850* (1964).

Roberts, D. *How Cruel was the Victorian Poor Law?* Historical Journ VI (1963).

Simon, B. *Studies in the History of Education 1780-1870* (1960). [The emphasis is on the impact of education on the working class].

Taylor, A.J. *Progress and Poverty in Britain 1780-1850. A reappraisal.* History XLV. No. 153 (Feb. 1960).

Agriculture

General

Curtler, W.H.R. *A Short History of English Agriculture* (1909).

Curtler, W.H.R. *The Enclosure and Redistribution of our Land* (1920).

Ernle, Lord (Prothero, R.E.) *The Land & its People* (1925).

Ernle, Lord (Prothero, R.E.) *English Farming Past & Present* (5th edn. 1936).

Franklin, T.B. *History of Agriculture* (1948).

Fussell, G.E. *The Old English Farming Books 1523-1730* [a critical bibliography] (1947).

Fussell, G.E. *More Old English Farming Books from Tull to the Board of Agriculture* (1950).

Gonner, E.K.C. *Common Land & Inclosure* (1912).

Gray, H.L. *English Field Systems*. (Harvard Hist. Studies xxii, 1915).

Hoskins, W.G. *Essays in Leicestershire History* (1950). [important for effects of enclosure and the fate of the yeoman].

Orwin, C.S. *English Farming Past & Present* (1949).

Riston, A.G. & Witney, D. *Hooton Pagnell. The Agrarian Evolution of a Yorkshire Village* (1934).

Rodgers, J. Thorold. *History of Agriculture & Prices in England* (1882).

Slater, Dr. G. *English Peasantry and the Enclosure of the Common Fields* (1907).

Tate, W.E. *The English Village Community and the Enclosure Movements* (1967).

Thirsk, J. *Content and Sources of English Agrarian History after 1500*. Agric. Hist. Rev. Vol. iii (1955). Lincs. Hist. ii (1955) 31-44.

Thirsk, J. *English Peasant Farming. The Agrarian History of Lincolnshire from Tudor to Recent Times* (1957).

Thirsk, J. *The Common Fields*. Past and Present 29 (1964).

16th & 17th Centuries

Leonard, G.M. *Inclosure of Common Fields in the 17th Century*. (Trans. Royal Hist. Soc. N.S. Vol. 19. 1905).

Orwin, C.S. & C.S. *Open Fields* (2nd edn. 1954).

Tawney, R.H. *The Agrarian Problem in the 16th Century* (1912).

Thirsk, J. *Tudor Enclosures* (Hist. Assoc. Pamphlet 1958).

Thirsk, J. (ed) *The Agrarian History of England and Wales.* Vol.4 (Tudor Period) (1967).

18th & 19th Centuries

Adams, L.P. *Agricultural Depression and Farm Relief in England 1813-1852* (1932).

Chambers, J.D. *Enclosure and the Small Landowner*. Ec. Hist. Rev. 1st Ser. X. No. 2 (Nov. 1940) p. 118.

Chambers, J.D. *Enclosure and Labour Supply during the Industrial Revolution*. Ec. Hist. Rev. 2nd. Ser. V. No. 3 (1953).

Franklin, T.B. *Enclosures in the Nineteenth Century*. Amat. Hist. Vol.1. No.6 June – July 1953.

Hunt, H. G. *Landownership and Enclosure.* Ec. Hist. Rev. 2nd Ser. Xl (1958-9) p. 497.

John, A. H. *The Course of Agricultural Change 1660-1760* in *Studies in the Industrial Revolution.* ed. L. S. Pressnell (1960).

Jones, E. L. *English Farming before and during the Nineteenth Century.* Econ. Hist. Rev. 2nd. Ser. XV. No. 1 (Aug. 1962) p.145.

Mingay, G. E. *The Size of Farms in the 18th Century.* Ec. Hist. Rev. 2nd. Ser. 14. No. 1 (Aug. 1961) p. 71.

Parker, R. A. C. *Enclosures in the 18th Century.* Hist. Assoc. Aids for Teachers.

Slater, Dr. G. *The English Peasantry & the Enclosure of the Common Fields* (1907).

Tate, W. E. *Enclosure Awards and Acts.* Short Guides to Records 14. History LI. No. 172 (June 1966).

Tate, W. E. *The English Village Community and the Enclosure Movements* (1967).

Towns, Trade and Industry

The majority of the General works listed above deal with aspects of Industry, and especially with the Industrial Revolution. Further works will be found in the bibliographies compiled by T. S. Ashton, Judith Williams and Pargellis & Medley. Some of the more important works on particular industries are listed by Philip A. M. Taylor (see below) p. 89.

General

Chaloner, W. H. *People and Industries* (1963).

Nef, J. U. *Cultural Foundations of Industrial Civilization* (1958).

Thirsk, J. *Industries in the Countryside* in *Essays in Honour of R.H. Tawney* (1961).

16th and 17th Centuries

Hoskins, W. G. *English Provincial Towns in the early 16th Century.* Trans. Royal Hist. Soc. 5th Ser. VI (1956) pp. 1-19.

Nef, J. U. *The Progress of Technology and the Growth of Large-Scal Industry in Great Britain 1540-1640.* Ec. Hist. Rev. V. No. 1 (1934).

18th and 19th Centuries

Ashton, T. S. *The Industrial Revolution* (1948).

Beales, H. L. *The Industrial Revolution 1750-1850, an Introductory Essay.*

Bythell, D. *The Handloom Weavers in the English Cotton Industry during the Industrial Revolution. Some Problems.* Ec. Hist. Rev. 2nd Ser. XVII No. 2 (Dec 1964) p. 339.

Clark, G.N. *The Idea of the Industrial Revolution* (1953).

Coleman, D.C. *The Domestic System in Industry* (1960).

Collier, F. *The Family Economy of the Working Class in the Cotton Industry 1784-1833* (1965).

Hammond, J.L. & B. See *The Poor - 18th & 19th Centuries,* above p.415.

Hartwell, R.M. *Interpretations of the Industrial Revolution in England.* Journ. Econ. Hist. XIX. No. 2 (1959).

Hoffmann, W. *British Industry 1700-1850* (English Translation 1955).

Mann, Julia de L. *The Cotton Trade and Industrial Lancashire 1600-1780* (1931).

Mantoux, P. *The Industrial Revolution* (English Translation, 1928).

Mayhew, H. See *The Poor - 18th & 19th Centuries,* above p.416.

Moir, E.A.L. *The Industrial Revolution - A Romantic View.* History Today IX 9 (1959).

Pinchbeck, Ivy. *Women Workers and the Industrial Revolution* (1930).

Taylor, Philip A.M. (ed) *The Industrial Revolution in Britain. Triumph or Disaster?* (1958).

Wood, H.T. *Industrial England in the Middle of the 18th Century.*

Other Occupations

Clergy and Parish Officers

Brooks, F.W. *The Social Position of the Parson in the 16th Century.* Journ. Brit. Arch. Assoc. 3rd Ser. X (1945-7).

Ditchfield, P.H. *The Old Time Parson* (1908).

Ditchfield, P.H. *The Parish Clerk* (1913).

Foster, Canon. *The State of the Church in the Reigns of Elizabeth and James I.* Lincoln Rec. Soc. 23 (1926).

Hart, A.T. *The 18th Century Country Parson* [c. 1689-1830] (1955).

Hart, A.T. *The Country Priest in English History* (1959).

Hartridge, R.A.R. *A History of Vicarages in the Middle Ages* (1930).

Johnson, W. Branch. *The Parish Constable in 1830.* Amat. Hist. Vol. IV. No. 8 (Summer 1960) p. 325.

Mayo, C.H. *The Social Status of the Clergy in the 17th & 18th Centuries.* Eng. Hist. Rev. XXXVII (Apr. 1922).

Prideaux, H. *Practical Guide to the Duties of Churchwardens* (16th edn. 1895).

Savidge, A. *The Parsonage in England* (1964).

Professions

Hamilton, Bernice. *The Medical Professions in the 18th Century.* Ec. Hist. Rev. 2nd Ser. IV. No. 2 (1951) p. 141.

Ives, E.W. *The Reputation of the Common Lawyer in English Society 1450-1550.* Univ. of Birmingham Hist. Journal VII. No. 2 (1960) p. 130.

Robson, R. *The Attorney in 18th Century England* (1959).

Servants

Hecht, J.J. *The Domestic Servant Class in 18th Century England* (1956).

Ketchley, C.P. *The Law as to Servants in the 18th Century.* Amat. Hist. II. No. 11 (Apr/May 1956).

Marshall, D. *The English Domestic Servant in History* (1949).

Marshall, D. *The Domestic Servants of the 18th Century.* Economica IX (1929) 15-40.

Others

Lewis, R.A. *Edwin Chadwick and the Railway Labourers.* Ec. Hist. Rev. 2nd. Ser. II (1950-1) p. 107.

Robins, F.W. *The Smith* (1954).

Stern, W.M. *The Porters of London* (1960).

Historical Demography

Bibliography

Eldridge, H.T. *The Materials of Demography. A Selected and Annotated Bibliography* (1951 revd. E. Grebenik 1959).

Wrigley, E.A. (ed) *An Introduction to English Historical Demography* pp. 241-263.

General

Brownlee, *The History of the Birth and Death Rates in England and Wales taken as a whole from 1570 to the present time.* Pub. Health xxix (1915-16) 211-22, 228-38.

Buckatzsch, E.J. *The Constancy of Local Populations and Migration in England before 1800.* Pop. Studies V. Pt. 1 (Jan 1951) p. 6?

Chambers, J.D. *The Vale of Trent 1670-1890.* Ec. Hist. Rev. Suppl No. 3.

Cipolla, Carlo. *The Economic History of World Population* (1962).

Coale, A. J. & others. *Aspects of the Analysis of Family Structure* (1965).

Drake, M. *An Elementary Exercise in Parish Register Demography.* Ec. Hist. Rev. 2nd Ser. 14 (Apl. 1962) pp. 427-45.

Goode, W. J. *World Revolution and Family Patterns* (1963).

Glass, D. V. (ed) *Social Mobility in Britain* (1954).

Glass, D. V. and Eversley, D. E. C. (eds)*Population in History* (1965).

Goubert, P. *Beauvais et le Beauvaisis de 1600 à 1730* (Paris 1959).

Greenwood, Major. *English Death Rates, Past, Present and Future.* Royal Stat. Journ. New Ser. XLIX (1936) 674-707.

Hollingsworth, T. H. *A Demographic Study of the British Ducal Families, 1330-1954.* Population Studies (July 1956) pp. 4-26.

Hollingsworth, T. H. *The Demography of the British Peerage.* Suppl. to Population Studies xviii. No. 2 (1965).

Hoskins, W. G. *Local History in England* (1959). Chap. X. Health, Disease and Population. pp. 139-152.

Hoskins, W. G. *The Population of an English Village 1086-1801.* Trans. Leics. Arch. & Hist. Soc. Vol. XXXIII (1957).

Krause, J. T. *Some Implications of Recent work in Historical Demography.* Comp. St. Soc. Hist. 1 (1958) 164-188.

Langer, W. L. *Europe's Initial Population Explosion.* Amer. Hist. Rev. XIX i 1963.

Laslett, P. *The World We Have Lost* (1965). [Describes some of the conclusions reached as a result of demographic studies on Parish Registers. Detailed criticism in *The Historical Journal.* Vol. 9 (1966) pp. 374-379.]

Ohlin, G. *Mortality, Marriage and Growth in Pre-Industrial Populations.* Pop. Studies XIV (1961).

Rehfisch, F. *Marriage and the Elementary Family among the Scottish Tinkers.* Scottish Studies VII (1961).

Thirsk, Joan. *The Family.* Past & Present 27 (1964).

Thirsk, Joan. *Sources of Information on Population.*Amat. Hist. IV Nos. 4 and 5 (1959) 129-33 and 182-5.

Tontain, J. C. *La Population de la France de 1700 à 1959.* Pub. in Bull. de l'Institut de Science Economique Appliquée. Suppl. No. 133. Jan. 1963. Ser. AF. No. 3.

Tucker, G. S. L. *English Pre-Industrial Population Trends.* Ec. Hist. Rev. 2nd Ser. XVI. No. 2 (1963).

Wrigley, E. A. (ed) *An Introduction to English Historical Demography* (1966). [The first publication of the Cambridge Group for the History of Population and Social Structure.]

Wrigley, E. A. *Parish Registers & Population History I & II.* Amat. Hist. VI. Nos 5 & 6 (Autumn 1964, Spring 1965).

Wrigley, E.A. *Family Limitation in Pre-Industrial England.* Ec. Hi
Rev. 2nd Ser. XIX (1966) pp. 82-109.

Mediaeval

Bean, J.M.W. *Plague, Population and Decline in the Later Middle
Ages.* Ec. Hist. Rev. 2nd Ser. 15. No. 3 (Apl. 1963) p. 423.

Hallam, H.E. *Some Thirteen Century Censuses.* Ec. Hist. Rev. 2nd
Ser. 10 (1957-8) p. 343.

Hallam, H.E. *Population Density in Mediaeval Fenland.* Ec. Hist.
Rev. 2nd Ser. 14. No. 1 (Aug. 1961) p. 71.

Harley, J.B. *Population Trends and Agricultural Developments from
the Warwickshire Hundred Rolls of 1279.* Ec. Hist. Rev. 2nd
Ser. 11 (1958-9) p. 8.

Harley, J.B. *The Hundred Rolls of 1279.* Amat. Hist. V.1 (1961).

Postan, M.M. *Some Economic Evidence of Declining Population in th
later Middle Ages.* Ec. Hist. Rev. 2nd Ser. II (1950) p. 236.

Russell, J.C. *British Mediaeval Population* (U.S.A. 1948).

Russell, J.C. *Late Mediaeval Population Patterns.* Speculum XX.
No. 2 (Apr-1945) pp. 157-171.

Russell, J.C. *Demographic Limitations of the Spalding Serf Lists.*
Ec. Hist. Rev. 2nd Ser. X. No. 1 (Aug. 1962) p. 138.

Russell, J.C. *A Quantitative Approach to the Mediaeval Population
Change.* Journ. Econ. Hist. XXIV (Mar. 1964) No. 1. p. 1.

Titow, J.Z. *Some Evidence of the 13th Century Population Increase.*
Econ. Hist. Rev. 2nd Ser. XIV. No. 2 (Dec. 1961) p. 218.

16th and 17th Centuries

Allison, K.J. *An Elizabethan Village "Census".* Bull. Inst. Hist.
Res. XXXVI (1963).

Brown, E.H. Phelps and Hopkins, Sheila V. *Wage Rates and Prices.
Evidence for Population Pressure in the 16th Century.*
Economica N.S. XXIV (1957) 289-306.

Chambers, J.D. Review of B. Frith's *Gloucestershire Marriage
Allegations* 1637-80. Ec. Hist. Rev. 2nd Ser. 9 (1956-7) p. 145.

Cornwall, J. *A Tudor Domesday. The Musters of 1522.* Journ. Soc.
Archivists III. No. 1 (Apl. 1965).

Cornwall, J. *An Elizabethan Census.* Records of Bucks XVI, 4 (1959)

Garside, B. *People and Homes in Hampton-on-Thames in the 16th and
17th Centuries* (1956).

Glass, D.V. *Gregory King and the Population of England and Wales
at the end of the 17th Century.* Eugenics Review Vol. xxxvii 4
(Jan. 1946) pp. 170-183.

Glass, D.V. *Gregory King's Estimate of the Population of England
and Wales,* 1695. Pop. Stud. iii (1949-50) pp.338-374.

Howson, W. G. *Plague, Poverty and Population in parts of North-West England 1580-1720.* Trans. Hist. Soc. of Lancs. & Chesh. CXII (1961).

Jones, P. E. and Judges, A. V. *The Population of London in the Late 17th Century.* Ec. Hist. Rev. VI (1935-6) p. 45.

Laslett, P. *The Gentry of Kent in 1640.* Camb. Hist. Journ. (1948).

Peyton, S. A. *The Village Population in the Tudor Lay Subsidy Rolls.* Eng. Hist. Rev. XXX (1915) pp. 234-50.

Rich, E. E. *The Population of Elizabethan England.* Econ. Hist. Rev. 2nd Ser. II (1949) pp. 247-265.

Styles, P. *A Census of a Warwickshire Village in 1698.* Univ. of Birmingham Historical Journal. Vol. iii (1951) p. 33.

Tawney, A. J. and R. H. *An Occupational Census of the Seventeenth Century.* Ec. Hist. Rev. 1st Ser. V. No. 1 (Oct. 1934) p. 25.

18th and 19th Centuries

Banks, J. A. *Prosperity and Parenthood. A Study of Family Planning among the Victorian Middle Classes* (1954).

Banks, J. A. and Olive. *Feminism and Family Planning in Victorian England* (1964).

Bartel, R. *Suicide in 18th Century England. The Myth of a Reputation.* Huntingdon Lib. Quart. XXIII. 2 (1960).

Blacker, J. G. C. *Social Ambitions of the Bourgeoisie in 18th Century France and their Relation to Family Limitation.* Pop. Studies XI. Pt. 1. p. 46.

Buer, M. C. *Health, Wealth and Population in the Early Days of the Industrial Revolution* (1926).

Chambers, J. D. *Population Change in Nottingham 1700-1800* in *Studies in the Industrial Revolution* (1960).

Caminos, P. T. *Late Victorian Sexual Respectability and the Social System.* Intern. Rev. Social Hist. VIII (1963).

Eversley, D. E. C. *A Survey of Population in an Area of Worcestershire from 1660-1850 on the Basis of Parish Registers.* Pop. Studies X (1957) pp. 253-279.

Eversley, D. E. C. *Mortality in Britain in the 18th Century: Problems and Prospects.* Conference on Historical Demography. Paper 20 (Liège 1963).

Glass, D. V. *The Population Controversy in 18th Century England.* Pop. Stud. VI (1952-3) pp. 69-91.

Gonner, E. C. K. *The Population of England in the 18th Century* Journ. Roy. Stat. Soc. lxxvi (1913) pp. 261-303).

Griffith, G. T. *Population Problems in the Age of Malthus* (1926).

Habbakuk, H. J. *The Economic History of Modern Britain.* Journ. Econ. Hist. XVIII (1939) [on population since the 18th century].

Habbakuk, H.J. *English Population in the 18th Century*. Econ. Hist. Rev. 2nd Ser. Vol. 6. No. 2 (Dec. 1953) p. 117.

Habbakuk, H.J. *Family Structure and Economic Change in 19th Centu* *Europe*. Journ. Econ. Hist. XV. 1. 1.

Hammond, B.L. *Urban Death Rates in the Early 19th Century*. Econ. Hist. 1 (1926-9) 419-28.

Hammond, J.L. *The Movement of Population during the Industrial Revolution History* XII *(1927)* pp. 146-8).

Hoskins, W.G. *Industry, Trade and People in Exeter 1688-1800* (193

House, J.W. *North-Eastern England: Population Movements and the Landscape since the Early 19th Century* (1956).

Krause, J.T. *Some Neglected Factors in the English Industrial Revolution*. Journ. Econ. Hist. XIX IV (1959).

Krause, J.T. *Changes in English Fertility and Mortality 1781-1850* Ec. Hist. Rev. 2nd Ser. Vol. XI. No. 1 (Aug. 1958) p. 52.

Marshall, T.H. *The Population of England and Wales from the Industrial Revolution to the World War*. Ec. Hist. Rev. 1st Ser Vol. 5. No. 2 (Apr. 1935) p. 65.

Morley, C.D. *Population of Northampton and the Ise Valley 1801-1951*. East Midland Geographer XI (1959).

Redford, A. *Labour Migration in England 1800-1850* (2nd edn. 1964)

Smith, C.T. *The Movement of Population in England and Wales in 1851 and 1861*. Geog. Journ. CXVII (1951).

Sogner, S. *Aspects of the Demographic Situation in 17 Parishes in Shropshire 1711-60*. Population Studies XVII (1963) pp. 126-146

Wrigley, E.A. *Industrial Growth and Population Change. A Regional Study of the Coalfield Areas of North West Europe in the later 19th Century* (1959).

B. HISTORICAL GEOGRAPHY

General

Darby, H.C. (ed) *Historical Geography of England before 1800* (1936 new edn. 1948).

Darby, H.C. *An Historical Geography of England. 20 Years After*. G Journ CXXVI 2 (1960).

East, N.G. *Geography Behind History* (1938).

Hoskins, W.G. *Making of the English Landscape* (1965).

Mitchell, J.B. *Historical Geography* (1954).

Shepherd, W. *The Living Landscape of Britain*.

Trent, C. *The Changing Face of England* (1956).

Ward, E.M. *English Coastal Evolution* (1922).

Towns

Checkland, S.G. *English Provincial Cities* [a bibliographical survey] Ec. Hist. Rev. 2nd Ser. VI. No. 2 (Dec 1953). p. 195.

Savage, Sir. W. *The Making of Our Towns* (1952).

Smailes, A.E. *The Geography of Towns* (1953).

Maps

Baker, A.R.H. *Local History in Early Estate Maps.* Amat. Hist. V. No. 2 (1962) p. 66.

Chubb, T. *Printed Maps and Atlases of Great Britain & Ireland. A Bibliography* (1927).

Gardner, D.E., Harland D. and Smith, F. *A Genealogical Atlas of England & Wales* (1960).

Harley, J.B. *Historian's Guide to Ordnance Survey Maps.* National Council of Social Service (1964).

Harley, J.B. *A Guide to Ordnance Survey Maps as Historical Sources.* Amat. Hist. V Nos 5-8 (1962).

Harley, J.B. *Maps & Plans of Towns.* Amat. Hist. Vol. 7. No. 6 (1967) p. 196. The first of a series of articles of maps for the Local Historian. The others will deal with Estate, Enclosure and Tithe Maps, Transport maps and County & Regional Maps. They will be reprinted in booklet form with an introduction, classified bibliographies and a note on the main map repositories in Britain.]

Institute of Heraldic and Genealogical Studies. County Maps. These show Parish Boundaries, Dioceses, Peculiars etc. and the starting dates of original registers. Most counties are now available.

Lynam, E. *British Maps and Map Makers 1250-1935* (1944).

Taylor, E.G.R. *Speed's Atlas of Tudor England* (1951).

Estate Maps and Surveys. Short Guides to Records 4. History XLVIII No. 162.

Gazetteers

Bartholemew's *Survey Gazetteer of the British Isles* (1932).

Lewis's *Topographical Dictionary of England.* 4 vols (edns 1831, 1833, 1835, 1840, 1842, 1849).

Moule, T. *The English Counties Delineated.* 2 vols (1837).

Place-Names

Place-Name Society. *Introduction to the Study of Place-Names* (1925).

Anderson, O.S. *English Hundred-Names.* 3 vols 1934-9.

Cameron, K. *English Place Names* (1961).

Ekwall, B.O.E. *Oxford Dictionary of English Place-Names* (4th edn. 1966).

Prickard, H.G. *Origin of Farm Names* (Country Life, 1954).

Reaney, P.H. *Origin of English Place-Names* (1960).

Stokes, H.G. *English Place-Names* (1949).

Wainwright, F.T. *Field Names* (Antiquity Vol. 17, 1943).

Transport

Carter, E.F. *A Historical Geography of the Railways of the British Isles* (1959). [An encyclopaedic account arranged chronologically of all the Railways of the British Isles].

De Mare, E. *Canals of England* (1950).

Duckham, B.F. *Transport and the Local Historian.* Amat. Hist. VII. No. 3 (1966) p. 84.

Elliot, Sir. J. *The Early Days of the Southern Railway.* Journal of Transport History IV. No. 4 (1960).

Ellis, C.H. *British Railway History 1830-1947.* 2 vols (1954-9).

Fowkes, E.H. *Railway History and the Local Historian.* East Yorks Local Hist. Soc. Pub. No. 16 (1963).

Hadfield, E. *British Canals* (1950).

Hadfield, E. *Canals of Southern England* (1955).

Hadfield, E. *Canals of South Wales and the Border* (1960).

Harper, C.G. *Stage Coach and Mail Coach.* 2 vols (1903).

Jackman, W.T. *The Development of Transportation in Modern England.* (2nd edn. 1962).

Stenton, F.M. *The Road System of Mediaeval England.* Ec. Hist. Rev. VII. No. 1 (Nov 1936) p. 1.

Thomas, David St. John. *A Regional History of the Railways of Great Britain.* Vol. I. *The West Country* (1960).

White, H.P. *A Regional History of the Railways of Great Britain.* Vol. II *Southern England* (1960).

C. LOCAL HISTORY

Bibliography

Anderson, J.P. *Book of British Topography* (1881).

Checkland, S.G. *English Provincial Cities.* Ec. Hist. Rev. 2nd. Ser. VI. No. 2 (Dec. 1953) p. 195.

Daniell, W.V. & Nudd, F.J. *Manual of British Topography. A Catalogue of County and Local Histories* (1909).

Hoskins, W.G. *Local History in England* (1959) [Useful comments are included on most works mentioned in the text or in the supplementary list].

Humphreys, A. L. *A Handbook to County Bibliography* (1917). A Bibliography of bibliographies relating to the counties and towns of Great Britain and Ireland.

Kuhlicke, F. W. and Emmison, F. G. (ed) *English Local History Handlist*. (Hist. Assoc. Helps for Students of History No. 69. 3rd ed 1965).

Library Association. *Subject Index to Periodicals* (annual 1915-) *Regional lists* (annual 1954-).

Nichols, J. *Bibliotheca Topographia Britannica*. 8 vols. (1780-90). Contd. in *Misc. Antiquities*. 2 vols (1791-1800) includes histories of Manors, Parishes etc.

Nichols, J. G. *Collectanea Topographia et Genealogica*. 8 vols (1834-43) contd. in the *Topographer and Genealogist*. 3 vols (1846-58).

Thompson, A. H. *A Short Bibliography of Local History*. Hist. Assoc. Leaflet No. 72 (London 1928).

Upcott, W. *A Bibliographical Account of the Principal Works relating to English Topography*. 3 vols (1818).

Readers' Guide on the Sources of Local History. Library Assoc. 2nd edn 1959.

Methods, Sources etc.

Armstrong, J. B. and Hopkins, P. G. M. *Local Studies* (1955).

Beresford, M. *History on the Ground* (1957).

Booth, T. and Carnell, H. A. (eds) *Local History in Bedfordshire. A Handbook of Guidance upon Sources and Materials available for Teachers and Historians* (Beds. C. C. 1960).

Celoria, F. *Teach Yourself Local History* (1959).

Clark, G. Kitson. *Guide for Research Students working on Historical Subjects* (1958).

Cox, J. C. *How to Write the History of a Parish* (1879 and edns).

Dale, J. K. *Introducing Local Studies* (1956).

Douch, R. *Local History and the Teacher* (1967).

Douch, R. and Steer, F. W. *Local History Essays. Some Notes for Students* (1960).

Finberg, H. P. R. *The Local Historian and his Theme* (1952).

Galbraith, V. H. *The Historian at Work* (1962).

Hobbs, J. L. *Libraries and the Materials of Local History* (1948).

Hoskins, W. G. *Local History in England* (1959) [The most comprehensive survey of the subject].

Hoskins, W.G. *The Writing of Local History.* History Today Vol. ii (1952).

Humphreys, A.L. *How to Write a Village History* (1930).

Humphreys, D.H. and Emmison, F.G. *Local History for Students* (1965)

Iredale, D. *How Can I Trace the History of My House.* Amat. Hist. Vol. 7. No. 6 (1967) p. 182.

Mills, D. *English Villages in the 18th and 19th Centuries.* 2. A Survey of the Main Types of Source Material. Amat. Hist. Vol. 7. No. 1. (1966) p. 7.

Morris, J.E. and Jordan, H.R. *Introduction to the Study of Local History and Antiquities* (1910).

Powell, W.R. *Local History in Theory and Practice.* Bull. Inst. Hist. Res. Vol. xxxi (1958).

Pugh, R.B. *How to Write a Parish History* (1954) [Based on J.C. Cox but brought up to date].

Wake, Miss J. *How to Compile a History and Present Day Record of Village Life* (1935).

Weaver, F.J. *The Material of English History* (1938).

General

Brown, A.F.J. *English History from Essex Sources 1750-1900* (1952).

Edwards, A.C. *English History from Essex Sources 1550-1750* (1952).

Pevsner, N. (ed) *Buildings of England.* [Volumes have now been published for all English counties]

Royal Commission on Historical Monuments – Inventory Volumes.

Simmons, J. (ed) *A New Survey of England.* Middlesex (1953), Devon (1954).

Tate, W.E. County Handlists of Enclosure Awards.

Victoria County Histories.

Webb, S. & B. *English Local Government.* 8 vols (1906-29).

Parish, Village and Manor

Addy, S.O. *Church and Manor* (1913).

Baker, W.P. *The English Village* (1953).

Banks, F.R. *English Villages* (1963).

Bullard, J.V. *The English Parish and Diocese* (1936).

Cox, J.C. *The English Parish Church* (1914).

Cox, J.C. & Ford, C.B. *The Parish Churches of England* (1935). [An abridgment of the above with additional chapters by C.B. Ford.]

Darton, F.J.H. *English Fabric: A Study of Village Life* (1935).

Ditchfield, P.H. *English Villages* (1901).

Ditchfield, P.H. *The Charm of the English Village* (1908).

Finberg, J. *Exploring Villages* (1958).

Gardiner, C.H. *Your Village and Mine* (1944).

Gras, N.S.B. and E.C. *Economic and Social History of an English Village: Crawley, Hants* (1930).

Havinden, M.A. *Estate Villages. A Study of the Berkshire Villages of Ardington and Lockinge* (1966).

Hone, N.J. *The Manor and Manorial Records* (1925).

Latham, L.C. *The Manor and Village* in G. Barraclough (ed) *Social Life in Early England* (1960).

Levett, Miss A.E. *Studies in Manorial History* (1938. New edn. 1963).

Packington, H. *English Villages and Hamlets* (1936).

Shaw, James. *The Parochial Lawyer* (1833).

Shaw, Joseph. *The Parish Lawyer* (1736).

Smith, Joshua Toulmin. *The Parish* (1854).

Thomson, P.D. *Parish and Parish Church* (1948).

D. BIOGRAPHY

Bibliography

Matthews, W. *British Autobiographies to 1951* (1955).

Matthews, W. *British Diaries 1442-1942*. Univ. of Calif. Press & C.U.P. (1950).

Riches (afds Sutton) Phyllis M. *An Analytical Bibliography of Universal Collected Biography* (1934).

County Biographical Dictionaries 1890-1937. Bull. Inst. Hist. Research XXIV (1961) p. 55.

Methods etc.

Hamilton-Edwards, G.K.S. *Genealogy and Biography*. Gen. Mag XV. p. 68 June 1965.

Iredale, D.A. *Organization of Biographical Material for Use in Village Histories*. Amat. Hist. Vol. 6. No. 5 (Autumn 1964).

Biographical Dictionaries

General

Dictionary of National Biography. 22 vols to 1901. Supplements to 1950. Additions and Corrections in Bulletin of Institute of Hist. Research included in Index to vols 1-25 (1954).

Boase, F, *Modern English Biography*. 6 vols. 1892-1921. reprinted 1965.

Hyamson, A.M. *A Dictionary of Universal Biography* (2nd edn, 1951).

Specialised

Colvin, H.M. *A Biographical Dictionary of English Architects 1660-1840* (1954).

Delany, J. and Tobin, J.E. *Dictionary of Catholic Biography* (1962).

Foster, J. *Alumni Oxonienses*. 8 vols (1887-92).

Foster, J. *Index Ecclesiasticus* [1800-1840] (1890).

Gillow, J. *A Literary and Biographical History or Bibliographical Dictionary of English Catholics*. 5 vols (1885-1902).

Grove, Sir G. *Dictionary of Music and Musicians*. 5th edn 9 vols (1954).

James, G.F. *Collected Naval Biography*. Bull. Inst. Hist Research XV 162 (1937-8)

Judd, G.P. *Members of Parliament 1734-1832* (1955).

Kirk, J. *Biographies of English Catholics in the 18th Century* (ed. J.H. Pollen & E. Burton) (1909).

Ralfe, J. *The Naval Biography of Great Britain*. 4 vols (1828).

Redgrave, S. *Artists of the English Schools* (1878).

O'Byrne, L.R. *A Naval Biographical Dictionary* [of officers serving in 1845] (1849).

O'Byrne, L.R. *Naval Biographical Dictionary*. Vol. I and part of Vol. II (1861).

Slonimsky, N (ed) *Baker's Biographical Dictionary of Musicians* (1958).

Venn, J. & J.A. *Alumni Cantabrigienses*. 10 vols (1922-54).

E. HERALDRY

Boutell, C. *English Heraldry*. rev. by C.W. Scott-Giles and J.P. Brooke-Little (1965).

Burke, Sir J.B. *The General Armory of England, Scotland, Ireland and Wales* (1842. Enlarged edn. 1878. new edn with supplement 1883).

Fox-Davies, A.C. *A Complete Guide to Heraldry* (1961).

Papworth, J.W. & Morant, A.W.W. *Ordinary of British Armorials* (1874). Repr. 1961 with introduction by G.D. Squibb and A.R. Wagner.

Pine, L.G. *Teach Yourself Heraldry and Genealogy* (1957).

Pine, L.G. *Family History from Heraldry*. Amat. Hist. Vol. I. No. 8. Oct/Nov 1953.

Scott-Giles, C.W. *The Romance of Heraldry* (1951).

Summers, P.G. *Harchments*. Amat. Hist. V. No. 5. (Autumn 1962) p. 145.

Wagner, Sir A.R. *Heraldry in England* (1949).

F. GENETICS

Altenburg, E. *Genetics* (1957).

Bacon, J.S.D. *The Science of Heredity* (1951).

Bonner, D.M. & Mills, S.E. *Heredity* (1964).

Encylopaedia Britannica. Article on *Heredity*.

Kallmann, F.J. *Heredity in Health and Mental Disorder* (1955).

Kalmus, H. *Genetics*. (Pelican, 1948).

Macbride, E.W. *An Introduction to the Study of Heredity* (1924).

Mottram, V.H. *The Physical Basis of Personality* (1944).

Mourant, A.E. *Distribution of Human Blood Groups* (1954).

Neel, J.V. & Schull, W.J. *Human Heredity* (1954).

Newman, H.H., Freeman, F.N. & Holzinger, K.J. *Twins – A Study of Heredity & Environment* (1937).

Race, R.C. & Sanger, Ruth. *Blood Groups in Man* (1962).

Ridge, C.H. *Scientific Genealogy*. Gen. Mag. Vol. 11. No. 4 (Dec. 1951).

Ridge, C.H. *How Many Ancestors Have We?* Amat. Hist. Vol. 1. No. 1 (Aug/Sept 1952)

Roberts, J.A.F. *Introduction to Medical Genetics* (1940).

Scheinfeld, A. *You and Heredity* (1952).

Sinnott, E.W., Dunn, L.C., & Dobzhansky, T. *Principles of Genetics* (5th edn. 1958).

Snyder, L.H. & David, P.R. *The Principles of Heredity* (5th edn. 1957).

Stahl, F.W. *The Mechanics of Inheritance* (1964).

Stern, C. *Principles of Human Genetics.* 2nd edn. 1960.

White, H.C. *More Scientific Genealogy.* Gen. Mag. Vol. 11. No. 5 (March 1952).

G. LAW

General

Blackstone, Sir W. *Commentaries on the Laws of England.* 4 vols (1793-95). Esp. Vol. 2 *"The Rights of Things"*. 1811 edn. contains Blackstone's latest corrections.

Halsbury's *Laws of England.* 37 vols. 2nd edn.

Holdsworth, Sir W.S. *History of English Law.* 16 vols (1931-52).

Jacob's *Law Dictionary.* Sets out forms of documents. 1st edn 1729 gives them in Latin. 2nd edn 1736 gives them in English.

Johnson, G.D. *Legal Terms and Phrases.* Amat. Hist. III p. 249 (1957-8).

Madox, T. *Formulare Anglicanum* (1702).

Maitland, F.W. *Forms and Actions at the Common Law* (1936).

Plucknett, T.F.T. *A Concise History of Common Law* (4th edn. 1948)

Potter, H. *An Historical Introduction to English Law and its Institutions* (3rd edn. 1948).

Radcliffe, G.R.Y. and Cross, G. *The English Legal System* (2nd edn Repr. 1948).

Ruegg, Judge. *Elementary Commentary on English Law* (1920).

Tomlin, Sir Thomas. *The Law Dictionary* (many old edns).

Wharton, J. *Law Lexicon* (various edns).

Ecclesiastical Law

Burn, R. *Ecclesiastical Law* (1760).

Cripps, C.A. *A Practical Treatise on the Law Relating to Church and Clergy* (6th edn. 1886).

Dale, W.L. *The Law of the Parish Church* (3rd edn. 1957).

Phillimore, Sir R.J. *Ecclesiastical Law in the Church of England* (2nd edn. 1895).

Law of Names

Linell, A. *The Law of Names, Public, Private and Corporate* (1938).

Marriage Law

Chanter, H. Prosser. *18th Century Marriage Law.* N & Q 22 Aug. 1936 pp. 139-140.

Hammick, J. T. *The Marriage Law of England* (1873. 2nd edn. 1887).

Property Law

Cheshire, G. C. *The Modern Law of Real Property* (7th edn. 1954 pp. 1-104. 8th edn. 1958).

Coke, Sir Edward. *The Complete Copyholder* (1673).

Hargreaves, A. D. *An Introduction to the Principles of Land Law* (3rd edn. 1952).

Holdsworth, Sir W. S. *An Historical Introduction to the Land Law* (repr. 1935).

Megarry, R. E. *Manual of the Law of Real Property* (2nd edn. 1955).

Megarry, R. E. and Wade, H. W. R. *The Law of Real Property* (1957).

Pollock, Sir Frederick. *The Land Laws* (1883 3rd edn. 1896).

Radcliffe, G. R. Y. *Real Property Law* (2nd edn. 1948).

Sandford-Thompson, W. A. C. *A Sidelight on Customary Tenure in the 17th Century.* Gen. Mag. Vol. 5. No. 5 (Mar. 1930) p. 134.

Simpson, A. W. B. *An Introduction to the History of the Land Law* (1961).

Law of Property (Personalty)

Bailey, S. J. *The Law of Wills* (5th edn. 1957).

Mustoe, N. E. *Executors and Administrators* (1952).

Parry, Sir O. H. *Law of Succession, testate or intestate* (3rd edn. 1953).

Vaines, J. C. *Personal Property* (2nd edn.)

Conveyancing

British Records Association Reports from Committees 1938. No. 4 *Cataloguing of Deeds* Part 3. pp. 20-26.

Burnett, J. F. R. *Elements of Conveyancing* (8th edn. 1952). chap. 1.

Foster, Amy G. *Conveyancing Practice from Local Records* (1948).

Pugh, R. B. *Calendar of Antrobus Deeds before 1625.* Wilts Arch. & Nat. Hist. Soc. Records Branch (1947). Introduction. Part III deals with some of main types of conveyancing in family muniments.

Pugh, R.B. *Abstracts of Feet of Fines relating to Wiltshire.....*
Edw. I and Edw. II (1939) Introduction.

Topham, A.F. *Real Property* (10th edn. 1947).

Criminal Law

Radzinowicz, L. *History of English Criminal Law from 1750* (3 vols. 1948-56).

Stephen, Sir J.F. *History of Criminal Law.* 3 vols (1883).

H. TECHNICAL AIDS ETC.

General

Ellis, R. *Select Bibliography of Archive Administration.* Journ. Soc. Archivists II. No. 2. Oct. 1960. p. 67.

Illustrations

Nunn, G.W.A. *British Sources of Photographs and Pictures* (1952).

Priestley, E.A. *Illustrating Local History.* Amat. Hist. Vol. 7. No. 2 (1966).

Document Photography

Bensusan, A.E. *Document Copying.* Amat. Hist. V. No. 2 (1962) p.77.

Born, L.K. *The Literature of Microreproduction 1950-55.* American Documentation. Vol. 7. No. 3 (1956) pp. 167-187.

Bradford, S.C. *Document Photography and Research.* Nature CXCIII (11 March 1939) pp. 393-95.

Burkett, J. *Microrecording in Libraries.* Library Assn. Pamphlet No. 17 (1957).

De Sola, R. *Microfilming* (1944).

Focal Press Ltd. *The Focal Encyclopaedia of Photography* (1956).

Greenwood, H.W. *Document Photography* (1947).

Hartley, W.C.E. *Document Copying.* Amat. Hist. II. p. 311 (Feb/Mar 1956).

Horder, A. (ed) *The Ilford Manual of Photography* (1958).

International Federation for Documentation. *Manual of Document Reproduction and Selection.* 2 vols (1954).

Jenkinson, Sir H. *Microphotography and Archives. A Memorandum from the Public Record Office.* Archivum Vol. 3. 1953. pp. 81-6.

McCrum, B.P. *Microfilms and Microcards, Their Use in Research* (1950).

Smith, A.H. *The Photography of Manuscripts.* London Mediaeval Studies 1. pt. 2 (1938) 179-201. reprinted Univ. Coll. London (1938).

Verry, H.R. *Document Copying and Reproduction Processes* (1958).

Printing

Hamilton-Edwards, G. *The Physical Side of Genealogy.* Gen. Mag. 10. No. 7. Sept. 1948. p. 225.

Minto, C.S. *Reflex Printing.* Library Assoc. Record May & June 1942.

Computers

Dodd, K.N. *Computers* (Pan Books, 1966).

Vine, R.E. *Printing and Indexing Parish Registers by Computer* Gen. Mag. Vol.15. No.12 (Dec. 1967) pp.461-468.

III MAGAZINES AND PERIODICALS

Genealogy

Current

The Genealogists' Magazine 1925 – date.

Family History 1962 – date.

Most of the regional family history societies publish their own
magazines. For a list of these societies see page xxii.

Extinct

The Ancestor. Vols 1-12, 1902-1905.

Collectanea Genealogica. Vols. 1-20, 1881-5. Also 4 vols 1887.

Collectanea Topographica et Genealogica. Vols. 1-8, 1834-43. Then
renamed *Topographer & Genealogist.* Vols. 1-3, 1846-58.

Fragmenta Genealogica. 13 Vols. 1889-1910.

Genealogical Quarterly. (formerly *Genealogical Monthly*).   1913.
1929.   1932–1975.

Genealogical Queries & Memoranda. 1896-1900. 2 Vols.

Genealogical Magazine. 8 Vols, 1897-1904.

The Genealogist. 7 Vols. New Ser. Vols. 1-38 with 5 vols of
supplements 1877-1922.

Genealogists' Reference Journal. 1935-37. 6 parts.

Herald & Genealogist. Vols. 1-8. 1862-74.

Miscellanea Genealogica et Heraldica. 1866-1938. 31 Vols.

The Northern Genealogist. 1895-1903.

The Pedigree Register. 1907-16.

Researches respecting Family History. Nos 1-28. 1866-69.

Archives

Current

Archives (Journal of BRA) 1949 – date.

Journal of the Society of Archivists. 1955-date.

National Register of Archives, *Bulletin* 1948 – date.
Historical Manuscripts Commission, *Reports* 1870 – date.
Council for the Preservation of Business Archives. Publications (Irregular).
Public Record Office. Annual Reports.
Archivum 1951- (An international UNESCO publication).

Extinct

The *British Archivist*. Nos. 1-24. 1913-20.

Monumental Inscriptions

Monumental Brass Soc. *Transactions* 1887-1914, 1935 – date.
Monumental Journal (Formerly *Monumental-Architectural Stone Journal*, then *Monumental and Architectural Journal*) 1934 – date.

General Antiquarian Subjects

Amateur Historian 1952 – date.
Antiquarian Notes 1898-1906.
Antiquarian Communications 1859-1864; then Cambridge Antiquarian Communications 1864-88; then Proc. of Cambridge Antiquarian Soc. 1888-
Antiquarian Magazine and Bibliographer 1882-1885. Then *Walford's Antiquarian* 1885-7.
Society of Antiquaries *Proceedings* 1843-1920. Then became the *Antiquaries Journal* 1921-date.
Journal of the Antiquarian Assoc. of the British Isles 1930-32.
The Antiquary 1880-1915.
Blackmansbury (Notes & Queries for the Genealogist etc.) 1964 – date.
The Manorial Society Monographs 1907-10. *Publications* 1909-29.
Midland Antiquary 1882-1887.
Notes & Queries 1849 – date.
The Reliquary 1860-94. *Reliquary & Illustrated Archaeologist* 1895-1909.
St. James Magazine & Heraldic & Historical Register 1849-50.
The Topographer. 4 vols. 1789-91 (then *Topographia Miscellania* 1791-2, Issue 1821).

Publication of Documents

Anglo-Norman Text Society 1939 – date.

Camden Society (now published by Royal Historical Soc.) 1900 – dat

Chetham Society (Lancs. & Cheshire) 1844-86, 1883-date.

Dugdale Soc. 1921 – Occasional Papers 1924 – date.

Harleian Society. Visitation Section 1869 – date. Parish Register
Section 1877-

Index Society. Occasional Indexes 1885-7. Publications 1878-91.
merged in index Library.

Index Library 1888 – date.

Parish Register Society 1896 onwards. 84 vols.

Pipe Roll Soc. 1884-date.

St. Anthony Hall Publications (renamed *Borthwick Papers*) 1951 – da

Selden Society. Publications 1887 – date.

Thoresby Socy. 1889, 1891 – date.

Thoroton Socy. Record Series 1903 – date. *Transactions* 1898 – date.

History

Annual Bulletin of Historical Literature (Historical Association)
1912-date.

English Historical Review 1886-

History Today 1951 – date.

Bulletin of Institute of Historical Research 1922 – date.

Economic History Review 1927 – date.

Royal Historical Society Transactions 1869-date.

History (Historical Association) 1916-date.

Agricultural History Review 1953-date.

Business History 1958-date.

Historical Journal 1958 – date. (formerly *Cambridge Historical
Journal*)

Past and Present 1952-date.

Population Studies 1947-date.

Journal of Economic History [New York] 1941 – date.

Victorian Studies [Indiana University] 1957 – date.

University of Birmingham Historical Journal 1947-date.

Local History

The Local Historian 1952 – date (formerly *Amateur Historian,* renamed since Vol. 8, 1968)

Heraldry

The Armorial (International Quarterly of Heraldry. Genealogy etc.) 1959 – date.

Coat of Arms 1950 – date.

Heraldry Gazette 1957 – date (official organ of the Heraldry Society).

Army and Navy

Journal of Society for Army Historical Research 1921-date.

Navy Records Society. Publications. 1894-date.

Others

Eugenics Review 1909 – date.

The Indexer 1958 – date.

Population Studies 1947 – date.

Local Population Studies 1968 – date.

Transactions of Ancient Monuments Society 1953 – date.

Journal of Documentary Reproduction. Washington 1938-1942. *American Documentation* 1950-date.